OCÉANO ATLÁNTICO

○La Habana

CUBA

Santiago •

PENÍNSULA DE YUCATÁN

REPÚBLICA
DOMINICANA

San Juan
○
● Ponce

HAITÍ

PUERTO RICO

Santo Domingo
○

JAMAICA

MAR CARIBE

elmopan
ELIZE

ONDURAS

egucigalpa

Caracas
○

León

NICARAGUA

Managua
○

Lago de
Nicaragua

Río Orinoco

VENEZUELA

COSTA RICA

Canal de Panamá

San José
○

Panamá
○

PANAMÁ

Río Magdalena

○Bogotá

COLOMBIA

BRASIL

¿QUÉ TAL?

Thalia Dorwick

Martha Alford Marks

Marty Knorre

Bill VanPatten
University of Illinois, Urbana-Champaign

Hildebrando Villarreal
California State University, Los Angeles

¿QUÉ TAL?

AN INTRODUCTORY COURSE

THIRD EDITION

McGraw-Hill, Inc.
New York St. Louis San Francisco Auckland Bogotá
Caracas Lisbon London Madrid Mexico Milan
Montreal New Delhi Paris San Juan Singapore
Sydney Tokyo Toronto

This is an  book.

¿Qué tal?
An Introductory Course

Copyright © 1991, 1987, 1983 by McGraw-Hill, Inc. All rights reserved. Portions of this book have been taken from *Puntos de partida: An Invitation to Spanish*, Third Edition, by Marty Knorre et al., copyright © 1989 by McGraw-Hill, Inc. Printed in the United States of America. Except as permitted under the United States Copyright Act of 1976, no part of this publication may be reproduced or distributed in any form or by any means, or stored in a data base or retrieval system, without the prior written permission of the publisher.

5 6 7 8 9 0   VNH   VNH   9 5 4 3 2

ISBN 0-07-557419-5

This book was set in Palatino by Graphic Typesetting Service.
The editors were Charlotte Jackson, Richard Mason, and Kathleen Kirk.
The design manager was Francis Owens.
The designer and cover designer was Juan Vargas.
The production supervisor was Tanya Nigh.
The photo researcher was Judy Mason.
Chapter-opening drawings were rendered by Allan Eitzen; other drawings were done by Axelle Fortier, Judith Macdonald, and Katherine Tillotson.
Production assistance was provided by Edie Williams and Anne Eldredge.
Von Hoffmann Press was printer and binder.

The cover illustration is a reproduction of *Encantamiento antillano*, 1949, by Cuban artist Mario Carreño. Collection of the Museum of Modern Art of Latin America, OAS, Washington, D.C.

Library of Congress Cataloging-in-Publication Data
¿Qué tal? : An Introductory Course / Thalia Dorwick . . . [et al.]—3rd ed.
    p. cm.
  English and Spanish.
  "This is an EBI book"—T.p. verso.
  Includes index.
  ISBN 0-07-557419-5
  1. Spanish language—Textbooks for foreign speakers—English.
I. Dorwick, Thalia, 1944–
PC4129.E5Q4 1991   90-47513
468.2'421—dc20   CIP

Grateful acknowledgment is made for use of the following:

Photographs *page 1* © Ulrike Welsch; *10 (top)* © Robert Frerck/Odyssey; *10 (middle left)* © Beryl Goldberg; *10 (bottom left)* © Stuart Cohen/COMSTOCK; *10 (bottom right)* © Sharon Chester/COMSTOCK; *11 (top)* © Wide World Photos; *11 (left)* © Wide World Photos; *11 (bottom middle)* © G. Rancinian/SYGMA; *11 (bottom right)* © Alan D. Levenson; *12* © Chip and Rosa María de la Cueva Peterson; *16* © Paul Conklin/Monkmeyer Press Photo; *25 (middle left)* © Robert Frerck/Odyssey; *25 (right)* © Peter Menzel; *25 (bottom)* © D. Donne Bryant; *26* © Bob Daemmrich/Stock, Boston; *29 (top)* © Peter Menzel; *29 (left)* © Hugh Rogers/Monkmeyer; *29 (bottom)* © Luis Martin/DDB Stock Photo; *29 (middle right)* © R. J. Dunitz/DDB Stock Photo; *36* © Chip and Rosa María de la Cueva Peterson; *39* © Robert Frerck/Odyssey; *66* © Stuart Cohen/COMSTOCK; *67* © Stuart Cohen/ COMSTOCK; *85* © Robert Frerck/Odyssey; *91* © Robert Frerck/Odyssey; *92 (top)* © D. Donne Bryant; *92 (middle)* © Milton Toby/DDB Stock Photo; *92 (bottom)* © Matthew Naythons/Stock, Boston; *99* © Robert Frerck/Odyssey; *100* © Chip and Rosa María de la Cueva Peterson; *118* © Robert Frerck/Odyssey; *136* © Peter Menzel; *146* © Robert Frerck/ Odyssey; *150* © Grant LeDuc/Monkmeyer; *154* © Beryl Goldberg; *158 (top)* © Courtesy of Susana Rendon; *158 (left)* © Robert Frerck/Odyssey Productions; *158 (right)* © Bob Daemmrich/Stock, Boston; *159 (top left)* © Bettmann Newsphotos; *159 (top right)* © Bob Daemmrich/Stock, Boston; ("Cakewalk") *159 (middle)* © Carmen Lomas Garza; *159 (bottom)* © Fabio Nosotti/LGI; *170* © Robert Frerck/Odyssey; *184* © Chip and Rosa María de la Cueva Peterson; *195* © Stuart Cohen/COMSTOCK; *212 (top)* © Peter Menzel; *212 (middle)* © Audrey Gottlieb/Monkmeyer; *218* © Paul Conklin/Monkmeyer; *219 (top)* © Mario Ruiz/*Time* Magazine; *219 (middle)* © Wide World Photos; *220 (top)* © Max & Bea Hunn/DDB Stock Photo; *220 (middle)* © Alan Carey/The Image Works; *230* © Renate Hiller/

(Continued on p. 470)

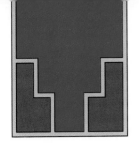

CONTENTS

CULTURAL MATERIAL	SKILLS PRACTICE

CULTURAL MATERIAL	SKILLS PRACTICE

CULTURAL MATERIAL	SKILLS PRACTICE

CULTURAL MATERIAL	SKILLS PRACTICE

CULTURAL MATERIAL	SKILLS PRACTICE

CULTURAL MATERIAL	SKILLS PRACTICE

PREFACE

The coauthors of *¿Qué tal? An Introductory Course* set about work on the third edition with appreciation for the many instructors who have found the text to be an appropriate vehicle for implementing a communicative approach, but who also seek a brief, manageable book. Based on the highly successful *Puntos de partida*, this third edition continues to emphasize functional material, concentrating on essential vocabulary and grammar and on teaching for communication through pair and group activities. We believe that the text continues to provide a flexible framework adaptable to individual teaching situations and goals—among them, a proficiency orientation and teaching for communicative competence.

The aims of the third edition are identical to those of the first: *to help students develop proficiency in the four language skills essential to truly communicative language learning.* The text was prepared with students in mind—to help them learn *how* to learn Spanish, and to give them the opportunity to use it and enjoy it.

Organization of the Third Edition

The chapter organization has been slightly altered in this edition of *¿Qué tal?* The text begins with three mini-lessons, the **Pasos preliminares,** which provide a functional introduction to Spanish language and culture that enables students to express themselves on a wide variety of topics before the formal presentation of grammar begins. The **Pasos preliminares** also explain the structure of the text itself.

Capítulos 1–27 are organized as follows:

- **Vocabulario** This section opens each chapter. It practices the thematic vocabulary and other simple structures that students will need for self-expression as they progress through the chapter. Another **Vocabulario** section appears in the middle of most chapters.

- **Pronunciación** This section, a feature of the first five chapters, focuses on individual sounds that are particularly difficult for native speakers of English.

- **Estructuras** This heading presents grammar topics, each introduced by a minidialogue, cartoon, or brief narrative, and followed by a series of contextualized exercises and activities (**Práctica**) that progress from more controlled to open-ended. Practice materials, carefully sequenced to lead students from guided to free responses, include story sequences, paraphrase, interview, partner, role-playing, and self-expression activities.

- **Un poco de todo** (formerly **Repaso**) These exercises and activities combine and review grammar presented in the chapter with previous chapters.

- **Un paso más** In alternating chapters, these sections consist of cultural readings (**Lectura cultural**) with prereading exercises (**Antes de leer**) and postreading comprehension and writing activities, or dialogues (**Situaciones**) that illustrate functional language and practical situations related to the chapter theme. Most **Situaciones** dialogues are followed by **Notas comunicativas sobre el diálogo** or other **Notas...,** boxes that highlight aspects of language and culture or aspects of particular interest in the dialogues.

- **Vocabulario** This end-of-chapter vocabulary list includes all important words and expressions considered active.

The text concludes with **Capítulo 28 (En el extranjero),** which explores the experiences of students studying abroad.

Additional features of importance include:

- **Notas (comunicativas, lingüísticas, culturales)** New to this edition, these boxes highlight functional language and cultural material at logical points throughout the text.
- **Al tanto...** Also new to this edition, these boxes highlight up-to-date vocabulary and expressions from all parts of the Hispanic world, with special emphasis on those used by young people.
- **¿Recuerda Ud.?** These brief review boxes provide a link between previous grammar points and new material that builds on those grammar points.
- **Study Hints** These boxes give students specific advice about how to acquire language skills: how to learn vocabulary, how to use a bilingual dictionary, and so on. They occur at logical points throughout the text.
- **Repaso/Voces del mundo hispánico** New to this edition, these cultural sections occur after every fourth chapter.

¿Qué tal? and Developing Language Proficiency

All exercises and activities in the program have been designed to help students develop proficiency in Spanish rather than simply display their grammatical knowledge. The authors believe that students' attempts to *use* language will provide them with the best language-learning situation—one that will prepare them to function autonomously in Spanish in the situations they are most likely to encounter outside the classroom.

Instructors whose classes are proficiency-oriented should note, in particular, the following features of *¿Qué tal?*:

- an insistence on the acquisition of vocabulary during the early stages of language learning—**Pasos preliminares**—and then in each chapter throughout the text
- an emphasis on personalized and creative use of language to perform various functions or achieve various goals
- careful attention to skills development rather than just grammatical knowledge

- a cyclical organization in which vocabulary, grammar, and language functions are consistently reviewed and re-entered
- an integrated cultural content that embeds practice in a variety of culturally significant contexts
- content that aims to raise student awareness of the interaction between language, culture, and society

Within each chapter, text materials follow each other in a way that facilitates and maximizes progress in communication skills: from vocabulary acquisition activities to grammar practice to various activities that stimulate student creativity. The overall text organization progresses from a focus on formulaic expressions, to vocabulary and structures relevant to the "here and now" (descriptions, student life, family life), to survival situations (ordering a meal, travel-related activities), to topics of broader conceptual interest (current events, the environment). Some material (such as the preterite) is introduced functionally in small chunks before the entire paradigm is presented. Major grammar topics such as the past tenses and the subjunctive are introduced, then re-entered later in the text; most grammar topics and language functions are continually reviewed and re-entered throughout the text and its ancillaries.

Major Changes in the Third Edition

Somewhat modifying the chapter structure of the first and second editions, the authors have thoroughly revised all features of the text.

Language: Skills Development and Content

- The **Pasos preliminares** have been shortened from four to three.
- **Vocabulario** sections and **Notas lingüísticas** boxes alternate with **Estructuras** sections in most chapters (rather than all **Vocabulario** sections coming at the beginning of the chapter, as in previous editions). By breaking up chapter material into more manageable "bites," we hope to provide greater variety for those instructors

who teach through the chapters in sequence.

- Starting with **Capítulo 17,** instructors will find the grammar sequence to be simplified and more coherently organized.
- More thought has been given to the conceptual "fit" between a chapter's vocabulary, grammar, and cultural themes, so that these elements work better together as integrated units.
- Grammar sections are more functionally oriented. Some points have been omitted, others treated as lexical items, some for recognition only. Many structures are used passively, in controlled situations, before their formal introduction.
- Many exercises have been rewritten to tell a story or form a logical sequence. Inferential follow-up activities will allow students to verify their comprehension of the content of such exercises and also serve as a starting point for discussion. Interview, partner, role-playing, and realia-based exercises and activities have been added throughout. Emphasis is on meaningful use of language. Pattern practice has been moved to the *Instructor's Manual.* Most fill-in activities now appear in the *Workbook* or in transparency-master format in the *Instructor's Resource Kit.*
- Review and re-entry continue to be emphasized, especially in the synthesizing **Un poco de todo** sections. Major topics that receive continuous attention in the exercises and activities include usages of **ser** and **estar,** preterite and imperfect, gender and gender agreement, and indicative and subjunctive.
- New **Situaciones** dialogues (replacing the **Imágenes del mundo hispánico** sections) together with the functional minidialogues serve as models of functional language usage.

Culture: An Integral Part of Language Learning

- New **Al tanto...** boxes allow instructors who wish to do so to make up-to-date vocabulary part of the text's active material.
- Most of the cultural readings have been replaced with two kinds of material. One kind takes the form of authentic materials or "realia": brief magazine or newspaper articles, a selection from

a driver-training manual, and so on. These are all accessible to beginning students within the context of the comprehension tasks that follow them. Another kind, amounting to a third of the cultural readings, are now "testimony": brief paragraphs written by Hispanics in answer to surveys conducted by the coauthors. Thus, here we have avoided interpreting the "Hispanic reality" of some cultural topics and instead have let Hispanic individuals speak for themselves.

- Realia (often in full color) from all parts of the Spanish-speaking world appear throughout the text. We have made no attempt to simplify or correct the language in these authentic pieces. Some are merely decorative, others serve as the basis for activities.
- The new **Repaso/Voces del mundo hispánico** sections vividly present the wide variety of people, places, activities, and ideas in the Hispanic world. Here (and in the essays in the **Pasos preliminares**) the main Hispanic groups are presented, with special emphasis on Hispanic communities within the United States. These groups have not been characterized for student readers; rather, the groups are permitted to speak for themselves in excerpts that are historically significant, timely, and—we hope—provocative.

Supplementary Materials for the Third Edition

The effectiveness of *¿Qué tal?* will be enhanced by combining it with any of the following components.

- The *Workbook* by Alice Arana (Fullerton College) and Oswaldo Arana (California State University, Fullerton) continues the format of previous editions, providing additional practice with vocabulary and structures through a variety of controlled and open-ended exercises, review sections, and guided compositions. The third edition has added realia-based exercises and review materials, especially review exercises that correspond to the **Repaso** sections in the student text.

- The *Laboratory Manual* and *Tape Program* by María Sabló-Yates (Delta College) continues to emphasize listening comprehension activities. The third edition makes more effective use of dialogue materials, and each chapter now contains a number of interview and dialogue activities in which students interact with speakers. More activities may now be answered in written form, to be collected if the instructor so wishes. Realia-based listening and speaking activities and more review materials have been added, in particular (as with the *Workbook*) review activities that correspond to the **Repaso** sections in the student text. A *Tapescript* is also available. Cassette tapes are free to adopting institutions and are also made available for student purchase upon request. Reel-to-reel tapes are available for copying.

- The *Instructor's Manual* contains section-by-section teaching suggestions, many supplementary exercises for developing listening, reading, and speaking skills (including conversation cards), and abundant variations and follow-ups on student text materials, especially the **Un paso más: Situaciones/Lectura cultural** and **Repaso** sections. It also offers an extensive introduction to teaching techniques, general guidelines for instructors, suggestions for lesson planning and for writing semester/quarter schedules, sample tests (one per chapter), and quizzes.

- Also available for instructors—and new to the third edition—is a *listening comprehension tape*, with an accompanying manual of comprehension and follow-up activities by María José Ruiz Morcillo. The tape, coordinated chapter by chapter with the student text, provides additional listening practice with major vocabulary groups and structures.

- The *Instructor's Resource Kit*, coordinated with chapters of the student text, offers additional optional activities, transparency masters of realia, and transparency masters of text visuals.

- *Juegos comunicativos* (a set of interactive, problem-solving modules for Apple IIe and IIc formats) and MHELT (the McGraw-Hill Electronic Language Tutor for IBM-PC, Apple IIe and IIc, and Apple Macintosh computers), includes most of the more controlled activities from the student text. Both are available free to adopting institutions.

- Ordering information for the *Random House Video Program for Spanish* by Total Video and *España y las Américas* (a monthly video magazine) by Eagle Multimedia Services Inc. is available upon request from your local McGraw-Hill representative.

- There are three slide sets from various parts of the Spanish-speaking world, with activities for classroom use. One set is available free to adopting institutions.

- A *training-orientation manual* for use with teaching assistants by James F. Lee (University of Illinois, Urbana-Champaign) is free to adopting institutions.

- *A Practical Guide to Language Learning* by H. Douglas Brown (San Francisco State University) is available free to adopting institutions or for purchase by individual students.

Finally, instructors will wish to examine the intermediate texts designed to follow up *¿Qué tal?* and *Puntos de partida*, namely, *Un paso más: An Intermediate Spanish Course* (Gene S. Kupferschmid and Thalia Dorwick) and *¡A leer! Un paso más: Reading Strategies and Conversation* (Hildebrando Villarreal and Gene S. Kupferschmid).

Acknowledgments

The coauthors would like to acknowledge the friends, students, and colleagues who contributed materials for the **Lectura cultural** sections that we referred to above as "testimony" by Hispanic individuals. These individuals are cited alongside most of their contributions to those sections. Also, although the following individuals are not included as coauthors of this third edition, the authors would especially like to acknowledge their contributions of ideas, realia, and dialogues: Ruth Ordás, Leslie J. Ford (Graceland College), Laura Chastain, María José Ruiz Morcillo. The thoughtful review of *¿Qué tal?* by Professor A. L. Prince (Furman University) also provided food for thought.

Special thanks go to the following instructors who participated in various types of reviews of the third edition. The appearance of their names does not constitute an endorsement of the text.

Ruth L. Allen
South Mountain Community College

Eloise G. Andries
Louisiana State University at Alexandria

Merlin Bradshaw
American River College

Aristeo Brito
Pima College

William H. Brow
Coker College

Linda J. Burk
Manchester Community College

Ann Stewart Caldwell
Auburn University at Montgomery

Guillermo Campos
San Antonio College

Joan Ciruti
Mount Holyoke College

S. Catherine Coupé
Mt. St. Clare College

Mark Couture
Michigan State University

Richard K. Curry
Texas A & M University

Carol D'Lugo
Clark University

Eileen Doll
Tulane University

Cynthia Duncan
University of Tennessee

Mario A. Faye
Tacoma Community College

Luis F. Fernández
Western Illinois University

Dolores Fischer
Napa Valley College

Margaret Florio
College of DuPage

Deanne K. Flouton
Nassau Community College

G. Ron Freeman
California State University, Fresno

Jesús García-Varela
Indiana University, Bloomington

Roger H. Gilmore
Colorado State University

Linda Gresham
Minot State University

Renato de Guzmán Rosales
Briar Cliff College

Carolyn J. Halstead
West Virginia State College

Tom Hinderliter
Friends Bible College

Corinne J. Huisman
Dordt College

Hilary W. Landwehr
Northern Kentucky University

Bari S. Levin
University of Massachusetts, Amherst

Domenico Maceri
Allan Hancock College

John D. Nesbitt
Eastern Wyoming College

Esther Plaza
Northern Kentucky University

Harriet N. Poole
Lake City Community College

Rita T. Prado
Cypress College/California State University, Fullerton

Gilbert Ranjel
University of New Mexico, Gallup

Rhea Rehark-Griffith
West Hills College

Stewart Robertson
SUNY College, Plattsburgh

Delia E. Sánchez
Phoenix College

Sister Grace Schiarone
Immaculata College

Debra Sommer
Santa Fe Community College

Eligio A. Velásquez
Santa Rosa Junior College

Myrna Vélez
Dartmouth College

Ana B. Waisman
Olympic College

Beth Wellington
Simmons College

Dewayne Winterlin
Fort Hays State University

Janice Wright
The University of Kansas

Dolly G. Young
University of Texas, Austin

Many other individuals deserve our thanks and appreciation for their help and support. Among them are the people who, in addition to the coauthors, read the manuscript to ensure its linguistic and cultural authenticity and pedagogical accuracy: Alice Arana (United States), Oswaldo Arana (Perú), Laura Chastain (El Salvador), María José Ruiz Morcillo (España), and María Sabló-Yates (Panamá). Eduardo Cabrera (Uruguay) read manuscript in earlier drafts.

Special thanks are also due our superb project editorial and production teams at McGraw-Hill (acknowledged individually on the copyright page).

We would like in particular to acknowledge the work of Richard Mason, for his cheerful and thoughtful handling of all aspects of the production process, including managing the authors, who were able to relax and let him do his work! Thanks also to Tim Stookesberry and the rest of the McGraw-Hill marketing and sales staff, for their continuing support and encouragement; and to Charlotte Jackson, Judy Getty, Kathleen Kirk, Heidi Clausen, and Sharla Volkersz for their help on various aspects of the third edition that most people will never know about, but without which a textbook—this textbook, at least—could not come to be.

PASOS PRELIMINARES

UNAM: Universidad Nacional Autónoma de México

¿Qué tal? means *"Hi, how are you doing?"* in Spanish. This textbook, called *¿Qué tal?*, will provide you with a way to begin to learn the Spanish language and to become more familiar with the many people here and abroad who use it.

Language is the means by which humans communicate with one another. To learn a new language is to acquire another way of exchanging information and of sharing your thoughts and opinions with others. *¿Qué tal?* will help you use Spanish to communicate in various ways—and function in many kinds of real-life situations—to understand Spanish when others speak it, to speak it yourself, and to read and write it. This text will also help you to communicate in Spanish in nonverbal ways through an awareness of cultural differences.

Learning about a new culture is an inseparable part of learning a language. "Culture" can mean many things: everything from great writers and painters to what time people usually eat lunch. Throughout *¿Qué tal?* you will have the opportunity to find out about the daily lives of Spanish-speaking people and the kinds of things that are important to them. Knowing about all these things will be important to you when you visit a Spanish-speaking country, and it may also be useful to you here. If you look around, you will see that Spanish is not really a foreign language, but rather a widely used language in the United States today.

Pasos preliminares *(First Steps)*, a three-part chapter, will introduce you to the Spanish language and to the format of *¿Qué tal?*

1

PASO UNO

 ## SALUDOS° Y EXPRESIONES DE CORTESÍA

Greetings

Here are some words, phrases, and expressions that will enable you to meet
and greet others appropriately in Spanish.

1. ANA: Hola, José.
   JOSÉ: ¿Qué tal, Ana? (¿Cómo estás?)
   ANA: Así así. ¿Y tú?
   JOSÉ: ¡Muy bien! Hasta mañana, ¿eh?
   ANA: Adiós.

2. SEÑOR ALONSO: Buenas tardes, señorita López.
   SEÑORITA LÓPEZ: Muy buenas, señor Alonso. ¿Cómo está?
   SEÑOR ALONSO: Bien, gracias. ¿Y usted?
   SEÑORITA LÓPEZ: Muy bien, gracias. Adiós.
   SEÑOR ALONSO: Hasta luego.

¿Qué tal?, **¿Cómo estás?**, and **¿Y tú?** are expressions used in informal situations with people you know well, on a first-name basis.

¿Cómo está? and **¿Y usted?** are used to address someone with whom you have a formal relationship.

---

[1]ANA: Hi, José. JOSÉ: How are you doing, Ana? (How are you?) ANA: So-so. And you? JOSÉ: Fine!
(Very well!) See you tomorrow, OK? ANA: 'Bye.
[2]MR. ALONSO: Good afternoon, Miss López. MISS LÓPEZ: Afternoon, Mr. Alonso. How are you?
MR. ALONSO: Fine, thanks. And you? MISS LÓPEZ: Very well, thanks. Good-bye. MR. ALONSO: See
you later.

3.   MARÍA: Buenos días, profesora.
     PROFESORA: Buenos días. ¿Cómo se llama usted?
        MARÍA: (Me llamo) María Sánchez.
     PROFESORA: Mucho gusto.
        MARÍA: Igualmente. (Encantada.)

¿Cómo se llama usted? is used in formal situations. **¿Cómo te llamas?** is
used in informal situations—for example, with other students. The phrases
mucho gusto and **igualmente** are used by both men and women when
meeting for the first time. In response to **mucho gusto**, a woman can also
say **encantada**; a man can say **encantado**.

Otros saludos y expresiones de cortesía

buenos días	good morning (*used until the midday meal*)
buenas tardes	good afternoon (*used until the evening meal*)
buenas noches	good evening, good night (*used after the evening meal*)
señor (Sr.)	Mr., sir
señora (Sra.)	Mrs., ma'am
señorita (Srta.)	Miss

Note that there is no standard Spanish equivalent for *Ms.* Use **Sra.** or **Srta.**,
as appropriate.

Notas comunicativas: Speaking Politely

The material in this recurring section of *¿Qué tal?* will help you deal with
everyday situations in Spanish: how to accept or decline an invitation, how to
order in a restaurant, and so on. Here are some words and phrases that will
help you speak politely.

gracias	thanks, thank you
muchas gracias	thank you very much
de nada	you're welcome
por favor	please (*also used to get someone's attention*)
perdón	pardon me, excuse me (*to ask forgiveness or to get someone's attention*)
con permiso	pardon me, excuse me (*to request permission to pass by or through a group of people*)

Con permiso.

---

[3]MARÍA: Good morning, professor. PROFESORA: Good morning. What's your name? MARÍA: (My
name is) María Sánchez. PROFESORA: Pleased to meet you. MARÍA: Likewise. (Delighted.)

Práctica

A.   Practice Dialogues 1 through 3 several times with another student, using your own names.

B.   How many different ways can you respond to the following greetings and phrases?

1. Buenas tardes.
2. Adiós.
3. ¿Qué tal?
4. Hola.
5. ¿Cómo está?
6. Buenas noches.
7. Muchas gracias.
8. Hasta mañana.
9. ¿Cómo se llama usted?
10. Mucho gusto.

C.   Situaciones. If the following persons met or passed each other at the times given, what might they say to each other? Role-play the situations with a classmate.

1. Mr. Santana and Miss Pérez, at 5:00 P.M.
2. Mrs. Ortega and Pablo, at 10:00 A.M.
3. Ms. Hernández and Olivia, at 11:00 P.M.
4. you and a classmate, just before your Spanish class

D.   Are these people saying **por favor**, **con permiso**, or **perdón**?

E.   Entrevista (*Interview*). Turn to the person sitting next to you and do the following.

- Greet him or her appropriately.
- Find out his or her name.
- Ask how he or she is.
- Conclude the exchange.

Now have a similar conversation with your instructor, using the appropriate formal forms.

EL ALFABETO ESPAÑOL

There are thirty letters in the Spanish *alphabet* (**el alfabeto**)—four more than in the English alphabet. The **ch**, **ll**, and **rr** are considered single letters even though they are two-letter groups; the **ñ** is the fourth extra letter. The letters **k** and **w** appear only in words borrowed from other languages.

Listen carefully as your instructor pronounces the names listed with the letters of the alphabet.

LETTERS	NAMES OF LETTERS	EXAMPLES		
a	a	Antonio	Ana	(la) Argentina
b	be	Benito	Blanca	Bolivia
c	ce	Carlos	Cecilia	Cáceres
ch	che	Pancho	Concha	Chile
d	de	Domingo	Dolores	Durango
e	e	Eduardo	Elena	(el) Ecuador
f	efe	Felipe	Francisca	(la) Florida
g	ge	Gerardo	Gloria	Guatemala
h	hache	Héctor	Hortensia	Honduras
i	i	Ignacio	Inés	Ibiza
j	jota	José	Juana	Jalisco
k	ca (ka)	(Karl)	(Kati)	(Kansas)
l	ele	Luis	Lola	Lima
ll	elle	Guillermo	Guillermina	Sevilla
m	eme	Manuel	María	México
n	ene	Nicolás	Nati	Nicaragua
ñ	eñe	Íñigo	Begoña	España
o	o	Octavio	Olivia	Oviedo
p	pe	Pablo	Pilar	Panamá
q	cu	Enrique	Raquel	Quito
r	ere	Álvaro	Clara	(el) Perú
rr	erre *or* ere doble	Rafael	Rosa	Monterrey
s	ese	Salvador	Sara	San Juan
t	te	Tomás	Teresa	Toledo
u	u	Agustín	Lucía	(el) Uruguay
v	ve *or* uve	Víctor	Victoria	Venezuela
w	doble ve, ve doble, *or* uve doble	Oswaldo	(Wilma)	(Washington)
x	equis	Xavier	Ximena	Extremadura
y	i griega	Pelayo	Yolanda	(el) Paraguay
z	ceta (zeta)	Gonzalo	Esperanza	Zaragoza

Práctica

A. The letters below represent the Spanish sounds that are the most different from their English counterparts. You will practice the pronunciation of some of these letters in upcoming sections of *¿Qué tal?* For the moment, pay particular attention to their pronunciation when you see them. Can you match the Spanish spelling with its equivalent pronunciation?

SPELLING

PRONUNCIATION

1. __ **ch**
2. __ **g** before **e** or **i**; also **j**
3. **h**
4. __ **g** before **a**, **o**, or **u**
5. __ **ll**
6. __ **ñ**
7. **r**
8. __ **r** at the beginning of a word or **rr** in the middle of a word
9. __ **v**

a. __ like the *g* in English *garden*
b. similar to *dd* of *caddy* or *tt* of *kitty* when pronounced very quickly
c. __ like *ch* in English *cheese*
d. __ like Spanish **b**
e. __ similar to a "strong" English *h*
f. __ like *y* in English *yes* or like the *li* sound in *million*
g. __ a trilled sound, several Spanish **r**'s in a row
h. __ similar to the *ny* sound in *canyon*
i. never pronounced

B. Spell your own name in Spanish, and listen as your classmates spell their names. Try to remember as many of their names as you can.

C. Identify as many of your classmates as you can, using the phrase **Te llamas...** (*Your name is . . .*). Then spell the name in Spanish.

MODELO: Te llamas María: **M** (eme) **A** (a) **R** (ere) **Í** (i acentuada) **A** (a).

D. Spell these U.S. place names in Spanish. All of them are of Hispanic origin: Toledo, Los Angeles, Texas, Montana, Colorado, El Paso, Florida, Las Vegas, Amarillo, San Francisco. Pronounce the names in Spanish before you begin to spell them.

. . . .

 SPANISH AS A WORLD LANGUAGE

Although no one knows exactly how many languages are spoken around the world, linguists estimate that there are between 3,000 and 6,000. Spanish, with 296 million native speakers, is among the top five languages. It is the language spoken in Spain, in all of South America (except Brazil and the Guyanas), in most of Central America, in Cuba, in Puerto Rico, and in the Dominican Republic—in approximately twenty countries in all.

Like all languages spoken by large numbers of people, modern Spanish varies from region to region. The Spanish of Madrid is different from that spoken in Mexico City or Buenos Aires, just as the English of London differs from that of Chicago or Dallas. Although these differences are most noticeable in pronunciation ("accent"), they are also found in vocabulary

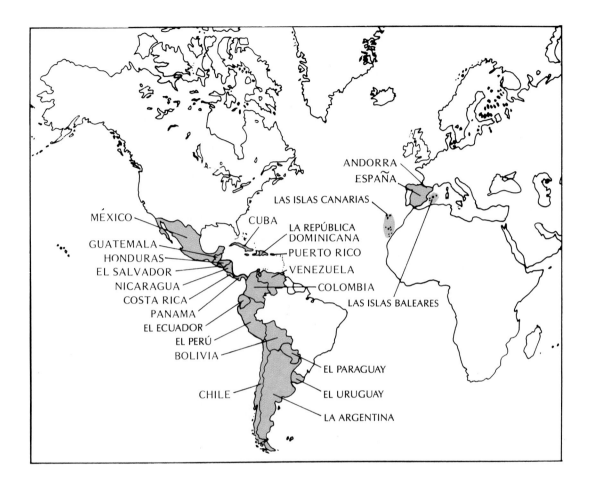

and special expressions used in different geographical areas. In Great Britain one hears the word *lift,* but the same apparatus is called an *elevator* in the United States. What is called an **autobús** (*bus*) in Spain may be called a **gua-gua** in the Caribbean. Although such differences are noticeable, they result only rarely in misunderstandings among native speakers, since the majority of structures and vocabulary are common to the many varieties of each language.

 LOS COGNADOS

Many Spanish and English words are similar or identical in form and meaning. These related words are called *cognates* (**los cognados**). Spanish and English share so many cognates because a number of words in both languages are derived from the same Latin root words and also because Spanish and English are "language neighbors," especially in the southwestern

United States. Each language has borrowed words from the other and adapted them to its own sound system. Thus, the English word *leader* has become Spanish **líder**, and Spanish **el lagarto** (*the lizard*) has become English *alligator.* The existence of so many cognates will make learning some Spanish vocabulary words easier for you and increase the number of words that you can recognize immediately. Many cognates are used in the **Pasos preliminares**. Don't try to memorize all of them—just get used to the sound of them in Spanish.

Here are some Spanish adjectives (words used to describe people, places, and things) that are cognates of English words. Practice pronouncing them, imitating your instructor. These adjectives can be used to describe either a man or a woman.

cruel	independiente	pesimista
eficiente	inteligente	realista
egoísta	interesante	rebelde
elegante	liberal	responsable
emocional	materialista	sentimental
idealista	optimista	terrible
importante	paciente	valiente

The following adjectives change form. Use the **-o** ending when describing a man, the **-a** ending when describing a woman.

extrovertido/a	introvertido/a	serio/a
generoso/a	religioso/a	sincero/a
impulsivo/a	romántico/a	tímido/a

Práctica

A. Describe Don Juan, the famous lover, in simple Spanish sentences that begin with **Don Juan es** (*is*)... or **Don Juan no es** (*is not*)...

B. Think of a well-known person—real or imaginary—and describe him or her. Try to describe as many qualities of the person as you can. For example:

El presidente es/no es...
Meryl Streep es/no es...

C. **El Supertest** is a true/false quiz from the Sunday supplement section of a Spanish newspaper. It includes items about historical events, general knowledge, and current issues. Although you will not be able to understand everything in it, there are many words and phrases that *will* be familiar to you! Focus on the cognates you can recognize—not on what you do not know—as you scan through the twelve items of the test. Answer *yes* (**sí**) or *no* (**no**) only if you think you understand enough about an item to make an educated guess. Remember! Your real task is to find cognates, not to do the test yourself. Later, your instructor may wish to work through the items with the whole class.

EL SUPERTEST

Las preguntas de nuestro Supertest de enero son bastante fáciles. ¡Pon a prueba tus conocimientos y contesta rápidamente!

Enunciado	Sí	No
1. Los habitantes de Teruel son turolenses	__	__
2. Camacho fue el capitán de la selección española en el Mundial 86 de México	__	__
3. La «Rendición de Breda» fue pintada por Goya	__	__
4. Marco Polo escribió «El libro de las maravillas»	__	__
5. La última Olimpiada se celebró en San Francisco	__	__
6. El chihuahua es la raza de perro más pequeña	__	__
7. El archipiélago canario se compone de nueve islas	__	__
8. Berlín es la capital de la RFA	__	__
9. Los nacidos entre el 20 de febrero y el 20 de marzo pertenecen al signo de Picis ..	__	__
10. El jugador de ajedrez Karpov es soviético	__	__
11. El caballo de Alejandro Magno se llamaba Bucéfalo	__	__
12. Saturno es el segundo planeta más grande del sistema solar	__	__

Note: Due to recent events, the answer to one of the test items is out of date. Can you find it?

Soluciones del supertest:
1. Sí. – 2. Sí. – 3. Velázquez.
– 4. Sí. – 5. En Los Ángeles.
– 6. Sí. – 7. De siete. – 8. Bonn.
– 9. Sí. – 10. Sí. – 11. Sí. – 12. Sí.

◆ ¿CÓMO ES USTED?°

¿Cómo... *What kind of person are you?*

You can use these forms of the verb **ser** (*to be*) to describe yourself and others.

(yo)	**soy**	*I am*
(tú)	**eres**	*you* (familiar) *are*
(usted)	**es**	*you* (formal) *are*
(él, ella)	**es**	*he/she is*

Práctica

A.   ¿Cómo es usted? Describe yourself, using adjectives from **Los cognados: Yo soy... Yo no soy...**

B.   Entrevista. Use the following adjectives, or any others you know, to find out what a classmate is like. Follow the model.

MODELO: —¿Eres generoso? (¿Eres generosa?)
—¿Sí, soy generoso/a. (No, no soy generoso/a.)

Adjetivos: sincero/a, eficiente, emocional, inteligente, impulsivo/a, liberal

Now find out what kind of person your instructor is, using the same adjectives. Use the appropriate formal forms.

MODELO: ¿Es usted optimista (generoso/a)?

HISPANICS IN THE UNITED STATES

You don't need to go abroad to find evidence of the importance of Spanish. The Spanish language and people of Hispanic descent have been an integral part of United States life for centuries, and Hispanics are currently one of the fastest-growing cultural groups in this country. In fact, based on information obtained from the 1980 census, the United States is now the sixth largest Spanish-speaking country in the world!

Who are the almost 19 million people of Hispanic descent living in the United States today? If we are tempted to think of all U.S. Hispanics as similar, we soon discover that nothing could be farther from the truth! In fact, they are characterized by great diversity, the result of their ancestors' or their own country of origin, the area of this country in which they live, socio-economic-professional factors, and, of course, individual talents and aspirations.

People of Hispanic origin were among the first colonizers of what is now the United States. A visitor to the states of Montana, Idaho, and Nevada, for example, would meet many descendants of Spanish settlers—as well as many Basques, more recent immigrants—and in the Southwest many Mexican-Americans can trace their ancestors back several centuries.

Niños mexicanoamericanos y puertorriqueños, en un barrio (*neighborhood*) de Chicago

Bailadoras de la República Dominicana, en un desfile (*parade*) de Nueva York

Comparing origins of U.S. Hispanic population

Total estimated population as of 1990: 25 million

Percentages:

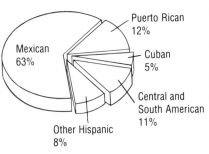

Mexican 63%

Puerto Rican 12%

Cuban 5%

Central and South American 11%

Other Hispanic 8%

Mural de la Pequeña Habana, el barrio cubano de Miami

Bailadores colombianos, en San Mateo, California

Large groups of more recent arrivals can be found in New York (where the Puerto Rican population is the largest) and in Florida (the home of many Cubans and Central Americans). And there has been a substantial increase in the number of Hispanics even in areas not usually thought of as having large Hispanic populations—Minneapolis–St. Paul, Seattle, Chicago, and New Orleans, to name only a few. Political and social changes in Central America have produced a recent influx of Nicaraguans and Salvadorans, who have established large communities in many U.S. cities, among them San Francisco and Los Angeles. Predominant among people of South American descent in this country are Colombians, Argentines, and Ecuadorans.

Many U.S. Hispanics strive to maintain aspects of their unique heritage while entering the mainstream of American culture at the same time. Although not all people of Hispanic origin speak Spanish, many are in fact bilingual and bicultural, able to move back and forth between their own and the mainstream culture with ease. This dual cultural identity is being increasingly recognized by the media and by the business community. Many major U.S. cities have one or more Spanish-language newspapers as well as television and radio stations. A wide variety of businesses are of course owned and operated by Hispanics, and major corporations in the food, clothing, entertainment, and service fields appeal to Hispanic clients . . . in both English and Spanish!

Perhaps the most important contributions of Hispanic culture to the United States come from individuals who make up the actual Hispanic population. It is easy to call to mind Hispanics who have achieved national prominence in all walks of life, but we should also keep in mind the many Hispanics, not in the public eye, who regularly make meaningful contributions in the fields of education, law, science, social work, and so on. Their efforts to create a better world are an integral part of the fabric of this country.

How many of these Mexican-Americans can you identify?

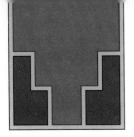

Al tanto...°   *Al... Up-to-date*

Here are some additional ways to greet people and say good-bye to them in Spanish. All of them are very informal.

¿Qué pasa? (¿Qué pasó?) ⎱
¿Qué hay? (¿Qué hay   ⎰   *What's up?*
  de nuevo?)
¡Chau!   *Bye.*
Nos vemos.   *See you.* (lit., *We'll*
                 see each other.)

Madrid, España

◆ MÁS COGNADOS

Although some English and Spanish cognates are spelled identically (*idea, general, gas, animal, motor*), most will differ slightly in spelling: *position*/**posición**, *secret*/**secreto**, *student*/**estudiante**, *rose*/**rosa**, *lottery*/**lotería**, *opportunity*/**oportunidad**, *exam*/**examen**.

The following exercises will give you more practice in recognizing and pronouncing cognates. Remember: Don't try to learn all of these words. Just get used to the way they sound.

Práctica

A. Pronounce each of the following cognates and give its English equivalent.

Naciones: la Unión Soviética, el Japón, Italia, Francia, España, el Brasil, la China, el Canadá

Personas: líder, profesor, actriz, pintor, político, estudiante

Lugares:° restaurante, café, museo, garaje, banco, hotel, oficina, océano, parque   *Places*

Conceptos: libertad, dignidad, declaración, contaminación

Cosas:° teléfono, fotografía, sofá, televisión, radio, bomba, novela, diccionario, dólar, lámpara, yate   *Things*

Animales: león, cebra, chimpancé, tigre, hipopótamo

Comidas y bebidas:° hamburguesa, cóctel, patata, café, limón, banana   *Comidas...* *Food and drink*

Deportes:° béisbol, tenis, vólibol, fútbol americano   *Sports*

Instrumentos musicales: guitarra, piano, clarinete, trompeta, violín

**Monolith
70-490 NIC**

**Técnica fascinante y línea
clara con perfiles
estrechos: esto es un
televisor al más alto nivel.
2 × 50 W Hifi stereo a
través de dos cajas
acústicas exponenciales.
Doble reproducción del
sonido stereo/dual
(Nicam 728 y sistema
alemán).**

B. Many of the Spanish words used to talk about technology and recent inventions, including the latest in electronic equipment, are cognates of English words. What piece of equipment is this ad for? Can you find the Spanish word for it? How many cognates are there in the text of the ad?

C. **¿Qué es esto?** (*What is this?*) Being able to tell what something is or to identify the group to which it belongs is a useful conversation strategy that will come in handy when you don't know the specific word for something in Spanish. Begin to practice this strategy by pronouncing these cognates and identifying the category from **Práctica A** to which they belong. Use the following sentences as a guide.

> Es **un** lugar (concepto, animal, deporte, instrumento musical).*
> Es **una** nación (persona, cosa, comida, bebida).*

> MODELO: béisbol → Es un deporte.

1. calculadora	8. limonada	15. turista
2. burro	9. elefante	16. rancho
3. sándwich	10. refrigerador	17. serpiente
4. golf	11. universidad	18. chocolate
5. México	12. fama	19. básquetbol
6. actor	13. terrorista	20. acordeón
7. clase	14. Cuba	21. democracia

D. With a classmate, practice identifying words, using the categories given in **Práctica C**.

> MODELO: —¿Qué (*What*) es un hospital? →
> —Es un lugar.

1. un saxofón	4. un doctor	7. una enchilada
2. un autobús	5. Bolivia	8. una jirafa
3. una estación	6. una Coca-Cola	

---

*The English equivalent of these sentences is *It is a place* (*concept* . . .); *It is a country* (*person* . . .). Note that Spanish has two different ways to express *a* (*an*): **un** and **una**. All nouns are either masculine (*m.*) or feminine (*f.*) in Spanish. **Un** is used with masculine nouns, **una** with feminine nouns. You will learn more about this aspect of Spanish in **Capítulo 1**. Don't try to learn the gender of nouns now, and note that you do not have to know the gender of nouns to do this activity.

Irene es un nombre griego que significa «paz».
Rafael es un nombre de origen hebreo que significa «Dios ha sanado».
Cora es un nombre griego que significa «bella, adornada».
Guillermo es un nombre de origen germánico que significa «voluntad y yelmo» y que podría interpretarse como «protector voluntarioso».

E.   ¿Quién (*Who*) **es usted?** With a classmate, assume the identity of one of these figures from the Spanish-speaking world. Your classmate will try to guess your identity based on the clues you provide according to the model. Use the names, categories, and countries given below as a guide. Use **Soy...** to identify yourself and **Soy de...** to tell where you are from.

MODELO: ESTUDIANTE 1 (uno): ¿Quién es usted?
　　　　　ESTUDIANTE 2 (dos): Soy rey (*king*).* Soy de España.
　　　　　　　ESTUDIANTE 1: Ah, usted es (se llama) Juan Carlos.
　　　　　　　ESTUDIANTE 2: Sí, soy (me llamo) Juan Carlos.
　　　　　　　　　　　　　　(No, no soy [No, no me llamo]...)

PERSONAS	CATEGORÍAS	NACIONES
Diego Rivera	actor (actriz)	México
Fernando Valenzuela	primer ministro	España
Gloria Estefan	cantante (*singer*)	los Estados
Fidel Castro	muralista	Unidos
Rita Moreno	jugador (*player*)	Puerto Rico
Ricardo Montalbán	de béisbol	Cuba
Lee Treviño	jugador de golf	
Julio Iglesias	reportero	
Severiano Ballesteros		

◆ PRONUNCIACIÓN

You have probably already noted that there is a very close relationship between the way Spanish is written and the way it is pronounced. This makes it relatively easy to learn the basics of Spanish spelling and pronunciation.

　　Many Spanish sounds, however, do not have an exact equivalent in English, so you should not trust English to be your guide to Spanish pronunciation. Even words that are spelled the same in both languages are usually pronounced quite differently. It is important to become so familiar with Spanish sounds that you can pronounce them automatically, right from the beginning of your study of the language.

Las vocales (*Vowels*): a, e, i, o, u

Unlike English vowels, which can have many different pronunciations or may be silent, Spanish vowels are always pronounced, and they are almost always pronounced in the same way. Spanish vowels are always short and tense. They are never drawn out with a *u* or *i* glide as in English: **lo** ≠ *low*; **de** ≠ *day*.

---

*Note that the indefinite article (**un**, **una**) is not used before unmodified nouns of profession.

¡OJO!   The *uh* sound or schwa (which is how all unstressed vowels are pronounced in English: c*a*nal, wait*e*d, at*o*m) does not exist in Spanish.

  a: pronounced like the *a* in *father*, but short and tense
  e: pronounced like the *e* in *they*, but without the *i* glide
  i: pronounced like the *i* in *machine*, but short and tense*
  o: pronounced like the *o* in *home* but without the *u* glide
  u: pronounced like the *u* in *rule*, but short and tense

Práctica

A.   Pronounce the following Spanish syllables, being careful to pronounce
each vowel with a short, tense sound.

1. ma fa la ta pa	4. mo fo lo to po	7. su mi te so la
2. me fe le te pe	5. mu fu lu tu pu	8. se tu no ya li
3. mi fi li ti pi	6. mi fe la tu do	

B.   Pronounce the following words, paying special attention to the vowel
sounds.

1. hasta	tal	nada	mañana	natural	normal	fascinante
2. me	qué	Pérez	usted	rebelde	excelente	elegante
3. así	señorita	así así	permiso	diligente	imposible	tímido
4. yo	con	cómo	noches	profesor	señor	generoso
5. uno	usted	tú	mucho	Perú	Lupe	Úrsula

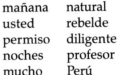

C.   Here is part of a rental car ad in Spanish. Can you find the
following information in it?

*   How many cars does the agency have available?
*   How many offices does the agency have?
*   What Spanish word expresses the English word
    immediately?
*   If not confirmed immediately, when are reservations
    confirmed by the agency?

---

*The word **y** (*and*) is also pronounced like the letter **i**.

LOS NÚMEROS 0–30

Una clase bilingüe en Virginia

Canción infantil*
Dos y dos son cuatro,
cuatro y dos son seis,
seis y dos son ocho,
y ocho dieciséis.

0 cero		
1 uno	11 once	21 veintiuno
2 dos	12 doce	22 veintidós
3 tres	13 trece	23 veintitrés
4 cuatro	14 catorce	24 veinticuatro
5 cinco	15 quince	25 veinticinco
6 seis	16 dieciséis[†]	26 veintiséis
7 siete	17 diecisiete	27 veintisiete
8 ocho	18 dieciocho	28 veintiocho
9 nueve	19 diecinueve	29 veintinueve
10 diez	20 veinte	30 treinta

The number *one* has several forms in Spanish. **Uno** is the form used in
counting. **Un** is used before masculine singular nouns, **una** before feminine
singular nouns: **un señor, una señora.** Note also that the number **veintiuno**
becomes **veintiún** before masculine nouns and **veintiuna** before feminine
nouns: **veintiún señores, veintiuna señoras.**

Use the word **hay** to express both *there is* and *there are* in Spanish. **No
hay** means *there is not* and *there are not.* **¿Hay... ?** asks *Is there . . . ?* or *Are
there . . . ?*

¿Cuántos estudiantes **hay** en la
  clase?—**(Hay)** Treinta.

*How many students are there in
  the class?—(There are) Thirty.*

¿**Hay** osos panda en el zoo?
  —**Hay** veinte osos, pero **no
  hay** osos panda.

*Are there any panda bears at the
  zoo?—There are twenty bears,
  but there aren't any pandas.*

***A children's song**   Two and two are four, four and two are six, six and two are eight, and
  eight (makes) sixteen.
[†]The numbers 16 to 19 and 21 to 29 can be written as one word (**dieciséis... veintiuno**) or as
  three (**diez y seis... veinte y uno**).

Práctica

A.   Practique los números.

1. 4 señoras	6. 1 clase (*f.*)	11. 28 bebidas
2. 12 noches	7. 21 ideas (*f.*)	12. 5 guitarras
3. 1 café (*m.*)	8. 11 tardes	13. 1 león (*m.*)
4. 21 cafés (*m.*)	9. 15 estudiantes	14. 30 señores
5. 14 días	10. 13 teléfonos	15. 20 oficinas

B.   Problemas de matemáticas: + (y)   − (menos)   = (son)

MODELO: $2 + 2 = 4 \rightarrow$ Dos y dos son cuatro.
$4 - 2 = 2 \rightarrow$ Cuatro menos dos son dos.

1. $2 + 4 = ?$	5. $9 + 6 = ?$	9. $9 - 9 = ?$
2. $8 + 17 = ?$	6. $5 + 4 = ?$	10. $13 - 8 = ?$
3. $11 + 1 = ?$	7. $1 + 13 = ?$	11. $14 + 12 = ?$
4. $3 + 18 = ?$	8. $15 - 2 = ?$	12. $23 - 13 = ?$

C.   **Preguntas** (*Questions*)

1.   ¿Cuántos estudiantes hay en la clase de español? ¿Cuántos estudiantes hay en clase hoy (*today*)? ¿Hay tres profesores o un profesor?

2.   ¿Cuántos días hay en una semana (*week*)? ¿Hay seis? (No, no hay...) ¿Cuántos días hay en un fin de semana (*weekend*)? Hay cuatro semanas en un **mes**. ¿Qué significa **mes** en inglés? ¿Cuántos días hay en el mes de febrero? ¿en el mes de junio? ¿Cuántos meses hay en un año?

3.   Hay muchos (*many*) animales en un zoo. ¿Hay un zoo en esta ciudad (*this city*)? ¿Cuántos elefantes hay en el zoo? ¿cuántas jirafas? ¿cuántos osos? ¿cuántos osos panda? ¿Hay muchos animales exóticos?

4.   Hay muchos edificios (*buildings*) en una universidad. En esta (*this*) universidad, ¿hay una cafetería? ¿un teatro? ¿un cine (*movie theater*)? ¿un laboratorio de lenguas? ¿un bar? ¿una clínica? ¿un hospital? ¿un museo? ¿muchos estudiantes? ¿muchos profesores?

Here is a page from a Spanish child's workbook. Can you find the Spanish word for *arithmetic*? What numbers are written differently in Spain? The letter **B** was written twice by the child's teacher. What do you think it stands for?

GUSTOS° Y PREFERENCIAS

Likes

—¿Te gusta el béisbol?
—¿Sí, me gusta, pero (*but*) me gusta más (*more*) el vólibol.

To indicate that you like something in Spanish, say **Me gusta**… . To indicate that you don't like something, use **No me gusta**… . Use the question **¿Te gusta**… ? to ask a classmate if he or she likes something. Use **¿Le gusta**… ? to ask your instructor the same question.

In the following conversations, you will use the word **el** to mean *the* with masculine nouns and the word **la** with feminine nouns. Don't try to memorize which nouns are masculine and which are feminine. Just get used to using the words **el** and **la** before nouns.

You will also be using a number of Spanish verbs in the infinitive form, which always ends in **-r**. Here are some examples: **estudiar** = *to study*; **comer** = *to eat*. Try to guess the meanings of the infinitives used in these activities from context. If someone asks you, for instance, **¿Te gusta beber Coca-Cola?**, it is a safe guess that **beber** means *to drink*.

Práctica

A. Indicate whether you like the following things or like to do the following activities.

MODELOS: ¿la clase de español? → (No) Me gusta la clase de español.

¿estudiar mucho? → (No) Me gusta estudiar mucho.

1.   ¿la música moderna? ¿la música clásica? ¿la música punk?
2.   ¿la universidad? ¿la cafetería de la universidad? ¿la librería (*bookstore*)?
3.   ¿la actriz Joan Collins? ¿el actor Emilio Estévez? ¿la cantante Madonna? ¿el grupo U2? ¿el presidente de los Estados Unidos?
4.   ¿estudiar español? ¿estudiar en la cafetería? ¿estudiar en la residencia (*dorm*)? ¿en la biblioteca (*library*)?
5.   ¿esquiar (*to ski*)? ¿jugar al tenis? ¿jugar al fútbol americano? ¿jugar al golf? ¿jugar a la lotería?
6.   ¿beber vino? ¿beber café? ¿beber té? ¿beber limonada? ¿beber chocolate?

B.   Entrevista. Ask another student if he or she likes the following activities.

MODELO: nadar (*to swim*) en el océano →
—¿Te gusta nadar en el océano?
—Sí, me gusta nadar en el océano.
(No, no me gusta nadar.)
(Sí, pero me gusta más jugar al tenis.)

1. ¿comer piza? ¿comer hamburguesas? ¿comer en la cafetería? ¿comer en un restaurante elegante?
2. ¿hablar (*to speak*) español? ¿hablar otras lenguas? ¿hablar por teléfono? ¿hablar ante (*in front of*) muchas personas?
3. ¿tocar la guitarra? ¿tocar el piano? ¿tocar el violín?
4. ¿ir a (*to go to*) clase? ¿ir al cine? ¿ir al bar? ¿ir al parque? ¿ir al museo?

Now use the preceding cues to interview your instructor about his or her likes and dislikes.

MODELO: ¿Le gusta comer piza?

◆ EL MUNDO° HISPÁNICO (PARTE 1)   *world*

Antes de leer:° Recognizing Interrogative Words and *estar*

Antes... *Before reading*

In the following brief reading, note that the word **está** means *is located*; **está** and other forms of the verb **estar** (*to be*) are used to tell where things are. You will learn more about the uses of **estar** in **Capítulo 5.**

The reading also contains a series of questions with interrogative words. You are already familiar with **¿cómo?**, **¿qué?**, and **¿cuántos?** (and should be able to guess the meaning of **¿cuántas?** easily). The meaning of other interrogatives may not be immediately obvious to you, but the sentences in which the words appear may offer some clues to meaning. You probably do not know the meaning of **¿dónde?** and **¿cuál?**, but you should be able to guess their meaning in the following sentences.

Cuba está en el Mar Caribe. ¿<u>Dónde</u> está la República Dominicana? Managua es la capital de Nicaragua. ¿<u>Cuál</u> es la capital de México?

Use the statements in the reading as models and the geographical and population information in the maps to answer the questions.

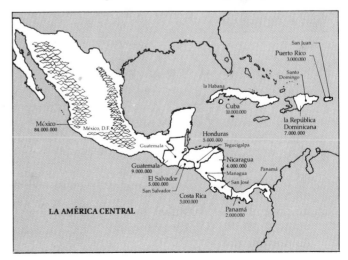

LA AMÉRICA CENTRAL

LAS NACIONES DEL MUNDO HISPÁNICO

¿En cuántas naciones de la América Central se habla español? Hay ochenta y cuatro (84) millones de habitantes en México. ¿Cuántos habitantes hay en Guatemala? ¿en El Salvador? ¿en las demás (*other*) naciones de la América Central? ¿Cuál es la capital de México? ¿de Costa Rica?

Cuba está en el Mar Caribe. ¿Dónde está la República Dominicana? ¿Qué parte de los Estados Unidos está también (*also*) en el Mar Caribe? ¿Dónde está el Canal de Panamá?

¿En cuántas naciones de Sudamérica se habla español? ¿Se habla español o portugués en el Brasil? ¿Cuántos millones de habitantes hay en Venezuela? ¿en Chile? ¿en las demás naciones? ¿Cuál es la capital de cada (*each*) nación?

España está en la Península Ibérica. ¿Qué otra nación está también en esa (*that*) península? ¿Cuántos millones de habitantes hay en España? No se habla español en Portugal. ¿Qué lengua se habla allí (*there*)? ¿Cuál es la capital de España? ¿Está en el centro de la Península?

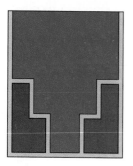

PASO TRES

¿QUÉ HORA ES?

On page 21 you will see part of a TV listing from Spain for a Monday. Scan the listing, then respond to these statements and questions.

Dé (*Give*) el nombre de…

un programa infantil
un melodrama
un programa de aventuras
un programa de deportes (*sports*)
un documental

¿Qué significa en inglés… ?

dibujos animados (dibujo = *drawing*)
telediario (diario = *newspaper*)
territorial
nacional

Es la una.   **Son** las dos.   **Son** las cinco.

¿Qué hora es? is used to ask *What time is it?* In telling time, one says *Es la una* but *Son las dos* (**las tres, las cuatro,** and so on).

Es la una **y** $\begin{cases} \textbf{cuarto.} \\ \textbf{quince.} \end{cases}$ Son las dos **y** $\begin{cases} \textbf{media.} \\ \textbf{treinta.} \end{cases}$

Son las cinco **y diez.**   Son las ocho **y veinticinco.**

Note that from the hour to the half-hour, Spanish, like English, expresses time by adding minutes or a portion of an hour to the hour.

Son las dos **menos** $\begin{cases} \textbf{cuarto.} \\ \textbf{quince.} \end{cases}$ Son las ocho **menos diez.**   Son las once **menos veinte.**

From the half-hour to the hour, Spanish usually expresses time by subtracting minutes or a part of an hour from the *next* hour.

Otras expresiones útiles

de la mañana	A.M., in the morning	**¿a qué hora?**	(at) what time?
de la tarde (noche)	P.M., in the afternoon (evening)	**a la una (las dos, ...)**	at 1:00 (2:00, . . .)
en punto	exactly, on the dot, sharp		

Son las cuatro de la tarde **en punto.**

It's exactly 4:00 P.M.

¿A qué hora es la clase de español?

(At) What time is Spanish class?

Hay una recepción **a las once de la mañana.**

There is a reception at 11:00 A.M.

¡OJO!   Don't confuse **Es/Son la(s)**… with **A la(s)**… The first is used for telling time, the second for telling when something happens (when class starts, when one arrives, and so on).

Práctica

A.   ¿Qué hora es?

1. 1:00
2. 6:00
3. 11:00
4. 1:30
5. 3:15
6. 6:45
7. 4:15
8. 11:45 exactly
9. 9:10 on the dot
10. 9:50 sharp

B.   Exprese la hora, usando de la mañana (tarde, noche).

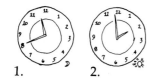

1.

3.

4.

5.

6.

7.

8.

C.   Situaciones. You are a travel agent. Your clients want to know when (**¿cuándo?**) they're going to arrive at their destinations. With a classmate, role-play this situation, according to the model.

> MODELO: Guanajuato / 9:00 A.M. →
> —¿Cuándo llegamos a (*do we get to*) Guanajuato?
> —A las nueve de la mañana.

1. Sevilla / 11:00 A.M.
2. Buenos Aires / 11:54 P.M.
3. Los Ángeles / 1:15 P.M.
4. Miami / 8:31 P.M.
5. Málaga / 5:35 A.M.
6. Cali / 2:30 A.M. exactly

D.   Entrevista. Ask a classmate what time the following events or activities take place. He or she will answer according to the cue or will provide the necessary information.

> MODELO: la clase de español / 10:00 A.M. →
> —¿A qué hora es la clase de español?
> —A las diez de la mañana… ¡en punto!

1. la clase de francés / 1:45 P.M.
2. la sesión de laboratorio / 3:10 P.M.
3. la excursión / 8:45 A.M.
4. el concierto / 7:30 P.M.

Now ask what time your partner likes to perform these activities. He or she should provide the necessary information.

> MODELO: estudiar español →
> —¿A qué hora te gusta estudiar español?
> —Me gusta estudiar español a las ocho de la noche.

1. cenar (*to have dinner*)
2. mirar (*to watch*) la televisión
3. jugar al (vólibol, tenis, …)
4. ir (*to go*) a la cafetería

E.   Situaciones. How might the following people greet each other if they met at the indicated time? With a classmate, create a brief dialogue for each situation.

1.   el profesor Martínez y Gloria, a las diez de la mañana
2.   la Sra. López y la Srta. Luna, a las cuatro y media de la tarde
3.   usted y su (*your*) profesor(a) de español, en la clase de español
4.   Jorge y María, a las once de la noche

LAS PALABRAS INTERROGATIVAS
Un resumen

You have already used a number of interrogative words and phrases to get information. (You will learn more in subsequent chapters of *¿Qué tal?*) Note the accent over the vowel you emphasize when you say the word, and the use of the inverted question mark. In this list only **¿cuánto?** is new.

¿a qué hora?	¿A qué hora es la clase?
¿cómo?	¿Cómo estás? ¿Cómo es don Juan?
	¿Cómo te llamas?
¿cuál?*	¿Cuál es la capital de Colombia?
¿cuándo?	¿Cuándo es la fiesta?
¿cuánto? (*how much?*)	¿Cuánto es?
¿cuántos?, ¿cuántas?	¿Cuántos días hay en una semana?
	¿Cuántas naciones hay en Sudamérica?
¿dónde?	¿Dónde está España?
¿qué?*	¿Qué es un hospital? ¿Qué es esto?
	¿Qué hora es?
¿quién?	¿Quién es usted?

Note that in Spanish the voice falls at the end of questions that begin with interrogative words.

¿Qué es un tren?   ¿Cómo estás?

Práctica

A.   What interrogative words do you associate with the following information?

1.   ¡A las tres en punto!
2.   En el centro de la península.
3.   Soy profesor.
4.   Muy bien, gracias.
5.   ¡Es muy arrogante!
6.   Hay 5 millones (de habitantes).
7.   Dos dólares.
8.   (La capital) Es Caracas.
9.   Es un instrumento musical.
10.   Mañana, a las cinco.
11.   Son las once.
12.   Soy Roberto González.

---

*Use **¿qué?** to mean *what?* when you are asking for a definition or an explanation. Use **¿cuál?** to mean *what?* in all other circumstances. See also Grammar Section 19.

B. Now ask the questions that would result in the answers given in **Práctica A.**

C. What question is being asked by each of the following persons?

> MODELO: El hombre pregunta (*is asking*): ¿_____?
>
> La mujer (*woman*) pregunta: ¿_____?

1. ¿la película (*movie*)?

2. ¿el libro?

3. ¿el regalo (*gift*)?

4. ¿la capital de España?

5. ¿el libro?

6. ¿el fantasma?

EL MUNDO HISPÁNICO (PARTE 2)

Antes de leer: Guessing Meaning from Context

You will recognize the meaning of a number of cognates in the following reading about the geography of the Hispanic world. In addition, you should be able to guess the meaning of the underlined words from the context (the words that surround them); they are the names of geographical features. The photo captions at the bottom of the page will also be helpful. You have learned to recognize the meaning of the word **¿qué?** in questions; in this reading, **que** (with no accent mark) means *that* or *which*.

LA GEOGRAFÍA DEL MUNDO HISPÁNICO

La geografía del mundo hispánico es impresionante y muy variada. En algunas° **some**
regiones hay de todo.° Por ejemplo, en la Argentina hay <u>pampas</u> extensas en **de... a bit of everything**
el <u>sur</u>° y la <u>cordillera</u> de los Andes en el oeste. En partes de Venezuela, Co- **south**
lombia y el <u>Ecuador</u>, hay regiones tropicales de densa selva, y en el Brasil está
el famoso <u>río</u> Amazonas. En el centro de México y también en El Salvador,
Nicaragua y Colombia, hay <u>volcanes</u> activos que a veces° producen erupciones **a... sometimes**
catastróficas. El Perú y Bolivia <u>comparten</u>° el enorme <u>lago</u> Titicaca, situado en **share**
una <u>meseta</u> entre los dos países.° **naciones**

<u>Cuba</u>, Puerto Rico y la República Dominicana son tres <u>islas</u> situadas en el
<u>Mar</u> Caribe. Las <u>bellas</u>° <u>playas</u>° del Mar Caribe y de la <u>península</u> de Yucatán **beautiful / beaches**
son populares entre° los turistas de todo el mundo. **among**

España, que comparte la Península Ibérica con Portugal, también tiene° **has**
una geografía variada. En el norte están los Pirineos, la <u>cordillera</u> que separa
a España del° resto de Europa. Madrid, la capital del país, está situada en la **from the**
meseta central, y en las <u>costas</u> del sur y del este hay playas tan bonitas como
las de° Latinoamérica y el Caribe. **tan... as pretty as those of**

Es importante mencionar también la gran diversidad de las ciudades del
mundo hispánico. En la Argentina está la gran° ciudad de Buenos Aires. Muchos **great**
consideran a Buenos Aires «el París» o «la Nueva York» de Sudamérica. En
Venezuela está Caracas, y en el Perú está Lima, la capital, y Cuzco, una ciudad
antigua de origen indio.

En fin,° el mundo hispánico es diverso **En... In short**
respecto a la geografía. ¿Y Norteamérica?

La ciudad de Montevideo, Uruguay

Una meseta cerca de (*close to*) Salamanca, España

El lago Atitlán y el volcán
San Pedro, en Guatemala

Comprensión

Demonstrate your understanding of the words underlined in the
reading and other words from the reading by giving an example
of a similar geographical feature found in the United States or
close to it. Then give an example from the Spanish-speaking world.

MODELO: un río → *the Mississippi*, el río Orinoco

1. un lago
2. una cordillera
3. un río
4. una isla
5. una playa
6. una costa
7. un mar
8. un volcán
9. una península
10. una meseta

MANDATOS Y FRASES COMUNES EN LA CLASE

Here are some phrases that you will hear and use frequently during class. Don't try to memorize all of them. You will learn to recognize them gradually, with practice.

Los estudiantes

Practice saying these sentences aloud. Then try to give the Spanish as you look at the English equivalents.

Tengo una pregunta (que hacer).	*I have a question (to ask).*
¿Cómo se dice *page* en español?	*How do you say "page" in Spanish?*
Otra vez, por favor. No entiendo.	*(Say that) Again, please. I don't understand.*
¡(Espere) Un momento, por favor!	*(Wait) Just a minute, please!*
No sé (la respuesta).	*I don't know (the answer).*
(Sí,) Cómo no.	*(Yes,) Of course.*

Los profesores

After you read these Spanish sentences, cover the English equivalents and say what each expression means.

¿Hay preguntas?	*Are there any questions?*
¿Qué opina (cree) usted?	*What do you think?*
Escuche. Repita.	*Listen. Repeat.*
Lea (en voz alta).	*Read (aloud).*
Escriba/Complete (la siguiente oración).	*Write/Complete (the next sentence).*

Conteste en español.	*Answer in Spanish.*
Prepare (el ejercicio) para mañana.	*Prepare (the exercise) for tomorrow.*
Abra el libro en la página ____.	*Open your book to page ____.*
Cierre el cuaderno.	*Close your notebook.*
Saque (un papel).	*Take out (a sheet of paper).*
Levante la mano si…	*Raise your hand if . . .*
Levántese y pase a la pizarra.	*Get up and go to the blackboard.*
Pregúntele a otro estudiante ____.	*Ask another student ____.*
Déle ____ a ____.	*Give ____ to ____.*
Busque un compañero.	*Look for a partner.*
Haga la actividad con dos compañeros.	*Do the activity with two classmates.*
Formen grupos de cinco estudiantes.	*Get into groups of five students.*

Una profesora bilingüe en Austin, Texas

VOCABULARIO

Although you have used and heard many words in this preliminary chapter of *¿Qué tal?*, the following words are the ones considered to be active vocabulary. Be sure that you know all of them before beginning **Capítulo 1**.

Saludos y expresiones de cortesía

**Buenos días. Buenas tardes.
    Buenas noches.
Hola. ¿Qué tal? ¿Cómo está(s)?
Así así. (Muy) Bien.
¿Y tú? ¿Y usted?
Adiós. Hasta mañana. Hasta
    luego.
¿Cómo te llamas? ¿Cómo se llama
    usted? Me llamo... .
señor (Sr.), señora (Sra.), señorita
    (Srta.)
(Muchas) Gracias. De nada.
Por favor. Perdón. Con permiso.
Mucho gusto. Igualmente.
    Encantado/a.**

¿Cómo es usted?

soy, eres, es

Los números

**cero, uno, dos, tres, cuatro, cinco,
    seis, siete, ocho, nueve, diez,
    once, doce, trece, catorce,
    quince, dieciséis, diecisiete,
    dieciocho, diecinueve, veinte,
    treinta**

Gustos y preferencias

**¿Te gusta... ? ¿Le gusta... ? Sí, me
    gusta... . No, no me gusta... .**

Palabras interrogativas

**¿cómo?, ¿cuál?, ¿cuándo?,
    ¿cuánto?, ¿cuántos/as?,
    ¿dónde?, ¿qué?, ¿quién?**

¿Qué hora es?

**Es la... , Son las... y/menos
    cuarto, y media, en punto, de
    la mañana (tarde, noche).
¿A qué hora... ? A la(s)...**

Palabras adicionales

sí yes
no no
hay there is/are
no hay there is not/
    are not
está is (*located*)
y and
o or
a to; at (*with time*)
de of; from
en in; at
hoy today
mañana tomorrow
que that; which
también also

INTRODUCTION TO *¿QUÉ TAL?*

¿Qué tal? is divided into twenty-eight chapters. Each chapter has its own theme—university life here and abroad, travel, foods, and so on. Important vocabulary and expressions related to these situations are included in the **Vocabulario** sections, which appear at the beginning of each chapter and often in between individual grammar sections (**Estructuras**) as well. **Pronunciación** (in the first five chapters) will introduce you to more aspects of the Spanish sound system.

   Estructuras sections are introduced with brief dialogues, drawings, realia, or readings. The grammar explanations are followed by exercises and activities (**Práctica**) that will help you function in realistic situations in Spanish, and express yourself creatively by answering questions, describing pictures and cartoons, completing sentences, and so on. You have already seen materials such as these in the **Pasos preliminares**. You will often be asked to work with another student or in small groups.

Throughout the text, the word **¡OJO!** (*Watch out!*) will call your attention to areas where you should be especially careful when using Spanish. Brief sections called **¿Recuerda Ud.?** (*Do you remember?*) will help you review structures you have already studied before you learn new structures based on these points.

¿Qué tal? presents several types of dialogue that serve as models for conversation throughout the text. 1) Minidialogues introduce many of the grammar topics by showing how a structure can be used in an everyday situation. 2) Functional minidialogues (accompanied by a photo) appear in different locations, as appropriate, to demonstrate brief conversational exchanges in specific situations. 3) The **Un paso más: Situaciones** dialogues at the end of most even-numbered chapters deal with more extended interaction between people. While containing much familiar material, they also include new material that is particularly useful for handling situations you might encounter in a Spanish-speaking country or area of the United States. The **Notas comunicativas** sections that accompany the dialogues will highlight this new material for easy reference.

Throughout the text you will find real materials from Spanish-speaking countries—ads, tickets, forms, clippings from newspapers and magazines, and the like. (You have already seen authentic materials of this kind in the **Pasos preliminares**, and you may have been surprised by how much in them you could understand!)

Also, various types of boxed material occur throughout the text. The brief sections called **Notas...** include **Notas comunicativas**, which suggest hints for communicating more successfully with people in Spanish; **Notas lingüísticas**, which offer insights into interesting aspects of the Spanish language; **Notas culturales**, which provide additional cultural information; and **Notas comunicativas sobre el diálogo**, which highlight aspects of language and culture of particular interest in the **Situaciones** dialogues. **A propósito...** boxes provide additional hints for successful communication. The boxes called **Al tanto...** present vocabulary and phrases that are currently in use in everyday speech in the Hispanic world.

The **Un poco de todo** sections present exercises and activities that combine and review all grammar presented in the chapter, and important grammar from previous chapters. The **Un paso más** sections at the end of each chapter offer two kinds of material. 1) **Un paso más: Lectura cultural** (*Cultural Reading*) contains narratives and authentic reading materials as well as brief segments that invite you to "listen in" to real people telling about some of their experiences, opinions, and beliefs. 2) **Un paso más: Situaciones** (mentioned earlier) illustrates functional language and practical situations related to the chapter theme. Each chapter ends with **Vocabulario**, a list of all important words and expressions actively used in the chapter.

. . . .

UNA INVITACIÓN AL MUNDO HISPÁNICO

One aspect of understanding another people's culture is understanding what they do all the time without thinking about it. Many times a familiar action—a particular gesture, for example—has a different meaning in another culture. Sometimes you see people doing things that just seem "wrong" to you. You will find shops closed when your culture tells you they "should" be open, and open when they "should" be closed.

In learning about another culture, you also learn more about your own. A culture is a structure that provides for basic human needs: personal safety, making and maintaining friendships, dealing with strangers, and so on. Each culture meets these needs

El Perú

in its own way. Your job as a visitor to another culture is to learn to observe this structure without immediately judging it, to compare by using the terms "same/different" and not "right/wrong." As you do this, your understanding and appreciation of yourself and of other people will continually grow, and you will be increasingly able to participate actively in many new and exciting experiences.

The photographs, dialogues, **Lectura cultural** sections, and authentic materials in *¿Qué tal?* will help you develop your understanding of Hispanic cultures. In addition, **Voces del mundo hispánico** in the **Repaso** sections that occur every four chapters will focus on specific areas of the Spanish-speaking world and on ethnic groups that speak Spanish.

España

La Argentina

México

EN LA UNIVERSIDAD

VOCABULARIO: ESCENAS UNIVERSITARIAS

En la librería

En la clase

el lápiz

la profesora

la pizarra

el papel

el dinero

el libro

la silla

el diccionario

la calculadora

el estudiante

el escritorio

la estudiante

el cuaderno

la mochila

el bolígrafo

¿Dónde? La universidad

la biblioteca library
el edificio building
la oficina office
la residencia dormitory

¿Quién? Personas

el consejero the (male) advisor
la consejera the (female) advisor

el estudiante the (male) student
la estudiante the (female) student
el profesor the (male) professor
la profesora the (female) professor
el secretario the (male) secretary
la secretaria the (female) secretary

¿Qué? Cosas

la mesa table
el papel (sheet of) paper

1.

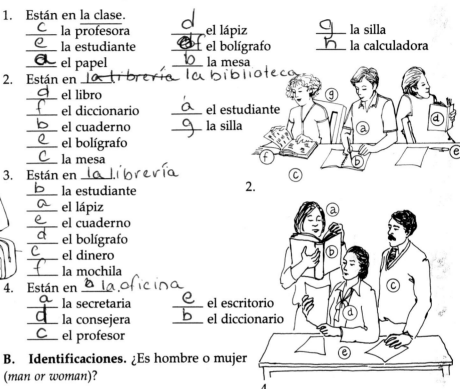

A. ¿Dónde están? (*Where are they?*) Tell where the following scenes are taking place. Then identify the people and items you see in them, using the letters in the drawings.

1. Están en la clase.
    _c_ la profesora   _d_ el lápiz   _g_ la silla
    _e_ la estudiante   _f_ el bolígrafo   _h_ la calculadora
    _a_ el papel   _b_ la mesa

2. Están en ~~la librería~~ la biblioteca
    _d_ el libro
    _f_ el diccionario   _a_ el estudiante
    _b_ el cuaderno   _g_ la silla
    _e_ el bolígrafo
    _c_ la mesa

3. Están en _la librería_
    _b_ la estudiante
    _a_ el lápiz
    _e_ el cuaderno
    _d_ el bolígrafo
    _c_ el dinero
    _f_ la mochila

4. Están en _b la oficina_
    _a_ la secretaria   _e_ el escritorio
    _d_ la consejera   _b_ el diccionario
    _c_ el profesor

2.

3.

4.

B. Identificaciones. ¿Es hombre o mujer (*man or woman*)?

MODELO: ¿La consejera? → Es mujer.

1. ¿El profesor?   2. ¿La estudiante?   3. ¿El secretario?   4. ¿El estudiante?

Al tanto...

In informal speech, Spanish speakers abbreviate some words, using only the first few syllables rather than the complete word. Can you guess what the boldfaced words refer to in these sentences?

Necesito (*I need*) un **boli**.
¿Quién es el **profe** en la clase de historia?
Necesito hablar con la **secre**.

Another useful word to know when talking about university life is **la facultad**, roughly the equivalent of English campus but implying primarily the classrooms of one's own school (Law, Liberal Arts, and so on), not the dorms and green spaces that typify many U.S. residential campuses. As you might expect, **la facultad** is also frequently abbreviated.

Nos vemos en la **facu**. (Latin America)
Nos vemos en la **fácul**. (Spain)

Study Hint: Learning New Vocabulary

Vocabulary is one of the most important tools for successful communication in a foreign language. What does it mean to "know vocabulary"? And what is the best way to learn vocabulary?

1. Memorization is only part of the learning process. Using new vocabulary to communicate requires practicing that vocabulary in context. What do you associate with this word? When might you want to use it? Create a context—a place, a situation, a person, or a group of people—for the vocabulary that you want to learn, or use a context from the text. The more associations you make with the word, the easier it will be to remember. Practice useful words and phrases over and over—thinking about their meaning—until you can produce them automatically. You may find it useful to "talk to yourself," actually saying aloud the words you want to learn.

2. Carefully study the words in vocabulary lists and drawings. If a word is a cognate or shares a root with an English word, be especially aware of differences in spelling and pronunciation. For example, note that **clase** is spelled with only one *s*; that

there is no *th* in **matemáticas**; and that **ciencias** does not begin with an *s*. Keep in mind that an "almost but not quite perfect" spelling may lead to a miscommunication: **el libro** (*the book*) versus **la libra** (*the pound*); **la mesa** (*the table*) versus **el mes** (*the month*); **el consejero** (*male advisor*) versus **la consejera** (*female advisor*). You also need to remember which words require **el** and which require **la** to express *the,* as well as which words require a written accent—**el lápiz, el bolígrafo,** for example—and where the accent occurs.

3. After studying the list or drawing, cover the English and give the English equivalent of each Spanish word.

4. When you are able to give the English without hesitation and without error, reverse the procedure; cover the Spanish and give the Spanish equivalent of each English word. Write out the Spanish words (using **el** or **la** where appropriate) once or several times and say them aloud.

5. Vocabulary lists and flash cards can be useful as a review or as a self-test.

PRONUNCIACIÓN: Diphthongs and Linking

Two successive weak vowels (**i, u**) or a combination of a strong vowel (**a, e,** or **o**) and a weak vowel (**i** or **u**) are pronounced as a single syllable, forming a *diphthong* (**un diptongo**): L**ui**s, s**ie**te, b**ue**no.

　　When words are combined to form phrases, clauses, and sentences, they are linked together in pronunciation. In spoken Spanish, it is usually impossible to hear the word boundaries—that is, where one word ends and another begins.

A.　Más práctica con las vocales.

1.	hablar	pagar	cantar	trabajar
2.	trece	clase	papel	general
3.	dinero	oficina	bolígrafo	libro
4.	hombre	profesor	dólares	los
5.	universidad	gusto	lugar	mujer

B.   Practique las siguientes palabras.

1.   residencia   secretaria   gracias   estudiante   Bolivia
2.   bien   Oviedo   siete   eficiente   diez
3.   secretario   biblioteca   adiós   diccionario   Antonio
4.   cuaderno   Eduardo   el Ecuador   Guatemala   Managua
5.   bueno   nueve   Puerto Rico   pueblo   Venezuela

C.   Practice saying each phrase as if it were one long word, pronounced without a pause.

1.   el papel y el lápiz   5.   la secretaria y el profesor
2.   la profesora y la estudiante   6.   la clase en la biblioteca
3.   el bolígrafo y el cuaderno   7.   el libro en la librería
4.   la calculadora y el dinero   8.   la oficina en el edificio

---

En *la clase*: *el* primer *día*

PROFESORA: ...y para *mañana,* es necesario traer *los libros* de texto, *papel, un cuaderno* y *un diccionario.*

ANA: Perdón, *profesora,* pero... ¿ya están *los libros* para esta *clase* en *la librería?*

PROFESORA: Creo que sí.

ANA: ¿Y *diccionarios?*

PROFESORA: ¿No hay en *la librería?*

PEDRO: Sí, hay... pero *el problema* es *el precio.*

Complete las oraciones lógicamente.
1.   Para mañana es necesario traer ____.   3.   El problema con (*with*) los diccionarios es ____.
2.   En la librería hay ____.

ESTRUCTURAS

. . . .
1 . IDENTIFYING PEOPLE AND THINGS
Singular Nouns: Gender and Articles*

To name persons, places, things, or ideas, you need to be able to use nouns. In Spanish, all *nouns* (**los sustantivos**) have either masculine or feminine *gender* (**el género**). This is a purely grammatical feature of nouns; it

---

In class: the first day INSTRUCTOR: . . . and for tomorrow, it's necessary to bring the textbooks, paper, a notebook, and a dictionary. ANA: Pardon me, ma'am [professor], but . . . are the books for this class in the bookstore already? INSTRUCTOR: I think so. ANA: And (what about) dictionaries? INSTRUCTOR: Aren't there any in the bookstore? PEDRO: Yes, there are . . . but the problem is the price.

*The grammar sections of *¿Qué tal?* are numbered consecutively throughout the book. If you need to review a particular grammar point, the index will refer you to its page number.

does not mean that Spanish speakers perceive things or ideas as having male or female attributes.

	MASCULINE NOUNS		FEMININE NOUNS	
Definite Articles	**el** hombre **el** libro	*the man* *the book*	**la** mujer **la** mesa	*the woman* *the table*
Indefinite Articles	**un** hombre **un** libro	*a (one) man* *a (one) book*	**una** mujer **una** mesa	*a (one) woman* *a (one) table*

A.   Nouns that refer to male beings and most nouns that end in **-o** are *masculine* (**masculino**) in gender: **hombre, libro.**

Nouns that refer to female beings and most nouns that end in **-a, -ción, -tad,** and **-dad** are *feminine* (**femenino**): **mujer, mesa, nación** (*nation*), **libertad** (*liberty*), **universidad.**

¡OJO!   A common exception is the word **día,** which ends in **-a** but is masculine in gender: **el día.** Many words ending in **-ma** are also masculine: **el problema, el programa, el drama,** and so on.

Nouns that have other endings and that do not refer to either males or females may be masculine or feminine. Their gender must be memorized: **el lápiz, la clase, la tarde, la noche,** and so on.

B.   In English, *the* is the *definite article* (**el artículo definido**). In Spanish, the definite article for masculine singular nouns is **el**; for feminine singular nouns it is **la.**

C.   In English, the singular *indefinite article* (**el artículo indefinido**) is *a* or *an*. In Spanish, the indefinite article, like the definite article, must agree with the gender of the noun: **un** for masculine nouns, **una** for feminine nouns. **Un** and **una** can also mean *one* as well as *a* or *an*. Context determines the meaning.

[Práctica A–B][†]

D.   Some nouns that refer to persons indicate gender according to the following patterns:

If the masculine ends in **-o**, the feminine ends in **-a**:

el niño	*the boy*	→	**la** niña	*the girl*	
el amigo	*the (male) friend*	→	**la** amiga	*the (female) friend*	

If the masculine ends in a consonant, the feminine has a final **-a**:

un profesor   *a (male) professor* →   **una** profesora   *a (female) professor*

[†]This type of reference is a feature of some grammar sections of *¿Qué tal?* This reference means that you are now prepared to do exercises A and B in the **Práctica** section.

Many other nouns that refer to people have a single form. Gender is indicated by the article: **el estudiante, la estudiante; el cliente** (*the male client*), **la cliente** (*the female client*). A few nouns that end in **-e** have a feminine form that ends in **-a: el dependiente** (*the male clerk*), **la dependienta** (*the female clerk*).

E. Since the gender of all nouns must be memorized, it is best to learn the definite article along with the noun; that is, learn **el lápiz** rather than just **lápiz**. The definite article will be given with nouns in vocabulary lists in this book.

[Práctica C–E]*

Práctica

A. Dé el artículo definido (**el, la**).

1. escritorio	5. hombre	9. mujer
2. biblioteca	6. diccionario	10. nación
3. bolígrafo	7. universidad	11. secretario
4. mochila	8. dinero	12. calculadora

Dé el artículo indefinido (**un, una**).

13. día	16. lápiz	19. papel
14. mañana	17. clase	20. condición
15. problema	18. noche	21. programa

B. Escenas de la universidad. Haga una oración con las palabras indicadas. Luego (*Then*) haga otra oración lógica, cambiando (*changing*) el lugar.

MODELO: estudiante / librería → Hay un estudiante en la librería.
Hay un estudiante en la residencia.

1. consejero / oficina	4. cuaderno / escritorio	7. palabra / papel
2. profesora / clase	5. libro / mochila	8. oficina / biblioteca
3. lápiz / mesa	6. bolígrafo / silla	9. pizarra / clase

C. ¿Quién es? Give the male or female counterpart of each of the following persons.

MODELO: Pablo Ortiz es consejero. (Paula Delibes) →
Paula Delibes es consejera también.

1. Camilo es estudiante. (Conchita)
2. Carmen Leal es profesora. (Carlos Ortega)
3. Juan Luis es dependiente. (Juanita)
4. Josefina es mi amiga. (José)

Now identify as many people as you can in your class and on your campus.

---

*You are now prepared to do activities C–E in the **Práctica** section.

D.   Definiciones. Con un compañero (una compañera), defina estas palabras en español según el modelo.

MODELO: biblioteca / edificio → —¿La biblioteca?
                                   —Es un edificio.

1.   cliente / persona   4.   dependiente / ¿ ?   6.   calculadora / ¿ ?
2.   bolígrafo / cosa   5.   hotel (*m.*) / ¿ ?   7.   ¿ ? / ¿ ?
3.   residencia / edificio

Notas comunicativas: Working with a Partner

As you have already seen, many of the exercises and activities in *¿Qué tal?* work well with a classmate. It is likely that you did the preceding partner activity with the person sitting next to you. This time, when your instructor says "Busque un compañero", find a different partner. Here are some phrases to use.

¿Tienes compañero?   *Do you have a partner?*
   —Todavía no.   *—Not yet.*
¿Deseas   ⎫   *Do you want*   ⎫
¿Te gustaría ⎬ trabajar conmigo?   *Would you like* ⎬ *to work with me?*
   —Sí, cómo no.   *—Yes, of course.*

You and your partner will probably feel comfortable talking at a distance of two or three feet from each other. If you were native speakers of Spanish, you would probably stand closer together. Spanish speakers generally maintain less distance between themselves and the person to whom they are speaking, often as little as 12 to 16 inches.

E.   Entrevista. ¿Te gusta... ? Find out whether a classmate likes the following things. Remember to use the definite article.

MODELO: comida (*food*) en la residencia →
                  —¿Te gusta **la** comida en la residencia?
                  —Sí, me gusta. (No, no me gusta.)

1.   comida en la residencia (en la cafetería, en...)
2.   música rock (clásica, ...)
3.   programa *General Hospital* (*All My Children*, . . .)
4.   drama *Dallas* (*L.A. Law*, . . .)

En la Facultad
—Por favor, ¿dónde está la librería?
—Está en el edificio Bolívar... allí mismo.°   allí... *right over there*
—Gracias, ¿eh?
—De nada.

Sevilla, España

ESTRUCTURAS

2. IDENTIFYING PEOPLE AND THINGS
Nouns and Articles: Plural Forms

What part of the newspaper do you think this clipping is from? How many nouns can you recognize in it? You have already seen some of these nouns, and many others are cognates.

CLASES-LECCIONES

SE DAN clases de Peluquería. Plazas limitadas, matrículas gratuitas 100%. Prácticas reales de 3 a 7 en la c/ Antonio Susillo, 25.

● DOY clases, de parapsicología y control mental, experiencia, alto nivel. 27 21 25

● UNIVERSITARIO, daría clases particulares EGB, BUP y F.P. 36 30 07

● ESTUDIANTE universitario, daría clases particulares EGB, horas comidas. José Luis. 21 77 25

● DARIA clases de inglés, profesor titulado con experiencia. De 2 a 5 h. 63 55 98

● ESTUDIANTE Filología, da clases de inglés, 250 ptas/h. Experiencia. Traducciones. 41 59 91

● ESTUDIANTE de COU, se ofrece para dar clases. EGB y BUP. Barato. 61 50 02

● CLASES de Astrología. 62 55 52

● SE DAN clases de sevillanas y palillos. 51 50 35 - 76 15 01

● PARA chicos/as de EGB. Clases particulares. Exito seguro. 45 33 04

● SE DAN clases de Francés, con 22 años de experiencia. 57 12 16

● PROFESOR EGB daría clases particulares. Económico. 64 11 10

● DOY CLASES a domicilio de EGB, mañanas y tardes. 41 86 90

● PROFESOR titulado da clases de guitarra clásica en mi domicilio. Sector Macarena. 38 35 25

● ESTUDIANTE de Filología da clases de inglés, 250 ptas/h. Experiencia. También traducciones. 41 59 91

● SE DAN clases particulares zona Nervión desde 225 ptas/H a 400 ptas/h. EGB y BUP. Especialidad en Ciencias. 63 14 60

● PROFESOR titulado da clases de inglés, BUP y COU. Experiencia. Economía. De 3 a 5 horas. 41 90 56

● DOY clases de inglés a nivel de EGB y 1º de BUP. Sábados por la mañana, 500 pts. Grupos reducidos. Esther. De 3 a 6 h. 62 66 25

● PROFESOR de informática daría clases particulares. 43 26 53

● ESTUDIANTE de Empresariales da clases de Matemáticas hasta 3º de BUP. Pedro. 21 75 95

● PROFESORA de EGB daría clases particulares. 35 93 11

● PROFESOR titulado nativo con experiencia. 63 55 98

	SINGULAR	PLURAL	
Nouns Ending in a Vowel	**el** libro **la** mesa **un** libro **una** mesa	**los** libros **las** mesas **unos** libros **unas** mesas	*the books* *the tables* *some books* *some tables*
Nouns Ending in a Consonant	**la** universidad **un** papel	**las** universidad**es** **unos** papel**es**	*the universities* *some papers*

A. Spanish nouns that end in a vowel form plurals by adding **-s.** Nouns that end in a consonant add **-es.** Nouns that end in the consonant **-z** change the **-z** to **-c** before adding **-es: lápiz** → **lápices.**

B. The definite and indefinite articles also have plural forms: **el** → **los, la** → **las, un** → **unos, una** → **unas. Unos** and **unas** mean *some, several,* or *a few.*

C. In Spanish, the masculine plural form of a noun is used to refer to a group that includes both males and females.

los amigos	*the friends* (both male and female)
unos extranjeros	*some foreigners* (males and females)

Práctica

A.   Dé la forma plural.

1. la mesa
2. el libro
3. el amigo

4. la oficina
5. un cuaderno
6. un lápiz

7. una extranjera
8. un bolígrafo
9. un edificio

Dé la forma singular.

10. los profesores
11. las calculadoras
12. las niñas

13. los lápices
14. unos papeles
15. unas tardes

16. unas residencias
17. unas sillas
18. unos escritorios

B.   Identificaciones. Which of the words listed to the right might be used to refer to the person(s) named on the left?

1. Ana María: consejero   mujer   dependiente   estudiante
2. Tomás: niño   consejera   profesor   secretaria
3. Margarita y Juan: extranjeros   amigos   hombres   estudiantes

C.   ¿Cómo se dice en español? Express in Spanish these phrases that describe people and buildings that you might see on your campus.

1. the (male and female) students
2. some dormitories
3. a (female) clerk in the bookstore

4. the foreigners
5. the (male) secretaries
6. some (female) professors

D.   Identifique las personas, las cosas y los lugares.

MODELO: Hay _____ en _____ . → Hay unos estudiantes en la clase.

1.   2.   3.   4.   5.

E.   ¿Qué hay en el cuarto (*room*) de Ernesto? Use el artículo indefinido.

MODELOS: Hay _____ en el cuarto de Ernesto.

En el escritorio hay _____.

¿Qué hay en su propio (*your own*) cuarto?

MODELOS: Hay _____ en mi cuarto.

En mi escritorio hay _____.

Palabras útiles: la computadora, la máquina de escribir (*typewriter*), la cama (*bed*), la lámpara

El patio de la Universidad de Salamanca, España

F. Working with your classmates, give as many nouns as you can that fit into these categories. Before you begin, you may wish to review the cognates presented in the explanations and exercises in the **Pasos preliminares.**

1. lugares de la universidad
2. cosas en una librería
3. personas en una librería
4. cosas en una clase típica
5. problemas de los estudiantes

Notas culturales: The Hispanic Educational System

The educational system in Hispanic countries differs considerably from that of the United States. The **escuela primaria**—sometimes called the **colegio**—corresponds to our elementary school and consists of from five to seven years of instruction. The **escuela secundaria** (also called **liceo, instituto,** or **colegio**) provides secondary education. Students who complete their secondary education receive the **bachillerato.** In some countries, students attend an additional year or two of **preparatorio** before entering the university.

At the university, students immediately begin specialized programs leading to a professional degree (**título**) in areas such as law, medicine, engineering, or the humanities. These university-level programs of study are established by ministries of education, and there are almost no electives. Students are required to take as many as eight different subjects in a single academic term. The lecture system is even more prevalent than it is in the United States, and university students take oral exams as well as written ones. In most countries, performance is evaluated on a scale of one to ten, with seven considered passing.

A number of universities in Spain and Latin America have arranged special courses for foreign students (**cursos para extranjeros**). Such courses are designed for students whose special interest is the study of Spanish language, literature, and culture.

UN POCO DE TODO

Asociaciones. Your instructor will name a place and a student will mention a noun at random. React by saying whether or not it is likely that the person or thing would be found in the place mentioned.

MODELOS: cafetería… exámenes… →
¡Imposible! (No. Creo que no.) No hay exámenes en la cafetería.

biblioteca… libros… →
Sí. (Creo que sí.) Hay libros en la biblioteca.

UN PASO MÁS: Lectura cultural

Antes de leer: More on Guessing Meaning from Context

As you learned in **El mundo hispánico** (**Paso dos** and **Paso tres**), you can often guess the meaning of unfamiliar words from the context (the words that surround them) and by using your knowledge about the topic in general. Making "educated guesses" about words in this way will be an important part of your reading skills in Spanish.

What is the meaning of the underlined words in these sentences?

1.   En una lista alfabetizada, la palabra **grande** aparece <u>antes de</u> la palabra **grotesco.**
2.   El edificio no es moderno; es <u>viejo.</u>

The position of a word in a sentence can also provide a clue as to its meaning. It is a safe bet that the word underlined in the following sentence, located between two phrases that contain nouns, is a verb. Can you guess its meaning?

3.   Los estudiantes <u>viven</u> en residencias.

Now try to guess the meaning of the words underlined in this sentence.

4.   Me gusta <u>estudiar</u> español, pero <u>detesto</u> la biología.

Some words are underlined in the following reading (and in the readings in subsequent chapters). Try to guess their meaning from context.

LAS UNIVERSIDADES HISPÁNICAS

En el mundo hispánico—y en los Estados Unidos—hay universidades grandes y <u>pequeñas</u>, públicas, religiosas y privadas, modernas y antiguas. Pero el concepto de «vida° universitaria» es diferente.

Por ejemplo, en los países° hispánicos la universidad no es un centro de actividad social. No hay muchas residencias estudiantiles. En general, los estudiantes <u>viven</u> en pensiones* o en casas particulares° y <u>llegan</u> a la universidad en coche o en autobús. En algunas° universidades hay un *campus* similar a los de° las universidades de los Estados Unidos. En estos casos se habla° de la «ciudad° universitaria». Otras universidades ocupan sólo un edificio grande, o posiblemente varios edificios, pero no hay zonas verdes.

life
naciones

casas... private homes
unas
los... those of / se... one speaks
city

---

*A **pensión** is a boarding house where students rent bedrooms and share a common bathroom with other boarders. Many students take their meals at the **pensión** as well.

Otra diferencia es que en la mayoría° de las universidades hispánicas no   *majority*
se da° mucha importancia a los deportes. Si los estudiantes desean practicar   *se... is given*
un deporte—el tenis, el fútbol° o el béisbol—hay clubes deportivos pero éstos°   *soccer / they (lit. these)*
no forman parte de la universidad.

Como se puede ver,° la forma y la organización de la universidad son   *Como... As you can see*
diferentes en las dos culturas. Pero los estudiantes estudian y se divierten° en   *se... have a good time*
todas partes.° A los estudiantes hispanos—así como° a los norteamericanos—   *en... everywhere / así... like*
les gusta mucho toda clase de música: la música moderna, la nacional° y la   *(music) from their own country*
importada (y hay para todos: Madonna, Durán-Durán, Ray Charles...), la
música clásica y la música con raíces° tradicionales. Otras diversiones prefe-   *roots*
ridas por los estudiantes son las discotecas y los cafés. Hay cafés ideales para
hablar con los amigos. También hay exposiciones de arte, obras de teatro y
películas° interesantes.   *movies*

Los días favoritos de muchos jóvenes° hispánicos son los fines de semana.   *young people*
¿Realmente son muy distintos los estudiantes hispanos?

Comprensión

¿Cierto o falso? Corrija (*Correct*) las oraciones falsas. Todas las oraciones se
refieren a la vida universitaria y a los estudiantes hispánicos.

1. La vida universitaria es similar a la (*that*) de los Estados Unidos.
2. Hay pocas (*few*) residencias para los estudiantes.
3. Una «ciudad universitaria» es una ciudad grande donde hay una
    universidad.
4. Siempre (*Always*) hay un equipo (*team*) de fútbol.
5. No hay interés en la música norteamericana.
6. Hay pocas diversiones culturales.

Para escribir

In this exercise, you will write a description of your own **vida universitaria.**
First, complete the following paragraph by selecting the appropriate word
or phrase from the possibilities given in parentheses, and by filling in the
blanks. You may wish to refer to the reading again to reacquaint yourself
with its vocabulary.

Mi universidad es (*grande/pequeña*). Es una universidad (*privada/pública*).
Hay _____ residencias en el *campus*. En general, los estudiantes viven (*en
residencias / en apartamentos / con su [their] familia*). Los edificios más
grandes (*biggest*) son (*la biblioteca, la administración, ...*) y (*el* student
union, *...*). (No) Se da mucha importancia (*a los deportes, a la música, al
teatro*).

Now rewrite the paragraph, using your own responses.

VOCABULARIO

Lugares

la biblioteca library
la clase class
el cuarto room
el edificio building
la librería bookstore
la oficina office
la residencia dormitory
la universidad university

Personas

el/la amigo/a friend
el/la cliente client
el/la consejero/a advisor
el/la dependiente/a clerk
el/la estudiante student

el/la extranjero/a foreigner
el hombre man
la mujer woman
el/la niño/a boy/girl
el/la profesor(a) professor
el/la secretario/a secretary

Cosas

el bolígrafo (ballpoint) pen
la calculadora calculator
el cuaderno notebook
el diccionario dictionary
el dinero money
el escritorio desk
el lápiz (*pl.* **lápices***)* pencil
el libro (de texto) (text)book
la mesa table

la mochila backpack
el papel (piece of) paper
la pizarra chalkboard
la silla chair

Otros sustantivos

el día day
la noche night
el problema problem
la tarde afternoon; evening

Palabras adicionales

luego then, next
para (intended) for; in order to
pero but

Frases útiles para la comunicación

creo que sí (no)   I think so (don't think so)

el piano

¿QUÉ ESTUDIA USTED?

VOCABULARIO: LAS MATERIAS

las ciencias sociales

la literatura

las matemáticas

el comercio

la sicología

la historia

las ciencias naturales

la computación

las lenguas

Las lenguas
- **el alemán** German
- **el chino** Chinese

el español Spanish
el francés French
el inglés English

el italiano Italian
el japonés Japanese
el ruso Russian

A.   Identifique los libros.

MODELO: *Los insectos de Norteamérica* → Es para una clase de ciencias.

1. *El cálculo I*
2. *Romeo y Julieta*
3. *México en crisis*
4. *Programación básica*
5. *Skinner y Freud*
6. *¿Qué tal?*
7. *Don Quijote*
8. *Análisis crítico de la economía mexicana*
9. *La caída* (fall) *del imperio romano*
10. *Los verbos irregulares italianos*

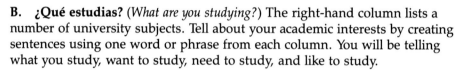

B.   **¿Qué estudias?** (*What are you studying?*) The right-hand column lists a number of university subjects. Tell about your academic interests by creating sentences using one word or phrase from each column. You will be telling what you study, want to study, need to study, and like to study.

(No) Estudio _____.
(No) Deseo estudiar _____.
(No) Necesito estudiar _____.
(No) Me gusta estudiar _____.

español, francés, inglés
arte, filosofía, literatura, música
ciencias políticas, historia, sicología, sociología
biología, física, química
comercio, matemáticas, computación

Matrícúlate
en nuestra Universidad

Elige entre las carreras de mayor demanda en el mundo profesional de hoy

BACHILLERATOS Y/O GRADOS ASOCIADOS

ADMINISTRACION COMERCIAL
  Computadoras
  Banca
  Contabilidad
CIENCIAS SECRETARIALES
  Líneas-Aéreas
ARTES LIBERALES
  Ciencias Policiales
  Justicia Penal (Criminología)

Pre-Legal
Pre-Médica
Comunicaciones
Tecnología de Ingeniería
Ciencias Naturales
EDUCACION ELEMENTAL Y/O SECUNDARIA
ENFERMERIA
CIENCIAS DE LA INFORMATICA
(Computadora)

C.   **¿Qué estudian los otros?** (*What are others studying?*) As you listened while other students described their academic interests in Exercise B, you learned a lot about what they are studying, want to study, and so on. How much do you remember? When your instructor asks about people in the class, give as much information as you can recall, following these models.

MODELOS: —¿Qué estudia Jorge?
        —Él estudia historia.*
        —¿Y Paula?
        —Ella desea estudiar computación.*
         Necesita estudiar ciencias.

---

*Note the use of the words **él** (*he*) and **ella** (*she*) for emphasis in these sentences.

When information is given about you, be sure it is correct.

> MODELO: —¿Y Ted?
> —Él estudia literatura.
> —¿Yo?[†] No estudio literatura. Estudio programación.

Al tanto...

Can you guess how **las matemáticas** is often shortened in casual speech? Right! **las mates.**

If you wanted to get together with Spanish-speaking friends after class, you would probably not go to **la cafetería**, as in the United States, but would extend the invitation in this way.

¿Nos vemos en **el bar** de la facultad?

In most Spanish-speaking cultures, **el bar** does not have the connotations it has in English. While alcoholic beverages are certainly served there, **un bar** is a place where all kinds of people can get together to chat and have a snack.

To talk about something that is "a real pain," you might say:

La historia? —¡Es **un rollo!**
¿Y la profe de historia? —¡Es **un rollo** también!

PRONUNCIACIÓN: Stress and Written Accent Marks

In the words **profes*o*r**, **l*á*piz**, **alem*á*n**, and **com*e*rcio**, the italicized vowel is stressed (given more emphasis than the others). In Spanish, *stress* (**la acentuación**) can be predicted based on the written form of the word.

- If a word ends in a *vowel*, *n*, or *s*, stress normally falls on the next-to-the-last syllable.

  ru-so   **co**-sa   **cla**-se   e-**xa**-men   o-**ri**-gen   **gra**-cias   **len**-guas

- If a word ends in any other consonant, stress normally falls on the last syllable.

  us-**ted**   es-pa-**ñol**   mu-**jer**   doc-**tor**   ac-**triz**   lu-**gar**   pa-**pel**

- Any exception to these two rules will have a *written accent mark* (**un acento ortográfico**) on the stressed vowel.

  a-le-**mán**   na-**ción**   fran-**cés**   **lá**-piz   **dó**-lar   bo-**lí**-gra-fo

Note in particular words that end in -**ía**.

  dí-a   si-co-lo-**gí**-a   lo-te-**rí**-a

[†]Note that Spanish uses **¿Yo** (*I*)**?** in this context to express English (*Who*) *Me?*

- When one-syllable words have accents, it is to distinguish them from other words that sound like them. For example: **tú** (*you*)/**tu** (*your*); **él** (*he*)/**el** (*the*); **sí** (*yes*)/**si** (*if*).
- Interrogative and exclamatory words have a written accent on the stressed vowel. For example: **¿quién?** (*who?*); **¿dónde?** (*where?*); **¡cómo no!** (*of course!*).

A. Practique las siguientes palabras.

1. chino	ruso	clase	mesa	silla	libro
italiano	consejero	literatura	interesante		
Carmen	origen	examen	lenguas	cursos	clientes
2. señor	mujer	favor	profesor	popular	
libertad	universidad	papel	español	general	sentimental
3. bolígrafo	matemáticas	romántico	librería	sicología	sociología
José	así así	Ramón	nación	perdón	
adiós	francés	inglés			
lápiz	Gómez	Pérez	Ramírez	Jiménez	

B. Indicate the stressed vowel of each word in the list that follows. Give the rule that determines the stress of each word.

1. examen	5. actitud	9. palabras	13. lugar
2. lápiz	6. acción	10. hombre	14. plástico
3. superior	7. japonés	11. peso	15. natural
4. margen	8. mujer	12. secretario	16. bolígrafos

ESTRUCTURAS

3. EXPRESSING ACTIONS
Subject Pronouns; Present Tense of *-ar* Verbs; Negation

Una fiesta para los estudiantes extranjeros

CARLOS: ¿No *desean* Uds. *bailar*?
ALFONSO: ¡Cómo no! Yo *bailo* con Mary. Ella *habla* inglés.
TERESA: Yo *hablo* francés y *bailo* con Jacques.
CARLOS: Y yo *bailo* con Gretchen.
GRETCHEN: Sólo si *pagas* las cervezas. ¡*Bailas* muy mal!

Who made—or might have made—each of the following statements?
1. Yo bailo con Jacques.
2. Yo hablo inglés.
3. Yo hablo alemán.
4. Nosotros (*We*) hablamos francés.
5. Yo bailo con Alfonso.
6. ¡Yo no bailo mal!

A party for foreign students   CARLOS: Don't you want to dance? ALFONSO: Of course! I'll dance with Mary. She speaks English. TERESA: I speak French and I'll dance with Jacques. CARLOS: And I'll dance with Gretchen. GRETCHEN: Only if you buy (pay for) the beers. You dance very badly!

In the **Pasos preliminares** and **Capítulo 1**, you used a number of Spanish verbs—and some subject pronouns—to talk about actions and states of being. In this section you will learn more words for expressing actions.

hablar (*to speak*): habl-		
Singular		*Plural*
(*I*) yo hab**lo**	(*we*) nosotros / nosotras } hab**lamos**	
(*you*) tú hab**las**	(*you*) vosotros / vosotras } habl**áis**	
(*you*) usted (Ud.)* (*he*) él } hab**la** (*she*) ella	(*you*) ustedes (Uds.)* ellos } hab**lan** (*they*) ellas	

Subject Pronouns

The preceding chart shows a number of Spanish subject pronouns you already know (**yo, tú, usted, él, ella**) with the corresponding forms of **hablar**. Here are some additional comments about these *pronouns* (**los pronombres**).

- Several subject pronouns have masculine and feminine forms: **nosotros, nosotras** (*we*); **vosotros, vosotras** (*you*); **ellos, ellas** (*they*). The masculine plural form is used to refer to a group of males as well as to a group of males and females.
- Spanish has two different words for *you* (singular): **tú** and **usted**. **Usted** is generally used to address persons with whom the speaker has a formal relationship. Use **usted** with people whom you call by their title and last name (**Sr. Gutiérrez, profesora Hernández**), or with people you don't know very well. Students generally address their instructors with **usted**. In some parts of the Spanish-speaking world, children use **usted** with their parents.

      Tú implies a familiar relationship. Use **tú** when you would address a person by his or her first name, with close friends or relatives, and with children and pets. Students usually address each other as **tú**. If you are unsure about whether to use **tú** or **usted**, it is better to use **usted**. The native speaker can always suggest that you use **tú** if that form is more appropriate.
- The plural of **usted** is **ustedes**. In Latin America, as well as in the United States, **ustedes** also serves as the plural of **tú**. In Spain, however, the

---

*Usted and **ustedes** are frequently abbreviated in writing as **Ud.** or **Vd.**, and **Uds.** or **Vds.**, respectively. *¿Qué tal?* will use **Ud.** and **Uds.**

plural of **tú** is **vosotros/vosotras**, which is used when speaking to two or more persons whom you would call **tú** individually.

Subject pronouns are not used as frequently in Spanish as they are in English. You will learn more about the uses of Spanish subject pronouns in **Capítulo 4**.

¿Qué... What the devil is that?
vos = tú en la Argentina y el Uruguay

¿Comprendes?

Infinitives and Personal Endings

A.   The *infinitive* (**el infinitivo**) of a verb indicates the action or state of being, with no reference to who or what performs the action or when it is done (present, past, or future). In English the infinitive is indicated by the word to: *to run*, *to be*. In Spanish all infinitives end in **-ar**, **-er**, or **-ir**.

B.   To *conjugate* (**conjugar**) a verb means to give the various forms of the verb with their corresponding subjects: *I speak, you speak, he (she, it) speaks*, and so on. All regular Spanish verbs are conjugated by adding *personal endings* (**las terminaciones personales**) that reflect the subject doing the action. These are added to the *stem* (**la raíz** or **el radical**): the infinitive minus the infinitive ending (**hablar** → **habl-**). These personal endings are added to the stem of all regular **-ar** verbs: **-o, -as, -a, -amos, -áis, -an.**

C.   Some important **-ar** verbs in this chapter include:

bailar	to dance	**hablar**	to speak; to talk
buscar	to look for	**necesitar**	to need
cantar	to sing	**pagar**	to pay (for)
comprar	to buy	**practicar**	to practice
desear	to want	**regresar (a)**	to return (to) (*a place*)
enseñar	to teach	**tomar**	to take; to drink
estudiar	to study	**trabajar**	to work

¡OJO!   In Spanish the meaning of the English word *for* is included in the verbs **pagar** (*to pay for*) and **buscar** (*to look for*).

D.   As in English, when two Spanish verbs are used in sequence and there is no change of subject, the second verb is usually in the infinitive form.

Necesito **trabajar**.   *I need to work.*
También desean **bailar**.   *They want to dance too.*

English Equivalents for Present Tense

In both English and Spanish, conjugated verb forms also indicate the *time* or *tense* (**el tiempo**) of the action: *I speak* (present), *I spoke* (past).

The present tense forms of Spanish verbs correspond to three English equivalents.

hablo	I speak	Simple present tense
	I am speaking	Present progressive to indicate an action in progress
	I will speak	Near future action

Note that another word or phrase may indicate future time when the present is used to describe near future actions.

Hablo con Juan **mañana**.   *I'll speak with John tomorrow.*
¿Estudiamos **por la noche**?   *Shall we study at night?*

Negation

A Spanish sentence is made negative by placing the word **no** before the conjugated verb. No equivalent for the English words *do* or *does* in negative sentences exists.

El señor **no** habla inglés.   *The man doesn't speak English.*
No, **no** necesitamos dinero.   *No, we don't need money.*

Práctica

A.   Mis compañeros y yo. Form complete sentences about yourself, your classmates, and your professor, based on the cues given. When the subject pronoun is given in parentheses, do not use it in the sentence. If any statement is not true for you or your class, make it negative or change it to make it correct.

1. (yo) necesitar / mucho dinero
2. (nosotros) cantar / en francés
3. (nosotros) desear / practicar español
4. (yo) trabajar / en la biblioteca
5. profesor(a), Ud. / enseñar / muy bien
6. (nosotros) tomar / cerveza en clase
7. (yo) tomar / ocho clases este (*this*) semestre / trimestre
8. profesor(a), Ud. / hablar / muy bien el alemán

B.   En la residencia. Complete the following paragraph with the correct form of the infinitives.

Esta noche° hay una fiesta en el cuarto de Marcos y Julio. Todos° los estudiantes (*cantar*[1]) y (*bailar*[2]), Jaime (*buscar*[3]) una Coca-Cola. Marta (*hablar*[4]) con un amigo. María José (*desear*[5]) enseñarles a todos° un baile° de Colombia. Todas las estudiantes desean (*bailar*[6]) con el estudiante mexicano—¡él (*bailar*[7]) muy bien! La fiesta es estupenda, pero todos (*necesitar*[8]) regresar a casa° o a sus° cuartos temprano.° ¡Hay clases mañana!

Esta... *Tonight* / *All*

enseñarles... *to teach everyone* / *dance*

a... *home* / *their* / *early*

Tell whether these statements are probably true (**cierto**) or false (**falso**), based on information in the paragraph.

1.   Marcos es un profesor de alemán.
2.   A Jaime le gusta la cerveza.
3.   María José es de Colombia.
4.   A los estudiantes les gustan las fiestas.

C.   Form complete sentences by using one word or phrase from each column. The words and phrases may be used more than once, in many combinations. Be sure to use the correct form of the verbs. Make any of the sentences negative, if necessary.

MODELO: Susana, tú no estudias francés.

yo	comprar	en el edificio de ciencias
(estudiante), tú	regresar	en la cafetería, en la universidad
nosotros (los miembros de esta [*this*] clase)	buscar	en una oficina, en una librería
los estudiantes de aquí (*here*)	trabajar	a casa por la noche
el extranjero	hablar	a la biblioteca a las dos
	(no) enseñar	francés, italiano, ruso
un secretario	pagar	bien el español
un profesor de español	tomar	los libros de texto con un cheque
un dependiente	estudiar	libros y cuadernos en la librería
	desear	tomar una clase de computación
	necesitar	hablar bien el español
		estudiar más (*more*)
		comprar una calculadora, una mochila
		pagar la matrícula (*tuition*) en septiembre

D.   Preguntas

1.   ¿Ud. estudia mucho o poco (*little*)? ¿Dónde estudia, en casa (*at home*), en la residencia o en la biblioteca? ¿Cuándo estudia, por la tarde o por la noche? ¿Con quién practica español? ¿Con quién desea practicar?

2.   Preguntas «indiscretas»: ¿Canta Ud. muy bien o muy mal? ¿Baila muy bien o muy mal? ¿Toma mucho o poco? ¿Regresa a casa tarde (*late*) o temprano?

3.   En una fiesta, ¿qué *no* desean Uds. hacer (*to do*)? ¿Desean estudiar? ¿cantar? ¿trabajar? ¿bailar con el profesor (la profesora)?

4. ¿Cuántas lenguas habla el profesor (la profesora)? ¿Qué lenguas enseña? ¿Trabaja en una oficina de la universidad? ¿Siempre (*Always*) está en su oficina? ¿Enseña por la mañana o por la tarde?

5. ¿Quién paga la matrícula, los estudiantes o los profesores? ¿Qué más necesitan pagar los estudiantes? ¿los libros de texto? ¿También necesitan comprar lápices? ¿diccionarios? ¿calculadoras?

E. Tell where these people are (using **está** or **están**) and what they are doing. Note that the definite article is used with titles—**el señor, la señora, la señorita, el profesor, la profesora**—when you are talking about a person.

MODELO: La señora Martínez _____. →
La señora Martínez está en la oficina.
Busca un libro, trabaja…

1. Los estudiantes extranjeros _____.

2. La cliente _____.

3. La profesora Gil _____.

4. Los amigos _____.

5. El Sr. Miranda _____.

6. Los estudiantes _____.

Notas comunicativas: Expressing Preferences

In the **Pasos preliminares** you learned to combine the phrases **me gusta** and **te gusta** with infinitives to express what you like—or don't like—to do. In this chapter, you have seen that verbs like **desear** and **necesitar** can also be followed by infinitives. Here are two other verbs to express preferences that are followed by infinitives. Learn to use their **yo** forms now.

(no) quiero + *infinitive*	I (don't) want to . . .
prefiero + *infinitive*	I prefer to . . .
Quiero comprar una calculadora.	I want to buy a calculator.
Prefiero estudiar más tarde.	I prefer to study later.

F.   Gustos y preferencias. Complete the following sentences by using infinitives you have learned plus any other necessary words. You may also wish to look back at the infinitives you used in the exercise on pages 18–19 in the **Pasos preliminares** before you begin this exercise.

1.   Siempre prefiero _____ temprano. No me gusta _____ tarde.
2.   No quiero _____ hoy. Prefiero _____.
3.   Me gusta _____ los fines de semana (*weekends*), pero este (*this*) fin de semana necesito _____.
4.   Quiero tomar _____ (materia), pero necesito tomar _____.
5.   No quiero tomar más clases de _____ (materia).

Hablando° de clases   *Speaking*
—¿Cuántos estudiantes hay en tu° clase de física?   *your*
—Creo que hay quince o dieciséis.
—Y ¿quién es el profesor?
—La doctora Ortega.

Bogotá, Colombia

ESTRUCTURAS

. . . .

4. GETTING INFORMATION
Asking Yes/No Questions

En una universidad: La oficina de matrícula
ESTUDIANTE: Necesito una clase más. ¿Hay sitio en la clase de sicología 2?
CONSEJERO: Imposible, señorita. No hay.
ESTUDIANTE: ¿Hay un curso de historia o de matemáticas?
CONSEJERO: Sólo por la noche. ¿Desea Ud. tomar una clase por la noche?
ESTUDIANTE: Trabajo por la noche. Necesito una clase por la mañana.
CONSEJERO: Pues... ¿qué tal el francés 10? Hay una clase a las diez de la mañana.
ESTUDIANTE: ¿El francés 10? Perfecto. Pero, ¿no necesito tomar primero el francés 1?

At a university registration office   STUDENT: I need one more class. Is there space in Psychology 2? COUNSELOR: Impossible, Miss. There's no room. STUDENT: Is there a history or math class? COUNSELOR: Only at night. Do you want to take a night course? STUDENT: I work at night. I need a class in the morning. COUNSELOR: Well . . . what about French 10? There's a class at ten in the morning. STUDENT: French 10? Perfect. But don't I need to take French 1 first?

1. ¿Necesita la señorita dos clases más?
2. ¿Hay sitio en sicología 2?
3. ¿Hay cursos de historia o de matemáticas por la mañana?
4. ¿A qué hora es la clase de francés 10?
5. ¿Cuál es el problema con la clase de francés 10?

There are two kinds of questions: information questions and yes/no questions. Questions that ask for new information or facts that the speaker does not know often begin with *interrogative words* such as *who, what,* etc. (You learned many interrogative words in the **Pasos preliminares**.) Yes/no questions are those that permit a simple *yes* or *no* answer.

Do you speak French? → No, I don't (speak French).

Rising Intonation

A common way to form yes/no questions in Spanish is simply to make your voice rise at the end of the question.

STATEMENT

Ud. trabaja aquí todos los días.   El niño regresa a casa hoy.
You work here every day.   *The boy is returning home today.*

QUESTION

¿Ud. trabaja aquí todos los días?   ¿El niño regresa a casa hoy?
Do you work here every day?   *Is the boy returning home today?*

There is no Spanish equivalent to English *do* or *does* in questions. Note also the use of an inverted question mark (¿) at the beginning of a question.

Inversion

Another way to form yes/no questions is to invert the order of the subject and verb, in addition to making your voice rise at the end of the question.

STATEMENT: **Ud.** trabaja aquí todos los días.   **El niño** regresa a casa hoy.

QUESTION: ¿Trabaja **Ud.** aquí todos los días?   ¿Regresa **el niño** a casa hoy?

Práctica

A.   En la librería (Parte 1). With a classmate, look carefully at the following drawing. Then, as your classmate looks away from the drawing, ask him or her questions about it based on the following statements. Your classmate should try to answer without looking at the drawing.

MODELO: El dependiente toma café. →
          —¿El dependiente toma café? (¿Toma café el dependiente?)
          —No. Ramón toma café.

1. Miguel habla con el dependiente.
2. Irma desea pagar la mochila.
3. Hildebrando busca un libro de historia.
4. Irma también busca un libro de historia.
5. Alicia estudia historia.
6. Ramón es una persona impaciente.
7. Hay tres dependientes en la librería hoy.

B.   En la librería (Parte 2). Ask the questions that lead to the following answers you have just overheard. Follow the model.

MODELO: Sí, estudio con él (*him*). → ¿Estudia Ud. con Guillermo?
                                       ¿Estudias (tú) con Guillermo?

1. No, no trabajo aquí todos los días.
2. Sí, ella habla muy bien.
3. No, no regreso a casa hoy.
4. Sí, estudiamos mucho para esa (*that*) clase.
5. Sí, él busca un diccionario español-inglés.
6. Pues… no, no necesitamos lápiz.

C.   Entrevista. Find out some information about a classmate, using the following cues as a guide.

1. estudiar en la biblioteca con frecuencia
2. practicar español con un amigo
3. tomar café por la mañana
4. bailar mucho en las fiestas
5. regresar a clase mañana
6. regresar a casa muy tarde a veces (*sometimes*)

Now find out the same information from your Spanish instructor. Begin each question with "**Profesor(a)** _____, ..." Remember to use **usted**.

D.   Entrevista. Without taking notes, interview a classmate by asking the following questions or any others that occur to you. Then present as much of the information as you can to the class.

MODELO: David toma cuatro clases. Prefiere la clase de literatura. Trabaja en McDonald's.

1.   ¿Cuántas clases tomas este (*this*) semestre/trimestre?
2.   ¿Estudias matemáticas? ¿literatura? ¿sicología? ¿comercio?
3.   ¿Qué clase te gusta más? ¿Qué clase te gusta menos (*least*)?
4.   ¿Quieres estudiar ciencias naturales? ¿computación? ¿japonés? ¿ruso? ¿chino?
5.   ¿Practicas español fuera de (*outside of*) la clase? ¿con quién?
6.   ¿Trabajas? ¿Dónde? ¿Te gusta el trabajo (*job*)?

UN POCO DE TODO

A.   Conversaciones en la cafetería. Form complete questions based on the words given, in the order given. Conjugate the verbs and add other words if necessary. Do not use the subject pronouns in parentheses.

1.   ¿buscar (tú) / diccionario?
2.   ¿no trabajar / Paco / aquí / en / cafetería?
3.   ¿necesitar / Uds. / calculadora / para / clase de cálculo?
4.   ¿qué tal si / tomar (nosotros) / Coca-Cola?
5.   ¿no desear (tú) / estudiar / minutos / más?

Now answer the questions in the negative, incorporating the following information into your responses.

1.   mi mochila   4.   no quiero / prefiero
2.   biblioteca   5.   quiero / regresar a casa
3.   matemáticas

B.   Describe the following persons by telling what they do and, if possible, where they do it.

1.   un secretario   3.   un estudiante   5.   Julio Iglesias
2.   una profesora   4.   una dependienta   6.   Madonna

UN PASO MÁS: Situaciones

En la biblioteca: Estudiando° con un amigo   *Studying*
—Oye,° ¿cuándo es tu clase de cálculo?   *Hey*
—A las once. ¿Qué hora es?
—Son las diez y veinte.
—Hay tiempo° todavía.° ¿No quieres estudiar diez minutos más?   *time / still*
—Está bien. Entonces,° ¿qué tal si tomamos un café antes de° tu clase?   *Then / antes... before*
—¡De acuerdo!

Notas comunicativas sobre el diálogo

To get a friend's attention: **Oye**...   To express agreement or
To suggest activities to a friend: to accept an invitation:

    ¿Quieres + *infinitive*   **Está bien.**
    ¿No quieres + *infinitive*   **De acuerdo.**
    ¿Qué tal si + **nosotros** *verb form*

Conversación

Practice the dialogue with a classmate. When you are familiar with it, vary some of the details:

- Mention a class you are taking this term.
- Give the time the class meets.
- Invite your friend to have a soft drink (**un refresco**) or an ice cream (**un helado**).

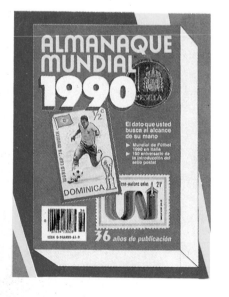

VOCABULARIO

Verbos

bailar to dance
buscar to look for
cantar to sing
comprar to buy
desear to want
enseñar to teach
estudiar to study
hablar to speak; to talk
necesitar to need
pagar to pay (for)
practicar to practice
regresar to return (*to a place*)
  regresar a casa to go home
tomar to take; to drink
trabajar to work

Materias y cursos

las ciencias (naturales,
  sociales) (natural, social)
  sciences
el comercio business
la computación computer science
la historia history
la literatura literature
las matemáticas mathematics
la sicología psychology

Lenguas

el alemán, el chino, el español, el
  francés, el inglés, el italiano,
  el japonés, el ruso

Cosas

la cerveza beer
la fiesta party
la matrícula tuition

¿Cuándo?

con frecuencia frequently
el fin de semana (on) the
  weekend
por la mañana (tarde, noche) in
  the morning (afternoon,
  evening)
siempre always
tarde late
  más tarde later
temprano early
todos los días every day

Palabras adicionales

aquí here
bien well
con with
en casa at home
mal badly
más more
mucho much, a lot
muy very
poco little; a little bit
pues... well . . .
si if
sólo only

Frases útiles para la comunicación

¡cómo no!   of course!
(no) quiero + *infinitive*   I want (don't want) to (*do
                                                           something*)

prefiero + *infinitive*   I prefer to (*do something*)

See also the words and phrases in **Notas comunicativas sobre el diálogo**.

¿CÓMO ERES?

VOCABULARIO: ADJETIVOS

guapo handsome, good-looking
bonito pretty
feo ugly

corto short (*in length*)
largo long

bueno good
malo bad

listo smart, clever
tonto silly, foolish

casado married
soltero single

simpático nice, likeable
antipático unpleasant

rico rich
pobre poor

delgado thin, slender
gordo fat

To describe a masculine singular noun, use **alto**, **bajo**, etc.; use **alt*a***, **baj*a***, etc., for feminine singular nouns.

A.   Preguntas. Conteste según los dibujos.

1.   Einstein es listo.
¿Y el chimpancé?

2.   Roberto es trabajador.
¿Y José?

3.   Pepe es bajo.
¿Y Pablo?

4.   Ramón Ramírez es casado.
También es viejo.
¿Y Paco Pereda?

5.   El ángel es bueno y
simpático. También es
guapo. ¿Y el demonio?

6.   El libro es viejo
y corto.
¿Y el lápiz?

7.   Elena es gorda y morena.
¿Y Marta? (¡OJO!)

8.   La familia Pérez es
grande y rica. ¿Y la
familia Gómez? (¡OJO!)

B.   ¿Cómo son? Your elderly uncle Guillermo is not familiar with these
famous personalities. Describe them to him, using as many adjectives as
possible. Don't forget to use cognate adjectives you have seen in the **Pasos
preliminares** and in previous chapters.

1. Michael J. Fox   2. J. R. Ewing   3. la princesa Diana   4. Martina
Navratilova

PRONUNCIACIÓN: *d*

Some sounds, such as English [b], are called *stops* because, as you pronounce them, you briefly stop the flow of air and then release it. Other
sounds, such as English [f] and [v], pronounced by pushing air out with a
little friction, are called *fricatives*.

Spanish **d** has two basic sounds. At the beginning of a phrase or sentence or after **n** or **l**, it is pronounced as a stop [d] (similar to English *d* in
dog). Like the Spanish [t], it is produced by putting the tongue against the
back of the upper teeth. In all other cases, it is pronounced as a fricative [d̶],
that is, like the *th* sound in English *they* and *another*.

A.   Practique las siguientes palabras y frases.

1. [d]   diez   dos   docena   doctor   ¿dónde?   el doctor
         el dinero   grande
2. [d̶]   mucho dinero adiós   usted   casado   ¿adónde?
         la doctora   gordo   todo

B.   Pronuncie.

¿Dónde está el dinero?   Dos y diez son doce.   Delia es delgada,
David Dávila es doctor.   ¿Qué estudia Ud.?   ¿verdad (*right*)?

Study Hint: Learning Grammar

Learning a language is similar to learning any other
skill; knowing *about* it is only part of what is involved.
Consider how you would acquire another skill—
swimming, for example. If you read all the available
books on swimming, you would probably become an
expert in talking *about* swimming and you would know
what you *should* do in a pool. Until you actually got
into a pool and practiced swimming, however, you
would probably not swim very well. In much the same
way, if you memorize all the grammar rules but spend
little time *practicing* them, you will not be able to communicate very well in Spanish.

As you study each grammar point in *¿Qué tal?*,
you will learn how the structure works; then you need
to put your knowledge into practice. First, read the
grammar discussion, study and analyze the examples,
and pay special attention to any **¡OJO!** sections, which
will call your attention to problem areas. Then begin
the **Práctica** section. Do the exercises. When you are
certain that your answers are correct, practice doing

each exercise several times until the answers sound
and "feel" right to you. As you do each item, think
about what you are conveying and the context in which
you could use each sentence, as well as about spelling
and pronunciation. Then you will be well prepared to
conclude the **Práctica** section with the more open-ended
situations in which, in general, there are no "right" or
"wrong" answers.

Always remember that language learning is
cumulative. This means that you are not finished with
a grammar point when you go on to the next chapter.
Even though you are now studying the material in
Capítulo 3, you must still remember how to conjugate
-ar verbs and how to form yes/no questions, because
Capítulo 3 builds on what you have learned in the
previous chapters—just as all subsequent chapters will
build on the material leading up to them. A few minutes spent each day reviewing "old" topics will increase
your confidence—and success—in communicating in
Spanish.

¿Recuerda Ud.?

Before beginning Grammar Section 5, review the forms and uses of **ser** that you have already learned by answering these questions.

1. ¿Eres estudiante o profesor(a)?
2. ¿De dónde eres?
3. ¿Eres una persona sentimental?
4. ¿Cómo es el profesor (la profesora) de español? ¿Es inteligente? ¿paciente? ¿elegante?
5. ¿Qué hora es? ¿A qué hora es la clase de español?
6. ¿Qué es un hospital? ¿Es una persona? ¿una cosa? ¿un edificio?

ESTRUCTURAS

5. EXPRESSING *to be*
Present Tense of *ser*; Summary of Uses

En la oficina de la profesora Castro

PROFESORA CASTRO: *¿Es* éste su examen, Sr. Bermúdez?
RAÚL BERMÚDEZ: *Es* posible. ¿*Es* el examen de Raúl Bermúdez o de Jaime Bermúdez? *Somos* hermanos.
PROFESORA CASTRO: *Es* de Jaime Bermúdez, y *es* un suspenso.
RAÚL BERMÚDEZ: Pues el suspenso *es* de Jaime. ¡Yo *soy* Raúl!

1. ¿Con quién habla Raúl Bermúdez?
2. ¿Raúl y Jaime son hermanos?
3. ¿Es Jaime profesor o estudiante?
4. ¿Es el examen de Raúl o de Jaime?

There are two Spanish verbs that mean *to be*: **ser** and **estar**. They are not interchangeable; the meaning that the speaker wishes to convey determines their use. In this chapter, you will review the uses of **ser** you already know and learn some new ones. Remember to use **está(n)** to express location. You will learn its complete conjugation and uses later.

In Professor Castro's office   PROFESSOR: Is this your exam, Mr. Bermúdez? RAÚL: It's possible. Is it Raúl Bermúdez's exam or Jaime Bermúdez's? We're brothers. PROFESSOR: It's Jaime Bermúdez's, and it's an F. RAÚL: Well, the F is Jaime's. I'm Raúl!

ser (*to be*)			
yo	**soy**	nosotros/as	**somos**
tú	**eres**	vosotros/as	**sois**
usted él ella	**es**	ustedes ellos ellas	**son**

Here are some basic language functions of **ser**. You have used all of them already in this and previous chapters.

- To *identify* people and things

    Yo soy **estudiante.**   **Alicia y yo** somos **amigas.**
    La doctora Ramos es   **Esto** es **un libro.**
    profesora.

- To *describe* people and things*

    Soy **sentimental.**   *I'm sentimental (a sentimental*
                                              person).
    El coche es **muy viejo.**   *The car is very old.*

- With **de**, to express *origin*

    Somos **de los Estados Unidos,**   *We're from the United States, but*
      pero nuestros padres son **de**   *our parents are from Argentina.*
      la Argentina. ¿De dónde es   *Where are you from?*
      Ud.?

                                              [Práctica A–B]

- With **para**, to tell *for whom or what something is intended*

    ¿Romeo y Julieta? Es **para la**   Romeo and Juliet? *It's for*
      clase de inglés.   *English class.*

    ¿Para quién son todos los rega-   *Who are all the presents for?*
      los? —(Son) **Para mi**   *—(They're) For my sister.*
      hermana.

                                              [Práctica C]

- To express *generalizations* (**es**)

    Es **importante** estudiar, pero   *It's important to study, but it's not*
      no es **necesario** estudiar   *necessary to study every day.*
      todos los días.

                                              [Práctica D]

---

*You will practice this language function of **ser** in Grammar Section 6 in this chapter and in subsequent chapters.

Here is an additional use of **ser**.

- In Spanish, **ser** is used with the preposition **de** to express *possession*

Es (el dinero) **de Carla**.	*It's Carla's (money).*
Son (las fotos) **de Jorge**.	*They're Jorge's (photos).*
¿**De quién** es el examen?	*Whose exam is it?*

Note that there is no *'s* in Spanish.

¡OJO!   The masculine singular article **el** contracts with the preposition **de** to form **del**. No other articles contract with **de**.

Es la casa **del** joven.	*It's the young man's house.*
Es la casa **de los** jóvenes.	*It's the young people's house.*

[Práctica E]

Práctica

A.   ¿De dónde son, según los nombres (*first names*) y apellidos (*last names*)?

Francia	Italia	Inglaterra (*England*)
México	los Estados Unidos	Alemania (*Germany*)

1.	John Doe	3.	Graziana Lazzarino	5.	Claudette Moreau
2.	Karl Lotze	4.	María Gómez	6.	Timothy Windsor

¿De dónde es Ud.? ¿de los Estados Unidos? ¿De qué país (*country*) son sus (*your*) padres? ¿Son norteamericanos? (Mis padres...) ¿sus abuelos (*grandparents*)? (Mis abuelos...)

B.   ¿Quiénes son, de dónde son y dónde trabajan ahora?

MODELO: Teresa: actriz / de Madrid / en Cleveland →
Teresa es actriz. Es de Madrid. Ahora trabaja en Cleveland.

1. Carlos Miguel: profesor / de Cuba / en Milwaukee
2. Maripili: extranjera / de Burgos / en Miami
3. Mariela: dependienta / de Buenos Aires / en Nueva York
4. Juan: dentista* / de Lima / en Los Ángeles

Now tell about a friend of yours, following the same pattern.

---

*A number of professions end in **-ista** in both masculine and feminine forms. The article indicates gender: **el/la dentista, el/la artista**, and so on.

Notas comunicativas: Explaining Your Reasons

In conversation, it is often necessary to explain a decision, tell why someone did something, and so on. Here are some simple words and phrases that speakers use to offer explanations.

porque because   **para** in order to   **por eso** that's why; for that reason

¿Por qué necesitamos un televisor
nuevo? ¡No comprendo!
—Pues... **para** mirar el partido de
fútbol... . ¡Es el campeonato!
—Ah, **por eso**.

*Why do we need a new TV set? I don't
understand!—Well . . . (in order) to
watch the soccer game . . . . It's the
championship!—Ah, that's why.*

¿Por qué trabajas tanto?
—¡**Porque** necesitamos el dinero!

*Why do you work so much?
—Because we need the money!*

Note the differences between **porque** (one word, no accent) and the interrogative **¿por qué?**

C. **¿Para quién son los regalos?** The first column lists gifts, the second friends and family members. Decide who receives which gift, then use the information about each person to explain your reasons.

MODELO: _____ es para _____. → El dinero es para mi hermana Anita.
Ella es estudiante. Por eso necesita dinero.

el dinero (para comprar una
  mochila, para pagar la matrícula, para ¿ ?)
la camioneta (*station wagon*)
el coche, un Mercedes
la cerveza
la silla mecedora (*rocking chair*)
los discos (*records*) de U2 y
  Bruce Springsteen
el televisor
los cien mil (*100,000*) dólares
¿ ?

Ernesto y Lupita: pasan todos
  los días en casa
Juan: le gusta mirar los parti-
  dos de fútbol
mi hermano Raúl y su esposa
  (*his wife*): ¡tienen (*they have*)
  seis niños!
mi hermana Anita: estudia en
  la universidad
Marcos: le gusta mucho la
  música moderna
Juana: es médica (*a doctor*)
mis padres: desean comprar
  una casa en Phoenix

D. **¿Qué crees?** (*What do you think?*) Exprese opiniones originales, afirmati-vas o negativas, con estas (*these*) palabras.

(No) {
Es importante
Es muy práctico
Es necesario
Es tonto
Es fascinante
Es posible
}

mirar la televisión todos los días
hablar español en la clase
comer (*to eat*) tres veces (*times*) al día
llegar (*to arrive*) a clase puntualmente
tomar cerveza en clase
hablar con los animales/las plantas
tomar mucho café y fumar (*to smoke*) cigarrillos
trabajar dieciocho horas al día

E.   ¡Seamos (*Let's be*) **lógicos!** ¿De quién son estas cosas? Con un compañero, haga y conteste preguntas según los modelos.

MODELOS: —¿De quién es el perro (*dog*)?
—Es de…

—¿De quién son las mochilas?
—Son de…

Personas: las estudiantes, la actriz, el niño, la familia con diez niños, el estudiante extranjero, los señores Schmidt

1. la casa en Beverly Hills
2. la casa en Viena
3. la camioneta

4. el gato (*cat*)
5. las fotos de la Argentina
6. las mochilas con todos los libros

VOCABULARIO

Los números 31–100

En casa, por la noche

treinta y uno, treinta y dos...

ochenta y cuatro, ochenta y cinco...

Continúe la secuencia:

treinta y uno, treinta y dos…
ochenta y cuatro, ochenta y cinco…

31	treinta y uno	36	treinta y seis	40	cuarenta
32	treinta y dos	37	treinta y siete	50	cincuenta
33	treinta y tres	38	treinta y ocho	60	sesenta
34	treinta y cuatro	39	treinta y nueve	70	setenta
35	treinta y cinco			80	ochenta
				90	noventa
				100	cien, ciento

Beginning with 31, Spanish numbers are *not* written in a combined form; **treinta y uno,*** **cuarenta y dos, sesenta y tres,** and so on, must be three separate words. **Cien** is used before nouns and in counting.

cien casas	*a (one) hundred houses*
noventa y ocho, noventa y nueve, **cien**	*ninety-eight, ninety-nine, one hundred*

---

*Remember that when **uno** is part of a compound number (**treinta y uno, cuarenta y uno,** and so on), it becomes **un** before a masculine noun and **una** before a feminine noun: **cincuenta y *una* mesas; setenta y *un* coches.**

A.   Más problemas de matemáticas

LA GUÍA TELEFÓNICA

LAZARO AGUIRRE, A. –Schez Pacheco, 17	415 0046
LAZCANO DEL MORAL, A. –E. Larreta, 14	215 8194
LAZCANO DEL MORAL, A. –Ibiza, 8	274 6868
	222 3894
LEAL ANTON, J. –Pozo, 8	
LIEBANA RODRIGUEZ, A.	463 2593
Guadarrama, 10	232 2027
LOPEZ BARTOLOME, J. –Palma, 69	407 5086
LOPEZ CABRA, J. –E. Solana, 118	776 4602
LOPEZ CABRA, J. –L. Van, 5	409 2552
LOPEZ GONZALEZ, J. A. –Ibiza, 27	478 8494
LOPEZ GUTIERREZ, G. –S. Cameros, 7	227 3570
LOPEZ LOPEZ, J. –Alamedilla, 21	218 6630
LOPEZ MARIN, V. –Illescas, 53	463 6873
LOPEZ MARIN, V. –N. Rey, 7	717 2823
LOPEZ MARIN, V. –Valmojado, 289	796 0035
LOPEZ NUÑEZ, J. –Pl. Pinazo, s/n	796 5387
LOPEZ NUÑEZ, J. –Rocafort, Bl. 321	429 3278
LOPEZ RODRIGUEZ, C. –Pl. Jesus, 7	239 4323
LOPEZ RODRIGUEZ, J. –Pl. Angel, 15	
LOPEZ RODRIGUEZ, M. E.	233 4239
B. Murillo, 104	462 5392
LOPEZ TRAPERO, J. –Cam. Ingenieros, 1	433 4646
LOPEZ VAZQUEZ, J. –A. Torrejón, 17	231 2131
LOPEZ VEGA, J. –M. Santa Ana, 5	252 2758
LORENTE VILLARREAL, G. –Gandia, 7	479 6282
LORENZO MARTINEZ, A. –Moscareta, 5	778 2800
LORENZO MARTINEZ, A. –P. Laborde, 21	
LORENZO MARTINEZ, A.	477 1040
Av. S. Diego, 116	276 9373
LOSADA MIRON, M. –Padilla, 31	431 7461
LOSADA MIRON, M. –Padilla, 31	
LOZANO GUILLEN, E.	250 3884
Juan H. Mendoza, 5	466 3205
LOZANO PIERA, F. J. –Pinguino, 8	273 3735
LUDEÑA FLORES, G. –Lope Rueda, 56	
LUENGO CHAMORRO, J.	471 4906
Gral Ricardos, 99	478 5253
LUQUE CASTILLO, J. –Pto Ariaban, 121	477 6644
LUQUE CASTILLO, L. –Cardeñosa, 15	
LLANES FERNANDEZ CAPALLEJA, R.	234 7204
Galilea, 93	433 6711
LLOMBART GALIANO, J. –Cavanilles, 37	
LLOVEZ FERNANDEZ, R.	461 7935
Av. N. Sra Fátima, 17	

1. 30 + 50 = ?
2. 45 + 45 = ?
3. 32 + 58 = ?

4. 77 + 23 = ?
5. 100 − 40 = ?
6. 99 − 29 = ?

7. 84 − 34 = ?
8. 76 − 36 = ?
9. 88 − 28 = ?

B.   Telephone numbers in many countries are written and said slightly differently than in the United States. Here are a number of listings from Hispanic telephone books. Following the model, give the phone numbers.

MODELO: 9-72-64-87 → nueve–setenta y dos–sesenta y cuatro–ochenta y siete.

Fierro Aguilar	Amalia	Avenida Juárez 86	7-65-03-91
Fierro Navarro	Teresa	Calle Misterios 45	5-86-58-16
Fierro Reyes	Gilberto	Avenida Miraflores 3	5-61-12-78
Figueroa López	Alberto	Calle Zaragoza 33	5-32-97-77
Figueroa Pérez	Julio	Avenida Iglesias 15	5-74-55-34
Gómez Pérez	Ana María	Calle Madero 7	7-94-43-88
Gómez Valencia	Javier	Avenida Córdoba 22	3-99-45-52
Guzmán Ávila	José Luis	Avenida Montevideo 4	6-57-29-40
Guzmán Martínez	Josefina	Avenida Independencia 25	2-77-22-70

Now give your phone number according to the model.

MODELO: —¿Cuál es tu teléfono?
—Es el siete–veinticuatro–ochenta y tres–sesenta y uno (724-8361).

Notas culturales: Hispanic Last Names

As you probably noted in the preceding excerpts from Hispanic telephone books, two last names (**apellidos**) were given for each entry: **Amalia** *Fierro Aguilar*. The first last name (**Fierro**) is that of the person's father; the second (**Aguilar**) is her mother's. This system for assigning last names is characteristic of all parts of the Spanish-speaking world, although it is not widely used by Hispanics living in the United States. You will learn more about this system in the **Lectura cultural** in this chapter.

Hablando° de fotos   *Talking*
—¿Quién es el joven alto y moreno en esta foto?
—Es mi hermano Julio.
—¡Qué guapo es!
—¿Te gustaría conocerlo?*
—¡Sí! ¡Claro que sí!°   *Of course!*

Bogotá, Colombia

---

*This sentence means: *Would you like to meet him?* To ask about a woman, change **-lo** to **-la**: ¿Te gustaría conocer*la*?

ESTRUCTURAS

6 . DESCRIBING
Adjectives: Gender, Number, and Position

Adjectives (**Los adjetivos**) are words used to talk about nouns or pronouns. Adjectives may describe (*large desk*, *tall woman*) or tell how many there are (*a few desks*, *several women*).

You have been using adjectives to describe people since the **Pasos preliminares**. In this section, you will learn more about describing the people and things around you.

Un poema sencillo

Amigo	Amiga
Fiel	Fiel
Amable	Amable
Simpático	Simpática
¡Bienvenido!	¡Bienvenida!*

Puerto Rico

According to their form, which of the adjectives below can be used to describe each person? Which can refer to you?

Marta: fiel   bienvenido   simpática   **Mario:** amable   simpático   bienvenida

Adjectives with *ser*

In Spanish, forms of **ser** are used with adjectives that describe basic, inherent qualities or characteristics of the nouns or pronouns they modify.

Antonio **es interesante**.   *Antonio is interesting. (He's an interesting person.)*

Tú **eres amable**.   *You're nice. (You're a nice person.)*
El disco **es barato**.   *The record is inexpensive.*

Forms of Adjectives

Spanish adjectives agree in gender and number with the noun or pronoun they modify. Each adjective has more than one form.

- Adjectives that end in **-e** (**inteligente**) or in most consonants (**fiel**) have only two forms, a singular form and a plural form. The plural of adjectives is formed in the same way as that of nouns.

*****A Simple Poem** Friend Loyal Kind Nice Welcome!

	MASCULINE	FEMININE
Singular	amigo inteligente amigo fiel	amiga inteligente amiga fiel
Plural	amigos inteligentes amigos fieles	amigas inteligentes amigas fieles

	MASCULINE	FEMININE
Singular	amigo alto	amiga alta
Plural	amigos altos	amigas altas

	MASCULINE	FEMININE
Singular	el doctor mexicano español alemán inglés	la doctora mexicana española alemana inglesa
Plural	los doctores mexicanos españoles alemanes ingleses	las doctoras mexicanas españolas alemanas inglesas

The names of many languages—which are masculine in gender—are the same as the masculine singular form of the corresponding adjective of nationality: **el español**, **el inglés**, **el alemán**, and so on. Note that in Spanish the names of languages and adjectives of nationality are not capitalized, but the names of countries are: **español**, but **España**.

[Práctica D]

Forms of *this/these*

The demonstrative adjective *this/these* has four forms in Spanish.[†]

este hombre	*this man*	esta mujer	*this woman*
estos hombres	*these men*	estas mujeres	*these women*

---

*Adjectives that end in **-dor**, **-ón**, **-án**, and **-ín** also have four forms: **trabajador**, **trabajadora**, **trabajadores**, **trabajadoras**.

[†]You will learn all the forms of the Spanish demonstrative adjectives (*this, that, these, those*) in Grammar Section 8.

You have already used the neuter demonstrative **esto**. It refers to something that is as yet unidentified: **¿Qué es esto?**

[Práctica E]

Placement of Adjectives

A.   Adjectives that describe qualities generally follow the noun they modify. Adjectives of quantity and demonstratives precede the noun.

Hay **cinco** sillas y **un** escritorio.	*There are five chairs and one desk.*
Y **este** edificio, ¿qué es?	*And this building, what is it?*
Busco **otro** coche.*	*I'm looking for another car.*

B.   The interrogative adjectives **¿cuánto/a?** and **¿cuántos/as?** also precede the noun: **¿cuánto dinero?**, **¿cuántas hermanas?**

C.   **Bueno**, **malo**, and **grande** may precede the nouns they modify. When **bueno** and **malo** precede a masculine singular noun, they shorten to **buen** and **mal**, respectively.

un perro **bueno** / un **buen** perro	*a good dog*
una niña **buena** / una **buena** niña	*a good girl*

D.   When **grande** appears after a noun, it means *large* or *big*. When it precedes a singular noun—masculine or feminine—it is shortened to **gran** and means *great* or *impressive*.

una ciudad **grande** / una **gran** ciudad	*a big city / a great (impressive) city*
un país **grande** / un **gran** país	*a large country / a great country*

[Práctica F–H]

Práctica

A.   Complete each sentence with all the adjectives that are appropriate according to form and meaning.

1.   Anita es _____. (morena / casado / jóvenes / lista / bonito / trabajadora)
2.   El padre de Ernesto es _____. (viejo / alto / nueva / grande / fea / interesante)
3.   Los clientes son _____. (rubio / antipático / inteligentes / viejos / ricos / práctica)
4.   Las niñas son _____. (malo / cortas / sentimental / buenas / casadas / joven)

*****Otro** by itself means *another* or *other*. The indefinite article is not used with **otro**.

B.   Descripciones. Describa a su (*your*) familia, a sus amigos y su universidad. Haga oraciones completas con estas palabras.

mi familia		interesante, importante,
mi padre/madre		amable, (im)paciente,
mi hermano/hermana		grande, ¿ ?
mi amigo/a (<u>nombre</u>)	(no) ser	intelectual, fiel, ¿ ?
mi perro/gato		nuevo, viejo, pequeño,
esta universidad		bueno, malo, famoso,
		¿ ?

C.   Juan and Juana, fraternal twins, are totally different. Tell what Juana is like, changing details as necessary.

Juan es soltero. Es alto y moreno y también muy guapo. Es muy perezoso—¡no le gusta estudiar! También es un poco gordo—¡no le gusta hacer ejercicio! No es como (*like*) su hermana Juana, pero es muy simpático de todos modos (*in any case*).

D.   Tell what nationality the following persons could be and where they might live: **Portugal, Alemania, Inglaterra, la China, España, Francia, Italia**.

1.   Monique habla francés; es _____ y vive (*she lives*) en _____.
2.   José habla español; es _____ y vive en _____.
3.   Greta y Hans hablan alemán; son _____ y viven en _____.
4.   Gilberto habla portugués; es _____ y vive en _____.
5.   Gina y Sofía hablan italiano; son _____ y viven en _____.
6.   Winston habla inglés; es _____ y vive en _____.
7.   Hai y Hau hablan chino; son _____ y viven en _____.

E.   Unas fotos interesantes. You and your friend Julio are looking at some photos of a party for your brother Manolo. Julio does not know any of the people. Point out some of them and tell him something about them. Begin each sentence with a demonstrative, as in the model, and use the correct form of **ser**. Add details if you can.

MODELO: fiesta / para mi hermano Manolo →
Esta fiesta es para mi hermano Manolo. Es profesor.

1.   mujer / la amiga de Manolo
2.   hombres / de San Francisco
3.   niñas / de California también
4.   joven morena / mi hermana Cecilia
5.   señor guapo / Julián Gutiérrez

F.   Variaciones. You have heard the following sentences in the places indicated. Who is most likely to have said each, **un empleado** (*employee*) or **un cliente**? After you have identified the speaker, create new sentences by inserting the adjectives in parentheses into them, one at a time. Can you add any other adjectives that are appropriate in meaning?

RICARDO MONTANER
Un toque de misterio – TH-Rodven
Ricardo Montaner, el joven cantante venezolano, es en este momento el número uno en ventas en su país. Ahora se presenta con un nuevo LP muy original, donde se destaca como tema promocional la canción "En la cima del cielo", que no para de escucharse en la radio venezolana y también en los Estados Unidos. Bajo el sello TH-Rodven, este LP llegará lejos.

1. En la agencia de automóviles: Busco un coche. (pequeño / francés / grande)
2. En la librería: Por favor, quiero comprar un diccionario. (completo / barato / nuevo)
3. En la biblioteca: Estas novelas son buenas. (alemán / nuevo / mexicano)
4. En la agencia de viajes (*travel agency*): ¿Buscan una excursión? (fascinante / largo / barato)

G.   Asociaciones. With several classmates, how many names can you associate with the following phrases? Everyone in the group must agree with the names you decide on. Use the words and phrases you know to agree with the suggestions of others. To disagree, simply say: **No estoy de acuerdo.**

1. una gran mujer
2. una buena clase
3. un gran hombre
4. una persona mala
5. un mal restaurante

H.   Entrevista. Ask a classmate questions that will elicit information to complete the following statements. Use adjectives, when appropriate, in your questions, and remember that you know a number of ways to ask questions. Another simple way to ask questions is to add the tag word **¿verdad?** (*right?*) to the end of a statement.

> MODELO: El profesor (La profesora) es _____. →
> —¿Cómo es la profesora? (¿Es inteligente la profesora? La profesora es simpática, ¿verdad?)
> —La profesora es inteligente. (Sí, es muy...)

1. El profesor (La profesora) es _____.
2. Por lo general (*In general*), las mujeres (madres, hermanas) son _____.
3. Por lo general, los hombres (padres, hermanos) son _____.
4. Los buenos amigos son _____.
5. Yo soy _____.
6. Mi mejor (*best*) amigo/a es _____.
7. Los padres de mi mejor amigo/a son _____.

Now compare your classmate's answers with those of other students. Is there general agreement on the adjectives used to complete these sentences?

UN POCO DE TODO

¿De dónde eres tú? With two classmates, ask and answer questions according to the model.

MODELO: Atlanta → ENRIQUETA: ¿De dónde eres tú?
AGUSTÍN: Soy de *Atlanta*.
EVA: Ah, eres *norteamericano*.
AGUSTÍN: Sí, por eso hablo *inglés*.

1. Guadalajara   2. París   3. Roma   4. San Francisco   5. Madrid
6. Londres   7. Berlín   8. Lima (peruano)   9. Tokio   10. Moscú

UN PASO MÁS: Lectura cultural

Antes de leer: Recognizing Cognate Patterns

You already know that cognates are words that are similar in form and meaning from one language to another: for example, English *poet* and Spanish **poeta**. The more cognates you can recognize, the more easily you will read in Spanish.

The endings of many Spanish words correspond to English word endings according to fixed patterns. Learning to recognize these patterns will increase the number of close and not-so-close cognates that you can recognize. Here are a few of the most common.

-dad → -ty	**-ción** → -tion	**-ico** → -ic, -cal
-mente → -ly	**-sión** → -sion	**-oso** → -ous

What are the English equivalents of these words?

1. unidad   4. idéntico   7. famoso   10. frecuentemente
2. reducción   5. dramático   8. reacción   11. religioso
3. explosión   6. estudioso   9. recientemente 12. religiosidad

Try to spot cognates in the following reading, and remember that you should be able to guess the meaning of underlined words from context.

LOS APELLIDOS HISPÁNICOS

En español, generalmente, las personas tienen° dos apellidos: el apellido   *have*
paterno y también el materno. Cuando un individuo usa solamente uno
de sus apellidos, casi siempre es el paterno.

Imagine que Ud. tiene una amiga, Gloria Gómez Pereda. El **nombre** de
esta persona es «Gloria» y sus **apellidos** son «Gómez» y «Pereda». «Gómez»
es el apellido paterno y «Pereda» es el materno. En situaciones oficiales o
formales, ella usa los dos apellidos. En ocasiones informales, usa solamente
el paterno. Cuando uno habla con ella, la llama° «Señorita Gómez» o «Señorita   *la... one calls her*
Gómez Pereda», pero nunca «Señorita Pereda».

Ahora imagine que su amiga Gloria va a casarse con un señor que se llama Eduardo Cabrera Meléndez. El nombre de casada° de Gloria será° Gloria Gómez de Cabrera, pues ella va a usar su apellido paterno (Gómez) y el apellido paterno de su esposo (Cabrera). En ocasiones formales Gloria será «la señora Gómez de Cabrera» o «la señora de Cabrera», pero nunca «la señora Gómez».

de... *as a married woman* / *will be*

Es importante comprender el sistema de apellidos cuando Ud. usa una lista alfabetizada. Lo primero° que determina el orden en la lista es el apellido paterno, y después el materno. En una guía telefónica, el señor Carlos Martínez Aguilar aparece cerca del comienzo° de la lista de todos los Martínez.* Su padre, el señor Alfonso Martínez Zúñiga, aparece cerca del final de la lista. En la guía telefónica de la Ciudad de México, hay más de veinticinco páginas— con más de 8.000° personas—que tienen el apellido paterno «Martínez». Si Ud. busca el número de teléfono de un señor Martínez y no sabe° su apellido materno, ¡va a tener° un gran problema!

Lo... *The first thing*
beginning
ocho mil
no... *you don't know*
¡va... *you're going to have*

Comprensión

Complete las oraciones 1 a 3 según la lectura. Después conteste la pregunta 4.

1. Un hispano tiene dos apellidos: _____.
   a. el paterno y el materno   c. dos maternos
   b. dos paternos
2. En una fiesta de amigos y colegas, una persona usa _____.
   a. su apellido materno   c. los dos apellidos
   b. su apellido paterno
3. Si Ud. busca el nombre de un amigo en la guía telefónica, necesita saber (*to know*) _____.
   a. solamente el apellido paterno   c. los dos apellidos
   b. solamente el apellido materno
4. ¿En qué orden aparecen estos nombres en una guía telefónica?
   _____ Benito Pérez Galdós   _____ Juan Pereda García
   _____ Jaime García Jiménez   _____ Virginia Pérez García
   _____ Baldomero Pérez Almena

Para escribir

Write a brief paragraph about the Hispanic system of names as it would apply to your own family. Use the following sentences as a guide.

1. Me llamo _____.
2. Mi apellido paterno es _____ y _____ es mi apellido materno.
3. En situaciones informales me llamo _____.

---

*Last names are made plural in Spanish simply by putting the plural definite article in front of the name: **los Martínez** (*the Martínez family*), **los García** (*the Garcías*), and so on.

4. ____ es el nombre completo de mi padre.
5. ____ es el nombre completo de mi madre.
6. Si me caso con (*If I marry*) Juan(a) García Sandoval, el nombre completo de mi hijo Carlos será (*will be*) Carlos ____.

VOCABULARIO

Verbo

ser (*irreg.*) to be

Adjetivos

alto/a tall
amable kind, nice
antipático/a unpleasant
bajo/a short (*in height*)
barato/a inexpensive
bienvenido/a welcome
bonito/a pretty
buen, bueno/a good
casado/a married
corto/a short (*in length*)
delgado/a thin, slender
este/a this
  estos/as these
feo/a ugly
gordo/a fat
gran(de) large, big; great
guapo/a handsome, good-looking
joven young
largo/a long

listo/a smart, clever
mal, malo/a bad
mejor best
moreno/a brunette
nuevo/a new
otro/a other, another
pequeño/a small
perezoso/a lazy
pobre poor
práctico/a practical
rico/a rich
rubio/a blond(e)
simpático/a nice, likeable
soltero/a single (*not married*)
todo/a all, every
tonto/a silly, foolish
trabajador(a) hardworking
viejo/a old

Sustantivos

el apellido last name
la camioneta station wagon

la casa house
la ciudad city
el coche car
el disco record
el ejercicio exercise
el examen test
la foto(grafía) photo(graph)
el gato cat
el/la hermano/a brother/sister
la madre mother
el nombre (first) name
el padre father
los padres parents
el país country, nation
el perro dog
el regalo gift

Los números

treinta, cuarenta, cincuenta, sesenta, setenta, ochenta, noventa, cien(to)

Frases útiles para la comunicación	
¿por qué?	why?
porque	because
por eso	that's why

NOSOTROS Y LOS DEMÁS

VOCABULARIO: LA FAMILIA Y LOS PARIENTES°

relatives

Joaquín

los abuelos

Josefina

Miguel

los padres

Mercedes

Juan

Carmen

Elena

Julio

los hijos

Manolo

Juanita

el abuelo grandfather	**el hijo** son	**el tío** uncle
la abuela grandmother	**la hija** daughter	**la tía** aunt
el padre (papá) father (dad)	**el nieto** grandson	**el sobrino** nephew
la madre (mamá) mother (mom)	**la nieta** granddaughter	**la sobrina** niece
el hermano brother	**el esposo** husband	**el primo** male cousin
la hermana sister	**la esposa** wife	**la prima** female cousin

A.   ¿Cierto o falso? Corrija las oraciones falsas.

1.   Juan es el hermano de Carmen.   4.   Elena y Juanita son hermanas.
2.   Josefina es la abuela de Juanita.   5.   Miguel es el tío de Manolo.
3.   Juanita es la sobrina de Joaquín.   6.   Miguel es el hijo de Julio.

B.   ¿Quiénes son? Identifique los miembros de cada (*each*) grupo, según el modelo.

> MODELO: los hijos → el hijo y la hija

1.   los abuelos   3.   los hermanos   5.   los tíos
2.   los padres   4.   los nietos   6.   los sobrinos

C.   ¿Quién es? Complete las oraciones lógicamente.

1.   La madre de mi* padre es mi _____.
2.   El hijo de mi tío es mi _____.
3.   La hermana de mi padre es mi _____.
4.   El esposo de mi abuela es mi _____.

Ahora (*Now*) defina estas personas, según el mismo (*same*) modelo.

5. prima 6. sobrino 7. tío 8. abuelo

D.   Una fiesta familiar. Imagine que Ud. está en una fiesta familiar, en la casa de sus (*your*) padres. ¿A qué hora llegan (*arrive*) todos? ¿Quién llega tarde? ¿Quién no llega? ¿Qué toman Uds.? ¿Es posible bailar? ¿cantar? ¿hablar con muchos (*many*) parientes? ¿Es necesario ser amable con todos? ¿Le gusta hablar con sus parientes? ¿A qué hora termina la fiesta?

Al tanto...

Hispanics use a number of terms to refer to spouses and loved ones with affection: **mi amor, mi vida** (*life*), **querido/a** (*dear*), **cielo** (*heaven*), **corazón** (*heart*). The members of a couple may also call each other **viejo/vieja** or even **mi hijo/mi hija**.

Just as in the English-speaking world, there is as yet no definitive Hispanic term to refer to a partner in a committed yet nonmarital relationship. The use of **compañero/a** is frequent, often shortened to **mi compa** or **un compa/una compa**.

INFORME ESPECIAL

De Amor y Amistad

19 de Septiembre, un día especial para recordar con un detalle y afirmar los sentimientos de amor y amistad.

---

*Use **mi** to mean *my* with singular nouns and **mis** with plural ones. You will learn more about using words of this type in Grammar Section 11.

PRONUNCIACIÓN: *r* and *rr*

Spanish has two *r* sounds, one of which is called a *flap*, the other a *trill*. The rapid pronunciation of *tt* and *dd* in the English words *Betty* and *ladder* produces a sound similar to the Spanish flap **r**: the tongue touches the alveolar ridge (behind the upper teeth) once. Although English has no trill, when people imitate a motor, they often produce the Spanish trill, which is a rapid series of flaps.

The trilled **r** is written **rr** between vowels (**carro**, **correcto**), and **r** at the beginning of a word (**rico**, **rosa**). Any other **r** is pronounced as a flap. Be careful to distinguish between the flap **r** and the trilled **r**. A mispronunciation will often change the meaning of a word—for example, **pero** (*but*) / **perro** (*dog*).

A.

inglés:	potter	ladder	cotter	meter	total	motor
español:	para	Lara	cara	mire	toro	moro

B.
1. rico
2. ruso
3. rubio
4. Roberto
5. Ramírez
6. rebelde
7. reportero
8. real
9. corro
10. carro
11. corral
12. error

C.
1. coro/corro
2. coral/corral
3. pero/perro
4. vara/barra
5. ahora/ahorra
6. caro/carro
7. cero/cerro

D.
1. el nombre correcto
2. un corral grande
3. una norteamericana
4. Puerto Rico
5. rosas grandes
6. un libro corto y barato
7. una mujer refinada
8. Enrique, Carlos y Rosita
9. El perro está en el corral.
10. Estos errores son raros.
11. Busco un carro caro (*expensive*).
12. Soy el primo de Roque Ramírez.

¿Recuerda Ud.?

The personal endings used with **-ar** verbs share some characteristics of those used with **-er** and **-ir** verbs, which you will learn in the next section. Review the endings of **-ar** verbs by telling which subject pronoun(s) you associate with each of these endings.

1. **-amos**   2. **-as**   3. **-áis**   4. **-an**   5. **-o**   6. **-a**

ESTRUCTURAS

7. EXPRESSING ACTIONS
Present Tense of *-er* and *-ir* Verbs; More About Subject Pronouns

Por la tarde, en casa de la familia Robles

SR. ROBLES: Paquita, *debes* estudiar más ahora. *Insisto* en eso.

PAQUITA: Pero, papá, *asisto* a todas mis clases y saco buenas notas. Además, todos mis amigos están en el centro comercial esta tarde.

SR. ROBLES: Tus amigos no son mis hijos. Nunca *abres* los libros en casa. Nunca *lees* el periódico. Nunca…

PAQUITA: ¡Ay, papá! ¡No me *comprendes*! ¡Eres terrible a veces!

¿Quién…

1. debe estudiar más hoy?
2. insiste en imponer su voluntad (*his or her will, way*)?
3. asiste a todas las clases?
4. nunca abre los libros en casa?
5. no comprende la situación?

Verbs that End in *-er* and *-ir*

comer (*to eat*)		**vivir** (*to live*)	
como	com**emos**	vivo	viv**imos**
comes	com**éis**	vives	viv**ís**
come	com**en**	vive	viv**en**

The present tense of **-er** and **-ir** verbs is formed by adding personal endings to the stem of the verb (the infinitive minus its **-er/-ir** ending). The personal endings for **-er** and **-ir** verbs are the same except for the first and second person plural.

Remember that the Spanish present tense has a number of present tense equivalents in English and can also be used to express future meaning:

como $\begin{cases} I\ eat \\ I\ am\ eating \\ I\ will\ eat \end{cases}$ simple present
present progressive
future

Afternoon at the Robles' house　MR. ROBLES: Paquita, you should study more now. I insist on that. PAQUITA: But, Dad, I go to all of my classes and I get good grades. Besides, all my friends are at the mall this afternoon. MR. ROBLES: Your friends aren't my children. You never open your books at home. You never read the newspaper. You never . . . PAQUITA: Oh, Dad! You don't understand me! You're terrible sometimes!

Some important **-er** and **-ir** verbs in this chapter include the following:

aprender	to learn *apprendre*	**abrir**	to open *ouvrir*
beber	to drink *boire*	**asistir (a)**	to attend, go (to) (*a class, function*) *assiste*
comer	to eat *Manger*	**escribir**	to write *écrire*
comprender	to understand *comprendre*	**insistir (en** + *inf.*)	to insist (on *doing something*) *insister*
creer (en)	to think, believe (in) *croire*	**recibir**	to receive *recevoir*
deber (+ *inf.*)	should, must, ought to (*do something*) *doire*	**vivir**	to live *vivre*
leer	to read *lire*		
vender	to sell *vendre*		

[Práctica A–C]

Use and Omission of Subject Pronouns

In English, a verb must have an expressed subject (a noun or pronoun): *he/ she/the train returns.* In Spanish, however, as you have probably noticed, an expressed subject is not required. Verbs are accompanied by a subject pronoun only for clarification, emphasis, or contrast.

*   *Clarification:* When the context does not make the subject clear, the subject pronoun is expressed **Ud./él/ella** *vende;* **Uds./ellos/ellas** *venden.* This happens most frequently with third person singular and plural verb forms.
*   *Emphasis:* Subject pronouns are used in Spanish to emphasize the subject when in English you would stress it with your voice.

> **¡Yo** no leo el periódico!   *I don't read the newspaper!*

*   *Contrast:* Contrast is a special case of emphasis. Subject pronouns are used to contrast the actions of two individuals or groups.

> **Ellos** comen mucho; **nosotros** comemos poco.   *They eat a lot; we eat little.*

[Práctica D–G]

Práctica

A.   En casa, con la familia. Form complete sentences about a Saturday morning spent at home with the family, based on the cues given and adding words when needed. When the subject pronoun is given in parentheses, do not use it in the sentence.

1.   (yo) leer / periódico / como siempre
2.   niños / insistir / en / mirar (*to watch*) / la televisión: ¡hay / dibujos animados!
3.   Paquita / escribir / ejercicios / para / clase de español
4.   hoy por / tarde / (ella) asistir / a / fiesta / en casa / de / amigos
5.   por eso / (ella) deber / estudiar / por / mañana

6. (yo) creer / que / Paquita / aprender / a* / ser / más responsable... ¡por fin (*finally*)!
7. mi esposa / abrir / carta (*letter*) / de / abuelo
8. él / vivir / otro / ciudad
9. (nosotros) creer / que / (él) deber / pasar (*to spend*) las vacaciones / con nosotros / este año
10. a las doce y media / todos / (nosotros) comer / juntos (*together*)... ¡En total, una mañana estupenda!

From whose point of view is the story told? Now retell it as if you were Paquita, using the same cues as a guide and making the necessary adjustments: **1. Mi padre lee...**

B.   Unas diferencias familiares: Habla Paquita. The following paragraphs tell Paquita's side of the disagreement you read about in the minidialogue. Complete them with the correct form of the infinitives.

Según° mi padre, los jóvenes (*deber*[1]) asistir a clase todos los días. Papá también (*creer*[2]) que nosotros (*deber*[3]) estudiar con frecuencia. Papá (*insistir*[4]) en que no es necesario mirar la televisión. Según él, es más interesante (*leer*[5]) el periódico. Él sólo trabaja, (*comer*[6]) y (*leer*[7]) .

    Yo no soy como papá. Prefiero mirar la televisión todas las noches. (*Yo: abrir*[8]) los libros a veces° y (*leer*[9]) cuando es necesario, pero... tengo muchos amigos y (*creer*[10]) que es más interesante estar con ellos.

According to

a... at times

Based on the preceding paragraphs and the minidialogue, who would have made the following statements, Paquita or her father (**su padre**)?

1. ¡No comprendo tu obsesión con los centros comerciales! *Su padre*
2. ¡Los programas de televisión son fascinantes! *Paquita*
3. ¡No comprendes a los jóvenes de hoy! *Paquita*
4. Esta noche quiero leer un buen libro. *Su padre*

C.   Las obligaciones familiares. ¿Qué deben o no deben hacer (*do*) los hijos de una familia?

1. escribir muchas cartas a los abuelos
2. *No* comer siempre en casa de los amigos
3. regresar a casa para (*by*) las once todas las noches
4. ser buenos con todos

¿Y qué deben o no deben hacer los padres?

5. pagar la matrícula de sus (*their*) hijos
6. abrir las cartas que llegan para sus hijos
7. comprender que sus hijos necesitan amigos
8. asistir a todas las fiestas de sus hijos

D.   ¿Cómo se dice en español?

---

*Note: **aprender** + **a** + *infinitive*

[handwritten: Comprende español   Creo que no y ella no comprende español]

1. "Does *he* understand Spanish?" "I don't believe so, and *she* doesn't *[inglés]* understand English." "What language should we speak, then (**entonces**)?" *[handwritten: ¿Cuál lenguas debemos hablar?]*

2. Anita has (**tiene**) two children, Pablo and Teresa. He doesn't believe in Santa Claus, but she still (**todavía**) believes in him (**él**). *[handwritten: Anita tiene dos hijos. Él cree a Santa Claus, pero ellas cree todavía a él.]*

E. Form complete sentences using one word or phrase from each column. Be sure to use the correct form of the verbs. Make any sentence negative.

yo	abrir	muchas/pocas (*few*) cartas
nosotros	leer	los problemas de los estudiantes
(estudiante), tú	escribir	el periódico/una revista (*magazine*)
Ud., profesor(a)	beber	todos los días
los esposos típicos	vender	Coca-Cola/café todos los días
mi padre/madre	comprender	llegar a casa temprano esta noche
mi abuelo/a	recibir	los libros al final del semestre/ trimestre
	vivir	mirar mucho la televisión
me gusta	deber	regalos
	¿ ?	muchos/pocos ejercicios
		(en) una casa/un apartamento/¿ ?
		la puerta (*door*) para las mujeres

F. **Una noche en casa.**
¿Quiénes son estas personas? ¿Cómo son? ¿Qué hacen (*do they do*)?

Palabras útiles:
el refrigerador, la comida (*food*)

◆ ## Notas comunicativas: Telling How Frequently You Do Things

Use the following words and phrases to tell how often you perform an activity.

todos los días	every day
con frecuencia	frequently
a veces	at times
una vez/dos veces a la semana/al mes	once/twice a week/month
casi nunca	almost never
nunca	never

Hablo con mis amigos **todos los días**. Hablo con mis padres **una vez a la semana**. **Casi nunca** hablo con mis abuelos. Y **nunca** hablo con mis tíos que viven en Italia.

Use the expressions **casi nunca** and **nunca** only at the beginning of a sentence. You will learn more about how to use them in Grammar Section 16.

G.   ¿Cómo pasa Ud. el tiempo? How frequently do you do each of the following things?

1.   Escribo una carta.
2.   Hablo por teléfono.
3.   Leo novelas.
4.   Como con todos los parientes.
5.   Miro la televisión.
6.   Bebo Coca-Cola.
7.   Leo el periódico.
8.   Aprendo palabras nuevas en español.
9.   Compro regalos para papá y mamá (mi esposo/a).
10.   Escribo un poema.
11.   Insisto en hablar inglés en esta clase.
12.   Recibo un suspenso (*F*) en un examen.

Now interview another student, asking him or her questions based on the sentences given above. Begin each question with **¿Con qué frecuencia... ?**

MODELO: ¿Con qué frecuencia escribes una carta?

Now use the same phrases to describe the activities of at least one member of your family.

MODELO: Mi padre nunca escribe cartas. Habla por teléfono con frecuencia...

Study Hint: Studying and Learning Verbs

Knowing how to use verb forms quickly and accurately is one of the most important parts of learning how to communicate in a foreign language. These suggestions will help you recognize and use verb forms.

1.   Study carefully any new grammar section that deals with verbs. Are the verbs regular? What is the stem? What are the personal endings? Don't just memorize the endings (**-o, -as, -a,** and so on). Practice the complete forms of each verb (**hablo, hablas, habla,** and so on) until they are "second nature" to you. Be sure that you are using the appropriate endings: **-ar** endings with **-ar** verbs, for example. Be especially careful when you write and pronounce verb endings, since a misspelling or mispronunciation can convey inaccurate information. Even though there is only a one-letter difference between **hablo** and **habla** or between **habla** and **hablan,** that single letter makes a big difference in the information communicated.

2.   Are you studying irregular verbs? If so, what are the irregularities? Practice the irregular forms many times so that you "overlearn" them and will not forget them: **soy, eres, es, son.**

3.   Once you are familiar with the forms, practice asking short conversational questions using **tú/Ud.** and **vosotros/Uds.** Answer each question, using the appropriate **yo** or **nosotros** form.

¿Hablas español?
¿Habla español?   } Sí, hablo español.

¿Comen Uds. en clase?
¿Coméis en clase?   } No, no comemos en clase.

4.   It is easy to become so involved in mastering the *forms* of new verbs that you forget their *meanings.* However, being able to recite verb forms perfectly is useless unless you also understand what you are saying. Be sure that you always know both the spelling *and* the meaning of all verb forms, just as you must for any new vocabulary word. Practice new verb forms in original sentences.

5.   Practice the forms of all new verbs given in the vocabulary lists in each chapter. Any special information that you should know about the verbs will be indicated in the vocabulary list.

VOCABULARIO

Las relaciones sentimentales

el novio	boyfriend; fiancé; groom
la novia	girlfriend; fiancée; bride
la iglesia	church
cariñoso/a	affectionate

la amistad

amiga/o

la cita

enamorado/a =) herdialect

el amor

el noviazgo

Novio/a

la boda

la luna de miel

el matrimonio

el divorcio

A. **Definiciones.** Match these words with their definitions.

1. el matrimonio
2. el amor
3. el divorcio
4. la boda
5. la amistad

a. relación cariñosa entre (*between*) dos personas *5*
b. posible resultado de un matrimonio desastroso *3*
c. relación sentimental y especial entre dos personas *2*
d. una ceremonia (religiosa o civil) en que la novia a veces lleva un vestido blanco (*wears a white dress*) *4*
e. relación legal entre dos personas *1*

B. Complete las oraciones lógicamente.

1. Mi abuelo es el _____ de mi abuela. *esposo*
2. Muchos novios tienen (*have*) un largo _____ antes de (*before*) la boda. *Noviazgo*
3. María y Julio tienen _____ para comer en un restaurante. *la cita*
4. La _____ de Juan y Marta es (*is taking place*) en la iglesia de San Martín. *boda*
5. La _____ entre estos ex esposos es imposible. No son amigos. *amistad*
6. A Ramón no le gusta la idea del _____; no desea tener esposa. *Matrimonio*
7. ¡El _____ es ciego! *amor*

Notas culturales: Relaciones de la vida social

Dos palabras españolas que no tienen equivalente exacto en inglés son **amigo** y **novio**. En el diagrama se indica cuándo es apropiado usar estas palabras para describir relaciones sociales en la cultura hispana y en la norteamericana.

friend	*girl/boyfriend*	*fiancée/fiancé*	*bride/groom*
amiga/amigo		novia/novio	

C.   ¿Cierto o falso? Conteste cierto, falso o depende.

1. El amor verdadero (*real*) no existe.   2. El matrimonio es una institución social necesaria.   3. Un novio / Una novia es una limitación.   4. Las bodas grandes y formales son una tontería (*foolish thing*).   5. Un novio debe ser alto, moreno y guapo.   6. La luna de miel es un concepto anticuado.

Notas comunicativas: Expressing Age

—¿Cuántos años tienes,° abuela?   *¿Cuántos... How old are you?*
—Setenta y tres, Nora.
—¿Y cuántos años tiene el abuelo?
—Setenta y cinco, mi amor. Y ahora, dime,° ¿cuántos años tienes tú?   *tell me*
—Pues... creo que tengo tres.

In Spanish, age is expressed with the phrase **tener... años** (literally, *to have . . . years*). You have now seen all the singular forms of **tener: tengo, tienes, tiene.**

D.   Complete las oraciones lógicamente.

1. Un hombre que (*who*) tiene noventa años es muy _____.
2. Un niño que tiene sólo un año es muy _____.
3. La persona más vieja (*oldest*) de mi familia es mi _____. Tiene _____ años.

E.   Entrevista. Use the phrases in **Notas comunicativas** to ask at least six classmates how old they are and how old their grandparents are. (If one's grandmother or grandfather is no longer living, one can say _____ **ya no vive.**) Then, based on the information you have learned, complete the following sentences. Compare your answers with those of other classmates to find the correct answers for the class as a whole.

1. La persona más vieja (*oldest*) de esta clase es _____. Tiene _____.
2. El abuelo de _____ es el más viejo de la clase. Tiene _____.
3. La abuela de _____ es la más vieja de la clase. Tiene _____.

España

Hablando° de la familia   *Speaking*
—Tienes una familia muy grande. ¿Cuántos son?
—Bueno, tengo seis hermanas y un hermano.
—Y ¿cuántos primos?
—¡Uf! Tengo un montón. Más de veinte.

ESTRUCTURAS

8. POINTING OUT PEOPLE AND THINGS
Demonstrative Adjectives

Depende del punto de vista...

Delante de una iglesia

PANCHITO: Pero no quiero asistir a *esta* boda, papá. Las bodas son
una tontería.

SR. MARTÍNEZ: Basta ya, Panchito. Todos entran ya en la iglesia y tú
debes entrar conmigo.

En la iglesia, un poco más tarde

SR. MARTÍNEZ: Mira, Panchito, *esas* mujeres son las damas de honor y
aquella señorita del vestido blanco es la novia.

PANCHITO: ¿Y *aquel* hombre mayor? ¿Es su padre? ¿Por qué está con ella?

SR. MARTÍNEZ: Porque su padre también es el padrino y los padrinos
siempre acompañan a la novia* al altar.

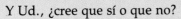

Y Ud., ¿cree que sí o que no?
1. Las bodas son una tontería.
2. La novia siempre debe llevar un vestido blanco.

3. Los niños deben asistir a las bodas con sus padres... aun
(*even*) cuando no conocen (*they don't know*) a los novios.

It depends on your point of view *In front of a church* PANCHITO: But I don't want to go to this
wedding, Papa. Weddings are silly (a foolish thing). MR. MARTÍNEZ: That's enough, Panchito.
Everyone is going into the church now and you must go in with me. *In the church, a bit later.* MR.
MARTÍNEZ: Look, Panchito, those women are the maids of honor and that young woman in the
white dress is the bride. PANCHITO: And that older man? Is that her father? Why is he with her?
MR. MARTÍNEZ: Because her father is also the best man and the best men always take the bride to
the altar.

*Note the use of the word **a** before a direct object that refers to a specific person, in this case, **la
novia.** As you can see in the translation of the minidialogue, this **a** has no equivalent in
English. You will learn more about this use of **a** in Grammar Section 17.

DEMONSTRATIVE ADJECTIVES		
this	este libro	esta mesa
these	estos libros	estas mesas
that	ese libro aquel libro (allí)	esa mesa aquella mesa (allí)
those	esos libros aquellos libros (allí)	esas mesas aquellas mesas (allí)

Demonstrative Adjectives

Demonstrative adjectives (**Los adjetivos demostrativos**) are used to point out or indicate a specific noun or nouns. In Spanish, demonstrative adjectives precede the nouns they modify. They also agree in number and gender with the nouns. You have already learned to use forms of **este**.

- **este, esta, estos, estas** (*this, these*)

Este coche es de Francia.	*This car is from France.*
Estas señoritas son argentinas.	*These women are Argentine.*

  Forms of **este** are used to refer to nouns that are close to the speaker in space or time.

- **ese, esa, esos, esas** (*that, those*)

Esos padres son cariñosos.	*Those parents are affectionate.*
Ese hombre (cerca de Ud.) es el novio.	*That man (close to you) is the groom.*

  Forms of **ese** are used to refer to nouns that are *not* close to the speaker. Sometimes nouns modified by forms of **ese** are close to the person addressed.

- **aquel, aquella, aquellos, aquellas** (*that* [over there], *those* [over there])

Aquel coche (allí en la calle) es rápido.	*That car (there in the street) is fast.*
Aquella casa (en las montañas) es del hermano de Ramiro.	*That house (in the mountains) belongs to Ramiro's brother.*

  Forms of **aquel** are used to refer to nouns that are even farther away.

Note that Spanish speakers use forms of **ese** and **aquel** interchangeably to indicate nouns that are at some distance from them: **esa/aquella casa en las montañas, esa/aquella ciudad en Sudamérica.** However, if a form of **ese** has been used to indicate a distant noun, a form of **aquel** must be used to indicate a noun that is even farther away in comparison: **esa señora allí y aquel hombre en la calle.**

[Práctica A–B]

Neuter Demonstratives

The neuter demonstratives **esto, eso,** and **aquello** mean *this*, *that* (not close), and *that* (farther away), respectively.

¿Qué es **esto**?	*What is this?*
Eso es todo.	*That's all.*
¡**Aquello** es terrible!	*That's terrible!*

They refer to a whole idea, concept, situation, or statement, or to an as yet unidentified object. They never refer to a specific noun. Compare: **este libro y ese bolígrafo, esa mesa y aquella silla**, and so on.

[Práctica C]

Práctica

A.   Comentarios en la boda y en la recepción. Haga oraciones completas para describir lo que se escucha (*what is overheard*).

SOCIALES

Enlace Ruiz-Pierluisi

En emotiva misa de esponsales, oficiada por Monseñor Arenas, unieron sus vidas Eloy Ruiz Calderón y Caridad Pierluisi Urrutia, en la Iglesia San Jorge, en Santurce. Los contrayentes son hijos, respectivamente, del Ing. Jorge Antonio Pierluisi y Doris Urrutia; Dr. Eloy Ruiz y Cuqui Calderón. Apadrinaron el enlace Doris Pierluisi de Lubke y Francisco Mirandés, hijo. Terminada la ceremonia, los invitados se trasladaron al Patio del Fauno, del Hotel Condado Beach, donde disfrutaron de la música de Chupi Porrata y Los Latinos. Además, fueron obsequiados con una serigrafía del artista Paul Kuchno. El brindis fue pronunciado por los hermanos de la novia: Jorge, Pedro y José Jaime.

Arriba: Primer plano de la bella novia
Caridad Pierluisi Urrutia.

1. este / iglesia / ser / muy bonito
2. ¡este / regalos / deber / ser / de / familia / de / novio!
3. este / recepción / ser / muy elegante
4. ese / jóvenes / ser / amigos / de / novia
5. ese / señora / no / bailar / muy bien
6. ese / niñas / no / desear / asistir / recepción
7. ese / niños / ser / malos: ¡comer demasiado (*too much*)!
8. ese / novios / desear / salir (*to leave*) pronto

B.   Situaciones. Imagine that you are one of the **novios** from the wedding in Exercise A. With another student, ask and answer questions about your **luna de miel** in Mexico, using the cues in parentheses. Follow the model.

MODELO: —¿Recuerdas (*Do you remember*) cómo es el restaurante La Buena Amistad? (excelente)
—¡Ah, **aquel** restaurante es excelente!

1.   Y el Hotel Libertad, ¿recuerdas qué tal es? (muy bueno)
2.   ¿Y los dependientes del hotel? (simpáticos)
3.   ¿Recuerdas cómo son los periódicos de la capital? (magníficos)
4.   ¿Y los programas de televisión mexicanos? (interesantes)
5.   ¿Total que te gusta mucho el país? (fenomenal)

C.   Match these questions or statements with the situations described below them.

1.   ¿Qué es esto?
2.   ¿Todo eso?

3.   Eso es terrible.
4.   ¿Qué es aquello?

a.   Ud. no puede ver (*You can't see*) bien el altar porque hay mucha gente (*people*) y unas velas (*candles*) muy altas.

b. El padre de la novia dice (*says*), «Para mi hija, una boda grande, una luna de miel en Europa, un coche nuevo y una casa grande. ¿Creen que es demasiado?»

c. Los novios abren un regalo y descubren una cosa interesante y curiosa.

d. La hermana del novio está en el hospital por (*because of*) un accidente de coche.

UN POCO DE TODO

La familia del nuevo nieto. The following sentences will form a description of a family in which there is a new grandchild. The name of the person described is given in parentheses after each description (if necessary). Form complete sentences based on the words given, in the order given. Conjugate the verbs and add other words if necessary.

As you create the sentences, complete the family tree given below with the names of the family members. Hint: Hispanic families pass on family names just like families in the United States.

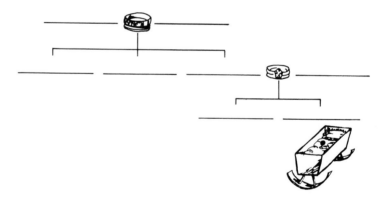

1. yo / ser / abuela / panameño (Anita)
2. nuevo / nieto / ser / de / Estados Unidos (Juan José)
3. Juan José / ser / padre / nieto
4. Juan José / también / ser / abuelo / panameño
5. uno / de / tías / de / nieto / ser / médico (Pilar)
6. otro / tía / ser / profesor / famoso (Julia)
7. madre / niño / ser / norteamericano (Paula)
8. hermana / niño / se llama / Concepción

Ahora conteste estas preguntas según la descripción de la familia.

1. ¿De dónde son los abuelos y tías?
2. ¿De dónde es la madre del niño?

UN PASO MÁS: Situaciones

Presentaciones

En casa…

—Abuelo, quiero presentarle a Adolfo… Adolfo Álvarez Montes.
Somos compañeros de clase en la universidad.

—Encantado, don Antonio.*

—Igualmente, Adolfo. Bienvenido a nuestro° casa.   *our*

En clase…

—Profesora Benítez, quisiera presentarle a Laura Sánchez Trujillo.
Es mi amiga salvadoreña.°   *de El Salvador*

—Mucho gusto, Laura.

—El gusto es mío, profesora.

En la cafetería…

—Quico, te presento a Adela. Es amiga de Julio, ¿sabes?°   *you know?*

—Mucho gusto, Adela.

—Igualmente.

—¿Qué tal si tomamos un café?

—¡De acuerdo!

Notas comunicativas sobre el diálogo

In the **Pasos preliminares** you learned some basic phrases to use when meeting someone for the first time. Here are some phrases to use to make introductions in formal and informal situations, as well as some additional responses.

Quiero }	presentar**le** (*form.*) a . . .[+]	*I want* } *to introduce you to. . .*
Quisiera }	presentar**te** (*fam.*) a . . .	*Allow me* }

Mucho gusto.   *Pleased to meet you.*
El gusto es mío.   *The pleasure is mine.*

Conversación

With other students, practice making the following introductions, using **le** (*formal*) or **te** (*informal*), as appropriate. Tell something about the person you are introducing.

---

*Note the use of the title **don** with a man's first name to express respect. **Doña** is used with a woman's name.

[+]Note again the use of the word **a** before a direct object that refers to a specific person or persons: **presentarle a Adolfo… presentarle a Laura Sánchez….**

1. You are at home, and a good friend stops by for a few minutes. Introduce him or her to your family.
2. You are in the library and happen to run into two of your professors at the circulation desk. Introduce them to each other.
3. You are at a party. Introduce one good friend to another.
4. Introduce the student next to you to another student.

VOCABULARIO

Verbos

abrir to open *ouvrir*
aprender to learn *apprendre*
asistir (a) to attend, go (to) (*a class, function*) *assister*
beber to drink *boire*
comer to eat *manger*
comprender to understand *comprendre*
creer (en) to think; to believe (in) *croire (en)*
deber (+ *inf.*) should, must, ought to (*do something*) *devoir*
escribir to write *écrire*
insistir (en + *inf.*) to insist (on *doing something*) *insister*
leer to read *lire*
llegar to arrive *arriver*
mirar to look (at); to watch *regarder*
pasar to spend (*time*) *passer*
recibir to receive *recevoir*
vender to sell *vendre*
vivir to live *vivre*

La familia y los parientes

el/la abuelo/a grandfather/ grandmother *grandpère/mère*
los abuelos grandparents *grandsparents*
el/la esposo/a husband/wife *époux/épouse*
el/la hijo/a son/daughter *fils/fille*
los hijos children *enfants*
mamá mom *maman*
el/la nieto/a grandson/ granddaughter *grandfils/fille*
papá dad *papa*
el/la primo/a cousin *cousin (e)*
el/la sobrino/a nephew/niece
el/la tío/a uncle/aunt *oncle/tante*

Las relaciones sociales

la amistad friendship
el amor love
la boda wedding
la cita date; appointment

el divorcio divorce
la iglesia church
la luna de miel honeymoon
el matrimonio marriage
el noviazgo courtship, engagement
el/la novio/a boy/girlfriend; fiancé/ fiancée; groom/bride

Otros sustantivos

la carta letter *la lettre*
la palabra word *le mot*
el periódico newspaper *le journal*
la tontería foolishness
la vida life *la vie*

Adjetivos

aquel, aquella that
  aquellos, aquellas those
cariñoso/a affectionate
ese, esa that
  esos, esas those
familiar family-related, of the family
mucho/a a lot of, many
norteamericano/a North American; from the U.S.
poco/a a little (*in amount*), few

Palabras adicionales

ahora now *maintenant*
allí there *là*
casi almost *presque*
tener . . . años to be... years old *avoir . . . . . ans*

Frases útiles para la comunicación

¿con qué frecuencia?	how often?
a veces	sometimes, at times
nunca	never
una vez/dos veces...	once/twice . . .
a la semana	a week
al mes	a month
tengo, tienes, tiene	I have, you have, he/she/it has

See also the words and phrases in the **Notas comunicativas sobre el diálogo.**

México y la América Central

¿Cuánto sabe Ud. (*do you know*) de la geografía de esta región? Identifique los siguientes países en el mapa: **México, Honduras, Costa Rica, Guatemala, Nicaragua, Panamá, El Salvador.** Luego ponga los nombres de estas capitales con sus países respectivos: **Managua, San José, la Ciudad de Panamá, la Ciudad de México, la Ciudad de Guatemala, San Salvador, Tegucigalpa.**

Ahora use la siguiente lista para nombrar los habitantes de cada país: **mexicano/a, hondureño/a, guatemalteco/a, salvadoreño/a, panameño/a, costarricense, nicaragüense.** Siga el modelo.

MODELO: Una persona de _____ es _____.

La ciudad de Tenochtitlán, con 300.000 (trescientos mil) habitantes, fue (*was*) la capital del imperio azteca. Fue destruida por los españoles en 1521 (mil quinientos veintiuno). Sobre (*On top of*) sus ruinas se fundó la moderna Ciudad de México. Lo siguiente (*The following*) es parte de la descripción de Tenochtitlán por Hernán Cortés, en una carta al rey español.

La llegada de Cortés a Tenochtitlán, mural de Diego Rivera

Esta gran ciudad de Tenochtitlán está fundada en esta laguna salada,° y desde° la tierra firme hasta el cuerpo° de la ciudad… hay dos leguas°… Es tan° grande la ciudad como Sevilla y Córdoba. Son las calles° de ella muy anchas° y muy derechas°… Tiene esta ciudad muchas plazas, donde hay continuos mercados y trato° de comprar y vender.

salty
from / body / legua = 5572 meters
as / streets
wide / straight
dealings

Ciudad de México: ¿la urbe más grande del mundo?

Carlos Brambila Paz

El propósito° de este ensayo es analizar la información disponible sobre la población de las principales metrópolis mundiales y ubicar° a la ciudad de México dentro de esta jerarquía urbana. La importancia de este análisis radica en el hecho de que, de acuerdo con las proyecciones internacionales más recientes, la ciudad de México será la metrópoli más poblada del mundo a finales del presente siglo.°

°*purpose*

°*locate, place*

will be
century

De acuerdo con las proyecciones de la ONU,° las metrópolis más pobladas en 1990 serán Tokio, con 23.4 millones de habitantes; la ciudad de México, con 22.9; Nueva York, con 21.8; São Paulo, con 19.9, y Shanghai, con 17.7. Otras ciudades con más de 10 millones de habitantes serán Beijing, Río de Janeiro, Bombay, Calcuta, Seúl, Buenos Aires, Yakarta y El Cairo, dentro de los países subdesarrollados.° En los países desarrollados se contarán Los Ángeles, París, Osaka-Kobe y Londres.

Organización de
Naciones Unidas

underdeveloped

Finalmente, de acuerdo con las estimaciones de la ONU que se reportan en el cuadro 1, las aglomeraciones más pobladas en el año 2000 serán la ciudad de México, con 31 millones de habitantes; São Paulo, con 25.8, y Tokio, con 24.2. Según las mismas proyecciones, las tasas de crecimiento° de las metrópolis de los países desarrollados deben de ser cercanas a cero, de modo que se espera que Nueva York sea la segunda metrópoli desarrollada que exceda los 20 millones de habitantes. [...]

tasas... growth rate

La gran Ciudad de México

Oscar Arias

Semblanza de Oscar Arias Premio Nobel de la Paz

SAN JOSE, Costa Rica (UPI) — Oscar Arias Sánchez, un abogado° y escritor elegido el año pasado como el presidente más joven de Costa Rica, que ayer° ganó el Premio Nobel de la Paz, comenzó su lucha° por la paz en Centroamérica desde el momento mismo que asumió su cargo.°

lawyer

yesterday

fight

position

Después de varias tentativas fracasadas,° los presidentes de El Salvador, José Napoleón Duarte; de Guatemala, Vinicio Cerezo Arevalo; de Honduras, José Azcona Hoyo; de Nicaragua, Daniel Ortega Saavedra y el propio Arias acordaron° reunirse en Guatemala el 6 y 7 de agosto para discutir el plan de paz.

failed

agreed

Tras la reunión presidencial, Arias declaró que 'éste es uno de los días más felices° de mi vida'. 'Para muchos esto era° un sueño° irrealizable, una utopía, una quijotada, una ilusión...pero, hay momentos en que las ideas tienen tanta fuerza° que llegan a plasmarse en realidad'.

más... happiest
was / dream

force

Arias está casado con Margarita Penon. La pareja tiene dos hijos, Eugenia, de 9 años, y Oscar Felipe, de 7.

Manifestación en Nicaragua

«A Roosevelt»

... esa América

que tiembla de huracanes y que vive de amor: hombres de ojos° sajones y alma bárbara,° vive. Y sueña.° Y ama, y vibra; y es la hija del Sol.° Tened cuidado.° ¡ Vive la América española!

eyes

alma... wild soul / it dreams
Sun / Tened... Be careful.

Rubén Darío, poeta nicaragüense
(1867–1916)

¿QUÉ LLEVAS HOY?

VOCABULARIO: LA ROPA

la chaqueta · el impermeable · la corbata · la camisa · el sombrero · la blusa · los bluejeans · el abrigo · la bolsa · el suéter · el traje · el cinturón · el reloj · el vestido · la camiseta · la cartera · la falda · los calcetines · las medias · los pantalones · los zapatos · las botas · las sandalias · el traje de baño

un par de (zapatos, medias...) a pair of (shoes, stockings, . . .)

es de (lana, algodón, seda)* it is made of (wool, cotton, silk)

¡Está muy de moda! It's the latest style!

llevar to wear; to carry; to take

*Note another use of **ser** + **de**: to tell what material something is made of.

A. ¿Qué ropa llevan estas personas?

1. El Sr. Rivera lleva _____.

2. La Srta. Alonso lleva _____.
   El perro lleva _____.

3. Sara lleva _____.

4. Alfredo lleva _____.
   Necesita comprar _____.

Generalmente, ¿qué artículos de ropa son para los hombres? ¿para las mujeres? ¿para hombres *y* mujeres?

B. Complete las oraciones lógicamente.

1. Para ir a bailar (*To go dancing*) a una discoteca me gusta llevar _____.
2. A una fiesta de etiqueta (*formal*) llevo _____.
3. En las playas (*beaches*) de Acapulco los turistas llevan _____ todos los días.
4. Muchos ejecutivos llevan _____.
5. Muchas ejecutivas llevan _____.
6. Nunca llevo _____ a clase.
7. En casa siempre llevo _____.
8. La ropa de _____ es muy elegante. La ropa de _____ es muy práctica.

Al tanto...

Here are some additional phrases to use to talk about what's in . . . and what's not!

In: Está en onda.
Es el último grito...
de la moda (francesa, italiana...)
en (ropa, música...)

Out: Está muy visto.
Está pasado de moda.

Finally, although the adjectives **guapo** and **chulo** have traditionally been used to describe handsome people, in contemporary usage they often describe things as well: **¡Qué vestido más chulo! Es una camiseta guapa.**

VOCABULARIO

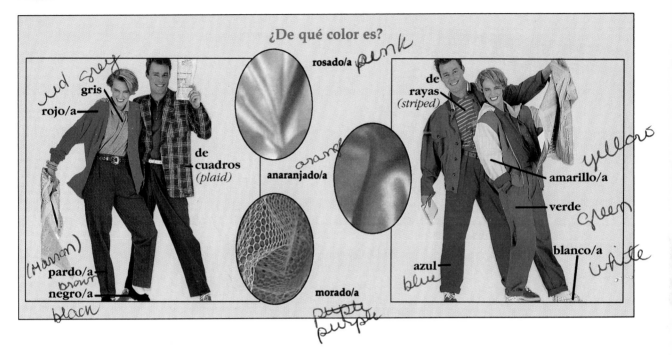

¿De qué color es?

rosado/a *pink*

gris *red grey*

rojo/a

de rayas *(striped)*

de cuadros *(plaid)*

anaranjado/a *orange*

amarillo/a *yellow*

verde *green*

pardo/a *(Maroon) brown*

negro/a *black*

morado/a *purple purple*

azul *blue*

blanco/a *white*

A.   Asociaciones. ¿Qué colores asocia Ud. con... ?

¿el dinero? ¿la una de la mañana? ¿una mañana bonita? ¿una mañana fea? ¿el demonio? ¿los Estados Unidos? ¿una jirafa? ¿un pingüino? ¿un limón? ¿una naranja? ¿un elefante? ¿las flores (*flowers*)?

B.   ¿De qué color es? Tell the color of things in your classroom, especially the clothing your classmates are wearing.

MODELOS: El bolígrafo de Anita es amarillo.

Los calcetines de Roberto son azules. Los de Jaime* son pardos.
Los de Julio...

Now describe what someone is wearing, without revealing his or her name. Using your clues, can your classmates guess whom you are describing?

---

*You can avoid repeating the noun **calcetines** just by dropping it and retaining the definite article. Here are some other examples of the same construction: **la camisa de Janet y la camisa de Paula** → **la camisa de Janet y** *la de* **Paula**; **el sombrero del niño y el sombrero de Pablo** → **el sombrero del niño y** *el de* **Pablo.** For more information on this topic, see Appendix 1, Using Adjectives as Nouns.

Briefly scan the text that accompanies these clothing ads. You will not be able to understand every word, but you should be able to identify some words related to clothing and colors. Can you find the Spanish words and phrases that express . . .)?

appealing accessories
flat heels
polka dots
long earrings

Seductora... ¡irresistible!

Si la ocasión es informal, con los mismos pantalones, esta vez con una blusa negra, accesorios tan llamativos como éstos, y unas sandalias de tacón plano ¡se verá regia!

LO «IN»... PUESTO

Lo que más domina e incluso manda este año en la moda veraniega son, sin duda, los colores blanco y negro. La verdad es que para lucir la piel morena no hay nada como el blanco, con la ventaja de que se puede mezclar con casi todos los colores. Los naranjas y amarillos también están en alza, y los lunares que no falten. Las faldas son estrechas, minis o largas, acompañadas de grandes chaquetas con solapas. Los pantalones ceñidos y estrechos, en los bajos, con camisas grandes, blusones y túnicas que se deben llevar siempre con cinturón, porque estilizan la figura. Los vestidos muy «sexy», por encima de la rodilla, y con los hombros descubiertos, o bien camiseros. Son imprescindibles los pendientes muy largos, con el pelo muy corto y llevar muchas pulseras y collares dorados...

PRONUNCIACIÓN: b/v

In Spanish, the pronunciation of the letters **b** and **v** is identical. At the beginning of a phrase or sentence—that is, after a pause—or after *m* or *n*, the letters **b** and **v** are pronounced just like the English stop [b]. Everywhere else they are pronounced like the fricative [b̪], produced by creating friction when pushing the air through the lips. This sound has no equivalent in English.

Practique las siguientes palabras y frases.

1. [b] bueno   viejo   verde   veinte   barato   Vicente
        boda   bota   también   hombre   sombrero
        bienvenido
2. [b̪] novio   llevar   libro   pobre   abrir   abrigo
        universidad   abuelo

3. [b/ƀ]   bueno / es bueno   busca / Ud. busca   bien / muy bien
en Venezuela / de Venezuela   vende / se vende
en Bolivia / de Bolivia

4. [b/ƀ]   beber   bebida   vivir   biblioteca   Babel   vívido

ESTRUCTURAS

9 . EXPRESSING ACTIONS AND STATES
Tener, venir, preferir, querer, and *poder*; Some Idioms with *tener*

tener *(to have)*	venir *(to come)*	preferir *(to prefer)*	querer *(to want)*	poder *(to be able, can)*
tengo	vengo	prefiero	quiero	puedo
tienes	vienes	prefieres	quieres	puedes
tiene	viene	prefiere	quiere	puede
tenemos	venimos	preferimos	queremos	podemos
tenéis	venís	preferís	queréis	podéis
tienen	vienen	prefieren	quieren	pueden

Querer es poder.

You have been using forms of some of these verbs for several chapters. The **yo** forms of **tener** and **venir** are irregular: **tengo, vengo.** In other forms of **tener, venir, preferir,** and **querer,** when the stem vowel **e** is stressed, it becomes **ie**: **t*ie*nes, v*ie*nes, pref*ie*res, qu*ie*res,** and so on. Similarly, the stem vowel **o** in **poder** becomes **ue** when stressed. In vocabulary lists these changes are shown in parentheses after the infinitive: **poder (ue).** You will learn more verbs of this type in Grammar Section 14.

Some Idioms with *tener*

An *idiom* (**Un modismo**) is a group of words that has meaning to the speakers of a language but that does not necessarily appear to make sense when examined word by word. Idiomatic expressions are often different from one language to another. For example, in English, *to pull Mary's leg* usually means *to tease her,* not *to grab her leg and pull it.* In Spanish, *to pull Mary's leg* is **tomarle el pelo a María** (literally, *to take María's hair*).

Many ideas expressed in English with the verb *to be* are expressed in Spanish with idioms using **tener.** You have already used one **tener** idiom: **tener... años.** Here are some additional ones. Note that they describe a condition or state that a person can experience.

tener miedo (de)	to be afraid (of)
tener prisa	to be in a hurry

tener razón	to be right
no tener razón	to be wrong
tener sueño	to be sleepy

Other **tener** idioms include **tener ganas de** (*to feel like*) and **tener que** (*to have to*). The infinitive is always used after these two idiomatic expressions.

Tengo ganas de trabajar.	*I feel like working.*
¿No tienes ganas de descansar?	*Don't you feel like resting?*
Tienen que ser prácticos.	*They have to be practical.*
¿No tiene Ud. que estudiar ahora mismo?	*Don't you have to study right now?*

Práctica

A.   Es la semana de los exámenes. Haga oraciones con las palabras indicadas para describir un día de Sara.

Sara…
1. tener / mucho / exámenes
2. por eso / (ella) venir / a / universidad / todo / días
3. (ella) preferir / estudiar / en / biblioteca / porque / allí / no / hay / mucho ruido (*noise*)
4. hoy / trabajar / hasta / ocho / noche
5. querer / leer / más / pero / no / poder
6. por eso / regresar / a / residencia
7. tener / mucho / sueño / y / tener / ganas / de / descansar / un poco…
8. …pero / ser / imposible / porque / uno / amigos / venir a mirar / la tele

Now retell the same sequence of events twice, first as if they had happened to you, then as if they had happened to you and your roommate, using **nosotros/as.** Supply an appropriate name for your roommate.

B.   Listen as a classmate reads the following paragraphs to you and complete them with the appropriate **tener** idioms.

1. De repente (*Suddenly*) hay un terremoto (*earthquake*). Todos tienen _____.
2. Ernesto regresa a la universidad. Son las tres menos cinco y tiene una clase de matemáticas a las tres. Ernesto tiene _____.
3. Hay una fiesta porque hoy es el cumpleaños (*birthday*) del primo Antonio. Tiene 29 _____. Todos tienen _____ de ir a la fiesta.
4. En la fiesta, hay muchos paquetes para Antonio. Son regalos para él y por eso tiene _____ abrir los regalos.
5. PROFESOR: ¿Y la capital de la Argentina?
   MARCIA: Buenos Aires.
   CELIA: Cuzco.
   Marcia tiene _____ y Celia no tiene _____. Celia tiene _____ estudiar más.
6. ¿Los exámenes de la clase de español? ¡Son siempre muy fáciles (*easy*)! Yo no tengo _____.

C.   Give advice to this person, who needs to make some clothing purchases immediately.

¡Qué horror! Tiene que comprar…
No puede asistir a…

Notas comunicativas: More About Getting Information

You have already used the tag phrase **¿verdad?** at the end of statements to change them into questions. Another common Spanish tag phrase is **¿no?**

Venden de todo aquí, $\begin{cases} \textbf{¿no?} \\ \textbf{¿verdad?} \end{cases}$ *They sell everything here, right? (don't they?)*

No necesito impermeable hoy,   *I don't need a raincoat today, do I?*
   ¿verdad?

¿Verdad? is found after affirmative or negative statements; **¿no?** is usually found after affirmative statements only. The inverted question mark comes immediately before the tag question, not at the beginning of the statement.

D.   Entrevista: Preferencias. Using question tags, try to predict the way your instructor will complete these sentences. He or she will answer as truthfully as possible.

1.   Ud. prefiere…
        los gatos / los perros
        la ropa elegante / la ropa informal
2.   Ud. quiere comprar…
        un coche deportivo, por ejemplo, un Porsche / una camioneta
        un abrigo / un impermeable
3.   Ud. viene a la universidad…
        todos los días / sólo tres veces a la semana
        en coche / en autobús
4.   Esta noche Ud. tiene ganas de…
        mirar la tele / leer
        comer en un restaurante / preparar la cena (*dinner*)
5.   Esta noche Ud. *no* puede…
        asistir a una fiesta / descansar

Barcelona, España

En la calle°   *street*
—Oye, quiero hablar un momento contigo.°   *with you*
—No puedo ahora… tengo prisa… ¡Hay unas rebajas°   *sales*
  estupendas en Celso García! Hasta luego, ¿eh?
—¡Hombre, siempre tienes prisa!
—¡Tú, tranquila! ¡Nos vemos° mañana!   *See you*

VOCABULARIO

¿Cómo estás? ¿Dónde estás?

estar (*to be*)	
estoy	estamos
estás	estáis
está	están

You have been using forms of the verb **estar** from the beginning of *¿Qué tal?* Note their use in the following brief dialogue, which shows how to invite someone to go and have coffee with you.

DESPUÉS DE (*AFTER*) CLASE

—¿Tienes tiempo para tomar un café?
—Gracias, pero no puedo.

- No estoy muy bien hoy y quiero regresar a casa.
- Tengo un examen mañana y tengo que estudiar.
- Ya tengo otros planes. Lo siento. (*I'm sorry.*)
- Estoy citado/a (*I've got a date*) con unos amigos en la biblioteca.
- Tengo que estar en el centro (*downtown*) a las tres.

—Tal vez (*Perhaps*) mañana, ¿eh?
—Sí, cómo no.

Universidad de los Andes, Bogotá, Colombia.

You need to use forms of **estar** to tell where someone or something is located and to describe someone's feelings, state of health, or other conditions.

¿Dónde **está** la camiseta de Diego?	*Where's Diego's T-shirt?*
—**Está** allí, en la mesa.	*—It's over there, on the table.*
¿Cómo está Ud. hoy?	*How are you today?*
—Estoy bien (mal, enfermo).	*—I'm fine (not well, sick).*

Estar is also used in a number of fixed expressions, such as **¡está muy de moda!**, which you saw earlier in this chapter, and **estar de acuerdo (con)**, which means *to be in agreement (with)*.

¿No están Uds. de acuerdo con Pablo?	*Don't you agree with Pablo?*
—¡De ninguna manera!	*—No way!*

You will work with additional uses of **estar** later in this chapter.

A.   Un día de compras. Form complete sentences about a day spent shopping with a friend, based on the cues given. When the subject pronoun is in parentheses, do not use it in the sentence.

1. (yo) estar / en la residencia / por la mañana
2. (yo) leer / en / periódico / que / hay / grande / rebajas (*sales*) / hoy
3. (yo) no / querer / estar / en / cuarto / todo / día
4. por eso / (yo) llamar / a* una amiga: «Anita, / ¿cómo / estar?»
5. (ella) estar / en casa / porque / estar / enfermo
6. luego / (yo) hablar / por teléfono / con / Carlos
7. él / estar / libre (*free*) / este / mañana
8. ¡(nosotros) estar / en / centro / a / diez!
9. rebajas / ser / estupendo / y / a / una / ya (*already*) / (nosotros) estar / cansado (*tired*)
10. a / una y media / tarde / (nosotros) ya estar / en / café / para / tomar / cerveza

Now retell the story as if you were Carlos, using the same cues as a guide and making the necessary adjustments: **1. Mi amiga está en la residencia...** In number 6, use **...conmigo** (*with me*).

B.   Situaciones. ¿Qué hacemos? (*What are we doing?*) With another student, form sentences that tell where you are and one thing you are doing there. Follow the model.

MODELO: en la clase → —Estamos en la clase.
                              —Cantamos en español.

1.   en una boda (fiesta)   3.   en casa (la residencia)
2.   en un restaurante (bar)   4.   en la librería

Now reverse the situation. Tell what you are doing, then tell where you are.

MODELO: cantar en español →
                              —Cantamos en español.
                              —Estamos en la cafetería con unos amigos colombianos.

1.   descansar   3.   comer espaguetis
2.   celebrar una fiesta   4.   hablar por teléfono

C.   ¿Con qué o con quién está Ud. de acuerdo?

1.   (No) Estoy de acuerdo con las ideas políticas de... (el presidente, los republicanos, los demócratas, el senador _____, Karl Marx, los capitalistas, ¿ ?)
2.   (No) Estoy totalmente de acuerdo con las ideas de... (mis padres, mis abuelos, mis profesores, todos mis amigos, las instituciones religiosas, ¿ ?)

---

*Note again the use of the word **a** before a direct object that refers to a specific person or persons: **llamar a una amiga.** This **a** has no equivalent in English. You will learn to use the word **a** in this way in Grammar Section 17.

ESTRUCTURAS

10. ¿SER O ESTAR?
Summary of the Uses of *ser* and *estar*

Aquí hay un lado (*side*) de una conversación entre una esposa que está en un viaje de negocios (*business trip*) y su (*her*) esposo, que está en casa. Habla el esposo.

Aló [...] ¿Cómo *estás*, mi amor? [...] ¿Dónde *estás* ahora? [...] ¿Qué hora *es* ahí? ¡Uyy!, *es* muy tarde. Y el hotel, ¿cómo *es*? [...] ¿Cuánto cuesta por noche? [...] *Es* bien barato. Oye, ¿qué haces ahora? [...] Ay, pobre, lo siento. *Estás* muy ocupada. ¿Con quién *estás* citada mañana? [...] ¿Quién *es* el dueño de esa tienda? [...] Ah, él *es* de Cuba, ¿verdad? [...] Bueno, mi vida, ¿dónde *estás* mañana? [...] ¿Y cuándo regresas? [...] *Está* bien, querida. Hasta luego, ¿eh? [...] Adiós.

Ahora imagine las palabras de la otra esposa.

Aló. [...] → **Aló, buenas noches, querido.** → ¿Cómo estás, mi amor? [...] etcétera.

Summary of the Uses of *ser*

- To *identify* people and things
- To express *nationality*; with **de** to express *origin*
- With **de** to tell of what *material* something is made
- With **para** to tell *for whom something is intended*.
- To tell *time*
- With **de** to express *possession*
- With *adjectives* that describe *basic, inherent characteristics*
- To form many *generalizations*

Ella **es doctora.**
Son cubanos. Son de la Habana.

Este bolígrafo **es de plástico.**
El regalo **es para** Sara.

Son las once. Es la una y media.
Es de Carlota.
Ramona **es inteligente.**

Es necesario llegar temprano. **Es importante** estudiar.

Hello . . . How are you, dear? . . . Where are you now? . . . What time is it there? . . . My, it's very late. And how's the hotel? . . . How much is it per night? . . . It's very inexpensive. Hey, what are you doing now? . . . Poor dear, I'm sorry. You're very busy. Whom do you have an appointment with tomorrow? . . . Who is the owner of that store? . . . Ah, he's from Cuba, isn't he? . . . Well, dear, where will you be tomorrow? . . . And when are you coming home? . . . OK, dear. Talk to you soon . . . 'Bye.

Summary of the Uses of *estar*

• To tell *location*	El libro **está en la mesa.**
• To describe *health*	Paco **está enfermo.**
• With *adjectives* that describe *conditions*	**Estoy** muy **ocupada.**
• In a number of *fixed expressions*	**(No) Estoy de acuerdo. Está bien. Está claro.**

Ser and *estar* with Adjectives

Ser is used with adjectives that describe the fundamental qualities of a person, place, or thing.

La amistad es **importante.**	*Friendship is important.*
¡Sus calcetines son **morados**!	*Her socks are purple!*
Esta chaqueta es muy **larga.**	*This jacket is very long.*

Estar is used with adjectives to express conditions or observations that are true at a given moment but that do not describe inherent qualities of the noun.

furioso/a	furious	**sucio/a**	dirty
nervioso/a	nervous	**limpio/a**	clean
cansado/a	tired	**abierto/a**	open
ocupado/a	busy	**cerrado/a**	closed
aburrido/a	bored	**triste**	sad
preocupado/a	worried	**alegre, contento/a**	happy

Many adjectives can be used with either **ser** or **estar**, depending on what the speaker intends to communicate. In general, when *to be* implies *looks, tastes, feels,* or *appears,* **estar** is used. Compare the following pairs of sentences:

Daniel **es** guapo.	*Daniel is handsome. (He is a handsome person.)*
Daniel **está** muy guapo esta noche.	*Daniel looks very nice (handsome) tonight.*
Este plato mexicano **es** muy rico.	*This Mexican dish is very delicious.*
Este plato mexicano **está** muy rico.	*This Mexican dish is (tastes) great.*
¿Cómo **es** Amalia? —**Es** simpática.	*What is Amalia like (as a person)?—She's nice.*
¿Cómo **está** Amalia? —**Está** enferma todavía.	*How is Amalia (feeling)? —She's still feeling sick.*

Práctica

A.   ¡Una tienda desastrosa! Cambie por antónimos los adjetivos indicados para describir la tienda.

1.   Cuando los clientes llegan a la tienda, ya no (*no longer*) está *abierta*; está _____.
2.   Los impermeables no están *limpios*; están _____.
3.   Una dependienta no está *bien*; está _____.
4.   El dueño (*owner*) de la tienda no está *contento*; está _____.
5.   Por eso los otros dependientes no están muy *tranquilos*; están _____.

B.   Haga oraciones completas con una palabra o frase de cada grupo.

1.   Hay algo (*something*) en la mesa. ¿Qué es? Es una camisa.

La camisa	es	muy de moda / de Celso García / sucia
	está	de algodón / de cuadros / roja y verde
		en una caja (*box*) bonita / un regalo para...

2.   Hay también una fotografía en la mesa de su (*your*) cuarto. ¿Quiénes son los jóvenes que aparecen en la foto?

Los jóvenes	son	mis primos argentinos / de Buenos Aires
	están	con los abuelos en la foto / muy simpáticos / en San Francisco esta semana
		muy contentos con el viaje (*trip*) en general / un poco cansados después (*after*) del viaje

C.   Actividades sociales. Complete the following description with the correct form of **ser** or **estar**, as suggested by the context.

LAS FIESTAS: Las fiestas (*ser/estar*[1]) populares entre los jóvenes de todas partes del mundo°. Ofrecen una buena oportunidad para (*ser/estar*[2]) con los amigos y conocer° a nuevas personas. Imagine que Ud. (*ser/estar*[3]) en una fiesta con muchos hispanos en este momento: todos (*ser/estar*[4]) muy alegres. Comen, hablan y bailan... ¡Y (*ser/estar*[5]) los dos de la mañana!

world
to meet

LA PANDILLA:° Hoy en el mundo hispánico ya no (*ser/estar*[6]) necesario tener chaperona. Muchas de las actividades sociales se dan° en grupos. Si Ud. (*ser/estar*[7]) miembro de una pandilla, sus° amigos (*ser/estar*[8]) el centro de su vida social y Ud. y su novio o novia salen° frecuentemente con otras parejas° o personas del grupo.

group of friends
se... ocurren
your
go out
couples

¿Sí o no? ¿Son éstas las opiniones de un joven hispánico?

1. Me gustan mucho las fiestas.
2. Nunca bailamos en las fiestas.
3. Todavía es necesario salir con chaperona.
4. La pandilla tiene poca importancia.

D. Haga oraciones completas. Use las palabras entre paréntesis y la forma correcta de **ser** o **estar**, según el modelo.

> MODELO: ¿El vestido de Delia (muy elegante) →
> Es muy elegante.

1. ¿John? (norteamericano)
2. ¿Mi otro suéter? (sucio)
3. ¿Los Hernández? (ocupados esta noche)
4. ¿Yo? (muy bien hoy)
5. ¿Su abuelo? (viejo, muy viejo)
6. ¿El problema? (muy difícil)
7. ¿La clase de computación? (muy interesante)
8. ¿Maricarmen? (no de acuerdo con nosotros)
9. ¿Los hijos de Francisco? (rubios y cariñosos)
10. ¿La tienda? (abierta esta tarde)

E.   Escenas de la primera (*first*) cita. ¿Cómo se dice en español?

1. These flowers (**flores**, *f.*) are for you.
2. I'm a little nervous.
3. You look very pretty tonight!
4. It's necessary to be home by (**para**) 12:00. Is that clear?
5. Oh, the restaurant is already closed.
6. These tacos are (taste) good!
7. The movie (**película**) is excellent, isn't it?
8. It's 11:00, but I'm not tired yet.

F.   Describa este dibujo de un cuarto típico de la residencia. Invente los detalles necesarios. ¿Quiénes son las dos compañeras de cuarto? ¿De dónde son? ¿Cómo son? ¿Dónde están en este momento? ¿Qué hay en el cuarto? ¿En qué condición está el cuarto? ¿Están ordenadas o desordenadas las dos?

G.   Sentimientos. Complete the following sentences by telling how you feel in the situations described. Then ask questions of other students in the class to find at least one person who completed a given sentence the way you did.

> MODELO: Cuando saco (*I get*) una A en un examen, estoy
> _____. →
> ¿Cómo te sientes (*do you feel*) cuando tienes una A en un examen?

1. Cuando saco una A en un examen, estoy _____.
2. Cuando tengo mucho trabajo, estoy _____.
3. Cuando no puedo estar con mis amigos, estoy _____.
4. Por lo general, cuando estoy en clase, estoy _____.
5. Los lunes (*Mondays*) por la mañana, estoy _____.
6. Los viernes (*Fridays*) por la noche, estoy _____.

UN POCO DE TODO

A.   Se busca dependiente. (*Clerk needed.*) Form complete questions based on the words in the order given. Conjugate the verbs and add other words if necessary. Use subject pronouns only when needed.

INTERVIEWER:

1. ¿tener / Ud. / experiencia / trabajando (*working*) / en / tienda de ropa?
2. ¿cuánto / años / tener / Ud.?
3. Ud. / asistir / clases / en / universidad / todo / mañanas / ¿no?

APPLICANT:

a. ¿poder / yo / trabajar / siempre / por / noche?
b. ¿hora / abrir / Uds. / almacén?
c. yo / no / tener / llegar / ocho / ¿verdad?

Now answer the questions.

Notas lingüísticas: Using *mucho* and *poco*

In the first chapters of *¿Qué tal?* you have used the words **mucho** and **poco** as both adjectives and adverbs. *Adverbs* (**Los adverbios**) are words that modify verbs, adjectives or other adverbs: *quickly*, *very smart*, *very quickly*. In Spanish and in English, adverbs are invariable in form.

Adverb:	Rosario estudia **mucho** hoy.	*Rosario is studying a lot today.*
Adjective:	Rosario tiene **mucha** ropa.	*Rosario has a lot of clothes.*
	Sobre todo tiene **muchos** zapatos.	*She especially has a lot of shoes.*

B.   Entrevista: Más preferencias. With a classmate, explore preferences in a number of areas by asking and answering questions based on the following cues. Form your questions with expressions like these:

¿Prefieres… o… ?
¿Te gusta más (*infinitive*) o (*infinitive*)?

If you have no preference, express that by saying **No tengo preferencia**. Be prepared to report some of your findings to the class. If you both agree, you will express this by saying **Preferimos…** If you do not agree, give the preferences of both persons: **Yo prefiero… pero Cecilia prefiere…**

1. Los animales: ¿los gatos siameses o los persas?* ¿los perros pastores alemanes o los perros de lanas (*poodles*)? ¿tener muchos o pocos animales?

---

*Note the *article + adjective* or *demonstrative + adjective* combination that can be used as a noun: **los gatos persas** (*Persian cats*) → **los persas** (*Persians*); **aquellos pantalones azules** (*those blue pants*) → **aquellos azules** (*those blue ones*). For more information on this topic, see Appendix 1, Using Adjectives as Nouns.

2. El color de la ropa informal: ¿el color negro o el blanco? ¿el rojo o el azul?
3. La ropa informal: ¿las camisas de algodón o las de seda? ¿los *bluejeans* de algodón o los pantalones de lana? ¿tener mucha o poca ropa?
4. La ropa de mujeres: ¿las faldas largas o las minifaldas? ¿los pantalones largos o los pantalones cortos?
5. La ropa de hombres: ¿las camisas de cuadros o las de rayas? (¿o las camisas de un solo (*a single*) color?) ¿chaqueta y pantalón o un traje formal?
6. Las actividades en casa: ¿mirar mucho la televisión o leer una novela? ¿escribir muchas cartas o hablar con unos amigos?

UN PASO MAS: Lectura cultural

Antes de leer: Finding the Main Parts of a Sentence

When reading Spanish, it's easy to "get lost" in long sentences. Here is a way to get around that difficulty. First omit the words and information set off by commas and concentrate on the main verb and its subject. Try this strategy in the following sentence.

En muchos lugares del mundo hispánico, especialmente en las tierras templadas o frías, los hombres casi siempre llevan una camisa con corbata y una chaqueta.

Once you have located the subject and verb (**los hombres**, **llevan**), you can read the sentence again, adding more information to the framework provided by the phrase *men wear*. . . Men from what part of the world? What, specifically, do they wear? Try the strategy again in this sentence.

Aunque mi mamá parece tímida, es una mujer independiente con ideas fijas que no tiene miedo de ofrecer su opinión.

Now apply the strategy to the reading.

LAS MODAS

Por lo general, los hispanos desean lucir bien.° Claro que los *bluejeans* son muy populares <u>entre</u> los jóvenes de todo el mundo. Pero para casi toda ocasión los hispanos se visten° con más esmero que° los norteamericanos. Cuando uno está en la calle, es decir,° cuando no está en casa, es preferible estar elegante.

En muchos lugares del mundo hispánico, especialmente en las tierras <u>templadas</u> o frías, los hombres por lo general llevan camisa con corbata y una <u>chaqueta</u>. Los colores preferidos para los pantalones y las chaquetas son azul, negro o gris, y las camisas son casi siempre blancas. <u>En cambio</u>, las mujeres usan ropa de colores vivos y alegres.

lucir... look nice

se... dress / con... more carefully than

es... that is

En los climas cálidos, el estilo de ropa se relaciona con el tiempo.° En ciudades como Cartagena, Veracruz o Guayaquil, por ejemplo, no todos los hombres llevan siempre chaqueta y corbata. Es muy común en estos lugares llevar una guayabera* para ir a la oficina o la universidad. Las guayaberas pueden ser muy elegantes; hay algunas muy bonitas, bordadas a mano.° También son muy cómodas.°

weather

bordadas... hand-embroidered
comfortable

Si usted visita un país hispánico, debe llevar ropa apropiada. Así° usted siempre puede causar una buena impresión.

That way

Comprensión

¿Cierto o falso? Corrija las oraciones falsas.

1. Los hispanos tienen poco interés en lucir bien.
2. A veces el clima determina el tipo de ropa que una persona lleva.
3. Al hombre hispano típico le gusta llevar ropa de colores vivos.
4. Cartagena y Veracruz son ciudades con un clima templado.
5. La guayabera es una camisa que se lleva solamente en casa.

Para escribir

Complete el siguiente párrafo sobre las modas en los Estados Unidos.

En los Estados Unidos la individualidad es importante en las modas. Por ejemplo, los estudiantes llevan _____, pero los profesores _____. También son diferentes los estilos de los jóvenes y los viejos. Las madres llevan _____ y los padres _____. Pero yo, cuando bailo en una discoteca (estudio en la biblioteca, trabajo en casa), llevo _____.

VOCABULARIO

Verbos

descansar to rest
estar (*irreg.*) to be
llevar to wear; to carry; to take
poder (**ue**) to be able, can
preferir (**ie**) to prefer
querer (**ie**) to want
tener (*irreg.*) to have
venir (*irreg.*) to come

La ropa

el abrigo coat
los *bluejeans* jeans
la blusa blouse
la bolsa purse
la bota boot
los calcetines socks
la camisa shirt
la camiseta T-shirt
la cartera wallet

el cinturón belt
la corbata tie
la chaqueta jacket
la falda skirt
el impermeable raincoat
las medias stockings
los pantalones pants
el par pair
el reloj watch
la sandalia sandal

*A **guayabera** is a man's shirt made to wear outside the trousers, not tucked in.

el **sombrero** hat
el **suéter** sweater
el **traje** suit
el **traje de baño** swimsuit
el **vestido** dress
el **zapato** shoe

Otros sustantivos

la **calle** street
la **película** movie
el **ruido** noise
la **tienda** store

Los colores

amarillo/a yellow
anaranjado/a orange
azul blue
blanco/a white
gris gray
morado/a purple
negro/a black
pardo/a brown Marron
rojo/a red
rosado/a pink
verde green

Materiales

es de... it is made of . . .
   algodón cotton
   lana wool
   seda silk

Adjetivos

abierto/a open
aburrido/a bored
alegre happy
cansado/a tired
cerrado/a closed
contento/a content, happy
difícil difficult, hard
enfermo/a sick
fácil easy
furioso/a angry
limpio/a clean
nervioso/a nervous
ocupado/a busy
preocupado/a worried
querido/a dear; beloved
sucio/a dirty
triste sad

Palabras adicionales

ahora mismo right now
de cuadros plaid
de rayas striped
en este momento right now, at this
   very moment
todavía still
ya already
   ya no no longer

estar citado/a to have a date, an
   appointment
estar de acuerdo (con) to be in
   agreement (with)

no tener razón to be wrong
tener...
   ganas de + *inf.* to feel like
      (*doing something*)
   miedo (de) to be afraid (of)
   prisa to be in a hurry
   que + *inf.* to have to (*do
      something*)
   razón to be right
   sueño to be sleepy

Frases útiles para la comunicación	
Está bien.	It's O.K. (fine).
Está claro.	It's clear.
¡Está muy de moda!	It's the latest style!
Lo siento.	I'm sorry.
¿no? ⎫ **¿verdad?** ⎭	right?, don't they (you, *etc.*)?
¡Nos vemos!	See you around!

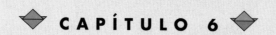

◆ C A P Í T U L O 6 ◆

DE COMPRAS

VOCABULARIO: ¿DÓNDE VENDEN... ?

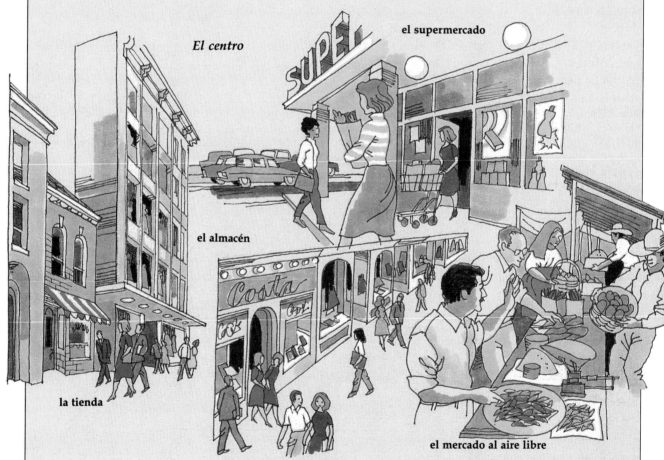

El centro

el supermercado

el almacén

la tienda

el centro comercial

el mercado al aire libre

comprar to buy
regatear to haggle, bargain
vender to sell
¡Venden de todo! They sell everything!

el precio (fijo) (fixed, set) price
las rebajas sales, reductions

barato/a inexpensive
caro/a expensive

110

A.   Complete las oraciones lógicamente.

1.   Un _____ es una tienda grande.
2.   No es posible _____ cuando hay precios fijos.
3.   Quiero _____ el coche, pero el _____ es muy alto.
4.   En la librería _____ de todo: textos y otros libros, cuadernos, lápices... Y siempre hay grandes _____ al final del semestre/trimestre.
5.   _____ de una ciudad es la parte céntrica.
6.   Siempre hay *boutiques* en los _____.
7.   Es fácil regatear en un _____ al aire libre.
8.   No puedo comprar esa blusa. Es demasiado (*too*) _____.

B.   **Preguntas.** Using tag questions (**¿no?, ¿verdad?**) ask a classmate questions based on the following statements. He or she will answer, based on general information, or as truthfully as possible, if the question is about aspects of his or her life.

1.   En un almacén hay precios fijos.
2.   Regateamos mucho en los Estados Unidos.
3.   En México no hay muchos mercados al aire libre.
4.   Los *bluejeans* Calvin Klein son muy baratos.
5.   Es necesario llevar traje y corbata a clase.
6.   Sólo compras ropa cuando hay rebajas.
7.   No hay centros comerciales en el mundo hispánico.
8.   Venden de todo en un *boutique*.

SUPERMERCADO

BOUTIQUES DE ALIMENTACION

MODA

EQUIPAMIENTO PERSONAL
Y DEPORTES

SERVICIOS

DECORACION Y HOGAR

RESTAURANTES

APERTURA 7 DE NOVIEMBRE

ABIERTO DESDE LAS 9 DE LA MAÑANA

ARTURO SORIA, 126

ARTURO SORIA
PLAZA

Al tanto...

Here are some more ways to talk about prices.

barato:	¡Es/Fue...	It is/was . . .
	una ganga!	a bargain!
	regalado/a!	a gift (so cheap that it was given away!)
caro:	¡Cuesta/Costó...	It costs/cost . . .
	un dineral!	a fortune!
	un ojo de la cara!	an arm and a leg! (lit., *an eye from my face!*)

What stores and services are available at the Arturo Soria Plaza? Make a list of as many as you can find, then compare your list with those of other classmates. Note: in this context, **servicios** is a false cognate. Can you guess what it means?

¿Recuerda Ud.?

Before beginning Grammar Section 11, review what you already know about expressing possession. Use **de** + *noun* to express these sentences in Spanish.

1.   Whose presents are these?
2.   They're Carmen's.
3.   Carmen's wedding is *today?!*

4.   Yes, and all of Miguel's relatives are coming.

ESTRUCTURAS

11. EXPRESSING POSSESSION
Possessive Adjectives (Unstressed)*

En el periódico

Querida Antonia,

Tengo un problema con <u>mis</u> padres. Me gusta ir de compras con <u>mi</u> hermana menor, pero <u>nuestros</u> padres creen que no se debe gastar dinero. ¡<u>Nuestra</u> situación es desesperante! ¿Cuál es <u>tu</u> consejo?

Sin Zapatos

Querida Sin Zapatos,

<u>Tu</u> situación es difícil pero no es imposible de solucionar. Debes contraer matrimonio con un ladrón porque casi siempre son ricos y no les importa gastar mucho dinero. Por otro lado, casi siempre tienen un par de esposas...†

Antonia

¿Qué escribe Sin Zapatos, **mi** o **mis**?
1.   _____ padres tienen mucho dinero.
2.   _____ hermana también quiere ir de compras.
3.   ¡_____ situación es terrible!

¿Qué contesta Antonia, **tu** or **tus**?
4.   _____ zapatos son muy viejos.
5.   _____ padre no tiene razón.
6.   _____ problema tiene solución.

In the newspaper   Dear Antonia, I have a problem with my parents. I like to go shopping with my younger sister, but our parents think that one should not spend money. Our situation is desperate! What is your advice? Shoeless

Dear Shoeless, Your situation is difficult but not impossible to solve. You should marry a thief because they're almost always rich and they don't mind spending a lot of money. On the other hand, they almost always have a couple of wives (handcuffs†) . . . Antonia

*There is another set of possessives called the Stressed Possessive Adjectives. They can be used as nouns. For information on them, see Appendix 1, Using Adjectives as Nouns.

†The plural form **esposas** means *handcuffs* as well as *wives*.

You have already used **mi(s)**, one of the possessive adjectives in Spanish. Here is the complete set.

POSSESSIVE ADJECTIVES				
my	**mi** libro/mesa **mis** libros/mesas	*our*	nuest**ro** libro nuest**ros** libros	nuest**ra** mesa nuest**ras** mesas
your	**tu** libro/mesa **tus** libros/mesas	*your*	vuest**ro** libro vuest**ros** libros	vuest**ra** mesa vuest**ras** mesas
your, his, *her, its* }	**su** libro/mesa **sus** libros/mesas	*your,* *their* }	**su** libro/mesa **sus** libros/mesas	

In Spanish, the ending of a possessive adjective agrees in form with the person or thing possessed, not with the owner/possessor. Note that unstressed possessive adjectives are placed before the noun.

$$\text{Son} \begin{Bmatrix} \text{mis} \\ \text{tus} \\ \text{sus} \end{Bmatrix} \text{zapatos.} \qquad \text{Es} \begin{Bmatrix} \text{nuestra} \\ \text{vuestra} \\ \text{su} \end{Bmatrix} \text{tienda.}$$

The possessive adjectives **mi(s)**, **tu(s)**, and **su(s)** show agreement in number only with the nouns they modify. **Nuestro/a/os/as** and **vuestro/a/os/as**, like all adjectives that end in **-o**, show agreement in both number and gender.

Notas lingüísticas: Clarifying Meaning with Possessives

Su(s) can have several different equivalents in English: *your* (sing.), *his, her, its, your* (pl.), *their*. Usually its meaning will be clear in context. For example, if you are admiring the car of someone whom you address as **Ud.** and ask, **¿Es nuevo su coche?**, it is clear from the context that you mean *Is your car new?* When context does not make the meaning of **su(s)** clear, **de** and a pronoun are used instead, to indicate the possessor.

el sombrero
la chaqueta
los calcetines
las sandalias } de él (de ella, de Ud., de ellos, de ellas, de Uds.)

¿Son jóvenes los hijos **de él**?	*Are his children young?*
¿Dónde vive el abuelo **de ellas**?	*Where does their grandfather live?*

Práctica

A. Which nouns can these possessive adjectives modify without changing form?

1. **su:** almacén / precios / tiendas / cartera / traje de baño / bolsas / esposo
2. **tus:** camisetas / zapatos / chaqueta / corbata / abrigo / hermanas
3. **mi:** pantalones / suéter / impermeable / zapatos / amor / vestido / prima

4. **sus:** trajes / centros comerciales / sandalias / almacén / reloj / precios
5. **nuestras:** blusa / botas / padres / camisas / vestidos / noviazgo / ropa
6. **nuestro:** calcetines / pariente / tacos / camiseta / coche / mamá / almacén

B.   ¿Cómo es la tienda del Sr. Alberti? Conteste según el modelo.

MODELO: tienda / grande → Su tienda es grande.

1. edificio / viejo
2. dependientes / muy trabajador
3. precios / fijo
4. ropa / muy de moda
5. abrigos / caro
6. botas / barato

Ahora imagine que Ud. es el Sr. Alberti. Describa su tienda con las mismas palabras como guía.

MODELO: tienda / grande → Mi tienda es grande.

C.   ¡Propaganda! Your store has the following characteristics. Explain them to a prospective client, following the model.

MODELO: tienda / extraordinario → ¡Nuestra tienda es extraordinaria!

1. precios / bajo
2. ropa / elegante
3. dependientes / amable
4. estacionamiento (*parking*) / gratis

Notas comunicativas: Asking for Repetition

As the exchanges you are able to have with others in Spanish become more complex, there is a greater chance that you will not always understand completely what the person you are speaking to has said. In the **Pasos preliminares** you learned to use the following sentences in that context: **Otra vez, por favor. No entiendo.** Here are some additional simple phrases you can use to ask for a repetition or to express a lack of understanding.

Repite,* por favor. No entendí.	*Repeat, please, I didn't get it.*
Favor de repetir.	*Please repeat.*
¿Cómo?	*What? I didn't catch that.*

Note in particular the use of **¿Cómo?** (and not **¿Qué?**) to indicate a real lack of understanding.

D.   Entrevista. You have already learned a great deal about the families of your classmates and instructor. This interview will help you gather more information. Use the questions as a guide to interview your instructor or a classmate and take notes on what he or she says. Then report the information to the class.

1. ¿Cómo es su familia? ¿grande? ¿pequeña? ¿Cuántas personas viven en su casa?
2. ¿Son norteamericanos sus padres? ¿hispanos? ¿De dónde son?

---

*Repite is the informal command form. Use it with a classmate or with someone you know well. **Repita** is the formal command.

3. ¿Son simpáticos sus padres? ¿generosos? ¿cariñosos?

4. ¿Trabaja su padre (madre)? ¿Dónde?   1 hermana - 24

5. ¿Cuántos hijos tienen sus padres? ¿Cuántos años tienen?

6. ¿Cómo son sus hermanos? ¿listos? ¿traviesos (*mischievous*)? ¿trabajadores? Si son muy jóvenes, ¿prefieren estudiar o mirar la televisión? Si son mayores (*older*), ¿trabajan o estudian? ¿Dónde?

7. ¿Viven sus padres en una casa o en un apartamento? ¿Cómo es su casa/apartamento?

8. ¿Sus abuelos/tíos viven también en la casa (el apartamento)?

9. ¿De dónde son sus abuelos? ¿Cuántos años tienen? ¿Cuántos hijos tienen?

10. ¿Tiene Ud. esposo/a o novio/a? ¿Cómo se llama? ¿Cuánto tiempo lleva con él/ella? ¿Cómo es? ¿Trabaja o estudia?

mediana: middle

VOCABULARIO

¿Qué día es hoy?

lunes	Monday	viernes	Friday
martes	Tuesday	sábado	Saturday
miércoles	Wednesday	domingo	Sunday
jueves	Thursday		

el lunes, el martes...	on Monday, on Tuesday . . .
los lunes, los martes...	on Mondays, on Tuesdays . . .
Hoy (Mañana) es viernes.	Today (Tomorrow) is Friday.
el fin de semana	(on) the weekend
pasado mañana	the day after tomorrow
el próximo (martes, miércoles, ...)	next (Tuesday, Wednesday, . . .)
la próxima semana	next week

Except for **el sábado/los sábados** and **el domingo/los domingos,** all the days of the week use the same form for the plural as they do for the singular. The definite articles are used to express *on* with the days of the week. The days are not capitalized in Spanish.

A.   Preguntas

1. ¿Qué día es hoy? ¿Qué día es mañana? Si hoy es sábado, ¿qué día es mañana? Si hoy es jueves, ¿qué día es mañana? ¿Qué día fue ayer?

2. ¿Qué días de la semana tenemos clase? ¿Qué días no?

3. ¿Estudia Ud. mucho durante el fin de semana? ¿y los domingos por la noche?

4. ¿Qué le gusta hacer (*to do*) los viernes por la tarde? ¿Le gusta salir (*to go out*) con los amigos los sábados por la noche?

B. Tell at least one thing you want, need, have to, like to, or can do each day this week. Then tell about next week.

MODELO: El lunes quiero (necesito, tengo que, puedo) asistir a clase.
Los lunes me gusta estudiar en la biblioteca por la noche.
El próximo lunes tengo que...

Palabras útiles: dormir (*to sleep*) hasta muy tarde, jugar (*to play*) al tenis (al golf, al vólibol, al...), ir al cine (*to go to the movies*), ir al bar (al parque, al museo, a...), ¿ ?

ESTRUCTURAS

12. EXPRESSING DESTINATION AND FUTURE ACTIONS
Ir; ir + a + Infinitive

Un regalo para la «mamá» ecuatoriana

ALLEN: El sábado *voy a ir* de compras. ¿Quieres *ir* conmigo?

LORENZO: Sí, con mucho gusto. ¿Qué *vas a comprar*?

ALLEN: Un regalo para mi mamá ecuatoriana... algo bueno pero barato—como una tostadora, por ejemplo.

LORENZO: Los aparatos eléctricos son muy caros aquí, Allen. ¿Por qué no compras una blusa bordada a mano?

ALLEN: Todos los artículos hechos a mano son también muy caros, ¿no?

LORENZO: Pues... no. Normalmente aquí son muy baratos.

¿Qué va a pasar el sábado? Complete las oraciones.
1. Allen y Lorenzo van a ir _____.
2. Allen va a buscar _____.
3. Allen no va a comprar _____.
4. Sí va a comprar _____ porque _____.

A gift for one's Ecuadorian "mother"   ALLEN: I'm going to go shopping on Saturday. Do you want to go with me? LORENZO: Yes, I'd really like to (*lit*. With much pleasure). What are you going to buy? ALLEN: A present for my Ecuadorian mother . . . something nice but inexpensive, like a toaster, for example. LORENZO: Electrical appliances are very expensive here, Allen. Why don't you buy a hand-embroidered blouse? ALLEN: All handmade things are also very expensive, aren't they? LORENZO: Well . . . no. Normally they're very inexpensive here.

Forms and uses of *ir*

ir (*to go*)	
voy	vamos
vas	vais
va	van

The first person plural of **ir**, **vamos** (*we go, are going, do go*), is also used to express *let's go*.

    Vamos a clase ahora mismo.   *Let's go to class right now.*

Ir + **a** + *infinitive* is used to describe actions or events in the near future.

    Van a venir a la fiesta esta   *They're going to come to the party*
      noche.   *tonight.*
    Voy a ir de compras esta tarde.   *I'm going to go shopping this*
                                          afternoon.

The Contraction *al*

In Chapter 3 you learned about the contraction **del**, formed by combining **de** with the masculine singular article **el**. There is one other contraction in Spanish: **al** is formed by combining **a** with **el**. Both contractions are obligatory. No other articles contract with **de** or **a**.

    Voy **al** centro comercial.   *I'm going to the mall.*
    ¡Vamos **a la** tienda de la Señora   *Let's go to Mrs. Hernandez's store!*
      Hernández!

Práctica

A. ¿Adónde van Uds. los viernes después de (*after*) la clase? Haga oraciones completas con **ir**.

1. yo / cine
2. Francisca / almacén para trabajar
3. tú / otra clase
4. Jorge y Carlos / café (*m.*)
5. nosotros / biblioteca
6. el profesor (la profesora) / ¿ ?

B. **¡Vamos de compras!** Describa esta excursión al centro. Use **ir** + **a** + el infinitivo, según el modelo.

    MODELO: Raúl compra un regalo para Estela. →
                Raúl va a comprar un regalo para Estela.

1. Llegamos al centro a las diez de la mañana.
2. Los niños comen algo.

3.   Compro unas medias para Lupita.
4.   Raúl busca una blusa de seda.
5.   No compras esta falda de rayas, ¿verdad?
6.   Tenemos que buscar algo más barato.
7.   ¿Puedes ir de compras mañana también?

C.   ¡Qué negativos! Exprese en español con **ir** + **a** + el infinitivo.

1.   I'll go to the market with you (**Uds.**), but I'm not going to bargain!
2.   We'll sell the old car, but we won't buy another, right?
3.   You'll look for bargains, but the things won't be cheap.

D.   ¿Adónde vas si...? ¿Cuántas oraciones puede Ud. hacer?

Me gusta
⎰
leer revistas (*magazines*).
ir de compras—¡no importa el precio!
buscar gangas y regatear.
bailar.
comer en restaurantes elegantes.
mirar programas de detectives.
⎱

Por eso voy a _____.

E.   Entrevista: ¿Qué hay en tu futuro? Complete las oraciones lógicamente.
Luego úselas (*use them*) para entrevistar a un compañero (una compañera)
de clase.

1.   Un día voy a tener (ser, comprar, poder) _____. (¿Qué vas a tener tú? ...)
2.   Esta noche voy a regresar a casa a las _____. Voy a estudiar _____. Voy a
     comer en _____. Y voy a mirar _____ en la tele. (¿Qué vas a... ?)
3.   Mañana voy a llegar a la universidad a la(s) _____. Voy a tener mi pri-
     mera clase a la(s) _____. A la(s) _____ voy a asistir a la clase de español.
     (¿A qué hora... ?)

España

¡Vamos de compras!
—Necesito comprar un abrigo nuevo.
—¿Adónde vas? ¿Al centro comercial?
—Sí. ¿Quieres ir conmigo°?   *with me*
—¡Cómo no! ¿A qué hora vas?
—Pues... a las tres. ¿Qué te parece?°   *¿Qué... What do you think?*
—Perfecto. Nos vemos a las tres.

VOCABULARIO

Los números 100 y más

Continúe la secuencia: cien, ciento uno, ciento dos, ...
mil, dos mil, ...
un millón, dos millones, ...

100	cien, ciento		700	setecientos/as
101	ciento uno/una		800	ochocientos/as
200	doscientos/as		900	novecientos/as
300	tresceintos/as *tresceintos/as*	1.000*	mil
400	cuatrocientos/as		2.000	dos mil
500	quinientos/as		1.000.000	un millón
600	seiscientos/as		2.000.000	dos millones

- **Ciento** is used in combination with numbers from 1 to 99 to express the numbers 101 through 199: **ciento uno, ciento dos, ciento setenta y nueve**, and so on. **Cien** is used in counting and before numbers greater than 100: **cien mil, cien millones**.
- When the numbers 200 through 900 modify a noun, they must agree in gender: **cuatrocientas niñas, doscientas dos casas**.
- **Mil** means *one thousand* or *a thousand*. It does not have a plural form in counting, but **millón** does. When used with a noun, **millón** (**dos millones**, and so on) must be followed by **de**.

1.899	mil ochocientos noventa y nueve
3.000 habitantes	tres mil habitantes
14.000.000 de habitantes	catorce millones de habitantes

A. ¿Cuánto es? Diga los precios.

el dólar (los Estados Unidos, Canadá)
el peso (México)

el bolívar (Venezuela)
la peseta (España)
el quetzal (Guatemala)

1. 7.345 pesetas
2. $100
3. 5.710 quetzales
4. 670 bolívares
5. 2.486 pesetas
6. $1.000.000

7. 528 pesos
8. 836 bolívares
9. 101 pesetas
10. $4.000.000,00
11. 6.500.000,00 pesos
12. 25.000.000,00 pesetas

B. Situaciones. Imagine that you have recently made a number of purchases. With a classmate, ask and answer questions about the amount you paid. Follow the model, using the prices indicated or inventing your own.

---

*In many parts of the Spanish-speaking world, a period is used in numerals where English uses a comma and a comma is used to indicate the decimal where English uses a period: **$10,45**.

Palabras útiles: pagaste (*you paid*), una compra (*purchase*), una ganga, fue

MODELO: el radio ($100) →
—¿Cuánto pagaste por el radio?
—Cien dólares.
—¡Uy! ¡Qué (*How*) cara!
¡Es/Fue una ganga!
Fue una buena compra.

1. la calculadora ($20)
2. tu coche nuevo ($5,600)
3. tu estéreo ($1,500)
4. la computadora ($2,400)

5. el coche usado ($1,850)
6. el reloj ($350)
7. ¿ ?

ESTRUCTURAS

13. DESCRIBING
Comparisons

Tipos y estereotipos

Adolfo es muy atlético y extrovertido, pero estudia poco.

- Es una persona **más** atlética **que** Raúl y Esteban.
- Es **menos** estudioso **que** Raúl.
- Es **tan** extrovertido **como** Esteban.

Y Raúl, ¿cómo es?

- Es menos extrovertido que _____.
- Es más estudioso que _____.
- No es una persona tan atlética como _____.

Esteban trabaja en la cafetería y también estudia—tiene cinco clases este semestre.

- Tiene **tantas** clases **como** Raúl.
- No tiene **tanto** tiempo libre **como** Adolfo.
- Tiene **más** amigos **que** Raúl pero **menos** amigos **que** Adolfo.

Y Adolfo, ¿cómo es?

- No tiene tantas clases _____.
- Tiene más tiempo libre _____.
- Tiene más amigos _____.

As you have just seen while you were describing Adolfo, Raúl, and Esteban, comparative forms enable you to compare and contrast people, things, and characteristics or qualities. Similar—but not identical—forms are used with adjectives and nouns.

WITH ADJECTIVES	WITH NOUNS
más/menos… que	más/menos… que
tan… como	tanto/a/os/as… como

Regular Comparisons of Adjectives*

Alicia es **más perezosa que** Marta.	*Alicia is lazier than Marta.*
Julio es **menos listo que** Pablo.	*Julio is less bright than Pablo.*
Enrique es **tan trabajador como** Alicia.	*Enrique is as hardworking as Alicia.*

The *comparative* (**El comparativo**) of most English adjectives is formed by using the adverbs *more* or *less* (***more** intelligent,* ***less** important*), or by adding *-er* (*tall**er**, long**er***).

In Spanish, unequal comparisons are usually expressed with **más** (*more*) + *adjective* + **que** or **menos** (*less*) + *adjective* + **que**.

Equal comparisons are expressed with **tan** + *adjective* + **como**.

[Práctica A–B]

Comparison of Nouns

Alicia tiene **más/menos** bolsas **que** Susana.	*Alicia has more/fewer purses than Susana.*
Nosotros tenemos **tantas** revistas **como** ellas.	*We have as many magazines as they (do).*

Nouns are compared with the expressions **más/menos** + *noun* + **que** and **tanto/a/os/as** + *noun* + **como**. **Más/menos** *de* is used when the comparison is followed by a number: **Tengo más *de un* hijo. Tanto** must agree in gender and number with the noun it modifies.

[Práctica C–F]

Práctica

A. Conteste según el dibujo.

1. Emilia, ¿es más alta o más baja que Sancho?
2. ¿Es tan tímida como Sancho? ¿Quién es más extrovertido?
3. Sancho, ¿es tan atlético como Emilia?
4. ¿Quién es más intelectual? ¿Por qué cree Ud. eso?
5. ¿Es Emilia tan estudiosa como Sancho? ¿Es tan trabajadora?
6. ¿Quién es más listo? ¿Por qué cree Ud. eso?

*Irregular comparative forms of adjectives are presented in Grammar Section 15.

B.   Opiniones. Cambie (*Change*) las oraciones. Exprese su opinión personal:
tan... como → más/menos que.

1.   Las botas son tan cómodas (*comfortable*) como las sandalias.
2.   Los niños siempre están tan ocupados como sus padres.
3.   También siempre están tan preocupados como sus padres.
4.   El dinero es tan importante como la amistad.
5.   El vólibol es tan difícil como el golf.
6.   Ir de compras es tan interesante como estudiar para un examen.

C.   Compare las cosas de Alfredo con las de Gustavo. Conteste según el
modelo.

ALFREDO   GUSTAVO

MODELO: —tiene tanto/a/os/as _____ como _____.
             —tiene más/menos _____ que _____.

1.   ¿Cuánta ropa tiene Alfredo?
2.   ¿Cuántas camisas tiene Gustavo?
3.   ¿Cuántos pantalones tiene Alfredo?
4.   ¿Cuántos abrigos tiene Gustavo?
5.   ¿Cuántas chaquetas tiene Gustavo?
6.   ¿Cuántos zapatos tiene Alfredo?

D.   Más opiniones. Cambie las oraciones para expresar su opinión personal: **tanto... como → más/menos... que**, o viceversa.

1.   Los profesores trabajan más horas que los estudiantes.
2.   En esta universidad las artes son tan importantes como las ciencias.
3.   Aquí el béisbol es tan importante como el fútbol americano.
4.   Hay más hombres que mujeres en esta clase.
5.   Hay tantos exámenes en la clase de español como en la clase de historia.
6.   En esta ciudad hay tantos cafés al aire libre como en Madrid.
7.   Yo bebo menos café (*coffee*) que el profesor (la profesora).
8.   Las mujeres pueden practicar tantos deportes (*sports*) como los hombres.

E.   ¿Cómo se dice en español?

1.   more than $1.000
2.   fewer than 100 students
3.   fewer than 20 chairs
4.   Are you over 18 years old?
5.   She's over 90 years old!

F.   Conteste las preguntas lógicamente. ¿Es Ud...

1.   tan guapo/a como Tom Cruise/Christie Brinkley?
2.   tan rico/a como los Rockefeller?
3.   tan inteligente como Einstein?
4.   tan romántico/a como su novio/a (esposo/a, amigo/a)?

¿Tiene Ud...

5.   tanto dinero como los Ford?
6.   tantos tíos como tías?
7.   tantos amigos como amigas?
8.   tantas ideas buenas como _____?
9.   tantos años como su profesor(a)?

UN POCO DE TODO

Pero, ¿no se puede regatear? Complete the following paragraph with the correct form of the words in parentheses, as suggested by the context. When two possibilities are given in parentheses, select the correct word.

Cuando Ud. va (*de/a*[1]) compras en (*un/una*[2]) ciudad hispánica, (*ir*[3]) a ver° una (*grande*[4]) variedad de tiendas. Hay almacenes (*elegante*[5]) como (*los/las*[6]) de los Estados Unidos, donde los precios siempre (*ser/estar*[7]) (*fijo*[8]). También hay (*pequeño*[9]) tiendas que se especializan° en un solo° producto. En (*un/una*[10]) zapatería, por ejemplo, venden solamente zapatos. (*El/La*[11]) sufijo **-ería** se usa° para formar el nombre (*del/de la*[12]) tienda. ¿Dónde (*creer*[13]) Ud. que venden papel y (*otro*[14]) artículos de escritorio? ¿A qué tienda (*ir*[15]) Ud. a comprar fruta?

 Si Ud. (*poder*[16]) pagar el precio que piden,° (*deber*[17]) comprar los recuerdos° en (*los/las*[18]) almacenes o *boutiques*. Pero si (*tener*[19]) ganas o necesidad de (*regatear*[20]), tiene (*de/que*[21]) (*ir*[22]) a un mercado: un conjunto° de tiendas (*pequeño*[23]) o locales° donde el ambiente° es más (*informal*[24]) que en los (*grande*[25]) almacenes. Ud. no (*deber*[26]) (*pagar*[27]) el primer° precio que mencione (*el/la*[28]) vendedor°—¡casi siempre va (*de/a*[29]) ser muy alto!

to see

se... specialize / single

se... is used

they ask
souvenirs
grupo
stalls / atmosphere
first
seller

¿Cierto o falso? Corrija las oraciones falsas.

1. En el mundo hispánico, todas las tiendas son similares.
2. Uno puede regatear en un almacén hispánico.
3. Es posible comprar limones en una papelería.
4. En un mercado, el vendedor siempre ofrece un precio bajo al principio (*beginning*).

UN PASO MÁS: Situaciones

En una tienda de ropa

—¿Le atienden°? ¿Qué desea?
—Hola, buenas. Busco un pantalón de algodón de color oscuro,° para mí.
—¿Qué talla° usa?
—La trece, por lo general.
—¿Qué le parece este pantalón negro?
—No está mal. Y ¿qué tal una blusa de seda también?
—Cómo no. En su talla tenemos blusas de seda en color beige, rojo y gris perla. Son perfectas para este pantalón.
—¿Dónde me los puedo probar°?
—Allí están los probadores.° Si necesita algo, mi nombre es Méndez.
—Gracias.

¿Le... Is someone waiting on you?
¿ ? (Guess the meaning.)
size

me... can I try them on?
¿ ? (Guess the meaning.)

Más tarde, hablando° con una amiga

—¿Cuánto pagaste por esta blusa?

—Fue muy barata… sólo mil pesetas. ¿Te gusta?

—Sí, me gusta mucho.

—¿Verdad? Pues… yo creo que el color no me va° muy bien.

—¡Qué va°! Te va estupendamente.

speaking

no… doesn't suit me

¡Qué… Nonsense!

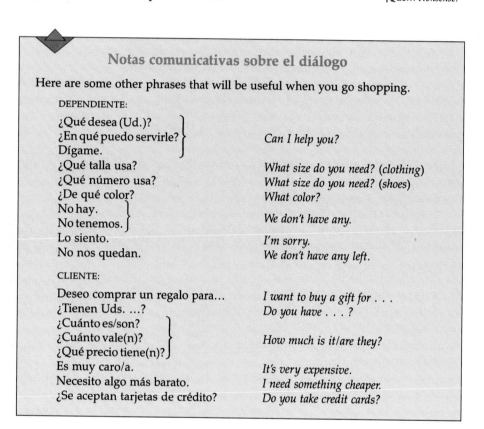

Notas comunicativas sobre el diálogo

Here are some other phrases that will be useful when you go shopping.

DEPENDIENTE:

¿Qué desea (Ud.)? ⎫	
¿En qué puedo servirle? ⎬	*Can I help you?*
Dígame. ⎭	
¿Qué talla usa?	*What size do you need? (clothing)*
¿Qué número usa?	*What size do you need? (shoes)*
¿De qué color?	*What color?*
No hay. ⎫	
No tenemos. ⎭	*We don't have any.*
Lo siento.	*I'm sorry.*
No nos quedan.	*We don't have any left.*

CLIENTE:

Deseo comprar un regalo para…	*I want to buy a gift for . . .*
¿Tienen Uds. …?	*Do you have . . . ?*
¿Cuánto es/son? ⎫	
¿Cuánto vale(n)? ⎬	*How much is it/are they?*
¿Qué precio tiene(n)? ⎭	
Es muy caro/a.	*It's very expensive.*
Necesito algo más barato.	*I need something cheaper.*
¿Se aceptan tarjetas de crédito?	*Do you take credit cards?*

Conversación

Although it is often possible—and lots of fun—to bargain over the price of an item in a shop or open-air market, merchandise is normally sold at a fixed price in many, if not most, Hispanic stores. With another student, take the roles of customer and salesperson in the following situations. Use the phrases from **Notas comunicativas** as well as strategies that you learned from listening to the preceding dialogues.

1. En la librería de la universidad: Ud. desea comprar dos cuadernos pequeños.

2. En una tienda pequeña: Ud. desea comprar una blusa azul para su hermana (madre, amiga, tía).
3. En un almacén: Ud. quiere comprar un regalo para un amigo.
4. En una tienda de flores: Ud. necesita comprar seis rosas rojas.

VOCABULARIO

Verbos

gastar to spend (money)
ir (*irreg.*) to go
 ir a + *inf.* to be going to
  (*do something*)
regatear to bargain

De compras

el precio (fijo) (fixed) price
las rebajas sales, reductions

Los lugares

el almacén department store
el café café, coffee shop; coffee
el centro downtown
el centro comercial shopping mall
el cine movie theater
el mercado (al aire libre)
  (outdoor) market(place)
el supermercado supermarket

Otros sustantivos

el consejo (piece of) advice
la revista magazine

Adjetivos

caro/a expensive
cómodo/a comfortable
próximo/a next (*in time*)

Formas posesivas

mi(s), tu(s), su(s),
  nuestro/a(s), vuestro/a(s)

Los números

cien(to), doscientos/as, trescientos/as, cuatrocientos/as, quinientos/as, seiscientos/as, setecientos/as, ochocientos/as, novecientos/as, mil, un millón

¿Cuándo?

pasado mañana the day after
  tomorrow
la próxima semana next week
el próximo (martes,
  miércoles, ...) next (Tuesday,
  Wednesday, . . .)

Los días de la semana

lunes, martes, miércoles, jueves,
  viernes, sábado, domingo

Palabras adicionales

de todo everything
ir de compras to go shopping
más/menos... que more/
  less . . . than
tan... como as . . . as
tanto/a/os/as... como as much/
  many . . . as

Frases útiles para la comunicación

Repite. (*fam.*)	Repeat.
¿Cómo?	What? I didn't catch that.
Favor de repetir.	Please repeat.
¿Cuánto pagaste (por...)?	How much did you pay (for . . .)?
Fue una ganga.	It was a bargain.

See also the words and phrases in **Notas comunicativas sobre el diálogo.**

LAS ESTACIONES Y EL TIEMPO

VOCABULARIO: ¿QUÉ TIEMPO HACE HOY?°

¿Qué... *What's the weather like today?*

Hace frío.

Hace calor.

Hace viento.

Hace sol.

Está (muy) nublado.

Llueve.

Nieva.

Hay mucha contaminación.

Hace (mucho) frío (calor, viento, sol). It's (very) cold (hot, windy, sunny).
Hace fresco. It's cool.
Hace (muy) buen/mal tiempo. It's (very) good/bad weather.
The weather is (very) good/bad.

la lluvia rain
la nieve snow

In Spanish, many weather conditions are expressed with **hace**. Note that the adjective **mucho** is used with the nouns **frío, calor, viento,** and **sol** to express *very*.

Pronunciation: In most parts of the Spanish-speaking world, **ll** is pronounced like **y: llueve, la lluvia.**

A.   Diga qué tiempo hace, según la ropa de cada persona.

1.   San Diego: María lleva pantalones cortos y una camiseta.
2.   Madison: Juan lleva suéter, pero no lleva chaqueta.
3.   Toronto: Roberto lleva suéter y chaqueta.
4.   Guanajuato: Ramón lleva impermeable y botas y también tiene paraguas (*umbrella*).
5.   Buenos Aires: Todos llevan abrigo, botas y sombrero.

B.   **¿Dónde debe vivir Joaquín?** Joaquín es de Valencia, España. El clima allí es moderado y hace mucho sol. Hay poca contaminación. Va a venir a los Estados Unidos y quiere vivir en un lugar con un clima similar. ¿Dónde debe—o *no* debe—vivir?

MODELO: Joaquín, (no) debes vivir en _____ porque allí _____.

1.   Seattle   3.   Phoenix   5.   Buffalo
2.   Los Ángeles   4.   New Orleans   6.   ¿ ?

Notas lingüísticas: More *tener* Idioms

Several other conditions expressed in Spanish with **tener** idioms—not with *to be*, as in English—include the following.

tener (mucho) calor	to be (very) warm
tener (mucho) frío	to be (very) cold

These expressions are used to describe people or animals only. To be comfortable—neither hot nor cold—is expressed with **estar bien.**

C.   **¿Tienen frío o calor? ¿Están bien?** Describe the following weather conditions and tell how the people pictured are feeling.

Al tanto...

Here are some colorful expressions for commenting on the weather.

Llueve a cántaros.	*It's pouring* (lit., *raining jugfuls*).
Estoy calado/a hasta los huesos.	*I'm soaking wet* (lit., *soaked to the bones*).
Hace un frío/calor de morirse.	*It's extremely cold/hot* (lit., *so cold/hot you could die*).
Hace un frío/calor espantoso.	*It's awfully (frightfully) cold/hot.*

EL TIEMPO

Aumentan las lluvias

J. L. RON

Las bajas presiones se extienden a todo el país, con una borrasca moderada en el noroeste de Galicia, y asociado a ella un frente frío que a mediodía estará sobre Portugal. Esto dará una situación de lluvias que en los próximos días afectarán a todo el país, siendo éstas débiles en el noreste, en Baleares y en el Cantábrico oriental y fuertes en la vertiente atlántica. La borrasca tiende a profundizarse, y terminará extendiéndose y desplazándose hacia el Este, con lo cual aumentarán las precipitaciones en la vertiente mediterránea.

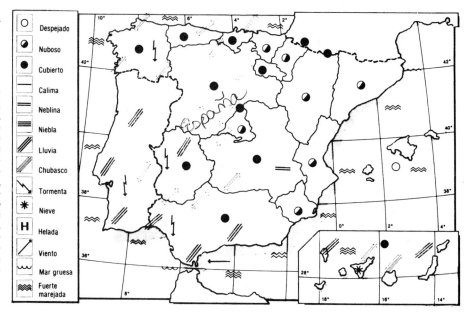

○	Despejado
◑	Nuboso
●	Cubierto
▬	Calima
═	Neblina
≡	Niebla
▨	Lluvia
▨	Chubasco
⚡	Tormenta
✳	Nieve
H	Helada
↗	Viento
∿	Mar gruesa
≋	Fuerte marejada

VOCABULARIO

Expressing Actions—*hacer*, *poner*, and *salir*

hacer (to do; to make)		**poner** (to put; to place)		**salir** (to leave; to go out)	
hago	hacemos	pongo	ponemos	salgo	salimos
haces	hacéis	pones	ponéis	sales	salís
hace	hacen	pone	ponen	sale	salen

- *hacer:* ¿Por qué no **haces** los ejercicios?   *Why aren't you doing the exercises?*

Two common idioms with **hacer** are **hacer un viaje** (*to take a trip*) and **hacer una pregunta** (*to ask a question*).

Quieren **hacer un viaje** al Perú.	*They want to take a trip to Peru.*
Los niños siempre **hacen muchas preguntas**.	*Children always ask a lot of questions.*

- *poner:* Siempre **pongo** mucho azúcar en el café.   *I always puts a lot of sugar in my coffee.*

Many Spanish speakers use **poner** with appliances to express *to turn on.*

Voy a **poner** el televisor.   *I'm going to turn on the TV.*

- *salir:* **Salen de** la clase ahora.   *They're leaving class now.*

Note that **salir** is always followed by **de** to express leaving a place. **Salir para** expresses destination. **Salir con** can mean *to go out with, to date.*

Salimos para la playa mañana.	*We're leaving for the beach tomorrow.*
Salgo con el hermano de Cecilia.	*I'm going out with Cecilia's brother.*

Sortir de la maison

A.   ¿Qué hacemos esta noche? Haga oraciones completas con una palabra o frase de cada grupo.

yo
mi amigo/a (nombre)   (no)
profesor(a), Ud.

- hacer   ejercicio en el gimnasio
- poner   el televisor a las seis para las noticias (*news*)
- salir   con unos amigos, con…
   ejercicios para la clase de español
   para la casa hasta (*until*) las siete o las ocho
   para la universidad otra vez, para estudiar en la biblioteca

B.   Consecuencias lógicas. ¿Qué va a hacer Ud. en estas condiciones? Use las siguientes (*following*) frases en su respuesta.

poner el aire acondicionador / la calefacción (*heat*)
poner el televisor / el radio

salir de / para…
hacer un viaje a…
hacer una pregunta

1.   Me gusta esquiar. Por eso…
2.   Tengo frío y hace frío afuera (*outside*). Por eso…
3.   Tenemos calor y hace calor afuera. Por eso…
4.   Hay un programa interesante en la televisión.
5.   ¡Estoy cansada de trabajar!
6.   Estamos aburridos. → *bored*
7.   Quiero escuchar (*to listen to*) música y bailar.
8.   No comprendo.

C.   Preguntas

1.   ¿Qué pone Ud. en el café? ¿en el té? ¿en una limonada? ¿Pone Ud. hielo (*ice*) en los refrescos (*soft drinks*)?
2.   ¿Qué hace Ud. el día de su cumpleaños (*birthday*)? ¿en septiembre? ¿los sábados?
3.   ¿Qué quiere Ud. hacer esta noche? ¿Qué necesita hacer? ¿Qué va a hacer? ¿Va a salir con sus amigos? ¿Adónde van?
4.   ¿A qué hora sale Ud. de la clase de español? ¿de otras clases? ¿A veces sale tarde de clase? ¿Por qué? ¿Le gusta salir temprano? ¿Siempre sale Ud. temprano para la universidad? ¿Sale tarde a veces?

¿Recuerda Ud.?

The change in the stem vowels of **querer** and **poder** (**e** and **o**, respectively) follows the same pattern as that of the verbs in the next section. Review the forms of **querer** and **poder** before beginning that section.

querer: **e** → ¿ ?	qu__ro	queremos	poder: **o** → ¿ ?	p__do	podemos
	qu__res	queréis		p__des	podéis
	qu__re	qu__ren		p__de	p__den

ESTRUCTURAS

14. EXPRESSING ACTIONS
Present Tense of Stem-Changing Verbs

Haciendo planes

PADRE: Mira, Esteban, *empiezo* a perder la paciencia contigo. No comprendo por qué no *quieres* hacer el viaje a Chile con nosotros.

ESTEBAN: Estoy muy bien aquí...

MADRE: Pero, hijo, aquí *nieva* todos los días y allí hace muy buen tiempo ahora. ¡Con lo que a ti te gusta nadar... !

ESTEBAN: Pero es que aquí *jugamos* al básquetbol en invierno y si nosotros no *volvemos* hasta febrero *pierdo* el campeonato. *Prefiero* no ir.

PADRE: Lo *siento*,* Esteban, pero no *pensamos* dejarte aquí. ¡Y se acabó!

Making plans   FATHER: Look, Esteban, I'm starting to lose patience with you. I don't understand why you don't want to take the trip to Chile with us. ESTEBAN: I'm just fine here . . . MOTHER: But son, here it's snowing every day, and there the weather is very nice now. Considering how much you like to swim . . . ! ESTEBAN: But it's just that we play basketball here in the winter and if we don't come back until February, I'll miss the championship game. I'd rather not go. FATHER: I'm sorry, Esteban, but we don't intend to leave you here. And that's that!
*** Siento** is the first person singular form of the stem-changing verb **sentir** (*to regret*). You will learn to use other forms of **sentir** in later chapters.

1. ¿Adónde va la familia?
2. ¿Qué tiempo hace ahora donde viven? ¿Y en Sudamérica?
3. ¿A qué juegan los amigos de Esteban en invierno?
4. ¿Qué va a perder Esteban si acompaña a sus padres?
5. En la opinión de Ud., ¿qué va a decir (*to say*) ahora Esteban?
   - Bueno, está claro que no tengo alternativa.
   - ¿No puedo volver un poco antes que Uds.?
   - ¡No quiero ir y no voy!

e → ie	o (u) → ue	e → i
pensar (ie) (*to think*)	**volver (ue)** (*to return*)	**pedir (i)** (*to ask for; order*)
pienso pensamos	vuelvo volvemos	pido pedimos
piensas pensáis	vuelves volvéis	pides pedís
piensa piensan	vuelve vuelven	pide piden

study

You have already learned three *stem-changing verbs* (**los verbos que cambian el radical**): **querer**, **preferir**, and **poder**. In these verbs the stem vowels **e** and **o** become **ie** and **ue**, respectively, in stressed syllables. The stem vowels are stressed in all present tense forms except **nosotros** and **vosotros**. All three classes of stem-changing verbs follow this regular pattern in the present tense. In vocabulary lists, the stem change will always be shown in parentheses after the infinitive: **volver (ue)**.

Some stem-changing verbs practiced in this chapter include the following.

e → ie		o (u) → ue		e → i	
cerrar (ie)	to close	**almorzar (ue)**	to have lunch	**pedir (i)**	to ask for; to order
empezar (ie)	to begin	**dormir (ue)**	to sleep	**servir (i)**	to serve
entender (ie)	to understand	**jugar (ue)***	to play (a game, sports)		
pensar (ie)	to think				
perder (ie)	to lose; to miss (a function)	**volver (ue)**	to return		

- When used with an infinitive, **empezar** is followed by **a**.

  Uds. **empiezan a hablar** muy bien el español.

  You're beginning to speak Spanish very well.

- When followed directly by an infinitive, **pensar** means *to intend, plan to*.

  ¿Cuándo **piensas contestar** la carta?

  When do you intend to answer the letter?

---

*Jugar is the only **u → ue** stem-changing verb in Spanish. **Jugar** is often followed by **al** when used with the name of a sport: **Juego al tenis**. Some Spanish speakers, however, omit the **al**.

Práctica

A.   Una tarde magnífica. Hace buen tiempo hoy. ¿Cuáles son las activi-dades de estas personas? Haga oraciones completas con una palabra o frase de cada grupo.

yo		almorzar	descansar en la playa, en el patio
el equipo (*team*)		volver	en el parque, en el patio
mi padre/madre		preferir	toda la tarde
los niños	(no)	perder	varios partidos (*games*)
mi amigo/a ____		jugar	al golf (tenis, vólibol...)
y yo		pedir	muchos refrescos
los perros		dormir	a casa muy tarde
			afuera
			la siesta
			helados (*ice-cream cones*)

B.   ¿Qué prefieren?

MODELO: Ignacio pide café, pero nosotros <u>pedimos</u> un refresco.

1. Tomás y Julia piensan viajar (*to travel*) a Sudamérica, pero nosotros ____ viajar a España.
2. Tú vuelves a la estación (*station*) mañana, pero nosotros ____ allí el jueves.
3. Nosotros empezamos a trabajar a las ocho, pero Reynaldo ____ a las nueve.
4. Nosotros dormimos ocho horas todas las noches, pero Lucía sólo ____ seis horas.
5. Nosotros servimos comida (*food*) mexicana en casa y Susana también ____ comida mexicana, especialmente en las fiestas.
6. Nosotros jugamos al tenis hoy y Paula ____ con nosotros.
7. Tú cierras la tienda a las ocho, pero nosotros no ____ hasta las diez.
8. María y Teresa prefieren esquiar en Vail, pero nosotros ____ ir a Aspen. Ellas no entienden por qué vamos a Aspen, y nosotros no ____ por qué van a Vail.

C.   Using the following verbs as a guide, tell about a visit to a restaurant. Use **yo** as the subject except where otherwise indicated.

1. pensar comer comida española
2. entrar en un restaurante en la calle Bolívar
3. pedir el menú
4. preferir comer paella, un plato español
5. (ellos) no servir comida española
6. pedir tacos y un refresco
7. (ellos) servir la comida en diez minutos
8. comer y volver a casa
9. dormir un poco porque hace calor

D. Preguntas

1. ¿A qué hora cierran la biblioteca? ¿A qué hora cierran la cafetería?
   ¿Están abiertas toda la noche durante el semestre/trimestre? ¿Y durante
   la época de los exámenes finales?
2. ¿Almuerza Ud., por lo general? ¿A qué hora? ¿Dónde le gusta almorzar?
   ¿Con quién? ¿Piensa Ud. almorzar hoy? ¿mañana? Cuando almuerza en
   la cafetería de la universidad, ¿qué pide? ¿una hamburguesa? ¿un taco?
   ¿una ensalada? ¿un refresco? ¿Sirven la comida en la cafetería o hay
   auto-servicio?
3. ¿Es Ud. un poco olvidadizo/a? Es decir, ¿pierde las cosas con frecuencia? ¿Qué cosa pierde Ud.? ¿el dinero? ¿su cuaderno? ¿su mochila? ¿sus
   llaves (keys)?
4. Los días de entresemana, ¿a qué hora sale Ud. de casa (de su cuarto/
   apartamento), por lo general? ¿A qué hora vuelve? ¿A qué hora
   empieza a comer? ¿a estudiar? ¿a mirar la tele? Y los fines de semana,
   ¿en qué forma es diferente su rutina?

Notas comunicativas: What Do You Think About . . . ?

One way to ask for someone's opinion with the verb **pensar** is to use the phrase
¿Qué piensas de... ? (*What do you think about . . . ?*). The answer can begin with
Pienso que... (*I think that . . .*).

—¿**Qué piensas de** la clase de matemáticas?
—¡**Pienso que** es muy difícil!

E. Entrevista: Otras preferencias.

With a classmate, explore preferences in
a number of areas by asking and answering questions based on the following cues. Form your questions with expressions like these:

¿Prefieres... o... ?	¿Qué piensas de... ?
¿Te gusta más (*infinitive*) o (*infinitive*)?	¿Piensas que... o... ?

If you have no preference or opinion, express that by saying **No tengo pre-
ferencia/opinión**. Be prepared to report some of your findings to the class.
If you both agree, you will express this with phrases like: **Pensamos que**...
Preferimos... . If you do not agree, give the preferences of both persons: **Yo
prefiero/pienso**... **pero Gustavo prefiere/piensa**...

1. Las clases: ¿las clases fáciles o las difíciles? ¿las clases que empiezan a las
   ocho o las que empiezan a la una? ¿hacer preguntas o contestar en clase?
   ¿hablar en inglés o en español en la clase de español? (¿o no hablar?)
2. Las bebidas: ¿el café con azúcar o sin azúcar? ¿el café con o sin cafeína?
   ¿la Coca-Cola con hielo o sin hielo? ¿los refrescos con calorías o los dietéticos? ¿los refrescos con o sin cafeína?
3. Cuando hace mucho calor: ¿beber agua (*water*), refrescos o cerveza?
   ¿estar en casa o estar afuera? ¿estar en el parque o en la playa? ¿jugar al
   tenis (al golf, ...) o dormir?

4. Los viajes: ¿hacer un viaje largo en autobús o en tren? ¿en tren o en avión (*plane*)? ¿en avión o en coche? ¿hacer los viajes en invierno o en verano? ¿tomar las vacaciones en invierno o en verano? ¿ir de vacaciones con su familia o con sus amigos?

VOCABULARIO

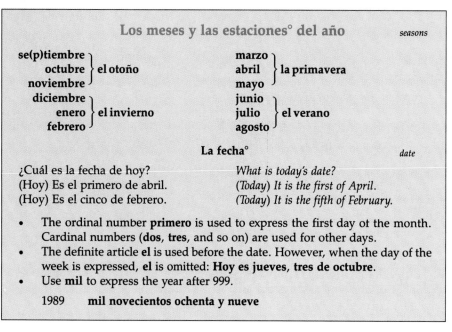

Los meses y las estaciones° del año   *seasons*

se(p)tiembre		marzo	
octubre	el otoño	abril	la primavera
noviembre		mayo	
diciembre		junio	
enero	el invierno	julio	el verano
febrero		agosto	

La fecha°   *date*

¿Cuál es la fecha de hoy?   *What is today's date?*
(Hoy) Es el primero de abril.   *(Today) It is the first of April.*
(Hoy) Es el cinco de febrero.   *(Today) It is the fifth of February.*

*   The ordinal number **primero** is used to express the first day of the month. Cardinal numbers (**dos, tres,** and so on) are used for other days.
*   The definite article **el** is used before the date. However, when the day of the week is expressed, **el** is omitted: **Hoy es jueves, tres de octubre.**
*   Use **mil** to express the year after 999.

    1989   **mil novecientos ochenta y nueve**

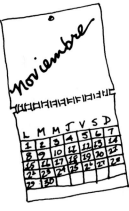

A.   ¿Qué día de la semana es el 12 (1, 20, 16, 11, 4, 29) de noviembre?

B.   Exprese estas fechas en español.

1. March 7
2. August 24
3. December 1

4. June 5
5. May 30, 1842
6. September 19, 1989

7. January 31, 1660
8. July 4, 1776

C.   Lea los siguientes años en español. ¿A qué dato (*fact, event*) corresponden?

1. 1492
2. 1776
3. 1945
4. 2001
5. 1963

a. el año de mi nacimiento (*my birth*)
b. la Declaración de la Independencia
c. el asesinato de John F. Kennedy
d. Cristóbal Colón descubre América
e. la bomba atómica

6. 1984   f. una película famosa
7. ¿ ?   g. la novela de George Orwell

                 h. este año

D. ¿Cuándo se celebran?*

1. el Día de la Raza (*Columbus Day*)
2. el Día del Año Nuevo
3. el Día de los Enamorados (de San Valentín)
4. el Día de la Independencia de los Estados Unidos
5. el Día de los Inocentes (*Fools*) en los Estados Unidos
6. la Navidad (*Christmas*)

E. Preguntas

1. ¿Cuál es la fecha de su cumpleaños? ¿del cumpleaños de su mejor amigo/a? ¿de su novio/a (esposo/a)? ¿Cuándo se celebran los cumpleaños de Lincoln y Washington? (Se celebran...)
2. ¿Cuándo tenemos el examen final en esta clase? ¿en su clase de _____? ¿Cuál es la fecha del próximo examen de español? ¿Tiene Ud. una prueba (*quiz*) mañana? ¿pasado mañana?
3. ¿Cuándo entra el verano? ¿el invierno? ¿y la primavera? ¿Cuál es su estación favorita? ¿Por qué?

F. ¿Cómo se siente Ud. (*do you feel*) **cuando... ?** Complete las oraciones lógicamente.

1. En otoño generalmente estoy _____ porque _____.
2. Cuando hace frío (calor) estoy _____ porque _____.
3. En verano estoy _____ porque _____.
4. Cuando llueve (nieva) estoy _____ porque _____.

Notas culturales: The Southern Hemisphere

As you know, seasons are reversed in the Southern Hemisphere, where many Spanish-speaking countries lie. This means, of course, that when it is summer in the United States, it is winter in Argentina, and vice versa. You may never have thought about the effect of this phenomenon on the celebration of many traditional holidays. Christmas and New Year's Eve, winter holidays for residents of the United States, are generally associated with snow and ice, snow figures, winter sports, and so on. What does this ad for a Chilean hotel reveal about the kind of holiday New Year's Eve is in the Southern Hemisphere?

---

*¡OJO! Note that the word **se** before a verb changes the verb's meaning slightly. **¿Cuándo se celebran?** = *When are they celebrated?* You will see this construction throughout *¿Qué tal?* Learn to recognize it, for it is frequently used in Spanish.

¡Hablemos° del tiempo!   *Let's talk*
—De todas las estaciones, ¿cuál es tu favorita?
—Creo que el otoño.
—¿El otoño? ¿Por qué?
—Porque hace calor durante el día y fresco durante
  la noche. Y porque llueve… ¡Me gusta la lluvia!

Santiago, Chile

ESTRUCTURAS

15. DESCRIBING
Irregular Comparative Adjectives

In the last chapter you learned to form comparisons
using **más** and **menos** + *adjective* + **que.**

> La biología es **más difícil que** la sociología.
> Las perros son **menos inteligentes que** los gatos.

Spanish also has four irregular comparative forms.

mejor(es)	better	**mayor(es)**	older
peor(es)	worse	**menor(es)**	younger

Estos televisores son buenos, pero ésos son **mejores.**
El clima de Alaska es malo, pero el de Siberia es **peor.**
Mi tío Juan es **mayor** que mi padre,
   pero mi padre es más grande que mi tío.
Mis hermanos son **menores** que yo. Son más
   pequeños también.

   Note that **mayor** and **menor** refer to age. When referring to size, the
comparative forms are regular: **más/menos grande, más/menos pequeño.**

Práctica

A.   ¿Quién diría (*would say*) lo siguiente, Esteban (minidiálogo, página 130)
o su padre?

1.   Es mejor ir de vacaciones a Sudamérica en invierno cuando hace mal
     tiempo aquí.
2.   Este mes el clima de Sudamérica es mejor que el de aquí.
3.   Para mí, los mejores deportes (*sports*) son los de invierno.
4.   Soy mayor que tú; por eso voy a tomar la decisión.
5.   ¡Es horrible ser el menor de la familia!

B. Complete las oraciones lógicamente con una comparación.

1. La comida italiana es buena, pero la mexicana es _____.
2. Las pruebas son malas, pero los exámenes son _____.
3. Esteban tiene 14 años y su hermano Demetrio tiene 20 años. Demetrio es el hermano _____.
4. Luisita es muy joven; el bebé de la familia es su hermano _____.
5. La Argentina es grande, pero el Brasil es aun (*even*) _____.
6. El elefante es grande. El chimpancé es _____.

UN POCO DE TODO

A.   Rosario y sus compañeros. Take the role of Rosario as she compares herself and her study habits to those of her classmates. Form complete sentences based on the words given, in the order given. Conjugate the verbs and add other words if necessary. Use subject pronouns only when needed.

1. yo / empezar / ser / estudiante / ejemplar (*exemplary*)
2. yo / volver / casa / con / más / libros / Elena
3. yo / no / perder / tanto / tiempo / cafetería / Raúl
4. próximo / semestre / yo / pensar / tomar / tanto / cursos / difícil / Estela
5. yo / pedir / menos / consejos / Felipe
6. yo / hacer / mejor / preguntas / Antonio

Marta and Solimar, Rosario's friends, are not good students at all. Describe them, using the preceding cues and changing the information as needed. Here are the first two items.

1. Rosario / empezar / ser / estudiante / ejemplar / pero / ¡nosotras, no!
2. (nosotras) volver / casa / con / menos / libros / Elena

B.   Dos hemisferios. Complete the following paragraphs with the correct forms of the words in parentheses, as suggested by the context. When two possibilities are given, select the correct word.

Hay (*mucho*[1]) diferencias entre el clima del hemisferio norte y el del hemisferio sur. Cuando (*ser/estar*[2]) invierno en los Estados Unidos, por ejemplo, (*ser/estar*[3]) verano en la Argentina, en Bolivia, en Chile… . Cuando yo (*salir*[4]) para la universidad en enero, con frecuencia tengo que (*llevar*[5]) abrigo y botas. En (*los/las*[6]) países del hemisferio sur, un estudiante (*poder*[7]) asistir (*a/de*[8]) clases en enero llevando° sólo pantalones (*corto*[9]), camiseta y sandalias.   *wearing*
En (*mucho*[10]) partes de los Estados Unidos, durante las vacaciones en diciembre, casi siempre (*hacer*[11]) frío y a veces (*nevar*[12]). En (*grande*[13]) parte de Sudamérica, al otro lado° del ecuador, hace calor y (*muy/mucho*[14]) sol durante (*ese*[15]) mes. A veces en enero hay fotos, en los periódicos, de personas que (*tomar*[16]) el sol y nadan° en las playas sudamericanas.   *side*   *swim*

Tengo un amigo que (*ir*[17]) a (*hacer/tomar*[18]) un viaje a Buenos Aires. Él me dice° que allí la Navidad (*ser/estar*[19]) una fiesta de verano y que todos (*llevar*[20]) ropa como la que° llevamos nosotros en julio. Parece increíble, ¿verdad?

Él... He tells me

la... that which

¿Probable o improbable? Conteste según el párrafo.

1. Los estudiantes argentinos están en la playa en julio.
2. Muchos sudamericanos hacen viajes de vacaciones en enero.
3. Hace frío en Santiago (Chile) en diciembre.

UN PASO MÁS: Lectura cultural

Antes de leer: Getting a General Idea About Content

Before starting a reading, it is a good idea to try to get a general sense of the content. The more you know about the reading before you begin to read, the easier it will seem to you. Here are some things you can do to prepare yourself for readings.

1. Make sure you understand the title. Think about what it suggests to you and what you already know about the topic. Do the same with any subtitles that the reading contains.
2. Look at the drawings, photos, or other visual cues that accompany the reading. What do they indicate about the content?
3. Read the comprehension questions before starting to read the text. They will tell you what kind of information you should be looking for.

The reading in this chapter is taken from a grade school geography book from Venezuela. No words have been changed in the reading to make it easier for you. You should be able to get the general meaning if you apply the preceding strategies and keep in mind some important information.

The title and subtitles. The reading, **Las Américas**, is divided into two subsections. You already know most of the words in the subtitles. Guess the meaning of **Lo que...** from context.

Lo que América debe a Europa
Lo que el mundo debe a América

If you guessed *what*, you are correct.

The art. The reading is accompanied by a drawing and a brief caption. What information is communicated by the drawing? As you do the reading, check the drawing periodically to see whether the items in it give you clues to the meanings of words you will find in the reading text.

The tense. Now that you have a sense of where the reading is going, can you predict what tense (present or past) the majority of the reading will be written in? Most of the reading is written in the past tenses of Spanish. You already know the Spanish past tense verb form **fue**. If you pay attention to the root meaning of other verbs and ignore the verb endings, many of which will be unfamiliar to you, you should be able to derive meaning from the forms themselves. You probably do not know the meaning of the word **colonizaron**, but you probably recognize its root in *to colonize*. If you see the verb in this context and you know the reading is talking about the past, what does the verb mean?

Los europeos <u>colonizaron</u> las Américas.

The comprehension questions. Finally, scan the items in **Comprensión**. What clues do they give you about some of the information contained in the reading?

LAS AMÉRICAS

Lo que América debe a Europa

Read for 10-29

América fue colonizada por europeos, como ya sabes. El traspaso° de las lenguas, religiones, costumbres y formas de vida de Europa a América se realizó con relativa facilidad, pues todos los pueblos° indígenas americanos sumaban apenas° diez millones en la época del descubrimiento. Sólo algunos° pueblos, como los mayas, los mexicas o aztecas, los chibchas y los quechuas, poseían un alto nivel de civilización. Por el resto de las tierras de América había numerosas tribus dispersas cuya existencia era pobre, debido a su atraso° cultural.

transfer

peoples

barely / some

backwardness

Los españoles, los ingleses, los portugueses, los franceses y los demás europeos que colonizaron las Américas, comenzaron la explotación de los grandes recursos naturales de nuestras tierras, mejoraron° la agricultura, crearon industrias y establecieron el comercio con Europa y demás partes del mundo.

improved

Entre los grandes aportes° traídos a América por los europeos figuran muchas plantas útiles, originarias del Viejo Mundo, como el trigo, el arroz, la caña de azúcar y el café, y también animales como el caballo, la vaca, el cerdo, el carnero y numerosas especies de aves de corral.

contribuciones

Tres siglos° después de comenzada la colonización europea, casi todos los pueblos de América se independizaron, pero la labor realizada por los europeos ha sobrevivido,° ya que de Europa nos llegaron nuestros idiomas, nuestras creencias religiosas y los otros elementos fundamentales de nuestra cultura actual.

un siglo = cien años

survived

Lo que el mundo debe a América

América no se ha limitado a recibir la herencia de la cultura europea. Nuestros pueblos han contribuido al progreso del mundo, provocando cambios° en la forma de vivir de los pueblos de Europa y de otros continentes.

changes

En los primeros tiempos coloniales fueron llevadas de América a Europa muchas plantas útiles que hoy cultivan los pueblos de varios continentes.

Entre estas plantas figuran la papa, el maíz, el caco, el tomate, la vainilla y la quina. El caucho,° uno de los más valiosos productos forestales del mundo actual, es también americano.

El tabaco, cuyo uso se ha generalizado° en todo el mundo, es originario de América, y fue descubierto en Cuba durante el primer viaje de Colón.°

En los tiempos más recientes se han logrado o han sido perfeccionados en América, especialmente en Estados Unidos, numerosas invenciones que hoy disfrutan° todos los pueblos del mundo. Entre estas invenciones pueden citarse el buque° de vapor, la luz eléctrica, el fonógrafo, el telégrafo, el teléfono, el avión, la radio y la televisión.

rubber

spread

Columbus

enjoy

boat

Algunas de las valiosas plantas oriundas de América, cuyo cultivo se ha extendido por todo el mundo.

Comprensión

A.   Complete la siguiente tabla según la lectura.

Lo que América debe a Europa

1. Número aproximado de habitantes indígenas en 1492: _____.
2. Nombres de algunas civilizaciones indias importantes: _____, _____, _____, _____.
3. Nombres de algunos países colonizadores: _____, _____, _____, _____.
4. Contribuciones de los europeos a América: ¿Sí o no? Conteste exclusivamente según la lectura.

       _____ algunas plantas   _____ la religión
       _____ el sistema de educación   _____ el idioma
       _____ aspectos de la agricultura   _____ el concepto de la explota-
       _____ el sistema político   ción de la tierra
       _____ algunos animales

Lo que Europa debe a América

Nombres de algunas contribuciones de América a Europa:
       algo que se come: _____.
       una planta que era (*was*) importante para los coches: _____.
       una planta que forma la base de una industria norteamericana muy
          importante: _____.
       dos invenciones modernas: _____, _____.

B.   Según la lectura, ¿en qué consiste América?

       _____ sólo los países de habla española
       _____ sólo los países de Norteamérica
       _____ todos los países de los dos continentes del hemisferio

Cuando *Ud.* usa la palabra **América**, ¿qué quiere decir (*what do you imply*)?

Study Hint: Using a Bilingual Dictionary

A Spanish–English/English–Spanish dictionary or vocabulary list is an excellent study aid, but one that should be used very carefully. Follow these guidelines to minimize the pitfalls.

1. If you are looking for a Spanish word in the Spanish-English part of the dictionary, remember that in the Spanish alphabet the letters **ch**, **ll**, and **ñ** follow the letters **c**, **l**, and **n**, respectively. The word **coche** is found after the word **cocina**; **calle** comes after **calma**; and **cañón** follows **cansado**.

2. When you look in the English-Spanish section for the Spanish equivalent of an English word, keep in mind the part of speech—noun, verb, adjective, and so on—of the word you are looking for. By doing so, you will avoid many mistakes. Imagine the confusion that would arise if you chose the wrong word in the following cases:

   can: **lata** (noun, *tin can*), but **poder** (verb, *can, to be able*)

   light: **luz** (noun, *electric light, daylight*), but **ligero** (adjective, *light, not heavy*), and **claro** (adjective, *light in color*).

3. If the Spanish word that you find is not familiar to you, or if you simply want to check its meaning and usage, look up the new word in the Spanish-English section. Do the English equivalents given there correspond to the meaning you want to convey?

4. Remember that there is rarely a one-to-one equivalency between Spanish and English words. **Jugar** means *to play* a sport or game, but the verb **tocar** must be used to talk about *playing* a musical instrument. **Un periódico** is a paper (a *news*paper) and **un papel** is a *sheet* of paper.

5. Minimize the number of "dictionary words" you use when writing in Spanish. It is best to limit yourself to words you know because you have used them in class. And when you do have to use the dictionary, try to check your word choice with your instructor or someone else who knows Spanish.

Para escribir

A. Write a brief paragraph about your favorite season by completing the following sentences. Describe your attitudes and activities during this season, as well as the weather.

Yo prefiero _____ porque _____. Durante esta estación....

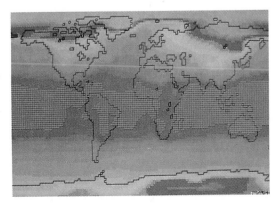

Estos programas permiten conocer el promedio de la temperatura del aire al nivel de la superficie de la Tierra, en grados centígrados, para el periodo que va de diciembre a febrero; las áreas más calientes se representan en rojo, y las frías en azul.

VOCABULARIO

Verbos

almorzar (ue) to have lunch *déjeuner*
cerrar (ie) to close *fermer*
contestar to answer *répondre à*
dormir (ue) to sleep *dormir*
empezar (ie) to begin *commencer*
  empezar a + *inf.* to begin to (*do
  something*)
entender (ie) to understand *comprendre*
hacer (*irreg.*) to do; to make *faire*
jugar (ue) (al) to play (*a game, pues
  sports*) *jouer*
pedir (i) to ask for; to order *demander*
pensar (ie) to think; to intend *penser*
perder (ie) to lose; to miss (*a
  function*) *perdre*
poner (*irreg.*) to put; to place *mettre*
salir (*irreg.*) (de) to leave, (*a place*);
  to go out *sortir de*
servir (i) to serve *servir*
tocar to play (*music*) *jouer*
viajar to travel *voyager*
volver (ue) to return *retourner*

Sustantivos

el agua (*f.*) water *l'eau*
el azúcar sugar *le sucre*
el clima climate
la comida food *la nourriture*
el hielo ice *la glace*
el parque park *le parque parc?*
la playa beach *la plage*

la prueba quiz *le contrôle*
el radio radio (*set*) *la radio*
el refresco soft drink *la boisson*
el televisor television (*set*) *la télé*
el tiempo weather; time *le temps*

Adjetivos

mayor older *année*
mejor better *meilleure*
menor younger *cadet*
peor worse *mal*
siguiente next, following *prochaine
  suivant*

¿Qué tiempo hace?

está (muy) nublado it's (very)
  cloudy, overcast
hace... (muy) buen/mal tiempo it's
  (very) good/bad weather *il fait beau/mal*
(mucho) calor it's (very) hot *il fait chaud*
fresco it's cool
(mucho) frío it's (very) cold *froid*
(mucho) sol it's (very) sunny *du soleil*
(mucho) viento it's (very) windy *du vent*
hay (mucha/poca) contaminación
  there's (a lot of/little) pollution, smog

llover (ue) to rain *pleuvoir*
  la lluvia rain *la pluie*
nevar (ie) to snow *neige*
  la nieve snow *la neige*

¿Cuál es la fecha?

l'anniversaire
el cumpleaños birthday
el primero de... the first of . . .
  le premier de

Los meses del año

avril
janvier, février, mars, août
enero, febrero, marzo, abril, *août*
  mayo, junio, julio, agosto, *mai, juin, juillet*
  se(p)tiembre, octubre, *septembre octobre*
  noviembre, diciembre *novembre décembre*

Las estaciones del año

le printemps l'été l'automne
la primavera, el verano, el otoño,
  el invierno
  l'hiver

Palabras adicionales

afuera outside *dehors*
hacer un viaje to take a trip *faire un voyage*
hacer una pregunta to ask a
  question *poser une*
hasta until *jusqu'à question*
ir de vacaciones to go on vacation
  aller en vacances

Frases útiles para la comunicación

tener calor	to be warm/hot
tener frío	to be cold
estar bien	to be comfortable (*temperature*)
¿Qué piensas de... ?	What do you think of . . . ?
Pienso que...	I think that . . .

EN UN RESTAURANTE

VOCABULARIO: ¡QUE APROVECHEN!°

¡Que... ! *Enjoy your meal*

el cocinero

el camarero

la cuenta

el dinero
en efectivo

los Ramírez

la vela

los González

la tarjeta de crédito

la bandeja

el menú

los
Fuentes

la servilleta

el cuchillo

la cuchara

la botella   la copa   el plato

el jarro

el tenedor

el vaso

el mantel

la cucharita

Las comidas

desayunar: el desayuno to have breakfast:
   breakfast

almorzar (ue): el almuerzo to have lunch: lunch
cenar: la cena to have dinner: dinner

¡OJO! The Spanish equivalents for *breakfast/lunch/dinner* given here do not express exactly the U.S. concept of these meals, nor are the meals eaten at the same time of day. See **Notas culturales** (page 144) for more information about mealtimes in Hispanic countries.

A.   Cuestiones de servicio. ¿Qué objeto(s) se usa(n) para… ?

1.   tomar agua o leche (*milk*)
2.   llevar los platos a la mesa
3.   llevar el vino (*wine*) a la mesa
4.   indicar cuánto tienen que pagar los clientes
5.   indicar todos los platos que se sirven en el restaurante
6.   tomar vino o champán
7.   tomar sopa (*soup*)
8.   comer helado (*ice cream*)
9.   iluminar la mesa
10.   pagar la cuenta

B.   ¿Quién habla, el dueño (*owner*) del restaurante, el cocinero, el camarero o el cliente? A veces hay más de una respuesta posible.

1.   Psst. En esa mesa necesitan una silla pequeña para un niño.
2.   Otra servilleta, por favor, cuando pueda (*whenever you have a second*).
3.   Aquí tienen Uds. el menú.
4.   Señor, este tenedor está sucio.
5.   ¡Imposible! No puedo preparar ese plato esta noche. No tengo todos los ingredientes…
6.   Si me permiten, voy a encender (*light*) las velas ahora.
7.   No, señor, no puedo llevar esta bandeja con tantos platos.
8.   La cuenta, por favor.
9.   No tengo dinero en efectivo esta noche. Voy a usar mi tarjeta de crédito.
10.   Lo siento, pero no aceptamos esa tarjeta de crédito.
11.   Me gusta mucho este restaurante. Creo que debemos cenar aquí otra vez (*again*). Y tú, ¿qué crees?
12.   Lo siento, pero no abrimos hasta la hora del almuerzo.

Notas culturales: Meals in the Spanish-Speaking World

Hispanic eating habits are quite unlike those in the United States. Not only does the food itself differ somewhat, but the meals occur at different times.

There are three fundamental meals: **el desayuno**, **la comida/el almuerzo** (*midday meal*), and **la cena**. Breakfast, which is eaten around seven or eight o'clock, is a very simple meal, frugal by most U.S. standards: **café con leche** or **chocolate** (*hot chocolate*) with a plain or sweet roll or toast; that is all. The **café con leche** is heated milk with very strong coffee to add flavor and color.

The main meal of the day, **la comida/el almuerzo**, is frequently eaten as late as two P.M., and is a much heartier meal than the average U.S. lunch. It might consist of soup, a meat or fish dish with vegetables and potatoes or rice, a green salad, and then dessert (often fruit or cheese). Coffee is usually served after the meal.

The evening meal, **la cena**, is somewhat lighter than the noon meal. It is rarely eaten before eight o'clock, and in Spain is commonly served as late as ten or eleven P.M. Because the evening meal is served at such a late hour, it is customary to eat a light snack (**una merienda**) about five or six P.M. The **merienda** might consist of a sandwich or other snack with **café con leche** or **chocolate**. Similarly, a snack is often eaten in the morning between breakfast and the midday meal.

VOCABULARIO

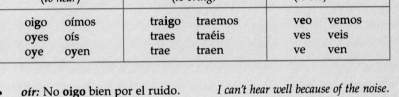

Expressing Actions—*oír*, *traer*, and *ver*

oír (to hear)		traer (to bring)		ver (to see)	
oigo	oímos	traigo	traemos	veo	vemos
oyes	oís	traes	traéis	ves	veis
oye	oyen	trae	traen	ve	ven

- *oír:* No **oigo** bien por el ruido.   *I can't hear well because of the noise.*

English uses *listen!* or *hey!* to attract someone's attention. In Spanish the command forms of **oír** are used: **oye (tú), oiga (Ud.), oigan (Uds.).**

Oye, Juan, ¿vas a la fiesta así?   *Hey, Juan, are you going to the party like that?*
¡Oiga Ud., por favor!   *Listen (Pay attention), please!*

- *traer:* ¿Por qué no **trae** la cuenta el camarero?   *Why doesn't the waiter bring the check?*
- *ver:* No **veo** bien por la contaminación.   *I can't see well because of the pollution.*

A.   ¡Qué restaurante más raro! Haga oraciones completas con una palabra o frase de cada grupo.

el dueño		los gritos (*shouts*) de los cocineros
los camareros		los menús
los otros clientes	traer	los manteles sucios
yo	(no) oír	nuestra cuenta
tú	ver	una botella de vino
nosotros	¿ ?	las voces (*voices*) de los clientes
		una tarjeta de crédito
		al camarero
		¿ ?

B.   ¡Un restaurante desastroso! You're eating dinner with friends at a new restaurant . . . and things are not working out well. Describe what is happening by completing the following sentences in as many ways as you can, using forms of **oír, traer,** and **ver**, when appropriate.

1.   Hay mucho ruido. Por eso yo no… .
2.   Hay muy poca luz (*light*). Por eso es imposible… .
3.   ¿Dónde está… ? El camarero debe… .
4.   ¡Qué desgracia! Aquí está la cuenta y yo no… .

Palabras útiles: mi cartera, la música, a mis amigos, la conversación, los platos, los platos del día (*specials*), el menú, el vino, la comida, dinero.

Al tanto...

Having something to eat or drink before dinner is a custom common to both U.S. and Hispanic cultures. The names for appetizers, however, vary considerably from one part of the Spanish-speaking world to another.

- In Spain, if someone invites you to have **un aperitivo**, you will probably order **un vermut** (*vermouth*) or **un** (**vino**) **fino** (*sherry*).
- In Latin America, **tomar un aperitivo** implies having a snack as well as a drink: olives, bits of cheese or sausage, and so on.
- In Spain, snacks of that kind are called **tapas**, a term also used in parts of the United States. There are many kinds of **tapas**, and people often make a full meal of them: **aceitunas** (*olives*), pieces of **chorizo** (*sausage*), **tortilla española** (*potato and onion omelette*), **croquetas**, and many more.
- In Mexico, appetizers are called **antojitos** or **bocadillos**.

Tapas en un bar madrileño

ESTRUCTURAS

peritivo

16. EXPRESSING NEGATION
Indefinite and Negative Words

Imagine que Ud. vive en Lima este año. ¿Cómo contesta Ud. en estas situaciones?

SU AMIGO ALFONSO: Ya son las diez de la noche. Vamos a comer *algo* en El Cebiche. ¡Tengo hambre!

USTED:
- No, gracias, casi *nunca* ceno fuera.
- Pero... ¡*nadie* cena a estas horas!
- Sí, pero... ¿*no* hay *ningún* otro restaurante cerca de la facultad?

EL CAMARERO: *También* tenemos cebiche, camarones...

USTED:
- Pues... creo que *no* voy a comer *nada*, gracias.
- ¡Qué bien! Quiero probar *algunos* platos típicos.
- Aquí *siempre* pido el cebiche.

YOUR FRIEND ALFONSO: It's already ten P.M. Let's go eat something at El Cebiche. I'm hungry! YOU: • No, thanks, I almost never have dinner out. • But . . . nobody eats dinner at this hour! • OK, but . . . isn't there any other restaurant close to campus? WAITER: We also have ceviche (*raw marinated fish*), shrimp . . . YOU: • Well . . . I don't think I'll have anything, thank you. • Great! I want to try some typical dishes! • I always order the ceviche here.

Aquí hay otras situaciones. ¿Qué respuestas puede Ud. improvisar, según el modelo de las respuestas anteriores (*preceding*)?

SU AMIGA ROSA: ¿Algo para beber? Pues, tienen agua mineral… y también hay vino, si quieres.

SU AMIGO RAÚL: ¿Tienes tu tarjeta de crédito? No traigo dinero en efectivo.

SU ABUELO: ¿No quieres venir para almorzar con nosotros el domingo? Tu abuelita siempre prepara una torta (*cake*) de chocolate ese día.

Here is a list of the most common indefinite and negative words. You have been using a number of these words since the early chapters of *¿Qué tal?*

algo	something, anything	**nada**	nothing, not anything
alguien	someone, anyone	**nadie**	no one, nobody, not anybody
algún, alguno/a/os/as	some, any	**ningún, ninguno/a**	no, none, not any
siempre	always	**nunca, jamás**	never
también	also	**tampoco**	neither, not either

Casi **nunca** ceno fuera los días de entre semana.	*I almost never have dinner out on weekdays.*
Queremos comer **algo** diferente esta noche.	*We want to have (eat) something different tonight.*
¿**Nadie** trae dinero?	*No one has (Doesn't anyone have) any money?*

Pronunciation hint: The **d** in **nada** and **nadie** is a fricative: **na da, na die**.

Pay particular attention to the following aspects of using negative words.

- When a negative word follows the main verb, Spanish requires that another negative word—usually **no**—be placed before the verb. When a negative word precedes the verb, **no** is not used.

¿**No** estudia **nadie**? ¿**Nadie** estudia?	*Isn't anyone studying?*
No estás en clase **nunca**. **Nunca** estás en clase.	*You're never in class.*
No quieren cenar aquí **tampoco**. **Tampoco** quieren cenar aquí.	*They don't want to have dinner here, either.*

- The adjectives **alguno** and **ninguno** shorten to **algún** and **ningún**, before a masculine singular noun, just as **uno** shortens to **un** and **bueno** to **buen**. The plural forms **ningunos** and **ningunas** are rarely used.

¿Hay **algunas** cartas para mí hoy? —Lo siento, pero hoy no hay **ninguna** carta para Ud.	*Are there any letters for me today?—I'm sorry, but there are no letters for you today. (There is not a single letter for you today.)*

Práctica

A.   ¡Por eso no come nadie allí! Exprese negativamente, con la negativa doble.

1. Hay algo interesante en el menú.
2. Tienen algunos platos típicos.
3. El profesor cena allí también.
4. Mis amigos siempre almuerzan allí.
5. Preparan algo especial para grupos grandes.
6. Siempre hacen platos nuevos.
7. Y también sirven paella, mi plato favorito.

B.   ¿Cómo se dice en español?

A la hora de la cena

1. Are there any napkins on the table?
2. They serve dinner at six at (**en**) their house, too.
3. No one is eating at home tonight, right?
4. We don't want to order anything right now.
5. There's no restaurant on that street.

En la residencia, antes del examen

1. No one understands that.
2. Marcos can't answer that question either.
3. You never study with Carmen. Why not?
4. No one is as tired as I am!
5. Doesn't anybody feel like sleeping?

C.   Rosa es una persona muy positiva, pero su hermano Rodolfo tiene ideas muy negativas. Aquí hay unas oraciones que expresan las ideas de Rosa sobre varios temas. ¿Cuáles son las opiniones de Rodolfo?

Sobre las clases y la vida universitaria

- Hay algunos estudiantes excelentes en mi clase de sicología.
- Algunas personas en mi clase de español son muy listas.
- Por lo general, ¡me gusta muchísimo (*very much*) mi compañera de cuarto!
- Salgo con mis amigos con frecuencia.

Las actividades de esta noche

- ¿Por qué no comemos algo?
- Vamos a beber algo antes de cenar.
- Sirven algunos platos estupendos aquí.
- Hay algo interesante en la tele esta noche.

Ahora invente Ud. algunos comentarios de Rodolfo sobre su familia y la ciudad donde vive. ¿Cómo reacciona Rosa?

D.   Preguntas

1.   ¿Vamos a vivir en la luna algún día? ¿Vamos a viajar a los otros plane-
     tas? ¿Vamos a vivir allí algún día? ¿Vamos a establecer contacto con seres
     (*beings*) de otros planetas algún día?

2.   ¿Algunos de los estudiantes de esta universidad son de países extran-
     jeros? ¿De dónde son? ¿Algunos de sus amigos son de habla española?
     ¿De dónde son?

3.   En esta clase, ¿quién… ? ¿siempre tiene algunas ideas buenas? ¿tiene
     algunos amigos españoles? ¿no entiende nada nunca? ¿no trae nunca su
     libro? ¿va a ser muy rico/a algún día? ¿nunca tiene tiempo para tomar
     un café después de (*after*) la clase? ¿nunca ve la televisión?

V O C A B U L A R I O

El infinitivo—Preposition + Infinitive

Acaban de pedir el desayuno.	*They've just ordered breakfast.*
Acabo de almorzar con Tina.	*I've just had lunch with Tina.*
La niña **vuelve a pedir** dulces.	*The little girl is asking for candy again.*
¡Nunca **vuelvo a comer** allí!	*I'll never eat there again!*

The infinitive is the only verb form that can follow a preposition in Spanish. You have already
learned to use the following constructions in which prepositions are followed by an infinitive: **ir
a, empezar a, tener ganas de.** Two other useful expressions with prepositions are **acabar de** +
infinitive (*to have just done something*) and **volver a** + *infinitive* (*to do something again*).

A.   Situaciones. Pregúntele a otro/a estudiante…

•   qué acaba de hacer si sale de los siguientes lugares

    MODELO: un restaurante →
              —Si sales de un restaurante, ¿qué acabas de hacer?
              —Acabo de comer.

1.   un mercado
2.   una discoteca
3.   una librería
4.   una tienda de ropa

•   dónde está si acaba de hacer las siguientes cosas

    MODELO: almorzar →
              — ¿Dónde estás si acabas de almorzar?
              — Estoy en la cafetería.

1.   cenar con su familia
2.   pedir la cuenta
3.   tomar una cerveza
4.   dormir ocho horas
5.   hacer una pregunta en español
6.   salir para la universidad

B.   Reacciones. Ud. está en los siguientes lugares o situaciones. ¿Qué quiere volver a hacer?

> MODELO: Ud. está en una discoteca con unos amigos. Hablan ahora, pero empiezan a tocar una música encantadora. → ¡Quiero volver a bailar!

1. Ud. está en las montañas. Acaba de esquiar cuatro horas y ahora descansa. Empieza a nevar.
2. Ud. está en la playa. Acaba de nadar (*to swim*) un poco, pero ahora toma el sol. ¡Hace mucho calor!
3. Ud. está en la cama (*bed*). Son las seis de la mañana y acaba de oír el despertador (*alarm clock*). Ud. quiere descansar un poco más.
4. En la clase de historia, Ud. acaba de sacar (*to receive*) una D en un examen.
5. Ud. mira un programa interesante en la tele cuando su amigo Julio llama por teléfono. Ud. contesta.
6. Ud. acaba de salir del cine. No vio (*You didn't see*) los primeros diez minutos de la película.

ESTRUCTURAS

17. ¿QUÉ SABES Y A QUIÉN CONOCES?
Saber and *conocer*; Personal *a*

Colinda, México

Delante de un restaurante

AMALIA: ¿Dónde vamos a almorzar?
ERNESTO: (Entrando en el restaurante.) ¿Por qué no aquí mismo?
AMALIA: ¿*Conoces* este restaurante?
ERNESTO: Sí, lo *conozco* y *sé* que es excelente.
AMALIA: ¿Y cómo *sabes* que es tan bueno?
ERNESTO: *Conozco* muy bien a la dueña. ¡Es mi tía! ¿Nos sentamos?

1. ¿Qué hora es, aproximadamente?
2. ¿Conoce Ernesto el restaurante?
3. ¿Cuál es su opinión del restaurante?
4. ¿Cómo sabe Ernesto que el restaurante es muy bueno?
5. ¿Por qué conoce a la dueña del restaurante?

In front of a restaurant   AMALIA: Where are we going to have lunch? ERNESTO: (Entering the restaurant.) Why not right here? AMALIA: Do you know (Are you familiar with) this restaurant? ERNESTO: Yes, I know it, and I know that it's excellent. AMALIA: And how do you know that it's so good? ERNESTO: I know the owner very well. She's my aunt! Shall we sit down?

Saber and *conocer*

(handwritten: wissen / savou   Kennen / connaître)

(handwritten: co/ca/cu => "k"   ce/ci/z => "th" in Sp   everywhere else it is as the same)

saber *(to know)*		conocer *(to know)*	
sé	sabemos	conozco	conocemos
sabes	sabéis	conoces	conocéis
sabe	saben	conoce	conocen

Saber means *to know* facts or pieces of information. When followed by an infinitive, **saber** means *to know how to* do something.

(handwritten: preparar)

No **saben** el teléfono de Alejandro.	*They don't know Alejandro's phone number.*
¿**Saben** Uds. dónde vive Carmela?	*Do you know where Carmela lives?*
¿**Sabes** tocar el piano?	*Do you know how to play the piano?*

Conocer means *to know* or *to be acquainted (familiar) with* a person, place, or thing. It can also mean *to meet*. Note the **a** used before a specific person.

(handwritten: conoces a (a person))

No **conocen** a la nueva estudiante todavía.	*They don't know the new student yet.*
¿**Conocen** Uds. el restaurante mexicano en la calle Goya?	*Are you familiar with (Have you been to) the Mexican restaurant on Goya Street?*
¿Quieren **conocer** a aquel joven?	*Do you want to meet that young man?*

[Práctica A–B]

Personal *a*

A.   In English and in Spanish, the *direct object* (**el complemento directo**) of a sentence answers the question *what?* or *whom?* in relation to the subject and verb.

Ann is preparing dinner.   { Ann is preparing *what?* / *What* is Ann preparing? }   *dinner*

They can't hear the baby.   { They can't hear *whom?* / *Whom* can't they hear? }   *the baby*

Indicate the direct objects in the following sentences:

1. I don't see Betty and Mary here.
2. Give the dog a bone.
3. No tenemos dinero.
4. ¿Por qué no pones la copa en la mesa?

B. In Spanish, the word **a** immediately precedes the direct object of a sentence when the direct object refers to a specific person or persons. This **a**, called the **a personal**, has no equivalent in English.*

Vamos a visitar **al profesor**.   *We're going to visit the professor.*
   but
Vamos a visitar **el museo**.   *We're going to visit the museum.*
Necesitan **a la camarera**.   *They need the waitress.*
   but
Necesitan **la cuenta**.   *They need the bill.*

¡OJO!   The verbs **esperar** (*to wait for*), **escuchar** (*to listen to*), **mirar** (*to look at*), and **buscar** (*to look for*) include the sense of the English prepositions *for*, *to*, and *at*. These verbs take direct objects in Spanish (not prepositional phrases, as in English).

Busco **mi abrigo**.   *I'm looking for my overcoat.*
Espero **a mi hijo**.   *I'm waiting for my son.*

C. The personal **a** is used before the interrogative words **¿quién?** or **¿quiénes?** when these words function as direct objects.

¿A quién llama?   *Whom are you calling?*
¿Quién llama?   *Who is calling?*

D. The personal **a** is used before **alguien** and **nadie** when these words function as direct objects.

¿Vas a invitar **a alguien**?   *Are you going to invite someone?*
¿A quién llamas?   *Whom are you calling?*
—No llamo **a nadie**.   *—I'm not calling anyone.*

[Práctica C–D]

Práctica

A.   ¿Qué saben hacer estas personas famosas?

Gloria Estefan	jugar al béisbol, al tenis
Mikhail Baryshnikov	hacer ejercicios gimnásticos
Fernando Valenzuela	cantar (en español), bailar
Mary Lou Retton **sabe**	cocinar (*to cook*) bien
James Michener	escribir novelas
Chris Evert	actuar (en español)
Julia Child	
James Edward Olmos	

---

*The personal **a** is not generally used with **tener: Tengo cuatro hijos.**

B. Parejas famosas. ¿A quién conoce... ?

Adán		Marta
Romeo		Cleopatra
Rhett Butler	conoce a	Eva
Antonio		Julieta
Jorge Washington		Scarlett O'Hara

C. ¿Qué hace Roberto los martes? Haga oraciones según las indicaciones para describir su rutina.

1. martes / Roberto / nunca / salir / temprano / apartamento
2. esperar / su amigo Samuel / en su casa
3. los dos / esperar / juntos / autobús (*m.*)
4. cuando / (ellos) llegar / universidad, / buscar / su amiga Ceci / en / cafetería
5. ella / acabar / empezar / estudios / allí / y / no / conocer / mucha gente (*people*) / todavía
6. a veces / (ellos) ver / profesora de historia en / cafetería / y / hablar / un poco / con ella
7. (ella) ser / persona / muy interesante / que / saber / mucho / de / ese / materia
8. a / dos / todos / tener / clase / de / sicología
9. siempre / (ellos) oír / conferencias (*lectures*) / interesante / y / hacer / alguno / pregunta
10. a veces / tener / oportunidad de / conocer / conferenciante (*m.*) (*lecturer*)
11. las cinco / Roberto y Samuel / volver / esperar / autobús
12. cuando entrar / apartamento, / Roberto / siempre / buscar / su compañero Raúl / para / hablar / un poco / con / él
13. los dos / preparar / cena / juntos / y / luego / mirar / televisión

¿Quién habla?

1. Quiero conocer a más gente. ¡Casi no conozco a nadie todavía!
2. Algunos estudiantes hacen buenas preguntas.
3. ¡Acabo de llegar! ¿Dónde estás?
4. ¡Ay! Ya veo a Roberto por la ventana (*window*) y todavía tengo que buscar mis libros.

Ahora vuelva a contar (*to tell*) la historia desde el punto de vista de Roberto. Use **yo** o **nosotros** como sujeto donde sea apropiado.

D. Preguntas

1. ¿Qué restaurantes conoce Ud. en esta ciudad? ¿Cuál es su restaurante favorito? ¿Por qué es su favorito? ¿Es buena la comida de allí? ¿Qué tipo de comida sirven? ¿Es agradable el ambiente (*atmosphere*)? ¿Come Ud. allí con frecuencia? ¿Conoce a los dueños del restaurante? ¿De dónde son?
2. ¿Conoce Ud. a alguna persona famosa? ¿Quién es? ¿Cómo es? ¿Qué detalles sabe Ud. de su vida?

3. ¿Qué platos sabe Ud. preparar? ¿tacos? ¿enchiladas? ¿pollo frito (*fried chicken*)? ¿hamburguesas? ¿Le gusta cocinar? ¿Cocina con frecuencia? ¿Por qué sí o por qué no?

4. ¿Qué habilidades especiales tiene Ud.? ¿Sabe jugar al tenis? ¿a otros deportes (*sports*)? ¿Sabe tocar un instrumento musical? ¿bailar muy bien? ¿cantar? ¿hablar otra lengua?

5. ¿Espera Ud. a alguien para ir a la universidad? ¿Espera a alguien después de (*after*) la clase? ¿A quién llama cuando necesita ayuda (*help*) con el español? ¿Dónde busca a sus amigos por la noche?

¿Dónde vamos a comer?
—Vamos al Mesón de las Tres Hermanas.
—No conozco ese restaurante.
—Pues allí sirven un bistec exquisito.
—¿Y no es muy caro?
—Al contrario. Los precios son muy razonables.
—¡Eso espero!° ¡A comer!   ¡Eso... *I hope so!*

Buenos Aires, Argentina

UN POCO DE TODO

A.   Con un compañero (una compañera), haga y conteste las siguientes preguntas. Puede contestar negativa o afirmativamente. La persona que contesta debe añadir (*add*) más información para explicar la respuesta.

Para hablar de la clase y de los estudiantes

1. ¿Ves algo en la pizarra en este momento?
2. ¿Traes algunos libros a clase hoy?
3. ¿Ves a alguien nuevo en la clase?
4. ¿Sabes algo de la historia de Puerto Rico?
5. ¿Sabes algo de la comida de Sudamérica?
6. ¿Qué clase no vuelves a tomar nunca?

Para hablar de sus amigos

7. ¿Conoces a alguien de la Argentina? ¿de Cuba?
8. ¿Conoces a algunos atletas?
9. ¿Tienes algunos amigos de habla española?
10. ¿Acabas de conocer a alguien interesante?

B.   ¡Firma (*Sign*) aquí, por favor! Find someone in the class about whom the following descriptions are true; have that person sign his or her name.

MODELO: Conozco a mucha gente latina. →
—¿Conoces a mucha gente latina?
—¡Sí! Tengo amigos argentinos, bolivianos,…
—Firma aquí, por favor.

Nombres

1. Conozco a mucha gente latina.
2. Sé hablar *muy muy* bien el español.
3. No me gusta nada comer.
4. Nunca tengo muchas ganas de trabajar.
5. Siempre traigo mucho dinero a la clase.
6. Veo *Roseanne* con frecuencia.
7. Conozco a una persona famosa, ____.
8. Oigo las noticias (*news*) en la radio; nunca las veo en la televisión.

UN PASO MÁS: Situaciones

En un restaurante español

MANUEL:	¿Nos sentamos°? Creo que aquí se está bien.°
ANA MARÍA:	Perfecto. Aquí viene el camarero. ¿Por qué no pides tú la cena ya que° conoces este restaurante?
CAMARERO:	Buenas noches, señores. ¿Desean algo de aperitivo?
MANUEL:	Para la señorita un vermut; para mí un fino. Los trae con jamón, queso y anchoas,° por favor. ¿Y qué recomienda Ud. de comida?
CAMARERO:	El solomillo a la parrilla° es la especialidad de la casa. Como plato del día hay paella°…
MANUEL:	Bueno. De entrada, el gazpacho.° De plato fuerte,° el solomillo con patatas y guisantes. Ensalada de lechuga y tomate.° Y de postre, flan.° Vino tinto° y, al final, dos cafés.
ANA MARÍA:	Manolo, basta° ya. ¡Estoy a dieta y he merendado más de la cuenta°!
MANUEL:	Chica,* ¿qué importa? Luego vamos a bailar.

¿Nos… *Shall we sit down?* / se… *we'll be comfortable*

ya… *since*

jamón… *ham, cheese, and anchovies*

solomillo… *grilled filet mignon*
Spanish dish of rice, seafood, often chicken; flavored with saffron
chilled tomato soup / plato… *main dish*

Ensalada… *Green salad*

de… *for dessert, custard* / *red*

enough

he… *I snacked more than I should have*

---

*Note that Manolo calls Ana María **chica**. The words **chico/chica** (*boy/girl*) are commonly used in Spanish by friends of all ages.

Notas comunicativas sobre el diálogo

Here are some useful words and expressions related to eating at home and in restaurants. You will be familiar with many of them already.

El camarero/La camarera:

¿Qué desea Ud. de aperitivo? ¿de
  plato principal? ¿de postre?
  ¿para beber?
¿Algo más?

*What would you like as an appetizer?
  as a main course? for dessert? to
  drink?*
Something else?

El/La cliente:

Favor de traerme un(a)...
¿Me trae un(a)... , por favor? }

¿Qué recomienda Ud.?
Un(a)... más, por favor.

Psst. Oiga. Señor/Señorita.

La cuenta, por favor.

Would you please bring me a . . . ?

What do you recommend?
One more . . . , please.
{ Used to get a waiter's/waitress's
   attention.
 Psst is not used in formal settings.
The check, please.

Conversación

You and a friend are dining at El Charro restaurant. During the meal, you call on the waiter/waitress a number of times. With your instructor acting as waiter/waitress, explain the following situations, using expressions from the **Notas comunicativas sobre el diálogo** as appropriate.

- You would like another napkin/knife/plate.
- You can't read the menu because there is no light.
- You need ice/a clean glass for your Coke.
- Your fork/teaspoon is dirty and you want another one.
- You are going to order another bottle of wine/pitcher of beer.
- You want your check.
- You can't pay because you don't have cash/a credit card.
- You want to speak with the chef/owner of the restaurant to explain the situation.

La tecnología más avanzada.

MICROONDAS, GRATINADO Y CONVECTOR

MOD R-8480
Dentro de la variable gama de los hornos microondas, SHARP une en este horno microondas la técnica ya conocida de la cocción por convección a la más reciente de cocción por microondas, lo cual reduce considerablemente el tiempo necesario para cocinar, mientras que las resistencias de la parrilla producen el gratinado apetecido. El plato giratorio consigue una cocción uniforme y el control variable de cocción, permite la selección de la potencia de microondas necesaria para una cocción rápida.

VOCABULARIO

Verbos

acabar de (+ *inf.*) to have just
  (*done something*)
cenar to have dinner
cocinar to cook
conocer (*irreg.*) to know, be
  acquainted with
desayunar to have breakfast
escuchar to listen (to)
esperar to wait (for); to hope
llamar to call
oír (*irreg.*) to hear
saber (*irreg.*) to know; to know
  how
traer (*irreg.*) to bring
ver (*irreg.*) to see
volver (**ue**) **a** (+ *inf.*) to do some-
  thing) again

Las comidas

el almuerzo lunch
la cena dinner, supper
el desayuno breakfast

En el restaurante

la bandeja tray
la botella bottle
el/la camarero/a waiter/waitress
el/la cocinero/a cook, chef
la copa wine glass, goblet
la cuenta bill, check
el dinero en efectivo cash
el/la dueño/a owner
el jarro pitcher
el mantel tablecloth
el menú menu
el plato plate; dish (*food*)
la servilleta napkin
la tarjeta (**de crédito**) (credit) card
el vaso (drinking) glass
la vela candle

Utensilios de comer

la cuchara (soup)spoon
la cucharita teaspoon
el cuchillo knife
el tenedor fork

Otros sustantivos

el detalle detail
la gente people
la respuesta answer

Adjetivos

algún, alguno/a/os/as some, any
juntos/as together
ningún, ninguno/a no, none, not
  any

Palabras adicionales

algo something
alguien someone, anyone
jamás never
nada nothing, not anything
nadie no one, nobody, not
  anybody
otra vez again
tampoco neither, not either

Frases útiles para la comunicación

cuando pueda   whenever you have a second (can)
¡Que aproveche(n)!   Enjoy your meal!

See also the words and phrases in **Notas comunicativas sobre el diálogo**.

LOS HISPANOS EN LOS ESTADOS UNIDOS
La comunidad mexicanoamericana

La gran mayoría de los mexicanoamericanos viven a lo largo de (*along*) la frontera (*border*) de los Estados Unidos y México—de Texas a California—y también en otros estados del oeste. Los antepasados (*ancestors*) de algunos fueron (*were*) los dueños de estos territorios muchos años antes de que (*before*) llegaran (*arrived*) los anglosajones. De

hecho (*In fact*), la patria (*home*) legendaria de los aztecas, la «tierra blanca» de Aztlán, hoy forma parte del sudoeste de los Estados Unidos. La frontera es solamente una línea artificial para la gente de la región fronteriza; es una realidad política, pero no divide dos pueblos.

SUSANA RENDON

Presidenta y Directora del Consejo Ejecutivo, Empresas Rendon Ltda. Publicidad/Promociones/Mercadotecnia.°   *Marketing*

Northwestern Univ., Evanston, Ill.

Comenzó° su trayectoria profesional como ingeniera en la industria de la televisión, 1976 - Publicista de TV   *She began*

Primera Ingeniera Telefónica con licencia de FCC

Fundó REL en 1982.

Miembro de la Asociación Latina de Negocios,° Cámara° de Comercio Hispano-Americana, Consejo Consultor de la Asociación México-Americana de Almacenes, Club de Publicidad de Los Ángeles y Consulado de la Archidiócesis de Los Ángeles, Parroquia San Vincente.   *Business / Chamber*

Las Posadas, San Antonio, Texas

La tradición oral: Refranes y adivinanzas (*riddles*)

- Plata° no es. Oro° no es. ¿Qué es?   *Silver / Gold*
- A buen hambre,° no hay pan duro.°   *hunger / pan... hard bread*
- Más vale° un hoy que diez mañanas.   *Más... is worth more*

Las posadas:° Una tradición navideña   *inn; lodging*

¿Quién les da° posada   *les... gives*
a estos peregrinos,°   *pilgrims*
que vienen cansados
de andar caminos°?   *andar... walking the roads*

Unos niños juegan con una piñata en Texas.

César Chávez

¡Viva la Causa! ¡Viva la Raza! ¡Viva la UFWA (*United Farm Workers Association*)!

Dos tradiciones… y ahora una tercera (*third*)

Yo soy hijo de la tierra,
y heredero° de la raza°;   *heir / Spanish-speaking people*
tengo rasgos° de españoles   *traces*
y de aztecas en mi alma.°   *soul*

Mario A. Benítez, poeta chicano,
«Yo soy hijo de la tierra»

De colores, de colores se visten° los   *se… dress*
   campos° en la primavera   *fields*
De colores, de colores son los pajaritos°   *little birds*
   que vienen de afuera
De colores, de colores es el arco iris°   *arco… rainbow*
   que vemos lucir°   *to shine*
Y por eso los grandes amores de muchos
   colores me gustan a mí.

Una tradición mexicana continúa en los Estados Unidos.

«Cuando el sol se baja° y los bolillos° dejan°   *se… sets / Anglos / leave*
sus tiendas, el pueblo americano se duerme
para no despertar° hasta el día siguiente.   *to wake up*

Cuando el sol se baja y la gente ha ce-
nado,° el pueblo mexicano se aviva y se   *ha… have had dinner*
oyen las voces del barrio: la gente mayor, los
jóvenes, los chicos, los perros…

El barrio puede llamarse el Rebaje, el de
las Conchas, el Cantarranas, el Rincón del
Diablo, el Pueblo Mexicano—verdaderamente los títulos importan poco.

Lo importante, como siempre, es la
gente.

Rolando Hinojosa, «Voces del barrio»

«Cake-Walk», de Carmen Lomas Garza, pin-
tora mexicanoamericana de Kingsville, Texas,
que ahora vive en San Francisco

Richard "Cheech" Marin

Richard «Cheech» Marin, actor, cómico, director de cine y de vídeo; su última película es «Nacido (*Born*) en el este de Los Ángeles».

«Nacido en el este de Los Ángeles» es una parodia del éxito (*success*) de Bruce Springsteen «Nacido en Los Estados Unidos». Y está basada en un incidente verdadero que ocurrió en 1984 cuando un ciudadano (*citizen*) americano de ascendencia mexicana fue aprehendido en una redada de migra (*immigration raid*) y fue deportado a México por no tener ningún docu-mento de identificación.

CHEECH: «[En "Nacido en el este de Los Ángeles"] Sólo estoy presentándolas [cuestiones] para que la gente tome sus propias (*own*) decisiones. Estas cuestiones no son tan claras como lo blanco y lo negro. Alguna gente del I.N.S. (*Immigration and Naturalization Service*) es buena y otra no tanto, y algunos se quedan (*are*) atrapados entre la espada y la pared (*a rock and a hard place*).»

Américas 2001

¿QUÉ VAMOS A PEDIR?

VOCABULARIO: LA COMIDA Y LAS BEBIDAS

¿Prefieres... ?
¿un desayuno estilo norteamericano?

el jugo de fruta
el café
los huevos
el jamón
el pan tostado

¿una comida rápida?

la hamburguesa
las papas fritas
la cerveza
el helado

¿o un típico desayuno hispánico?

un bollo
las galletas
un café o un café con leche

¿una cena elegante?

la langosta
el vino blanco
el pan
la sopa
el pastel
la ensalada de lechuga y tomate

las arvejas
el arroz
el pollo
la manzana
el agua mineral*

¿o un menú ligero?

Las bebidas
la leche milk
el refresco soft drink
el té tea
el vino tinto red wine

La carne
el bistec steak
las chuletas (de cerdo) (pork) chops

Los mariscos
los camarones shrimp

El pescado
el atún tuna
el salmón salmon

Las verduras
los frijoles beans
la zanahoria carrot

Otros platos y comidas
el queso cheese
el sándwich sandwich

La fruta
la banana banana
la naranja orange

Los postres
el flan custard
la galleta cookie; cracker

*The noun **agua** (*water*) is feminine, but the masculine articles are used with it in the singular: **el agua**. This phenomenon occurs with all feminine nouns that begin with a stressed **a** sound: **el ama de casa** (*the homemaker*).

Cruciletras

En este cruciletras deberás encajar los siguientes nombres: ajo -
apio - haba - brecol - tomate - rábano - judías - acelgas - puerro -
lechuga - lenteja - cebolla - zanahoria.

A.   Definiciones. ¿Qué es esto?

1. un líquido caliente (*hot*) que se toma* con cuchara
2. un plato de lechuga y tomate
3. una bebida alcohólica blanca o roja
4. una verdura anaranjada
5. la carne típica para barbacoa en los Estados Unidos
6. una comida muy común en China y en Japón
7. la comida favorita de los ratones
8. una verdura frita que se come con las hamburguesas
9. una fruta roja o verde
10. una fruta amarilla de las zonas tropicales
11. un líquido de color blanco que se sirve especialmente a los
    niños
12. la bebida tradicional de los ingleses
13. se usa para preparar sándwiches
14. un postre muy frío
15. un postre que se sirve en las fiestas de cumpleaños
16. una cosa que se come y que tiene el centro amarillo y el
    resto blanco

Notas lingüísticas: More *tener* idioms

Here are two additional **tener** idioms related to foods and eating.

tener (mucha) hambre	*to be (very) hungry*
tener (mucha) sed	*to be (very) thirsty*

B.   Consejos a la hora de comer. ¿Qué debe Ud. comer o beber en las siguientes situaciones?

1. Ud. quiere comer algo ligero (*light*) porque no tiene hambre.
2. Ud. quiere comer algo fuerte (*heavy*) porque tiene mucha hambre.
3. Ud. tiene un poco de sed y quiere tomar algo antes de (*before*) la comida.
4. Ud. quiere comer algo antes del plato principal.
5. Ud. quiere comer algo después del (*after*) plato principal.
6. Después de jugar al tenis, Ud. tiene mucha sed.
7. Ud. está a dieta.
8. Ud. es vegetariano/a; come en un restaurante con unos amigos.
9. Ud. está de vacaciones en Maine (o Boston).
10. Ud. está enfermo/a.

---

*Remember that placing **se** before a verb form can change its English equivalent slightly: **toma**
(*he/she/it drinks*) → **se toma** (*is drunk*).

C.   Asociaciones. ¿Qué palabras asocia Ud. con estas frases y oraciones?

1.   comer bien
2.   un bistec
3.   cenar

4.   engordar (*to gain weight*)
5.   el desayuno
6.   el almuerzo

D.   Entrevista. Use the following patterns to find out what several class-mates had to eat last night. Take notes on what you learn.

MODELO: —¿Qué *comiste* anoche?
          —*Comí* una hamburguesa con papas fritas.

Now use this pattern to report what you learned to the class and to add information about what you had to eat.

MODELO: Juanita *comió* una hamburguesa con papas fritas anoche.
          Yo *comí* pescado.

Notas comunicativas: Expressing Likes and Dislikes

You have been using the phrase **me gusta/no me gusta** since the beginning of this text. Here are two simple ways to express *intense* likes and dislikes.

¡Me gusta **muchísimo**!	*I like it a lot!*
¡No me gusta **(para) nada**!	*I don't like it at all!*

COMER VERDURA CRUDA

*P*ARA preparar las verduras en crudo lo más impor-tante es el lavado, pues hay que eliminar cualquier pará-sito o bichito. Las lechugas, es-carolas, berros, etc., se ponen en un colador, bajo el cho-rro del agua fría, para qui-tarles la tierra. Luego, se inspecciona hoja por hoja y se lavan también al chorro. Se pican a continua-ción en un recipiente hondo lleno de agua con unas gostas de lejía –una gota por cada litro de agua– y se dejan un rato. La le-jía es un desinfectante muy efi-caz. Pasado este tiempo se escu-rre y se prepara como más guste. Las zanahorias crudas no necesitan ponerse en lejía, pues ya se pelan o raspan. Las ver-duras, una vez en casa, hay que consumirlas en el día o, a lo sumo, en dos. Conservarlas en la parte baja del frigorífico. Tam-bién se pueden conservar en ca-charros de plástico que cierren bien. En ellos, la lechuga limpia y lavada dura cua-tro o cinco días.

E.   Una encuesta. Read the following categories and jot down your answers. Then pick the four items that interest you the most and ask questions of four classmates to determine how they answered each one. Try to get additional information and be prepared to share your answers with the class.

MODELO: un restaurante que no me gusta nada →
          ¿Qué restaurante no te gusta nada?
          ¿Acabas de comer en ese restaurante?
          ¿Qué comiste allí?
          ¿Vas a volver a comer allí?

1.   un programa de televisión que veo con frecuencia y que me gusta muchísimo
2.   un programa de televisión que no me gusta nada
3.   una película (nueva o vieja) que acabo de ver y que es estupenda
4.   una película nueva que quiero ver
5.   una estación de radio que escucho con frecuencia
6.   un restaurante estupendo donde comí recientemente / donde acabo de comer
7.   un restaurante que no me gusta nada
8.   un plato que no vuelvo a comer nunca

Desayuno: 1 vaso de jugo de naranja, un emparedado compuesto por una rebanada de pan untada con 1 quesito desnatado cubierta con otra rebanada untada con mostaza de semillas y tostado, así como 1 café o té sin azúcar. Total, 200 Calorías.

Comida: ensalada verde, filete de ternera a la plancha y 1 racimo de uvas. Total, 360 Calorías.

Cena: zanahorias estofadas, 2 lonchas de jamón cocido y 1 manzana. Total, 390 Calorías.

Zanahorias estofadas. Por persona se necesitan 200 g de zanahorias, 100 g de brotes de soja, 1 cubito Maggi, 1 cucharadita de azúcar, sal y perejil fresco. Pelar las zanahorias y cortarlas en rebanadas finas. Disolver el cubito de caldo en 1/4 de taza de agua caliente, añadir las zanahorias y los brotes de soja y cocer a fuego suave hasta que las zanahorias estén tiernas. Sazonar con el azúcar y una pizca de sal y espolvorear con perejil.

Nuestro consejo: los brotes de soja son nutritivos, están repletos de vitaminas y aportan escasas calorías. Constituyen, pues, un excelente recurso. Se encuentran en tiendas de verduras y supermercados pero conviene recordar que son un producto perecedero. Para conservarlos cierto tiempo hay que recurrir a las conservas.

Especial para: los días en que podemos permitirnos frenar un poco la marcha, ya sea durante el fin de semana o en vacaciones. Aunque la composición del menú garantiza la aportación de proteínas, los platos no tienen excesivo poder saciante.

Al tanto...

Here are some phrases that you can use at mealtimes.

• apetecer	¿Qué te apetece?	*What do you feel like (having)?*
	Me apetece tomar...	*I'd like (to have) . . .*
• picar	¿Vamos a picar algo?	*Shall we nibble a bit?*
• un hambre de lobos	¡Tengo un hambre de lobos!	*I'm as hungry as a bear (lit., I have the hunger of wolves)!*

Study Hint: Practicing Spanish Outside of Class

The few hours you spend in class each week are not enough time for practicing Spanish. But once you have done your homework and gone to the language lab (if one is available to you), how else can you practice your Spanish outside of class?

1. Practice "talking to yourself" in Spanish as you walk across campus, wait for a bus, and so on. Have an imaginary conversation with someone you know, or simply practice describing what you see or what you are thinking about at a given moment. Write notes to yourself in Spanish.

2. Hold a conversation hour—perhaps on a regular basis—with other students of Spanish. Or make regular phone calls to practice Spanish with other students in your class. It is difficult to communicate on the phone, because you can't rely on gestures and facial expressions, but it's an excellent way to improve your skill.

3. See Spanish-language movies when they are shown on campus or in local movie theaters. Check local bookstores, libraries, and record stores for Spanish-language newspapers, magazines, and music. Read the radio and television listings. Are there any Spanish-language programs or any stations that broadcast partially or exclusively in Spanish?

4. Practice speaking Spanish with a native speaker—either a Hispanic American or a foreign student. Is there an international students' organization on campus? An authentic Hispanic restaurant in your town? Spanish-speaking professors at your university? Try out a few phrases—no matter how simple—every chance you get. Every bit of practice will enhance your ability to speak Spanish.

ESTRUCTURAS

 18. EXPRESSING *WHAT* OR *WHOM*
Direct Object Pronouns

¿Dónde vamos a comer?

AGUSTÍN: Empiezo a tener hambre. ¿Qué te parece si cenamos fuera esta noche?

MARIELA: ¡Buena idea! A propósito, ¿conoces a los Velázquez?

AGUSTÍN: Claro que sí. Hace años que *los* conozco. ¿Por qué me *lo* preguntas?

MARIELA: Pues acabo de oír que tienen un restaurante en la Avenida Bolívar.

AGUSTÍN: ¡Qué suerte! ¡A ver si *nos* invitan* a comer!

1. ¿Quién tiene hambre?
2. ¿Quién conoce a los Velázquez?
3. ¿Por qué habla Mariela de ellos?
4. ¿Quiere pagar la comida Agustín?

DIRECT OBJECT PRONOUNS			
me	*me*	**nos**	*us*
te	*you* (fam. sing.)	**os**	*you* (fam. pl.)
lo[†]	*you* (form. sing.), *him, it* (m.)	**los**	*you* (form. pl.), *them* (m., m. + f.)
la	*you* (form. sing.), *her, it* (f.)	**las**	*you* (form. pl.), *them* (f.)

A.   Like direct object nouns, *direct object pronouns* (**los pronombres del complemento directo**) answer the questions *what?* or *whom?* in relation to the subject and verb. Direct object pronouns are placed before a conjugated verb and after the word **no** when it appears. Direct object pronouns are used only when the direct object noun has already been mentioned.

Where are we going to eat?   AGUSTÍN: I'm starting to get hungry. What do you think about eating out tonight? MARIELA: Great! By the way, do you know the Velázquezes? AGUSTÍN: Of course I do. I've known them for years. Why do you ask? MARIELA: Well, I've just heard that they have a restaurant on Bolívar Avenue. AGUSTÍN: What luck! Let's see if they treat us to a meal!

*¡OJO!   **Invitar** is a cognate that has somewhat different connotations in Spanish and in English. In English, *to invite* someone is to request that person's company. In Spanish, **te invito, nos invitan,** and similar phrases imply that the person who is inviting will also pay.
†In Spain and in other parts of the Spanish-speaking world, **le** is frequently used instead of **lo** for the direct object pronoun *him*. This usage will not be followed in *¿Qué tal?*

¿El libro? Diego no **lo** necesita.   *The book? Diego doesn't need it.*
¿Dónde están la revista y el   *Where are the magazine and the*
   periódico? **Los** necesito   *newspaper? I need them now.*
   ahora.
Ellos **me** ayudan.   *They're helping me.*

B. The direct object pronouns may be attached to an infinitive.

Las tengo que leer. ⎫
Tengo que leer**las**. ⎭   *I have to read them.*

Práctica

A. Situaciones. Imagine you are in the following situations, performing the indicated tasks. A friend asks you about particular items. Answer logically—you will not need some items at all! Follow the models.

1. Ud. hace la maleta (*You're packing*) para un viaje a Acapulco.
   ¿El traje de baño? —¡Claro que *lo* necesito!

Artículos: las sandalias, las gafas de sol (*sunglasses*), los pantalones cortos, las camisetas, la crema bronceadora (*suntan lotion*), el reloj

2. Ud. prepara un pastel para el cumpleaños de un amigo.
   ¿La harina (*flour*)? —Sí, tengo que usar*la*.

Ingredientes: los huevos, la leche, el azúcar, el chocolate, la vainilla

3. Ud. está en un restaurante y es hora de pedir.
   ¿El vino blanco? —Sí, voy a pedir*lo*.

Platos: la sopa de espárragos, el pan, las chuletas de cerdo, las papas fritas, el café, el helado de vainilla

B. Agustín y Mariela cenan fuera. The following description of Agustín and Mariela's dinner out is very repetitive. Rephrase the sentences, changing direct object nouns to pronouns as needed.

1. El camarero trae los vasos y pone los vasos en la mesa.
2. Luego trae el menú y Agustín y Mariela leen el menú.
3. «¿Los platos del día? Voy a explicar los platos del día ahora mismo.»
4. A Agustín le gusta el bistec y va a pedir el bistec.
5. Mariela prefiere el pescado fresco pero hoy no tienen pescado fresco.
6. «Agustín, no debes comer el postre antes del plato principal. ¿Por qué no comes el postre después?»
7. Agustín necesita un tenedor y el camarero trae el tenedor.
8. Los dos prefieren vino tinto. Por eso Agustín pide vino tinto.
9. «¿La cuenta? El dueño acaba de preparar la cuenta.»
10. Agustín quiere pagar con tarjeta de crédito pero no trae su tarjeta de crédito.
11. Por fin Mariela toma la cuenta y paga la cuenta.

C. Más invitaciones. Con otro/a estudiante, haga y conteste preguntas según el modelo.

> MODELO: comer en tu casa → —¿Cuándo *me* invitas a comer en tu casa?
> —*Te* invito a comer el sábado.

1. cenar fuera
2. almorzar
3. nadar (*to swim*) en tu piscina (*pool*)
4. ver una película
5. ir contigo a la playa

Ahora repita el ejercicio en plural, según el modelo.

> MODELO: comer en tu casa → —¿Cuando *nos* invitas a comer en tu casa?
> —*Los* invito a comer el sábado.

D. ¿Qué comiste anoche? Con otro/a estudiante, haga y conteste preguntas según el modelo.

> MODELO: tacos → —¿Comiste tacos anoche?
> —Sí, *los* comí. (No, *no los* comí.)

1. jamón
2. zanahorias
3. papas fritas
4. salmón
5. enchiladas
6. helado

E. Your roommate (**compañero/a de cuarto**) is constantly suggesting things for you to do, but you've always just finished doing them. How will you respond to each of the following suggestions? Follow the model.

> MODELO: —¿Por qué no escribes la composición para la clase de español?
> —¡Porque *acabo de* escribir*la*!

1. ¿Por qué no estudias la lección ahora?
2. ¿Por qué no visitas el museo conmigo?
3. ¿Por qué no aprendes las palabras nuevas?
4. ¿Por qué no compras el periódico de hoy?
5. ¿Por qué no pagas las cervezas?
6. ¿Por qué no preparas las arvejas?
7. ¿Por qué no compras agua mineral?
8. ¿Por qué no me ayudas más?

Hazlo
adelgazar a *él*:
tu perrito

Los animales domésticos de las personas con exceso de peso tienden a engordar mucho (en los Estados Unidos, uno de cada cuatro perros es obeso). Ahora que estás poniéndote como una sílfide, ayuda a tu perro o gato a sentirse feliz con su cuerpo, en lugar de apenado. Dale alimentos de pocas calorías. ¿Y por qué no llevar al perrito en tus caminatas para adelgazar? Así se pondrán lindos los dos y te sentirás muy bien acompañada.

F. Una encuesta sobre la comida. Haga preguntas a sus compañeros de clase para saber si comen las comidas indicadas y con qué frecuencia. Deben explicar también por qué comen o *no* comen cierta comida.

> MODELO: la carne →
> —¿Comes carne?
> —*No la* como casi nunca porque tiene mucho colesterol.

1. la carne
2. los mariscos
3. el yogur
4. la piza
5. las hamburguesas
6. el pollo
7. el café
8. el vino
9. el alcohol
10. el atún

Palabras útiles: la grasa (*fat*), el colesterol, las calorías, la cafeína, la salud (*health*), ser alérgico/a a, me pone (*it makes me*) nervioso/a, me hace engordar, estar a dieta

VOCABULARIO

¿Dónde está?—Las preposiciones

Prepositions express relationships in time and space:

The book is *on* the table.   The food is *for* tomorrow.

- Some common Spanish prepositions you have already used include **a**, **con**, **de**, **en**, and **para**. Here are some others in addition to those illustrated in the drawing.

antes de	before
después de	after
entre	between, among
durante	during
sin	without

lejos de

cerca de la pimienta

la sal detrás de / delante de

encima de

debajo de el platillo

a la izquierda de / a la derecha de

- In Spanish, the pronouns that serve as objects of prepositions are identical in form to the subject pronouns, except for **mí** and **ti**.

Ella va a comprar un regalo para **mí**.   *She's going to buy a gift for me.*
Buscamos algo para **ti**.   *We're looking for something for you.*

- **Conmigo** expresses *with me*. Use **contigo** to express *with you* (*fam. sing.*).

No puedo hablar **contigo** ahora.   *I can't talk with you now.*

- As you know, the infinitive is the only verb form that can follow a preposition.

¿Adónde vas **después de estudiar**?   *Where are you going after you study?*

A.   ¿Dónde está? Con un compañero (una compañera), explique dónde están los siguientes objetos en el dibujo.

> MODELO: la copa → —¿La copa?
> —Está cerca de la botella de vino.

1. el plato	4. el jarro	7. el tenedor
2. el cuchillo	5. el vaso	8. la pimienta
3. el pan	6. el platillo	9. la servilleta

B.   Preguntas. ¿Qué hace Ud. antes de la clase de español? ¿y durante la clase? ¿y después? ¿Quién está delante de Ud. durante la clase? ¿Tiene otra clase después de ésta? ¿Adónde va Ud. después de estudiar en la biblioteca toda la tarde? ¿Qué hace antes de un examen? ¿y después? ¿Con quién estudias para los exámenes?

C.   Situaciones. You and a friend are discussing what is easy (**fácil**) and difficult (**difícil**) for each of you to do. Ask and answer questions according to the model, adding more information when possible.

MODELO: hablar en público →
—Para ti, ¿es fácil o difícil hablar en público?
—Para mí es difícil hablar en público.
—Pues, para mí es muy fácil. ¡Me gusta hablar en público!

1. asistir a clase todos los días
2. aprender el vocabulario
3. comer menos
4. estudiar los sábados por la noche
5. gastar menos dinero en (ropa, libros, discos...)

ESTRUCTURAS

19. GETTING INFORMATION
Summary of Interrogative Words

¿Cómo?	How?	¿Quién(es)?	Who?
¿Cuándo?	When?	¿De quién(es)?	Whose?
¿A qué hora?	At what time?	¿Dónde?	Where?
¿Qué?	What? Which?	¿De dónde?	From where?
¿Cuál(es)	What? Which one (ones)?	¿Adónde?	Where (to)?
		¿Cuánto/a?	How much?
¿Por qué?	Why?	¿Cuántos/as?	How many?

You have been using interrrogative words to ask questions and get information since the preliminary chapter of *¿Qué tal?* The preceding chart shows all of the interrogatives you have learned so far. Be sure that you know what they mean and how they are used. If you are not certain, the end vocabulary will help you find where they are first introduced. Only the specific uses of **¿qué?** and **¿cuál?** represent "new" material.

Using *¿qué?* and *¿cuál?*

¿Qué? asks for a definition or an explanation.

¿Qué es esto?	*What is this?*
¿Qué quieres?	*What do you want?*
¿Qué tocas?	*What are you playing?*

¿Qué? can be directly followed by a noun.

¿**Qué traje** necesitas?	*What (Which) suit do you need?*
¿**Qué playa** te gusta más?	*What (Which) beach do you like most?*
¿**Qué instrumento** musical tocas?	*What (Which) musical instrument do you play?*

¿**Cuál(es)?** expresses *what?* or *which?* in all other cases.*

¿**Cuál** es la clase más grande?	*What (Which) is the biggest class?*
¿**Cuáles** son tus verduras favoritas?	*What (Which) are your favorite vegetables?*
¿**Cuál** es la capital de Uruguay?	*What is the capital of Uruguay?*
¿**Cuál** es tu teléfono?	*What is your phone number?*

Práctica

A.   ¿Qué? o ¿cuál(es)?

1. ¿_____ es esto? —Una tortilla de patatas.   *Qué   defin*
2. ¿_____ es Sacramento? —Es la capital de California.   *Qué defin*
3. ¿_____ es tu pescado favorito? —Pues, yo creo que es el atún.   *Cuál*
4. ¿_____ postre vas a tomar? —El flan.   *Qué / (st. Cuál)*
5. ¿_____ son los cines más modernos? —Los del centro.   *Cuáles*
6. ¿_____ camisa debo llevar? —La azul.   *Qué*
7. ¿_____ galletas vas a comprar? —Las italianas.   *Qué*
8. ¿_____ es el novio de Alicia? —Es el hombre moreno.   *Cuál / Quién*

B.   Una tarjeta postal de Buenos Aires. Here is a postcard that Sara has sent to Alfonso in the United States. Read the postcard. Then, using interrogative words, form as many questions as you can about its content to ask your classmates. You can ask questions about what it actually says as well as about what it implies.

Alfonso:
Hola, ¿qué tal? Katia y yo acabamos de llegar a la Argentina Hace mucho frío porque es agosto— en el hemisferio sur° los meses de invierno son junio, julio y agosto. Los argentinos piensan que somos turistas porque llevamos camisetas y sandalias. Tienen razón... ¡y nosotras tenemos frío! ¡Qué mal escogimos° la ropa para este viaje! Ahora ... tomamos café en el hotel. Mañana pensamos comprar ropa abrigada.° Bueno, eso es todo por ahora.
Un abrazo° de
Sara

Alfonso Solís

145 Elm Street

Hudson, Ohio 44236

USA

southern

¡Qué... How badly we chose

warm

hug

---

*The ¿**cuál(es)?** + *noun* structure is not used by many speakers of Spanish, but rather ¿**cual(es) de?** + noun: ¿**Cuál de los dos libros** quieres? *Which of the two books do you want?* Accepted by all speakers is ¿**qué?** + noun: ¿**Qué libro** quieres? *Which (What) book do you want?*

C.   Entrevista. Without taking notes, interview another student by asking the following questions or any others like them that occur to you. Then present as much of the information as you can to the class.

1. ¿De dónde eres? ¿Dónde vives ahora? ¿Quién vive contigo? ¿Por qué vives allí?
2. ¿Qué materias tienes este semestre/trimestre? ¿Por qué estudias español? ¿Lo entiendes todo en clase?
3. ¿Cuántos primos tienes? ¿Cuántos tíos?
4. ¿Qué tipo de persona eres?
5. ¿Qué platos prefieres?
6. ¿Cuál es tu color favorito? ¿Tienes mucha ropa de ese color?
7. ¿Tienes novio/a (esposo/a)? ¿un amigo (una amiga) especial? ¿Cómo es?
8. ¿Con quién te gusta salir los sábados? ¿Adónde van?
9. ¿Adónde quieres viajar algún día? ¿Por qué quieres hacer un viaje a ese lugar?

Córdoba, España

Oiga, señor...
—Camarero, esta sopa está fría.
—No es posible, señor. Si acaban de prepararla.
—De todas maneras, está fría.
—Lo siento (Disculpe), señor. Le traigo otro plato inmediatamente.

UN POCO DE TODO

A.   Comentarios de un camarero. Complete the following paragraphs with the correct forms of the words in parentheses, as suggested by the context. When two possibilities are given in parentheses, select the correct word.

(Yo: *ser/estar*[1]) camarero en un excelente restaurante mexicano que se llama El Charro. El dueño del restaurante (*ser/estar*[2]) mi tío Rodrigo. (Él: *llegar*[3]) al restaurante cada° mañana (*son/a*[4]) las siete en punto. (*Nada/Nunca*[5]) puede llegar tarde porque él tiene (*que/de*[6]) (*abrir*[7]) las puertas° y (*hacer*[8]) los preparativos para el día. Entra en la oficina y (*cerrar*[9]) la puerta tan pronto como llega. Nunca lo (yo: *ver*[10]) salir antes de (*los/las*[11]) once y media.

    Necesita tres horas y media para (*preparar*[12]) el menú del día. Todo depende de° los productos disponibles° en el mercado. En primavera y verano, por ejemplo, hay más verduras y frutas frescas (*como/que*[13]) en las otras estaciones. Durante el otoño hay mucho guajolote o carne de res.° Los vendedores° del mercado (*conocer/saber*[14]) que (*nosotros/nuestros*[15]) clientes esperan° lo mejor° que hay.

every

doors

on / available

carne... beef
merchants
expect / lo... the best

Durante todas las estaciones del año (nosotros: *ofrecer*[16]) platos tradicionales de (*nuestro*[17]) país: tacos con salsa picante, mole poblano, enchiladas de pollo, guacamole… (*Este*[18]) platos (*ser/estar*[19]) los favoritos de todos. Si los clientes (*ser/estar*[20]) satisfechos, nosotros (*ser/estar*[21]) contentos también.

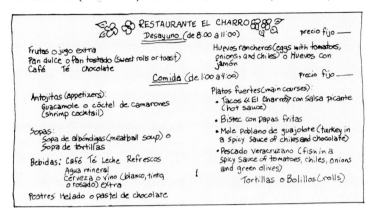

¿Probable o improbable?

1. Al camarero le gusta trabajar en el restaurante de su tío.
2. El camarero es un trabajador entusiasta.
3. El trabajo del dueño de un restaurante es muy duro (*hard*).
4. El restaurante de la historia es uno de los más baratos de la ciudad.
5. El menú es igual todos los días.

B. Una encuesta. Practice getting information from others by getting the following information from at least three classmates. You may want to compare the results obtained to see if there is a consensus in the class on any of these topics. Note that you will be asking two different kinds of questions: one to determine a preference between two options, the other to determine a general preference. Following the model, ask questions based on the cues suggested, then invent a category of your own.

MODELO: grupos musicales: U2 / los Beatles →
            ¿Cuál prefieres, el grupo U2 o los Beatles?
            ¿Qué grupo musical prefieres entre todos?

Hint: If you like neither of the choices offered in the first question when you are being interviewed, simply answer by saying: **Ninguno/a** (*Neither*).

1. grupo musical: U2 / los Beatles
2. tipo de música: la música clásica / la música rock
3. bebida en la mañana: el café / el té
4. bebida con el almuerzo: un refresco / una limonada
5. deporte individual: el esquí / el tenis
6. deporte de equipo: el béisbol / el fútbol americano
7. equipo de fútbol americano: los _____ / los _____
8. estación del año: el otoño / el verano
9. ¿ ?

UN PASO MÁS: Lectura cultural

Read

Antes de leer: Words with Multiple Meanings

It is easy to get "off the track" while reading if you assign the wrong meaning to a word that has multiple English equivalents. The word **como** can cause confusion because it can mean *how, like, the way that, as, since,* or *I eat,* depending on the context in which it occurs. Other common words with multiple meanings include **que** (*what, that, who*), **clase** (*class meeting, course, kind* or *type*), and **esperar** (*to wait for, to hope, to expect*).

You must rely on the context to determine which meaning is appropriate. Practice by telling what **como** means in each of the following sentences.

1. En España, como en Francia, se come mucho pescado.
2. No me gusta como habla el profesor; necesita hablar más despacio.
3. Como tú no deseas estudiar, ¿por qué no tomamos una cerveza?

The readings in this **Un paso más** section consist of recipes (**recetas**) taken from Spanish and Latin American magazines. Scan this vocabulary list before you begin the readings. You will not find all the words in exactly the same form in the recipes as in the list, but in most cases you should be able to infer their meanings. As you read, think about the verb form that is characteristic of recipes in English. You will find two different ways of expressing that verb form in these recipes, but you need only to recognize the action indicated in Spanish to understand the recipes.

el aceite	oil	**agregar**	to add
la cebolla	onion	**asar**	to roast
el chorizo	sausage	**bajar**	to turn down
la morcilla	blood sausage	**colocar**	to put, place
la olla	pot	**espolvorear**	to sprinkle
		extender (ie)	to spread
dorado/a	browned	**mezclar**	to mix
hecho/a	done, cooked	**quitar**	to remove
		remover (ue)	to stir

ALGUNAS RECETAS HISPÁNICAS

L as dos recetas que se presentan aquí nos demuestran que hoy en día, aunque hay muchas diferencias entre la cocina° de los países del mundo, hay muchas semejanzas también. Con frecuencia, para dar un sabor° nuevo a los platos tradicionales, se incorporan elementos de la cocina de otros países. El arroz con pollo es una receta típica de muchos países hispánicos. Aquí se presenta con una pequeña diferencia. ¿Puede Ud. encontrar el ingrediente nuevo? El asado, una de las comidas más típicas de la Argentina, se parece a° una costumbre norteamericana, pero también hay una diferencia. ¿Cuál es?

cooking

flavor

se... resembles

ASADO ARGENTINO

Para seis personas

Tiempo de preparación:
Cinco minutos más el tiempo de la preparación de la barbacoa, más una media hora de cocción.

Dificultad:
Ninguna. Para principiantes.

Ingredientes:
— Dos kilos y medio de tira de falda de buey (o pedir al carnicero carne para el asado argentino), chorizo y morcillas frescos a gusto. Orégano; sal.

Modo de hacerlo:
1.—En una barbacoa con las brasas candentes, pero sin llamas, asar la carne a la que habremos espolvoreado orégano, así como los chorizos y morcillas por ambos lados al principio para que no se escapen los jugos. Luego dejarlo hacerse más lentamente. El tiempo de cocción variará según nos guste la carne a punto, poco hecha o más hecha. Salar la carne después de asada. Servir en seguida con una ensalada verde.

ARROZ CON POLLO A LA ITALIANA

300 g (10 onzas ap.) de arroz
12 tazas ap. de agua
El jugo de medio limón
Sal a gusto
8 muslos de pollo con el encuentro (puede usar 8 medias pechugas)
6 cdas. de aceite de oliva
100 g (3.5 oz ap.) de cebolla
2 cdtas. de polvos de curry
350 g (11.6 onzas ap.) de pulpa de tomate
6 cucharadas de leche

En una olla del tamaño apropiado, cocine el arroz en el agua, con sal a gusto y el jugo de limón (este último para que los granos queden blancos). Quítele la piel a las piezas de pollo, y cocínelas por unos minutos. Agregue la cebolla triturada, y continúe cocinando hasta que el pollo esté dorado (debe remover con frecuencia para que la cebolla no se queme). Agregue los polvos de curry, la pulpa de tomate, la leche caliente y sal a gusto. Mezcle bien, baje el fuego y cocine a calor bajo removiendo de vez en cuando alrededor de media hora, o hasta que al pinchar el pollo con un tenedor la masa esté suave y no salga sangre. Extienda el arroz ya cocido en una fuente o molde que pueda llevarse a la mesa, y coloque encima las piezas de pollo con la salsa. Si lo desea, espolvoree encima un poco de polvos de curry adicionales.

Comprensión

A. ¿A qué categoría general pertenecen (*belong*) estas recetas?

_____ un plato principal   _____ un postre
_____ una tapa o un antojito   _____ una ensalada

B. **Arroz con pollo a la italiana**

1. ¿Qué ingrediente no contiene el arroz con pollo, generalmente?
   a. el limón   b. el curry   c. la cebolla
2. ¿Qué significan las palabras indicadas?
   a. sal *a gusto*   d. *polvos* de curry
   b. 6 *cucharadas* de leche   e. baje *el fuego*
   c. *pulpa* de tomate

C. **Asado argentino**

1. ¿En qué se parecen y en qué son diferentes el asado argentino y una barbacoa estilo norteamericano?
   a. los tipos de carne que se usan   b. la manera de prepararlos
2. ¿Qué significan las palabras indicadas?
   a. una media hora de *cocción*   d. *salar* la carne
   b. para *principiantes*
   c. en una barbacoa con *las brasas candentes*

Para escribir

Write a brief paragraph about your eating preferences or those of your family. Use the following questions as a guide in developing your paragraph.

1. ¿Cuántas veces comen al día? ¿A qué horas?
2. ¿Comen juntos?
3. ¿Quién(es) prepara(n) la comida?
4. ¿Qué prepara(n)? ¿Es excelente la comida? ¿buena? ¿mala? ¿regular?
5. ¿Qué comida prefieren cuando comen en un restaurante? ¿comida china? ¿mexicana? ¿italiana? ¿hamburguesas? ¿En qué restaurantes comen?
6. ¿Comen allí con frecuencia? ¿Cuántas veces al año? ¿Cuándo van a volver?

VOCABULARIO

el jarro/la jarra (Perú): pitcher

Verbos

ayudar to help
engordar to gain weight

La comida

el agua (*f.*) **(mineral)** (mineral) water
el arroz rice
las arvejas peas
el atún tuna
la bebida drink, beverage
el bistec steak
los camarones shrimp
la carne meat
la chuleta (de cerdo) (pork) chop
el flan custard
los frijoles beans
la galleta cookie; cracker
el helado ice cream
el huevo egg
el jamón ham

el jugo juice
la langosta lobster
la leche milk
la lechuga lettuce
la manzana apple
los mariscos shellfish
la naranja orange
el pan bread
   el pan tostado toast
la papa (frita) (French fried) potato
el pastel cake; pie
el pescado fish
el pollo chicken
el postre dessert
el queso cheese
la sopa soup
las verduras vegetables
el vino (blanco, tinto) (white, red) wine
la zanahoria carrot

Cognados

la banana, la ensalada, la fruta, la hamburguesa, el salmón, el sándwich, el té, el tomate

Preposiciones

a la derecha de to the right of
a la izquierda de to the left of
antes de before (*in sequence*)
cerca de close to, near
debajo de under(neath)
delante de in front of
después de after (*in sequence*)
detrás de behind
durante during
encima de on top of
entre between; among
lejos de far from
sin without

Otro sustantivo

el/la compañero/a de cuarto roommate

Palabras adicionales

anoche last night
conmigo with me
contigo with you (*fam.*)
fuera out (*as in* **cenar fuera**)

Frases útiles para la comunicación

estar a dieta	to be on a diet
tener (mucha) hambre	to be (very) hungry
tener (mucha) sed	to be (very) thirsty
comí, comiste, comió	I ate, you ate, he/she/it ate
¡me gusta muchísimo!	I like it a lot!
¡no me gusta (para) nada!	I don't like it at all!

¡BUEN VIAJE!

VOCABULARIO: EN EL AEROPUERTO

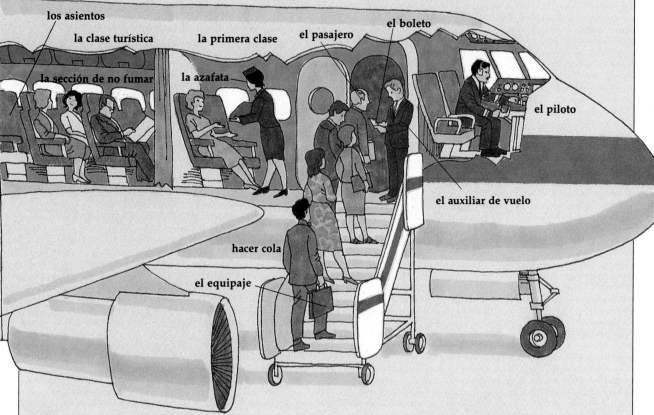

el avión

los asientos
la clase turística
la sección de no fumar
la azafata
la primera clase
el pasajero
el boleto
el piloto
el auxiliar de vuelo
hacer cola
el equipaje

el boleto/el billete* ticket	**el pasaje** passage, ticket	**bajar (de)** to get off (of), down (from)
de ida one-way	**el pasaporte** passport	**despegar** to take off (*airplane*)
de ida y vuelta round-trip	**la sala de espera** waiting room	**estar atrasado/a** to be late
la demora delay	**la salida** departure	**facturar el equipaje** to check one's bags
la llegada arrival	**el vuelo** flight	**guardar (un puesto)** to save (a place)
la maleta suitcase		**hacer escalas** to have/make stopovers
		subir (a) to get (on) (*a vehicle*)

*Throughout Spanish America, **boleto** is the word used for a *ticket for travel*. **Billete** is commonly used in Spain. The words **entrada** and **localidad** are used to refer to tickets for movies, plays, or similar functions.

A. Ud. va a hacer un viaje en avión. El vuelo sale a las siete de la mañana. Use los números 1 a 10 para indicar en qué orden van a pasar las siguientes cosas.

_8_ Subo al avión.
_5_ Voy a la sala de espera.
_3_ Hago cola para comprar el boleto de ida y vuelta y facturar el equipaje.
_2_ Llego al aeropuerto a tiempo (_on time_) y bajo del taxi.
_10_ Despega el avión.
_7_ Por fin se anuncia la salida del vuelo.

_1_ Estoy atrasado/a. Salgo para el aeropuerto en taxi.
_9_ La azafata me indica el asiento.
_4_ Pido asiento en la sección de no fumar.
_6_ Hay demora. Por eso todos tenemos que esperar el vuelo allí antes de subir al avión.

B. ¿Cuántas cosas y acciones puede Ud. identificar o describir en este dibujo?

C. ¿A quién se describe, a don Gregorio, vicepresidente de la IBM, o a Harry, típico estudiante universitario?

1. Siempre viaja en clase turística porque es más económica. A Harry
2. No le (_to him_) importan nada las demoras; no tiene prisa. A Harry
3. Nunca hace cola para comprar el billete porque su secretaria le arregla (_arranges for him_) todo el viaje. A don Gregorio
4. Cuando viaja en avión, es porque está de vacaciones. A Harry
5. Por lo general, prefiere viajar en tren porque es más económico. A Harry
6. Muchas veces no lleva equipaje porque hace viajes de un solo día. A don Gregorio
7. Siempre que (_Whenever_) viaja, lleva traje y corbata. A Don Gregorio

D.   Preguntas

1. Imagine que Ud. va a viajar en avión. ¿Pide primera clase o clase turística? ¿Por qué? ¿Pide asiento en la sección de fumar o en la de no fumar? ¿Pide asiento en la cola (_tail_) o lo más adelante posible (_as far forward as possible_)? ¿Le guarda el puesto a alguien?
2. ¿Cómo paga el pasaje? ¿con cheque? ¿con tarjeta de crédito? ¿Paga al contado (_in cash_)?
3. Imagine que la aerolínea pierde su equipaje. ¿Cómo reacciona Ud.?

Al tanto...

Here are some additional terms related to flying and airline fares. What are their English equivalents?

- descuentos en los billetes...
  para menores (= menores de 18 años)
  para la «tercera edad» (= mayores de 65 años)
  para grupos (más de 10 personas)

- un billete de ida y vuelta, con vuelta abierta
  (= con fecha de regreso sin determinar)
- la tarifa (= el costo del billete)
- la visa (Latinoamérica), el visado (España)

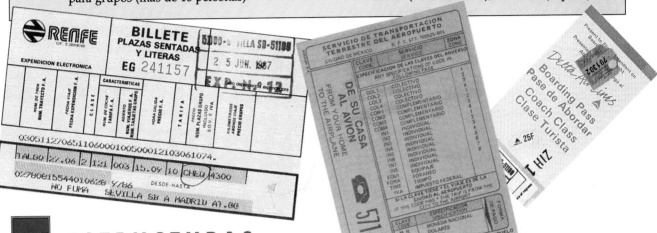

ESTRUCTURAS

20. EXPRESSING *TO WHOM* OR *FOR WHOM*
Indirect Object Pronouns; *dar* and *decir*

En la sala de espera del aeropuerto

HIJO: Mamá, tengo hambre. *¿Me das* un caramelo?

MAMÁ: No, hijo. No *te* voy a *dar* un caramelo. Acabas de comer.

HIJO: Mamá, quiero leer. *¿Me* compras un librito?

MAMÁ: No, no *te* voy a comprar más libros. Ya tienes tres.

HIJO: Mamá...

MAMÁ: No, hijo. Te quiero mucho, pero no *te doy* nada más.

HIJO: Pero mamá...

MAMÁ: ¡*Te digo* que no!

HIJO: Pero mamá, ¿no oyes? ¡Acaban de anunciar nuestro vuelo!

In the airport waiting room SON: Mom, I'm hungry. Will you give me a piece of candy? MOM: No, son. I will not give you a piece of candy. You just ate. SON: Mom, I want to read. Will you buy me a little book? MOM: No, I'm not going to buy you any more books. You already have three. SON: Mom . . . MOM: No, son. I love you a lot, but I'm not giving you anything else. SON: But Mom . . . MOM: I'm telling you no! SON: But Mom, don't you hear? They've just announced our flight!

¿Qué dicen el niño y su mamá, **me** o **te**?

EL NIÑO:
1. ¿_me_ das un caramelo?
2. ¿_me_ compras un librito?
3. ¿_me_ quieres mucho?

LA MAMÁ:
No, no _te_ doy más dulces (*sweets*).
No, no _te_ voy a comprar nada más.
¡Claro que _te_ quiero!, pero _me_ haces demasiadas (*too many*) preguntas.

Indirect Object Pronouns

me	*to, for me*		**nos**	*to, for us*
te	*to, for you* (fam. sing.)		**os**	*to, for you* (fam. pl.)
le	*to, for you* (form. sing.), him, her, it		**les**	*to, for you* (form. pl.), *them*

A.   *Indirect object* nouns and pronouns usually answer the questions *to whom?* or *for whom?* in relation to the verb. The word *to* is frequently omitted in English. Note that indirect object pronouns have the same form as direct object pronouns, except in the third person: **le**, **les**.

Indicate the direct and indirect objects in the following sentences.

1. I'm giving her the present tomorrow.
2. Could you tell me the answer now?
3. El profesor nos va a hacer algunas preguntas.
4. ¿No me compras el librito ahora?

B.   Like direct object pronouns, *indirect object pronouns* (**los pronombres del complemento indirecto**) are placed immediately before a conjugated verb. They may be attached to an infinitive.

No, no **te** presto el coche.   *No, I won't lend you the car.*
Voy a guardar**te** el asiento.
Te voy a guardar el asiento.   *I'll save your seat for you.*

C.   Since **le** and **les** have several different equivalents, their meaning is often clarified or emphasized with the preposition **a** and the pronoun objects of prepositions (see **Las preposiciones, Capítulo 9**).

Voy a mandar**le** un telegrama **a Ud.** (**a él, a ella**).   *I'm going to send you (him, her) a telegram.*
Les hago una comida **a Uds.** (**a ellos, a ellas**).   *I'm making you (them) a meal.*

D.   Even when there is an indirect object noun in a sentence, the indirect object pronoun is almost always used in addition. This construction is very common in Spanish.

Vamos a decir**le** la verdad **a Juan**.	*Let's tell Juan the truth.*
¿**Les** guardo los asientos **a Jorge y Marta**?	*Shall I save the seats for Jorge and Marta?*

E.   Verbs frequently used with indirect objects include **dar** (*to give*), **decir** (*to say; to tell*), **escribir**, **explicar**, **hablar**, **mandar**, **pedir**, **preguntar** (*to ask*), **prestar**, **regalar** (*to give a gift*), and **servir**.

Dar and *decir*

dar (*to give*)		decir (*to say; to tell*)	
doy	damos	digo	decimos
das	dais	dices	decís
da	dan	dice	dicen

Dar and **decir** are almost always used with indirect object pronouns in Spanish.

¿Cuándo **me das** el dinero?	*When will you give me the money?*
¿Por qué no **me dice** Ud. la verdad, señor?	*Why don't you tell me the truth, sir?*

¡OJO!   In Spanish it is necessary to distinguish between the verbs **dar** (*to give*) and **regalar** (*to give as a gift*). Do not confuse **decir** (*to say* or *to tell*) with **hablar** (*to speak*).

Práctica

A.   **¿Quién te... ?** Who does the following things for you? Follow the model.

MODELO: En el restaurante: traer el menú (camarero) →
En el restaurante, el camarero *me* trae el menú.

1.   En el restaurante: traer el menú (camarero), explicar los platos del día (camarero), preparar la comida (cocinero), servir la comida (camarero), dar la cuenta (dueño)
2.   En clase: explicar la gramática (profesor[a]), hacer preguntas (otros estudiantes), dar exámenes (profesor[a]), prestar un lápiz o un papel (un compañero)

Now repeat the same items, using **nos**: **En el restaurante, el camarero *nos* trae el menú.**

B.   Your friends the Padillas, from Guatemala, need help arranging for and getting on their flight back home. Explain how you will help them, using the cues as a guide.

MODELO: comprar el boleto → *Les* compro el boleto.

1. llamar un taxi
2. bajar (*to carry down*) las maletas
3. guardar el equipaje
4. facturar el equipaje
5. guardar el puesto en la cola
6. guardar el asiento en la sala de espera
7. buscar los pasaportes
8. por fin decir adiós

Now explain the same sequence of actions as if you were talking about your friend Guillermo: *Le* **compro el boleto.** Then tell your friend Guadalupe how you will help her: *Te* **compro el boleto.**

C.   ¿Qué va a pasar? Dé varias respuestas.

Palabras útiles: medicinas, Santa Claus, tarjetas navideñas (*Christmas cards*), flores (*flowers*), juguetes (*toys*)

1. Su amiga Elena está en el hospital con un ataque de apendicitis. Todos le mandan… Le escriben… Las enfermeras (*nurses*) le dan… De comer, le sirven…
2. Es Navidad. Los niños les prometen (*promise*) a sus padres… Les piden… También le escriben… Le piden… Los padres les mandan… a sus amigos. Les regalan…
3. Hay una demora y el avión no despega a tiempo. La azafata nos sirve… El auxiliar de vuelo nos ofrece… El piloto nos dice…
4. Mi coche no funciona hoy. Mi amigo me presta… Mis padres me preguntan… Luego me dan…
5. Es la última semana de clases y hay exámenes finales la próxima semana. En la clase de computación, todos le preguntan al profesor… El profesor les explica a los estudiantes…

D.   Your little cousin Benjamín has never eaten in a restaurant before. Explain to him what will happen, filling in the blanks with the appropriate indirect object pronoun.

Primero el camarero _____ indica una mesa desocupada. Luego tú _____ pides el menú al camarero. También _____ haces preguntas sobre los platos y las especialidades de la casa y _____ dices tus preferencias. El camarero _____ trae la comida. Por fin papá _____ pide la cuenta al camarero. Si tú quieres pagar, _____ pides dinero a papá y _____ das el dinero al camarero.

E.   Entrevista. Find out to whom or for whom a classmate does the following things. Then find out who does them to or for him or her.

MODELO: darle consejos →
—¿A quién le das consejos?
—Pues… con frecuencia le doy consejos a mi compañero de cuarto.
—Y ¿quién te da consejos a ti?
—¡Mis padres me dan muchos consejos! Mi mejor amiga también…

1. darle consejos (dinero)
2. pedirle ayuda académica (dinero)
3. prestarle la ropa (el coche, dinero)
4. mandarle flores (dulces)
5. decirle secretos (mentiritas [*little white lies*])
6. hacerle favores (regalos especiales)
7. escribirle cartas románticas (tarjetas postales)

¿Recuerda Ud.?

You have already used forms of **gustar** to express your likes and dislikes (**Paso dos**). Review what you know by answering the following questions. Then use them, changing their form as needed, to interview your instructor.

1. ¿Te gusta el café (el vino, el té, …)?
2. ¿Te gusta jugar al béisbol (al golf, al vólibol, al…)?
3. ¿Te gusta viajar en avión (fumar, viajar en tren, …)?
4. ¿Qué te gusta más, estudiar o ir a fiestas (trabajar o descansar, cocinar o comer)?

ESTRUCTURAS

21. EXPRESSING LIKES AND DISLIKES
Gustar

1. ¿Dónde están sentados (*seated*) los dos hombres?
2. Al hombre de la derecha, ¿qué le gusta hacer?
3. ¿Qué cosa no le gusta al hombre de la izquierda?
4. ¿Dónde debe estar sentado el hombre de la izquierda?
5. ¿Les gusta a todos el humo de los cigarrillos?
6. ¿A Ud. le gusta fumar?

Parece que à Ud. no le gusta el humo.

Constructions with *gustar*

SPANISH	EQUIVALENT	ENGLISH
Me gusta la playa.	The beach is pleasing to me.	*I like the beach.*
No le gustan sus cursos.	His courses are not pleasing to him.	*He doesn't like his courses.*
Nos gusta correr.	Running is pleasing to us.	*We like to run.*

As you already know, the verb **gustar** is used to express likes and dislikes. However, **gustar** does not literally mean *to like*. **Gustar** means *to be pleasing* (to someone).

Gustar is always used with an indirect object pronoun: someone or something is pleasing *to* someone else. It is most commonly used in the third person singular or plural (**gusta/gustan**), and must agree with its subject, which is the person or thing liked, *not* the person whose likes are being described. Note that an infinitive (**correr** in the final sentence in the preceding box) is viewed as a singular subject in Spanish.

A mí me gustan las arvejas. **A Ud.** no **le** gustan, ¿verdad?	*I like peas. You don't like them, do you?*
¿**A ellos les** gusta nadar?	*Do they like to swim?*

As in the preceding sentences, **a mí** (**a ti**, **a Ud.**, and so on) may be used in addition to the indirect object pronouns for clarification or emphasis.

The indirect object pronoun *must* be used with **gustar** even when an indirect object noun is expressed. A common word order is as follows:

a + PRONOUN/ NOUN	INDIRECT OBJECT PRONOUN	*gustar* + SUBJECT
A Juan	le	gustan las fiestas.
(A ellas)	Les	gusta esquiar.

Would Like/Wouldn't Like

What one *would* or *would not* like to do is expressed with the form **gustaría*** + *infinitive* and the appropriate indirect objects.

A mí me gustaría viajar al Perú.	*I would like to travel to Peru.*
Nos gustaría despegar a tiempo.	*We would like to take off on time.*

Práctica

A.   Gustos y preferencias. ¿Le gusta o no le gusta? Siga los modelos.

MODELOS: ¿el café? → (No) Me gusta el café.

¿los pasteles? → (No) Me gustan los pasteles.

1. ¿el vino?
2. ¿los niños pequeños?
3. ¿la música clásica?
4. ¿los discos de Madonna?
5. ¿el invierno?
6. ¿hacer cola?
7. ¿las clases que empiezan a las ocho?
8. ¿el chocolate?
9. ¿las películas de horror?
10. ¿cocinar?
11. ¿las clases de este semestre/ trimestre?
12. ¿la gramática?
13. ¿los vuelos con muchas escalas?
14. ¿bailar en las discotecas?

---

*This is one of the forms of the conditional of **gustar**. You will study all of the forms of the conditional in Grammar Section 49.

B. **De viaje.** ¿Cómo se dice en español?

1. My mother likes to fly (to travel by plane), but she doesn't like long flights. She wouldn't like to go to China (**la China**) by plane.
2. My father doesn't like to wait in line, and he doesn't like delays.
3. My brothers like to get on the plane right away (**en seguida**), but they don't like to save a place for anyone.
4. And I like to travel with the whole family!

Escriba Ud. en español un párrafo parecido sobre los gustos y preferencias de los miembros de su familia (sus compañeros de clase, de la residencia, etcétera).

C. **Los gustos de los señores Trujillo.** ¿Qué les gusta hacer a los señores Trujillo? Conteste según el dibujo. ¿Puede Ud. inventar otros detalles sobre su vida? Por ejemplo: ¿Cuántos años tienen? ¿Tienen niños? ¿Dónde viven? etcétera.

D. **Entrevista: ¿Qué te gusta más?** Use the following cues to determine what another student likes or dislikes about the topics, asking him or her to give reasons, if possible. When the interview is over, report the most interesting information you have learned to the class.

MODELO: el rojo, el azul o el verde →
—¿Qué color te gusta más—el rojo, el azul o el verde?
—Pues… yo creo que me gusta más el azul.
—¿Puedes explicarme por qué te gusta más ese color?
—Sí, me gusta porque es el color de los ojos (*eyes*) de mi novio/a (esposo/a,…).

1. el cine o la televisión
2. el verano, el invierno, el otoño o la primavera
3. vivir solo/a o vivir con un compañero (una compañera)
4. viajar en clase turística o en primera
5. vivir en la residencia, en un apartamento o en la casa de sus padres
6. las fiestas grandes o las pequeñas
7. comer en casa o cenar fuera
8. ir de compras a un almacén o a una tienda especializada

E.   ¿Qué te gusta? ¿Qué no te gusta para nada? (*What do you really dislike?*) Almost every situation has aspects that one likes or dislikes—even hates. React to the following situations by telling what you like or don't like about them. Follow the models and the cues, but add your own words as well and expand your responses, using **me gustaría** if you can.

MODELOS: En la playa: el agua, el sol, nadar (*to swim*), la arena (*sand*) →
Me gusta mucho el agua pero no me gusta nada el sol. Por eso no me gustaría pasar todo el día en la playa.

Me gusta nadar pero no me gusta la arena. Por eso me gustaría más nadar en una piscina (*pool*).

1. En el avión: viajar en avión, la comida, las películas, la música
2. En la discoteca: la música, bailar, el ruido, el humo
3. En el parque: los animales, los insectos, las flores, la hierba (*grass*)
4. En el coche: manejar (*to drive*), el tráfico, los camiones (*trucks*), los policías, el límite de velocidad
5. En el hospital: las inyecciones, los médicos, los enfermeros (las enfermeras) (*nurses*), los visitantes, recibir flores

Otros sitios: en una fiesta; en la biblioteca; en clase; en una cafetería; en un gran almacén; en casa, con sus padres; en un autobús/tren

---

En el aeropuerto
—Perdón, ¿sabe Ud. si el vuelo 638 va a salir a tiempo?
—Sí, eso dicen. A las tres y cuarto.
—Pues, ¡qué bien! Así tengo tiempo para tomar algo.
—Si quiere, deje° sus cosas aquí. Le   *leave* puedo guardar el puesto.
—Muchísimas gracias. ¿Quiere algo?
—No, nada. Gracias.

Bogotá, Colombia

UN POCO DE TODO

Recomendaciones para las vacaciones. Complete the following vacation suggestion with the correct form of the words in parentheses, as suggested by the context. When two possibilities are given in parentheses, select the correct word.

(*Les/Los*[1]) quiero decir (*algo/nada*[2]) sobre (*el/la*[3]) ciudad de Machu-Picchu. ¿Ya
(*lo/la*[4]) (*saber/conocer*[5]) Uds.? (*Ser/Estar*[6]) situada en los Andes, a unos ochenta kilómetros° de la ciudad de Cuzco (Perú). Machu-Picchu es conocida°   50 millas / known
como (*el/la*[7]) ciudad escondida° de los incas. (Ellos: *decir*[8]) que (*ser/estar*[9])   hidden
una de las manifestaciones (*más/tan*[10]) importantes de la arquitectura
incaica. Era° refugio y a la vez ciudad de vacaciones de los reyes° (*incaico*[11]) .   It was / kings
    Uds. deben (*visitarla/la visitar*[12]). (*Le/Les*[13]) gustaría porque (*ser/estar*[14])
un sitio inolvidable.° Es mejor (*ir/van*[15]) a Machu-Picchu en primavera o ve-   unforgettable
rano—son las (*mejor*[16]) estaciones para visitar este lugar. Pero es necesario
(*comprar/compran*[17]) los boletos pronto, porque (*mucho*[18]) turistas de todos los
(*país*[19]) del mundo (*visitar*[20]) este sitio extraordinario. ¡(Yo: *saber/conocer*[21])
que a Uds. (*los/les*[22]) va a (*gustar*[23]) el viaje!

¿Cierto o falso? Conteste según la descripción.

1. Machu-Picchu está en Chile.
2. Fue un lugar importante en el pasado.
3. Todavía es una atracción turística de gran interés.
4. Sólo los turistas latinoamericanos conocen Machu-Picchu.

UN PASO MÁS: Situaciones

Un fin de semana en el
AL ANDALUS EXPRESO.
Madrid-Córdoba-Sevilla con
toda la magia y esplendor de un tren fantástico que pone
a su disposición todos los medios del más lujoso hotel.
Haga este itinerario por gusto. Viaje en un maravilloso hotel
sobre raíles. Es un placer que Ud. recordará siempre.

Se busca transporte

En el aeropuerto

—Buenas tardes, señor.
—Muy buenas. Aquí están
  mi boleto y mi pasaporte.
—Perfecto. ¿Éste es todo el
  equipaje que va a facturar?
—Sí, sólo esas dos maletas.
—Y ¿dónde quiere sentarse°?   *to be seated*
—Me gustaría estar en la sección de los no fumadores.
  Quiero la ventanilla° y lo más adelante posible,° por favor.   *window seat / lo . . . ¿ ?*
—Muy bien. Tiene el asiento 23A. Ya puede seguir a la puerta de embarque°   ¿ ?
  número 7. El vuelo está atrasado veinticinco minutos solamente.

UN FIN DE SEMANA INOLVIDABLE.
Desde 39.000 pts. Infórmese en su agencia de viajes.

En la estación del tren

—Quisiera° un billete Madrid–Sevilla.　　　　　　　　　　　*I would like*
—¿Para qué tren?
—Quiero viajar de noche.
—En ese caso tiene un expreso a las 20:45,° y otro a las 23.°　　*las nueve menos cuarto de la noche /*
—Bien. Déme° uno para el tren de las 23.　　　　　　　　　　　*las once de la noche*

　　　　　　　　　　　　　　　　　　　　　　　　　　　　　　　　¿ ?

En la estación de autobuses

—Por favor, un boleto para Guanajuato.
—Ya no quedan° boletos para esta mañana. Tiene que esperar hasta la tarde.　*¿ ?*
—¿A qué hora sale el primero?
—Tiene autobús a las cuatro y media, a las seis, a las siete, a las nueve y a
　las diez y cuarto.
—Muy bien. Déme un boleto para las cuatro y media. ¿Puedo comprar
　ahora un boleto de regreso° para esta misma noche?　　　　　　*vuelta*
—Por supuesto.° El último sale de Guanajuato a las diez.　　　　*Por... Of course.*

Notas comunicativas sobre el diálogo

In class you are frequently asked to use complete sentences. But when you speak Spanish outside of the classroom, you don't always speak in complete sentences—sometimes because you do not know or cannot remember how to say something. And when you try to say a long sentence, such as *"Would you be so kind as to tell me how I can get to the train station?"*, it is easy to get tongue-tied, to omit something, or to mispronounce a word. When this happens, the listener often has trouble understanding. A shorter, more direct phase or sentence often yields more effective results. A simple **perdón** or **por favor** followed by **¿la estación del tren?** is both adequate and polite.

To accomplish something more complicated, such as buying two first-class tickets on Tuesday's 10:50 A.M. train for Guanajuato, you might begin by saying, **«Dos boletos para Guanajuato, por favor.»** After that you can add other information, often in response to the questions that the ticket agent will ask you. By breaking the message down into manageable bits you simplify the communication process for both parties.

A word of caution, though: You may streamline your message, but native speakers may answer using complex sentences and words that are unfamiliar to you. Be prepared to guess, relying on context and on real-world information. You can also use the following phrases.

Repita, por favor. No comprendo.	*Repeat, please. I don't understand.*
Por favor, repita...	*Please, repeat . . . (Repeat or approximate what you didn't "catch".)*
Más despacio, por favor.	*More slowly, please.*
¿Me lo escribe, por favor?	*Will you write it down for me, please?*

Conversación

How would you go about getting the following information? Prepare a series of short statements and questions that will help you get all the information you need. Your instructor will play the role of ticketseller, travel agent, or flight attendant.

MODELO: You need to buy two first-class tickets on Tuesday's 10:50 A.M. flight for Guanajuato. → Dos boletos para Guanajuato, por favor. Para el martes, el vuelo de las 10:50. De primera clase, por favor.

1. You need to buy two tourist-class tickets for today's 2:50 P.M. flight to Barcelona.
2. You are at the airport and need to find out how to get to the university—which you understand is quite some distance away—by (**para**) 10:00 A.M.
3. The flight you are on is arriving late, and you will probably miss your connecting flight to Mexico City. You want to explain your situation to the flight attendant and find out how you can get to Mexico City by 7:00 this evening.
4. You are talking to a travel agent and want to fly from Santiago, Chile, to Quito, Ecuador. You are traveling with two friends who prefer to travel first class, and you need to arrive in Quito by Saturday afternoon.

VOCABULARIO

Verbos

anunciar to announce
bajar to carry down
  bajar (de) to get off (of), down (from)
dar (*irreg.*) to give
decir (*irreg.*) to say; to tell
despegar to take off (*airplane*)
explicar to explain
facturar to check (*baggage*)
fumar to smoke
guardar to watch over; to save (*a place*)
gustar to be pleasing
mandar to send
preguntar to ask (*a question*), inquire
prestar to lend
regalar to give (*as a gift*)
subir (a) to get (on) (*a vehicle*)

Los viajes

el aeropuerto airport
el asiento seat
el auxiliar de vuelo male flight attendant
el avión airplane
la azafata female flight attendant
el billete/el boleto ticket
  de ida one-way
  de ida y vuelta round-trip
la demora delay
el equipaje baggage, luggage
la llegada arrival
la maleta suitcase
el pasaje passage, ticket
el/la pasajero/a passenger
el pasaporte passport
el/la piloto/a pilot

el puesto place (*in line, etc.*)
la sala de espera waiting room
la salida departure
el vuelo flight

Otros sustantivos

la flor flower
el humo smoke

Adjetivo

atrasado/a (*with* **estar**) late

Palabras adicionales

a tiempo on time
la clase turística tourist class
hacer cola to stand in line
hacer escalas to have/make stopovers
la primera clase first class
la sección de (no) fumar (non)smoking section

Frases útiles para la comunicación

me gustaría (+ *inf.*)   I would like to (*do something*)

See also the words and phrases in **Notas comunicativas sobre el diálogo.**

DE VACACIONES

VOCABULARIO: ¡VAMOS DE VACACIONES!

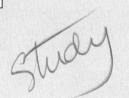

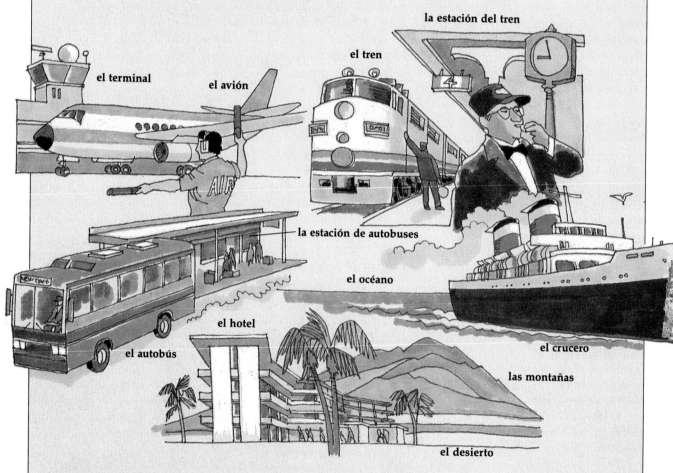

la estación del tren

el tren

el terminal

el avión

el crucero

las montañas

la estación de autobuses

el océano

el hotel

el autobús

el desierto

esquiar* to ski
estar/ir de vacaciones to be/go on vacation
hacer *camping* to go camping
hacer las maletas to pack one's bags
jugar (ue) al (tenis, golf) to play (tennis, golf)
montar a caballo to ride horseback

nadar to swim
navegar en barco to travel by boat
pasarlo bien/mal to have a good/bad time
tomar el sol to sunbathe
volar (ue) en avión to fly

*Note the accentuation patterns in the forms of **esquiar: esquío, esquías, esquía, esquiamos, esquiáis, esquían.**

A.   Definiciones. Defina Ud. los siguientes lugares según lo que (*what*) pasa allí. Siga el modelo.

MODELO: un terminal → Los aviones salen de un terminal.

1.   una estación del tren
2.   el océano
3.   un hotel

4.   una estación de autobuses
5.   el cielo (*sky*)
6.   una playa

B.   Gustos y preferencias. ¿Adónde prefieren ir de vacaciones las siguientes personas? Haga oraciones completas con una palabra o frase de cada grupo. Luego explique cada respuesta con otra oración, según el modelo.

MODELO: (A mí) Me gusta tomar el sol. Por eso me gustaría ir a Acapulco este año.

a mi familia		navegar en barco
a mi (pariente)		montar a caballo
a mi mejor amigo/a		jugar al…
a mí	(no) me gusta	hacer *camping*
al presidente de los	le	nadar
Estados Unidos	les	esquiar
al profesor/a la		viajar
profesora		estar en casa / en un gran hotel
¿ ?		pasar (un mes) en la
		playa / las montañas
		¿ ?

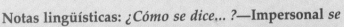

Notas lingüísticas: ¿*Cómo se dice… ?*—Impersonal *se*

Se estudia mucho aquí, ¿verdad?   *You (They) study a lot here, right?*

In English several subjects—*you, one, people, they*—can refer to people in general instead of to one person in particular. In Spanish these impersonal subjects are commonly expressed by using the word **se** followed by the third person singular of the verb.* There is no expressed subject.

C.   Situaciones. ¿Qué se hace en los siguientes lugares? ¿Qué no se hace? Conteste con un compañero (una compañera).

MODELO: en la biblioteca → En la biblioteca se estudia, se lee, se escribe… No se habla en voz alta (*loudly*), no se habla con los amigos…

1.   en un crucero por el mar Caribe
2.   en las montañas de Chile
3.   en el desierto

4.   en una playa del océano Atlántico
5.   en un hotel de lujo (*luxury*)
6.   en un campo de golf

***Se habla español (aquí)** is a similar construction: *Spanish is spoken here; One speaks Spanish here.*

D.   Se usa la expresión **¿Cómo se dice... ?** cuando se quiere aprender una palabra nueva. Repase Ud. (*Review*) el vocabulario nuevo de esta lección. Pregunte a las otras personas de la clase, **¿Cómo se dice... en inglés?** o **¿Cómo se dice... en español?**

Al tanto...

Here are some additional terms and expressions related to traveling.

- *to hitchhike* = hacer autostop (España)
  hacer dedo (Latinoamérica)
  pedir un aventón (México: ¿Me das un aventón?)
- en el tren   viajar en primera o en segunda
  viajar en coche cama (*sleeping car*) o en litera (*berth*)
- el autobús = el autocar (España)
  el camión (México)

Notas comunicativas: Se habla de los viajes

Here are a few phrases that will enable you to talk about some aspects of trips you have taken in the past.

¿Adónde **fuiste/fue** (el verano pasado)?   *Where did you go (last summer)?*
    —**Fui** a...   *—I went to . . .*
¿Adónde (¿Cómo) **has/ha viajado?**   *Where (How) have you traveled?*
    —**He viajado** a/en...   *—I've traveled to/in . . .*

Lo que no debe hacer durante el verano: dejar que se le acumule el correo, mantener el garaje abierto, dejar cubos de basura vacíos a la puerta de su vivienda, dejar ventanas y persianas abiertas, fijar notas o avisos en la puerta de su domicilio, olvidar una escalera de mano fuera de la casa.

E.   Preguntas

1.   Por lo general, ¿cuándo está Ud. de vacaciones? ¿en invierno? ¿en verano? En las vacaciones, ¿le gusta viajar o prefiere no salir de su ciudad? ¿Le gusta ir de vacaciones con su familia? ¿Prefiere ir solo/a, con un amigo (una amiga) o con un grupo de personas?

2.   ¿Cuáles son las actividades que Ud. normalmente asocia con las vacaciones? ¿En qué mes fue de vacaciones el año pasado? ¿Adónde fue? ¿Con quién(es) fue?

3.   De los medios de transporte mencionados en **Vocabulario: ¡Vamos de vacaciones!** ¿cuáles conoce Ud. personalmente? Conteste con esta oración: He viajado en (avión, tren, autobús, barco, coche). De estos medios de transporte, ¿cuál es el más

rápido? ¿el más económico? ¿Cuáles hacen más escalas o paran (*stop*) con más frecuencia? ¿Cómo prefiere Ud. viajar?

4. Por lo general, cuando Ud. viaja en avión (tren, autobús), ¿cómo pasa el tiempo durante el viaje? ¿Habla con los otros pasajeros? ¿Lee? ¿Duerme? ¿Mira el paisaje (*scenery*)? ¿Trabaja? ¿Estudia? ¿Escribe cartas? ¿Mira la película? ¿Escucha música?

ESTRUCTURAS

. . . .

22. INFLUENCING OTHERS
Present Subjunctive: An Introduction

Un pasajero distraído

AZAFATA: *Pase* Ud., señor. Bienvenido a bordo.

PASAJERO: Gracias. Éste es mi asiento, ¿verdad?

AZAFATA: Sí, es el 5A. Es necesario que *tome* asiento ahora mismo. Y, por favor, no *olvide* el cinturón de seguridad.

PASAJERO: ¿Puedo fumar?

AZAFATA: Se puede fumar en esta sección, pero no queremos que *fume* ahora. Vamos a despegar pronto para Quito y...

PASAJERO: ¿Para Quito? Pero... el vuelo ciento doce va a Cuzco.

AZAFATA: Sí, señor, pero éste es el vuelo ciento dos. ¡*Baje* Ud. ahora mismo! Todavía es posible que *llegue* a su avión a tiempo.

1. ¿Qué dice la azafata cuando el pasajero entra en el avión?
2. ¿El pasajero encuentra (*finds*) su asiento? ¿Cuál es?

3. ¿Por qué no debe fumar ahora el pasajero?
4. ¿Cuál es el error del pasajero?
5. ¿Qué debe hacer el pasajero?

Subjunctive: An Overview

The present tense forms you have already learned are part of a verb system called the *indicative mood* (**el indicativo**). In both English and Spanish, the indicative is used to state facts and to ask questions. It is used to express objectively most real-world actions or states of being.

An absent-minded passenger FLIGHT ATTENDANT: Come in, sir. Welcome aboard. PASSENGER: Thank you. This is my seat, isn't it? FLIGHT ATTENDANT: Yes, it's 5A. You must take your seat (It's necessary that you take your seat) right now. And, please, don't forget your seat belt. PASSENGER: Can I smoke? FLIGHT ATTENDANT: Smoking is permitted (One can smoke) in this section, but we don't want you to smoke now. We're going to take off soon for Quito and . . . PASSENGER: For Quito? But . . . flight 112 goes to Cuzco. FLIGHT ATTENDANT: Yes, sir, but this is flight 102. Get off right now! It's still possible for you to get to your plane on time.

She's writing the letter.
We are already there!

Both English and Spanish have another verb system called the *subjunctive mood* (**el subjuntivo**). The subjunctive is used to express more subjective or conceptualized actions or states: things we want to happen, things we try to get others to do, and events that we are reacting to emotionally.

*I recommend that **she write** the letter immediately.*
*I wish (that) **we were** already there.**

In later chapters, you will learn more about the concepts associated with the Spanish subjunctive as well as about the structure of sentences in which it is used. This chapter focuses on the forms of the subjunctive and on a use of the subjunctive with which you are already familiar. In Spanish, many command forms are part of the subjunctive, identical in form to the third person singular and plural. You have seen command forms in several contexts: in **Mandatos y frases comunes en la clase** (**Pasos preliminares**) and in direction lines throughout the chapters of this text (**Haga**... , **Complete**... , **Conteste**... , and so on).

Forms of the Present Subjunctive

PRESENT SUBJUNCTIVE OF REGULAR VERBS					
hablar **habló → habl-**		**comer** **comó → com-**		**vivir** **vivó → viv-**	
hable	hablemos	coma	comamos	viva	vivamos
hables	habléis	comas	comáis	vivas	viváis
hable	hablen	coma	coman	viva	vivan

- The personal endings of the present subjunctive are added to the first person singular of the present indicative minus its **-o** ending. **-Ar** verbs add endings with **-e**, while **-er/-ir** verbs add endings with **-a**.
- Verbs ending in **-car**, **-gar**, or **-zar** have a spelling change in all persons of the present subjunctive, in order to preserve the **-c-**, **-g-**, or **-z-** sounds.

  -car: c→ **qu**   buscar: bus**que**, bus**ques**, ...
  -gar: g→ **gu**   pagar: pa**gue**, pa**gues**, ...
  -zar: z→ **c**   empezar: empie**ce**, empie**ces**, ...

- Verbs with irregular **yo** forms show the irregularity in all the persons of the present subjunctive.

---

*Subjunctive has lessened in modern English, and many English speakers no longer use it.

conocer: **conozca**, ...   poner: **ponga**, ...   traer: **traiga**, ...
decir: **diga**, ...   salir: **salga**, ...   venir: **venga**, ...
hacer: **haga**, ...   tener: **tenga**, ...   ver: **vea**, ...
oír: **oiga**, ...

- A few verbs have irregular present subjunctive forms.

dar: **dé, des, dé,**   ir: **vaya**, ...
              demos, deis,   saber   **sepa**, ...
              den   ser: **sea**, ...
estar: **esté**, ...
haber (hay): **haya**

- **-Ar** and **-er** stem-changing verbs follow the stem-changing pattern of
  the present indicative:

pensar (ie):   **pie**nse, **pie**nses, **pie**nse, pensemos, penséis, **pie**nsen
poder (ue):   **pue**da, **pue**das, **pue**da, podamos, podáis, **pue**dan

- **-Ir** stem-changing verbs show the main stem change in four forms and a
  second stem change in the **nosotros** and **vosotros** forms.

dormir (ue, u):   **due**rma, **due**rmas, **due**rma, d**u**rmamos, d**u**rmáis, **due**rman
preferir (ie, i): pref**ie**ra, pref**ie**ras, pref**ie**ra, pref**i**ramos, pref**i**ráis, pref**ie**ran

[Práctica A]

Meanings of the Present Subjunctive; Use with *querer*

Like the present indicative, the Spanish present subjunctive has several
English equivalents: **(yo) hable** can mean *I speak, I am speaking, I may speak,*
or *I will speak.* The exact English equivalent of the Spanish present subjunctive depends on the context.

An English infinitive is frequently used to express the Spanish
subjunctive.

Quieren que **estemos** allí a las   *They want us **to be** there (that we*
dos.   *be there) at 2:00.*
Quiero que **hables** con él en   *I want you **to speak** (that you*
seguida.   *speak) to him immediately.*

Note that there are two conjugated verbs in the preceding sentences. The
subjunctive form is the second of the two verbs, while a form of the verb
querer occurs at the beginning of the sentence.

This use of the verb **querer** is one of the cues for the use of the subjunctive in the second part of the sentence. In this section you will practice the
forms of the subjunctive mainly with **querer**. You will learn additional frequent uses of the subjunctive in the remaining chapters of this book and will
see still other instances of the Spanish subjunctive wherever appropriate,
though you may not know the rule or generalization that governs a particular
occurrence. Now that you know how the subjunctive is formed, however,
you will *always* be able to recognize it and understand its general meaning.

[Práctica B–C]

Práctica

A.   Al aeropuerto, por favor. ¡Tenemos prisa! En el siguiente diálogo, identifique los verbos del subjuntivo.

ESTEBAN: ¡Más rápido, Carlota! ¡Quiero que <u>lleguemos</u> al aeropuerto a
tiempo!

CARLOTA: ¿Quieres que te <u>ayude</u> con las maletas?

ESTEBAN: No. Quiero que <u>subas</u> al taxi. Estamos atrasados. No quiero que
<u>perdamos</u> el vuelo, como la última vez.

CARLOTA: ¡Y yo no quiero que esto te <u>dé</u> un ataque al corazón (*heart*)! Si el
avión despega sin nosotros, ¿qué importa? Tomamos el próximo
vuelo y llegamos unas horas más tarde.

Ahora, conteste según el diálogo.

1. Esteban quiere que (ellos)…
   a. lleguen a tiempo.
   b. lleguen en dos horas.
2. Según Esteban, parece que Carlota…
   a. no tiene prisa
   b. no encuentra sus maletas
3. Esteban quiere que Carlota…
   a. suba al taxi   b. suba al autobús
4. No quiere que Carlota…
   a. lo ayude con las maletas   b. lo ayude con el taxista
5. No quiere que (ellos)…
   a. pierdan el taxi   b. pierdan el vuelo
6. Según Carlota, es más importante…
   a. estar tranquilo   b. estar en el aeropuerto a tiempo

Y Ud., ¿es como Carlota o como Esteban?

B.   Haga oraciones según las indicaciones. **¡OJO!** Cambie sólo el infinitivo.

1. Quiero que (tú)… (bailar, cenar, mirar esto, llegar a tiempo, buscar a
   Anita)
2. ¿Quieres que el niño… ? (aprender, escribir, leer, responder, asistir a
   clases)
3. Ud. quiere que (yo)… , ¿verdad? (empezar, jugar, pensarlo, servirlo,
   pedirlo)
4. No quieren que (nosotros)… (pedir eso, almorzar ahora, perderlos, dormir allí, cerrarla, encontrarlo aquí)
5. Queremos que Uds… (conocerlo, hacerlo, traerlo, saberlo, decirlo)
6. Yo no quiero que Ana… (venir, salir ahora, ponerlo, oírlo, ser su amiga)
7. ¿Quieres que (yo)… ? (tenerlo, verlo, estar allí, dar una fiesta, ir al cine
   contigo)

C.   Más sugerencias para las vacaciones. Aquí están los miembros de la
familia Soto. ¿Qué quiere cada uno que hagan todos de vacaciones? Haga
oraciones según el modelo.

MODELO: papá: ir a la playa → Papá quiere que *vayamos* a la playa.

1. hermanitos: ir a la playa también
2. Ernesto: volver a hacer *camping* en las montañas
3. abuelos: no salir de la ciudad en todo el verano
4. mamá: sólo hacer unas excursiones cortas
5. Elena: visitar Nueva York

Y Ud., ¿adónde quiere que su familia vaya este verano?

VOCABULARIO

Expressing wishes—¡*Ojalá!*

¡Ojalá que yo gane la lotería algún día!

The word **ojalá** means *I wish* or *I hope*. It never changes form. It is used with the subjunctive to express wishes or hopes. The use of **que** is optional.

¡Ojalá (que) haya paz en el mundo algún día!   *I hope (that) there is peace in the world someday!*
Ojalá (que) no pierdan su equipaje.   *I hope (that) they don't lose your luggage.*

It is also used alone as an interjection in response to a question.

—¿Están bien tus abuelos? —**¡Ojalá!**

Tres deseos... Imagine que Ud. desea tres cosas: una para Ud. personalmente, otra para algún miembro de su familia y otra para el país o la humanidad. ¿Qué desea Ud.? Exprese sus deseos con **Ojalá (que)...** .

Palabras útiles: terminar (*to end*), la guerra (*war*), las elecciones, el partido (*game*), el millonario (la millonaria), resolver (ue), el hambre, la gente que no tiene hogar (casa), la pobreza

Bogotá, Colombia

¡Por fin° estamos de vacaciones!   Por... *Finally*
—¿Cuántos días te dan de vacaciones?
—Este año, tres semanas.
—¿Vas a ir a algún lugar?
—¡Claro! Es posible que vayamos a la playa.

ESTRUCTURAS

23. ASKING SOMEONE TO DO SOMETHING
Formal Commands

- ¿Cuántas formas subjuntivas puede Ud. encontrar en el siguiente anuncio para una excursión? ¿Qué cree Ud. que significan?
- ¿Qué significa C.R.? (= un país)
- La tortuga es un animal que camina muy lento (*slowly*). ¿Qué cree Ud. que significa «la temporada (*season*) del *desove* de la Tortuga Verde»?
- Busque un sinónimo de...
  excursión
  transporte
  reservas

Conozca la zona más exótica de C.R.
LOS CANALES DE TORTUGUERO
a bordo del

MAWAMBA
Tour de 3 días - 2 noches
SALIDAS: TODOS LOS VIERNES

Haga sus reservaciones con anticipación para la temporada del desove de la Tortuga Verde.
O su **Agencia de viajes** favorita
El tour incluye: traslados, alojamiento, todas las comidas. Lláme-nos y consulte nuestro programa.

Formal Commands

Commands (imperatives) are verb forms used to tell someone to do something. In Spanish, the *formal commands* (**los mandatos formales**) are used with people whom you address as **Ud.** or **Uds.** The command forms for **Ud.** and **Uds.** are the corresponding forms of the present subjunctive.

	hablar	**comer**	**escribir**	**volver**	**decir**
Singular	hable (Ud.)	coma (Ud.)	escriba (Ud.)	vuelva (Ud.)	diga (Ud.)
Plural	hablen (Uds.)	coman (Uds.)	escriban (Uds.)	vuelvan (Uds.)	digan (Uds.)
English equivalent	*speak*	*eat*	*write*	*come back*	*tell*

Using **Ud.** or **Uds.** after the command form makes the command somewhat more formal or more polite. Since the formal commands are part of the subjunctive system, they reflect all the changes and irregularities you have seen listed on pp. 192–193.

- Formal commands of stem-changing verbs will show the stem change.

  piense Ud.   **vue**lva Ud.   **pi**da Ud.

- Verbs ending in **-car**, **-gar**, or **-zar** have a spelling change.

  buscar: bus**que** Ud.   pagar: pa**gue** Ud.   empezar: empie**ce** Ud.

- The **Ud./Uds.** commands for verbs that have irregular **yo** forms will reflect the irregularity: **conozca Ud., diga Ud.**, and so on.

- A few verbs have irregular **Ud./Uds.** command forms. What are the forms for **dar, estar, ir, saber,** and **ser**?

[Práctica A–B]

Position of Object Pronouns with Formal Commands

Direct and indirect object pronouns must follow affirmative commands and be attached to them. In order to maintain the original stress of the verb form, an accent mark is added to the stressed vowel if the original command has two or more syllables.

Léa**lo** Ud.	*Read it.*
Búsque**le** el bolígrafo.	*Look for the pen for him.*

Direct and indirect object pronouns must precede negative commands.

No lo lea Ud.	*Don't read it.*
No le busque el bolígrafo.	*Don't look for the pen for him.*

[Práctica C–E]

Práctica

A. El Sr. Casiano no se siente (*feel*) bien. Lea la descripción que él da de algunas de sus actividades.

«*Trabajo* muchísimo—¡me gusta trabajar! En la oficina, *soy* impaciente y *critico* bastante (*a good deal*) a los otros. En mi vida personal, a veces *soy* un poco impulsivo. *Fumo* bastante y también *bebo* cerveza y otras bebidas alcohólicas, a veces sin moderación... *Almuerzo* y *ceno* fuerte, y casi nunca *desayuno.* Por la noche, con frecuencia *salgo* con los amigos—me gusta ir a las discotecas—y *vuelvo* tarde a casa.»

¿Qué *no* debe hacer el Sr. Casiano para estar mejor? Aconséjele sobre lo que no debe hacer. Use los verbos indicados o cualquier (*any*) otro, según los modelos.

MODELOS: *trabajo* → Señor Casiano, no trabaje tanto.

soy → Señor Casiano, no sea tan impaciente.

B. Imagine que Ud. es el profesor (la profesora) hoy. ¿Qué mandatos debe dar a la clase?

MODELOS: hablar español → Hablen Uds. español.

hablar inglés → No hablen Uds. inglés.

Un bronceador natural

La zanahoria posee más vitamina A que cualquier otra hortaliza conocida. De cara al verano, y para los amantes del bronceado que reniegan de cremas y potingues, tiene tam-

La zanahoria acelera el proceso del bronceado.

bién la propiedad de activar la producción de melanocitos, responsables del «moreno» como respuesta a la agresión del sol.

1. llegar a tiempo
2. leer la lección
3. escribir una composición
4. abrir los libros
5. pensar en inglés
6. estar en clase mañana
7. traer los libros a clase
8. olvidar los verbos nuevos
9. ¿ ?

C.   Situaciones. El Sr. Casiano ha decidido (*has decided*) adelgazar (*to lose weight*). ¿Debe o no debe comer o beber las siguientes cosas? Con otro estudiante, haga y conteste preguntas según los modelos.

MODELOS: ensalada → —¿Ensalada?   postres → —¿Postres?
                            —Cóma*la*.   —*No los* coma.

1. alcohol (*m.*)
2. verduras
3. pan
4. dulces (*candy, m.*)
5. leche
6. hamburguesas con queso
7. frutas
8. refrescos dietéticos
9. pollo
10. carne

D.   Situaciones. You are a clerk at a ticket counter (**el mostrador**) in a small airport. Someone has asked you how to get to the waiting room for Gate 2. Give him or her directions in Spanish.

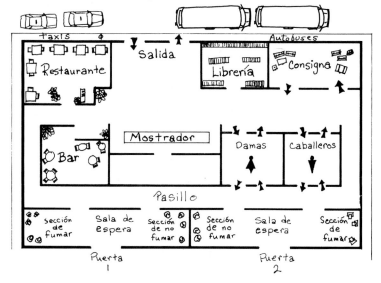

Frases útiles: ir: vaya Ud., doblar: doble Ud. (*turn*), seguir (i, i): siga Ud. (*continue*), pasar: pase Ud. por (*pass through/by*), (todo) derecho (*straight [ahead]*), a la derecha, a la izquierda, el pasillo (*the hall, corridor*)

Now, if you are in/at . . .

la sala de espera
la consigna (*baggage claim area*)
el restaurante
la puerta 2

tell someone how to get to . . .

el bar
la librería
los servicios (*restrooms*)
la parada (*stand*) de taxis/de autobuses

Notas culturales: Los mandatos

Los mandatos formales son de verdad mandatos, y a veces pueden parecer (*to seem*) un poquito bruscos. Si usted está en un restaurante, por ejemplo, es importante no ofender al camarero para no quedar mal (*to make a bad impression*). Si le dice, «Tráigame otra cerveza», puede resultar maleducado (*impolite*).

Hay varias maneras de suavizar (*softening*) un mandato. La más fácil es la de decir también «por favor» o «si me hace el favor». Otra forma es la de usar simplemente el presente del verbo: «Me trae, por favor, otra cerveza». Más suave aún es la forma interrogativa: «¿Me trae otra cerveza, por favor?» Si usted quiere estar seguro de no ofender a nadie, pregúntele: «¿Puede Ud. traerme otra cerveza, por favor?»

E. En la oficina del consejero. Imagine that you are a guidance counselor. Students consult you with questions of all kinds, some trivial and some important. Offer advice to them in the form of affirmative or negative commands. How many different commands can you invent for each situation?

1. EVELIA: No me gusta tomar clases por la mañana. Siempre estoy muy cansada durante esas clases y además (*besides*) a esa hora tengo hambre. Pienso constantemente en el almuerzo… y no puedo concentrarme en las explicaciones.
2. FABIÁN: En mi clase de cálculo, ¡no entiendo nada! No puedo hacer los ejercicios que el profesor nos da de tarea (*as homework*) y durante la clase tengo miedo de hacerle preguntas, porque no quiero parecer tonto.
3. FAUSTO: Fui a México el verano pasado y me gustó (*I liked it*) mucho. Quiero volver a México este verano. Ahora que lo conozco mejor, quiero manejar (*to drive*) mi coche y no ir en autobús como el verano pasado. Desgraciadamente no tengo dinero para hacer el viaje.
4. PILAR: Mis padres no están muy contentos conmigo. Dicen que no los llamo nunca, que no les escribo y que los visito con poca frecuencia.

UN POCO DE TODO

A. Preparativos para un viaje. ¿Cómo se dice en español?

1. Pack (**Ud.**) your bags. I want you to (**Quiero que…**) pack your bags.
2. Don't forget your wallet. I don't want you to (**No quiero que…**) forget your wallet.
3. Go to the airport. I want you to (**Quiero que…**) go to the airport.
4. Don't be (**llegar**) late. I don't want you to be late.
5. Buy your round-trip ticket. I want you to buy your round-trip ticket.
6. Check your bags. I want you to check your bags.
7. Stand in line. I want you to stand in line.

8.   Give your ticket to the flight attendant. I want you to give your ticket to
     the flight attendant.
9.   Get on the plane. I want you to get on the plane.
10. Find your seat. I want you to find your seat.

B.   ¿Has viajado a Machu-Picchu? Do you know where your classmates
have traveled and how they have traveled? Interview a classmate to find out
the following information.

1.   una gran ciudad o centro turístico de los Estados Unidos a la que (*which*)
     fue una vez (o varias veces)
2.   una ciudad o centro turístico que le gustaría visitar
3.   si ha viajado a Europa (¿A qué país?), a Latinoamérica (¿A qué país?),
     a Asia, África, Centroamérica, otro país de Norteamérica
4.   el país que más le gustaría visitar y por qué

After completing the survey, compile the results of all of the interviews to
determine the following:

1.   el lugar visitado por la mayoría (*majority*) de la gente
2.   el lugar que la mayoría de la gente quiere visitar
3.   la persona que ha visitado el mayor número de continentes

UN PASO MÁS: Lectura cultural

Antes de leer: Accessing Background Information

Before beginning a reading, it is sometimes helpful to think about the information the reading might contain in order to review important background
information you already know about the topic. For example, if you are reading a newspaper account of a traffic accident, what kinds of information and
details would you expect to find in it? What kinds of information would you
find in a magazine article about drugs? In a manual for the owner of a car or
a computer?

    Working with a partner, spend three minutes "brainstorming" about
ideas and information you think will be presented in the following adver-
tisements about vacation spots. You can talk in English or in Spanish. Then,
working as a class, share your ideas and select the ten most frequently mentioned ideas. How many of the ideas actually appear in the reading?

¡VENGA CON NOSOTROS A... !

Los siguientes anuncios son de revistas y periódicos sudamericanos y
caribeños. Léalos para saber dónde y cómo la gente latinoamericana puede
pasar sus vacaciones.

CANCUN $234*
ida y vuelta sin escala, desde San Juan

Donde hasta los dioses descansan

- Un verdadero paraíso en el Caribe mexicano; de cautivante belleza de día y fabulosa vida nocturna.
- ¡Por algo era el lugar de veraneo favorito de los emperadores mayas!
- Salidas: martes, jueves y domingos a las 4:45 P.M.
- Con Servicio Azteca de Oro: dos menús a escoger, con quesos y frutas, champán y vinos franceses ¡gratis!

Para más información, llama a tu Agente de Viajes o a Mexicana al 721-2323

Te estamos esperando.
Ya es hora de que vuelvas...¡por Mexicana!

*Por persona. Efectivo el 1ro de septiembre hasta el 14 de diciembre de 1986. Sujeto a cambio sin previo aviso.

mexicana
La primera línea aérea de Latinoamérica

Comprensión

A.   ¿Cuál de los tres sitios de los anuncios...

- se caracteriza por sus fenómenos naturales?
- tiene interés histórico?
- es un lugar de veraneo muy moderno?

B.   ¿Adónde van a querer viajar las siguientes personas? Conteste según los anuncios. Algunas preguntas tienen más de una respuesta correcta.

1.   una persona a quien le interesa mucho la antropología
2.   una persona a quien le gusta practicar varios deportes
3.   una persona que tiene pasión por el juego (*gambling*)
4.   un matrimonio que tiene que pasar las vacaciones con sus niños
5.   una persona que sobre todo (*especially*) quiere pasar el tiempo en la playa
6.   una persona para quien los aspectos culturales del lugar son de gran importancia

este verano
viva la naturaleza
en
TERMAS de CHILLAN

SALUD, DESCANSO Y ENTRETENCION PARA TODA LA FAMILIA

NATURALEZA Y ENTRETENCION
- PISCINA
- PASEOS A CABALLO
- CAMINATAS A PRECIOSOS LUGARES
- TENIS
- PASEOS EN TELESILLA
- JUEGOS INFANTILES
- ASADOS

EXCELENTE HOTEL
- TELEVISION Y VIDEO-CINE
- JUEGOS ELECTRONICOS
- PARVULARIA
- ORQUESTA
- DISCOTHEQUE

SALUD Y TERMALISMO
- BAÑOS TERMALES DE AZUFRE, FIERRO Y VAPOR NATURAL
- FANGOTERAPIA
- SAUNA, HIDROMASAJES
- COSMETOLOGIA
- MASAJES KINESICOS
- SERVICIO MEDICO

ACTIVIDADES CULTURALES
- OBRAS DE TEATRO
- CONCIERTOS
- RECITALES
- MUSICA CLASICA
- EXPOSICIONES
- CHARLAS CULTURALES Y CIENTIFICAS

VENGA CON SU FAMILIA Y VIVA LA NATURALEZA EN TERMAS DE CHILLAN.

CREDITO HASTA 12 MESES

COMPLEJO TURISTICO TERMAS de CHILLAN

SANTIAGO: PROVIDENCIA 2237 LOCAL P. 41 ☎ 2515776-2512685.
CONCEPCION: O'HIGGINS 734 LOCAL 14 ☎ 234981.
CHILLAN: ARAUCO 600 ☎ 223664.

Disfrute con Lan Chile las mejores vacaciones de su vida.

Programa Espectacular incluye:
- Recepción y traslados aeropuerto-hotel-aeropuerto.
- Alojamiento por 7 noches con desayuno, en hotel de su elección.
- City tour.
- Opcional/arriendo de auto (kilometraje ilimitado).
- Seguro médico y asistencia jurídica gratuita los tres primeros días. I.T.C. (Travellers Assistance Ltd.).
* Precio por persona en base habitación doble.

Punta del Este, un lugar pleno de atracciones para usted y su familia. Maravillosas playas, casino, vida nocturna. Un lugar que usted y los suyos pueden disfrutar ahora intensamente con Lan Chile y su programa espectacular.
Consulte a su Agente de Viajes o a Lan Chile.

LanChile
Una buena razón para ser los mejores.

Para escribir

Imagine you are writing out some travel tips for a Spanish-speaking friend who is going to visit the United States. How will you complete each sentence?

1. Si quieres visitar una gran ciudad, te recomiendo la ciudad de ＿＿＿. Allí puedes ver ＿＿＿.
2. Si te interesa nadar y pasar el tiempo en la playa, ¿por qué no vas a ＿＿＿? Tiene ＿＿＿.
3. Entre las atracciones turísticas de este país, la que más me gusta es ＿＿＿. Te recomiendo este lugar porque ＿＿＿.
4. Una vez fui a ＿＿＿ y no me gustó. Por eso no te recomiendo que vayas allí.
5. Un fenómeno natural que tienes que ver es ＿＿＿ porque ＿＿＿.

VOCABULARIO

Verbos

doblar to turn (*a corner*)
encontrar (ue) to find
esquiar to ski
manejar to drive
nadar to swim
olvidar to forget
parecer to seem
seguir (i, i) to continue; to follow
volar (ue) to fly

Los medios de transporte

el autobús bus
el barco boat, ship
el crucero cruise ship; cruise
el taxi taxi
el tren train

Actividades

estar/ir de vacaciones to be/go on vacation
hacer *camping* to go camping
hacer las maletas to pack one's bags
hacer una excursión to take a trip
montar a caballo to ride horseback
navegar en barco to travel by boat
pasarlo bien/mal to have a good/bad time
tomar el sol to sunbathe

Otros sustantivos

el desierto desert
la estación station
  de autobuses bus station
  del tren train station
el golf golf
el hotel hotel
la montaña mountain
el océano ocean
el tenis tennis
el terminal terminal

Adjetivos

impaciente impatient
tranquilo/a calm, tranquil

Palabras adicionales

(todo) derecho straight (ahead)
lo que what; that which

Frases útiles para la comunicación	
fui, fuiste, fue	I, you, he/she/it went
he, has, ha + viajado	I, you have traveled, he/she/it has traveled
ojalá (que)...	I wish, I hope (that) . . .

LO QUE TENGO Y LO QUE QUIERO

VOCABULARIO: TENGO... NECESITO... QUIERO... LOS BIENES PERSONALES°

Los... *Possessions*

- el grabador de vídeo
- el equipo estereofónico
- la pintura
- el pájaro
- el cartel
- el trofeo
- el pez
- el acuario
- el radio portátil
- el equipo fotográfico
- el compact disc
- el televisor
- la computadora/ el ordenador*
- la máquina de escribir
- la camioneta
- la impresora
- la moto(cicleta)
- el coche descapotable
- la bici(cleta)

En la oficina

el aumento raise	**el sueldo** salary
el cheque check	**el trabajo** job, work; written work; (term) paper
los impuestos taxes	
el/la jefe/a boss	

Verbos útiles

cambiar (de cuarto, de puesto, de ropa...) to change (rooms, jobs, clothing . . .)
conseguir (i, i) to get, obtain
dejar to leave (behind)

funcionar to function, operate, work
ganar to earn; to win
manejar to drive
sacar fotos to take photos

*****La computadora** is the term most commonly used in Hispanic America. **El ordenador** is used primarily in Spain.

A.   ¿Qué acción o descripción corresponde a los sustantivos que están a la izquierda?

1. el grabador de vídeo
2. el cartel
3. el aumento de sueldo
4. el trabajo
5. el acuario
6. el equipo fotográfico
7. el trofeo
8. los impuestos

a. Es necesario si queremos combatir la inflación.
b. Son todas las cosas que necesitamos si nos gusta sacar fotos.
c. Es la parte de nuestro sueldo que le pagamos al gobierno (*government*).
d. Lo que nos dan cuando ganamos una competencia.
e. El lugar donde viven los peces que tenemos en casa.
f. Algo que colgamos (*we hang*) en la pared (*wall*).
g. Lo usamos cuando hay un programa de televisión que queremos ver pero estamos ocupados en ese momento.
h. Puede tener mucho prestigio y ser muy interesante o puede ser algo monótono.

Notas comunicativas: More About Expressing Interests

You already know how to use the verb **gustar** to talk about what you and others like. Here are some additional verbs that are used in exactly the same way.

interesar: No **me interesa** nada el arte moderno.   encantar: ¡**Me encanta** sacar fotos!
            Me interesan mucho las ciencias.   **Me encantan** las películas extranjeras.

B.   ¿Qué tienen las siguientes personas en casa, en su cuarto o en su oficina? Con otros dos compañeros, contesten, inventando (*inventing*) todos los detalles posibles. Luego comparen sus descripciones con las de otros grupos. Estén preparados para explicar sus respuestas. Si dicen que una persona tiene un equipo fotográfico, tienen que decir por qué: le gusta sacar fotografías, lo necesita para su trabajo, etcétera.

1. Maripepa tiene un trabajo de tiempo parcial por las tardes, en el centro. Hace la correspondencia para un dentista y les manda las cuentas a sus pacientes. Por las mañanas toma clases en un «community college» que está en los suburbios. Este semestre estudia literatura inglesa. Tiene que leer mucho y hacer muchos trabajos académicos. Le interesa mucho la fotografía.

2. Teresa tiene una vida muy activa. Le gusta participar en los deportes (*sports*) y también sigue los deportes profesionales con gran interés. Le encanta pasar tiempo fuera de casa, en el campo (*country*) o en el parque. También escucha mucho la música y le encanta visitar el zoo.
3. Francisco no tiene una vida muy activa. Es contador (*accountant*). Maneja su coche a la oficina por la mañana y regresa a casa por la noche. Le interesan mucho el arte y la música y también le encantan las telenovelas (*soap operas*).
4. Los Fuentes tienen cinco hijos. Aunque (*Although*) los dos esposos trabajan, pasan mucho tiempo con los niños por las noches y durante los fines de semana. Los ayudan mucho con su tarea (*homework*). No les gusta que los niños miren mucho la televisión pero sí les interesa que vean películas y vídeos de interés cultural. Creen que los niños deben llevar una vida muy activa y que es una buena experiencia para un niño tener la responsabilidad de cuidar de (*take care of*) un animal.

C. Escoja (*Choose*) el mejor consejo para cada (*each*) situación. Luego justifique su respuesta.

1. Su jefe es muy antipático.
    a. Cambie de puesto, porque los jefes no cambian nunca.
    b. Sea muy simpático/a para ver si él empieza a cambiar de actitud con Ud.
    c. ¿ ?
2. Su compañero/a de cuarto en la residencia es una persona muy desordenada... ¡y Ud. es todo lo contrario!
    a. Cambie de cuarto. No es posible que una persona desordenada aprenda a ser organizada.
    b. Insista en que su compañero/a cambie de cuarto, porque a Ud. le encanta el cuarto que tiene ahora.
    c. ¿ ?
3. Ud. gana un sueldo muy bajo.
    a. Explíquele su situación a su jefe y pídale un aumento.
    b. Consiga un trabajo de tiempo parcial por las noches.
    c. ¿ ?
4. Su coche es muy viejo y no funciona muy bien.
    a. Pídales dinero a sus padres para conseguir otro coche.
    b. No vuelva a manejarlo. Véndalo y empiece a tomar el autobús.
    c. ¿ ?

D.   Los bienes personales

1. ¿Qué tiene Ud. en su cuarto en su residencia (apartamento, casa)? Mencione todos los bienes personales que pueda en un minuto. Sus compañeros de clase van a escuchar con cuidado y luego tratar de escribirlos todos.
2. ¿Qué necesita Ud. con urgencia para su cuarto (apartamento, casa)? ¿Qué quiere tener algún día? Compare sus respuestas con las de los

VS 550 T

Multi-Audio-System
El VS 550 abre nuevas perspectivas a los amantes del video creativo. El sistema Multi-Audio conduce con sus posibilidades de sonorización a una nueva era de la videografía. El sistema Picture in Picture (PIP) o el Multi-Channel cuádruple posibilitan el control continuo sobre su pantalla de programas de televisión. Todo ello con un manejo fascinantemente simple.

otros estudiantes de la clase. ¿Hay algo mencionado por todos o casi
todos?

3. ¿Qué deja Ud. en el suelo con frecuencia? ¿Qué deja Ud. sin terminar a
veces?

Al tanto...

Here are the words for some **bienes personales** that have become
increasingly useful in recent years. Try to guess
their meanings:

> el (teléfono) inalámbrico (*Hint:* el alambre = *wire*)
> el contestador automático (*Hint: What does* contestar *mean?*)
> los juegos electrónicos

Given the tendency of some Spanish speakers to shorten words,
how do you think **la bicicleta** and **la motocicleta** are often abbreviated? If you said **la bici** and **la moto**, you are right!

*Es época de adviento navideño y, con toda seguridad,
usted quiere regalarse algo para disfrutarlo en familia...
Una buena posibilidad es incorporarse al mundo del
vídeo. Pensando en ello es que en esta edición le
entregamos una completa guía de compras de vídeo-
grabadores, vídeo-reproductores, cámaras y equipos de
grabación y cintas para su equipo. En suma, todo lo que
usted podrá encontrar de equipamiento de vídeos.*

ESTRUCTURAS

24. EXPRESSING DESIRES AND REQUESTS
The Subjunctive in Noun Clauses: Concepts; Influence

El viernes, por la tarde

JEFE: Tenemos que trabajar el sábado, señores, y tal vez el domingo. *Es necesario* que el inventario *esté* listo el lunes.

EMPLEADO: Ud. *quiere* que *lleguemos* a las ocho, como siempre, ¿verdad?

JEFE: No, una hora más temprano. Y si quieren comer, *recomiendo*
que *traigan* algo de casa. No va a haber tiempo para salir.

EMPLEADO: (A la empleada.) ¡Ay! Mis planes para el fin de semana...
Ojalá que el jefe *cambie* de idea.

EMPLEADA: ¡Lo más probable es que tengas que cambiar de planes!

Friday afternoon   BOSS: We'll have to work on Saturday, people, and maybe on Sunday. It's
necessary that the inventory be ready on Monday. EMPLOYEE: You're going to want us to be
here at eight as usual, right? BOSS: No, an hour earlier. And if you want to eat, I recommend
that you bring something from home. There won't be any time to go out. EMPLOYEE: (*To female
employee*.) Oh, my plans for the weekend! I hope that the boss changes his mind. FEMALE
EMPLOYEE: It's more likely that you'll have to change your plans!

¿Qué va a pasar este fin de semana? Use el subjuntivo de las palabras entre paréntesis.
1. El jefe quiere que los empleados (*preparar*)...
2. Va a ser necesario que todos (*llegar*)...
3. Va a ser necesario que los empleados (*traer*)...
4. Va a ser necesario que el empleado (*cambiar*)...

Subjunctive: Sentence Structure

INDEPENDENT CLAUSE		DEPENDENT CLAUSE
I recommend	that	she write the letter.
I wish	(that)	we were already there.

As you saw in Grammar Section 22 (**Capítulo 11**), the subjunctive is used in the preceding English sentences. In addition, the sentences share another characteristic. Each has two clauses: an independent clause with a conjugated verb and subject that can stand alone (*I recommend, I wish*), and a dependent (subordinate) clause that cannot stand alone (*that she write, that we were there*). The subjunctive is used in the dependent clause.

Indicate the independent and dependent clauses in the following sentences.

1. I don't think (that) they're very nice.
2. We feel (that) you really shouldn't go.
3. He suggests (that) we be there on time.
4. We don't believe (that) she's capable of that.

The Spanish subjunctive also occurs primarily in *dependent clauses* (**las cláusulas subordinadas**). Note that each clause has a different subject and that the clauses are linked by **que**.

INDEPENDENT CLAUSE		DEPENDENT CLAUSE
first subject + *indicative*	(that)	second subject + *subjunctive*
Quiero	**que**	subas al taxi.
No quiero	**que**	perdamos el vuelo.

Subjunctive: Concepts

In addition to the sentence structure typical of many sentences that contain the subjunctive in Spanish, the use of the subjunctive is associated with the presence, in the independent clause, of a number of concepts or conditions—influence, emotion, or doubt—that trigger the use of the subjunctive in the dependent clause.

- ***What** does the boss want?*
  Quiere que los empleados lleguen a tiempo. *(direct object)*
- ***What** does the boss like?*
  Le gusta que los empleados lleguen a tiempo. *(subject)*
- ***What** does the boss doubt?*
  Duda que los empleados siempre lleguen a tiempo. *(direct object)*

These uses of the subjunctive fall into the general category of the subjunctive in noun clauses. The clause in which the subjunctive appears functions like a noun (subject or direct object) in the sentence as a whole.

Subjunctive in Noun Clauses: Influence

INDEPENDENT CLAUSE		DEPENDENT CLAUSE
first subject + *indicative* (expression of influence)	**que**	second subject + *subjunctive*

La jefa **quiere** que los empleados **estén** contentos.	*The boss wants the employees to be happy.*
¿**Prefieres** tú que (yo) **compre** un compact disc o un grabador de vídeo?	*Do you prefer that I buy a compact disc player or a VCR?*
Es necesario que Álvaro **estudie** más.	*It's necessary that Álvaro study more.*

A.   Expressions of influence are those in which someone, directly or indirectly, tries to influence what someone else does or thinks: *I suggest that you be there on time; It's necessary that you be there.* In Spanish, expressions of influence, however strong or weak, are followed by the subjunctive mood in the dependent clause.

B.   Some verbs of influence include **desear, insistir (en), mandar** (*to order* or *to send*), **pedir (i, i), permitir** (*to permit* or *allow*), **preferir (ie, i), prohibir** (*to prohibit* or *forbid*), **querer (ie)**, and **recomendar (ie)**. Because it is impossible to give a complete list of all Spanish verbs of influence, remember that verbs that convey the sense of influencing—not just certain verbs—are followed by the subjunctive.

C.   Remember to use the infinitive—not the subjunctive—after verbs of influence when there is no change of subject:

> **Desean cenar** ahora.
>   *but*
> **Desean** que **Luisa y yo cenemos** ahora.

[Práctica A]

D.   As you know, generalizations are followed by infinitives: **Es necesario estudiar.** When a generalization of influence is personalized (made to refer to a specific person), it is followed by the subjunctive in the dependent

clause: **Es necesario** *que estudiemos*; **Es importante** *que consiga* **el puesto.**
Other generalizations of influence include **es urgente, es preferible**, and **es preciso** (*necessary*).

[Práctica B–E]

Práctica

A.   En la oficina. ¿Qué recomendaciones hace la jefa? Haga oraciones completas según el modelo. Use el pronombre sujeto sólo si es necesario.

> MODELO: Paco / trabajar el sábado →
> La jefa quiere que Paco trabaje el sábado.
>
> La jefa (no) quiere que…
> Recomienda que…
> Insiste en que…
> Pide que…
> Prohíbe que…

1.   yo / no hablar tanto por teléfono
2.   Alicia / empezar a llegar a las ocho
3.   el Sr. Morales / buscar otro puesto
4.   todos / ser más cuidadosos (*careful*) con los detalles
5.   nosotros / tener el inventario listo para el miércoles
6.   los empleados / fumar en su oficina
7.   la Sra. Medina / llevar un trabajo importante a casa este fin de semana
8.   los empleados / pedirle aumentos este año

¿Qué opina Ud. de esta jefa? ¿Qué tipo de persona es? ¿Es muy exigente (*demanding*)? ¿muy comprensiva? ¿Es una amiga para sus empleados? ¿Le gustaría tenerla como jefe? ¿Por qué sí o por qué no?

B.   Preparativos para una fiesta. Imagine que Ud. y un grupo de amigos van a dar una fiesta en su apartamento. ¿Qué es necesario hacer para tenerlo todo preparado? Haga oraciones con una palabra o frase de cada grupo.

			invitar a los otros amigos
			comprar los refrescos
es necesario		alguien	buscar unos discos nuevos
es preciso	que	tú	ayudarme a preparar la comida
quiero		¿ ?	traer un estéreo
			avisar a los vecinos (*neighbors*)
			sacar fotos durante la fiesta

C.   ¡Dos padres muy distintos! Nati y Tomás tienen dos hijos: una niña de ocho años que se llama Nora y un niño de nueve años que se llama Joaquín. A los dos padres les encantan sus hijos, pero tienen ideas muy distintas sobre la mejor manera de educarlos. Tomás tiene ideas muy tradicionales, pero Nati es más moderna: cree que los niños deben crecer (*grow up*) en un ambiente de libertad y con ciertas responsabilidades, para que (*so that*) aprendan a ser adultos responsables.

Describa las ideas de Nati y Tomás sobre los siguientes temas, usando las frases como guía. Empiece sus descripciones con frases como: **Nati quiere que...** , **Tomás prefiere que...** , **Nati nunca permite que...** , etcétera. Siga el modelo.

MODELO: Nora: jugar sólo con muñecas (*dolls*), tener coches también si los quiere → Tomás quiere que Nora juegue sólo con muñecas. Nati prefiere que tenga coches también, si los quiere.

1. Joaquín: tener muñecas, jugar con soldados y coches
2. Nora: ser profesora o médica algún día, ser esposa y madre
3. los niños: no tocar la computadora, aprender a usarla
4. los niños: tener animales en casa, no tener ningún animal
5. los niños: jugar en la piscina, no jugar allí solos
6. los niños: no tocar el grabador de vídeo, usarlo
7. Joaquín: aprender a cocinar, no aprender a hacerlo
8. Nora: aprender a arreglar (*repair*) el coche, no saber nada de coches
9. los niños: no ver la televisión nunca, verla cuando quieran
10. los niños: estar con ellos los fines de semana, estar con sus amigos

D.   Recomendaciones del director. ¿Cómo se dice en español?

1. I want you to do the inventory.
2. I insist that it be ready by (**para**) tomorrow.
3. If you can't do it by then (**para entonces**), I want you to work this weekend.
4. It's urgent that it be on my desk at 8 A.M.
5. I recommend that you begin it immediately (**en seguida**).

E.   ¿Qué cree Ud. que ocurre en cada una de las siguientes situaciones? Primero lea las oraciones incompletas. Luego, identifique el lugar y complete las oraciones lógicamente. Compare sus respuestas con las de otros compañeros de clase. ¿Vieron todos (*Did everyone see*) la misma cosa?

1. El cliente _____. No tiene _____.
   El dependiente _____.
   Siempre es preciso _____.

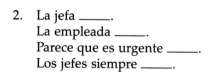

1.

2.   *¿Quieres que lo haga ahora o mañana?*

2. La jefa _____.
   La empleada _____.
   Parece que es urgente _____.
   Los jefes siempre _____.

3. La madre _____. Los niños _____.
   Yo creo que es necesario _____.
   Los padres siempre _____.

3.

Notas lingüísticas: More About Describing Things

You already know that the verb **ser** can be used with **de** + *a noun* to tell what something is made of: **La falda es** *de algodón.* **La camisa es** *de lana.* These descriptions could also be expressed in this way: **Es una falda de algodón. Es una camisa de lana.** Their English equivalent is *a cotton skirt, a wool shirt.*

As you can see in these examples, an English noun can modify another noun, to express the material of which something is made: *a gold watch.* The same *noun* + *noun* structure is used in English to describe the nature of a place or thing: *the language lab, a summer day.*

In Spanish, this structure can only be expressed by using a *noun* + **de** + *noun* phrase: **un reloj** *de* **oro, el laboratorio** *de* **lenguas, un día** *de* **verano.** You have seen this structure in some of the new vocabulary for this chapter: **un grabador de vídeo, una máquina de escribir.**

Zoquetes de streech femenino con logo. Artículo 038. Set de 4 pares de colores diferentes. Precio del set: ₳ 14.

Maletín. De goma negra, art. 011 precio: ₳ 160. De cocodrilo negro art. 012a y marrón 012b. Precio: ₳ 200.

A. ¿De quiénes son los siguientes objetos? Explique su respuesta.

Objetos: la alarma de seguridad, las piezas de cerámica, el acuario de agua salada, los trofeos de tenis, la tienda de campaña (*tent*), el saco de dormir

1. A Adela le encantan los deportes. De hecho (*In fact*), es campeona de golf, tenis y vólibol.
2. A Geraldo le gusta hacer *camping* en las montañas.
3. Los señores de Inza son muy ricos. Tienen una casa magnífica y una colección de pinturas de un valor incalculable.
4. Laura tiene una pequeña colección de figuras de animales.
5. A Ernestito le interesan mucho los peces. Tiene más de 100 peces tropicales.

B. Lo que me gustaría tener. Consulte la lista de **Palabras útiles** antes de contestar las siguientes preguntas.

1. ¿Qué hay en la casa de sus padres (de un amigo/una amiga) que a Ud. le gustaría tener? ¿Por qué quiere Ud. tenerlo/la?
2. Imagine que Ud. puede pedirle cualquier (*any*) cosa a un amigo (una amiga)… ¡y recibirla! ¿Qué le va a pedir?

   MODELO: _____, quiero que me des un(a) _____ de _____.

Palabras útiles:

Materiales: oro, plata (*silver*), diamantes, cristal, porcelana, cerámica, madera (*wood*); cuero (*leather*), ante (*suede*), pieles (*fur*); pana (*corduroy*), dril (*denim*), mezclilla (*tweed*).

Objetos: anillo (*ring*), cadena (*chain*), reloj, pendientes (*earrings*), pulsera (*bracelet*); pieza, figura, vaso, escultura

En la oficina

—¿Cuánto tiempo llevas en tu nuevo empleo?

—Casi dos meses.

—¿Y cómo te va?°   *And how's it going?*

—No muy bien. Me piden que trabaje los fines de semana... , y el sueldo no es muy bueno.

—Me imagino que vas a buscar otro puesto, ¿no?

—Sí. Sólo espero que termine el mes para hacerlo.

ESTRUCTURAS

Guadalajara, México

25. EXPRESSING FEELINGS
The Subjunctive in Noun Clauses: Emotion

Un futuro peatón

ANITA: ¿Qué tal el tráfico en la carretera esta mañana?

CARLOS: Un desastre, un verdadero desastre. Dos horas al volante, una multa y ahora un coche que no funciona como debe. *Tengo miedo* de que la transmisión no *esté* totalmente bien.

ANITA: ¡Hombre, parece que siempre tienes problemas de este tipo! *Me sorprende* que no *busques* un apartamento más cerca de la oficina.

JULIO: ... ¡o que no *compres* un carro nuevo!

Buenos Aires, la Argentina

1. Para Carlos, ¿es fácil llegar a la oficina?
2. ¿De qué tiene miedo Carlos ahora?
3. ¿Dónde vive Carlos, cerca o lejos de la oficina?
4. ¿Qué le recomiendan Anita y Julio?

INDEPENDENT CLAUSE		DEPENDENT CLAUSE
first subject + *indicative* (expression of emotion)	**que**	second subject + *subjunctive*
Esperamos que Ud. **pueda** asistir.		*We hope (that) you'll be able to come.*
Tengo miedo (**de**) que mi abuelo **esté** muy enfermo.		*I'm afraid (that) my grandfather is very ill.*

A future pedestrian   ANITA: What was the traffic like on the highway this morning? CARLOS: Terrible, just terrible. Two hours at the wheel, a ticket, and now a car that isn't working as it should. I'm afraid that the transmission isn't quite right. ANITA: Man, it seems as if you always have problems like these (of this kind). I'm surprised you don't look for an apartment closer to the office. JULIO: . . . or buy a new car!

> **Es lástima** que no **den** aumentos este año.
>
> *It's a shame (that) they're not giving raises this year.*

A. Expressions of emotion are those in which speakers express their feelings: *I'm glad you're here; It's good that they can come.* Such expressions of emotion are followed by the subjunctive mood in the dependent clause.

B. Some expressions of emotion are **esperar, gustar, sentir (ie, i)** (*to regret* or *feel sorry*), **me** (**te, le,** and so on) **sorprende** (*it is surprising to me* [*you, him, her*]), **temer** (*to fear*), and **tener miedo (de).** Since not all expressions of emotion are given here, remember that any expression of emotion—not just certain verbs—is followed by the subjunctive.

C. When generalizations of emotion are personalized, they are followed by the subjunctive in the dependent clause. Some expressions of emotion are **es terrible, es ridículo, es mejor/bueno/malo, es increíble** (*incredible*), **es extraño** (*strange*), **¡qué extraño!** (*how strange!*), **es lástima,** and **¡qué lástima!** (*what a shame!*).

Práctica

A. Sentimientos. ¿Cuáles son algunas de las cosas que le gustan o que le dan miedo a Ud.?

1. Me gusta mucho que _____. (*estar contentos mis amigos, funcionar bien mi equipo estereofónico, venir todos a mis fiestas, estar bien mis padres [hijos], ¿ ?*)
2. Tengo miedo de que _____. (*haber mucho tráfico en la carretera mañana, no venir nadie a mi fiesta, haber una prueba mañana, ocurrir una crisis internacional, no darme el jefe un aumento, ¿ ?*)

B. Chismes (*Gossip*) **de la oficina.** Haga oraciones completas de dos cláusulas, según el modelo.

MODELO: A Julio / no gustar / tenemos que trabajar los fines de semana
→ A Julio no le gusta que tengamos que trabajar los fines de semana.

1. Anita / esperar / le dan un aumento
2. a ti / sorprender / hay tanto trabajo
3. Carlos / temer / lo van a despedir (*fire*)
4. a nosotros / no gustar / son tan altos los impuestos
5. a mí / no gustar / nos dan sólo dos semanas de vacaciones
6. todos / tener miedo / no hay aumentos este año
7. director / sentir / tener / despedir / cinco / empleados

C. Complete las oraciones con la forma apropiada del verbo entre paréntesis.

1. Dicen en la agencia que mi carro nuevo es económico. Por eso me sorprende que (*usar tanta gasolina*). Temo que el coche (*no funcionar totalmente bien*).

2. ¡Qué desastre! El jefe dice que me va a despedir. ¡Es increíble que (*despedirme*)! Es terrible que (yo) (*tener que buscar otro puesto*). Espero que (él) (*cambiar de idea*).

3. Generalmente nos dan un mes de vacaciones, pero este año sólo tenemos dos semanas. Es terrible que sólo (*darnos dos semanas*). No nos gusta que (*ser tan breves las vacaciones*). Es lástima que (*no poder ir a ningún lugar*).

4. A los niños no les gustan sus regalos de Navidad este año. ¡Qué lástima que no (*gustarles los regalos*)! Siento que (ellos) (*estar tan triste*). Espero que (ellos) (*recibir lo que pidan*) el año que viene.

D.   Las siguientes personas piensan en otra persona o en algo que van a hacer. ¿Qué emociones sienten? ¿Qué temen? Conteste las preguntas según los dibujos.

1. Jorge piensa en su amiga Estela. ¿Por qué piensa en ella? ¿Dónde está? ¿Qué siente Jorge? ¿Qué espera? ¿Qué espera Estela? ¿Espera que la visiten los amigos? ¿que le manden algo? ¿que le digan algo?

2. Fausto quiere comer fuera esta noche. ¿Quiere que alguien lo acompañe? ¿Dónde espera que cenen? ¿Qué teme Fausto? ¿Qué le parecen los precios del restaurante? ¿Dónde quiere él que coman los dos?

1.   2.

UN POCO DE TODO

A.   Ud. es jefe/a de una oficina. Hoy viene un empleado a la oficina por primera vez. ¿Qué le va a decir? ¿Qué consejos le va a dar?

Recomiendo que Ud...	trabajar todos juntos (*together*) aquí
Espero que los otros empleados...	conocer a los otros empleados
	llegar puntualmente por la mañana
Es necesario que Ud...	no usar el teléfono en exceso
Me gusta que todos...	no dejar para mañana el trabajo de hoy
Es preferible que...	no estar ausente con frecuencia
Quiero que Ud...	hacer preguntas cuando no comprenda algo
Ojalá que...	no querer cambiar de puesto pronto

B.   Los valores de nuestra sociedad. Express your feelings about these situations by restating them, beginning with one of the following phrases or any others you can think of: **(No) Quiero que, Es necesario que, Es bueno/malo que, Es extraño/increíble que, Recomiendo que, Es lástima que.**

1.   Muchas personas viven para trabajar. No saben descansar.
2.   Somos una sociedad de consumidores.
3.   Siempre queremos tener el último modelo de todo... el coche de este año, el grabador de vídeo que acaba de salir...
4.   Juzgamos (*We judge*) a los otros por las cosas materiales que tienen.
5.   Las personas ricas tienen mucho prestigio en esta sociedad.
6.   Las mujeres generalmente no ganan tanto como los hombres cuando hacen el mismo trabajo.
7.   Los plomeros ganan más que los profesores.
8.   Los jugadores profesionales de fútbol norteamericano ganan salarios fenomenales.
9.   Muchas personas no tienen con quién dejar a los niños cuando trabajan.

UN PASO MÁS: Lectura cultural

Antes de leer: Word Families

Guessing the meaning of a word from context is easier if it has a recognizable root, or a relation to another word that you already know. For example, if you know **llover**, you should be able to guess the meaning of **lluvia** and **lluvioso** quite easily in context. Can you guess the meaning of these words?

la pobreza   La pobreza es un problema muy grave en muchas partes de la India y Latinoamérica.

la enseñanza   Mucho datos indican que la enseñanza actual en los Estados Unidos es inferior a la del año 1960.

If you know the following words, you will be able to guess the approximate meaning of the related words you will encounter in the reading: **el lápiz, estudiar, iluminar, marcar, la playa, la ingeniería, la formación, el papel, usar.**

«TENGO... NECESITO... QUIERO... »

En una de las primeras actividades del **Capítulo 12**, Ud. terminó° la serie de oraciones incompletas que constituye el título de esta lectura. Escuche ahora mientras° tres hispanos terminan las mismas oraciones. Tres estilos distintos... tres individuos. ¿Qué nos revelan estas respuestas sobre la vida de estas tres personas? ¿Son sus respuestas similares a las que Ud. dio°?

completed

as

las... those you gave

Margarita Cuesta, España

Tengo una casa donde vivir, un coche pequeño, bastante ropa, estatuillas de Italia, Guatemala y España, cacharros de cocina.° En cuanto a entretenimiento,° tengo una tienda de campaña con linternas, saco de dormir y cocina.

cooking / En… As for entertainment

Necesito una cuna muy grande para mi bebé, que se haga° cama cuando él sea mayor, pero como es bastante cara me tengo que conformar con una cuna normal y corriente.

se… can be made into

Quiero un Fiat descapotable rojo, un reloj y una pulsera de oro.

Marcial Beltrán, México

Tengo dos pantalones de mezclilla, ocho playeras,° dos camisas, diez calzoncillos,° diez pares de calcetines, un cinturón, tres pares de tenis, dos calzones para correr, muchas cosas de higiene personal, platos, vasos, cucharas, cuchillos y tenedores, dos ollas° para cocer° frijoles, una estufa, un refrigerador, un televisor, un sofá, una mesa con cuatro sillas, una lámpara y un «sleepbag», seis trofeos de carreras° y cinco medallas.

camisetas
shorts, underwear

pots / cocinar

racing

Necesito mucho, pero lo más importante es comprar material escolar para poder seguir mis estudios y un lugar seguro° donde vivir.

stable, permanent

También **quiero** mucho, pero hay tres cosas principales en mi vida. La primera, llegar a ser ingeniero. Segunda, formarme como individuo en la sociedad. Y tercera, correr en la Olimpiada.

María José Ruiz Morcillo, España

Tengo una cámara de fotos bastante buena pero todavía no tengo un equipo fotográfico muy completo. Tengo una buena colección de posters y de carteles (que ya no sé en dónde colgar). Tengo bastantes libros e° infinidad de artículos de papelería (cuadernos, lapiceros, bolígrafos, clips, carpetas,° etiquetas,° tarjetas, sobres° de distinto color y formato, marcadores de lectura…), ¡muchos de los cuales no he usado nunca!

y
files / labels
envelopes

Necesito una impresora y no es necesario que sea muy sofisticada (de lo que se deduce que tengo un ordenador personal). Necesito un buen traje de chaqueta pues casi toda mi ropa es bastante informal.

Me gustaría **tener** un buen equipo estereofónico y una buena colección de música. También **quiero** tener una casa no muy grande pero que sea tranquila y luminosa.

Comprensión

Hay más de una respuesta posible. De estas tres personas, ¿quién… ?

1. es esposa y madre   2. es estudiante ahora   3. escribe muchos trabajos académicos   4. lleva una vida muy activa   5. pasa mucho tiempo en la cocina   6. vive ahora en un apartamento   7. no está muy contenta con el sitio donde vive ahora   8. aspira a tener fama internacional

De las tres, ¿a quién le interesa(n)… ?

1. el arte   2. los deportes (*sports*)   3. estar fuera de casa   4. las diversiones que se hacen en casa   5. las matemáticas   6. sacar fotos

Para escribir

Vuelva Ud. a completar las tres oraciones del título de la lectura. Incorpore en sus respuestas algunas de las palabras y frases que acaba de leer. Por ejemplo:

En cuanto a… (*As far as . . . is concerned*)
Necesito… pero me tengo que conformar con…
Necesito mucho, pero lo más importante es…

Hay… cosas principales en mi vida: …
Necesito… pues…
Tengo… de lo que se puede deducir que (yo)…

VOCABULARIO

Verbos

cambiar (de) to change
conseguir (i, i) to get, obtain
dejar to leave (behind)
despedir (i, i) to fire, dismiss
funcionar to function, operate, work
ganar to earn; to win
mandar to order
permitir to permit, allow
prohibir to prohibit, forbid
recomendar (ie) to recommend
sentir (ie, i) to regret, feel sorry; to feel
temer to fear

Los bienes personales

el acuario aquarium
la bici(cleta) bicycle
el cartel poster
el compact disc compact disk (player)
la computadora computer (*L.A.*)
el equipo estereofónico stereo equipment

el equipo fotográfico photographic equipment
el grabador de vídeo VCR
la impresora printer
la máquina de escribir typewriter
la moto(cicleta) motorcycle
el ordenador computer (*Spain*)
el pájaro bird
el pez (*pl.* **peces**) fish
la pintura painting
el radio (portátil) portable radio
el trofeo trophy

El trabajo

el aumento raise, increase
el cheque check
el/la director(a) manager, director
el/la empleado/a employee
el impuesto tax
el inventario inventory
el/la jefe/a boss
el puesto job, position
el sueldo salary
el trabajo job, work; written work; (term) paper

Otros sustantivos

el campo country(side)
la carretera highway
el gobierno government

Adjetivos

cada (*inv.*) each, every
descapotable convertible (*with cars*)
listo/a (*with* **estar**) ready, prepared

Palabras adicionales

aunque although
de tiempo parcial part-time
es extraño it is strange
  ¡Qué extraño! How strange!
es…
  increíble incredible
  preciso necessary
  preferible preferable
  urgente urgent
es lástima it is a shame
  ¡Qué lástima! What a shame!
me (te, le…) sorprende it is surprising to me (you, him . . .)
sacar fotos to take pictures, photographs

Frases útiles para la comunicación

me interesa(n)…   . . . is/are interesting to me
me encanta(n)…   . . . is/are exciting to me

LOS HISPANOS EN LOS ESTADOS UNIDOS
La comunidad cubanoamericana*

En su mayoría (*majority*), los cubanos son un grupo inmigrante. Comenzaron a llegar a los Estados Unidos en gran número alrededor del año 1960 debido a (*due to*) la situación política existente en la isla de Cuba. Esta inmigración es, en cierto sentido, única (*unique*) en la historia de los Estados Unidos.

En la mayoría de los casos de las grandes inmigraciones a este país, la gente era (*was*) pobre y perteneciente a las clases más humildes. Pero en el caso de los cubanos, los inmigrantes de la década de los años 60 eran (*were*) en su mayoría profesionales de las clases media y alta. Llegaron sólo con su cultura y su educación.

En sólo una generación los inmigrantes cubanos han recuperado (*have gotten back*) casi todo lo que tuvieron que abandonar y ejercen ahora una enorme influencia en la vida del sur de la Florida en donde todavía están concentrados.

Cuba: Sube número de turistas extranjeros

Aproximadamente 250 mil turistas extranjeros visitaron Cuba el año pasado, un diez por ciento más que el año pasado. El Instituto Nacional de Turismo informó que se esperaba° que los ingresos devengados° alcancen a 120 millones de dólares.

La Época (Santiago de Chile)

se… *it was hoped* / ingresos… *revenue generated*

«Así, nos encontramos° con las familias Rodríguez y Montesino… El auto de la familia, casi tocando el mar de breves olas,° dos asientos bajo los pinos y la fresca brisa marina que resulta infantilmente acariciante proveen° a los Rodríguez y Montesino de ese ambiente° de paz revitalizante que tanto necesitan…
—¿De dónde son ustedes?
—De Pinar del Río.°
—Vinimos° porque el señor Montesino se está recuperando° y este lugar vale un millón.
—¿Acostumbran a venir con frecuencia?
—Sí. Este lugar es mejor que un tónico.»

Ralph Rewes, «El entrepuente del sol», *Miami Mensual*

nos… *we find ourselves*
waves

provide
atmosphere

ciudad de Cuba
pretérito de *venir*
se… *is convalescing*

Varadero, Cuba

«Yo soy un hombre sincero
de donde crece° la palma;
y antes de morirme,° quiero
echar mis versos del alma.

Mi verso es de un verde claro
y de un carmín encendido:°
mi verso es un ciervo herido°
que busca en el monte amparo.°»

José Martí (1853–1895), héroe nacional de Cuba y poeta, de *Versos sencillos*

grows
dying

fiery

ciervo… *wounded deer*
refugio

---

*A number of verbs in this section are in a past tense called the preterite. You have already learned some verb forms in this tense (**fui/fuiste/fue**, **pagaste**, **comí/comiste/comió**), and you will learn to form the complete conjugation in Chapter 13. For now, focus only on the stem of the verb. For example, you can guess that **comenzaron** is from **comenzar**, that **llegaron** is from **llegar**, and so on. Forms you cannot recognize in this way will be glossed.

Un son° para Celia Cruz

Celia Cruz canta que canta,
y de su canto diré°
que el son, de Cuba se fue
escondido° en su garganta.°

Hay en su voz, una santa
devoción por la palmera;
vibra en ella Cuba entera,
y es tan cubano su acento
que su voz, al darse al viento,°
flota como una bandera°…

Canta, Celia Cruz, en tanto,°
ya que° no hay nada que vibre
y recuerde° a Cuba libre
como el sabor de tu canto.

Ernesto Montaner, «El poeta del exilio», en *La Voz libre*, Los Ángeles, 11 de
septiembre de 1987

typically Hispanic musical form

I will say

hidden / throat

al… as it mixes with the wind
flag

en… a little
ya… for
brings to mind

La mundialmente famosa Celia Cruz, que ostenta
el honroso título de «La Guarachera de Cuba»
cuya estrella será (*will be*) colocada en el famoso
Bulevar de la Fama, el próximo jueves 17 del
actual, a las doce y media del día. Será un acontecimiento memorable.

Xavier Suárez, alcalde (*mayor*)
de Miami

- Nacido (*Born*) en Las Villas, Cuba, el noveno (*ninth*) de catorce hijos
- Llegó a los Estados Unidos, a los once años, después de la inva-
sión de la Bahía de los Cochinos
- Aprendió inglés en dos meses
- B.S. en ingeniería, Villanova University
- M.A. en administración pública, Harvard University
- Título de abogado (*lawyer*), Harvard University
- Cita de su discurso de inauguración: «Con los pobres de la tierra
quiero yo mi suerte echar (*cast my fate*)»—José Martí

«Miami esencialmente se ha profesionalizado en general. Esto se refleja inclusive en la manera en la que
visten las personas… Estamos llegando a nivel de gran
metrópolis internacional. Nosotros como arquitectos nos
damos cuenta de° eso… La combinación de idiomas, la
combinación de ideologías sociales y políticas… todo
esto ha hecho que° muchos describan a Miami como la
Suiza del Hemisferio.»

Hilario Candela, arquitecto cubano, en *Miami Mensual*

nos… we realize

ha… has made

La famosa Calle Ocho, Miami

«Ricco tiene 15 años, el cabello° rubio oscuro y los ojos color castaño.° Es un muchachón fuerte y ágil y habla ayudado con las manos, como cualquier otro latino...
—Y tú, ¿cómo te sientes, Ricco, americano o mia-mense?, le pregunto. Sin la menor vacilación, me con-testa con un fuerte acento cubano:
—Chico, a la verdad que yo me siento cubano.
—¿Cómo fue que te empezaste a interesar en hablar español? ¿Fue la curiosidad o qué?...
—Primero fue porque, yo parezco° cubano, tú sabes. Y todo el mundo me hablaba° en español. Empecé a entender ya mucho, pero no hablaba casi nada. Des-pués en la escuela me empecé a reunir con cubanitos, y me gustó el ambiente, tú sabes.»
Ralph Rewes, «El bilingüismo en Hialeah», *Miami Mensual*

hair
brown

look
would speak

«Hermanita nacida° en estas tierras»   *born*

...No es un reproche
hermana
hermanita nacida en estas tierras
Es que tú sólo tienes
la alegría°   *joy, happiness*
de los héroes de Disney
Porque sonreirás°   *you will smile*
cuando el señor genial
de los muñecos°   *dolls (from Disney movies)*
haga de ti
de cada niño
un payasito° plástico   *little clown*
y ridículo

Al escurrirte°   *Al... As you slip away*
lenta y cariñosa
sin poder inventarte
otra niñez°   *childhood*
regalarte la mía°   *regalarte... (I wish I could) give you mine*
que aunque también
se alimentó de héroes
tuvo sabor° a palma   *taste, flavor*
y mamoncillo°   *papaya*
Y no sufrió la burla°   *joke (in a negative sense)*
de los juguetes caros
que te regala
el fantasma engañoso°   *deceitful*
de diciembre

Elías Miguel Muñoz, novelista y poeta cuba-noamericano; poema de *En estas tierras/In This Land*, Bilingual Review Press, 1989

Niños cubanoamericanos, la Pequeña Habana, Florida

"It's one thing to speak English, even to require it. It's quite another to *think and feel English*, and *that* you can't legislate.

"I am blessed, and I mean that sincerely, in that I can think and feel in both circles. But I cannot, and I shall not, forget that my father died in Cuba because he loved it so, and that I am part of that land that he loved so much."

María C. García, periodista cubanoamericana, *Hispanic Link*, March 2, 1986

EN CASA

VOCABULARIO: LOS CUARTOS, LOS MUEBLES° Y LAS OTRAS PARTES DE UNA CASA

furniture

la cama de agua water bed
el estante bookshelf
la mesita end table

la pared wall
el sillón armchair

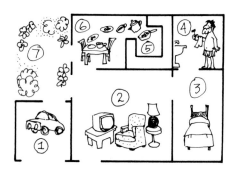

A.   Identifique las partes de esta casa y diga lo que hay en cada cuarto.

B.   ¿A qué parte de la casa se refiere? Identifique el lugar y luego explique quién habla y con quién habla. Invente todos los detalles necesarios.

Palabras útiles: la criada (*maid*), las visitas (*guests*)

1. Por favor, ponga la leche en el refrigerador.
2. Tu hermanito está afuera.
3. El niño duerme. Por favor, no hagan tanto ruido.
4. ¡Este perro está muy sucio! Tenemos que lavarlo (*to wash him*).
5. El médico quiere que hagas más ejercicio. Y aquí estás, sentado (*seated*) en el sofá como siempre.
6. Pasen Uds., por favor. ¡Bienvenidos a esta casa!
7. ¿Por qué no invitas a Carmen y Jorge a cenar el sábado?
8. ¿Cómo es posible? Todavía tienes las manos (*hands*) sucias y es la hora de comer.

C.   ¿Qué muebles o partes de la casa asocia Ud. con las siguientes actividades? Compare sus asociaciones con las de otros estudiantes. ¿Tienen todos las mismas costumbres?

1. estudiar para un examen importante
2. dormir la siesta por la tarde
3. pasar una noche en casa con la familia
4. comer con las visitas

Al tanto...

Spanish speakers in different areas express the names of rooms of a house in several ways. Here are some typical variations.

> *bedroom:* la alcoba, el dormitorio, la recámara, la habitación
> *living room:* la sala, la salita, el cuarto de estar, la sala de estar

Common to Spanish-speaking areas are these names for parts of a house. Can you match the definitions with the names?

la azotea	algo que abre la puerta de la calle desde
la despensa	el apartamento, sin necesidad de ir
el portero automático	a la calle
	terraza encima del techo (*roof*) del edificio
	lugar donde se almacena (*is stored*) la
	comida, en o cerca de la cocina

Las telas, en diferentes colores y estampados, se convierten en las auténticas protagonistas de la vivienda.

¿Recuerda Ud.?

Review the direct (Grammar Section 18) and indirect (Grammar Section 20) object pronouns before beginning Grammar Section 26. Remember that direct objects answer the questions *what* or *whom* and that indirect objects answer the questions *to whom* or *for whom* in relation to the verb.

| Direct: | me | te | **lo/la** | nos | os | **los/las** |
| Indirect: | me | te | **le** | nos | os | **les** |

Identifique los complementos directo e* indirecto en las siguientes oraciones.

1. Nos mandan los libros mañana.
2. ¿Por qué no los vas a comprar?
3. ¿Me puedes leer el menú?
4. Hágalo ahora, por favor.
5. Juan no te va a dar el dinero hoy.
6. Quiero que lo tenga para mañana, por favor.
7. Sí, claro que te voy a invitar.
8. ¿Me escuchas?

ESTRUCTURAS

26. EXPRESSING DIRECT AND INDIRECT OBJECTS TOGETHER[†]
Double Object Pronouns

Pedestrian!

When both an indirect and a direct object pronoun are used in a sentence, the indirect object pronoun (**I**) precedes the direct (**D**): **ID**. Note that nothing comes between the two pronouns. The position of double object pronouns with respect to the verb is the same as that of single object pronouns.

¿La fecha del examen? ¡Claro que la sé! —¿Por qué no **nos la** dices?

The date of the exam? Of course I know it! —Why don't you tell (it to) us?

---

*Note that the word **y** changes to **e** before the sound **i** (which can also be spelled **hi-**): **español e inglés, padres e hijos**.

[†]Note that the exercises and activities in *¿Qué tal?* do not place a lot of emphasis on producing this structure. However, it is important to become familiar with it so that you can learn to recognize it when you see it or hear it.

Mamá, ¿cuándo nos das la cena? —**Os la** preparo ahora mismo.	*Mom, when is (will you give us) dinner? —I'm getting it ready for you right now.*
¿Tienes el trofeo? —Sí, acaban de dár**melo**.	*Do you have the trophy? —Yes, they just gave it to me.*

When both the indirect and the direct object pronouns begin with the letter *l*, the indirect object pronoun always changes to **se**. The direct object pronoun does not change.

Le ↓ **Se** compra unos zapatos.	*He's buying her some shoes.*
los compra.	*He's buying them for her.*
Les ↓ **Se** mandamos la blusa.	*We'll send you the blouse.*
la mandamos.	*We'll send it to you.*

Since **se** stands for **le** (*to/for you* [sing.], *him, her*) and **les** (*to/for you* [pl.], *them*), it is often necessary to clarify its meaning by using **a** plus one of the pronoun objects of prepositions.

Se lo escribo (**a Uds., a ellos, a ellas...**).	*I'll write it to (you, them . . .).*
Se las doy (**a Ud., a él, a ella...**).	*I'll give them to (you, him, her . . .).*

Práctica

A. El jefe está muy exigente (*demanding*) hoy. ¿A qué se refiere (*What is he talking about*) cuando dice lo siguiente? Fíjese en (*Pay attention to*) los pronombres y en el sentido de la oración.

una computadora	unos contratos	una carta
un nuevo trabajo	un aumento	unas cuentas

1. ¡No! ¡No quiero que se lo expliquen ahora!
2. ¿Me los trae ahora, por favor?
3. ¡Es necesario que Ud. se las mande ahora mismo!
4. Prefiero que Ud. *no* me lo pida este mes.
5. Es necesario que me la escriba a máquina inmediatamente.
6. Es preciso que Ud. nos la arregle (*fix*) hoy. ¡La necesitamos!

B. Ud. acaba de comer pero todavía tiene hambre. Pida más comida, según el modelo. Fíjese en (*Note*) el uso del tiempo presente como sustituto para el mandato.

MODELO: ensalada → ¿Hay más ensalada? Me la pasas, por favor.

1. pan   2. tortillas   3. tomates   4. fruta   5. vino   6. jamón

C. En el aeropuerto. Cambie: sustantivos → pronombres para evitar (*to avoid*) la repetición.

1. ¿La hora de la salida? Acaban de decirnos la hora de la salida.
2. ¿El horario (*schedule*)? Sí, quiero que me leas el horario, por favor.
3. ¿Los boletos? No, no tiene que darle los boletos aquí.
4. ¿El equipaje? Claro que les guardo el equipaje.
5. ¿Los billetes? ¿No quieres que te compre los billetes?
6. ¿El puesto en la cola? No te preocupes. Yo te puedo guardar el puesto.
7. ¿La clase turística? Sí, les recomiendo la clase turística, señores.
8. ¿La cena? La azafata nos va a servir la cena en el avión.

D. Situaciones. La casa de su amigo Raúl es un desastre… y sus padres vienen a visitarlo este fin de semana. Un compañero (Una compañera) va a hacer el papel (*role*) de Raúl. Dígale cómo va a ayudar a poner la casa en orden. Use el verbo apropiado para cada caso.

MODELO: —¡Todos los platos están sucios! →
—¡No te preocupes! Yo te los lavo.

Los muebles de madera de estilo rústico predominan en la sala de estar y en los dormitorios de invitados.

Verbos: lavar, comprar, arreglar

1. También están sucias las paredes de la sala.
2. No hay refrescos en casa.
3. Tampoco hay leche.
4. Hay un montón de ropa sucia en la alcoba.
5. El televisor no funciona.
6. Tampoco funciona el refrigerador.

VOCABULARIO

¿Dónde vive Ud.? ¿Dónde quiere vivir?

las afueras	outskirts; suburbs	**la luz**	light; electricity
alquilar	to rent	**el/la portero/a**	building manager; doorman
el alquiler	rent		
el centro	downtown	**el/la vecino/a**	neighbor
la dirección	address	**la vista**	view
el/la dueño/a	owner; landlord, landlady		
el gas	gas; heat	**la planta baja**	ground floor
el/la inquilino/a	tenant; renter	**el primer (segundo, tercer) piso**	the second (third, fourth) floor

Notas culturales: Naming the Floors of a Building

In English the phrases *ground floor* and *first floor* are used interchangeably in most dialects. In Spanish, however, there are separate expressions for these concepts. **La planta baja** can refer only to the *ground floor*. **El primer piso** (literally, *the first floor*) refers to what English speakers call *the second floor*. **El segundo piso** (literally, *the second floor*) is actually *our third floor* of the building, and so on.

A. ¿Qué prefiere Ud.?

1. ¿vivir en una casa o vivir en un edificio de apartamentos?
2. ¿vivir en el centro o en las afueras? ¿o tal vez (*perhaps*) en el campo?
3. ¿alquilar una casa/un apartamento o comprar una casa?
4. ¿pagar el gas y la luz—o pagar un alquiler más alto con el gas y la luz incluidos?
5. ¿ser el dueño del apartamento o ser el inquilino?
6. ¿que el portero/la portera lo arregle todo o arreglarlo todo Ud. mismo/a (*yourself*)?
7. ¿vivir en la planta baja o en un piso más alto?
8. ¿un apartamento pequeño con una vista magnífica o un apartamento más grande sin vista?
9. ¿un apartamento pequeño con una dirección elegante o un apartamento grande con una dirección más modesta?

B. Definiciones

MODELO: la piscina → Allí nadamos. (Se nada en una piscina.)

1. el inquilino
2. el centro
3. el alquiler
4. el portero
5. el vecino
6. el dueño
7. la criada
8. las afueras

ESTRUCTURAS

27. TALKING ABOUT THE PAST (1)
Preterite of Regular Verbs and of *dar*, *hacer*, *ir*, and *ser*

Un problema con la agencia de empleos

SRA. GÓMEZ: ¡La criada que Uds. me *mandaron* ayer *fue* un desastre!

SR. PARDO: ¿Cómo que *fue* un desastre? ¿Qué *hizo*?

SRA. GÓMEZ: Pues, no *hizo* nada. *Pasó* todo el día en la casa, pero no *lavó* los platos, no *limpió* la bañera, ni *recogió* los juguetes de los niños. Y cuando *salió* a las tres, me *dio* las buenas tardes como si nada.

SR. PARDO: Trate de comprender, señora; cada persona tiene sus más y sus menos. Por lo menos esta criada *fue* mejor que la otra que le *mandamos* anteayer... que ni *llegó*.

A problem with the employment agency MRS. GÓMEZ: The maid you sent me yesterday was a disaster! MR. PARDO: What do you mean, a disaster? What did she do? MRS. GÓMEZ: Well, she didn't do anything. She spent all day at the house, but she didn't wash the dishes, clean the bathtub, or pick up the kids' toys. And when she left at 3:00, she said, "Good afternoon," as if nothing were wrong. MR. PARDO: Try to understand, madam; everyone has his or her good and bad points. At least this maid was better than the other one we sent you the day before yesterday—who didn't even arrive.

> Imagine que Ud. es la Sra. Gómez y descríbale al Sr. Pardo las acciones de la criada. Use el diálogo como guía.
> 1. Ella no... (lavar los platos, limpiar la bañera, recoger los juguetes)
> 2. Pero (ella) sí... (llegar temprano por la mañana, pasar todo el día en casa, salir a las tres)
> 3. Total que (ella)... (no hacer nada, ser un desastre)
>
> ¿Quiere la Sra. Gómez que esta criada vuelva mañana? ¿Va a querer que esta agencia le mande otra criada?

In previous chapters of *¿Qué tal?*, you have already used a few past tense forms: **¿Qué *comiste* anoche?**, *Fue* **una ganga**, and so on. To talk about all aspects of the past in Spanish, you need to know how to use two simple tenses (tenses formed without an auxiliary or "helping" verb): the preterite and the imperfect. You will focus on the forms and uses of these tenses beginning in this chapter and continuing through **Capítulos 14**, **15**, and **16**.

The *preterite* (**el pretérito**) has several equivalents in English. For example, **hablé** can mean *I spoke* or *I did speak*. The preterite is used to report finished, completed actions or states of being in the past. If the action or state of being is viewed as completed—no matter how long it lasted or took to complete—it will be expressed with the preterite.

Preterite of Regular Verbs

hablar		comer		vivir	
hablé	*I spoke (did speak)*	comí	*I ate (did eat)*	viví	*I lived (did live)*
hablaste	*you spoke*	comiste	*you ate*	viviste	*you lived*
habló	*you/he/she spoke*	comió	*you/he/she ate*	vivió	*you/he/she lived*
hablamos	*we spoke*	comimos	*we ate*	vivimos	*we lived*
hablasteis	*you spoke*	comisteis	*you ate*	vivisteis	*you lived*
hablaron	*you/they spoke*	comieron	*you/they ate*	vivieron	*you/they lived*

Note the accent marks on the first and third person singular of the preterite tense. These accent marks are dropped in the conjugation of **ver**: **vi**, **vio**.

Pronunciation hint: some English words are distinguished from each other solely by the position of stress: *objéct* (*to express disagreement*) or *óbject* (*thing*); *súspect* (*one who is suspected*) or *suspéct* (*to be suspicious*). The same is true in Spanish: **tomas** (*you take*) or **Tomás** (*Thomas*). It is particularly important to pay attention to stress in preterite verb forms since many of them are identical in form—except for the written accent—to other forms you have learned: **hablo** (*I speak*) versus **habló** (*he/she/it spoke*), **hable** (*speak*, **Ud.** command) versus **hablé** (*I spoke*), and so on.

Also, note the following about regular preterite forms.

- Verbs that end in **-car**, **-gar**, or **-zar** show a spelling change in the first person singular of the preterite.

> buscar: bus**qu**é, buscaste, …   empezar: empe**c**é, empezaste, …
> pagar   pa**gu**é, pagaste, …

- **-Ar** and **-er** stem-changing verbs show no stem change in the preterite: **desperté**, **volví**. **-Ir** stem-changing verbs do show a change.*
- An unstressed **-i-** between two vowels becomes **-y-**.

> creer: cre**y**ó, cre**y**eron   leer: le**y**ó, le**y**eron

Irregular Preterite Forms

dar		hacer		ir/ser	
di	dimos	hice	hicimos	fui	fuimos
diste	disteis	hiciste	hicisteis	fuiste	fuisteis
dio	dieron	hizo	hicieron	fue	fueron

The preterite endings for **dar** are the same as those used for regular **-er**/**-ir** verbs in the preterite, except that the accent marks are dropped. The third person singular of **hacer**—**hizo**—is spelled with a **z** to keep the [s] sound of the infinitive. **Ser** and **ir** have identical forms in the preterite. Context will make the meaning clear.

> **Fui** profesora.   *I was a professor.*
> **Fui** al centro anoche.   *I went downtown last night.*

Práctica

A.   El día de dos compañeras. Teresa y Evangelina comparten un aparta-mento en un viejo edificio de apartamentos. Ayer Teresa fue a la universi-dad mientras (*while*) Evangelina se quedó (*stayed*) en casa. Describa lo que hicieron, según la perspectiva de cada una.

TERESA:
1. (yo) salir / apartamento / las nueve
2. llegar / biblioteca / las diez
3. estudiar / toda la mañana / para / examen de química
4. escribir / todo / ejercicios / de / libro de texto
5. las doce y media / almorzar / con / amigos / en / cafetería
6. la una / ir / laboratorio
7. hacer / todo / experimentos / de / manual (*m.*) de laboratorio

---

*You will practice the preterite of most stem-changing verbs in **Capítulo 14.**

Tercera... *Senior Citizens*

Piso = Apartamento

Chalet = Casa

8. tomar / examen / las cuatro
9. comentarlo / con / amigos: ¡ser / horrible!
10. regresar / a casa / y / ayudar / a / Evangelina / preparar / cena

EVANGELINA:

1. (yo) pasar / casi todo / día / en casa
2. por la mañana / ver / que / portero / llegar / tarde
3. por eso / (yo) llamar / dueño / de / edificio
4. tomar / café / con / vecinos, / que / salir / las once y media
5. luego / hacer / cheques / para / pagar / luz / y gas
6. electricista / llegar / las dos
7. (él) arreglar / luz / de / sala
8. (yo) bajar / alguno / cajas (*boxes*) / planta baja
9. más tarde / ir / supermercado / y / comprar / comida
10. empezar / preparar / cena / las cinco

¿Quién lo dijo (*said*), Evangelina o Teresa?

1. Mi compañera de apartamento no asistió a clase hoy.
2. ¡El examen fue desastroso!
3. El portero es perezoso. Hoy llegó muy tarde.
4. ¿Qué compraste para la cena?
5. Por fin el electricista arregló la luz.
6. Pagué el gas y la electricidad.

Ahora vuelva a contar el día de Evangelina pero según la perspectiva de Teresa. Luego cuente el día de Teresa según Evangelina.

B.   ¿Qué hicieron ayer? Haga oraciones completas, con los verbos en el pretérito.

1. **Julián:** hacer cola para comprar una entrada (*ticket*) de cine / comprarla por fin / entrar en el cine / ver la película / gustarle mucho / encontrar a unos amigos frente (*opposite*) al cine / ir a un café con ellos / regresar a casa tarde
2. **mis compañeros de apartamento:** ir a la universidad por la mañana / asistir a todas sus clases / regresar temprano a casa / prepararlo todo para la fiesta de este fin de semana
3. **yo:** llegar a la universidad a las ¿ ? / asistir a clases / ir a la cafetería / almorzar con ¿ ? / prestarle un libro a ¿ ? / ¿ ?

C.   Un semestre en México. Cuente la siguiente historia según la perspectiva de la persona indicada. Use el pretérito de los verbos.

1. (yo) pasar un semestre estudiando (*studying*) en México.
2. mis padres: pagarme el vuelo…
3. …pero yo: trabajar para ganar el dinero para la matrícula y los otros gastos (*expenses*)
4. vivir con una familia mexicana encantadora
5. aprender mucho sobre la vida y la cultura mexicanas
6. visitar muchos lugares de interés turístico e histórico

7. mis amigos: escribirme muchas cartas
8. (yo) mandarles muchas tarjetas postales (*postcards*)
9. comprarles muchos recuerdos (*souvenirs*) a todos
10. volver a los Estados Unidos al final de agosto

D.   Preguntas

1. ¿Qué le dio Ud. a su mejor amigo/a (esposo/a, novio/a) para su cumpleaños el año pasado? ¿Qué le regaló a Ud. esa persona para su cumpleaños? ¿Alguien le mandó a Ud. flores el año pasado? ¿Le mandó Ud. flores a alguien? ¿Le gusta a Ud. que le traigan chocolates? ¿otras cosas?

2. ¿Dónde y a qué hora comió Ud. ayer? ¿Con quiénes comió? ¿Le gustaron todos los platos que comió? ¿Quién se los preparó? Si comió fuera, ¿quién pagó?

3. ¿Cuándo decidió Ud. estudiar el español? ¿Cuándo lo empezó a estudiar? ¿Va a estudiarlo el semestre (trimestre) que viene?

4. ¿Qué hizo Ud. ayer? ¿Adónde fue? ¿Con quién(es)? ¿Ayudó a alguien a hacer algo? ¿Lo/La llamó alguien? ¿Llamó Ud. a alguien? ¿Lo/La invitaron a hacer algo especial algunos amigos? Y anteayer, ¿qué hizo? ¿Lo mismo? (*The same thing?*)

5. ¿Qué programa de televisión vio anoche? ¿Qué película vio la semana pasada? ¿Qué libro/novela leyó el año pasado?

¡Qué apartamento más lindo°!   bonito
—¿Cuántos años llevas aquí?
—Casi tres. ¿Te gusta?
—¡Sí! ¡Es un apartamento fenomenal!
—Pues lo decoré yo misma y casi no gasté nada.

UN POCO DE TODO

A.   Situaciones: Se lo di a… (*I gave it to . . .*) Con otro/a estudiante, haga y conteste preguntas, según el modelo. Use el nombre de la persona más apropiada.

MODELO: discos de música punk →
          —Oye, ¿me prestas tus discos de música punk?
          —Lo siento, pero no puedo. Se los di a Roberto.

Amigos y parientes

- Susana tiene una nueva computadora que no funciona.
- A Hildebrando le gusta mucho la música… y especialmente las canciones en español.

- El televisor de sus padres no funciona.
- A Roberto le interesa mucho todo tipo de arte.
- Teresa piensa hacer un viaje.
- A su hermanito le encanta ir al campo.
- Su madre acaba de empezar a estudiar francés.

1. discos de Menudo o de Los Lobos	4. máquina de escribir vieja
2. bicicleta vieja	5. maleta vieja
3. libro de francés	6. televisor viejo

B.   Una cuestión de suerte (*luck*). Complete the following dialogue with the correct form of the words in parentheses, as suggested by the context. When two possibilities are given in parentheses, select the correct word.

CARLOS, estudiante colombiano que estudia comercio internacional en
    Arizona
FRED, estudiante estadounidense y compañero de Carlos
LA SRA. CARRILLO, empleada de una oficina de empleos

En la residencia

CARLOS: ¿(*Saber/Conocer*[1]), Fred? Va a (*ser/estar*[2]) necesario que (yo:
    regresar[3]) a Colombia sin (*terminar*[4]) el semestre. Temo que
    (*mí/mi*[5]) padres no me (*poder*[6]) ayudar más.

FRED: ¡Qué fatal, hombre! ¿Por (*que/qué*[7]) no buscas un trabajo (*en/
    de*[8]) tiempo parcial?

CARLOS: No (*saber/conocer*[9])... Hay (*tan/tanto*[10]) reglas° para los   *rules*
    extranjeros...

FRED: Sí, pero también hay excepciones. (*Sólo/Solo*[11]) tienes (*de/
    que*[12]) demostrar° que hay circunstancias excepcionales.   *to show*

CARLOS: ¡Ojalá que (tú: *tener*[13]) razón! ¿(*Mí/Me*[14]) acompañas a
    Inmigración?

FRED: Cómo no.

En la oficina de empleos

SRA. CARRILLO: No sé... Sin título,° experiencia ni recomendaciones, temo   *degree*
    que Ud. (*tener*[15]) muy (*poco*[16]) posibilidades de (*conseguir*[17])
    un buen trabajo. ¿Tiene (*alguno*[18]) oficio°?   *trade*

CARLOS: No, señora, ni carrera tampoco. Todavía (*ser/estar*[19]) estu-
    diante. Lo que necesito (*ser/estar*[20]) sólo un trabajo de tiempo
    parcial.

SRA. CARRILLO: Ah, ya comprendo. (*Esperar*[21]) Ud. un momento mientras
    veo en este fichero°... ¿(*Saber/Conocer*[22]) Ud. traducir contra-   *card file*
    tos del inglés (*al/a la*[23]) español y viceversa? Una empresa°   *compañía*
    mercantil (*buscar*[24]) traductor. Ud. (*poder*[25]) traducir los docu-
    mentos en (*tu/su*[26]) casa... y le pagan bastante (*bueno/bien*[27]).

CARLOS: ¡Creo que (*ser/estar*[28]) la persona para ese empleo! Estudio comercio internacional.

SRA. CARRILLO: Pues (*ir*[29]) Ud. a la Sección de Personal de la empresa con estos papeles. Es necesario que (*se los/se las*[30]) presente al jefe en mi nombre. ¡Buena suerte en la entrevista!

CARLOS: Se lo agradezco° enormemente, señora Carrillo. ¡Adiós!　　　*I thank*

¿Quién lo dijo (*said*), Carlos, sus padres, la Sra. Carrillo o Fred? Conteste según el diálogo.

1. ¡Ay! No quiero regresar tan pronto.
2. Nos gusta que Carlos sea tan independiente.
3. No te preocupes. Sé lo que puedes hacer.
4. No sé por qué no se me ocurrió antes buscar empleo.
5. Me gusta que el joven sea tan cortés.
6. Creo que Ud. es la persona para este puesto.

Notas culturales: Working Abroad

Carlos is able to get special permission from the Immigration Department to seek a job in the United States, but in many cases it is not easy for a foreigner to get a work permit in this country. Normally a student visa does not permit one to work, and other regulations make it difficult for skilled or semiskilled foreigners to support themselves in this country. The situation in Hispanic countries is even more strict, and in many nations foreigners are strictly prohibited from holding jobs at all. All employment possibilities are reserved for citizens.

UN PASO MÁS: Situaciones

En busca de un cuarto

—¿Qué te pasa?° Pareces muy preocupado.　　　　　　　　　　¿Qué... *What's wrong?*

—Llevo dos semanas buscando° cuarto y... ¡nada!　　　　　　　Llevo... *For two weeks I've been looking for*

—¿Qué tipo de cuarto buscas?

—Pues... quiero un cuarto para mí solo, que sea grande. Además,° necesito　　*Also*
muchos estantes para poner libros y un armario° bien grande. También　　*closet*
me gusta que el cuarto tenga mucha luz y que sea tranquilo.

—¿Nada más?

—Además quiero que esté cerca de la universidad, que tenga garaje, con
derecho° a usar la cocina, con teléfono... y ¡claro!, que sea barato.　　*right*

—Hombre, no pides mucho... Pero no te preocupes. Ahora que me lo dices,
creo que hay uno en el edificio donde vive Rosario. ¡No sé por qué no se
me ocurrió antes°! ¿Sabes dónde está?　　　　　　　　　　no... *I didn't think of it before*

—Creo que sí. La voy a llamar ahora mismo. Te lo agradezco, ¿eh?

Notas comunicativas sobre el diálogo

Many common expressions in Spanish contain double object pronouns that are used in a fixed pattern. Try to use them in conversation, without thinking about the specific meaning of the pronouns.

Ahora que **me lo** dices...	*Now that you mention it . . .*	**Se lo** agradezco. ⎫
No **se me** ocurrió.	*It didn't occur to me.*	**Te lo** agradezco. ⎬ *Thanks a lot.*
¿**Se te** ocurre algo?	*Does anything occur to you?*	⎭

Conversación

Think about the things you would want if you were looking for a room, apartment, or house to rent. Then, with a classmate, practice the preceding dialogue, substituting real information wherever possible.

VOCABULARIO

Verbos

alquilar to rent
arreglar to fix
lavar to wash
limpiar to clean
recoger to pick up

Los cuartos y las otras partes de una casa

la alcoba bedroom
la bañera bathtub
el baño bathroom
la cocina kitchen
el comedor dining room
el garaje garage
la pared wall
el patio patio; yard
la puerta door
la sala living room

Los muebles

la alfombra rug
la cama (de agua) (water) bed
la cómoda bureau
el estante bookshelf
la lámpara lamp
la mesita end table
el sillón armchair
el sofá sofa

¿Dónde vive Ud.?

las afueras outskirts, suburbs
el alquiler rent
la dirección address
el/la dueño/a landlord, landlady
el gas gas; heat
el/la inquilino/a tenant; renter
la luz (*pl.* **luces**) light; electricity

Los muebles

la planta baja ground floor, first floor
el/la portero/a building manager; doorman
el primer (segundo, tercer) piso second (third, fourth) floor
el/la vecino/a neighbor
la vista view

Otros sustantivos

el/la criado/a servant, maid
la entrada ticket (*for a performance*)
el juguete toy
la visita guest

¿Cuándo... ?

anteayer the day before yesterday
ayer yesterday
pasado/a past, last (*in time*)

Palabras adicionales

mientras while
por lo menos at least

Frases útiles para la comunicación

No te preocupes.   Don't worry.
Pase(n) Ud(s).   Come in.

See also the words and phrases in the **Notas comunicativas sobre el diálogo**.

LOS QUEHACERES DOMÉSTICOS

VOCABULARIO: LOS APARATOS DOMÉSTICOS

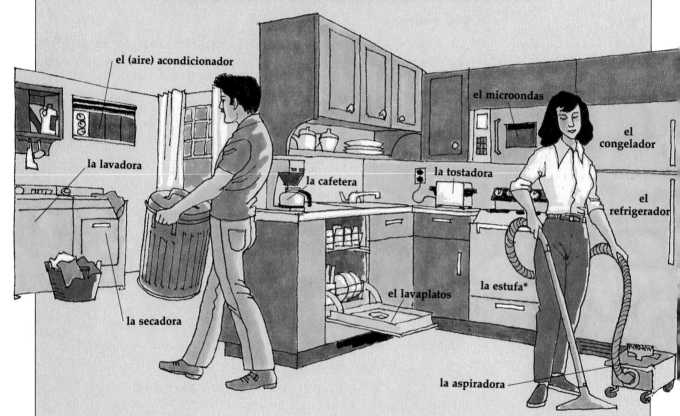

el (aire) acondicionador

el microondas

el congelador

la lavadora

la cafetera

la tostadora

el refrigerador

el lavaplatos

la estufa*

la secadora

la aspiradora

Los quehaceres domésticos

barrer (el suelo) to sweep (the floor)
hacer la cama to make the bed
lavar (las ventanas, los platos) to wash (the windows, dishes)
limpiar la casa (entera) to clean the (whole) house

pasar la aspiradora to vacuum
planchar la ropa to iron clothing
poner la mesa to set the table
preparar la comida/cocinar to prepare food/to cook
sacar la basura to take out the trash
sacudir los muebles to dust the furniture[†]

*The word for *stove* varies in the Hispanic world. Many Spanish speakers use **la cocina**. *Oven* is generally **el horno.**
[†]An alternative phrase used in some parts of the Spanish-speaking world is **quitar el polvo.**

LA COCINA

Los muebles de cocina se derivan
hacia un diseño moderno y sencillo.
Los materiales son las maderas
lacadas y melaminas. El color base,
el blanco y como detalle los
tenedores en colores vivos o como
en el caso de la imagen en un tono
discreto y fácilmente combinable:
el gris.

A. ¿En qué cuarto o parte de la casa se hacen las siguientes actividades?

1. Se hace la cama en _____.
2. Se pone la mesa en _____.
3. Se saca la basura de _____ y se deja en _____.
4. Se prepara la comida en _____.
5. Se sacude los muebles de _____.
6. Se duerme en _____.
7. Uno se baña (*bathes*) en _____. Uno baña al perro en _____.
8. Se barre el suelo de _____.
9. Se pasa la aspiradora en _____ y en _____.
10. Se lava la ropa en _____ y se plancha en _____.

B. ¿Para qué se usan los siguientes productos? Explíqueselo a su amigo hispano, que no los conoce.

1. Windex   3. Endust   5. Joy   7. Tide
2. Mr. Coffee   4. Glad Bags   6. Cascade   8. Lysol

C. **Familias de palabras.** Dé Ud. el verbo que corresponda al sustantivo indicado en cada oración.

> MODELO: **preparación** → **preparar**

1. La **secadora** sirve para _secar_ la ropa. La **plancha** sirve para _planchar_ la.
2. Es necesario _refrigerar_ la comida en un **refrigera**dor.
3. En la **cocina** se puede _cocinar_
4. La **lavadora** sirve para _lavar_ la ropa.
5. El **acondiciona**dor sirve para _acondicionar_ el aire.

cera = *wax*

VOCABULARIO

Más verbos útiles

acostar (ue)	to put to bed	**levantar**	to lift, raise
afeitar	to shave	**quitar**	to remove; take away
bañar	to bathe	**sentar (ie)**	to seat, lead to a seat
despertar (ie)	to wake	**vestir (i, i)**	to dress
divertir (ie, i)	to amuse, entertain		

Complete las oraciones lógicamente. Use estas palabras o cualquier otra.

- el televisor, el ruido, una buena película, el sol, la clase de español, el despertador (*alarm clock*), el estéreo
- mi compañero/a, la enfermera (*nurse*), el camarero, el barbero, el dueño, el padre, la madre, un estudiante

1. _____ me despierta.
2. _____ me divierte.
3. _____ baña al bebé.
4. _____ nos sienta en el restaurante.
5. _____ nos afeita en la barbería.
6. _____ acuesta a los niños en el hospital.
7. _____ quita los platos después de la comida.
8. _____ viste a los niños.
9. _____ levanta la mano (*hand*).

Madrid, España

¿A quién le toca?
—¿Quieres poner el televisor? Hay una película estupenda esta noche.
—Espérate. ¿A ti no te toca lavar los platos?
—A mí, no. Creo que le toca a Julio.
—Pero Julio no está. Ya salió.
—Vamos a dejarlos hasta que regrese.

ESTRUCTURAS

28. EXPRESSING -self/-selves
Reflexive Pronouns

Un día típico

1. *Me llamo* Alicia; mi esposo *se llama* Miguel.   2. *Me despierto* y *me levanto* temprano, a las seis. Él también *se levanta* temprano.   3. *Nos bañamos* y *nos vestimos*.   4. Luego yo pongo la mesa y él prepara el desayuno.   5. Después él hace la cama y yo lavo los platos.   6. ¡Por fin! Estamos listos para salir para la oficina.   7. Pero… un momentito. ¡Es sábado! ¿Es demasiado tarde para *acostarnos* otra vez? No, pero… desgraciadamente, ¡ya no tenemos sueño!

Imagine que Ud. es Alicia y complete las oraciones.
1. *Me* llamo Alicia y mi esposo *Se* llama Miguel.
2. *Me* levanto a las seis y Miguel *Se* levanta a las seis y diez.
3. *Me* baño; luego él *Se* baña.
4. *Me* visto y él *Se* viste al mismo tiempo.

Ahora imagine que Ud. es Miguel. Complete las oraciones para describir las acciones de los dos.
1. Alicia y yo *Nos* levantamos temprano.
2. *Nos* bañamos y *Nos* vestimos con prisa (*quickly*) por la mañana.
3. Casi siempre *Nos* acostamos temprano también.

Many English verbs that describe parts of one's daily routine—to get up, to take a bath, and so on—are expressed in Spanish with a reflexive construction: *I'm taking a bath* → **me baño** (literally, *I'm bathing myself*). In this section you will learn to use reflexive pronouns, as well as other verbs that are used reflexively, to talk about your daily routine.

A typical day   1. My name is Alicia; my husband's name is Miguel.   2. I wake up and get up early, at six. He also gets up early.   3. We bathe and get dressed.   4. Then I set the table, and he makes breakfast.   5. Next he makes the bed, and I wash the dishes.   6. Finally! We're ready to leave for the office.   7. But . . . just a minute. It's Saturday! Is it too late to go back to bed? No, but . . . unfortunately, we're not sleepy any more!

Uses of Reflexive Pronouns

bañarse (to take a bath)		
(yo)	**me** baño	*I'm taking a bath*
(tú)	**te** bañas	*you're taking a bath*
(Ud.)		*you're taking a bath*
(él)	**se** baña	*he's taking a bath*
(ella)		*she's taking a bath*
(nosotros/as)	**nos** bañamos	*we're taking baths*
(vosotros/as)	**os** bañáis	*you're taking baths*
(Ud.)		*you're taking baths*
(ellos)	**se** bañan	*they're taking baths*
(ellas)		*they're taking baths*

In Spanish, whenever the subject does anything to or for him/her/itself, a *reflexive pronoun* (**un pronombre reflexivo**) is used. The Spanish reflexive pronouns are **me**, **te**, and **se** in the singular; **nos**, **os**, and **se** in the plural. English reflexives end in *-self/selves*: *myself*, *yourself*, and so on.

The pronoun **se** at the end of an infinitive indicates that the verb is used reflexively. When the verb is conjugated, the reflexive pronoun that corresponds to the subject must be used: (*yo*) *me* **baño**, (*tú*) *te* **bañas**, and so on.

The following Spanish verbs, which you have already used nonreflexively, are also frequently used with reflexive pronouns.* Many of them are stem-changing.

acostarse (ue)	to go to bed	**lavarse**	to wash oneself, get washed
afeitarse	to shave	**levantarse**	to get up; to stand up
bañarse	to take a bath	**llamarse**	to be named, called
despertarse (ie)	to wake up	**ponerse**	to put on (*clothing*)
divertirse (ie, i)	to have a good time, enjoy oneself	**quitarse**	to take off (*clothing*)
dormirse (ue, u)	to fall asleep	**sentarse (ie)**	to sit down
irse	to leave, go away	**vestirse (i, i)**	to get dressed

¡OJO!   After **ponerse** and **quitarse**, the definite article—not the possessive—is used with one's own articles of clothing.

Se pone **el** abrigo.   *He's putting on his coat.*
Se quitan **el** sombrero.   *They're taking off their hats.*

Placement of Reflexive Pronouns

Like direct and indirect object pronouns, reflexive pronouns are placed before a conjugated verb but after the word **no** in a negative sentence: **No** *se* **bañan.** They may either precede the conjugated verb or be attached to an infinitive.

---

*Compare: **Juan se lava.** (*John gets washed/washes himself.*) **Juan lava la ropa.** (*John washes his clothing.*) **Juan la lava.** (*John washes it.*)

Me tengo que levantar temprano. ⎫
Tengo que levantar**me** temprano. ⎭ *I have to get up early.*

¡OJO!   Regardless of its position, the reflexive pronoun reflects the subject
of the sentence.

[Práctica A–C]

Reflexive pronouns are attached to affirmative commands, but they precede the verb in negative commands. When a reflexive and another object
pronoun are used together, the reflexive comes first.

Quíte**se** el suéter.   *Take off your sweater.*
Quíte**selo** Ud.   *Take it off.*

No **se** ponga esa blusa.   *Don't put on that blouse.*
No **se la** ponga Ud.   *Don't put it on.*

[Práctica D–G]

Práctica

A.   Hábitos y costumbres. ¿Qué acostumbran hacer los miembros de la
familia Hernández? Imagine que Ud. es el esposo (la esposa) y haga oraciones completas. Use el sujeto pronominal cuando sea necesario.

1.   yo / levantarse / a las siete
2.   mi esposo/a / levantarse / más tarde cuando puede
3.   nosotros / bañarse / por la mañana
4.   por costumbre / niños / bañarse / por la noche
5.   yo / vestirse / antes de desayunar
6.   mi / esposo/a / vestirse / después de tomar un café
7.   por la noche / niños / acostarse / muy temprano
8.   yo / acostarse / más tarde, a las once
9.   por lo general / mi esposo/a / acostarse / más tarde que yo

En la familia Hernández, ¿quién...

1.   se levanta primero?
2.   se acuesta primero?
3.   no se baña por la mañana?
4.   se viste antes de tomar
     el desayuno?

Ahora, con un compañero (una compañera), haga y conteste preguntas ba-
sadas en las frases anteriores, según el modelo. La persona que contesta
puede cambiar los detalles.

MODELO: yo / levantarse / a las siete → —¿A qué hora te levantas?
                                          —Me levanto a las ocho.

B.   Complete las oraciones con la forma correcta de los verbos de la
derecha.

1. En la escuela primaria los niños _____ en el suelo con frecuencia. Generalmente los maestros prefieren _____ en una silla.
2. ¡Hace calor! Yo voy a _____ el abrigo. ¿No vas a _____ la chaqueta?
3. Voy a _____ antes de acostarme esta noche. Mi esposo/a, en cambio, _____ en la mañana.
4. Nosotros _____ muy temprano, a las seis de la mañana. Y tú, ¿a qué hora te gusta _____?
5. Hace un poco de frío. Voy a _____ una chaqueta. Alfredo prefiere _____ un suéter.
6. ¡Siempre te gusta _____ en las fiestas! ¿Por qué no _____ ahora?
7. Yo _____ cuando tengo sueño; no importa la hora. En cambio (*On the other hand*) mi compañero/a de cuarto siempre _____ a las once.

lavarse
sentarse
acostarse
despertarse
ponerse
quitarse
divertirse
bañarse

C. Complete las oraciones lógicamente para describir su propia rutina diaria.

¡OJO! Después de una preposición, sólo puede usarse el infinitivo. Use pronombres reflexivos cuando sea posible.

1. Me levanto después de _____.
2. Me siento a la mesa antes de _____.
3. Me duermo después de _____.
4. Me baño antes de _____.
5. Me visto después de _____.
6. Me quito la ropa antes de _____.
7. Me pongo el abrigo antes de _____.
8. Por la noche, me divierto antes de _____.

D.   Consejos. Su vecino Pablo es una persona muy perezosa y descuidada (*careless*). No estudia mucho y tampoco hace los quehaceres en el apartamento donde vive con un compañero. Déle consejos lógicos con estos verbos, según el modelo.

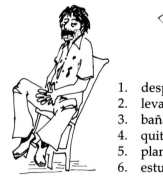

MODELO: afeitarse → Es necesario que se afeite. ¡Aféitese!

1. despertarse más temprano
2. levantarse más temprano
3. bañarse más
4. quitarse esa ropa sucia y ponerse ropa limpia
5. planchar su ropa y vestirse mejor
6. estudiar más
7. no divertirse tanto
8. ir más a la biblioteca
9. no acostarse tan tarde
10. ayudar con los quehaceres
11. sacar la basura, por lo menos
12. ¿ ?

E.   Situaciones: En el hospital. Con un compañero (una compañera), hagan los papeles (*play the roles*) de paciente y enfermero/a, según el modelo.

MODELO: los zapatos → —¿Quiere Ud. que me quite los zapatos ahora?
—Sí, quíteselos, por favor.

1. el suéter
2. la camisa/la blusa
3. los pantalones
4. la camiseta
5. los calcetines/las medias
6. toda la ropa

¿Qué otros mandatos le puede dar la enfermera (el enfermero) al paciente?

F. Aquí hay algunas escenas de un sábado típico de la vida de la familia Hernández. Describa los distintos momentos que se ven e invente otros detalles. Use pronombres reflexivos cuando sea posible. Por ejemplo:

Dibujo 1: Los padres se despiertan muy temprano. El bebé se despierta aun (*even*) más temprano. Va a la cama de sus padres y los despierta.

Conteste estas preguntas en su descripción.

1. ¿Quiénes son los miembros de la familia Hernández? (¿Cuántos hijos hay en total? ¿Vive alguien más con la familia? etcétera)
2. ¿Necesitan un despertador los señores Hernández? ¿Por qué sí o por qué no?
3. ¿Dónde duerme cada miembro de la familia? ¿Dónde es necesario que duerma la niña?
4. ¿Cuáles son los «juguetes» del bebé?
5. ¿Qué parece ser el centro de la vida doméstica de esta familia?

Palabras útiles: la bañera, la cuna (*crib, cradle*), el juguete, la pelota (*ball*), los anteojos (*eyeglasses*)

G.   Entrevista. Using the following verbs as a guide, ask another student what he or she does during a typical day, and, when appropriate, where. Note the answers; then tell the class about his or her day.

MODELO: despertarse → ¿Te despiertas temprano? ¿tarde? ¿fácilmente?
¿A qué hora te despiertas?

1. despertarse
2. levantarse
3. bañarse
4. afeitarse
5. vestirse
6. desayunar
7. salir para la universidad
8. asistir a clases
9. almorzar
10. divertirse
11. volver a casa
12. cocinar
13. cenar
14. lavar los platos
15. limpiar la cocina
16. sacar la basura
17. sentarse a ver la televisión
18. quitarse la ropa
19. acostarse
20. dormirse
21. dormir _____ horas

VOCABULARIO

Talking About Obligation

You already know several ways to express obligation, things you have to do.

Tengo que	⎫		*I have to*	⎫	
Necesito	⎬ barrer el suelo.		*I need to*	⎬ *sweep the floor.*	
Debo	⎭		*I should*	⎭	

Of the three alternatives, **tener que** + *infinitive* expresses the strongest sense of someone's obligation.

The concept *turn to do* (*something*) is expressed in Spanish with the verb **tocar** plus an indirect object.

¿A quién le toca lavar los platos esta noche?—**A mí me toca** solamente sacar la basura. Creo que **a papá le toca** lavar los platos.

Whose turn is it to wash the dishes tonight?—I only have to take out the garbage. I think it's Dad's turn to wash the dishes.

Entrevista. ¿Es Ud. buen(a) ama de casa (*housekeeper*)? ¿Con qué frecuencia hace Ud. los siguientes quehaceres? Si Ud. no los hace, ¿a quién le toca? Otro/a estudiante lo/la va a entrevistar para evaluar sus hábitos domésticos. Si Ud. vive en una residencia estudiantil, imagine que vive en una casa o en un apartamento.

MODELO: lavar las ventanas →
—¿Con qué frecuencia lavas las ventanas? (¿A quién le toca lavar las ventanas?)
—Nunca me toca a mí lavarlas. Me las lava la criada. (Las lavo frecuentemente. No me gusta que estén sucias.)

0 = nunca   1 = a veces   2 = frecuentemente   3 = todos los días

_____ 1. lavar las ventanas
_____ 2. hacer las camas
_____ 3. poner la mesa
_____ 4. preparar la comida
_____ 5. sacudir los muebles
_____ 6. lavar los platos
_____ 7. limpiar la casa entera

_____ 8. sacar la basura
_____ 9. pasar la aspiradora
_____ 10. limpiar el horno
_____ 11. planchar la ropa
_____ 12. barrer el suelo
_____ TOTAL

Interpretaciones

0–8 puntos: ¡Cuidado! (*Careful!*) Ud. estudia demasiado (*too much*). Por favor, ¡limpie su casa! O, por lo menos, haga que alguien se la limpie. ¡No lo deje para mañana!

9–17 puntos: Ud. puede vivir en su casa, pero no debe invitar a otras personas sin limpiarla bien primero.

18–27 puntos: Su casa, aunque no está perfecta, está limpia. Es un buen modelo para todos.

28–36 puntos: ¡Ud. es una maravilla y tiene una casa muy, muy limpia! Pero, ¿pasa Ud. todo el día limpiándola (*cleaning it*)? ¿Tiene Ud. una criada? ¿Le pide a la criada que le limpie todo?

ESTRUCTURAS

. . . .
29. TALKING ABOUT THE PAST (2)
Irregular Preterites; Stem-Changing Preterites

Pronóstico de un nombre

FÉLIX: ¿Por qué faltaste al bautizo de la nieta de don Pepe ayer?

BEGOÑA: *Quise* ir pero no *pude* por el trabajo. ¿Qué tal *estuvo*?

FÉLIX: La fiesta *estuvo* estupenda. ¡Cuánta gente! ¡Y todos *se divirtieron* tanto!

BEGOÑA: ¿Qué nombre le *pusieron* a la niña?

FÉLIX: Arántzazu Gazteizgogeascoa. Son vascos, sabes.

BEGOÑA: ¡Por dios! Con un nombre así, tiene que hacerse oculista. ¡No hay más remedio!

1. ¿Por qué faltó Begoña al bautizo?
2. ¿Qué tal estuvo la fiesta?
3. ¿Qué nombre le pusieron a la niña?
4. ¿Por qué es preciso que ella llegue a ser oculista?

Irregular Preterites

You have already learned the irregular preterite forms of **dar**, **hacer**, **ir**, and **ser**. The following verbs are also irregular in the preterite. Note that the first and third person singular endings, which are the only irregular ones, are unstressed, in contrast to the stressed endings of regular preterite forms.

estar: estuv-   ⎫ -e
poder: pud-   ⎪ -iste
poner: pus-   ⎬ -o
querer: quis-   ⎪ -imos
saber: sup-   ⎪ -isteis
tener: tuv-   ⎭ -ieron
venir: vin-

estar	
estuve	estuvimos
estuviste	estuvisteis
estuvo	estuvieron

decir: dij-   ⎫ -e, -iste, -o, -imos, -isteis, **-eron**
traer: traj- ⎭

When the preterite verb stem ends in **-j-**, the **-i-** of the third person plural ending is omitted: **dijeron**, **trajeron**.

The preterite of **hay** (**haber**) is **hubo** (*there was/were*).

"¿Sólo dijiste AT&T Español?..."

"Sí, y me ayudaron en español."

Prognosis for a name   FÉLIX: Why weren't you at the baptism of don Pepe's granddaughter yesterday? BEGOÑA: I tried to go, but I couldn't because of work. How was it? FÉLIX: The party was marvelous. So many people! And everyone had such a good time! BEGOÑA: What name did they give the child? FÉLIX: Arántzazu Gazteizgogeascoa. They're Basques, you know. BEGOÑA: Heavens! With a name like that, she has to become an eye doctor. She has no choice!

Several of these Spanish verbs have an English equivalent or implication in the preterite tense that is different from that of the infinitive.

saber:	Ya lo sé.	*I already know it.*
	Lo **supe** ayer.	*I found it out (learned it) yesterday.*
conocer:	Ya la conozco.	*I already know her.*
	La **conocí** ayer.	*I met her yesterday.*
querer:	Quiero hacerlo hoy.	*I want to do it today.*
	Quise hacerlo ayer.	*I tried to do it yesterday.*
	No quise hacerlo anteayer.	*I refused to do it the day before yesterday.*
poder:	Puedo leerlo.	*I can (am able to) read it.*
	Pude leerlo ayer.	*I could (and did) read it yesterday.*
	No pude leerlo anteayer.	*I couldn't (did not) read it the day before yesterday.*

[Práctica A–C]

Stem-Changing Preterites

As mentioned in **Capítulo 13**, the **-ar** and **-er** stem-changing verbs have no stem change in the preterite.

recordar (ue) *(to remember)*		**perder (ie)**	
recordé	recordamos	perdí	perdimos
recordaste	recordasteis	perdiste	perdisteis
recordó	recordaron	perdió	perdieron

The **-ir** stem-changing verbs have a stem change in the preterite, but only in the third person singular and plural, where the stem vowels **e** and **o** change to **i** and **u** respectively.

pedir (i, i)		**dormir (ue, u)**	
pedí	pedimos	dormí	dormimos
pediste	pedisteis	dormiste	dormisteis
pidió	pidieron	durmió	durmieron

These are the **-ir** stem-changing verbs you already know:

conseguir (i, i)	pedir (i, i)	sentir(se) (ie, i)
despedir (i, i)	preferir (ie, i)	servir (i, i)
divertir(se) (ie, i)	seguir (i, i)	vestir(se) (i, i)
dormir(se) (ue, u)		

On the next page you will find some additional **-ir** stem-changing verbs that you will use in the preterite in this chapter.

despedirse (i, i) (de) to say good-bye (to), take leave (of)

morir (ue, u)   to die

reírse (i, i)*   to laugh (at)
sonreír (i, i)†   to smile

[Práctica D–F]

Práctica

A. El primer cumpleaños de Arántzazu Gazteizgogeascoa. Haga el papel (*role*) de uno de los hijos mayores y describa lo que pasó en casa de los Gazteizgogeascoa. Haga oraciones en el pretérito según las indicaciones y use el sujeto pronominal cuando sea necesario.

1. todos / ya / estar / en nuestra casa / antes de / nueve
2. nosotros / poner / mucho / regalos / encima / mesa
3. tíos y abuelos / venir / con / comida y refrescos
4. niños / querer / abrir / paquetes (*m.*) / pero / no / poder
5. yo / tener / que / ayudar / a / preparar / comida
6. más tarde / alguno / vecinos / venir / a / cantar / «Las mañanitas»‡
7. niños / pequeño / ir / a / su / alcobas / diez / y / acostarse
8. papá / sacar / basura / y / pasar / aspiradora
9. mamá / barrer / suelo / y / lavar / platos
10. al día siguiente / todos / decir / que / fiesta / estar / estupendo

¿Cierto, falso o no lo dice? Corrija las oraciones falsas.

1. Hubo muy poca gente en la fiesta.
2. Sólo vinieron los parientes.
3. Todos comieron bien… ¡y mucho!
4. Los niños abrieron los regalos de la pequeña Arántzazu.

B. Un sábado por la tarde. Complete el siguiente diálogo con el pretérito de los infinitivos. Use el sujeto pronominal cuando sea necesario.

P1: Oye, ¿y dónde (*estar: tú*) toda la mañana?
P2: (*Yo: Tener*) que ir a la oficina a terminar un trabajo.
P1: ¿Por qué no me lo (*decir: tú*) antes de irte?
P2: ¡Qué memoria! ¿Nunca recuerdas nada? Te lo (*decir: yo*) anoche.
P1: Puede ser, pero se me olvidó (*I forgot*).
P2: ¿(*Venir*) tus padres?
P1: Sí, y los chicos y yo (*tener*) que arreglar la sala. ¡Qué lata (*pain*)!
P2: No te quejes. (*Don't complain.*) Tú también puedes hacer algunos de los quehaceres.
P1: ¿Por qué? Nunca los (*hacer: yo*) en casa de mis padres y no quiero empezar ahora.

---

*Note the simplification: **ri-ió → rió; ri-ieron → rieron; son-ri-ió → sonrió; son-ri-ieron → sonrieron.**

†Note the accentuation patterns in the present tense forms of **(son)reír: (son)río, (son)ríes, (son)ríe, (son)reímos, (son)reís, (son)ríen.**

‡A song traditionally sung for birthdays, especially in Mexican environments.

El sueño dorado

¿Quién lo dijo, la persona 1 o la persona 2?

1.   Mañana tengo que regresar a la oficina, aunque es sábado.
2.   Mis padres no me hicieron ayudar con los quehaceres.
3.   No me gustan los quehaceres domésticos, pero los hago.
4.   ¡Levántense, niños! Aquí están los abuelos... ¡y la casa es un desastre!

Es probable que hablen dos esposos, pero... ¿quién es la persona 1 y quién es la persona 2? Conteste y explique su respuesta.

C.   A la persona perezosa del diálogo anterior le tocó ayudar hoy con los quehaceres de la casa, pero se le olvidó hacer ciertas cosas. Hágale preguntas según el modelo.

> MODELO: estar: garaje / sacar la basura →
>   Estuviste en el garaje. ¿Por qué no sacaste la basura?

1.   estar: comedor / poner la mesa
2.   ir: garaje / sacar la ropa de la secadora
3.   pasar por: alcoba / hacer las camas
4.   estar: sala / poder pasar la aspiradora
5.   ir: cocina / poner los platos en el lavaplatos

D.   **Un día fatal.** En casa de sus amigos Alicia y Raúl, todos lo pasaron muy mal ayer. Describa lo que pasó. Haga oraciones según las indicaciones.

1.   niños / dormir / muy mal
2.   bebé / despertarse / tres / mañana
3.   tú / no recordar / traerme / libro / que / yo / pedirte
4.   Raúl / perder / llaves (*keys*, f.) / de / coche
5.   criada / les / servir / niños / pastel para la fiesta
6.   yo / empezar / perder / paciencia / con / ella
7.   Raúl / reírse / de / jefe / y / jefe / lo / despedir
8.   abuelos / no despedirse / hasta / once

E.   Cuente las siguientes historias breves en el pretérito. Luego continúelas, si puede.

1.   En un restaurante: Juan (*sentarse*) a la mesa. Cuando (*venir*) el camarero, le (*pedir*) una cerveza. El camarero no (*recordar*) lo que Juan (*pedir*) y le (*servir*) una Coca-Cola. Juan no (*querer*) beber la Coca-Cola. Le (*decir*) al camarero: «Perdón, señor. Le (*pedir*: yo) una cerveza.» El camarero le (*contestar*): _____.
2.   Un día típico: Rosa (*acostarse*) temprano y (*dormirse*) en seguida. (*Dormir*) bien y (*despertarse*) temprano, a las siete. (*Vestirse*) y (*salir*) para la universidad. En el autobús (*ver*) a su amigo José y los dos se (*sonreír*). A las nueve _____.
3.   Dos noches diferentes: Yo (*vestirse*), (*ir*) a una fiesta, (*divertirse*) mucho y (*volver*) tarde a casa. Mi compañero de cuarto (*decidir*) quedarse (*to stay*) en casa y (*ver*) la televisión toda la noche. No (*divertirse*) nada. (*Perder*) una fiesta excelente y lo (*sentir*) mucho. Yo _____.

Cafetera UFESA "COMBI",
con salida de vapor y agua caliente:
de 19.500 pts. a 14.750 pts.

F. Describa Ud. estos hechos (*events*) pasados. Use una palabra o frase de cada grupo. Use el pretérito de los verbos.

durante la primavera pasada	llover	buenos puestos después de graduarse
en 1969 los estadounidenses	traer	un hombre en la luna
Adán y Eva	saber	en Valley Forge con sus soldados
Jorge Washington	conocer	«que coman (*let them eat*) pasteles»
Romeo	recordar	en Acapulco
María Antonieta	poner	el caballo al Nuevo Mundo
Rip Van Winkle	dormir	por Julieta
los turistas	morir	muchos años
mis amigos	empezar	todo el vocabulario en el último examen
yo	conseguir	mucho
la segunda guerra mundial	nevar	en 1939
los europeos	divertirse	que las serpientes son malas
Stanley	decir	a Livingston en África
	estar	

G. Entrevista: Preguntas indiscretas. Hágale preguntas personales a un compañero (una compañera). Use estas frases como guía. Invente otras «preguntas indiscretas» si quiere. Luego dígale a la clase algo interesante sobre su compañero/a.

1. ¿a qué hora? despertarse esta mañana
2. ¿a qué hora? volver a casa el sábado pasado (anoche, …)
3. ¿por cuánto tiempo? mirar la televisión ayer
4. ¿a qué hora? acostarse anoche
5. ¿cuánto? pagar de gas (luz, alquiler) el mes pasado
6. ¿cuánto? pagar por la ropa que lleva hoy
7. ¿qué? comer anteayer
8. ¿de quién? enamorarse (*to fall in love*) el año pasado
9. ¿en qué clase? sacar (*to get*) una nota (*grade*) mala en la escuela secundaria
10. ¿qué? tocarle hacer ayer (anteayer, el mes pasado, …) pero que no hizo
11. ¿a qué hora? ¿dónde? dormirse ayer
12. ¿qué? ¿a quién? servir en su última fiesta (cena)
13. ¿de quién? ¿a qué hora? despedirse anoche
14. ¿ ?

UN POCO DE TODO

A. Un día en la vida de Domingo Meléndez. Domingo es un estudiante graduado en la Universidad de Sevilla. Los siguientes verbos sirven de base para hacer una descripción de un día típico de su vida. Úselos para describir lo que Domingo hizo ayer. Luego, con los mismos verbos, diga lo que Ud. hizo ayer. ¡OJO! Hay toda clase de verbos en la lista.

despertarse a las ocho
levantarse
bañarse
vestirse
desayunar
tomar sólo un café con leche
ir a la universidad
asistir a clases toda la mañana
almorzar con unos amigos a
   las tres en una cafetería
divertirse con ellos

despedirse de ellos
ir a la biblioteca
quedarse allí para estudiar toda
   la tarde
volver a casa a las ocho
ayudar a su madre a preparar
   la cena
poner la mesa
cenar con la familia
poner los platos en el lavaplatos
tratar de estudiar
no poder (estudiar)

mirar la televisión
decirle buenas noches a su madre
salir a las once a reunirse con unos
   amigos en un bar
tomar unas copas (*drinks*) con ellos
bailar un poco con una amiga
volver a casa a la una
quitarse la ropa y acostarse
leer un poco
poner el despertador
dormirse pronto

Notas comunicativas: Putting Events in Sequence

When telling about what we did, we often want to emphasize the sequence in which events took place. You can use these phrases to put events into a simple sequence in Spanish. You will learn additional words and phrases of this kind as you learn more about the past tenses.

Primero...	First . . .	**Después... y...**	Afterwards . . . and . . .
Luego... y...	Then . . . and . . .	**Finalmente (Por fin)...**	Finally . . .

B. **¿Por qué no sacudió Ud. los muebles?** The housekeeper will have to explain why she did not dust the furniture. An able excusemaker, she could point out all the other tasks that she *did* complete. She could also indicate the many unexpected complications that kept her from dusting.

—*Ah, pues...Naturalmente: ¡Si le pasa usted el dedoº!...*

le... you run your finger over it!

MODELO: ¿Por qué no sacudió Ud. los muebles? →
   —No fue posible, señora, pero sí hice muchas otras cosas.
    Primero hice todas las camas. Luego lavé las ventanas y
    saqué la basura. Después preparé la cena y...
   —No lo hice hoy, señora, porque—como Ud. sabe—llegó
    inesperadamente (*unexpectedly*) su hermana con sus diez
    niños. Primero les preparé el almuerzo. Luego los acom-
    pañé al museo de arte moderno. Después fui al mercado a
    comprar más carne y tuve que...

Following the model of the housekeeper's excuses, give the most elaborate excuses that you can in response to the following questions.

1. EL JEFE: ¿Por qué llegó Ud. tarde a la oficina?
2. LA PROFESORA: ¿Por qué no terminó Ud. los ejercicios de hoy?
3. SU MEJOR AMIGO: ¿Por qué no me llamaste la semana pasada?
4. SU COMPAÑERO/A: ¿Por qué no le ayudaste a Juan a limpiar el
                  apartamento?
                  ¿Por qué no comiste nada esta mañana?
                  ¿Por qué no fuiste a la fiesta anoche?
5. SUS PADRES: ¿Por qué no nos escribiste la semana pasada?

UN PASO MÁS: Lectura cultural

Antes de leer: Recognizing Derivative Adjectives

In previous chapters you learned to recognize cognates, word endings, and new words that are related to familiar words. Another large group of adjectives derived from verbs ends in **-ado** or **-ido**: you can often guess the meaning of these adjectives if you know the related verb. For example: **conocer** (*to know*) → **conocido** (*known, famous*); **preparar** (*to prepare*) → **preparado** (*prepared*). Can you guess the meaning of the following italicized adjectives based on verbs you already know?

1. unas ideas bien *explicadas*   2. una mujer *desconocida*   3. su libro *preferido*

In the following reading there are many **-do** adjectives. Try to guess their meaning from context.

«HOGAR, DULCE HOGAR»

«¿**Q**ué te sorprendió cuando llegaste a los Estados Unidos, sobre todo en lo que a las casas y a la manera de vivir se refiere?» Ésta fue la pregunta que les hicimos a varias personas de descendencia hispana que ahora viven en los Estados Unidos. Las respuestas son interesantes… y se le ofrecen a Ud. sin mencionar el nombre de la persona que habla, sólo el de su país de origen.

la calefacción central
el extremo confort (microondas, *freezer*, alfombrado en toda la casa, secarropa, etcétera)
los productos congelados
la cantidad de canales en la TV
las lámparas que tienen regulador de intensidad
la cantidad de objetos descartables°   *disposable*
los pequeños vasos descartables del baño
el papel higiénico perfumado
los garajes grandes con más de un auto
el autoservicio en la mesa
los «dips» para las papas fritas
la cantidad de enchufes° en cada pared   *electrical outlets*
   de la Argentina

A mi llegada a los Estados Unidos, el hecho de que° las casas estaban° cerradas,   el… *the fact that / were*
sin ventilación, en comparación con las de mi país, en donde siempre había°   *there was*
un patio lleno de plantas y flores, me sorprendió. Me parecía° que faltaba aire   Me… *It seemed to me*
y que uno estaba propenso a asfixiarse.
   de México

Una de las cosas que me sorprendió cuando vine por primera vez a los Estados Unidos fue el orden, aseo° y disciplina de esta gente. Me fue muy grato observar que los carros o más bien dicho el tráfico se paraba° para dejar que los peatones cruzaran las calles. También me sorprendió mucho ver las grandes calles solitarias y muertas° de ciudades como Beverly Hills.

cleanliness
se... stopped

dead, not lively

de El Salvador

El culto a los animales domésticos: perros, gatos, ¡ratones!, etcétera. Las industrias que se han originado° y se benefician de este culto: comidas especiales, juguetes, ropa, casas especiales para que vivan estos animales, hospitales, cementerios, agencias que se dedican a cuidar de estos animales cuando los dueños se ausentan, etcétera. El aspecto retraído,° serio y a veces sombrío de la gente en la calle. El aparente aislamiento en que vive la gente.

se... have come from

withdrawn

de El Salvador

Lo que más me sorprendió fue la preocupación y la necesidad de «privacidad»° de la gente. También es sorprendente el que° se espere que los hijos adolescentes se vayan de la casa familiar y tengan su propia casa a una edad relativamente temprana. También me impresionó la mobilidad, la frecuencia con que las personas cambian de casa, ciudad o estado. A otro nivel, me gustó la falta° de formalidad en las costumbres y en la vestimenta.°

vida privada
el... the fact that

lack / ropa

del Uruguay

Como en Panamá tenemos un clima tropical, las casas tienen más ventanas para que entre el aire fresco. Aunque las casas en los Estados Unidos tenían° muchas ventanas, eran° más pequeñas y algunas de ellas ni siquiera se podían° abrir.

had
they were / ni... couldn't even be

de Panamá

Las casas no suelen° tener tantos aparatos electrodomésticos como en los Estados Unidos, o por lo menos no son tan grandes, en particular las neveras° y congeladores, las lavadoras y las secadoras (aparato, este último, de uso no muy extendido verdaderamente). Otra cosa de la que suelen carecer° las cocinas hispanas medias° es del triturador de basuras. ¡Es todo un ingenio que tenemos que aprender a manejar al llegar a los Estados Unidos!

no... don't usually
refrigeradores

de... that is usually lacking in
average

de España

Comprensión

¿Dónde está Ud., en una casa hispana o en una norteamericana?

1. Antes de una cena elegante, le ofrecen a Ud. como *hors d'œuvre* unas patatas fritas con una salsa hecha (*made*) con crema agria (*sour cream*) y cebollas (*onions*)... y tiene que servirse a sí mismo (*yourself*).
2. En la cocina hay algunos aparatos eléctricos, pero no muchos.
3. Todos los cuartos de la casa están ubicados (*located*) alrededor de (*around*) un patio central, donde hay plantas, flores y pájaros.
4. Unos amigos llegan a la casa para cenar con la familia un domingo por la tarde. Llevan pantalones cortos, camiseta y sandalias.

Para escribir

Write two short paragraphs about your living accommodations. The first should give information about where you live: whether in a house, apartment, or dormitory; the number of rooms; a description of the furniture; and so on. You might also want to write about what you like or do not like about where you live. The second paragraph should include information about those you live with and about your and their personal habits: who gets up first, who takes care of domestic chores, who smokes and doesn't smoke, and so on.

VOCABULARIO

Verbos

acostar (ue) to put to bed
  acostarse to go to bed
afeitar to shave
  afeitarse to shave (oneself)
bañar to bathe
  bañarse to take a bath
despedirse (i, i) (de) to say good-
  bye (to), take leave (of)
despertar (ie) to wake
  despertarse to wake up
divertir (ie, i) to amuse, entertain
  divertirse to have a good time,
  enjoy oneself
dormirse (ue, u) to fall asleep
irse to leave, go away
lavarse to wash oneself, get
  washed
levantar to lift, raise
  levantarse to get up; to stand
  up
llamarse to be named, called
morir (ue, u) to die
ponerse to put on (*clothing*)
preparar to prepare
quedarse to stay, remain
quitar to remove; to take away

quitarse to take off (*clothing*)
recordar (ue) to remember
reírse (i, i) (de) to laugh (at)
sentar (ie) to seat, lead to a seat
  sentarse to sit down
sonreír (i, i) to smile
vestir (i, i) to dress
  vestirse to get dressed

Algunos quehaceres domésticos

barrer (el suelo) to sweep (the
  floor)
hacer la cama to make the bed
lavar las ventanas to wash the
  windows
limpiar la casa (entera) to clean
  the (whole) house
pasar la aspiradora to vacuum
planchar to iron
poner la mesa to set the table
sacar la basura to take out the
  garbage
sacudir los muebles to dust the
  furniture

Algunos aparatos domésticos

el (aire) acondicionador air
  conditioner
la aspiradora vacuum cleaner
la cafetera coffeepot
el congelador freezer
la estufa stove
el horno oven
la lavadora washing machine
el lavaplatos dishwasher
el microondas microwave oven
el refrigerador refrigerator
la secadora clothes dryer
la tostadora toaster

Otros sustantivos

el despertador alarm clock
el/la enfermero/a nurse

Palabras adicionales

demasiado too, too much
después later, afterward
en cambio on the other hand
finalmente finally

la cocina → range
el .

Frases útiles para la comunicación

tocarle a uno   to be someone's turn

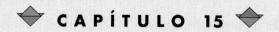

DÍAS FESTIVOS

VOCABULARIO: HABLANDO° DE FIESTAS...

Talking

el Día de los Muertos: el 2 de noviembre

la Navidad:
el 25 de diciembre

la Nochebuena:
el 24 de diciembre

la Noche Vieja:
el 31 de diciembre

el Día de los Reyes Magos:
el 6 de enero

el Día del Año Nuevo New Year's Day
la Pascua Passover
la Pascua (Florida) Easter
el Día de Gracias Thanksgiving

¡felicidades! congratulations!
los refrescos refreshments (drinks w/o alcohol)
la sorpresa surprise
las tapas hors d'œuvres

dar/hacer una fiesta to give/have a party
faltar to be absent, lacking
llorar to cry
pasarlo bien/mal to have a good/bad time
reírse (i, i) (de) to laugh (at)
sentirse (ie, i) feliz/triste to feel happy/sad
sonreír (i, i) to smile

ser + en + (lugar) to take place at (*location*)
   ¿Dónde es la fiesta? Where's the party?
   —**Es en casa de Julio.** —It's at Julio's house.

¡OJO! Note that not all the holidays are considered "active" vocabulary that you are expected to learn.

¿CUAL DE ESTAS FIESTAS ES MAS IMPORTANTE?		
	%	Total
Nochebuena		30,8
Navidad		19,4
Nochevieja		19,4
Año Nuevo ·		3,7
Reyes Magos		3,6
Todas por igual		21,2
NS/NC		2,0

ACTOS RELIGIOSOS		
Aparte de las celebraciones, ¿en estos días asiste usted a oficios religiosos navideños?		
	%	Total
Sí		42,7
No		55,2
NS/NC		2,2

¿QUE ES LA NAVIDAD?		
¿Cuál de estas frases se ajusta más a la forma en que usted pasa las Navidades?		
	%	Total
Es una fiesta fundamentalmente religiosa		9,5
Es una fiesta esencialmente familiar		73,6
Es una fiesta para consumir y gastar dinero		7,3
Son unas vacaciones de invierno, sin ningún otro significado		3,2
Es una época triste y deprimente que preferiría que no existiera		6,1
NS/NC		0,4

A. ¿Qué palabra corresponde a estas definiciones?

1. el día en que se celebra el nacimiento (*birth*) de Jesús
2. algo que alguien no sabe o no espera
3. algo de comer que se sirve en las fiestas (dos respuestas)
4. el día en que los hispanos visitan el cementerio para honrar la memoria de los difuntos (*deceased*)
5. reacción emocional cuando se reciben muy buenas noticias (*news*) (tres respuestas)
6. reacción emocional cuando se recibe la noticia de una tragedia (dos respuestas)
7. la noche en que se celebra el pasar de un año a otro
8. palabra que se dice para mostrar una reacción muy favorable, por ejemplo, cuando un amigo recibe un gran aumento de sueldo

B. Explique cómo se divierte Ud. en estas fiestas y en otras ocasiones. ¿Qué hace para pasarlo bien? ¿Qué desea Ud. que ocurra, idealmente?

1. el día de su cumpleaños
2. durante las vacaciones de invierno o de Semana Santa (*Holy Week*)
3. en una fiesta que dan sus padres (sus hijos)… y los amigos de ellos están presentes
4. los viernes por la noche
5. el Día de Gracias
6. la Navidad/la Pascua

Ahora describa una situación típica en la que Ud. lo pasa mal.

C. Explíquele a un amigo hispano los siguientes días festivos. ¿Qué hace la gente en estos días en los Estados Unidos?

Palabras útiles: el pavo (*turkey*), dar las doce (*to strike 12*), el trébol (*shamrock, clover*), hacerle una broma a alguien (*to play a trick on someone*), el corazón (*heart*), hacer un *picnic* (*to have a picnic*), el desfile (*parade*)

1. el Día de Gracias
2. *Labor Day*
3. *Saint Patrick's Day*
4. la Noche Vieja
5. el Día de los Enamorados
6. *April Fools' Day*

Notas comunicativas: Telling How Long Ago . . .

Tell how long ago something happened by using the word **hace** + *period of time.*

¿Cuándo fuiste a Bogotá con tu familia? —**Hace tres años.**	*When did you go to Bogotá with your family? —Three years ago.*

The preterite is the verb form most commonly used with **hace** to express *ago.* Note also the use of **que** when the **hace** phrase comes at the beginning of the sentence.

Fui a Bogotá con mi familia hace tres años.
Hace tres años **que** fui a Bogotá con mi familia.

D.   Entrevista. With another student, ask and answer questions to determine the first or last time the following situations occurred. Answer using the **hace** + *time* structure if possible and give some additional details.

MODELO: —¿Cuándo fue la última vez (la primera vez) que tú... ?
—Pues, la verdad es que, hace dos años, en...

1. decir tonterías (*silly things*) en una clase
2. estar muy contento/a
3. estar muy enfermo/a
4. tener que pedirle ayuda a alguien
5. traer mucho dinero a clase
6. dar una fiesta
7. ir a un centro comercial
8. enamorarse (*to fall in love*)
9. enojarse (*to get angry*)
10. faltar a una clase
11. quejarse (*to complain*) de algo
12. ¿ ?

Notas culturales: Celebraciones

En la vida de uno hay muchas ocasiones para dar fiestas. Claro que todos los años hay que celebrar el cumpleaños. Pero en partes del mundo hispánico se celebra también el día del santo. En el calendario religioso católico cada día corresponde al nombre de un santo. Si usted se llama Juan, por ejemplo, el día de su santo es el 24 de junio, y lo celebra igual que el día de su cumpleaños.

Para las señoritas, la fiesta de los quince años, la quinceañera, es una de las más importantes, porque desde esa edad a la niña se le considera ya mujer. Para los muchachos, la fiesta de los dieciocho o veintiún años representa la llegada a la mayoría de edad (*coming of age*).

ESPECIALMENTE PARA TI
En El Día
De Tu Santo

Deseando disfrutes todo
Cuanto pueda serte grato
Y te rodeen el cariño
Las atenciones y halagos
De familiares y amigos
En el día de tu santo.

Muchas Felicidades

Un brindis argentino

Al tanto...

In Spanish, *to toast* is **hacer un brindis**. Here are two common Spanish toasts.

- Salud, amor y pesetas... y (el) tiempo para gozarlos (*to enjoy them*).
- Arriba (*Up*), abajo, al centro y... ¡adentro!

"Hoy ¡ES MI CUMPLEAÑOS!"

Llegó el gran día... ¡Sorpréndalo con una fiesta bien linda!

ESTRUCTURAS

30. EXPRESSING *EACH OTHER*
Reciprocal Actions with Reflexive Pronouns

1. ¿Dónde se encuentran los dos pulpos?
2. ¿Cómo se saludan (*do they greet each other*)?
3. ¿Se conocen? ¿Cómo se sabe?

—¿Tú crees que cada vez que nos encontramos tenemos que saludarnos dándonos la mano?

The plural reflexive pronouns, **nos**, **os**, and **se**, can be used to express *reciprocal actions* (**las acciones recíprocas**). Reciprocal actions are usually expressed in English with *each other* or *one another*.

Nos queremos.	*We love each other.*
¿**Os** ayudáis?	*Do you help one another?*
Se miran.	*They're looking at each other.*

Práctica

A. Describa las siguientes relaciones familares o sociales. Haga oraciones completas con una palabra o frase de cada grupo.

los novios
los buenos amigos
los parientes
los esposos
los padres y los niños
los amigos que no viven en la misma ciudad
los profesores y los estudiantes
los jefes y los empleados

(no)

verse con frecuencia
quererse
ayudarse (con los quehaceres domésticos/con los problemas económicos/con los problemas personales)
hablarse (todos los días/con frecuencia/sinceramente)
respetarse
llamarse por teléfono (con frecuencia)
mirarse (en la clase/con cariño)
necesitarse
conocerse bien
casarse (*to get married*) en junio
escribirse
saludarse (en la clase/con cariño)
darse la mano

B. Preguntas

1. ¿Con qué frecuencia se ven Ud. y su novio/a (esposo/a, mejor amigo/a)? ¿Hace cuánto tiempo que se conocieron? ¿Con qué frecuencia se dan regalos? ¿se escriben? ¿se telefonean? ¿Le gusta a Ud. que se vean tanto (tan poco)? ¿Es lástima que no se vean con más frecuencia?

2. ¿Con qué frecuencia se ven Ud. y sus abuelos (primos)? ¿Por qué se ven Uds. tan poco (tanto)? ¿Cómo se mantienen en contacto? Por lo general, ¿es bueno que los abuelos y los nietos se vean con frecuencia? ¿Ocurre esto con frecuencia en la sociedad norteamericana? En su opinión, ¿es esto común entre los hispanos?

VOCABULARIO

Más emociones

enojarse	to get angry	**olvidarse (de)**	to forget (about)
portarse bien/mal	to behave well/badly	**quejarse**	to complain
		recordar (ue)	to remember

To Become (Get)

¿Por qué **te pones** tan furioso?	*Why are you getting (becoming) so angry?*
Vamos a **ponernos** muy tristes.	*We're going to get (become) very sad.*
Se hizo ⎱ directora de la **Llegó a ser** ⎰ compañía.	*She became director of the company.*
Quiere ⎰ **hacerse** ⎱ rico. ⎱ **llegar a ser** ⎰	*He wants to become rich.*

Ponerse + *adjective* is used to indicate physical, mental, or emotional changes. **Hacerse** and **llegar a ser** + *noun* indicate a change as the result of a series of events or effort. They are also frequently used with the adjectives **rico** and **famoso**.

Being Emphatic

To emphasize the quality described by an adjective or an adverb, speakers of Spanish often add **-ísimo/-a/-os/-as** to it, adding the idea *extremely* (*exceptionally; very, very; super*) to the quality. You have already used one emphatic form of this type: **Me gusta muchísimo.**

Estas tapas son **dificilísimas** de preparar.	*These hors d'œuvres are very hard to prepare.*
Durante la época navideña, los niños son **buenísimos**.	*At Christmastime, the kids are extremely good.*

If the adjective ends in a consonant, **-ísimo** is added to the singular form: **difícil → dificilísimo** (and any accents on the accent stem are dropped). If the adjective ends in a vowel, the final vowel is dropped before adding **-ísimo: bueno → buenísimo.** Spelling changes occur when the final consonant of an adjective is **c, g,** or **z: riquísimo, larguísimo, felicísimo.**

A. ¿Cómo reacciona o cómo se pone Ud. en estas situaciones? Use estos adjetivos o cualquier otro, y también los verbos que describen las reacciones emocionales. No se olvide de usar las formas enfáticas cuando sea apropiado.

serio/a	feliz/triste	avergonzado/a (*embarrassed*)
nervioso/a	furioso/a	contento/a

1. Es Navidad y alguien le regala a Ud. un reloj muy, muy caro.
2. Es Navidad y sus padres se olvidan de regalarle algo.
3. En una fiesta, alguien acaba de contarle (*to tell you*) un chiste (*joke*) muy cómico.
4. Ud. está completamente aburrido/a en una fiesta que sus amigos le dan. Tiene ganas de estar en otro lugar, pero no quiere ofender a sus amigos.
5. Ud. da una fiesta pero la gente no lo pasa bien, es decir, no se ríen, no sonríen, no cuentan chistes, están aburridos, etcétera.
6. Hay un examen muy importante esta mañana, pero Ud. no estudió nada anoche.
7. Ud. acaba de terminar un examen difícil (fácil) y cree que lo hizo bien (mal).
8. En un examen de química, Ud. se olvida de una fórmula muy importante.
9. Sin querer, Ud. se portó en una forma muy descortés con un buen amigo.
10. Se acaban (*run out*) las tapas durante su fiesta de Noche Vieja, y sólo son las diez de la noche.

B. ¿Qué ambiciones tiene Ud.? Complete las oraciones lógicamente. Luego explique sus decisiones. (Consulte la lista de profesiones y oficios de la página 395.)

Yo quiero hacerme _____ algún día.
Nunca quiero llegar a ser _____.

¿QUE DIA HACE USTED LOS REGALOS?		
	%	Total
Día de Reyes Magos		64,0
Día de Navidad		9,9
Días de Navidad y de Reyes Magos		6,8
No hay día fijo para dar regalos		9,3
No hacemos regalos		8,9
NS/NC		1,0

¿CON QUE FAMILIA CELEBRA USTED ESTAS FIESTAS?					
%	Nochebuena	Navidad	Nochevieja	Año Nuevo	Reyes Magos
Propia familia	67,1	66,2	62,5	67,1	72,3
Familia (padres)	17,5	15,9	11,6	12,5	12,4
Familia (suegros)	3,7	4,6	3,7	3,9	1,6
Todos juntos	5,7	6,2	6,1	5,6	3,9
No en familia	1,0	1,8	10,9	6,2	5,1
NS/NC	5,0	5,3	5,2	4,6	4,7

La Nochebuena
—¿Cómo pasaste la Nochebuena?
—Estuve en casa de unos amigos. Lo pasamos muy bien. ¿Y tú?
—Tuve una invitación de mis tíos y fui a cenar con ellos.
—¿Te divertiste?
—Sí. Comí, bailé y me reí mucho.

México, D.F.

ESTRUCTURAS

31. DESCRIPTIONS AND HABITUAL ACTIONS IN THE PAST
Imperfect of Regular and Irregular Verbs

La nostalgia

MATILDE: ...y todos los hijos *eran* chiquitos. *Entraban* y *salían* de casa como locos. ¡Qué ruido *había* siempre! ¿Te acuerdas?

ARMANDO: Sí, sí, sí, aquéllos *eran* otros tiempos.

MATILDE: Y luego en verano *íbamos* siempre a la playa con todos los tíos y tus padres y dos criados y los amigos de los niños. *Teníamos* aquella casita tan linda... ¡Casi la puedo ver! ¿No la ves?

ARMANDO: Sí, sí, sí, aquéllos *eran* otros tiempos.

MATILDE: Dime una cosa, Armando. De verdad, ¿qué prefieres, aquella época o estos tiempos más tranquilos?

ARMANDO: Sí, sí, sí, aquéllos *eran* otros tiempos.

Nuevo México

MATILDE: Ay, querido, parece que las cosas nunca cambian. ¡Tampoco me *escuchabas* en aquel entonces!

1. ¿Qué hacían los niños de Matilde y Armando?
2. ¿Su casa era muy tranquila?
3. ¿Adónde iban siempre en verano? ¿Iban solos?
4. ¿Qué le pregunta Matilde a Armando? ¿Cómo responde él?
5. ¿Armando escucha lo que Matilde dice? Y antes, ¿la escuchaba?

The *imperfect* (**el imperfecto**) is the second simple past tense in Spanish. In contrast to the preterite, which is used when you view actions or states of being as finished or completed, the imperfect tense is used when you view past actions or states of being as habitual or as "in progress." The imperfect is also used for descriptions.

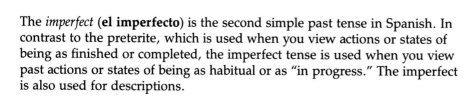

Nostalgia   MATILDE: . . . and all the kids were little. They went in and out of the house like mad. There was always so much noise! Remember? ARMANDO: Yes, yes, yes, those were different times. MATILDE: And then in the summer we would go to the beach with all the uncles and aunts and your parents and two servants and the kids' friends. We used to have that pretty little house . . . I can almost see it! Don't you see it? ARMANDO: Yes, yes, yes, those were different times. MATILDE: Tell me something, Armando. Honestly, which do you prefer—those times or these more peaceful times? ARMANDO: Yes, yes, yes, those were different times. MATILDE: Well, dear, I guess things never change. You never used to listen to me back then, either!

The imperfect has several English equivalents. For example, **hablaba**, the first person singular of **hablar**, can mean *I spoke, I was speaking, I used to speak*, or *I would speak* (when *would* implies a repeated action). Most of these English equivalents indicate that the action was still in progress or was habitual, except *I spoke*, which can correspond to either the preterite or the imperfect.

Forms of the Imperfect

hablar		comer		vivir	
hablaba	hablábamos	comía	comíamos	vivía	vivíamos
hablabas	hablabais	comías	comíais	vivías	vivíais
hablaba	hablaban	comía	comían	vivía	vivían

Stem-changing verbs do not show a change in the imperfect: **almorzaba**, **perdía**, **pedía**. The imperfect of **hay** is **había** (*there was, there were, there used to be*).

Only three verbs are irregular in the imperfect: **ir**, **ser**, and **ver**.

ir		ser		ver	
iba	íbamos	era	éramos	veía	veíamos
ibas	ibais	eras	erais	veías	veíais
iba	iban	era	eran	veía	veían

Uses of the Imperfect

The imperfect is used for the following.

- To describe *repeated habitual actions* in the past

| Siempre **nos quedábamos** en aquel hotel. | We always stayed (used to stay, would stay) at that hotel. |
| Todos los veranos **iban** a la costa. | Every summer they went (used to go, would go) to the coast. |

- To describe an *action that was in progress*

| **Pedía** la cena. | She was ordering dinner. |
| **Buscaba** el carro. | He was looking for the car. |

- To describe two *simultaneous past actions in progress*, with **mientras**

| Tú **leías mientras** Juan **escribía** la carta. | You were reading while John was writing the letter. |

- To describe ongoing *physical, mental,* or *emotional states* in the past

| **Estaban** muy distraídos. | They were very distracted. |
| La **quería** muchísimo. | He loved her a lot. |

- To tell *time* in the past and to express age with **tener**

Era la una.	*It was one o'clock.*
Eran las dos.	*It was two o'clock.*
Tenía dieciocho años.	*She was eighteen years old.*

¡OJO!   Just as in the present, the singular form of the verb **ser** is used with one o'clock, the plural form from two o'clock on.

Práctica

A.   De niño/a. (*As a child.*) La vida de Tina era muy diferente cuando tenía ocho años. Haga oraciones según las indicaciones.

1.   vivir / en / casa / de / padres
2.   todos los días / asistir / a / escuela primaria
3.   caminar / a / escuela / con / mejor / amigo
4.   por / mañana / aprender / a / leer / y / escribir / en / pizarra
5.   a / diez / beber / leche / y / dormir / un poco
6.   ir / a / casa / para / almorzar / y / regresar / escuela
7.   estudiar / geografía / y / hacer / dibujos
8.   jugar / vólibol / con / compañeros / en / patio / de / escuela
9.   camino de (*on the way*) casa / comprar / dulces (*candy*) / y / se los / comer
10. frecuentemente / pasar / por / casa / de / abuelos
11. cenar / con / padres / y / ayudar / a / lavar / platos
12. ver / tele / un rato (*short while*) / y / acostarse / a / ocho

¿Cierto, falso o no lo dice? Corrija las oraciones falsas.

1. Tina no tenía hermanos.   2. Iba a la escuela en autobús.   3. Tenía un perro que se llamaba Júpiter.   4. Generalmente, almorzaba y cenaba en casa.   5. Le gustaba estar con los abuelos.   6. Era una niña muy distraída.

Ahora vuelva a hacer la descripción con el sujeto **yo** para describir su propia (*own*) infancia.

B.   ¿Cómo eran o qué hacían estas personas de niños?

Joe Montana	ser	con frecuencia/siempre
Michael Jackson	cantar	fútbol americano/béisbol/tenis
Elizabeth Taylor	tocar	música moderna
José Canseco	estudiar	mucho/poco
Steffi Graf	jugar al/con	el piano/la guitarra
Ann Landers	creer en	el señor Wilson
Richard Gere	acostarse	temprano/tarde
Daniel el Travieso	(no) ⟨ equivocarse	guapo/a, pobre, rico/a
(*Dennis the Menace*)	(*to be wrong*)	tarde/temprano
todos	levantarse	Santa Claus/los Reyes Magos
yo	dar	consejos
	caerse	¿ ?
	(*to fall down*)	
	molestar	

C.   Descripciones

- **La vida en New Hampshire.** Complete la descripción con la forma correcta del imperfecto del verbo apropiado.

    Cuando (yo: _____^{1}) veinticinco años, (_____^{2}) en New Hampshire. Allí siempre (_____^{3}) mucho en invierno y en primavera, pero me (_____^{4}) mucho el clima. Además (*Besides*), las montañas (_____^{5}) cerca y me (_____^{6}) esquiar. En verano no (_____^{7}) muchísimo calor. (Nosotros: _____^{8}) a la playa con frecuencia.

- **Una noche tranquila en casa.** ¿Cómo se dice en español?
    It was eight o'clock, and I was reading while my friend was writing a letter. There was little noise, and it was snowing outside. We weren't expecting (**esperar**) anyone, and we thought that it was going to be a quiet evening.

D.   **Los tiempos cambian.** Muchas cosas y costumbres actuales son diferentes de las del pasado. Las oraciones siguientes describen algunos aspectos de la vida de hoy. Después de leer cada oración, invente Ud. otra para describir cómo eran las cosas antes, en otra época.

Ayer

MODELO: Ahora casi todos los bebés nacen en el hospital. →
              Antes casi todos los bebés nacían en casa.

1.   Ahora muchas personas viven en apartamentos.
2.   Se come con frecuencia en los restaurantes.
3.   Muchísimas mujeres trabajan fuera de casa.
4.   Muchas personas van al cine y miran la televisión.
5.   Ahora las mujeres—no sólo los hombres—llevan pantalones.
6.   Ahora hay enfermeros y maestros—no sólo enfermeras y maestras.
7.   Ahora tenemos coches pequeños que gastan (*use*) poca gasolina.
8.   Ahora usamos más máquinas y por eso hacemos menos trabajo físico.
9.   Ahora las familias son más pequeñas.
10.   Muchas parejas viven juntas sin casarse.

Hoy

ESTRUCTURAS

32. EXPRESSING EXTREMES
Superlatives

article + *noun* + **más/menos** + *adjective* + **de**

article + **mejor/peor** + *noun* + **de**

David es **el** estudiante **más inteligente de** la clase.	*David is the smartest student in the class.*
Son **los mejores** doctores **de** aquel hospital.	*They're the best doctors at that hospital.*

The *superlative* (**el superlativo**) is formed in English by adding *-est* to adjectives or by using expressions such as *the most, the least,* and so on, with the adjective. In Spanish, this concept is expressed in the same way as the comparative but is always accompanied by the definite article. In this construction **mejor** and **peor** tend to precede the noun; other adjectives follow. *In* or *at* is expressed with **de**.

A Fiesta de la Candelaria es una de las celebraciones paganas más exóticas del continente. Su origen se remonta a los mineros indígenas de Oruro, Bolivia, donde, según la leyenda, el bandido indio Chiru Chiru salvó de morir atrapado en un socavón cuando la Virgen intervino haciendo brotar de su candela una criatura fantástica y deslumbrante: ¡el diablo! Así apareció la diablada, interpretada primero por los indígenas mineros y después por lujosos conjuntos de 80 y 120 personas.

Práctica

A. Expand the information in these sentences, according to the model.

MODELO: Carlota es una estudiante muy inteligente. (la clase) →
          En efecto, es la estudiante más inteligente de la clase.

En la oficina

1. Olga y Paula son empleadas muy trabajadoras. (todas)
2. La Sra. Gómez es una secretaria muy buena. (la oficina)
3. Es una oficina muy eficiente. (la compañía)

En la excursión

4. Es una plaza muy pequeña. (la ciudad)
5. Son ciudades muy grandes. (el país)
6. Es un metro muy rápido. (mundo)

En la universidad

7. Son capítulos muy importantes. (el texto)
8. Es una residencia muy ruidosa. (la universidad)
9. ¡Es una clase muy mala! (el departamento)

B.   Situaciones. A su amigo Rodolfo le gusta exagerar. Cuando Ud. lo llama el día de Navidad, él contesta sus preguntas pero lo exagera todo, como de costumbre. Con un compañero (una compañera), haga y conteste preguntas. Invente las respuestas exageradas de Rodolfo. Luego compare sus respuestas con las de otros estudiantes. ¿Quién exageró más… pero sin salir de los límites de la realidad?

MODELO: —¿Es importante para tu familia la fiesta de este día? →
¡Hombre! ¡Es un día importantísimo! (Es la fiesta más importante del año.) (Es la única fiesta que celebramos en la familia.)

1. Tu árbol (*tree*) de Navidad, ¿cómo es? ¿Es grande? ¿elegante?
2. Tus hermanitos, ¿están felices?
3. Los platos que preparó tu mamá, ¿cómo son? ¿Son ricos? ¿Son difíciles de preparar?
4. ¿Hay muchos regalos para todos? ¿Cómo son? ¿Son caros?
5. Y tú, ¿cómo estás?

C.   Entrevista. With another student, ask and answer questions based on the following phrases. Then report your opinions to the class. Report any disagreements as well.

1. la persona más guapa del mundo
2. la noticia más seria de esta semana
3. un libro interesantísimo y otro pesadísimo (*very boring*)
4. el mejor restaurante de la ciudad y el peor
5. el cuarto más importante de la casa y el menos importante
6. un plato riquísimo y otro malísimo
7. un programa de televisión interesantísimo y otro pesadísimo
8. un lugar tranquilísimo, otro animadísimo y otro peligrosísimo (*very dangerous*)
9. la canción más bonita del año y la más fea
10. la mejor película del año y la peor

UN POCO DE TODO

Más días festivos. Complete the following paragraphs with the correct form of the words in parentheses, as suggested by context. When two possibilities are given in parentheses, select the correct word. Use the preterite of infinitives indicated with an asterisk.

La fiesta de la Virgen de Guadalupe

En (*alguno*[1]) países hispánicos los días de (*cierto*[2]) santos (*ser/estar*[3]) fiestas nacionales. El día 12 (*de/del*[4]) diciembre se (*conmemorar*[5]) a la santa patrona de México, la Virgen de Guadalupe. (*Mucho*[6]) mexicanoamericanos celebran (*este*[7]) fiesta también. Se (*creer*[8]) que la Virgen María se le (*aparecer*[9])* (*a/de*[10]) Juan, un humilde pastor,° en el pueblo (*a/de*[11]) Guadalupe. La Virgen (*dejar*[12])* su imagen en un rebozo° que todavía se puede (*ver*[13]) en la Catedral de la Ciudad de México.

shepherd

shawl

La fiesta de San Fermín

No (*todo*[14]) las fiestas hispánicas (*ser/estar*[15]) religiosas. Esta fiesta de Pamplona (España) lleva (*el/la*[16]) nombre de un santo y (*ser/estar*[17]) de origen religioso, pero es esencialmente secular. Durante diez días—entre (*el/la*[18]) 7 y (*el/la*[19]) 17 de julio—se interrumpe la rutina diaria° (*del/de la*[20]) ciudad.   *daily*
(*Llegar*[21]) personas de todas partes de España e inclusive de (*otro*[22]) países para beber, cantar, bailar... y (*pasarlo*[23]) bien en general. Todas las mañanas se (*permitir*[24]) que algunos toros (*correr*[25]) sueltos° por (*el/la*[26]) calle de la   *free*
Estafeta, en dirección (*al/a la*[27]) plaza de toros. (*Alguno*[28]) personas atrevidas° (*correr*[29]) delante de ellos. No (*haber*[30]) duda que (*este*[31]) demostración   *daring*
de brío° (*ser/estar*[32]) bastante peligrosa. Luego por (*el/la*[33]) tarde se celebra   *courage*
una corrida° en la famosa plaza de toros que (*describir*[34])* Ernest Hemingway   *bullfight*
en (*su*[35]) novela *The Sun Also Rises*. En Pamplona todavía (*ser/estar*[36]) posible (*hablar*[37]) con personas que (*saber/conocer*[38])* a este famoso escritor estadounidense que (*tener*[39])* tanto interés por las culturas (*hispánico*[40]).

¿Cierto o falso? Corrija las oraciones falsas.

1. Todas las fiestas hispánicas son religiosas.
2. Sólo los mexicanos celebran la fiesta de la Virgen de Guadalupe.
3. La fiesta de San Fermín es esencialmente para los niños.
4. Algunos españoles todavía recuerdan a Hemingway.

 UN PASO MÁS: Situaciones

En una fiesta de Navidad

A la llegada

—¡Chicos, cuánto gusto! ¡Felices Pascuas!* Pasen, pasen.

—¡Hola, Antonieta! ¡Felices Pascuas!

—¿Por qué no vino Alejandro?

—Se me olvidó° decirte que no pudo regresar. Perdió el vuelo de la tarde.   *Se... I forgot*

—Lo siento. Ahora pónganse cómodos y vamos a divertirnos. ¿Qué quieren tomar?

—Una bebida sin alcohol, por favor. Pero, primero, ¿dónde podemos dejar estas cosillas° que trajimos?   *little things (i.e., gifts of food)*

—¡Ay, muchas gracias! ¡Muy amables! Pueden dejarlas en la cocina. Ahora bien: José Antonio preparó un ponche muy rico que a todos nos gusta.

—Oye, esta fiesta está estupenda. La música es fabulosa y ¡cuánta comida deliciosa!

—¡Pobre Alejandro! Se va a perder la mejor fiesta del año.

---

*Although **Pascua** is the word for *Easter* or *Passover*, many Spanish speakers use the phrase **Felices Pascuas** as a holiday greeting at Christmas time.

A la despedida

—Muchas gracias por venir.

—Gracias a ti. ¡Lo pasamos estupendamente!

—Y, como ya te dijimos, mañana vamos a estar aquí a las nueve para ayu-
darte a limpiar la casa.

—No es necesario que se molesten.° Se lo agradezco,° de verdad.   se... *you go to that trouble / I thank*

—No es molestia.°   *a bother*

—Bueno, si insisten… Seguro que entre todos vamos a terminar pronto.

Conversación

With a classmate, repeat the first part of the dialogue with these variations.

- Imagine that the party is taking place at the apartment or home of a
  friend.
- Substitute the names of real people and other real information.

With another classmate, create a brief dialogue in which a friend of the
host(ess) asks how the party was. Base the details of the reply on the preceding dialogue and on the minidialogue on page 257. Use the preterite
tense as much as possible and keep sentences simple.

VOCABULARIO

Verbos

casarse (con) to get married (to)
celebrar to celebrate
contar (ue) to tell about
enojarse to get angry
faltar to be absent, lacking
hacerse (*irreg.*) to become
llegar (gu) a ser to become
llorar to cry
olvidarse (de) to forget (about)
ponerse (*irreg.*) to become, get
portarse to behave
quejarse to complain

saludar to greet
sentirse (ie, i) to feel

Sustantivos

el árbol tree
el chiste joke
el nacimiento birth
la noticia (piece of) news; *pl.* news
los refrescos refreshments
la sorpresa surprise
las tapas hors d'oeuvres

Adjetivos

avergonzado/a embarrassed
feliz (*pl.* **felices**) happy
peligroso/a dangerous
pesado/a boring

Palabras adicionales

además besides
dar/hacer (*irreg.*) **una fiesta** to
  give/have a party
en aquel entonces at that time,
  back then
¡felicidades! congratulations!
ser (*irreg.*) **en** + *place* to take place
  in/at (*place*)

Algunos días festivos

**la Noche Vieja, la Pascua (Flo-
  rida), la Nochebuena, la
  Navidad**

Frases útiles para la comunicación

hace + *time* (+ *preterite*)	(*time*) ago
Se fue hace dos años.	He left two years ago.

LA SALUD Y EL BIENESTAR

VOCABULARIO: PARA ESTAR EN FORMA°

en... *in good shape*

caminar

comer equilibradamente

correr

dormir lo suficiente

hacer ejercicios aeróbicos

practicar deportes

cuidarse to take care of oneself
dejar de + *inf.* to stop (*doing something*)
llevar gafas/lentes (de contacto) to wear (eye)glasses/contact lenses
llevar una vida tranquila (sana) to lead a calm (healthy) life

Algunas partes del cuerpo
la boca mouth
el corazón heart
el estómago stomach
la garganta throat
la nariz nose
los ojos eyes
los pulmones lungs

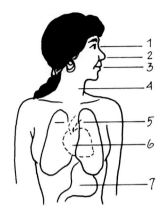

A. ¿Cómo se llaman las partes del cuerpo indicadas en el dibujo?

B. Imagine que Ud. es Richard Simmons; explique cada una de las siguientes oraciones.

> MODELO: Se debe comer equilibradamente. →
> RICHARD: ¡Sí, eso es! Eso quiere decir (*means*) que es necesario comer muchas verduras, que…

1. Se debe dormir lo suficiente todas las noches.
   RICHARD: ¡Exacto! Esto significa que… También…
2. Hay que hacer ejercicio.
3. Es necesario llevar una vida tranquila.
4. En general, uno debe cuidarse mucho.

C. Entrevista. Use las siguientes frases como guía para entrevistar a un compañero (una compañera) de clase. ¿Cree él/ella que estas acciones son buenas o malas para la salud? Pídale que explique su punto de vista. ¿Traen algún beneficio para la salud de uno? ¿Hacen algún daño? ¿En qué parte del cuerpo?

1. fumar tres o cuatro cigarrillos al día
2. fumar dos paquetes de cigarrillos al día
3. preocuparse mucho y no descansar
4. gritar (*to shout*) y enojarse con frecuencia
5. leer con poca luz
6. hacer ejercicio sin llevar zapatos
7. salir sin chaqueta cuando hace frío
8. no llevar las gafas—¡por vanidad!—aunque uno tiene miopía o astigmatismo
9. correr todos los días hasta el punto de agotarse (*to exhaust oneself*)
10. beber uno o dos vasos de vino al día
11. dejar de tomar bebidas alcohólicas por completo
12. dejar de comer por completo para adelgazar (*to lose weight*)

¿CUÁNTO SABES?

Las vitaminas son indispensables para nuestro organismo, pero lo son más en unos casos que en otros. ¿Cómo andas en conocimientos dietéticos! ¡Es importante!

ESTRUCTURAS

◆ ·
33. NARRATING IN THE PAST
Using the Preterite and Imperfect

No es para tanto...

CARMEN: Yo no *sabía* lo que *tenía*, pero la doctora me lo *diagnosticó* en seguida.

PILAR: ¿Y qué te *dijo* que *tenías*?

CARMEN: Pues... que tengo insomnio... y que tengo los ojos muy irrita-dos... Pero de todos modos todavía tengo que terminar las investigaciones para el proyecto que necesitan mañana en la oficina.

1. ¿Quién acaba de tener una consulta con la doctora?
2. ¿Pudo la doctora diagnosticar la enfermedad?
3. ¿Qué dijo la doctora que tenía Carmen?

Ahora invente respuestas para las siguientes preguntas.
1. ¿Cuándo empezó a no dormir bien Carmen?
2. ¿Por qué tiene los ojos muy irritados?
3. ¿Qué recomienda la doctora que haga?
4. ¿Qué quiere el jefe que Carmen haga?
5. ¿Qué cree Ud. que va a hacer ella?

When speaking about the past in English, you choose which past tense forms to use in a given context: *I wrote letters, I did write letters, I was writing letters, I used to write letters,* and so on. Usually only one or two of these options will convey exactly the idea you want to express. Similarly, in many Spanish sentences either the preterite or the imperfect can be used, but the meaning of the sentence will be different, depending on which tense you use. The choice between the preterite and imperfect depends on the speaker's perspective: how does he or she view the action or state of being?

A. The PRETERITE is used to report *completed* actions or states of being in the past, no matter how long they lasted or took to complete; focus may be on the beginning or end of the action or state. The IMPERFECT is used, how-ever, if the *ongoing* or *habitual nature* of the action is stressed, with no refer-ence to its beginning or termination.

Escribí las cartas.	*I wrote (did write) the letters.*
Escribía las cartas cuando...	*I was writing the letters when . . .*

It's not that serious...   CARMEN: I didn't know what I had, but the doctor diagnosed it for me immediately. PILAR: And what did she say you had? CARMEN: Well . . . that I have insomnia . . . and that my eyes are very irritated . . . But in any case I still have to finish the research for the project (that) they need at the office tomorrow.

Carlos **fue** estudiante.	*Carlos was a student* (at that time).
Carlos **era** estudiante.	*Carlos was* (*used to be*) *a student.*
Anita **estuvo** nerviosa.	*Anita was* (*became*) *nervous.*
Anita **estaba** nerviosa.	*Anita was* (*used to be*) *nervous.*

B. *A series of completed actions that take place in sequence* will be expressed in the PRETERITE (unless it refers to habitual actions).

Me **levanté**, me **vestí** y **desayuné**.	*I got up, got dressed, and ate breakfast.*

Actions or states *in progress* are expressed with the IMPERFECT. The IMPERFECT is also used to express most *descriptions*; *physical, mental, and emotional states*; *the time* (with **ser**); and *age* (with **tener**).

Escribía las cartas **mientras** Ana **leía**.	*I was writing letters while Ann was reading.*
Estaban cansados.	*They were tired.*
Eran las ocho.	*It was eight o'clock.*
Tenía ocho años.	*She was eight years old.*

C. Certain words and expressions are frequently associated with the preterite, others with the imperfect.

WORDS OFTEN ASSOCIATED WITH THE PRETERITE

ayer, anteayer, anoche	el año pasado, el lunes pasado,...
una vez, dos veces,...	de repente (*suddenly*)

WORDS OFTEN ASSOCIATED WITH THE IMPERFECT

en aquella época (*at that time*)
todos los días, todos los lunes,...
siempre, frecuentemente
de vez en cuando (*from time to time*)
mientras
de niño/a, de joven
was _____*-ing*, *were* _____*-ing* (in English)
used to, would (when *would* implies *used to* in English)

¡OJO!   The words do not automatically cue either tense, however. The most important consideration is the meaning that the speaker wishes to convey.

Ayer cenamos temprano.	*Yesterday we had dinner early.*
Ayer cenábamos cuando Juan llamó.	*Yesterday we were having dinner when Juan called.*
De niño jugaba al fútbol.	*He played football as a child.*
De niño empezó a jugar al fútbol.	*He began to play football as a child.*

[Práctica A–B]

D. Remember the special English equivalents of the preterite forms of **saber, conocer, poder,** and **querer: supe** (*I found out*), **conocí** (*I met*), **pude** (*I could and did*), **no pude** (*I couldn't and didn't*), **quise** (*I tried*), **no quise** (*I refused*).

[Práctica C]

E. The preterite and the imperfect frequently occur in the same sentence.

Miguel **estudiaba** cuando **sonó** el teléfono.	*Miguel was studying when the phone rang.*
Olivia **comió** tanto porque **tenía** mucha hambre.	*Olivia ate so much because she was very hungry.*

In the first sentence the imperfect tells what was happening when another action—conveyed by the preterite—broke the continuity of the ongoing activity. In the second sentence, the preterite reports the action that took place because of a condition, described by the imperfect, that was in progress or in existence at that time.

F. The preterite and imperfect are also used together in the presentation of an event. The preterite narrates the action while the imperfect sets the stage, describes the conditions that caused the action, or emphasizes the continuing nature of a particular action.

[Práctica D–G]

Práctica

A. Give the preterite or the imperfect of the verbs in parentheses, basing your decision on the clues in the sentences.

1. Cuando (*ser*) niños, Jorge y yo (*vivir*) en la Argentina. En aquella época (*ir*) al Mar del Plata para pasar la Navidad. Allí casi siempre (*quedarse*) en el Hotel Fénix.
2. (*Ser*) las once de la noche cuando de repente (*sonar*) el teléfono. (Yo: *dejar*) de leer y (*levantarse*) para contestarlo.
3. Antonio (*trabajar*) en aquella farmacia todos los lunes. ¿No lo (*ver*) tú allí alguna vez?
4. La tía Anita (*estar*) enferma la semana pasada, pero (*quedarse*) en casa y (*cuidarse*) y ahora se siente bastante (*a lot*) mejor.
5. ¡Qué mala suerte tengo! El año pasado (*perder*) mi cartera durante las vacaciones. (*Estar*) de muy mal humor durante todo el viaje.
6. El niño (*llorar*) bastante mientras la enfermera le (*hablar*). La madre del niño (*esperar*) pacientemente. Por fin (*venir*) la doctora. Le (*tomar*) la temperatura, le (*examinar*) la garganta y le (*dar*) a la madre una receta (*prescription*) para un antibiótico.

B.   Situaciones. With another student, ask and answer questions based on the cues. The questions ask for an explanation of an action. What tense should be used in them? The answers explain the reason for the actions. What tense do they require?

En un restaurante: El dueño habla con un camarero.

1. esos clientes, ¿por qué / irse / sin pedir nada ?
   porque / yo / no / atenderlos / como / deber
2. ¿por qué / no / traer / vasos ?
   porque / llevar / mucho / en / bandeja
3. ¿por qué / olvidarse / pedidos (*orders*) ?
   porque / no saber / bien / detalles / de / menú

En casa: Los padres de un niño le hablan sobre su comportamiento.

4. ¿por qué / dormirse / en clase / hoy ?
   porque / tener / mucho / sueño
5. ¿por qué / no / hacer / tarea (*homework*) / para hoy ?
   porque / estar / distraído / con / nuevo perrito
6. ¿por qué / reírse / tanto / que / maestra / mandarte / a / oficina / de / director ?
   porque / mi / amigos / hacer / cosas cómicas

C. **Los hijos de los Quintero.** ¿Cómo se dice en español?

1. When I met Mr. and Mrs. Quintero, I already knew their son.
2. He knew how to read when he was five.
3. And he could play the piano before starting (to go to) school (**la escuela**).
4. They tried to teach their daughter to play when she was five.
5. But she refused to practice ten hours a (**al**) day.
6. How did you find all of that (**todo eso**) out?

D. Explain the reasons for the use of the preterite or the imperfect for each verb in the following paragraph.

Cuando Carmen se levantó, hacía mucho frío en su apartamento. Cerró con cuidado todas las ventanas, pero todavía tenía frío. Parecía que la calefacción (*heat*) no funcionaba. Se preparó una taza de té, se puso otro suéter y llamó al dueño del edificio para decirle lo que pasaba. Éste le dijo que ya lo sabía y que un técnico iba a venir en seguida. Mientras Carmen lo esperaba, llamó a Pilar, que vivía en el apartamento vecino, para saber qué hacía para abrigarse (*keep warm*).

Which Spanish past tense should be used to express each verb in the following paragraph? Explain why in each case.

We were walking down Fifth Street when we caught sight of him. He looked very tired and his clothes were very dirty. He said he was hungry and he asked us for money. We gave him all the money that we had because he was an old friend.

E. Read the following paragraph at least once to familiarize yourself with the sequence of events in it. Then read it again, giving the proper form of the verbs in parentheses in the preterite or the imperfect, according to the needs of each sentence and the context of the paragraph as a whole.

Rubén (*estudiar*[1]) cuando Soledad (*entrar*[2]) en el cuarto. Le (*preguntar*[3]) a Rubén si (*querer*[4]) ir al cine con ella. Rubén le (*decir*[5]) que sí porque (*sentirse*[6]) un poco aburrido con sus estudios. Los dos (*salir*[7]) en seguida para el cine. (*Ver*[8]) una película cómica y (*reírse*[9]) mucho. Luego, como (*hacer*[10]) frío, (*entrar*[11]) en El Gato Negro y (*tomar*[12]) un chocolate. (*Ser*[13]) las dos de la mañana cuando por fin (*regresar*[14]) a casa. Soledad (*acostarse*[15]) inmediatamente porque (*estar*[16]) cansada, pero Rubén (*empezar*[17]) a estudiar otra vez.

Answer the following questions based on the paragraph about Rubén and Soledad. ¡OJO!   A question is not always answered in the same tense as that in which it is asked.

1.   ¿Qué hacía Rubén cuando Soledad entró?
2.   ¿Qué le preguntó Soledad a Rubén?
3.   ¿Por qué dijo Rubén que sí?
4.   ¿Les gustó la película? ¿Por qué?
5.   ¿Por qué tomaron un chocolate?
6.   ¿Regresaron a casa a las tres?
7.   ¿Qué hicieron cuando llegaron a casa?

F. Read the following paragraphs once for meaning. Then read them again, giving the proper form of the verbs in parentheses in the present, preterite, or imperfect.

Durante mi segundo año en la universidad, yo (*conocer*[1]) a Roberto en una clase. Pronto nos (*hacer*[2]) muy buenos amigos. Roberto (*ser*[3]) una persona muy generosa que (*organizar*[4]) una fiesta en su apartamento todos los viernes. Todos nuestros amigos (*venir*[5]). (*Haber*[6]) muchas bebidas y comida, y todo el mundo (*hablar*[7]) y (*bailar*[8]) hasta muy tarde.

Una noche algunos de los vecinos de Roberto (*llamar*[9]) a la policía y (*decir*[10]) que nosotros (*hacer*[11]) demasiado ruido. (*Venir*[12]) un policía al apartamento y le (*decir*[13]) a Roberto que la fiesta (*ser*[14]) demasiado ruidosa. Nosotros no (*querer*[15]) aguar (*to spoil*) la fiesta, pero ¿qué (*poder*[16]) hacer? Todos nos (*despedir*[17]) aunque (*ser*[18]) solamente las once de la noche.

Aquella noche Roberto (*aprender*[19]) algo importantísimo. Ahora cuando (*hacer*[20]) una fiesta, siempre (*invitar*[21]) a sus vecinos.

G.   **Caperucita Roja.** Retell this familiar story, based on the drawings and the cues that accompany each drawing. For the first four drawings, full sentences are given and you need only provide the correct verb forms. For the remaining drawings, you will need both to give the appropriate verb forms *and* add other elements to create complete sentences.

Be sure to scan the **Palabras útiles** before beginning the exercise. Also note the first words of the narrative. They are typically used to begin a tale in Spanish. Can you guess what they mean?

Palabras útiles: abalanzarse sobre (*to pounce on*), avisar (*to warn*), dispararle (*to shoot at someone/something*), esconderse (*to hide*), enterarse de (*to find out about*), huir (*to flee*), saltar (*to jump*)

Érase una vez una niña hermosa que (*llamarse*[1]) Caperucita Roja. Todos los animales del bosque (*ser*[2]) sus amigos y Caperucita Roja los (*querer*[3]) mucho.

Un día su mamá le (*decir*[4]): —Quiero que (*llevar*[5]) en seguida esta jarrita de miel a casa de tu abuelita. Ten cuidado con el lobo feroz.

En el bosque, el lobo (*salir*[6]) a hablar con la niña. Le (*preguntar*[7]): —¿Adónde vas, Caperucita? Ésta le (*contestar*[8]) dulcemente: —Voy a casa de mi abuelita.

—Pues, si vas por este sendero, vas a llegar antes. —(*decir*[9]) el malvado lobo, que (*irse*[10]) por otro camino más corto.

El lobo: (*llegar*[11]) primero a la casa de la abuelita / (*entrar*[12]) La abuelita: (*tener*[13]) mucho miedo / (*saltar*[14]) de la cama / (*correr*[15]) a esconderse

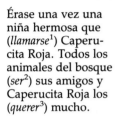     

Caperucita: (*llegar*[16]) por fin a la casa de la abuelita / (*encontrar*[17]) a su "abuelita" / (*decir*[18]) —¡Qué dientes tan largos tienes! —¡Son para comerte mejor!

Una ardilla del bosque: (*enterarse*[19]) del peligro que (*correr*[20]) Caperucita / (*avisar*[21]) a un cazador

El lobo: (*saltar*[22]) de la cama / (*abalanzarse*[23]) sobre Caperucita. Ella: (*salir*[24]) de la casa / (*empezar*[25]) / a correr (*pedir*[26]) socorro desesperadamente

El cazador: (*ver*[27]) lo que (*ocurrir*[28]) / (*dispararle*[29]) al lobo / (*hacerle*[30]) huir

Caperucita: (*regresar*[31]) a casa de su abuelita (*abrazarla*[32]) / (*prometerle*[33]) escuchar siempre los consejos de su mamá

Hay varias versiones del cuento de Caperucita Roja. La que Ud. acaba de leer termina felizmente, pero otras no. Con otros dos compañeros, vuelva a contar la historia. Empiece por el dibujo número 7. Invente un diálogo más largo entre Caperucita y el lobo y cambie por completo el final del cuento.

Más palabras útiles: comérselo/la (*to eat something up*), atacar, matar (*to kill*)

VOCABULARIO

En el consultorio° del médico   *office*

el/la enfermero/a	nurse
el/la paciente	patient
congestionado/a	congested, stuffed-up
mareado/a	dizzy, nauseated
el antibiótico	antibiotic
el jarabe	(cough) syrup
la pastilla	pill
la receta	prescription
el resfriado	cold (*illness*)
la tos	cough
doler (ue)	to hurt, ache
Me duelen los pies.	My feet hurt.
enfermarse	to get sick
guardar cama	to stay in bed
ponerle una inyección	to give (*someone*) a shot
resfriarse*	to get/catch a cold
respirar	to breathe
sacar (la lengua)	to stick out (one's tongue)
tener dolor (de)	to have a pain (in)

tener fiebre	to have a fever
tomarle la temperatura	to take (*someone's*) temperature
toser	to cough

Visadron®
Combate
el enrojecimiento y la
irritación ocular.

*Usar los medicamentos
adecuadamente y siguiendo
sus instrucciones.*

Visadron
846998-E.F.P.

16 ml Colirio

Boehringer
Ingelheim

TETANOS

Es una infección muy peligrosa que actúa sobre el sistema nervioso de forma generalizada y aguda a través de una toxina.

El tétanos sólo se reconoce cuando se manifiestan los síntomas externos. No hay ninguna otra alteración detectable mediante radiografía o análisis de sangre –a excepción de un ligero aumento de los leucocitos– que permita tomar medidas precoces.

F. Navarro

A.   Estudio de palabras. Complete las siguientes oraciones con una palabra de la misma familia de la palabra en *letras cursivas*.

1.   Si me *resfrío*, tengo _____.
2.   La *respiración* ocurre cuando alguien _____.
3.   Si me _____, estoy *enfermo/a*; un(a) _____ me toma la temperatura.
4.   Cuando alguien *tose*, se oye una _____.
5.   Si me *duele* el estómago, tengo un _____ de estómago.

*Note the accentuation patterns in the forms of **resfriarse: me resfrío, te resfrías, se resfría, nos resfriamos, os resfriáis, se resfrían.**

B.   Asociaciones. ¿Qué partes del cuerpo asocia Ud. con las siguientes palabras?

1. un ataque   3. comer   5. congestionado   7. mareado
2. la digestión   4. respirar   6. ver

C.   Describa Ud. la situación de estas personas. ¿Dónde están y con quiénes? ¿Qué síntomas tienen? ¿Qué les recomienda Ud.?

1. Anamari está muy bien de salud. Nunca le duele(n) _____.
    Nunca tiene _____. Siempre _____. Es bueno que _____.
2. Martín tiene un resfriado. Le duele(n) _____. Tiene _____.
    El médico le dice que _____. Le va a _____.
    Es mejor que _____.
3. Inés tiene apendicitis. Le duele(n) _____.
    Tiene _____. El médico y la enfermera
    mandan que _____. Es necesario que _____.

2.

1.

3.

D.   Ud. no se siente bien y va al consultorio del médico. Complete el diálogo entre Ud. y el médico.

PACIENTE: Buenas tardes, doctor.

DOCTOR: Buenas tardes. ¿Qué le pasa? ¿Qué tiene?

PACIENTE: Es que me _____ muy mal. Me _____ le cabeza y tengo una _____ muy alta.

DOCTOR: Entonces, ¿tiene un resfriado?

PACIENTE: Bueno, Ud. es el médico.

DOCTOR: ¿Se tomó la temperatura antes de venir?

PACIENTE: No, pero la _____ me la tomó y tenía 38,5.

DOCTOR: ¿Tiene dolor de estómago? ¿Se siente _____?

PACIENTE: No, pero respiro con dificultad; estoy muy _____. Toso tanto que me duelen también los _____. Es que me duele el _____ entero.

DOCTOR: Vamos a ver. Abra Ud. la _____, por favor, y _____ la lengua. Hmm… tiene la _____ bastante inflamada. Ahora la respiración… _____ Ud. profundamente… Me parece que está bien. ¿Tiene alergia a los antibióticos?

PACIENTE: No, no creo.

DOCTOR: Bueno, aquí tiene Ud. una _____. Vaya a la farmacia y compre este _____ para la tos. Tómeselo cuatro veces al día. Para la fiebre, tome un par de _____ cada cuatro horas y este _____ para combatir la infección. Si todavía se siente mal la semana que viene, venga a verme otra vez. Y cuídese, ¿eh?

PACIENTE: Muchas gracias, doctor. Adiós.

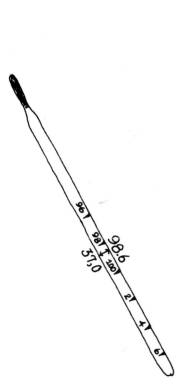

Notas comunicativas: The Good News . . . The Bad News . . .

Use **lo** with the masculine singular form of an adjective to describe general qualities or characteristics.

>   lo bueno / lo malo   lo más importante   lo mejor / lo peor   lo mismo

This structure has a number of English equivalents, especially in colloquial speech.

>   **lo bueno** = the good thing/part/news, what's good

E.   A nadie le gusta estar enfermo, pero también es cierto que, cuando no se trata de (*it's not a question of*) algo grave, el estar enfermo puede tener ventajas. Con un compañero (una compañera), conteste las siguientes preguntas. Luego compare sus respuestas con las de otros compañeros. ¿Quién pudo reunir el mayor número de ventajas y desventajas?

No le trate como a un perro.

Es de la familia

Mundocan

El cuidado más humanizado
para su perro

1.   En su opinión, ¿qué es lo bueno de tener un resfriado muy grave? ¿Y lo malo?
2.   Para un niño, ¿qué es lo bueno de tener fiebre y dolor de estómago? ¿Y lo malo?
3.   Para un niño, ¿qué es lo malo de tener amigdalitis (*tonsilitis*)? ¿Y lo bueno?
4.   ¿Qué es lo bueno de estar en el consultorio del médico / del dentista? ¿Y lo malo?

Notas culturales: La medicina en los países hispánicos

Como regla general los hispanos tienen como costumbre consultar no sólo a los médicos sino a otros profesionales con sus problemas de salud. Por ejemplo, ya que (*since*) muchas drogas se venden sin receta en los países hispánicos, es posible que una persona enferma le explique sus síntomas a un farmacéutico, que le pueda recomendar una medicina. Aun le puede recomendar y poner inyecciones al paciente. Los farmacéuticos reciben un entrenamiento riguroso y están al tanto en farmacología. También se puede consultar a un practicante. Éstos tienen tres años de entrenamiento médico y pueden aplicar una serie de tratamientos, incluso inyecciones.

   Otra característica del sistema médico hispánico es que es fácil y barato conseguir los servicios de una enfermera particular (*private*) que cuide a un enfermo, ya sea en la casa o en el hospital. Las enfermeras no tienen que tener tantos conocimientos teóricos como las de los Estados Unidos, pero tienen mucha experiencia en su campo.

Al tanto...

Here are some more useful terms for talking about health-related problems and situations.

- picar *to itch; to hurt* (colloquial)
  Me pica la espalda (*back*).
  Me pica la garganta.
- empastar una muela *to fill a tooth*
  el empaste *filling*
- el SIDA *AIDS*

Finally, can you guess what the colloquial term **matasanos** refers to? (Hint: **matar** = *to kill*)

FARMACIAS 4° turno
Abiertas de Sábado a Viernes de 8 a 22 hs.

CENTRO

ORIENTE

CAMBIO DE FIRMA
DESCUENTOS ESPECIALES
EN TODAS SUS COMPRAS

SAN JOSE 1350 esq. EJIDO

ENVIOS A DOMICILIO
SIN COSTO
TEL. 911165 y 911170

MASSONE

GABRIEL PEREIRA 3148 y 26 de MARZO
Teléfono de pedidos: 78.18.73

SERVICIO NOCTURNO DE 22 A 8
Para ser atendido toque timbre

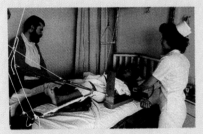

Bogotá, Colombia

En la sala de urgencia (de emergencias)
—¿Qué le ocurre?
—Me caí por la escalera (*staircase*) y ahora me duele mucho el tobillo (*ankle*).
—A ver… Lo tiene bastante inflamado… pero no parece que haya fractura.
—Lo peor es que no lo puedo mover.
—Bueno, lo voy a mandar a radiología para que le saquen una radiografía.

UN POCO DE TODO

A. Form complete sentences based on the words given in the order given. Conjugate the verbs in the preterite or the imperfect and add other words if necessary. Use subject pronouns only when needed.

1. cuando / yo / ser / niño / pensar / que / mejor / de / estar enfermo / ser / guardar cama
2. peor / ser / que / con frecuencia / yo / resfriarse / durante / vacaciones
3. una vez / yo / ponerme / muy / enfermo / durante / Navidad / y / mi / madre / llamar / a / médico / con / quien / tener / confianza
4. Dr. Matamoros / venir / casa / y / darme / antibiótico / porque / tener / mucho / fiebre
5. ser / cuatro / mañana / cuando / por fin / yo / empezar / respirar / sin dificultad
6. desgraciadamente / día / de / Navidad / yo / tener / tomar / jarabe / y / no / gustar / nada / sabor (*taste*)
7. bueno / de / este / enfermedad / ser / que / mi / padre / tener / dejar / fumar / mientras / yo / estar / enfermo

Ahora vuelva a contar la historia desde el punto de vista de la madre del niño.

B.   Entrevista. Use the following questions to interview another student about his or her childhood and about specific events in the past, as well as what is currently happening in his or her life. Report the most interesting information to the class.

1. ¿A qué escuela asistías (cuando tenías _____ años)? ¿Asististe a esta universidad el año pasado? ¿Hace cuánto tiempo que empezaste a estudiar aquí?
2. ¿Qué lenguas estudiabas? ¿Estudiaste latín en la secundaria? ¿Hace cuando (*How long ago?*) empezaste a estudiar español?
3. ¿Qué hacías cuando te enfermabas? ¿Cuántas veces te resfriaste el año pasado? ¿Es necesario que empieces ahora a llevar una vida más sana?
4. ¿Qué películas te gustaban más? ¿Te gustó la última película que viste? ¿Qué nueva película quieres ver este mes?
5. En la secundaria, ¿qué era lo más importante de tu vida? ¿Qué cosa importante te pasó el año pasado? ¿Qué esperas que pase este año?
6. ¿Qué hacías durante los veranos? ¿Qué hiciste el verano pasado? ¿Qué vas a hacer este verano?

UN PASO MÁS: Lectura cultural

¿Está Ud. resfriado/a?

No hay nada más común que el resfriado común… y nada más raro que un remedio seguro. Ya que, tarde o temprano, todos sufrimos los efectos de un resfriado, el folklore de todos los países del mundo ofrece varios remedios. Aquí se dan algunos remedios que se usan en el mundo hispano. ¿Cómo se comparan con los de su familia?

- Para los resfríos es bueno tomar antes de acostarse leche bien caliente con miel y alguna bebida fuerte.° Se abriga uno bien y se pone dos o tres frazadas° para transpirar° durante la noche.

  de la Argentina

  bebida… alcohol (in some form)
  blankets / sweat

- Para «sudar la calentura»° de una gripe, se usa una mezcla caliente de jugo de limón (con todo el bagazo°), canela,° miel y un poco de licor, con dos aspirinas, antes de acostarse.

  de El Salvador

  fiebre
  pulp / cinnamon

- Un remedio que se acostumbraba usar era el de la cáscara de naranja para bajar la fiebre. Se pone una porción de la cáscara en agua y se deja hervir.° Una vez hervida el agua, se separa la cáscara y se toma el agua más o menos caliente.

  de Panamá

  to boil

- Para los catarros:° leche caliente con miel. También puede tomarse café con leche, y es muy popular añadirle un poquito de coñac. Esto y una aspirina ayudan a sudar bastante, lo cual es muy recomendable cuando se tiene fiebre.

  de España

  resfriados

- Para curar el resfriado es bueno tomar una limonada caliente con bastante limón, con un poquito de tequila y unas dos aspirinas antes de acostarse.

  de México

Comprensión

¿Cierto o falso? Corrija las oraciones falsas.

1. En general los resfriados no se tratan con ningún tipo de medicina en el mundo hispánico.
2. Se recomienda con frecuencia tomar una bebida con un poco de alcohol como medicina (no para emborracharse).
3. Parece que los hispanos aguantan (*endure*) los resfriados sin acostarse.
4. Es frecuente el uso de las frutas tropicales como la papaya y la piña para curar un resfriado.

Study Hint: Writing

You can develop a more mature writing style in Spanish by using transition words to link shorter sentences. Follow these suggestions.

1. Write a first draft of your composition, trying to express your ideas in short, simple sentences. Be sure that each sentence contains at least a subject and a verb.
2. Determine which sentences have a logical relationship and can be linked together. Choose transition words that show these relationships.
3. Rewrite the composition, adding the transition words and making changes, if necessary. For example, if you link the following sentences together with **cuando**, the word **ella** will not be necessary.

> MODELO: Vimos a Jacinta. Ella estaba en la cafetería. →
>   Cuando vimos a Jacinta, estaba en la cafetería.
>
> Remember to use words with which you are familiar because you have used them before, and
> avoid using the dictionary too much (**Study Hint, Capítulo 7**).
>
> ## Transition Words
>
> | | | | |
> |---|---|---|---|
> | **además** | besides | **pero** | but |
> | **así** | thus, so | **por ejemplo** | for example |
> | **cuando** | when | **por eso** | therefore, for that reason |
> | **de vez en cuando** | from time to time | **por fin** | at last, finally |
> | **en cambio** | on the other hand | **pues** | well; since |
> | **es decir** | that is | **sin embargo** | nevertheless |
> | **luego** | then, next | **también** | also |
> | **mientras** | while | | |

LOS PROBLEMAS OCULARES NO SIEM-
PRE SE MANIFIESTAN EN UNA MALA VISION.
POR ELLO, Y POR MUCHAS OTRAS RAZO-
NES, DEBEMOS CONSULTAR CON EL MEDICO
OFTALMOLOGO AL MENOS UNA VEZ AL AÑO.

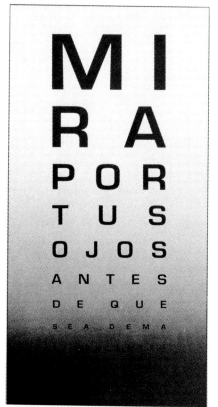

Desgraciadamente algunas enfermedades no dan síntomas
hasta fases muy tardías. Conozcamos cómo atajarlas.

Para escribir

Answer the following questions about your last visit to the doctor, adding as many details as possible. Then, using the words in
Study Hint: Writing and any others you know, join the sentences
together to form three paragraphs that flow smoothly.

Párrafo A

1.   ¿Cuándo fue la última vez que Ud. consultó con un médico?
2.   ¿Por qué lo hizo? ¿Cuáles eran sus síntomas?

Párrafo B

1.   En el consultorio, ¿tuvo Ud. que esperar mucho tiempo?
     ¿Esperaban también otros pacientes?
2.   Cuando por fin entró en el consultorio, ¿cuánto tiempo duró
     la consulta? ¿Qué actitud mostró el médico? ¿compasión?
     ¿humor? ¿preocupación? ¿indiferencia?
3.   ¿Le recetó alguna medicina? ¿Qué otras recomendaciones le
     dio? ¿Las siguió Ud.? ¿Por qué sí o por qué no?

Párrafo C

1.   ¿Cuándo se mejoró Ud. por fin?
2.   ¿Qué hace ahora para mantenerse en buen estado de salud?

VOCABULARIO

La salud y el bienestar

caminar to walk
comer equilibradamente to eat a well-balanced diet
cuidarse to take care of oneself
dejar de + *inf.* to stop (*doing something*)
doler (ue) to hurt, ache
enfermarse to get sick
examinar to examine
guardar cama to stay in bed
hacer ejercicio to exercise, get exercise
hacer ejercicios aeróbicos to do aerobic exercises
llevar una vida... to lead a . . . life
ponerle una inyección to give (*someone*) a shot, injection
practicar deportes to play sports
resfriarse to get/catch a cold
respirar to breathe
sacar to stick out (*one's tongue*)
tener dolor (de) to have a pain (in)
toser to cough

Algunas partes del cuerpo

la boca mouth
la cabeza head
el corazón heart
el estómago stomach
la garganta throat
la lengua tongue
la nariz nose
los ojos eyes
los pulmones lungs

Las enfermedades y los tratamientos

el antibiótico antibiotic
el consultorio (medical) office
la farmacia pharmacy, drugstore
la fiebre fever
las gafas (eye)glasses
el jarabe (cough) syrup
los lentes (de contacto) contact lenses
la medicina medicine
el/la médico/a doctor, physician
el/la paciente patient
la pastilla pill
la receta prescription
el resfriado cold (*illness*)
la sala de emergencias (de urgencia) emergency room
el síntoma symptom
la temperatura temperature
la tos cough

Otros sustantivos

la escuela school
la tarea homework

Adjetivos

congestionado/a congested
mareado/a nauseated
sano/a healthy

Palabras adicionales

bastante rather, quite; a lot
de joven as a youth
de niño/a as a child
de repente suddenly
de vez en cuando from time to time
en aquella época at that time
en forma in good shape

Frases útiles para la comunicación

lo + *adjective* (*masc. sing.*)   the . . . thing/part/news
  lo bueno/lo malo   the good news/the bad news
  lo suficiente   enough

LOS HISPANOS EN LOS ESTADOS UNIDOS
La comunidad puertorriqueña

«American Feast», pintado por Ibsen Espada

Como los mexicanoamericanos, los puertorriqueños no son extranjeros. La isla de Puerto Rico es un Estado Libre Asociado de los Estados Unidos, y las personas que allí nacen son ciudadanos (*citizens*) norteamericanos.

Las grandes concentraciones de puertorriqueños se encuentran en Nueva York, Nueva Jersey y Pensilvania. Hay mucho movimiento entre las ciudades del noreste de los Estados Unidos y la Isla (como los puertorriqueños llaman a Puerto Rico), ya que muchas personas tienen amigos y familiares en las dos partes.

La mayoría de los puertorriqueños que se han establecido (*have settled*) en el continente vinieron en busca de mejores condiciones económicas y educativas para ellos y sus hijos. Mientras muchos quieren que Puerto Rico se incorpore a los Estados Unidos, para ser el estado número cincuenta y uno, otros prefieren que se independice. Otros desean que se mantenga el *status quo*.

Cuando a sus playas llegó Colón,
exclamó, lleno de admiración,
¡Oh! ¡Oh! ¡Oh!
Ésta es la linda tierra
que busco yo,
es Borinquen,° la hija
del mar y el sol.

nombre indio de la isla de Puerto Rico

de «La borinqueña», himno nacional de Puerto Rico

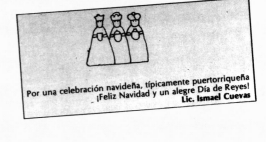

Por una celebración navideña, típicamente puertorriqueña
¡Feliz Navidad y un alegre Día de Reyes!
Lic. Ismael Cuevas

Una playa de Puerto Rico

Hermoso° *bouquet*,   Bonito
Aquí te traemos
Bellísimas flores
Del jardín riqueño.
De todas las flores
Yo te traigo un ramo.°   *bouquet*
Recíbelas bien
Que éste es mi aguinaldo.°   *Christmas gift*

de «El aguinaldo de las flores», canción de la tradición popular

282

El Festival de Música Casals

- Se celebra anualmente en San Juan
- Atrae a los mejores músicos del mundo
- Fundada por Pablo Casals (el famoso violoncelista que murió en 1973) y su esposa Marta Istomín (directora artística del *John F. Kennedy Center for the Performing Arts* hasta 1990)

El Maestro Rafael Frübeck de Burgos y la Orquesta Sinfónica de Puerto Rico, en el Festival Casals, 1986

Willie Colón

We drank hot cocoa and talked about summertime. Momma talked about Puerto Rico and how great it was, and how she'd like to go back one day, and how it was warm all the time there and no matter how poor you were over there, you could always live on green bananas, *bacalao*, and rice and beans. "*Dios mío*," she said, "I don't think I'll ever see my island again."

"Sure you will, Mommie," said Miriam, my kid sister. She was eleven. "Tell us, tell us all about Porto Rico."

"It's not Porto Rico, its Puerto Rico," said Momma.

"Tell us, Moms," said nine-year-old James, "about Puerto Rico. . ."

Moms copped that wet-eyed look and began to dream-talk about her *isla verde*, Moses' land of milk and honey.

"When I was a little girl," she said, "I remember getting up in the morning and getting the water from the river and getting the wood for the fire and the quiet of the greenlands, and the golden color of the morning sky, the grass wet from the *lluvia* . . . *ai, Dios*, the *coquís* and the *pajaritos* making all the *música*. . ."

Piri Thomas, autor puertorriqueño, *Down These Mean Streets*

Nueva York

Puerto Rico

ROGELIO NARANJO/*Actualidad, Mexico*

puerto rico 1974
this is not the place where i was born
remember—as a child the fantasizing images my mother planted
within my head—
the shadows of her childhood recounted to me many times
over welfare loan on *crédito* food from *el bodeguero*
i tasted *mango* many years before the skin of the fruit
ever reached my teeth . . .

i was born on an island where to be puerto rican meant to be
part of the land & soul & *puertorriqueños* were not the
minority
puerto ricans were first, none were second
no, i was not born here . . .
no, i was not born in the attitude & time of this place

Miguel Piñero, poeta puertorriqueño, «this is not the place
where i was born», de *La Bodega Sold Dreams*

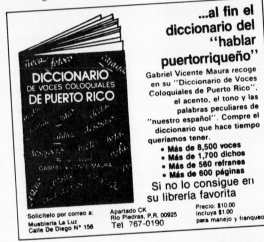

...al fin el diccionario del "hablar puertorriqueño"

Gabriel Vicente Maura recoge en su "Diccionario de Voces Coloquiales de Puerto Rico", el acento, el tono y las palabras peculiares de "nuestro español". Compre el diccionario que hace tiempo queríamos tener.

• Más de 8,500 voces
• Más de 1,700 dichos
• Más de 560 refranes
• Más de 600 páginas

Si no lo consigue en su librería favorita

Solicítelo por correo a:
Mueblería La Luz
Calle De Diego N° 156

Apartado CK
Río Piedras, P.R. 00925
Tel 767-0190

Precio: $10.00
Incluya $1.00
para manejo y franqueo

Carta a Los Hispanos
a mis alumnos

Quiero escribir un poema tipo colectivo
donde cada latino meta° mano   ponga
y recite sobre el papel veinticinco tristezas°   sorrows
o unos cuantos sueños ya olvidados.

Quiero redactar° un verso tipo cesta° abierta   escribir / basket
donde cada cual deposite lo que trajo
y se deshaga° con ello de limosnas cotidianas,   se... get rid of
welfare cards, los food-stamps, la yerba° y to's° los hang-ups. marihuana / todos

Quiero unos versos escritos por manos negras,
manos callosas y llenas de trabajo.
ni la tinta° ni el papel ya nos importan   ink
sino el relief de dejarlo todo a un lado.

Ay, quiero escribir un poema tipo colectivo.
Se solicitan escribientes,
Favor de contestarme para atrás,° HERMANO.   para... back

Luz María Umpierre, poeta puertorriqueña y
profesora de español, Western Kentucky University

Puertorriqueños en un
desfile en Nueva York

CAPÍTULO 17

¡HUY, PERDÓN!

VOCABULARIO: ME LEVANTÉ CON EL PIE IZQUIERDO° con... on the wrong side of the bed

¡Pobre Sr. Martínez!

la cabeza

el brazo

la mano

la pierna

el pie

Le duele la cabeza.

Se da con la puerta.

Se equivoca.

DAMAS

Se cae por la escalera.   Se hace daño en el pie.

Sufre muchas presiones.

Discúlpeme. Pardon me.
Fue sin querer. It was unintentional; I (he, we
. . .) didn't mean to do it.
¡Qué mala suerte! What bad luck!

acordarse (ue) (de) to remember
apagar to turn off (*lights or an appliance*)
caerse (me caigo) to fall down
equivocarse to make a mistake
morir(se) (ue, u) to die
pegar to hit, strike
romper to break

la aspirina aspirin
la llave key

distraído/a absent-minded
torpe clumsy

A. Indique una respuesta para cada pregunta o situación. Luego invente un contexto para cada diálogo. ¿Dónde están las personas que hablan? ¿en casa de un amigo? ¿en una oficina? ¿Qué van a decir después?

A

1. ¡Ay, sufro muchas presiones en el trabajo! H
2. Anoche no me acordé de poner el despertador.
3. ¡Ay! ¡Me pegaste! D
4. Nunca miro por donde camino (*I'm going*). Esta mañana me caí otra vez. E
5. Lo siento, señores, pero ésta no es la casa de Lola Pérez. B
6. No cambié de lugar el coche y el policía me puso una multa (*fine*). G
7. Anoche en casa de unos amigos rompí su lámpara favorita. A
8. ¿Sabes? Ayer se murió nuestro perro. F

B

a. ¿Vas a comprarles otra?
b. Perdón, señora. Nos equivocamos de casa.
c. ¿Otra vez? ¡Qué distraído eres! ¿Te hiciste daño?
d. Huy, perdón. Fue sin querer.
e. ¿Te olvidaste otra vez? ¿A qué hora llegaste a la oficina?
f. ¡Qué triste! Lo siento.
g. ¡Qué mala suerte! ¿Cuánto tienes que pagar?
h. ¿Sí? ¿Por qué no te tomas unos días de vacaciones?

B. **Asociaciones.** ¿Qué verbos asocia Ud. con estas palabras?

| la llave | la mano | la aspirina | la luz | el despertador |
| la pierna | el brazo | la cabeza | los pies | la presión |

Verbos útiles: despedirse, doler, apagar, caminar, levantar, correr, preguntar, pegar, escribir, pensar, tomar, caerse, hacerse daño, poner, darse con, perder

C. ¿Qué puede Ud. hacer o decir—o qué le puede pasar—en cada situación?

1. A Ud. le duele mucho la cabeza.
2. Ud. le pega a otra persona sin querer.
3. Ud. se olvida del nombre de otra persona.
4. Ud. está muy distraído/a y no mira por donde camina.
5. Ud. se hace daño en la mano/el pie.

D. ¿Se refieren a Ud. estas oraciones? Conteste con «**Sí, así soy**» o «**No, no soy así**».

1. Se me caen (*I drop*) las cosas de las manos con facilidad en el trabajo y en casa.
2. Con frecuencia no me acuerdo de hacer la tarea para la clase de español.
3. Cuando oigo el despertador, lo apago y me duermo otra vez.
4. Rompo los platos y los vasos cuando los lavo.
5. Se me pierden (*I misplace*) ciertos objetos, como las llaves, los cuadernos, la cartera…
6. Con frecuencia me doy con los muebles.
7. Algunas veces me hago daño en las manos mientras preparo la cena.
8. En las fiestas, me olvido de los nombres de las personas que acabo de conocer.

Study Hint: False Cognates

Not all Spanish and English cognates are identical in meaning. Here are a few important "traps" to be aware of: **sano** is *healthy*; **renta**, *income*; **pariente**, *relative*; **gracioso**, *funny*; **actual**, *current, up to date*; **fábrica**, *factory*; **colegio**, *elementary or secondary school*; **una molestia**, *a bother*; **sopa**, *soup*; **ropa**, *clothing*; **real**, *real or royal*; **sensible**, *sensitive*; **éxito**, *success*—and **constipado** means *suffering from a head cold*. These words are *false*, or misleading, *cognates* (**amigos falsos**).

Occasionally such words can lead to communication problems. The American tourist who, feeling embarrassed, describes himself or herself as **embarazado/a** may find people chuckling at the remark, since **embarazada** means not *embarrassed* but *pregnant*.

Al tanto...

Here are some additional expressions to use when talking about occasions on which things don't go quite right for you or someone else.

sale... *turns out right*

meter la pata	to make a bad mistake; to stick one's foot (*lit.* paw) in it
ponerse colorado/a	to blush, turn red
¿Dónde llevas la cabeza?	*Where's your head?*
¿En qué estarías pensando?	*What could you have been thinking about?*

estar en las nubes; ser despistado/a = estar/ir distraído/a

—¡Ay, chica! ¡No sabes cómo metí la pata con Francisco! Me puse colorada y todo...
—Pero ¿qué le dijiste?
—Pues, que _____.
—Pero... ¿dónde llevas la cabeza?
—Es que estaba en las nubes, como siempre. Ya sabes, soy muy despistada.

Discúlpeme, por favor
—Perdone, fue sin querer.
—No se preocupe.°
—De verdad, no lo vi. Déjeme ayudarlo.
—No, si no es nada ... Estoy bien.

No... *Don't worry.*

México, D.F. (Distrito Federal)

ESTRUCTURAS

34. ¿QUÉ ESTÁS HACIENDO?
Progressive Forms: *estar* + *-ndo*

The sentences in the left-hand column tell what the following persons are able to do or want to do. Following the example, tell what they *are doing* right now (**ahora mismo, en este momento**).

Dolores baila muy bien. → Dolores **está bailando** ahora mismo.

Soledad canta muy bien. → Soledad **está** _cantando_

Yo hablo español. → Yo _estoy hablando_

Santiago quiere comer algo. → Santiago **está comiendo** algo en este momento.

Nati quiere beber algo. → Nati _está_ bebiendo

Queremos escribir una carta. → (Nosotros) _estamos_ _escribiendo_

Now tell what *was happening* when Mr. Martínez arrived home.

MODELO: Cuando el señor Martínez llegó a casa, el bebé ... (llorar) →
el bebé **estaba llorando.**

(gritar) → la hija mayor _estaba gritando_
(ladrar) → el perro _estaba ladrando_
(correr) → el gato _estaba corriendo_

¡Y su esposa estaba desesperada!

Uses of the Progressive

As you saw in the two pairs of drawings that opened Grammar Section 34, you need to use special verb forms in Spanish to describe an *action in progress*—that is, something actually happening at the time it is being described. These Spanish forms, called **el progresivo**, correspond to the English *progressive: I am walking, we are driving, she is studying*. But their use is not identical. Compare the Spanish and English verb forms in the following sentences.

Estoy apagando las luces en este momento.	*I'm turning off the lights right now.*
Compramos la casa mañana.	*We're buying the house tomorrow.*
Adelaida **estudia** química este semestre.	*Adelaida is studying chemistry this semester.*

In Spanish, the progressive is used primarily to describe an action that is actually *in progress*, as in the first example. The simple Spanish indicative is used to express other English usages of the progressive: to tell what is going to happen (the second sentence), and to tell what someone is doing over a period of time but not necessarily at this very moment (the third sentence).

Formation of the Present Progressive

The Spanish present progressive is formed with **estar** plus the present participle (**el gerundio**), which is formed by adding **-ando** to the stem of **-ar** verbs and **-iendo** to the stem of **-er** and **-ir** verbs.* The present participle never varies; it always ends in **-o.**

pegar	→ **pegando**	*hitting, striking*
toser	→ **tosiendo**	*coughing*
salir	→ **saliendo**	*leaving*

Spelling hint: Unaccented **i** represents the sound [y] in the participle ending **-iendo**: **comiendo, viviendo.** Unaccented **i** between two vowels becomes **y**: **leyendo, oyendo.**

The stem vowel in the present participle of **-ir** stem-changing verbs also shows a change. This change is the second of those shown in parentheses for stem-changing verbs.†

preferir (ie, i)	→ **prefiriendo**	*preferring*
pedir (i, i)	→ **pidiendo**	*asking*
dormir (ue, u)	→ **durmiendo**	*sleeping*

[Práctica A]

---

*Ir, poder,** and **venir** have irregular present participles: **yendo, pudiendo, viniendo.** These three verbs, however, as well as **saber,** are seldom used in the progressive.
†This change is identical to the change you have already learned to use in the **nosotros** and **vosotros** forms of the present subjunctive, and in the third person singular and plural forms of the preterite.

Formation and Uses of the Past Progressive

As you saw in the drawings about Sr. Martínez at the beginning of Grammar Section 34, the progressive can also be formed in the past, with the imperfect of **estar**, to tell what was happening at a particular moment.*

> **Estábamos cenando** cuando llamaste.
> *We were having dinner when you called.*
>
> Yo **estaba corriendo** en el parque cuando me caí.
> *I was running in the park when I fell.*

The simple imperfect—**cenábamos, corría**—can also be used in the preceding sentences to express the ongoing actions. The use of the progressive emphasizes that the action was actually in progress.

[Práctica B]

Position of Pronouns

Direct object, indirect object, and reflexive pronouns can be attached to the end of the present participle, in which case a written accent must be added to maintain the proper stress. Of course, the pronouns can also precede the conjugated form of **estar**, as in the second example in each pair.

> ¿Tu blusa? Estoy planchándo**la** ahora.
> **La** estoy planchando ahora.
> *Your blouse? I'm ironing it now.*
>
> Estaban diciéndo**te** la verdad.
> **Te** estaban diciendo la verdad.
> *They were telling you the truth.*
>
> Su niño está portándo**se** muy bien.
> Su niño **se** está portando muy bien.
> *Your child is behaving very well.*

[Práctica C]

Práctica

A.   El sábado por la tarde. Haga oraciones según las indicaciones. Todos sus amigos están en el parque. Ud. quiere ir también. ¿Por qué?

todos		comer... , beber...
mi amigo/a (nombre)		hablar (mucho, acerca de...)
mucha gente	estar	preparar... , servir...
los demás		jugar al (tenis, vólibol, ...)
		celebrar...
		dormir (en... , debajo de...)

---

*A progressive tense can also be formed with the preterite of **estar**: *Estuvieron* **cenando hasta las doce.** The use of the progressive with the preterite of **estar**, however, is relatively infrequent and will not be practiced in *¿Qué tal?*

Pero Ud. no puede ir. ¿Por qué no?

yo	estar	trabajar (en...)	escribir...
		estudiar (para...)	leer (la lección para...)

B. ¡Qué suerte más buena! Imagine que Ud. tuvo la suerte de conocer a las siguientes personas famosas. Explique lo que cada una estaba haciendo cuando Ud. la conoció.

Julia Child
Clint Eastwood
los empleados de McDonald's
J.R. Ewing
Stephen King
el presidente
la esposa del presidente
David Letterman
el pobre Sr. Martínez
Rubén Blades

(i) sirviendo
servir hamburguesas
caerse en/por... cayendose
cantar una canción (en...) cantando
hablar (por teléfono) con... hablando
beber en un bar bebiendo → murderer
buscar a un asesino
conspirar con... conspirando
preparar una cena muy preparando
 elegante
¿ ?

C. Otro día desastroso. ¿Qué le pasa en este momento al pobre Sr. Martínez? Complete las oraciones con la forma correcta del progresivo del verbo entre paréntesis. ¡OJO! Hay pronombres con unos verbos.

1. El Sr. Martínez acaba de perder sus llaves. Por eso su hijo (*buscarlas*).
2. Martínez prefiere desayunar fuera, pero esta mañana (*desayunar en casa*).
3. Generalmente pide huevos fritos, pero hoy su esposa (*servirle cereal frío*).
4. El bebé ya no (*dormir / llorar muy fuerte* [loudly]).
5. A veces al pobre papá le duele mucho la cabeza. En este momento (*dolerle muchísimo*).
6. Por fin el hijo encuentra las llaves. Por fin Martínez (*despedirse de su familia*).
7. Generalmente va en coche a trabajar, pero hoy el coche no (*funcionar*).
8. Por eso tiene que tomar el coche de su mujer. Ahora mismo (*sacarlo del garaje*).
9. Cuando está distraído, se da con las cosas. ¡Mire! En este momento (*darse con un árbol*).
10. El pobre Sr. Martínez sufre muchas presiones en la vida. Es obvio que (*sufrirlas esta mañana*).

SEGURO ESPECIAL
ACCIDENTES

Puede ocurrirle esto...

O no ocurrirle nada...

...y suerte que está Asegurado

Porque si no lo estuviera, la solución sería más difícil y gravosa para su economía.

Con este Seguro Especial Accidentes la energía que gasta en preocuparse por lo que pueda pasar, la puede emplear en ocuparse de lo que está pasando.
Compruebe la diferencia y su tranquilidad se lo agradecerá. Téngalo por seguro.

Por lo que pueda pasar

V O C A B U L A R I O

Talking About How Things Are Done: Adverbs

You already know some of the most common Spanish *adverbs* (**los adverbios**): **bien, mal, mejor, peor, mucho, poco, más, menos, muy, pronto, a tiempo, tarde, temprano, siempre, nunca, sólo.** The form of adverbs is invariable.

Adverbs that end in *-ly* in English usually end in **-mente** in Spanish. The suffix **-mente** is added to the feminine singular form of adjectives. Adverbs ending in **-mente** have two stresses: one on the adjective stem and the other on **-mente**. The stress on the adjective stem is the stronger of the two.

ADJECTIVE	ADVERB	ENGLISH
rápido	**rápidamente**	*rapidly*
fácil	**fácilmente**	*easily*
valiente	**valientemente**	*bravely*

In Spanish, adverbs modifying a verb are placed as close to the verb as possible. When they modify adjectives or adverbs, they are placed directly before them.

Hablan **estupendamente** el español.   *They speak Spanish marvelously.*
Ese libro es **poco** interesante.*   *That book is not very interesting.*
Vamos a llegar **muy tarde**.   *We're going to arrive very late.*

A.   Complete estas oraciones lógicamente con adverbios basados en los siguientes adjetivos.

Adjetivos: directo, inmediato, paciente, posible, rápido, fácil, puntual, tranquilo, total, constante

1. La familia está esperando _____ en la cola.
2. Hay examen mañana y tengo que empezar a estudiar _____.
3. Se vive _____ en aquel pueblo en la montaña.
4. ¿Las enchiladas? Se preparan _____.
5. ¿El hombre va a vivir en la luna algún día? Mi hermana contesta, «_____».
6. ¿Qué pasa? Estoy _____ confundido.
7. Un vuelo que hace escalas no va _____ a su destino.
8. Cuando mira la tele, mi hermanito cambia el canal _____.
9. Es necesario que las clases empiecen _____.

B.   Entrevista. Con un compañero (una compañera), haga y conteste preguntas para obtener la siguiente información.

---

*Note that in Spanish one equivalent of *not very* + *adjective* is **poco** + *adjective*.

MODELO: algo que hace pacientemente →
—¿Qué haces pacientemente? (Dime [*Tell me*, fam.] algo que haces pacientemente.)
—Pues… espero a mi esposo pacientemente cuando se viste para salir. ¡Lo hace tan lentamente! También…

1. algo que hace pacientemente
2. algo que su (compañero/a, mejor amigo/a, esposo/a, …) hace constantemente y que le molesta muchísimo a la persona entrevistada (*interviewed*)
3. algo que le toca hacer inmediatamente
4. algo que hizo (comió, escuchó, …) solamente una vez y que no le gustó nada
5. algo que hacía (comía, escuchaba) frecuentemente de niño/a
6. algo que hace fácilmente pero que para los otros es difícil

ESTRUCTURAS

35. EXPRESSING UNPLANNED OR UNEXPECTED EVENTS
Another Use of *se*

Se me cayó el vaso.

A Mario se le perdieron los libros.

I dropped the glass. (The glass fell from my hands.)
Mario lost his books. (Mario's books were lost to him.)

Unplanned or unexpected events (*I dropped, we lost, you forgot*) are frequently expressed in Spanish with **se** and the third person of the verb. In this structure, the occurrence is viewed as happening *to* someone—the unwitting performer of the action. Thus the victim is indicated by an indirect object pronoun, often clarified by **a** + *noun* or *pronoun*. In such sentences, the subject (the thing that is dropped, broken, forgotten, and so on) usually follows the verb.

(**a** + NOUN OR PRONOUN)	**se**	INDIRECT OBJECT PRONOUN*	VERB	SUBJECT
(A mí)	Se	me	cayó	el vaso.
A Mario	se	le	perdieron	los libros.

*While the verb form is always third person singular or plural in this construction, all of the indirect object pronouns can be used: **¿A Uds.** *se les* **perdió todo el dinero?; A los niños** *se les* **perdió el perro.** However, the exercises in *¿Qué tal?* will focus on sentences containing **se me… , se te… ,** and **se le… .**

The verb agrees with the grammatical subject of the Spanish sentence (**el vaso, los libros**), not with the indirect object pronoun. **No** immediately precedes **se**: **A Mario** *no se* **le perdieron los libros.**

As with **gustar**, the clarification of the indirect object pronoun is optional. But the indirect object pronoun itself is always necessary whether or not the victim is named: *A la mujer* **se** *le* **rompió el plato**. Some verbs frequently used in this construction include the following.

acabar	to finish; to run out of	**perder (ie)**	to lose
caer	to fall	**quedar**	to remain, be left; to leave behind
morir (ue, u)	to die	**romper**	to break
olvidar	to forget		

Práctica

A. Hablando de desastres. Complete las siguientes descripciones con una frase de esta lista.

olvidó llenar (*to fill*) el tanque	rompió la pierna
quedó la cartera en casa	rompieron muchos platos y
murió el pájaro	vasos
perdieron las gafas	acabó el vino

1. ¡Pobre camarero! Lo despidieron porque se le _____.
2. Carmen no pudo pagar la cuenta en el restaurante anoche porque se le _____.
3. Tú esquías mucho, ¿no? ¿Se te _____ alguna vez?
4. Anoche tuve invitados (*guests*) para cenar y les serví champán porque se me _____.
5. Señor, el problema es que el coche no tiene gasolina. ¿Se le _____?
6. ¡Qué distraído eres, niño! ¿Se te _____ otra vez?
7. ¡Pobre Maribel! Está triste porque se le _____.

B. Pablo pasó un día fatal ayer. Lea la siguiente descripción de su día. Luego explique cada acción o circunstancia, usando la frase **porque se le...**

Pablo no se levantó a las siete, como siempre, sino (*but rather*) muy tarde, a las ocho. Se vistió rápidamente y salió de casa descalzo (*barefooted*). Entró en el garaje pero no pudo abrir la puerta del coche. Por eso trató de tomar el autobús para llegar a la oficina, pero cuando el conductor le pidió la tarifa, no tenía dinero. Por eso tuvo que irse caminando.

    Cuando por fin entró en la oficina, su jefe se ofendió porque Pablo lo trató descortésmente. Su primer cliente se enojó porque Pablo no tenía toda la información necesaria para resolver su caso. Para las diez de la mañana, Pablo tenía muchísima hambre. Por eso fue a la cafetería para comer algo. Se sentó con el vicepresidente de la compañía, quien se levantó furioso de la mesa, diciendo que Pablo le arruinó la chaqueta de su traje. Pablo se levantó y regresó a casa. ¡Ya no pudo más!

MODELO: Pablo se levantó tarde, a las ocho, porque se le...

	tomar el desayuno
	las llaves del coche
olvidar	la cartera
perder	todos los papeles en casa
caer	una taza (*cup*) de café
quedar	saludar al jefe
	poner el despertador
	ponerse los calcetines y zapatos

Ahora, déle un consejo a Pablo: Pablo, la próxima vez que Ud. se levante con el pie izquierdo, debe...

C.   Al mono más vivo se le cae la banana de vez en cuando. (*Even the brightest monkey drops his banana sometimes.*) ¿Qué desastres le han ocurrido (*have happened*) a Ud.? Después de completar las oraciones, use sus propias respuestas como guía para entrevistar a un compañero de clase.

MODELO: Una vez durante las vacaciones se me perdió/perdieron
_____. →

Una vez durante las vacaciones se me perdió el dinero. ¿Se te perdió el dinero alguna vez? ¿Qué te pasó?

1.   Una vez durante las vacaciones se me perdió/perdieron _____.
2.   Una vez se me cayó/cayeron _____.
3.   A veces se me olvida(n) _____. De niño/a, siempre se me olvidaba(n) _____.
4.   Nunca/Casi siempre se me acaba(n) _____.
5.   Una vez se me rompió/rompieron _____.
6.   A veces se me queda(n) _____ en casa.
7.   El año pasado se me perdió/perdieron _____.

· ·

UN POCO DE TODO

A.   Complete las oraciones lógicamente, usando un verbo para describir los sentimientos, la condición o las emociones de la persona nombrada.
¡OJO!   ¿Qué tiempo verbal se debe usar, el imperfecto o el pretérito? Use el progresivo cuando sea posible.

1.   A Cristina el trabajo para la clase de historia se le quedó en casa porque _____.
2.   Ayer Roberto se dio con un sillón y se cayó porque _____.
3.   Cuando se le murió la abuela, Leopoldo _____.
4.   Cuando se despidió de su novio, Ángela _____.
5.   Gregorio volvió temprano a casa anoche porque _____.
6.   A Angelito se le rompió el reloj que le regalaron sus padres. Por eso (él) _____.

7. El niño se hizo mucho daño cuando se cayó en la calle. Por eso _____.

8. Alfonso se tomó dos aspirinas porque _____.

B. Blancanieves y los siete enanitos. Complete the following fairy tale with the correct form of the infinitives—preterite or imperfect—as needed. When an adjective is given in parentheses, give the adverb derived from it. When two possibilities are given in parentheses, select the correct word. You should be able to guess the approximate meaning of the underlined words from context and on the basis of the drawings and your prior knowledge of the story.

Érase una vez una linda princesita blanca como la azucena, hija de un rey casado por segunda vez.

Su madrastra, la reina, (*tener*[1]) un espejo mágico. (*Diario*[2]) la reina le (*preguntar*[3]) al espejo: —¿Quién es la más hermosa?

Un día el espejo le (*contestar*[4]): —¡Blancanieves! Llena (*Full*) de envidia y de maldad la reina (*mandar*[5]) a un criado que matara (*to kill*) a la princesa.

El criado la (*llevar*[6]) al bosque y por compasión la (*dejar*[7]) abandonada. Una ardilla la (*llevar*[8]) (*alegre*[9]) a una casita.

En la casita (*vivir*[10]) siete enanitos. Cuando (ellos: *volver*[11]) a casa por la noche, (*encontrar*[12]) a Blancanieves dormida en sus camitas.

En el palacio, la madrastra (*volver*[13]) a consultar el espejo: —Y ahora, ¿quién es la más bella? El espejo le (*contestar*[14]) sin vacilar: —¡Blancanieves!

Por eso la reina (*planear*[15]) matarla. (*Llegar*[16]) a la casa de los enanitos una tarde, disfrazada de vieja, y le (*ofrecer*[17]) a Blancanieves una manzana envenenada.

Cuando (ella: *morderla*[18]), Blancanieves (*caer*[19]) desvanecida. Por la noche, los enanitos la (*encontrar*[20]) tendida (*lying*) en el suelo.

Un príncipe muy guapo, quien (*enterarse*[21]) de lo que (*ocurrir*[22]), (*ir*[23]) a verla. Cuando el príncipe la (*besar*[24]), Blancanieves (*recobrarse*[25]) (*inmediato*[26]).

Enamorados, los dos (*salir*[27]) (*feliz*[28]) hacia el castillo del príncipe, donde (*casarse*[29]) con gran alegría de los enanitos.

¿Quién lo dijo?

1. ¡Ay! ¿Qué vamos a hacer? ¡Parece que se murió!
2. Sé que no te gusta que me vuelva a casar. Lo siento sinceramente.
3. No sabía que la manzana estaba envenenada.
4. ¡Te quiero desesperadamente! Quiero que te cases conmigo.
5. Yo estaba más contenta antes de la segunda boda de papá.
6. Ay, aquí viene otra vez a hacerme la misma pregunta… ¡Qué molestia!
7. No importa lo que me diga la reina. No lo puedo hacer.
8. ¿Cómo es posible que me conteste de la misma manera? Debe ser que todavía está viva…
9. En esta casita viven unos amigos míos que te van a gustar.
10. No hay nadie más linda que nuestra Blancanieves.

 ·

UN PASO MÁS: Situaciones

Incidentes de la vida diaria

En una mesa o dondequiera° que sea — *wherever*
—¡Oh! Discúlpeme. ¡Qué torpeza°! Permítame que le limpie la camisa. — *clumsiness*
—No se preocupe. No es nada.
—Lo siento muchísimo.

En el autobús o en el metro
—Sígueme.° Hay un sitio en el fondo.° — *Follow me. / back*
—¡Hombre! Es imposible llegar allí.
—¿Tú crees? Mira… Con permiso… Disculpe, señora, fue sin querer… Con permiso… Perdone… Permiso, gracias… (Al pisar° a una señora.) ¡Huy! — *Al… Upon stepping on*
Perdón, lo siento, señora.
—¡Mal educado!° — *¡Mal… How rude!*

Al llegar tarde a una cita
—¡Uf! Lo siento. Créeme que no era mi intención llegar tan tarde. De verdad. Fue culpa° del autobús. — *fault*
—Anda°… No te voy a regañar° por diez minutos de retraso. No importa. — *Come on / scold*

Al olvidar° algo — *Al… When you forget*
—Oye, ¿trajiste los apuntes° que te pedí? — *(class) notes*
—¿Los apuntes? ¿Qué apuntes? ¡Ay! Si ya decía yo que se me olvidaba algo. Se me ha pasado por completo.° Lo lamento. Te los llevo el lunes, sin — *Se… I completely forgot about it.*
falla.° — *¿ ?*
—Bueno, bueno… No es para tanto.° — *para… ¿ ?*

Conversación

Con un compañero (una compañera) practique las conversaciones anteriores. Trate de variar las expresiones de cortesía. Si quiere, lea primero **A propósito…** en la página 298.

Notas culturales: Más sobre la cortesía

El pisarle los pies a alguien, sobre todo en el transporte público, es algo que ocurre todos los días. En **Situaciones**, la señora que llamó «¡Mal educado!» al joven que le pisó los pies tal vez se exaltó demasiado (*got too worked up*), pero usó una frase hispánica muy típica para expresar su disgusto con el comportamiento (*behavior*) de alguien. La frase **mal educado** significa *ill mannered, rude, poorly brought up*, lo opuesto de **educado**, que significa *well mannered, polite, cultured*.

A propósito... Extending and Accepting Apologies

Familiarity with the following expressions can help smooth over embarrassing moments. Use the expressions in the first two columns below when you need to apologize to someone. You can follow these phrases by a brief explanation of what caused the problem. To accept someone else's apology graciously, use one of the expressions on the right.

Perdón, me equivoqué.	Fue sin querer.	Está bien.
Perdón, es que...	Lo hice sin querer.	No se preocupe.
¿Me perdona(s)?	No quise decir eso.	No te preocupes.
Lo siento mucho.	Perdón. No sabía que...	No importa.
¡Cuánto lo siento!	No sé qué decirle.	Tranquilo/a.
Me equivoqué de...	Mil disciplas.	No es para tanto.

VOCABULARIO

Verbos

acabar to finish; run out of
acordarse (ue) (de) to remember
apagar to turn off (*lights or appliances*)
caer (caigo) to fall
  caerse to fall down
darse con to run, bump into
equivocarse to make a mistake
hacerse daño to hurt oneself
morir(se) (ue, u) to die
pegar to hit, strike
quedar to remain, be left; to leave behind

romper to break
sufrir to suffer

¡Huy, perdón!

discúlpeme pardon me
fue sin querer it was unintentional
levantarse con el pie izquierdo to get up on the wrong side of the bed
perdone pardon
¡qué mala suerte! what bad luck!

Más partes del cuerpo

el brazo arm
la mano hand
el pie foot
la pierna leg

Otros sustantivos

la aspirina aspirin
la escalera stairs, stairway
la llave key
la multa fine, penalty
la presión pressure
  sufrir muchas presiones to be under a lot of pressure
la taza cup

Adjetivos

distraído/a absent-minded
torpe clumsy

Frases útiles para la comunicación

Dime (algo, una cosa). (*fam.*)   Tell me (something, one thing).

LOS COCHES

VOCABULARIO: EN LA ESTACIÓN DE GASOLINA

la circulación

el camino

la esquina

el taller

el semáforo

la calle

Revisamos el aceite
y la batería.

la carretera

GASOLINERA GÓMEZ

Sí, señor, aquí
recibe Ud. un
servicio
completo.

el conductor

la autopista

Llenamos el tanque con gasolina.

Revisamos
las llantas.

los frenos brakes
la licencia (de manejar/conducir) (driver's)
  license
una llanta desinflada a flat tire

arrancar to start (*a motor*)
arreglar to fix, repair
contener (*like* **tener**) to contain, hold

chocar (con) to run into, collide (with)
doblar to turn (*a corner*)
estacionar(se) to park
gastar to use, expend
manejar, conducir (conduzco) to drive
parar to stop
seguir (i, i) (todo derecho) to keep on going; to
  go (straight ahead)

A.   Definiciones. Busque Ud. la definición de las palabras de la columna de la derecha.

1.   Se pone en el tanque. g
2.   Se llenan de aire. h
3.   Lubrica el motor. e
4.   Es necesaria para arrancar el motor. d
5.   Cuando se llega a una esquina hay que hacer esto o seguir todo derecho. b
6.   No contiene aire suficiente y por eso es necesario cambiarla. f
7.   Es un camino público ancho (*wide*) donde los coches circulan rápidamente C
8.   Se usan para parar el coche. a
9.   El policía nos la pide cuando nos para en el camino. j
10.   Allí se revisan y se arreglan los carros. e

a.   los frenos
b.   doblar
c.   la carretera
d.   la batería
e.   el taller
f.   una llanta desinflada
g.   la gasolina
h.   las llantas
i.   el aceite
j.   la licencia

Ahora, siguiendo el modelo de las definiciones anteriores, ¿puede Ud. dar una definición de las siguientes palabras?

1.   el semáforo
2.   la circulación
3.   estacionarse
4.   gastar gasolina
5.   la gasolinera
6.   la autopista

B.   En la gasolinera. Describa Ud. las cosas y acciones que se ven en el dibujo.

C.   Entrevista. Usando las siguientes frases como guía, entreviste a un compañero (una compañera) de clase para determinar con qué frecuencia hace las siguientes cosas.

1.   dejar la licencia en casa cuando va a manejar
2.   acelerar (*to speed up*) cuando ve a un policía
3.   manejar después de beber alcohol
4.   respetar o exceder el límite de velocidad
5.   estacionar el coche donde dice «Prohibido estacionarse»
6.   revisar el aceite y la batería
7.   seguir todo derecho a toda velocidad cuando no sabe llegar a su destino
8.   adelantar (*to pass*) tres carros a la vez (*at the same time*)

Ahora, según lo que Ud. averiguó (*learned*), describa la forma de manejar de su compañero/a. ¿Es un buen conductor (una buena conductora)?

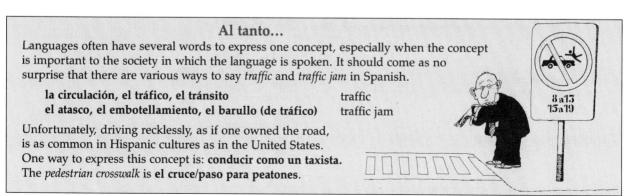

Al tanto...

Languages often have several words to express one concept, especially when the concept is important to the society in which the language is spoken. It should come as no surprise that there are various ways to say *traffic* and *traffic jam* in Spanish.

la circulación, el tráfico, el tránsito   traffic
el atasco, el embotellamiento, el barullo (de tráfico)   traffic jam

Unfortunately, driving recklessly, as if one owned the road, is as common in Hispanic cultures as in the United States. One way to express this concept is: **conducir como un taxista.** The *pedestrian crosswalk* is **el cruce/paso para peatones.**

ESTRUCTURAS

. . . .

36. EXPRESSING UNCERTAINTY
Use of the Subjunctive in Noun Clauses: Doubt and Denial

—*¡No es posible* que *pidan* diez mil!
—*Dudo* que *tenga* una batería nueva.
—*No creo* que el interior *esté* en buenas condiciones.
—Estoy seguro de que tiene más de 40 mil millas.

Continúe las especulaciones de los compradores.
* ¡Es imposible que...
* No creo que...
* Dudo que...
* Estoy seguro/a de que... (¡OJO!)

INDEPENDENT CLAUSE		DEPENDENT CLAUSE
first subject + *indicative* (expression of doubt or denial)	**que**	second subject + *subjunctive*

No creo que **sean** estudiantes.	*I don't believe they're students.*
No están seguros de que Roberto **tenga** razón.	*They're not sure that Roberto is right.*
Es imposible que **esté** con él.	*It's impossible for her to be with him.*

A. Expressions of doubt and denial are those in which speakers express uncertainty or negation: *I doubt he's right; It's not possible for her to be here.* Such expressions, however strong or weak, are followed by the subjunctive in the dependent clause in Spanish.

B. Expressions of doubt and denial include **no creer, dudar** (*to doubt*), **no estar seguro/a**, and **negar (ie)** (*to deny*). Not all Spanish expressions of doubt are given here. Remember that any expression of doubt is followed by the subjunctive in the dependent clause.

C. When generalizations of doubt are personalized, they are followed by the subjunctive in the dependent clause. Some generalizations of doubt and denial are **es posible, es imposible, es probable, es improbable, no es verdad, no es cierto** (*certain*), and **no es seguro** (*a sure thing*).*

---

*Generalizations that express certainty are not followed by the subjunctive: *Es verdad* que *cocina* **bien**; *No hay duda* de que el inquilino lo *paga.*

Indicative Versus Subjunctive

No creer, **dudar**, **no estar seguro/a** and **negar** are followed by the subjunctive. However, **creer**, **no dudar**, **estar seguro/a**, and **no negar** are usually followed by the indicative, since they do not express doubt, denial, or negation. Compare the following:

No niego (**No dudo**) que **es** simpático.	*I don't deny (doubt) that he's nice.*
Niego (**Dudo**) que **sea** simpático.	*I deny (doubt) that he's nice.*
Estamos seguros (**Creemos**) que el examen **es** hoy.	*We're sure (believe) the exam is today.*
No estamos seguros (**No creemos**) que el examen **sea** hoy.	*We're not sure (We don't believe) that the exam is today.*

Práctica

A.   ¡El coche no funciona! Ésta es una conversación que ocurrió ayer en el taller cuando Ud. llevó allí su «nuevo coche viejo». Haga oraciones según las indicaciones. Use el pretérito de los verbos marcados con asterisco (*).

1.   es verdad / que / (yo) sólo / pagar* / mil / dólar / por / coche
2.   es cierto / que / coche / funcionar* / bien / por / dos / mes
3.   ahora / dudo / que / carro / arrancar / otra vez
4.   ¿creer / Ud. / que / ser / transmisión?
5.   es mejor / que / Ud. / dejarlo / aquí / hasta / mañana
6.   (yo) no / estar / seguro / de que / (yo) poder / arreglarlo
7.   (yo) creer / que / es probable / que / Ud. / tener / que / comprar / otro / coche
8.   es posible / que / en / agencia / (ellos) darle / ciento / dólar / por / coche

¿Cierto, falso o no lo dice? Corrija las oraciones falsas.

1.   Es verdad que Ud. tiene un coche nuevo.
2.   Es seguro que Ud. tiene que comprar otro coche.
3.   Ud. manejó el coche a casa ayer.

B.   Escenas de la carretera. Describa lo que pasa en el siguiente dibujo, contestando las preguntas e inventando otros detalles.

Palabras útiles: el hombre/la mujer de negocios (*businessman/woman*), el recipiente (*container*)

¿Por qué hay tanto tráfico ahora? ¿Qué le pasa al coche de la señora? ¿Es posible que sea la transmisión? ¿Adónde iba la señora? ¿Qué pasa con el coche del señor? ¿Qué lleva el señor? ¿Es probable que tenga una llanta desinflada? ¿De dónde viene el señor? ¿Adónde iba? ¿Es probable que alguien pare para ayudarlos?

C.   Algunos creen que las oraciones siguientes describen el mundo de hoy.
¿Qué cree Ud.? Reaccione Ud. a estas oraciones, empezando con una de
estas expresiones:

Dudo que…	Es probable que…	Es increíble que…
(No) Es verdad que…	Es bueno/malo que…	(No) Me gusta que…
No hay duda que…	Es lástima que…	

1.   Los niños miran la televisión seis horas al día.
2.   Hay mucha pobreza (*poverty*) en el mundo.
3.   En los Estados Unidos, gastamos mucha energía.
4.   Hay mucho sexo y violencia en la televisión y en el cine.
5.   Se come poco y mal en muchas partes del mundo.
6.   Los temas de la música punk son demasiado violentos.
7.   Hay mucho interés en la exploración del espacio.
8.   El fumar no es malo para la salud.
9.   Los deportes para las mujeres no reciben tanto apoyo (*support*) finan-
     ciero como los de los hombres.
10.   No se permite el uso de la marihuana.

Indique Ud. soluciones para algunos de los problemas. Empiece las soluciones con estas frases:

Es urgente que…	Quiero que…	Es importante que…
Es preferible que…	Es necesario que…	Insisto en que…

LOS SEMAFOROS

Son dispositivos de control para regular el tránsito automotor y permitir el paso
seguro de los peatones.

La luz roja indica al conductor que debe detenerse.
La luz verde indica al conductor que
puede seguir.
La luz amarilla es una señal de prevención, debes disminuir la velocidad.

Semáforos Peatonales
El foco superior te muestra una persona en actitud de espera, tú debes hacer
lo mismo,
La señal inferior muestra a una persona caminando, te indica que puedes
cruzar.

Notas culturales: Variaciones lingüísticas

Las palabras que se usan para hablar de caminos y vehículos y de la acción de manejar varían en las diferentes partes del mundo de habla española. Aquí hay algunos ejemplos.

car =   coche, auto, automóvil (uso generalizado)
          carro (Centroamérica y los Estados Unidos)
              ¡OJO!   carro = *cart* en España
bus =   autobús (uso generalizado)
          guagua (Cuba y Puerto Rico)
          camión (México)
              ¡OJO!   camión = *truck* en la mayoría del mundo de habla española
tire =   llanta, neumático (uso generalizado)
          rueda (España)

VOCABULARIO

Putting Things in Rank Order: Ordinals

primer(o)	first	**quinto**	fifth	**octavo**	eighth
segundo	second	**sexto**	sixth	**noveno**	ninth
tercer(o)	third	**séptimo**	seventh	**décimo**	tenth
cuarto	fourth				

Ordinal numbers are adjectives and must agree in number and gender with the nouns they modify.* Ordinals usually precede the noun: **la cuarta lección, el octavo ejercicio.**

Like **bueno,** the ordinals **primero** and **tercero** shorten to **primer** and **tercer,** respectively, before masculine singular nouns: **el primer niño, el tercer mes.**

A.   ¿En qué grado están estos niños?

1. Manuel—5°
2. Teresa—3ᵉʳ

3. Eduardo—7°
4. Jesús—1ᵉʳ

5. Pablo—10°
6. Evangelina—2°

---

*Ordinal numbers are frequently abbreviated with superscript letters that show the adjective ending: **las 1ᵃˢ lecciones, el 1ᵉʳ grado, el 5° estudiante.**

B. Conteste las preguntas según el dibujo.

1. ¿Quién es la décima persona? ¿la quinta? ¿la tercera? ¿la segunda?
2. ¿En qué posición está Ángela? ¿Cecilia? ¿Juan? ¿Simón? ¿Linda?

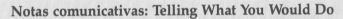

Notas comunicativas: Telling What You Would Do

You have already learned to use the form **me gustaría...** to talk about what you would like—or not like—to do. You can use a similar form, **sería** (*would be*), to talk about what you would do in a given situation.

El primer factor sería... El segundo sería...
Lo más importante para mí sería...
Para mí, la primera consideración sería...

C. Imagine que Ud. tiene que tomar las siguientes decisiones. ¿En qué orden de importancia colocaría (*would you put*) los siguientes factores? ¿Por qué?

MODELO: Lo más importante para mí sería la materia del curso.

1. Ud. tiene que elegir los cursos para el próximo semestre.
   _____ la hora de la clase
   _____ el profesor (la profesora)
   _____ la materia del curso
   _____ la posibilidad de sacar (*getting*) una buena nota.
2. Ud. tiene que escoger entre dos puestos.
   _____ el sueldo
   _____ el prestigio de la compañía
   _____ la ciudad
   _____ la posibilidad de ascenso (*promotion*)
   _____ la personalidad del jefe (de la jefa)
   _____ las condiciones físicas de la oficina

D. Su viejo coche no arrancó esta mañana y en el taller le dicen que no lo pueden arreglar. Es hora de comprar un coche nuevo. ¿Qué tipo de coche desea Ud.? Lea la siguiente lista de factores y póngalos en orden de importancia según sus preferencias. Luego describa el coche que va a comprar, según el modelo.

MODELO: Primero, deseo un coche _____ porque _____.
Segundo, ...
No me importan estos factores: si es grande o no, ...

_____ grande / económico
_____ nuevo / usado
_____ con una transmisión automática / de cambios (*manual shift*)
_____ con llantas convencionales / con llantas radiales
_____ con aire acondicionado / sin aire acondicionado
_____ con radio AM / con radio AM/FM / sin radio
_____ con frenos normales / con frenos de disco
_____ de color _____ / marca _____
_____ hecho (*made*) en USA / importado
_____ con cassette / sin cassette

ESTRUCTURAS

37. EXPRESSING INFLUENCE, EMOTION, DOUBT, AND DENIAL
Uses of the Subjunctive in Noun Clauses: A Summary

En el taller

CLIENTE: *Temo* que mi carro *tenga* algo serio. ¿Podría revisarlo, por favor?

EMPLEADO: Sí, señor. Entre por aquí y apague el motor, por favor.

CLIENTE: Esta mañana tuve dificultad en hacerlo arrancar.

EMPLEADO: Puede ser la batería.

CLIENTE: Pues... la verdad... *me sorprende* que *sea* la batería. Es nueva; la cambié hace dos semanas, ¿sabe?

EMPLEADO: En ese caso, le *recomiendo* que lo *deje* para poder revisarlo con cuidado.

CLIENTE: Está bien. También *quiero* que le *revise* las llantas delanteras y las bujías.

EMPLEADO: Sí, señor. Eso es parte de nuestro servicio normal.

CLIENTE: ¿Por cuánto tiempo debo dejar el carro aquí?

EMPLEADO: Lo puede venir a buscar en dos horas. *No creo* que *sea* nada que requiera más tiempo.

At the shop CLIENT: I'm afraid there is something seriously wrong with my car. Could you take a look at it, please? EMPLOYEE: Yes, sir. Come in through here and shut off the motor, please. CLIENT: I had trouble getting it to start this morning. EMPLOYEE: Maybe it's the battery. CLIENT: Well, actually . . . I'm surprised that it could be the battery. It's new; I changed it two weeks ago, you know? EMPLOYEE: In that case, I recommend that you leave it to be checked out carefully. CLIENT: O.K. I also want you to check the front tires and the spark plugs. EMPLOYEE: Yes, sir. That's part of our normal service. CLIENT: How long should I leave the car here? EMPLOYEE: You can come to get it in two hours. I don't think it will take any longer.

1. ¿Qué teme el dueño del carro?
2. ¿Está de acuerdo el empleado del taller?
3. ¿Qué posibilidad menciona el empleado?
4. ¿Cuál es la reacción del dueño?
5. ¿Qué recomienda el empleado?
6. ¿Cuánto tiempo se requiere para revisar el coche?

INDEPENDENT CLAUSE	DEPENDENT CLAUSE
first subject + *indicative*	**que** second subject + *subjunctive*
expression of { influence, emotion, doubt, denial	

Remember that, in Spanish, the subjunctive occurs primarily in two-clause sentences with a different subject in each clause. If there is no change of subject, an infinitive follows the first verb. Compare the following:

Quiero } que él revise el coche.
Es necesario }

I want } him to check the car.
It's necessary for }

Quiero } revisar el coche.
Es necesario }

I want } to check the car.
It's necessary }

The independent clause, in addition to fulfilling the preceding conditions, must contain an expression of influence, emotion, or doubt in order for the subjunctive to occur in the dependent clause. If there is no such expression, the indicative is used.* Compare the following:

Dicen que maneje Julio.
Dicen que Julio **maneja** muy mal; por eso **quieren que maneje** Carlota.

They say that Julio should drive.
They say that Julio drives very badly; that's why they want Carlota to drive.

Práctica

A.   Un coche: ¿Una compra esencial? Si Ud. quiere comprar un coche para su uso personal, tiene que ir a una agencia de automóviles. Allí va a ver todos los nuevos modelos. ¿Qué quiere Ud. que pase en la agencia?

Quiero que el vendedor...
- enseñarme los últimos modelos
- explicarme cómo funciona cada coche
- decirme cuáles son las ventajas y las desventajas de cada modelo

---

*See Grammar Sections 22, 24, 25, and 36 for a more detailed presentation of the uses of the subjunctive in noun clauses.

SEÑALES REGLAMENTARIAS
Son aquellas que limitan, prohiben o restringen el uso de las vías, desobedecerlas constituye una infracción de tránsito.

Claro está que Ud. va a aprender mucho. ¿Qué es lo que le va a sorprender?

Me va a sorprender que...
- costar tanto los coches hoy día
- ser tan fáciles de manejar
- haber tantos modelos distintos

Después de examinar muchos coches, es probable que Ud. por fin decida comprar uno. Si no puede pagar en efectivo, es posible que le hagan unas sugerencias en la agencia.

Es posible que el vendedor...
- proponerme un plan para pagar a plazos (*in installments*)
- pedirme mi tarjeta de crédito
- decirme que espere hasta el mes que viene, pues va a haber unas rebajas

SEÑALES PREVENTIVAS
Son aquellas que advierten sobre la existencia de un peligro, especificando su naturaleza.

Si Ud. decide pagar a plazos, firme los papeles necesarios y ya puede tener su coche nuevo. ¡Buena suerte!

B. Situaciones. Ud. es mecánico/a y encuentra muchos problemas con el coche de un cliente. ¿Cuáles son? Ud. y el cliente pueden hablar de los frenos de disco, la transmisión, el aire acondicionado, las llantas, la batería, el radiador, el aceite, etcétera. Use estas palabras como guía. ¿Cuántas oraciones puede Ud. inventar?

SEÑALES INFORMATIVAS
Son aquellas que indican la proximidad de sitios necesarios para el usuario de la vía.

Temo que	revisarme _____
Recomiendo que	su _____ estar roto/a (*broken*)
Me sorprende que	no funcionar bien _____
¿Cómo es posible que...?	poner un(a) _____ nuevo/a
Quiero que	arreglar _____
Le digo que...	ir a costarle _____
	usar un(a) _____ reconstruido/a (*rebuilt*)
	no hay _____ en _____
	¿ ?

Bogotá, Colombia

En la gasolinera
—Buenos días, señora.
—Hola, buenos. Lléneme el tanque, por favor. Aquí tiene la llave.
—¿Gasolina super o normal?
—Super. ¿Puede revisar el aceite?
—Sí. Ábrame el capó.°... Está un poco bajo, pero todavía tiene.   °hood
—Muy bien.

UN POCO DE TODO

A.   El coche nuevo: ¿una ganga o un desastre? Complete the following dialogue with the correct form of the words in parentheses, as suggested by the context. When two possibilities are given in parentheses, select the correct word. Begin with the present indicative.

Margarita, (un/una[1]) joven de veinticinco años que (acabar[2]) (de/que[3]) comprarse un carro nuevo

Alberto, un amigo de Margarita (quien/que[4]) sabe (mucho/muchos[5]) de coches

Camino a° una fiesta en casa de unos amigos   *Camino... On the way to*

A: (Al volante°) Margarita, perdona (que / lo que[6]) te interrumpa, pero a sólo   *wheel*
3 kilómetros de tu casa, no es posible que el termómetro (marcar[7]) una
temperatura (tan/tanto[8]) alta en el motor. Ya (ser/estar[9]) en la zona roja.

M: No te (preocupar[10]); deber (que/—[11]) estar roto como el cuentakilómetros y
(el/la[12]) reloj, que tampoco (funcionar[13]).

A: Pronto te vas a (quedas/quedar[14]) sin coche. Mira, en cosa de pocos minutos se (poder[15]) localizar (el/la[16]) problema. En (ese[17]) estación de servicio (haber[18]) un mecánico y un electricista. ¿Quieres que (yo: parar[19])?

M: ¡Ay, Alberto! Ahora no vamos a (un/una[20]) taller sino° a una fiesta. Con-   *but rather*
duce más (rápido[21]), por favor, o vamos a (llegamos/llegar[22]) tarde.

Ahora, con un compañero (una compañera), invente el resto de la conversación entre Margarita y Alberto.

B.   De vacaciones. Cuando menos se espera, las cosas pueden no ir bien—sobre todo cuando se trata de coches (*where cars are concerned*). La escena en este dibujo no es una excepción. Describa la situación, contestando las preguntas y añadiendo otros detalles cuando sea posible.

1. ¿Quiénes son estas personas?
2. ¿Adónde es probable que vayan?
¿De dónde vienen?
3. ¿Por qué tienen que empujar (*to push*) el coche?
4. ¿Qué se les cae del coche?
5. ¿Qué quiere cada miembro de la familia que hagan?
6. ¿Qué cree Ud. que deben hacer?
7. ¿Cómo va a terminar el episodio?

UN PASO MÁS: Lectura cultural

Manual para el conductor

Aunque los caminos y carreteras son diferentes en algunos aspectos en los distintos países del mundo de habla española, también es cierto que las normas generales de seguridad, dictadas por el buen sentido común al conducir, son universales. La siguiente página es de un manual de conductores de Nicaragua. Va a ver que Ud. tiene mucho en común con el típico conductor nicaragüense.

SIETE CONSEJOS PARA CONDUCIR BIEN

1.   Saber, cuidar y mantener el vehículo en condiciones mecánicas seguras y excelentes: Lubricación, frenos, llantas, volante, luces y amortiguadores.

2.-   Saber manipular el vehículo diestramente.

3.-   Conocer y usar las reglas y prácticas de conducir vehículos.

4.-   Saber como usar correctamente sus ojos.

5.-   Saber como conducir en toda clase de caminos, rectos, con curvas, pendiente, ascendente y descendente, secos, mojados, resbaladizos, con hojas mojadas, aceitosos.

6.-   Conocer los peligros y evitar el beber y conducir.

7.-   Sea un conductor que conduce a la defensiva; tenga buena actitud; asuma responsabilidad de conducir sin accidentes.

EL ACCIDENTE INEVITABLE

La gran mayoría de los accidentes que le ocurran a los vehículos de motor podrían llamarse colisiones-choques y los pocos restantes podrían considerarse más correctamente como accidentes. En este último grupo se incluyen los que realmente son accidentes por su naturaleza, los que son casi inevitables. En otras palabras, la inmensa mayoría de los choques son evitables, son innecesarios y reflejan errores o faltas de parte de los conductores afectados.

Comprensión

De los «Siete consejos para conducir bien», ¿cuál trata de (*deals with*)... ?

_____ el alcohol
_____ la condición física del vehículo
_____ la necesidad de ser un conductor responsable
_____ la vista (*vision*)
_____ el acto de manejar
_____ el conocimiento del reglamento de tránsito
_____ la condición del camino

Para escribir

¿Es Ud. un buen conductor (una buena conductora)? Conteste en tres párrafos.

Primer párrafo: ¿Cómo, cuándo y dónde aprendió Ud. a conducir? Añada algunos detalles interesantes.

Segundo párrafo: Evaluación de su estilo de manejar según los «Siete consejos para conducir bien». Añada los detalles necesarios.

Tercer párrafo: Su *record* de conducir: multas, accidentes, etcétera.

Si Ud. no sabe conducir, describa el estilo de conducir de otra persona.

VOCABULARIO

Hablando de coches

arrancar to start (*a motor*)
contener (contengo) to contain, hold
gastar to use, expend
llenar to fill (up)
revisar to check

el aceite oil
el automóvil car, automobile
la batería battery
la estación de gasolina gas station
los frenos brakes
la gasolina gasoline
la gasolinera gas station
la llanta tire
  una llanta desinflada a flat tire
el/la mecánico/a mechanic
el servicio service
el taller (repair) shop
el tanque tank

En el camino

conducir (conduzco) to drive
chocar (con) to run into, collide (with)
estacionar(se) to park
parar to stop

la autopista freeway
la circulación traffic
el/la conductor(a) driver
la esquina corner (*of a street*)
la licencia license
la milla mile
el/la policía police officer
el semáforo traffic signal
el tráfico traffic
la velocidad speed

Otros verbos

dudar to doubt
negar (ie) to deny

Otros sustantivos

la desventaja disadvantage
la ventaja advantage

Adjetivo

roto/a broken

Los adjetivos ordinales

primer(o/a), segundo/a, tercer(o/a), cuarto/a, quinto/a, sexto/a, séptimo/a, octavo/a, noveno/a, décimo/a

Palabras adicionales

a la vez at the same time
es cierto it's certain
es seguro it's a sure thing
estar seguro/a to be sure, certain

Frases útiles para la comunicación	
sería	it would be

CAPÍTULO 19

LA TECNOLOGÍA

VOCABULARIO: LAS COMPUTADORAS/LOS ORDENADORES

la máquina de escribir

la pantalla

el monitor

la impresora

las teclas
el teclado

el disco

la informática/computación data processing
el lenguaje (computer) language
el manejo/uso operation, use (*of a machine*)
la memoria memory
la microcomputadora microcomputer
el ordenador personal personal computer, PC

archivar la información to store information
diseñar programas to design, write programs
escribir a máquina to type
manejar/usar to use, operate (*a machine*)

INVES

PORQUE LE DA LA GAMA

Conozca la nueva gama de productos INVES. Soluciones que completan la actual serie de ordenadores, impresoras, monitores... Novedades como el INVES PC X-30 PLUS, tres veces más potente que los XT tradicionales.

Conozca las nuevas impresoras matriciales y láser que le sorprenderán por su alta calidad de impresión y por su precio.

Conozca los monitores monocromo, color, VGA (monocromo y color), CGA; diskettes de 3 1/2" y 5 1/4", discos duros de 20, 40, 80, 150 y 330 Mb de memoria, streamers, tarjetas de comunicación... y todo lo que Vd. pueda imaginar.

Venga a ver nuestras soluciones profesionales. INVESTRONICA le da la gama.

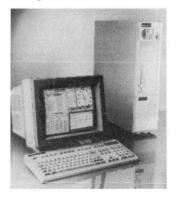

A.   ¿Está Ud. de acuerdo con las siguientes ideas? Defienda sus opiniones.

1.   Saber manejar una computadora es un requisito indispensable para conseguir un buen empleo hoy en día.
2.   Es difícil aprender a manejar un ordenador. Es mucho más fácil escribir a máquina.
3.   La informática es una ciencia muy útil. Saber algo de informática debe ser un requisito para graduarse en esta universidad.
4.   El precio de los microordenadores personales baja todos los años. Por eso no pienso comprarme uno todavía.
5.   Las computadoras nos controlan a nosotros; nosotros no las controlamos a ellas.
6.   Es bueno que tengamos acceso a información médica, bancaria y educativa por medio (*means*) de las computadoras.

B.   ¿Cómo se llaman las partes de la computadora que se ven en el dibujo?

C.   **Definiciones.** Dé Ud. una definición de estas palabras.

MODELO: la memoria → Es lo que se archiva en un ordenador.

1.   la pantalla   4.   la impresora
2.   las teclas   5.   el lenguaje
3.   el disco   6.   el programador

D.   **Preguntas.** De niño/a, ¿tenía Ud. mucho contacto con las computadoras? ¿Aprendió a manejar una computadora en la escuela primaria? ¿En la secundaria? ¿Es necesario que aprenda la informática en la universidad? ¿Qué lenguajes sabe Ud.? ¿PASCAL? ¿BASIC? ¿Tiene una computadora personal? ¿Cuánto le costó? ¿Cuándo la usa?

Al tanto...

There has been a rapid increase in Spanish-speaking areas in the amount of vocabulary and expressions relating to computers. As with vocabulary in other technological fields, the influence of English is strong. Can you guess the meaning of the following words and phrases? You have seen synonyms for some of them in the **Vocabulario** section at the beginning of this chapter.

un procesador de textos
un ordenador con disco duro
almacenar en la memoria
se me borró (el documento, el archivo)
salir del (programa, documento)

En una tienda de computadoras
—Quiero comprar una computadora personal, pero no sé cuál. ¿Puede recomendarme alguna?
—¿Tiene experiencia?
—Realmente no.
—Entonces le sugiero que compre este modelo. Es fácil de manejar y tiene muchas funciones.

España

ESTRUCTURAS

38. MÁS DESCRIPCIONES
Past Participle Used as an Adjective

Unos refranes y dichos en español

1. En boca *cerrada* no entran moscas.
2. *Aburrido* como una ostra.

3. Cuando está *abierto* el cajón, el más *honrado* es ladrón.

1. A veces, ¿es mejor no decir nada? ¿Qué le puede pasar a uno cuando tiene la boca abierta?
2. ¿Llevan una vida muy interesante las ostras? ¿Sufren de muchas presiones?
3. ¿Cometen todos los delitos (*crimes*) los criminales? ¿Es posible que una persona honrada llegue a ser criminal?

Forms of the Past Participle

hablar	comer	vivir
hab**lado** (*spoken*)	com**ido** (*eaten*)	viv**ido** (*lived*)

The past participle of most English verbs ends in -*ed*: for example, *to walk* → *walked; to close* → *closed*. Many English past participles, however, are irregular: *to sing* → *sung; to write* → *written*. In Spanish the *past participle* (**el participio pasado**) is formed by adding **-ado** to the stem of **-ar** verbs, and **-ido** to

---

A few Spanish proverbs and sayings   1. Into a closed mouth no flies enter.   2. As boring as an oyster.   3. When the drawer is open, the most honest person is (can become) a thief.

the stem of **-er** and **-ir** verbs. An accent mark is used on the past participle of **-er/-ir** verbs with stems ending in **-a, -e,** or **-o.**

caído	**creído**	**leído**	**oído**	**(son)reído**	**traído**

The following Spanish verbs that you already know have irregular past participles.

abrir:	**abierto**	hacer:	**hecho**	romper:	**roto**
decir:	**dicho**	morir:	**muerto**	ver:	**visto**
escribir:	**escrito**	poner:	**puesto**	volver:	**vuelto**

Three other common verbs also have irregular past participles.

cubrir (*to cover*)	**cubierto**
descubrir (*to discover*)	**descubierto**
resolver (ue) (*to solve, resolve*)	**resuelto**

The Past Participle Used as an Adjective

In both English and Spanish, the past participle can be used as an adjective to modify a noun. Like other Spanish adjectives, the past participle must agree in number and gender with the noun modified.

Tengo una bolsa **hecha** en El Salvador.	*I have a purse made in El Salvador.*
El español es una de las lenguas **habladas** en los Estados Unidos.	*Spanish is one of the languages spoken in the United States.*

The past participle is frequently used with **estar** to describe conditions that are the result of a previous action.

La puerta **está abierta**.	*The door is open.*
Todos los vasos **estaban rotos**.	*All the glasses were broken.*

¡OJO!   English past participles often have the same form as the past tense: *I* closed *the book. The thief stood behind the* closed *door.* The Spanish past participle is never identical in form or use to a past tense. Compare the following:

Cerré la puerta.	*I closed the door.*
Ahora la puerta está **cerrada**.	*Now the door is closed.*

Práctica

A.   Los siguientes consejos y recomendaciones son de un anuncio del Ministerio de Industria de España. Complételos con la forma correcta del participio pasado de los verbos indicados.

1. Las fuentes (*sources*) de energía no están _____ todavía. (*agotar = to exhaust*)
2. Pero las fuentes son _____. (*limitar*)
3. Todavía no estamos _____ a conservar energía diariamente. (*acostumbrar*)
4. Cuando nos servimos la comida, la puerta de la nevera (= refrigerador) debe estar _____. (*cerrar*)
5. Las luces de la casa deben estar _____ mientras vemos la televisión. (*apagar*)
6. El tocadiscos debe estar _____ y el termostato del radiador debe estar _____ cuando nos acostamos. (*desconectar, bajar*)

Consuma electricidad como si quedara poca.

Queda poca.
Es increíble. Dá la sensación de que el interruptor es una fuente inagotable de energía, ¿no es verdad?

No es verdad. Porque las fuentes de producción de energía eléctrica son limitadas. Bien es cierto que estamos aún muy lejos de un agotamiento, de una insuficiencia eléctrica. Pero prevenir es curar. Y prevenir es fácil en este caso.

Basta con acostumbrarnos a unos pequeños gestos cotidianos: cerrar las neveras mientras nos servimos

la cerveza, tener las luces de la casa apagadas mientras vemos a Kojak, desconectar el tocadiscos o bajar el termostato del radiador al acostarse.

Pequeños hábitos que asegurarán una vida más plena a nuestros hijos y unas facturas más llevaderas a nuestra economía. Moderémonos. Ahora.

**Campaña Nacional de Ahorro de Energía.
Centro de Estudios de la Energía.
Ministerio de Industria.**

Aunque usted pueda pagarla, España no puede.

B. Las siguientes oraciones describen las obligaciones o los deseos de algunas personas. ¿Cuál es la situación del momento presente? Conteste, siguiendo el modelo.

MODELO: Natalia les tiene que *escribir* una carta a sus abuelos. →
La carta no está *escrita* todavía.

1. Los señores García deben *abrir* la tienda más temprano. ¡Ya son las nueve!
2. David y Marta quieren *casarse*. Se conocieron hace dos años.
3. Pablo tiene que *cerrar* las ventanas; entra un aire frío.
4. Los niños siempre esperan que la tierra (*ground*) se *cubra* de nieve para la Navidad.
5. Los turistas tienen que *facturar* el equipaje. No les permiten llevarlo con ellos al avión.
6. Delia debe *poner* la mesa. Los invitados llegan a las nueve y ya son las ocho.
7. Se debe *resolver* pronto el problema con esa computadora.

C. Describa Ud. el siguiente dibujo, tratando de mencionar todos los detalles que han ocasionado (*have caused*) la situación presentada. Use el participio pasado donde sea posible.

MODELO: Todo está preparado para la cena…

 HUMOR   Por Herví

zona de desparramamiento nuclear

¡ALÉJESE!
BOMBA NEUTRONICA
EN PR[...]

¡no tocar los
cicloprotones!

acelerador
de particulas
en reparación

¡PELIGRO!
PLUTONIO
ALTAMENTE
RADIOAC[...]

*¡Ah! ¿Te acuerdas de esos viejos tiempos de
"Cuidado con el perro", o "No pisar el césped"?*

D.   Preguntas

1. ¿Tiene Ud. algo (ropa, perfume, un auto, …) hecho en Francia? ¿en un país latinoamericano? ¿en España? ¿en el Japón? ¿algo hecho a mano?

2. ¿Sabe Ud. el título de un libro escrito por un autor latinoamericano? ¿por un autor español?

3. En su casa o garaje, ¿hay algo roto? ¿algo sucio?

4. En su casa, ¿el televisor está puesto constantemente? ¿el estéreo? ¿el radio?

5. ¿El Nuevo Mundo ya estaba descubierto en 1700? ¿La penicilina ya estaba descubierta en 1960?

E.   Use **he** + el participio pasado para expresar algo inolvidable (*unforgettable*) que Ud. haya hecho (*have done*), siguiendo el modelo.

MODELO: ver → He visto un concierto de Bruce Springsteen.

1. oír	3. romper	5. leer	7. ¿?
2. comer	4. hacer un viaje	6. olvidar	

ESTRUCTURAS

. . . .

◆   **39. ¿QUÉ HAS HECHO?**
Present Perfect Indicative

¿Lo has leído ya?

AMALIA: *¿Has leído* este fascinante artículo acerca de una nueva computadora que puede… ?

ROGELIO: (Interrumpiéndola) ¿Para qué? Ya me *he cansado* de leer artículos sobre la tecnología. Soy muy conservador, ¿sabes? Si escribo, prefiero hacerlo a máquina. Es demasiado complicado usar una computadora.

AMALIA: Será que no *has tratado* de manejar una computadora últimamente. Las *han mejorado* muchísimo… y son más útiles que nunca. Mira, yo uso mi computadora personal casi todos los días. Y en la oficina, *he archivado* casi toda la información que necesito en mi trabajo. Eso me *ha ayudado* bastante.

ROGELIO: Todavía no me convence la idea… ¡Parece que tú—como todo el mundo—te *has vuelto* loca por la informática!

Have you read it yet?   AMALIA: Have you read this fascinating article about a new computer that can . . . ? ROGELIO: (*Interrupting her*) Why should I? I've already gotten tired of reading articles on technology. I'm very conservative, you know? When I write, I prefer to type. Using a computer is too complicated. AMALIA: It must be that you haven't tried to use a computer lately. They've improved them so much . . . and they're more useful than ever. Look, I use my personal computer almost every day. And at the office, I've stored almost all the information I need in my work. That has helped me a lot. ROGELIO: I'm still not convinced by the idea . . . It seems that you—like everyone else—have gone crazy for data processing!

¿Quién lo dice, Amalia o Rogelio?
1. He leído un artículo fascinante.
2. Siempre te han interesado los avances de la tecnología. A mí siempre me han aburrido.
3. En la oficina mis colegas y yo lo hemos archivado todo.
4. Últimamente he usado mi computadora personal mucho.
5. ¡Todo el mundo se ha vuelto loco por la computación!
6. Hasta luego, ¿eh? Tengo que irme. Todavía no he terminado de escribir a máquina el trabajo para mi clase de inglés...

Ordenadores
En el fantástico mundo de las imágenes animadas por ordenador no existen imposibles. Los chips se han convertido en los **nuevos ilusionistas**.
PAG. **4**

Aterrizaje simulado de un avion de caza.

Armamento
Los arsenales nucleares de las grandes potencias han ocultado durante años ese otro **horror secreto** ꞁe es la **guerra química.**

Psicología
¿Qué es el estrés? Una mezcla de angustia, presión y sobrecarga del organismo que nos aplasta.

he hablad**o**	*I have spoken*	**hemos** hablad**o**	*we have spoken*
has hablad**o**	*you have spoken*	**habéis** hablad**o**	*you (pl.) have spoken*
ha hablad**o**	*you have spoken, he/she has spoken*	**han** hablad**o**	*you (pl.) have spoken, they have spoken*

In English, the present perfect is a compound tense consisting of a present tense form of the verb *to have* plus the past participle: *I have written, you have spoken*, and so on.

Pretérito Perfecto = Present Perfect

In the Spanish *present perfect* (**el presente perfecto**) the past participle is used with present tense forms of **haber**, the equivalent of English *to have* in this construction. **Haber**, an auxiliary verb, is not interchangeable with **tener**.

In general, the use of the Spanish present perfect parallels that of the English present perfect.

No **hemos estado** aquí antes.   *We haven't been here before.*
Me he divertido mucho.   *I've had a very good time.*
Ya le **han escrito** la carta.   *They've already written her the letter.*

The form of the past participle with **haber** never changes, regardless of the gender or number of the subject. The past participle always appears immediately after the appropriate form of **haber** and is never separated from it. Object pronouns and **no** are always placed directly before the form of **haber**.

The present perfect of **hay** is **ha habido** (*there has/have been*).

¡OJO!   Remember that **acabar** + **de** + *infinitive*—not the present perfect tense—is used to state that something *has just* occurred.

Acabo de mandar la carta.   *I've just sent the letter.*

Práctica

~~A.~~ Ud. y su amigo/a trabajan en la misma compañía. ¿Qué han hecho Uds. hoy? Haga oraciones basándose en las siguientes frases. Use la forma **hemos...**

1. comprar una nueva micromputadora
2. subirla al tercer piso
3. enchufar (*to plug in*) la computadora
4. limpiar la pantalla y el teclado
5. buscar unos discos
6. leer el manual
7. tratar de usar la computadora
8. pedirle ayuda al técnico
9. volver a nuestros escritorios
10. escribir las cartas a máquina... ¡pero sólo para hoy!

B. Situaciones. Margarita lo/la llama a Ud. por teléfono. Quiere saber lo que Ud. está haciendo. Con otro/a estudiante, haga y conteste preguntas, según el modelo.

> MODELO: cenar → MARGARITA: Estás cenando, ¿no?
> UD.: No, ya he cenado.

1. cocinar	3. lavar los platos	5. poner la mesa
2. descansar	4. leer el periódico	6. usar la computadora

Ahora Margarita tiene unos recados (*messages*) de Jorge.

> MODELO: llamarlo → MARGARITA: Jorge dice que lo llames.
> UD.: Pero ya lo he llamado.

7. mandarle una invitación a Pablo	9. ir a su casa
8. hablar con Concepción	10. ver (película)
	11. escribir la composición esta tarde

C. Entrevista. Con un compañero (una compañera), haga y conteste preguntas con estos verbos. La persona que contesta debe decir la verdad.

> MODELO: visitar México → —¿Has visitado México?
> —Sí, he visitado México una vez. (No, no he visitado México nunca.) (Sí, he visitado México durante las últimas vacaciones.)

1. comer en un restaurante hispánico	6. escribir un poema
2. estar en Nueva York	7. actuar en una comedia
3. manejar un Alfa-Romeo	8. ver un monumento histórico
4. correr en un maratón	9. conocer a una persona famosa
5. abrir hoy tu libro de español	10. romperse la pierna alguna vez

Grid, una compañía de Tandy Corp. especializada en ordenadores portátiles, presentó un nuevo ordenador superligero sin teclado que reconoce escritos a mano y los traduce a textos computerizados. Con sus dos kilos de peso y un tamaño similar al folio, es capaz de leer en medio segundo lo escrito por un lápiz electrónico gracias a un sofisticado *software*. Este mecanismo supone un nuevo paso hacia la consecución del ordenador *secretaria de bolsillo*. Su precio en el mercado norteamericano es de dos mil quinientos dólares (unas trescientas mil pesetas) y puede trabajar hasta ocho horas con unas baterías alcalinas.

Gridpad: ordenador sin teclado

Notas lingüísticas: Talking About What You Had Done

Use the past participle with the imperfect form of **haber** (**había, habías,** …) to talk about what you had—or had not—done before a given time in the past. This form is called the past perfect.

Antes de graduarme en la escuela secundaria, no **había estudiado** español.

Before graduating from high school, I hadn't studied Spanish.

Antes de 1985, siempre **habíamos vivido** en Kansas.

Before 1985, we had always lived in Kansas.

D.   Entrevista. Use the following cues to interview a classmate about his or her activities before coming to this campus. Begin your questions with **Dime…**

MODELO: algo / no haber aprendido a hacer todavía →
—Dime algo que no habías aprendido a hacer todavía antes de estudiar aquí.
—Pues… no había aprendido a nadar. Aprendí a nadar en mi clase de natación.

1. algo / no haber aprendido a hacer todavía
2. una materia / no haber estudiado todavía
3. un deporte / haber practicado mucho
4. un viaje / haber hecho varias veces
5. un libro / no haber leído todavía
6. una decisión / no haber tomado todavía
7. ¿ ?

UN POCO DE TODO

A.   Dé Ud. el nombre de…

1. algo contaminado
2. una persona muy/poco organizada
3. un programa de computadora bien diseñado
4. un edificio bien/mal construido
5. un grupo humano explotado
6. algo que pueda estar cerrado o abierto
7. un curso acelerado
8. un servicio necesitado por muchas personas
9. un tipo de transporte usado por muchas personas
10. algo deseado por muchas personas
11. un programa visto por muchas personas
12. un problema resuelto por un árbitro

B.   Todos somos «diferentes» en el sentido de que hemos hecho algo que los otros no han hecho. Hemos visitado un sitio que los otros no conocen, ganado alguna vez un concurso (*contest*), inventado o preparado un plato especial (u otra cosa), etcétera. ¿Qué ha hecho Ud. que lo/la hace diferente? Complete la siguiente oración. Sus compañeros de clase le van a hacer preguntas para saber más detalles sobre lo que ha hecho: **Soy diferente. (No) He…**

Study Hint: Listening

When you are listening to someone speaking Spanish, try to pick out cognates and to guess the meaning of unfamiliar words from context, just as you do when you are reading. The following suggestions will also help you to understand more of what you hear.

1. Remember that it is not necessary to understand every word to get the gist of the conversation. You may feel uncomfortable if you cannot understand absolutely everything, but chances are good that you will still be able to handle the conversational situation.
2. Watch the speaker's facial expressions and gestures—they will give you a general idea about what he or she is saying. For example, if there is a pause and the speaker is looking at you expectantly, it is reasonable to guess that he or she has just asked you a question.
3. Use brief pauses in the conversation to digest the words that you have just heard.
4. The more familiar you are with the vocabulary being used, the easier it will be to understand

what you are hearing. Listen for familiar words—and be flexible: they may appear with a different meaning in a new context. Listen also for specific clues, such as the following.

- *gender of nouns and adjectives:* Is the speaker talking about **un chico alto** or **una chica alta**? Here you have three chances—with the article, the noun itself, and the adjective—to catch the gender of the person being described.
- *verb endings:* Who did what to whom? If you hear **habló**, for example, you know that the speaker is not talking about himself or herself, since the **-ó** ending signals another person.
- *object pronouns:* The sentence **La vi en el restaurante** can only refer to a woman or to a feminine noun.
- *intonation:* Did you hear a question or a statement?

Above all, if you really have not understood what someone said to you, react: ask questions, admit that you haven't understood, and ask him or her to repeat.

A propósito... More About Being Polite

When you are searching for words to express the exact nature of a problem or situation or when you are trying to make a request, it is possible to sound abrupt or impolite, even though that is not your intention. The uses of phrases such as **por favor**, **perdón**, and **con permiso** will show that you want to be polite, even when you may not be able to express yourself as precisely or as eloquently as a native speaker of Spanish.

In addition to direct commands—often with **por favor**—Spanish speakers use a number of other ways of expressing requests.

Quisiera + *infinitive*	*I would like to (do something)*
¿Podría Ud. + *infinitive*?	*Could you (do something)?*
Necesito que Ud. + *subjunctive*	*I need you to (do something)*

All of these alternatives are more polite than just saying **quiero** (*I want*).

UN PASO MÁS: Situaciones

La tecnología
En la oficina
—¿Sabes? Tengo que comprar un nuevo ordenador personal.
—¿Qué le pasó al ordenador que usabas?

—Pues… nada. Todavía funciona, pero necesito uno que tenga más memoria. El viejo ya no puede archivar toda la información que necesito.

—¿No puedes simplemente comprar más memoria? Sería mucho más barato.

—Supongo que sí, pero… para decirte la verdad, tengo ganas de comprar uno nuevo.

—Sí, chico, ya te entiendo… Otra vez esa necesidad tuya de tener el equipo más nuevo… más avanzado… Es que te gusta estar al tanto en todo. ¿Por qué no lo admites de una vez°?   de… *once and for all*

Un servicio extraordinario

—Buenas. ¿Qué desea?

—Necesito que alguien me arregle esta impresora.

—Bien. Puede dejarla y pasar mañana o pasado mañana a recogerla°.   *to pick it up*

—Pero… es que estoy haciendo un trabajo importante y… quisiera tenerla pronto, si fuera° posible.   *it were*

—Bueno, si se trata° de un caso de urgencia, de acuerdo. Llévela allí delante. Alguien la va a atender en seguida.   se… *es cuestión*

—Muchas gracias. Muy amable.

Conversación

Con un compañero (una compañera), practique las conversaciones anteriores. Trate de variar las expresiones de cortesía.

VOCABULARIO

Verbos

cubrir to cover
descubrir to discover
enchufar to plug in
resolver (ue) to solve, resolve

Las computadoras/Los ordenadores

el disco computer disc
la informática data processing
el lenguaje (computer) language
el manejo/uso operation, use (*of a machine*)

la memoria memory
la microcomputadora microcomputer
el monitor monitor, screen
la pantalla screen
el teclado keyboard
las teclas keys (*of computer, typewriter, etc.*)

archivar la información to store information
diseñar programas to design, write programs
escribir a máquina to type
manejar/usar to use, operate (*a machine*)

Otro sustantivo

la tierra earth, ground

Frases útiles para la comunicación

había (habías, había, …) + *past participle*	I (you, he/she/it . . .) had (*done something*)
Antes de 1985, yo no había estudiado español todavía.	Before 1985, I hadn't studied Spanish yet.
¿Podría Ud. + *inf.*?	Could you (*do something*)?
Quisiera + *inf.*	I would like to (*do something*)

EL MEDIO AMBIENTE

VOCABULARIO: ¿CUÁL PREFIERES, LA CIUDAD O EL CAMPO°?

country

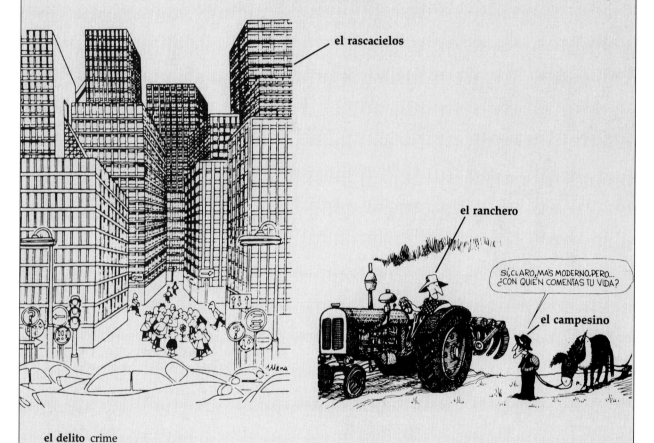

el rascacielos

el ranchero

SÍ, CLARO, MÁS MODERNO. PERO... ¿CON QUIÉN COMENTAS TU VIDA?

el campesino

el delito crime
la escasez scarcity, shortage
la finca, la hacienda farm
la naturaleza nature
la población population
el rancho ranch
el ritmo (acelerado) de la vida (fast) pace of life
los servicios públicos public services
la soledad solitude
el transporte transportation
la vivienda housing

bello/a beautiful
denso/a dense
puro/a pure

encantar to enchant
  me encanta(n) I like very much
madrugar to get up early
montar a caballo to ride horseback
recorrer to pass through; to cover (*territory, miles, etc.*)

A.   De las siguientes oraciones, ¿cuáles corresponden al campo? ¿a la ciudad?

1.   El aire es más puro y hay menos contaminación. *Ci*
2.   La naturaleza es más bella. *Ca*
3.   El ritmo de la vida es más acelerado. *Ci*
4.   Hay menos autopistas y menos tráfico. *Ca*
5.   Los delitos son más frecuentes. *Ci*
6.   Los servicios financieros y legales son más asequibles (*available*). *Ci*
7.   Hay pocos transportes públicos. *Ca*
8.   La población es menos densa. *Ca*
9.   Hay escasez de viviendas. *Ci*
10. Hay más árboles y zonas verdes. *Ca*

B.   **Definiciones.** Dé Ud. una definición de estas palabras.

MODELO: ranchero → Es el dueño de una finca (un rancho).

1. campo	3. delito	5. naturaleza	7. soledad
2. campesino	4. finca	6. población	8. rascacielos

C.   Pancho cree que la vida del campo es ideal. Para él, vivir en la ciudad no ofrece ni una sola ventaja. Gabriela, la amiga de Pancho, es una mujer muy cosmopolita. Le encanta la ciudad y no puede decir nada bueno de la vida del campo. ¿Quién dijo las siguientes oraciones? ¿Qué desventaja puede citar la otra persona en cada caso?

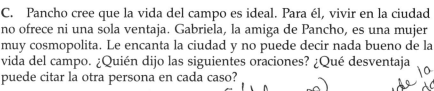

1.   No hay buenos servicios públicos. *G (del campo)*   *G (de la ciudad)*
2.   Hay más actividades culturales—teatro, conciertos y museos. *G*
3.   Allí es posible vivir en paz y en tranquilidad. *P (del campo)*
4.   No me gusta levantarme temprano; allí hay que madrugar para terminar el trabajo. *G (del campo)*
5.   Me encanta recorrer las autopistas de la ciudad por la noche.
6.   Necesito vivir en contacto con la naturaleza. *P (de la ciudad)*
7.   Cuando la nieve cubre las calles, las ciudades están paralizadas.
     P (de la ciudad)

Ahora adopte el punto de vista de Pancho/Gabriela. ¿Qué va Ud. a decir sobre los siguientes temas?

1. el ritmo de la vida	3. la gente/los vecinos
2. la explotación de la tierra	4. los delitos

Costa Rica

Ventajas y desventajas
—¿Prefieres vivir en el campo o en la ciudad?
—Me encantan las ciudades… el bullicio,° la animación…   *hubbub*
—También tienen sus inconvenientes, ¿no?
—¡Por supuesto! Por eso… vivo en el campo.

ESTRUCTURAS

40. DUDO QUE LO HAYAS HECHO
Present Perfect Subjunctive

¿Cambio de ritmo?

RAFAEL: Me parece increíble que *hayas vivido* siempre en grandes ciudades, entre ruidos y contaminación. ¡Es difícil creer que no
hayas tenido tiempo de apreciar la naturaleza! Que nunca *hayas
madrugado* al canto del gallo ni sepas montar a caballo. Me
extraña mucho la vida que Uds. llevan aquí.

AURELIA: Pues... como tú siempre has vivido en el campo, no has conocido otro estilo de vida. Me alegro de que por fin te *hayas
interesado* por la vida cultural de la ciudad.

RAFAEL: Bueno, como me has hablado tanto de ella, por fin decidí ver
lo que tiene de extraordinario. El campo tiene muchas ventajas, pero creo que voy a sentirme a gusto aquí.

AURELIA: ¡Ajá! ¡Y tú que me decías que jamás podrías acostumbrarte!

RAFAEL: Bueno, bueno... eso fue antes de mudarme aquí. ¡Por eso
nunca hay que decir «de esta agua no beberé»!

Exprese los pensamientos (*thoughts*) de Rafael y Aurelia.

RAFAEL: Me parece increíble que Aurelia siempre *haya...* (*vivir / ciudad*)

AURELIA: Es fenomenal que Rafael *haya...* (*montar / caballo*)

RAFAEL: Es terrible que ella no *haya...* (*tener tiempo / apreciar / naturaleza*)

AURELIA: Es lástima que él no *haya...* (*poder apreciar / vida cultural*)

RAFAEL: ¡Qué triste que ella nunca *haya...* ! (*madrugar / canto del gallo*)

AURELIA: Es bueno que él se *haya...* (*mudar / ciudad / por fin*)

haya hablado	**hayamos** hablado
hayas hablado	**hayáis** hablado
haya hablado	**hayan** hablado

The *present perfect subjunctive* (**el perfecto del subjuntivo**) is formed with the
present subjunctive of **haber** plus the past participle. It is used to express

---

A change of pace?   RAFAEL: It seems incredible that you've always lived in big cities amidst
noise and pollution. It's hard to believe that you haven't had time to appreciate nature! And
that you've never gotten up at dawn to the crowing of a rooster or learned to ride horseback.
The life you people lead here is very strange to me. AURELIA: Well . . . since you've always lived
in the country, you haven't known any other lifestyle. I'm glad that you've finally become interested in the cultural life of the city. RAFAEL: Well, since you've talked to me so much about it, I
finally decided to see what it has that's so special. The country has many advantages, but I
think I'm going to feel at home here. AURELIA: Aha! And you were the one that used to tell me
you would never be able to adjust! RAFAEL: OK, OK . . . that was before I moved here. That's
why one should never say never (*lit.* never say "I will not drink this water")!

I have spoken (*written,* and so on) when the subjunctive is required. Although its most frequent equivalent is *I have + past participle,* its exact equivalent in English depends on the context in which it occurs.

Es posible que lo **haya hecho.**	*It's possible (that) he may have done (he did) it.*
Me alegro de que **hayas venido.**	*I'm glad (that) you have come (you came).*
Es bueno que lo **hayan recorrido.**	*It's good that they passed through (have passed through) it.*

Note that the English equivalent of the present perfect subjunctive can be expressed as a simple or as a compound tense: *did/have done; came/have come; passed through/have passed through.*

Práctica

A. Imagine que Ud. es dueño/a de una casa de apartamentos. Conteste las siguientes preguntas, empezando sus respuestas con las palabras entre paréntesis.

1. ¿Han alquilado todos los apartamentos? (Dudo que…)
2. ¿Han vuelto de su viaje los inquilinos del primer piso? (Es posible que…)
3. ¿Se han mudado ya los inquilinos ruidosos? (Sí, y me alegro mucho de que…)
4. ¿Han pagado todos el gas y la luz este mes? (No creo que…)
5. ¿Se ha arreglado ya la ventana? (Es probable que…)
6. Se ha muerto la esposa del portero. (¡Ay, siento que… !)

B. Con un compañero (una compañera), reaccione a las siguientes oraciones. La persona que reaccione debe empezar con frases como **Lo siento, (nombre), pero dudo que… ; No, es imposible que… ; Estoy seguro/a que… ; Es obvio que… ;** etcétera.

> MODELO: —Anoche hice un viaje a la luna.
> —Lo siento, Harry, pero dudo que hayas hecho un viaje a la luna.

1. Escribí una novela este fin de semana.
2. Leí *Lo que el viento se llevó* (*Gone with the Wind*) en veinte minutos.
3. Anoche salí con Robert Redford/Emilio Estévez/Ally Sheedy/Madonna/¿ ?
4. Vi un OVNI (objeto volador no identificado) esta mañana.
5. Tom Selleck/Jessica Lange me mandó una carta de amor.
6. Hice algo estúpido en una ocasión.
7. En mi otra vida fui rey/reina de Inglaterra.
8. Anoche tomé ocho botellas de cerveza y una de vino.

VOCABULARIO

El medio ambiente°				*environment*
la energía	energy	**construir***	to build	
la fábrica	factory	**contaminar**	to pollute	
el gobierno	government	**desarrollar**	to develop	
los recursos naturales	natural resources	**destruir***	to destroy	
		evitar	to avoid	
acabar	to run out, use up completely	**proteger (protejo)**	to protect	
conservar	to save, conserve			

NO CONTAMINES A NUESTRA COSTA

Las costas y las playas necesitan cuidado, defensa y protección.
El Ministerio de Obras Públicas y Urbanismo, desde 1983 hasta 1986, ha destinado 12.000 millones de pesetas para la regeneración de playas, accesos a las mismas y paseos marítimos.
También desde 1983, en colaboración con el Instituto Nacional de Empleo, está llevando a cabo un Programa de Limpieza de playas y vigilancia de costas. Este verano se realiza en 331 municipios, lo que, además de mejorar la calidad de nuestras playas, supone la creación de nuevos puestos de trabajo.
Para que las costas y las playas no se deterioren, mantengan su atractivo y sean un lugar de descanso y recreo.
Pero todo esfuerzo resultaría inútil sin tu colaboración.
Porque proteger la costa cuesta dinero, porque es necesaria una conducta responsable con un bien que es de todos.

MOPU
Ministerio de Obras Públicas y Urbanismo.

A. Más definiciones. Dé Ud. una definición de estas palabras, usando los verbos indicados cuando sea necesario. Luego dé ejemplos de cada palabra.

1. la fábrica (fabricar)
2. el gobierno (gobernar [ie])
3. la conservación
4. la contaminación

B. ¿Está Ud. de acuerdo con las ideas siguientes? Defienda sus opiniones.

1. Para conservar energía debemos bajar la calefacción en invierno y usar menos el aire acondicionador en verano.
2. Es mejor calentar la casa con una estufa de leña (*wood stove*) que con gas o electricidad.
3. Debemos proteger nuestras «zonas verdes» y crear (*to create*) más parques públicos para las futuras generaciones.
4. Es más importante explotar los recursos naturales que proteger el medio ambiente.
5. Para gastar menos gasolina, debemos tomar el autobús, caminar más y formar *car pools*.
6. Sólo debemos importar petróleo de otros países si se acaban nuestras propias reservas.
7. El gobierno debe poner multas muy fuertes a las compañías y a los individuos que contaminen el aire.

---

*Note the present indicative conjugation of **construir: construyo, construyes, construye, construimos, construís, construyen. Destruir** is conjugated like **construir.**

8. Debemos adoptar una manera de vivir más sencilla.

9. No es necesario destruir la naturaleza para construir centros urbanos bien planeados. Se puede evitar eso.

10. Se deben explotar todos nuestros recursos naturales al máximo para satisfacer las necesidades que la población tiene en la actualidad (*right now*).

C. ¿Qué piensa Ud. de la tecnología? Express your opinions about this topic by completing the following sentences in a logical manner, selecting topics from the right-hand column and adding appropriate information. Then ask other students how they responded (**¿Qué esperas de... ?** etc.) until you find some who share your hopes and/or uncertainties.

MODELO: Espero que la tecnología ayude a resolver el problema del hambre mundial. Y tú, ¿qué esperas de la tecnología?

1. Espero que _____.	las computadoras
2. Estoy seguro/a de que _____.	el progreso científico
3. Dudo que _____.	la tecnología
4. Me alegro de que _____.	la energía nuclear
5. Tengo miedo de que _____.	la escasez de energía
6. Creo que _____.	la comunicación instantánea
	los robots
	¿ ?

Al tanto...

As with computer vocabulary, the vocabulary of ecology changes quickly and is often closely related to English terms. Can you guess the meaning of the following words and phrases?

los verdes	la capa de ozono
la comida natural	el efecto invernadero
las especies protegidas	el parque natural

Una selva tropical de Panamá

EMPRESA Y SOCIEDAD

FAPAS protege al oso y regala pegatinas

El Fondo para la Protección de los Animales Salvajes (FAPAS) ha comenzado una campaña de información sobre sus actividades, con el mensaje "Mis amigos los osos" y una atractiva pegatina que puedes pedir gratis a esta asociación ecologista dirigiéndote a: Fondo para la Protección de los Animales Salvajes. Apartado 106. 33500 Llanes (Asturias).

Mis amigos los osos

FONDO PARA LA PROTECCION DE LOS ANIMALES SALVAJES
Apdo.106 –33500 LLANES(ASTURIAS)

ESTRUCTURAS

41. EL INFINITIVO
Verb + Infinitive; Verb + Preposition + Infinitive

Ventajas y desventajas de la era de la tecnología

Algunos de los inventos del siglo (*century*) XX nos traen problemas a la vez que nos facilitan otros aspectos de la vida. Mire el dibujo y lea el comentario del señor. Luego, usando las frases como guía, invente la historia de este señor, que es una víctima del progreso. Use infinitivos con cada frase.

1. Este señor tenía que...
2. Quería...
3. Cuando llegó a la oficina, trató de...
4. Pero no pudo...
5. Por eso tuvo que...
6. Una vez en casa, decidió...
7. En este momento, acaba de...
8. El señor con quien habla va a...

—Yo quería ir a su oficina a pagar la tasa de estacionamiento, pero no pude hacerlo porque no encontré sitio para estacionar.

As you have already learned, when two verbs occur in a series, the second verb is usually in the infinitive form. The infinitive is also the only verb form that can follow a preposition. You have already used many of the constructions that are presented in this section.

A. Many Spanish verbs require no preposition before an infinitive.

| **Prefieren poner** la mesa. | *They prefer to set the table.* |

deber	esperar	parecer	preferir (ie)
decidir	gustar	pensar (ie) *to intend*	querer (ie)
desear	necesitar	poder (ue)	saber

B. Some Spanish verbs require a preposition or **que** before an infinitive.

1. Some verbs require **a** before an infinitive.

| La profesora nos **enseña a bailar**. | *The professor is teaching us to dance.* |

aprender a	empezar (ie) a	invitar a	venir (ie) a
ayudar a	enseñar a	ir a	volver (ue) a

2. Other verbs or verb phrases require **de** before an infinitive.

| Siempre **tratamos de llegar** puntualmente. | *We always try to arrive on time.* |

acabar de	dejar de	tener ganas de
acordarse (ue) de	olvidarse de	tratar de

Para que podamos circular mejor...

● **La bicicleta no contamina** y ocupa poco espacio. Su uso beneficia a todos. **No acose a los ciclistas.**

3. **Insistir**, a frequently used verb, requires **en** before an infinitive.

> **Insisten en venir** esta noche.   *They insist on coming over tonight.*

4. Two verbs require **que** before an infinitive: **haber que**, **tener que**.

> **Hay que sacar** la basura.   *It's necessary to take out the garbage.*

Práctica

A.   Complete las oraciones lógicamente usando infinitivos.

1. A un mecánico le gusta _____ con los coches. Trata de _____lo todo con cuidado y a veces tiene que _____ a arreglar algo si no le sale bien la primera vez. A veces nos dice que hay que _____ el coche hasta el día siguiente.

2. Un niño de un año empieza a _____ y a _____. Un niño de cinco años aprende a _____ y a _____ en la escuela. Le gusta _____ con sus amigos en el patio de la escuela. A los trece años, no tiene ganas de _____. Sólo quiere _____ con los amigos.

3. Si un estudiante sale de la biblioteca a las once de la noche, acaba de _____ mucho. Es probable que piense _____ a un bar estudiantil o al apartamento de unos amigos para _____. No va a volver a _____ esa noche.

4. Mi abuelo tiene que _____ a cuidarse mejor. Tiene que dejar de _____ y _____ tanto, y el médico le dijo que debe empezar a _____ ejercicio y _____ mejor. Espero que mi abuelo trate de _____ los consejos del médico.

5. Los novios acaban de _____. Piensan _____ a Hawai para su luna de miel. Allí desean _____ todo el día en la playa y por la noche van a _____ a comer y a _____.

6. En el avión, hay que _____ de fumar cuando el avión despega. Durante el vuelo, los pasajeros pueden _____ una película o _____ música. Algunos prefieren _____ revistas o periódicos y otros tienen que _____ porque están en un viaje de negocios (*business*).

B.   Imagine que se descubrió el año pasado un caso de contaminación ambiental en su ciudad. ¿Qué ha dicho la gente sobre el caso? Haga oraciones completas según las indicaciones. Use **ellos** como sujeto cuando sea necesario y el perfecto del subjuntivo en la cláusula dependiente.

1. es probable: ya / empezar / estudiar el problema
2. no creo: poder / descubrir la solución todavía
3. es posible: volver / consultar con unos expertos
4. es dudoso: las fábricas / dejar / echar contaminantes
5. espero: tratar / hablar con los dueños de las fábricas

> Sevilla es una ciudad hermosa.
>
> No contribuya a contaminarla.
>
> Utilice los transportes públicos.

C.   Entrevista. Use las frases como guía para entrevistar a un compañero (una compañera) de clase. Empiece sus preguntas con **Dime...**

1. algo que él/ella dejó de hacer el año pasado
2. algo que le gustaría aprender a hacer
3. algo que empieza a hacer muy bien
4. la razón por la cual (*the reason why*) tuvo que guardar cama una vez
5. algo que sus padres (hijos) le ayudan a hacer
6. algo que siempre se olvida de hacer (y que le molesta mucho a su compañero/a [esposo/a, madre/padre, …])
7. algo que piensa hacer después de graduarse
8. lo que prefería comer para el almuerzo cuando era niño/a
9. algo que le gusta hacer en la ciudad
10. algo que prefiere hacer en el campo

UN POCO DE TODO

A.   Cambio de ritmo. Complete the following paragraphs with the correct form of the words in parentheses, as suggested by the context. When two possibilities are given in parentheses, select the correct word.

Ayer yo decidí (∅/a¹) pasar el día recorriendo mi nueva finca. Toda la vida he (admirar²) la naturaleza, pero creo que (ser³) la primera vez que había (ver⁴) (tan/tanto⁵) belleza en (tan/tanto⁶) poco tiempo. En el lago había unos patitos° y sus padres (les/los⁷) estaban enseñando (de/a⁸) nadar. La buganvilla, que (florecer⁹) la semana pasada, estaba (cubrir¹⁰) de flores de colores (brillante¹¹). (Oír: yo¹²) la canción de un pájaro y (ver: yo¹³) que uno estaba (construir¹⁴) su nido° en (un/una¹⁵) árbol cerca del lago.

(Pasar: yo¹⁶) todo el día a caballo hasta la hora de (cenar¹⁷) y luego, después de (comer¹⁸) (descansar¹⁹) un rato bajo los árboles. Antes de (mudarse²⁰) al campo, (hablar: nosotros²¹) constantemente de las ventajas del aire puro y del ritmo lento° de la vida, pero no (pensar²²) en la tranquilidad y la belleza de las cosas (cotidiano²³). Ahora (ser/estar: nosotros²⁴) (tan/tanto²⁵) contentos que no es posible que nuestra decisión (haber ser²⁶) un error.

ducklings

nest

slow

B.   Entrevista. With two other students, react to the following statements by telling whether you believe them to be possible or not. Use the present perfect indicative or subjunctive, as needed.

MODELO: —Hoy tuve que madrugar. Me levanté a las cinco. →
—Bueno, yo creo que te has levantado hoy a las cinco.
—No, no te creo. Es imposible (No es probable) que te hayas levantado hoy a las cinco.

1. A veces digo cosas estúpidas y absurdas.
2. Nunco digo cosas estúpidas y absurdas.
3. Nunca duermo.
4. Hoy me levanté a las tres de la mañana.
5. Puedo leer quince libros en una hora.
6. He leído muchos libros este año.

7. Mis padres me mandaron mil dólares la semana pasada.
8. Fui al Japón el año pasado.
9. Fui a Nueva York el mes pasado.
10. Siempre salgo bien en los exámenes difíciles.

UN PASO MÁS: Lectura cultural

Estos consejos son de un folleto (*pamphlet*) de la Secretaría General de Turismo de España.

NORMAS BASICAS PARA LA PROTECCION DEL MEDIO AMBIENTE POR PARTE DEL TURISMO

Disfrute y observe la riqueza de fauna y flora españolas, pero no capture animales ni arranque plantas. No importe ni intente exportar objetos naturales sin autorización o información al respecto. • Visite nuestros nueve «Parques Nacionales» y once «Parques Naturales»: disfrute de ellos y evite su deterioro. • Los incendios forestales ocasionan en España graves pérdidas económicas y ecológicas. No encienda hogueras[a] en el campo, salvo en los lugares señalados para ello. Apague las colillas[b] y no las arroje por la ventanilla de su automóvil. • El agua es un bien escaso en la mayoría del territorio español. No la malgaste. • El vertido[c] de combustible y aceite de embarcaciones a motor es un importante factor de contaminación del agua. Mantenga en buen estado el motor de su embarcación. • Las aguas de lavado y desperdicios pueden contaminar gravemente los ríos. Evite realizar estas tareas fuera de las instalaciones adecuadas; en caso de que no le sea posible, vierta el agua sucia sobre el terreno. No acerque su vehículo a menos de 100 metros de arroyos, ríos, lagunas, etc. • El vertido de aceites de automóvil en el suelo puede producir una grave contaminación de aguas subterráneas. No cambie nunca el aceite de su vehículo en el campo. • Las rodaduras de automóvil son uno de los agentes de inicio de erosión más poderosas. No invada con su vehículo el césped y vegetación fuera de los caminos o carreteras. • Ochenta y tres decibelios es el nivel máximo de ruido permisible a un automóvil. Además es preciso mantener niveles mínimos de emisión de partículas y monóxido de carbono. Mantenga a punto[d]

el motor de su vehículo. • En sus viajes por carretera pare en las estaciones de servicio o puntos de estacionamiento señalados, donde podrá depositar basuras y residuos en los recipientes al efecto. Evite en todo caso arrojarlos en las márgenes de las carreteras. • El abandono de basuras en el medio natural constituye un atentado a la estética, además de un claro peligro en muchos casos. No deje jamás en el campo ningún tipo de residuo orgánico o inorgánico. Extreme su cuidado en zonas especialmente delicadas, como son las playas. • La excavación por parte de excursionistas en zonas naturales muy frecuentadas se traduce en notables alteraciones de la vegetación y de los horizontes superficiales del suelo. No excave nunca agujeros[e] en el suelo para ocultar residuos de ningún tipo. • La acampada libre es una de las causas más importantes de contaminación y deterioro del medio natural. No acampe fuera de las áreas dispuestas para ello. • El máximo nivel de ruido ambiental permisible es de cincuenta y cinco decibelios. Evite, en lo posible, elevar el volumen de su aparato de radio o TV., especialmente en lugares y transportes públicos, en el campo o medio natural, y siempre durante las horas de descanso. • Cumpla las normas sanitarias que afecten a los animales que traiga con Vd. Mantenga su perro sujeto por la correa en zonas públicas. Para hacer sus necesidades, condúzcalo a los desagües[f] practicados en los bordillos. • España es un país deficitario en energía. Sea moderado en el uso del agua caliente, luz y aparatos de calefacción y aire acondicionado. • Si adquiere Vd. terrenos o edificios en España, infórmese previamente de sus condiciones urbanísticas en los Ayuntamientos[g] respectivos. • Los monumentos y lugares históricos urbanos deben ser objeto de especial cuidado en cuanto al abandono de residuos. No arroje colillas, envoltorios u otros objetos que puedan deteriorarlos.

a. *bonfires* b. *butts* c. *spilling* d. a... *tuned up* e. *holes* f. *drains* g. *city governments*

Comprensión

1. ¿Cuántos parques nacionales hay en España? ¿Cuántos parques naturales?
   En su opinión, ¿cuál es la diferencia entre los dos tipos de parques?

2. Según el anuncio, ¿cuáles de los siguientes sitios de interés turístico hay en España?

_____ playas   _____ bosques (*forests*)
_____ volcanes   _____ monumentos en la ciudad
_____ sitios para hacer *camping* _____ cuevas (*caves*)
_____ lagos y ríos   _____ pirámides

3. Busque en el folleto algo que el turista sí debe hacer en relación con cada uno de los siguientes y algo que no debe hacer.

	SÍ	NO		SÍ	NO
los animales y las plantas	_____	_____	la basura	_____	_____
			los coches	_____	_____
los bosques	_____	_____			
el agua	_____	_____			

Para escribir

Describa la ciudad más grande que Ud. conoce. Su descripción debe incluir los siguientes detalles.

1. dónde está   2. su importancia nacional e internacional   3. población: tamaño (*size*), grupos étnicos o culturales   4. lugares de interés   5. industrias   6. política   7. si le gustaría a Ud. vivir allí y por qué (no)

VOCABULARIO

Verbos

conservar to save, conserve
construir (construyo) to build
contaminar to contaminate
desarrollar to develop
destruir (destruyo) to destroy
encantar to enchant
evitar to avoid
explotar to exploit
madrugar to get up early
mudarse to move, change location/residence
proteger (protejo) to protect
recorrer to pass through; to cover (*territory, miles, etc.*)

El medio ambiente

el aire air
la energía energy
la escasez (*pl.* **escaseces**) scarcity, shortage
la fábrica factory
la naturaleza nature
la población population
los recursos naturales natural resources

¿La ciudad o el campo?

el/la campesino/a farm worker; peasant

el delito crime
la finca farm
la hacienda ranch
el negocio business
el/la ranchero/a rancher
el rancho ranch
el rascacielos skyscraper
el ritmo rhythm, pace
los servicios públicos public services
la soledad solitude
el transporte (means of) transportation
la vivienda housing

Adjetivos

acelerado/a accelerated
bello/a beautiful
denso/a dense
público/a public
puro/a pure

Frases útiles para la comunicación	
en la actualidad	at the present time, right now
la razón por la cual	the reason why

VOCES DEL MUNDO HISPÁNICO

La América Latina

¿Cuánto sabe Ud. de la geografía de esta región del mundo de habla española (y también de habla portuguesa, porque en uno de los países latinoamericanos se habla ese idioma)? Identifique los siguientes países en el mapa: la Argentina, el Brasil, Bolivia, Colombia, Chile, el Ecuador, el Paraguay, el Perú, el Uruguay, Venezuela. Luego ponga estas capitales con sus respectivos países: Brasilia, Buenos Aires, Bogotá, Santiago, La Paz, Asunción, Quito, Caracas, Montevideo, Lima.

Ahora indique el nombre para los habitantes de cada país: paraguayo/a, brasileño/a, ecuatoriano/a, boliviano/a, argentino/a, peruano/a, uruguayo/a, colombiano/a, chileno/a, venezolano/a.

MODELO: Una persona de _____ es _____.

Himno de Manco Capac

El Cuzco, el Perú

Viracocha,°   *Supreme God*
poderoso cimiento del mundo,
Tú dispones:
«Sea éste varón,°   *hombre*
sea ésta mujer.»
Tú gobiernas
hasta° al granizo.°   *even / hail*
¿Dónde estás
—como si no fuera°   *no... I weren't*
yo hijo tuyo—
arriba,
abajo,
en el intermedio
o en tu asiento de supremo juez°?   *judge*
Óyeme,
Tú que permaneces°   *remain*
en el océano del cielo
y que también vives
en los mares de la tierra,
gobierno del mundo,
creador del hombre. [...]
Tú, que me mandaste
el cetro° real,   *scepter, staff*
óyeme
antes de que caiga
rendido o muerto.

Traducido del quechua, lengua del Perú incaico

Machu Picchu, el Perú

Niños venezolanos

LA HISTORIA OFICIAL

En 1986 obtuvo el Oscar a la Mejor Película Extranjera y recibió veintisiete premios internacionales. Quizás esta presentación baste para referirse al filme del argentino Luis Puenzo, quien, en casi dos horas, retrata[a] un período traumático de la vida de su país.

A través de la vida de "Alicia" (Norma Aleandro) –una profesora de historia estricta y conservadora– se va descubriendo lo que aconteció[b] en Argentina durante los regímenes militares. La maestra, casada con un próspero hombre de negocios, "Roberto" (Héctor Alterio), vive feliz junto a "Gaby", a quien adoptaron al verse impedida ella de tener hijos. Hasta ese momento, su situación es ideal. Los tres conforman un hogar[c] armónico, donde la niña es lo principal.

Sus angustias irrumpen cuando en la prensa abundan las informaciones respecto a menores, cuyos[d] padres por razones políticas han desaparecido, que fueron entregados en adopción. Desde ese momento, "Alicia" no descansará. Quiere llegar a la verdad, y una vez que la obtiene ya no puede vivir con ella. La dramática trama se combina con lo que acontece[e] en esos momentos en Buenos Aires, adquiriendo esta "Historia oficial" un carácter documental.

Argentina (1985)
Protagonistas: Norma Aleandro y Héctor Alterio
Director: Luis Puenzo
Censura: Mayores de 18 años
Duración: 112 minutos
Distribuidora: Villarrica Films Video
Hablada: En español

Videograma, Santiago (Chile)

a. *portrays*   b. pasó
c. casa   d. *whose*   e. pasa

Buenos Aires,
la Argentina

compañías

productivity

período de cinco años

successful ones

La semana,
Buenos Aires
(Argentina)

Retorno para 54

Angel Parra

La ola de rumores anunciando que el gobierno daría a conocer una nueva

a. *entry*   b. cantante

lista de exiliados a los cuales se les permitiría el ingreso[a] a Chile, tuvo su confirmación el miércoles pasado por la tarde. Ese día, el Ministerio del Interior hizo pública una cuartilla conteniendo 54 nombres de autorizados para volver, entre los cuales se cuentan los del cantautor[b] Angel Parra; el ex ministro del Trabajo del gobierno de Allende, Jorge Godoy; el ex senador radical Hugo Miranda; Viviana Corvalán Castillo, hija del secretario general del Partido Comunista, Luis Corvalán; y los ex diputados socialistas Alejandro Giliberto y Andrés Sepúlveda. •

APSI, Santiago (Chile)

Manifestación en
Santiago, Chile,
1988

Los ex Presidentes de la República de Colombia juegan un papel político vital

REUTER, Bogotá
Un puñado[a] de ex Presidentes colombianos juega un papel decisivo en la vida política del país, pero una nueva generación de dirigentes jóvenes y ambiciosos se encuentra impaciente por disputarles esa influencia. Estos veteranos estadistas pertenecen tanto al Partido Liberal como al Conservador.

handful

La Época, Santiago (Chile)

Verbo

Voy a arrugar° esta palabra   *wrinkle*
voy a torcerla,°   *twist it*
sí,
es demasiado lisa,°   *even, smooth*
como si un gran perro o un gran río
le hubiera repasado° lengua o agua   *le... had passed over it*
durante muchos años.

Quiero que en la palabra
se vea la aspereza,°   *harshness*
la sal ferruginosa,°   *iron-laden*
la fuerza desdentada°   *toothless*
de la tierra,
la sangre
de los que hablaron y de los que no hablaron.

Quiero ver la sed
adentro de las sílabas:
quiero tocar el fuego
en el sonido:
quiero sentir la oscuridad
del grito.° Quiero   *scream*
palabras ásperas
como piedras° vírgenes   *stones*

Pablo Neruda, poeta chileno, Premio Nobel de
literatura, 1971

La Época, Santiago (Chile)

Edificios modernos en
Buenos Aires, la Argentina

CONTAMINACION DE PLAYAS

El final de un problema

☐ **Autoridades de la quinta región analizan dos alternativas para terminar con la polución de las aguas del mar.**

Si bien el problema de contaminación que afecta a las playas de Viña del Mar aún no está solucionado en forma definitiva, la situación este año parece más auspiciosa que en temporadas pasadas. En 1986, la comisión encargada de estudiar tanto la contaminación de playas (arena) como la calidad del agua (mar), que es presidida por el gobernador de Valparaíso, determinó la clausura de nueve balnearios de la ciudad jardín.

La medida no afectó el flujo turístico hacia la zona, pero sí provocó una natural preocupación entre los veraneantes. Según expresó a ERCILLA el jefe subrogante del Departamento de Programas del Ambiente de la quinta región, doctor Cristián Gutiérrez, en la actualidad se están haciendo los estudios pertinentes en los diferentes balnearios de la región.

Explicó el funcionario que con los datos en la mano se podrá hacer una evaluación que permita entregar un diagnóstico sobre el estado de contaminación que las playas puedan presentar.

Gabriel García Márquez,
Premio Nobel de
literatura, 1982;
autor de *Cien años
de soledad*

La obra se instalará en la ciudad sede,° Barcelona   *site*

Fernando Botero construirá° una gran escultura para las Olimpíadas de 1992

will build

El artista, que vive entre París, Colombia y Nueva York, criticó los remates° de obras de arte que organizan las casas de Christie's y Sotheby's. Actualmente no expone en galerías de arte; dice preferir los espacios abiertos "pues hay que acercar las esculturas a las plazas públicas".

auctions

La Época, Santiago (Chile)

El petróleo, el «oro
negro» del lago
Maracaibo, Venezuela

LOS PASATIEMPOS Y LA VIDA COTIDIANA

VOCABULARIO: LOS PASATIEMPOS

las funciones
la taquilla

la acera   las entradas*

dar un paseo to take a walk
hacer *camping* to go camping
hacer planes para + *inf.* to make plans to (*do something*)
ir al teatro/a ver una película to go to the theater/to see a movie
jugar (ue) a las cartas/al ajedrez to play cards/chess

pasarlo bien, divertirse (ie, i) to have a good time
practicar un deporte to participate in a sport
ser divertido/a to be fun
tomar el sol to sunbathe
visitar un museo to visit a museum

la butaca seat (*in a theater*)
el cine movie theater
la comedia play; comedy
la función performance, show
la película (doblada) (dubbed) movie
la trama plot

los ratos libres free time

*The words **billete** and **boleto** can designate *tickets* for travel or theater tickets. **Entrada** (and its synonym **localidad**) can mean only *tickets* for an event or performance.

337

cerca
de
descansar

A.   Ud. quiere ir al cine. Usando los números del **1** al **9**, indique en qué orden va a hacer las siguientes cosas.

_____ Llamo a mi amigo/a para ver si quiere acompañarme.
_____ Cuando hago planes para ir al cine, lo primero que hago es consultar el periódico.
_____ Compramos las entradas en la taquilla.
_____ Subo al autobús para ir al centro, donde está el cine.
_____ Buscamos buenas butacas para poder ver bien.
_____ Compramos refrescos para tomar durante la película.
_____ Me fijo en (_I pay attention to_) la trama para tratar de adivinar (_to guess_) cómo va a terminar la película.
_____ Espero a mi amigo/a en la acera delante de la taquilla.
_____ Después de la función, vamos a un café a tomar algo.

B.   Describa los dibujos, contestando las preguntas e inventando otros detalles.

1.   VOCABULARIO: la pantalla, tener lugar (_to take place_)
¿Dónde tiene lugar esta escena? ¿Por qué han venido estas personas a este sitio? ¿Por qué están de pie esas dos personas? ¿Por qué han llegado tarde? ¿En qué país se hizo esta película? ¿Está doblada? ¿Por qué sí o por qué no? ¿Quiénes son el actor y la actriz principales? ¿Es una película de aventuras? ¿de horror? ¿romántica? Cuente Ud. un poco de la trama.

2.   VOCABULARIO: la plaza central
¿Tiene lugar esta escena en los Estados Unidos? Explique su respuesta. ¿Qué tiempo hace? ¿Qué hace la familia ahora? ¿Qué ha hecho ya hoy? ¿Qué planes tiene para el resto de la tarde? ¿Qué hace el resto de la gente? ¿Se está divirtiendo?

3.   VOCABULARIO: el río, el valle, el bosque (_forest_)
¿Qué hace esta familia? ¿Dónde están? ¿De dónde son? ¿Por qué han venido a este sitio? ¿Cuándo llegaron? ¿Cuánto tiempo van a pasar allí en total? ¿Por qué les gusta hacer esto? ¿En qué otros sitios lo han hecho?

4.   VOCABULARIO: la pareja (_couple_), la exposición de arte
¿En qué tipo de edificio está la pareja? ¿Por qué han venido a este lugar? ¿Dónde viven? ¿Por qué cree Ud. esto? ¿Qué día de la semana cree Ud. que es? ¿Por qué está aquí la pareja? ¿Qué otras cosas han hecho hoy? ¿Qué van a hacer después?

C.   Asociaciones. ¿Qué actividades o pasatiempos asocia Ud. con... ?

el verano, la primavera, el otoño, el invierno, una cita especial con (su novio/a, su esposo/a, ...), un día lluvioso

Notas culturales: La tertulia

Una costumbre muy común en muchas partes del mundo hispánico es la tertulia, que consiste en un grupo de amigos a quienes les gusta pasar el rato conversando. Los participantes se reúnen (*get together*) periódicamente, por ejemplo, a la misma hora de la tarde todos los días. Generalmente la tertulia se celebra en un bar o café donde se puede tomar vino o cerveza y hablar. Las conversaciones pueden abarcar (*cover*) muchos temas, pero sin duda dos de los más comunes son los deportes y la política. Ya que la gente hispánica se muda con menos frecuencia que en los Estados Unidos, muchos de estos grupos duran años y años, con los mismos amigos reuniéndose en el mismo sitio y a la misma hora.

Al tanto...

Here are some additional words and phrases to use to describe what you do in your free time.

dar un paseo	=	pasear
		dar una vuelta (con los compas [= compañeros])
		estirar (*to stretch*) las piernas
mirar la tele	=	tumbarse a ver la tele
dormir un poco	=	echarse una siesta
ir a bailar	=	ir a la disco(teca)

¿*T*e has preguntado por qué generación tras generación los jóvenes vienen coleccionando sellos?
  Seguramente porque hay gustos para todo. Temas no faltan: deporte, arte, ecología... Siempre hay una buena razón para empezar tu colección de sellos.
  En las expendedurías de Tabacalera especializadas en filatelia puedes encontrar las nuevas emisiones de sellos desde el primer día que se ponen en circulación. Durante 30 días reservan las series completas al coleccionista. Sin necesidad de anticipar ningún dinero. Sin esperas ni desplazamientos. Muy cerca de ti, tu expendedor filatélico.

BUSCA ESTE SÍMBOLO.
AQUÍ EL COLECCIONISTA ES EL PRIMERO.

¿Recuerda Ud.?

Ud. and **Uds.** commands (Grammar Section 23) are the third persons (singular and plural) of the present subjunctive. Object pronouns (direct, indirect, reflexive) must follow and be attached to affirmative commands; they must precede negative commands.

Affirmative: Háble**le** Ud.   Duérma**se**.   Díga**selo** Ud.
Negative: **No le** hable Ud.   **No se** duerma.   **No se lo** diga Ud.

¿Cómo se dice en español?
1. Bring me the book. (**Uds.**) Tráiganmelo.
2. Don't give it to her. (**Uds.**) No se lo den,
3. Sit here, please. (**Ud.**) Siéntese aquí, por favor.
4. Don't sit in that chair! (**Ud.**) ¡No se siente en esta silla!
5. Tell them the truth. (**Uds.**) Díganles la verdad.
6. Tell it to them now! (**Uds.**) ¡Dígansela ahora!
7. Never tell it to her. (**Uds.**) Nunca se la digan.
8. Take care of yourself (**Ud.**) Cuídese.
9. Lead a healthy life. (**Ud.**) Lleve una vida sana.
10. Listen to me. (**Ud.**) Escúcheme

ESTRUCTURAS

42. INFLUENCING OTHERS
Tú Commands

En la escuela primaria: frases útiles para la maestra
—Maritere, *toma* tu leche; *no tomes* la de Carlos.
—Cristina, *escribe* las oraciones en la pizarra; *no las escribas* en la pared.
—Joaquín, *escucha*; *no hables* tanto.
—Esteban, *siéntate* en tu silla; *no te sientes* en el suelo.
—Silvia, *quítate* el abrigo; *no te quites* el suéter.
—Graciela, *dale* el cuaderno a Ernesto; *no se lo des* a Joaquín.
—Mario, *ponte* el abrigo; *no olvides* tu calculadora.
—Ramón, *ten* cuidado; *no corras*, *no te caigas*.
—Juana, *no hagas* eso; *tráeme* el papel.

1. ¿Qué dice la maestra cuando Maritere no toma su leche? ¿cuando alguien debe escribir en la pizarra? ¿no escucha? ¿no se sienta en la silla? ¿no se quita el abrigo? ¿no le da el cuaderno a Ernesto? ¿no se pone el abrigo? ¿no tiene cuidado? ¿no trae el papel?
2. ¿Por qué la maestra da mandatos negativos? Por ejemplo, ¿por qué le dice la maestra a Maritere «no tomes la leche de Carlos»?
   • Porque Maritere tomó la leche de Carlos.
   • Porque no está tomando su propia leche.
   • Porque la maestra no quiere que Maritere la tome.

Informal commands (**los mandatos informales**) are used with persons whom you address as **tú**.

Negative *tú* Commands

-ar VERBS		**-er/-ir** VERBS	
No hables.	*Don't speak.*	**No comas.**	*Don't eat.*
No cantes.	*Don't sing.*	**No escribas.**	*Don't write.*
No juegues.	*Don't play.*	**No pidas.**	*Don't order.*

In grade school: Useful phrases for the teacher Maritere, drink your milk; don't drink Carlos's. Cristina, write the sentences on the board; don't write them on the wall. Joaquín, listen; don't talk so much. Esteban, sit in your chair; don't sit on the floor. Silvia, take off your coat; don't take off your sweater. Graciela, give the notebook to Ernesto; don't give it to Joaquín. Mario, put on your coat; don't forget your calculator. Ramón, be careful; don't run, don't fall. Juana, don't do that; bring me the paper.

Like **Ud.** commands (Grammar Section 23), the negative **tú** commands are expressed with the present subjunctive: **no hable Ud.**, **no hables (tú)**. The pronoun **tú** is used only for emphasis.

No cantes **tú** tan fuerte.	*Don't you sing so loudly.*

As with negative **Ud.** commands, object pronouns—direct, indirect, and reflexive—precede negative **tú** commands.

No lo mires.	*Don't look at him.*
No les escribas.	*Don't write to them.*
No te levantes.	*Don't get up.*

[Práctica A–B]

Affirmative *tú* Commands*

-ar VERBS		**-er/-ir** VERBS	
Habla.	*Speak.*	**Come.**	*Eat.*
Canta.	*Sing.*	**Escribe.**	*Write.*
Juega.	*Play.*	**Pide.**	*Order.*

Unlike the other command forms you have learned, most affirmative **tú** commands have the same form as the third person singular of the present *indicative*. Some verbs have irregular affirmative **tú** command forms.

decir:	**di**	poner:	**pon**	tener:	**ten**
hacer:	**haz**	salir:	**sal**	venir:	**ven**
ir:	**ve**	ser:	**sé**		

Sé puntual pero **ten** cuidado.	*Be there on time, but be careful.*

¡OJO! The affirmative **tú** commands for **ir** and **ver** are identical: **ve**. Context will clarify meaning.

¡**Ve** esa película!	*See that movie!*
Ve a casa ahora mismo.	*Go home right now.*

As in affirmative **Ud.** commands, object and reflexive pronouns follow affirmative **tú** commands and are attached to them. Accent marks are necessary except when a single pronoun is added to a one-syllable command.

Dile la verdad.	*Tell him the truth.*
Léela, por favor.	*Read it, please.*
Póntelos.	*Put them on.*

[Práctica C–E]

---

*Affirmative **vosotros** commands are formed by substituting **-d** for the final **-r** of the infinitive: hablar → hablad; comer → comed; escribir → escribid. There are no irregular affirmative **vosotros** commands. Negative **vosotros** commands are expressed with the present subjunctive: **no habléis/comáis/escribáis**. Placement of object pronouns is the same as with all other command forms: **Decídmelo; No me lo digáis.**

Práctica

A.   Un viaje con Raúl. Durante un viaje en coche, su amigo Raúl insiste en hacer cosas que a Ud. no le gustan. Dígale que no las haga, según el modelo.

MODELO: Raúl estaciona el carro en medio (*middle*) de la calle. →
Raúl, no lo estaciones aquí, por favor.

1. Raúl gasta mucho dinero en gasolina.
2. Raúl maneja rápidamente.
3. Cierra la ventana.
4. Dobla en la esquina.
5. Para en la esquina.
6. Lee el mapa.
7. Sigue todo derecho.
8. Dice que Uds. van a llegar tarde.
9. Es muy descortés con Ud.
10. Arranca rápidamente.

B.   Los señores Villarreal no están contentos con el comportamiento de su hija Julita. Continúe los comentarios de ellos con mandatos informales lógicos según cada situación. Siga los modelos.

MODELOS: *Hablaste* demasiado ayer. → No *hables* tanto hoy, por favor.

Dejaste tu ropa en el suelo anoche. → No la *dejes* allí hoy, por favor.

1. También *dejaste* tus libros en el suelo.
2. ¿Por qué *regresaste* tarde a casa hoy después de las clases?
3. Ayer *usaste* mi toalla.
4. Tampoco quiero que *entres* en nuestro cuarto de baño para nada.
5. No es bueno que *corras* y *juegues* en la calle.
6. ¿Por qué *vas* al parque todas las tardes?
7. No es bueno que *mires* la televisión constantemente. ¿Y por qué quieres *ver* todos esos programas de detectives?
8. ¿Por qué le *dices* mentiras (*lies*) a tu papá?
9. Siempre *te olvidas* de sacar la basura, que es la única tarea que tienes que hacer.
10. Ay, hija, no te comprendemos. ¡*Eres* tan insolente!

C.   La pobre Julita también escucha muchos mandatos de su maestra en clase. Invente Ud. esos mandatos según las indicaciones.

1. llegar / a / escuela / puntualmente
2. entrar / clase / sin / hacer tanto ruido
3. quitarse / abrigo / y / sentarse
4. sacar / libro de matemáticas / y / abrirlo / en / página 10
5. escribir / problema dos / en / pizarra
6. leer / nuevo / palabras / y / aprenderlas / para mañana
7. venir / aquí / a / hablar conmigo / sobre / este / composición
8. ayudar / Carlitos / con / su composición

¿Qué mandatos—positivos o negativos—recuerda Ud. de la escuela primaria?

D. En casa, otra vez las acciones de la pobre Julita siguen disgustando a todos, hasta a Eufemia, su hermana mayor. Continúe los comentarios de todos con mandatos informales lógicos—positivos o negativos—según cada situación.

1. Siempre entras en mi cuarto y usas mis cosas sin permiso. No quiero que toques nada en este cuarto, ¿comprendes?
2. No ayudas nunca con las tareas domésticas. Por lo menos puedes poner la mesa, ¿no?
3. Siempre quieres hacer las cosas rápidamente. Nunca tienes paciencia ni cuidado.
4. Tienes que desayunar. No puedes salir para la escuela sin tomar algo.
5. No me escuchas nunca. ¿Qué te pasa? ¿Por qué no puedes poner atención?
6. No debes contestarme con ese tono de voz. Y cuando te hablo, quiero que me mires.
7. No le dijiste la verdad a papá sobre el disco roto.
8. Nunca te acuestas cuando yo te lo digo. ¿Por qué no puedes ser obediente, como Eufemia?

E. Con dos compañeros, invente mandatos informales para las siguientes situaciones.

- para ser un esposo (una esposa) feliz
- para ser el compañero (la compañera) de cuarto ideal
- para estar en buena salud
- para divertirse con los amigos

Bogotá, Colombia

La vida de la gran ciudad
—¿Cómo pasas tus ratos libres aquí en la capital?
—A veces voy al teatro o a ver una película. Soy muy aficionado al cine.
—¿No te gusta visitar los museos?
—Eso también. Sobre todo el Museo de Arte Moderno.

ESTRUCTURAS

. . . .

43. ¿HAY ALGUIEN QUE...? ¿HAY UN LUGAR DONDE...?
Subjunctive After Nonexistent and Indefinite Antecedents

En la plaza central
Describa lo que pasa y lo que *no* ocurre en esta escena de la plaza principal de un pueblo mexicano.

- *Hay personas* que *conversan* con los amigos, que *pasan* aquí sus ratos libres todos los días, que... (jugar al ajedrez, vender/comprar periódicos/comida, tomar el sol, ¿ ?)
- *Hay niños* que *toman* helados, que... (jugar en la acera, dar un paseo con sus padres, ¿ ?)
- *No hay nadie* que *lleve* ropa de invierno, que *juegue* al vólibol, que... (ser aficionado al golf, ser de los Estados Unidos, escuchar la radio, ¿ ?)

In English and Spanish, statements or questions that give or ask for information about a person, place, or thing often contain two clauses:

> I have a **car** *that* **gets good mileage.**
> Is there a **house** for sale *that* **is closer to the city?**

Each of the preceding sentences contains a main clause (*I have a car . . .* ; *Is there a house for sale . . .*). In addition, each sentence also has a dependent clause (*. . . that gets good mileage; . . . that is closer to the city?*) that modifies a noun in the main clause: *car, house.* The noun (or pronoun) modified is called the *antecedent* (**el antecedente**) of the dependent clause, and the clause itself is called an adjective clause, since—like an adjective—it modifies a noun (or pronoun).

In Spanish, when the antecedent of an adjective clause refers to someone (something, someplace, and so on) that does not exist in the speaker's experience or whose existence is indefinite or uncertain, the subjunctive must be used in the adjective (dependent) clause.

EXISTENT ANTECEDENT:	**Hay algo** aquí que me **interesa**.	*There is something here that interests me.*
NONEXISTENT ANTECEDENT:	**No hay nada** aquí que me **interese**.	*There is nothing here that interests me.*

AJEDREZ
Por Román Torán

POSICION NUMERO 5.295

Blancas juegan y ganan

En la partida Apsheniek-Meingailis (Kemeri, 1939) se llegó a esta posición. En ella, ambos bandos tienen ataque y, por lo tanto, también están en peligro y deben maniobrar con precisión. Las blancas lograron imponerse con enérgica combinación. ¿Cuál es?

La solución, en el próximo número

DEFINITE ANTECEDENT:	**Hay muchos restaurantes** donde **sirven** comida mexicana auténtica.	*There are a lot of restaurants where they serve authentic Mexican food.*
INDEFINITE ANTECEDENT:	**Buscamos un restaurante** donde **sirvan** comida salvadoreña auténtica.	*We're looking for a restaurant where they serve authentic Salvadorean food.*

Note, as in the preceding examples, that adjective clauses of this type can be introduced with **donde...** rather than **que...**

¡OJO! The dependent adjective clause structure is often used in questions to find out information about someone or something the speaker does not know much about. Note, however, that the indicative is used to answer the question if the antecedent is known to the person who answers.

¿Hay algo aquí que te **guste**? —Sí, **hay varias cosas** que me **gustan** y que **creo** que las voy a comprar.	*Is there something here that you like? —Yes, there are several things that I like and I think I'm going to buy them.*

¡OJO! The personal **a** is not used with direct object nouns that refer to hypothetical persons.* Compare the use of the indicative and the subjunctive in the following sentences.

Busco **un señor** que lo **sepa**.	*I'm looking for a man who knows that (it).*
Busco **al señor** que lo **sabe**.	*I'm looking for the man who knows that (it).*

Práctica

A. Contradict the speakers in the following situations, using the cues in parentheses.

1. Ud. y su amigo Rodolfo están perdidos en un camino rural, por la noche. Además, parece que el coche empieza a fallar (*sputter*).
   RODOLFO: —Seguramente hay alguien en aquella casa que conoce el camino. (No, hombre, no hay nadie...)
   —Sin duda en aquella gasolinera hay alguien que puede arreglar el coche. (No, no hay nadie...)

2. En una oficina: son las cinco de la tarde y hay mucho trabajo que hacer todavía. Ud. habla con el jefe.
   JEFE: —Necesito al secretario que sabe chino. (Pero, señor, aquí no tenemos ningún...)
   —Claro que hay alguien que tiene tiempo de terminarlo para mañana. (Siento decírselo, pero no hay...)

---

*Remember that **alguien** and **nadie** always take the personal **a** when they are used as direct objects: **Busco a alguien que lo sepa. No veo a nadie que sea norteamericano.**

3. En la tienda de muebles: su esposo/a busca muebles para su casa.

ESPOSO/A: —Pues, sí, aquí hay algunas cosas que me gustan. (No hay nada…)

—Necesitamos un sillón que sea un poco más grande. (Pero si ya tenemos dos…)

B. Carmen acaba de llegar aquí de otro estado. Quiere saber algunas cosas sobre la universidad y la ciudad. Haga las preguntas de Carmen según el modelo.

MODELO: restaurantes / sirven comida latinoamericana →
¿Hay restaurantes que sirvan (donde sirvan) comida latinoamericana?

1. librerías / venden libros usados
2. tiendas / se puede comprar revistas de Latinoamérica
3. cafés cerca de la universidad / se reúnen muchos estudiantes
4. discotecas / se puede bailar
5. apartamentos cerca de la universidad / son buenos y baratos
6. cines / pasan (*they show*) películas en español
7. canchas (*courts*) de tenis / se puede jugar por la noche
8. un gimnasio en la universidad / se juega al ráquetbol
9. parques / la gente corre o da paseos
10. museos / hacen exposiciones de arte latinoamericana

Según las preguntas que ha hecho Carmen, ¿son ciertas o falsas las siguientes declaraciones?

1. A Carmen no le interesa la cultura hispánica.
2. Carmen es una persona muy deportista (*sports-minded*).
3. Es posible que sea estudiante.
4. Este año piensa vivir con unos amigos de sus padres.

Ahora conteste las preguntas de Carmen con información verdadera sobre la ciudad donde Ud. vive y su universidad.

C.   Una encuesta. Las habilidades o características de un grupo de personas pueden ser sorprendentes. ¿Qué sabe Ud. de los compañeros de su clase de español? Por turno, pregunte a la clase quién sabe hacer lo siguiente o a quién le ocurre lo siguiente. Deben levantar la mano sólo los que puedan contestar afirmativamente. Luego la persona que hizo la pregunta debe hacer un comentario apropiado. Siga el modelo.

MODELO: hablar chino → En esta clase, ¿hay alguien que hable chino? (Nadie levanta la mano.) No hay nadie que hable chino.

1. hablar ruso
2. saber tocar la viola
3. conocer a un actor (una actriz)
4. saber preparar comida vietnamita
5. tener el cumpleaños hoy
6. escribir poemas
7. ser muy deportista
8. ¿ ?

UN POCO DE TODO

Hablando de películas... Complete the following dialogue and movie reviews with the correct form of the words in parentheses, as suggested by the context. When two possibilities are given in parentheses, select the correct word. Use the past participle of infinitives indicated with an asterisk.

Saliendo del cine

—Bueno, ¿qué piensas (*de/en*[1]) la película? ¿Te gustó?

—Pues, (*ser/estar*[2]) muy (*divertir*[3])*... pero quizás un poco superficial.

—Ah, ¿sí? ¿Por qué (*reírse*[4]) tanto?

—Hombre, no hay (*alguien/nadie*[5]) que no lo (*pasar*[6]) bien viendo una de estas historietas de vez en cuando. Pero (*que/lo que*[7]) yo realmente (*preferir*[8]) son las películas sobre temas más (*profundo*[9]). Como, por ejemplo, (*ese*[10]) película francesa (*que/lo que*[11]) (*ver:* nosotros[12]) la semana (*pasar*[13])*.

—Bueno, la próxima vez es mejor que tú (*escoger*°[14]) la película; pero no me   *to select* (escojo)
(*llevar*[15]) a ver (*alguna/ninguna*[16]) película (*doblar*[17])*, ¿eh? Ya (*saber/conocer:* tú[18]) que éstas no me (*gustar*[19]) nada.

El regreso del Jedi

Esta película (*ser/estar*[20]) la tercera parte de una serie muy famosa que se (*iniciar*[21]) con *La guerra de las galaxias* y (*continuar*[22]) con *El imperio* (*contraatacar*[23]). El rasgo° principal de *El regreso del Jedi* (*ser/estar*[24]) la acción   *característica*
emocionante, (*caracterizar*[25])* por complejos efectos (*especial*[26]). En *Jedi*, los
personajes° principales, (*que/lo que*[27]) representan la Alianza Rebelde,   *characters*
(*volver*[28]) para enfrentarse° con las Fuerzas Imperiales de la Oscuridad,   *to confront*
(*encabezar*°[29])* por el malévolo° Darth Vader.   *to lead / malo*

La Bamba

Esta película, (*escribir*[30])* y (*dirigir*°[31])* por Luis Valdez, se (*basar*[32]) en la   *to direct*
vida de Ritchie Valens y (*los/las*[33]) ocho meses de su ascenso a la fama. *La
Bamba* trata de° los sueños° «rocanroleros» de un joven chicano y de cómo   *trata... deals with / dreams*
su trágica muerte, (*ocurrir*[34])* en un accidente de aviación a la edad de 17
años, lo (*cambiar*[35]) todo. En ese accidente (*morir*[36]) también Buddy Holly y
J. P. Richardson, más (*conocer*[37])* como «Big Bopper». Verdaderamente, *La
Bamba* es (*uno*[38]) película excelente que muestra° realidades de la vida que   *shows*
(*ir*[39]) más allá de° la historia de un joven chicano que logra° saborear las   *más... beyond / consigue*
agridulces° experiencias del estrellato.°   *bittersweet / stardom*

UN PASO MÁS: Situaciones

¿Qué quieres hacer?

Una tarde de verano

—Lo siento pero… no los puedo acompañar. Ya no tengo bicicleta.
—Pues, si quieres, puedes usar la de mi hermano.
—¿Qué te parece si vamos hasta el lago?
—¡Estupendo! …y podemos llevar la merienda.°   snack

Un fin de semana en la ciudad

—¿Qué hacen Uds. los fines de semana?
—Nos encanta pasear° por la mañana, cuando hay poco tráfico.   caminar
—Sí, y a veces visitamos alguna exposición de arte y después tomamos el
  aperitivo° en un café.   ¿ ?
—¿Me permiten ir con Uds. alguna vez?
—¡Encantados!

Delante del cine

—¡Hola, hombre! ¿Tú también vienes a ver *El museo de Drácula*?
—¡Qué va! Voy a ver *El sol de Acapulco*.
—¿Por qué no nos acompañas? Está con nosotros Marisa, la prima de
  Carlos.
—Lo siento, pero voy a encontrarme con Elena Ortega… y además a mí me
  parecen pesadísimas las películas de horror.
—Hasta luego, entonces. Que lo pases bien.°   Que… ¿ ?
—Chau. ¡Y que se diviertan°!   Que… ¿ ?

Notas lingüísticas: Indirect Commands

You should be able to guess from context the meaning of the last two phrases glossed
in the dialogue. They are both the approximate equivalent of English *"Hope you have
a good time!"* Note that the subjunctive is used in both expressions.

   Structures of this type are called indirect commands in Spanish. If they were
direct commands, they would be: **Pásalo bien, Diviértanse.** Instead, their structure
is like that of the dependent clause in a two-clause sentence that uses the subjunctive:

   (Espero) Que lo pases bien.
   (Ojalá) Que se diviertan.

Indirect commands of this kind are used frequently in Spanish. You should be able
to understand them easily whenever you hear or read them.

AGENDA

Cine en Valladolid

ENTRE el 20 y el 28 de este mes se celebra la 34 edición de la *Semana Internacional de Cine de Valladolid*. En la «Sección Oficial» compiten cerca de veinte largometrajes del mundo de la actualidad que, pese a su valor creativo, no suelen acceder a las pantallas españolas.

El Palmarés de la Semana de Valladolid se cierra con la entrega de la *Espiga de Oro* y la *Espiga de Plata* a las mejores películas que hayan concursado. ∎

Conversación

Con un compañero (una compañera), invente las siguientes conversaciones, siguiendo el modelo de los diálogos anteriores. Haga dos versiones de cada conversación: en una, la persona invitada acepta la invitación; en otra, dice que no, explicando por qué.

- invitar a un amigo a pasar la tarde en la playa
- invitar a un amigo a acompañarlo/la al cine con un pariente de su novio/a (esposo/a)

VOCABULARIO

Los pasatiempos

dar un paseo to take a walk
hacer planes para + *inf.* to make plans to (*do something*)
jugar (ue) a las cartas/al ajedrez to play cards/chess
visitar un museo to visit a museum

Otros verbos

acompañar to accompany
reunirse (con) to get together (with)

El cine y el teatro

la acera sidewalk
la butaca seat (*in a theater*)
la comedia play; comedy
la entrada ticket (*for performance*)
la función performance, show
la taquilla box office
la trama plot (*of a play or novel*)

Otro sustantivo

el rato libre free time; *pl.* spare, free time

Adjetivos

cotidiano/a daily
deportista sports-minded; athlete
divertido/a fun
doblado/a dubbed

Palabras adicionales

tener cuidado to be careful
tener lugar to take place

Frases útiles para la comunicación

Que + *subjunctive*
  Que lo pases bien.
  Que te diviertas.

I hope + *verb form*

(I hope you) Have a good time.

LOS DEPORTES

VOCABULARIO: ¿ERES DEPORTISTA?

jugar al fútbol norteamericano

jugar al fútbol

pasear en bici(cleta)

esquiar

patinar

nadar, la natación

correr

Otros deportes: el básquetbol, el béisbol, el golf, el hockey, el tenis, el vólibol

ganar to win
perder (ie) to lose
ser aficionado/a (a) to be a fan (of)

el campo (playing) field
la cancha (tennis) court
el equipo team; equipment
el estadio stadium

el gimnasio gymnasium
el juego play (*in a game*); (card, board) game
el/la jugador(a) player
el partido game, match ⟨w. sports⟩

los esquís skis
la pelota ball
la raqueta racket
la red net
el traje de baño bathing suit

el baloncesta: basketball
el balon: ball
el cesto: basket
el bañador: bathing suit

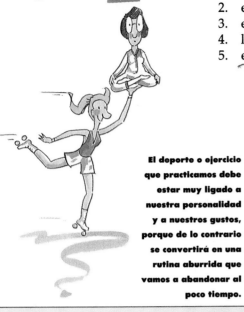

El deporte o ejercicio
que practicamos debe
estar muy ligado a
nuestra personalidad
y a nuestros gustos,
porque de lo contrario
se convertirá en una
rutina aburrida que
vamos a abandonar al
poco tiempo.

A. ¿Qué palabra o frase no pertenece al grupo? Explique por qué.

1. la cancha   la raqueta   el campo   la piscina
2. el ciclismo   el correr   el juego   la natación
3. el traje de baño   la pelota   el jugador   la raqueta
4. la red   los esquís   la bicicleta   el equipo
5. el campo   el equipo   los aficionados   los jugadores

(handwritten: cycling   running)

B. ¿Dónde y cuándo se practican estos deportes? ¿Cómo es el jugador típico de cada deporte? ¿Qué tipo de persona es? ¿Le gusta jugar con un equipo o practicar el deporte individualmente? ¿Le interesa la competencia o prefiere competir consigo mismo (*with himself*)? ¿Cómo es el aficionado típico? Conteste estas preguntas sobre uno o dos de los siguientes deportes.

1. el golf
2. el fútbol norteamericano
3. el correr
4. el béisbol
5. el básquetbol
6. la natación
7. pasear en bicicleta
8. el esquiar

Al tanto...

You know the names for many specific sports, but . . . what if you just want to go out and toss a ball around?

   jugar al balón (a la pelota) = jugar con una pelota de una manera informal, es decir, sin que sea un partido de fútbol, de básquetbol, ni de ningún deporte específico.

Be careful with the use of the adjective **deportista**, which refers to one's interests, *not* to one's ability. A skilled athlete (**un[a] atleta**) is **muy atlético/a.**

Carlos Di Laura en acción, mientras Yzaga lo observa. El dúo peruano aunque tuvo altibajos luchó por equilibrar el encuentro en el que los australianos Fitzgerald y Cahill se mostraron superiores.

El jugador argentino de fútbol Diego Maradona

¡Malas noticias!
—Lo siento, pero tu equipo volvió a perder.
—No me hables. 3 a 0... ¡y en casa!
—Si siguen así, es posible que pierdan la liga.°   *division title*
—¡La culpa es de los árbitros!
—¡Claro! Siempre que pierde tu equipo, la culpa es del árbitro.

ESTRUCTURAS

44. EXPRESSING CONTINGENCY AND PURPOSE
The Subjunctive After Certain Conjunctions

Unos verdaderos aficionados

SARA: No quiero ir al partido *a menos que juegue* David.

CARLOS: Estoy de acuerdo. *Antes de que compres* los boletos, pregunta si va a jugar.

JULIO: Y *en caso de que* no *juegue*, ¿qué?

CARLOS: ¡Hombre, pues entonces mejor nos quedamos en casa! Hay un estupendo partido en la televisión. Aquí tenemos cerveza y bocadillos y cojines y... ¡Y además está empezando a llover! ... ¿No es hora de poner la tele?

Busque en el diálogo el equivalente de las frases indicadas.
1. No voy al partido *si no juega David.*
2. *Antes de comprar* los boletos, quiero saber quién juega.
3. ¿Qué hacemos *si no juega*?

¿Son verdaderos deportistas Sara, Carlos y Julio? ¿Les interesa más el deporte o su amigo David? ¿Les interesa más el deporte o su propia comodidad (*comfort*)?

When one action or condition is related to another—X will happen provided that Y occurs; we'll do Z just in case A happens—we say that a relationship of *contingency* exists between the actions or conditions: one thing is contingent, or depends, on another.

The following Spanish *conjunctions* (**las conjunciones**) express relationships of contingency or purpose. The subjunctive always occurs in dependent clauses introduced by these conjunctions.

a menos que	unless	**en caso de que**	in case
antes (de) que	before	**para que**	so that
con tal (de) que	provided (that)		

Some real fans   SARA: I don't want to go to the game unless David is playing. CARLOS: I agree. Before you buy the tickets, ask if he's going to play. JULIO: And if (in case) he's not playing, what shall we do? CARLOS: Well, then it's better to stay home! There's a great game on TV. We've got beer and snacks and cushions here . . . And besides, it's starting to rain! . . . Isn't it time to turn on the TV?

Voy **con tal que** ellos me acompañen.	*I'm going, provided (that) they go with me.*
En caso de que llegue Juan, dile que ya salí.	*In case Juan arrives, tell him that I already left.*

Note that these conjunctions introduce dependent clauses in which the events have not yet materialized; the events are conceptualized, not real-world events. When there is no change of subject in the dependent clause, Spanish more frequently uses the prepositions **antes de** and **para**, plus an infinitive, instead of the corresponding conjunctions plus the subjunctive. Compare the following:

PREPOSITION:	Estoy aquí **para aprender**.	*I'm here to (in order to) learn.*
CONJUNCTION:	Estoy aquí **para que Uds. aprendan**.	*I'm here so that you will learn.*
PREPOSITION:	Voy a comer **antes de salir**.	*I'm going to eat before leaving.*
CONJUNCTION:	Voy a comer **antes (de) que salgamos**.	*I'm going to eat before we leave.*

Práctica

A. Siempre es buena idea llegar un poco temprano al teatro o al cine. Sin embargo (*However*), su amigo Julio, quien va al cine con Ud. esta tarde, no quiere salir con un poco de anticipación. Trate de convencerle de que Uds. deben salir pronto.

—No entiendo por qué quieres que lleguemos al teatro tan temprano.
—Pues, para que (nosotros)...

Sugerencias: poder estacionar el coche, no perder el principio de la función, poder comprar entradas, conseguir buenas butacas, no tener que hacer cola, comprar palomitas (*popcorn*) antes de que empiece la película, hablar con Raúl y Ceci, ¿ ?

B. **Un fin de semana en las montañas.** Hablan Manuel y su esposa Marta. Use la conjunción entre paréntesis para unir las oraciones, haciendo todos los cambios necesarios.

1. No voy. Dejamos a los niños en casa. (a menos que)
2. Yo también prefiero que vayamos solos. Pasamos un rato libre sin ellos. (para que)
3. Esta vez voy a aprender a esquiar. Tú me lo enseñas. (con tal que)
4. Quiero que salgamos temprano por la mañana. Nieva mucho. (a menos que)
5. Es importante que lleguemos a la cabaña. Empieza a nevar en las montañas. (antes de que)

6. Compra leña (*firewood*) aquí. No hay leña en la cabaña. (en caso de que)
7. Deja un recado (*message*). Tus padres nos llaman. (en caso de que)

¿Cierto, falso o no lo dice?

1. Manuel y Marta acaban de casarse.
2. Casi siempre van de vacaciones con los niños.
3. Los dos son esquiadores excelentes.
4. Son dueños de una cabaña que está en las montañas.

C.   Cualquier (*Any*) acción humana puede justificarse. Explique Ud. las siguientes situaciones tan lógicamente como sea posible.

1. Cuando la familia es muy grande, los padres trabajan mucho para (que)…
2. Los profesores les dan tarea a los estudiantes para que…
3. Tenemos que pagar los impuestos federales para que…
4. Los dueños de los equipos profesionales les pagan mucho a algunos jugadores para (que)…
5. Les compramos juguetes a los niños para que…
6. Se doblan las películas extranjeras para (que)…
7. Cambiamos de lugar los muebles de vez en cuando para (que)…
8. Los padres castigan (*punish*) a los niños para (que)…

Esta tarde los aurinegros contaron nuevamente con la presencia de Gerardo Rabajda en el arco, quien fuera figura en el clásico pasado por el Competencia.

—Gerardo, ¿cómo está Peñarol?

—Bien, estamos trabajando muy tranquilos y con muchas esperanzas de que salga un lindo partido y de poder obtener la victoria.

—Y para ti la oportunidad de tener nuevamente una gran actuación como en el clásico pasado.

—Sí, por supuesto que me gustaría repetir la actuación que tuve, pero el clásico pasado ya pasó, es otra historia y ahora hay que pensar en éste que es muy importante para muchos de nosotros ya que nos estamos jugando un puesto en el plantel principal.

¿Recuerda Ud.?

Review the forms and uses of possessive adjectives (Grammar Section 11) before beginning Grammar Section 45.

Singular:	mi	tu	su	nuestro/a	vuestro/a	su
Plural:	mis	tus	sus	nuestros/as	vuestros/as	sus

Son **mis** libros.   *They're my books.*
Es **su** gobierno.   *It's his (her, your, their) government.*
Son **nuestras** casas.   *They're our houses.*

¿Cómo se dice en español?

1. It's his racket.
2. What about (*¿Y…*) my skis?
3. It's our court.
4. It's your problem, too! (**Uds.**)
5. Their children don't do much exercise.
6. Our kids are pretty lazy too.
7. Your health is important. (**Ud.**)
8. Let's go to your gym. (**tú**)

ESTRUCTURAS

. . . .
45. MORE ABOUT EXPRESSING POSSESSION
Stressed Possessives

Algún día, hijo mío, todo esto va a ser tuyo.

1. ¿Quién es el dueño del mundo en esta visión del futuro?
2. ¿A quién le va a dar todo el padre robot?

When in English you would emphasize the possessive with your voice, or when you want to express English *of mine* (*of yours*, *of his*, and so on), you will use the *stressed forms* (**las formas tónicas**) of the possessive in Spanish. As the term implies, they are more emphatic than the *unstressed forms* (**las formas átonas**).

FORMS OF THE STRESSED POSSESSIVE ADJECTIVES			
mío/a/os/as	*my, (of) mine*	**nuestro/a/os/as**	*our, (of) ours*
tuyo/a/os/as	*your, (of) yours*	**vuestro/a/os/as**	*your, (of) yours*
suyo/a/os/as	*your, (of) yours; his, (of) his; her, (of) hers; its*	**suyo/a/os/as**	*your, (of) yours; their, (of) theirs*

Es **mi** amigo.

Es **un** amigo **mío**.

He's my friend.
{ He's **my** friend.
He's a friend of mine.

Es **su** perro.
Es **el** perro **suyo**.
Es **un** perro **suyo**. Es **suyo**.

It's her dog.
It's **her** dog.
It's a dog of hers. It's hers.

The stressed forms of the possessive adjective follow the noun, which must be preceded by a definite or indefinite article or by a demonstrative adjective. The stressed forms agree with the noun modified in number and gender. The stressed possessives are often used as pronouns: **la raqueta suya** → **la suya**; **el equipo tuyo** → **el tuyo**.*

———————————————————
*For more information, see Appendix 1, Using Adjectives as Nouns.

Práctica

A.   En el club de tenis. Complete el siguiente diálogo con las formas apropiadas del posesivo.

—Perdone, señor, pero esta raqueta que Ud. me ha dado no es (*mío*).
—¿No es (*suyo*)? ¿No es Ud. el señor García?
—Sí, soy yo, pero esta raqueta no es (*mío*). Ud. todavía tiene la (*mío*). Está allí a la derecha.
—Ah, me equivoqué. Ésta es del señor *Gracia*. Aquí tengo la (*suyo*). Lo siento, ¿eh?
—Pues, nada, hombre.

B. Ud. trata de encontrar una serie de objetos perdidos. ¿Son suyos los objetos que le ofrecen? Con un compañero (una compañera), haga y conteste preguntas según los modelos.

> MODELO: —Esta raqueta, ¿es *de Ud.*?
>   —No, no es *mía*.

1. de Juan   2. de Uds.   3. de Alicia   4. de Ud.   5. tuya

> MODELO: —¿Y esta *radio*?
>   —No, no es *mía*. *La mía* es (más pequeña, más grande, ...)

6. despertador   8. llave   10. pastillas
7. esquís   9. televisor   11. traje de baño

C.   Entrevista. Con un compañero (una compañera), haga y conteste las siguientes preguntas.

1. ¿Qué clases tienes este semestre (trimestre)? ¿Son interesantes? ¿Cuáles son más interesantes, mis clases o las tuyas?
2. ¿Cómo es tu horario (*schedule*) este semestre (trimestre)? ¿Cuál es más fácil, mi horario o el tuyo?
3. ¿Tienes coche? ¿Cómo es? ¿Prefieres mi coche o el tuyo?
4. ¿Vives en un apartamento? ¿Cuánto pagas al mes? ¿Cuál es más barato, mi apartamento o el tuyo?
5. ¿Cuántas personas hay en tu familia? ¿Cuál es más grande, mi familia o la tuya?
6. ¿Trabajas? ¿Dónde? ¿Te gusta ese trabajo? ¿Cuál es mejor, mi puesto o el tuyo?

Lord Aby venció a The Boss

Tatuaje ganó el premio 'Capitán FAP. Abelardo Quiñónez'

Lord Aby, respondiendo a nuestras simpatías, se impuso ayer de punta a punta en el clásico "Fuerza Aérea del Perú", derrotando por un cuerpo a The Boss.

El pupilo del stud "Polo Norte" marcó 1.32" para los 1500 metros.

Mientras tanto, en el premio especial "Capitán FAP. José Abelardo Quiñónez", le correspondió el triunfo a Tatuaje, marcando 1.32"1/5 para los 1500 metros.

UN POCO DE TODO

A.   La rutina y las diversiones. Form complete sentences based on the words given, in the order given. Give the informal command form of the verb in the main clause and add other words if necessary. Use subject pronouns only when needed.

1.   tratar / despertarse / antes de que / sonar (ue) / despertador / por favor
2.   buscar / alguien / que / levantarse / cinco / mañana / para correr
3.   poner / mesa / y / tener / comida / preparado / antes de que / empezar / noticiero (*news*) / de / seis
4.   en caso de que / tú / tener / rato libre / sábado, / comprar / entradas / para / cine
5.   dormir / con / ventanas / abierto / para que / entrar / aire

B.   Lea la siguiente sinópsis de algunas películas extranjeras que se exhibieron en Santiago (Chile) durante el mes de diciembre y complete las oraciones lógicamente, usando la información de la sinópsis o con información verdadera.

Sinopsis

● **Crónica de una muerte anunciada:** hermosa fotografía y ambientación, pero sin que el director Francesco Rosi logre recrear adecuadamente el libro de García Márquez. REGULAR.

● **Woodstock:** a más de un decenio de su estreno, mantiene su interés y sigue atrayendo a la juventud. RECOMENDABLE.

● **Robocop:** un policía, parte humano y parte robot, impone la ley y el orden; abundante violencia y acción. En su género, RECOMENDABLE.

● **Jardines de Piedra:** la guerra de Vietnam y la vida militar vistas desde una unidad ceremonial del ejército norteamericano. Dirigida por Coppola. RECOMENDABLE.

● **Tiempo de amar:** célebre violinista pierde su salud, su arte y su marido. A pesar de los esfuerzos de Julie Andrews, MENOS QUE REGULAR.

● **Mil veces adiós:** romance en tiempos de guerra (1942). Aviador norteamericano ama a hermosa sefardí en Jerusalén. La familia se opone. MENOS QUE REGULAR.

● **Camorra:** mujeres de Nápoles contra la mafia y las drogas, con la directora Lina Wertmuller en cuarto menguante. MENOS QUE REGULAR.

● **La familia:** ocho decenios de los placeres y pesares de una familia italiana. Muy buena interpretación de Vittorio Gassman. BUENA.

● **Los Intocables:** contra viento y marea, dos personajes muy disímiles imponen la ley en el Chicago de 1930, enviando a Al Capone a la cárcel. RECOMENDABLE.

● **Detective suelto en Hollywood:** Eddie Murphy otra vez hace de las suyas en Beverly Hills. Como entretención, sin mayores pretensiones. RECOMENDABLE.

● **Cita a ciegas:** farsa que no está a la altura de los buenos momentos en la trayectoria del realizador Blake Edwards. Con Kim Basinger. REGULAR.

● **"Cocodrillo" Dundee:** amena historia de un amable australiano dentro y fuera de su salsa. Con Paul Hogan. RECOMENDABLE.

Posibles terminaciones: italiano, francés, norteamericano

1.   Hay varias películas que (ser) _____.
2.   No hay ninguna película que (ser) _____.

Posibles terminaciones: recomendable, excepcional, bueno

3.   Hay muchas películas que (ser) _____.
4.   Hay pocas que (ser) _____.
5.   No hay ninguna que (ser) _____.
6.   Antes de que los niños (ir) _____ a ver una película, es bueno que los padres _____.
7.   De estas películas, he visto _____ (no he visto ninguna). (No) Le recomiendo que _____ porque _____.

UN PASO MÁS: Lectura cultural

LOS PASATIEMPOS

En el mundo hispánico las diversiones son tan variadas y numerosas como en los Estados Unidos. Las actividades pueden variar según la clase social y el lugar, pero hay aficiones que gozan de° gran aceptación popular en todas partes: el cine, las visitas y los deportes. Además, hay una serie de juegos o pasatiempos que se hacen en casa, para pasar el tiempo. Son populares, entre otros, el ajedrez, las damas,° las canicas,° los rompecabezas... Aquí les ofrecemos tres pasatiempos distintos: dos de niños y un juego de cartas. ¿Se parecen a algún juego norteamericano?

gozan... tienen

checkers / marbles

«Veo veo... »

Este juego de vocabulario es popular entre los niños. ¡También puede ayudar a los estudiantes de lenguas extranjeras!

El adulto (El profesor) dice: «Veo veo... » El niño (el estudiante) contesta: «¿Qué ves?» ADULTO: «Una cosita... » NIÑO: «¿Y qué cosita es?» ADULTO: «Empieza con la letra... » («Es de color... ») El niño tiene que pensar en las palabras que conoce que empiezan con la letra dada (y que son del color nombrado).

José Luis Suárez, España

«Los platillos»

Un pasatiempo muy popular cuando era niño era el juego de «platillos» (tapas° de botellas, especialmente las que encontramos en los refrescos como Coca-Cola). El juego consiste en marcar un círculo de tamaño° regular en la acera. Si el cemento es liso,° mejor todavía, porque de esta manera el platillo se desliza° fácilmente. Se colocan° los platillos de todos los jugadores en el centro del círculo y todos tratan de sacar del círculo, con su platillo, los platillos de los otros jugadores. Para impulsar el platillo, uno necesita colocar los dedos de tal forma que con un movimiento rápido de uno de los dedos el platillo se dirige al centro del círculo a fin de ir reduciendo gradualmente el número de platillos dentro del círculo. Al final, el jugador con el mayor número de platillos en su poder es el ganador.

Emilién Sabló, Panamá

caps

size / smooth

se... slides / Se... Se ponen

«La casita robada»

Se reparten° cuatro cartas a cada participante (no más de dos). Se ponen cuatro cartas boca arriba° sobre la mesa. El primer jugador ve si entre las cartas que tiene hay alguna igual a las que están sobre la mesa; si no hay, descarta° una carta suya. Ahora es el turno del otro jugador.

Si alguno encuentra en la mesa una carta igual a la suya, la toma mostrando la suya y se la lleva, poniéndola a su lado boca arriba. Si el compañero de turno tiene en su mano la misma carta que el otro tiene a su lado, se la puede robar («casita robada») y ponerla en el lado suyo. Se puede robar de la mesa o del compañero.

Cuando se acaban las cartas que se tienen en la mano, se reparten otras cuatro, y así hasta que se acabe el mazo.° Gana el que tiene la mayor cantidad de cartas al finalizar el juego. ¡OJO! Se juega con barajas° españolas (bastos, copas, oros y espadas).

Marianela Chaumiel, Argentina

Se... Are distributed

boca... face (lit. mouth) up

he discards

deck

cartas

Comprensión

Según la lectura, las siguientes observaciones sobre el mundo hispánico no son válidas. Explique brevemente por qué.

1. Las diversiones más populares del mundo hispánico son totalmente distintas a las de los Estados Unidos.
2. El juego de los platillos no se parece a ningún juego norteamericano.
3. Se pueden jugar todos los juegos hispánicos usando cartas norteamericanas.
4. Los hispanos no se interesan en los juegos que tienen que ver con palabras.

Para escribir

Describa un juego o pasatiempo que Ud. recuerde de su niñez. Su breve párrafo debe incluir los siguientes detalles.

1. con quién y dónde jugaba Ud.
2. el número de participantes
3. en qué consistía el juego y algunas de sus reglas (*rules*)

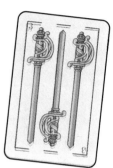

VOCABULARIO

Los deportes

la natación swimming
pasear en bicicleta to ride a bike
patinar to skate

Otros deportes: el básquetbol, el béisbol, el fútbol (norteamericano), el golf, el hockey, el tenis, el vólibol

Sustantivos

el/la aficionado/a fan, enthusiast
el campo (playing) field
la cancha (tennis) court
el equipo team
los esquís skis
el estadio stadium
el gimnasio gymnasium

el juego play (*in a game*); (card, board) game
el/la jugador(a) player
el partido game, match
la pelota ball
la raqueta racket
la red net

Conjunciones

a menos que unless
antes (de) que before
con tal (de) que provided (that)
en caso de que in case
para que so that

Frases útiles para la comunicación	
siempre que	whenever

LAS ÚLTIMAS NOVEDADES

VOCABULARIO: LAS NOTICIAS

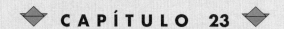

Asesinato de un dictador

Huelga de obreros en Alemania

Guerra en el Oriente Medio

**Erupción de un volcán
en Centroamérica**

Choque de trenes

Bombas en un avión

el/la ciudadano/a citizen
los demás others, other people
la prensa press; print medium
el/la reportero/a reporter
el/la testigo witness

el acontecimiento event
el barrio neighborhood
el derecho right

el desastre disaster
la esperanza hope
la ley law
la paz peace

enterarse (de) to find out, learn (about)
informar to inform
obedecer (obedezco) to obey
ofrecer (ofrezco) to offer

A.   Definiciones. ¿Qué palabra se asocia con cada definición?

1. un programa que nos informa de lo que pasa en nuestro mundo
2. la persona que está presente durante un acontecimiento y lo ve todo
3. un medio importantísimo de comunicación
4. la persona que nos informa de las novedades
5. la persona que gobierna un país de una forma absoluta
6. la persona que emplea la violencia para cambiar el mundo según sus deseos
7. cuando los obreros se niegan a (*refuse*) trabajar
8. la frecuencia en que se transmiten y se reciben los programas de televisión
9. la confrontación armada entre dos o más países

a. el noticiero
b. la guerra
c. el/la terrorista
d. el/la dictador(a)
e. el canal
f. el/la testigo
g. el/la reportero/a
h. la huelga
i. la prensa

Ahora diga las palabras que Ud. asocia con los siguientes conceptos o dé una definición de cada uno.

1. votar
2. obedecer
3. los demás
4. el desastre
5. la libertad

6. la desigualdad (*inequality*)

B.   Algunos creen que las siguientes declaraciones describen el estado del mundo actual. ¿Qué cree Ud.? Dé su opinión, empezando con una de estas expresiones.

TERRORISMO SENTIMENTAL

VICENTE Rodríguez, supuesto miembro de la Armada ecuatoriana, quería bailar, pero «ella» le negó la danza. Entonces, Rodríguez decidió que si no bailaba con él, aquella mujer no bailaba con ninguno, y lanzó una granada de mano contra la pista. El frustrado danzarín fue detenido por la policía nada más cumplido su acto de venganza contra el cabaret La Naranja Mecánica, de Guayaquil, donde trabajaba como camarera la mujer origen del ataque, en el que una persona resultó muerta y cinco heridas de gravedad. Después de la negativa de la camarera, Rodríguez se dirigió a la salida del cabaret, y al llegar a la puerta lanzó el explosivo contra la pista de baile, donde otros con más suerte aparente que el danzarín con sus parejas. No contento con eso, los policías que llegaron al lugar de los hechos para detenerle, se encontraron con que el despechado danzarín les recibió a tiros, lo que no impidió su captura.

(No) Dudo que…
(No) Es verdad que…
Es probable que…
Es bueno/malo que…
Es lástima que…
Es increíble que…
(No) Me gusta que…

1. En los Estados Unidos seguimos usando demasiado petróleo.
2. Debemos concederles todo lo que pidan a los terroristas que tienen rehenes (*hostages*).
3. Hay más catástrofes naturales actualmente que hace 50 años.
4. Es una buena idea asesinar a todos los dictadores del mundo.
5. No hay esperanza de una paz mundial.
6. En los Estados Unidos, la igualdad legal de todos los ciudadanos es una realidad, no sólo una esperanza.
7. Los policías, los bomberos (*firefighters*), los médicos y los enfermeros no tienen el derecho de declararse en huelga.
8. La guerra es un buen medio de resolver los conflictos internacionales.

Ahora invente una oración a la que van a responder sus compañeros de clase.

Premios Rey de España

S IETE periodistas de España e Iberoamérica recibieron de manos del rey Juan Carlos el premio internacional de Periodismo que lleva su nombre, establecido por la agencia EFE y el Instituto de Cooperación Iberoamericana. Entre ellos figura Daniel Samper Pizano, autor de informes especiales en CAMBIO16, tercero de derecha a izquierda en la fotografía de la ceremonia de entrega de premios en el Palacio de la Zarzuela el lunes pasado.

Samper Pizano, que escribe también para el diario *El Tiempo* de Colombia, su país natal, publicó en los números 859 y 860 (Mayo 16 y 23 de 1988 de CAMBIO16) un informe sobre «La lengua española, un imperio amenazado», que mereció el Premio V Centenario.

C. Indique la importancia que tienen para Ud. los siguientes acontecimientos: **1** = de poco o ningún interés   **2** = de interés   **3** = de gran interés

_____   1. el asesinato de un político estadounidense
_____   2. el asesinato de un dictador de otro país
_____   3. las noticias del continente africano
_____   4. un accidente de coches en una carretera que está cerca de su barrio
_____   5. una huelga de obreros en algún país europeo
_____   6. una huelga de obreros en el suroeste de los Estados Unidos
_____   7. una guerra en el Oriente Medio
_____   8. una guerra en Centroamérica o en Sudamérica
_____   9. una guerra en Europa
_____ 10. el precio de la gasolina

Ahora compare las respuestas de los miembros de la clase. ¿Qué indican sus respuestas sobre su interés en los acontecimientos mundiales?

D.   Preguntas

1. Para Ud., ¿es importante estar informado/a de lo que pasa en el mundo? ¿Cómo se entera de las noticias locales o regionales? ¿Cómo se entera de lo que pasa en su barrio? ¿en su familia?

2. ¿Qué canal de televisión prefiere Ud. para enterarse de las noticias? ¿Cree Ud. que en ese canal le informan mejor? ¿O es que le gusta el locutor (la locutora) que se las ofrece? ¿Le interesan a Ud. mucho o poco las noticias del estado de California? ¿de Nueva York? ¿Por qué sí o por qué no?

3. ¿Le importan más a Ud. su autonomía e individualismo o los sentimientos de los demás? En una tienda, ¿hace cola con paciencia o primero trata de atraer la atención del dependiente? En una parada de autobús, ¿hace cola o trata de subir primero?

4. Para Ud., ¿cuáles son los derechos más básicos de que todos debemos gozar (*enjoy*)? ¿Cuáles son las obligaciones de un buen ciudadano? ¿Es importante que todos votemos en todas las elecciones, sean nacionales o locales? ¿Por qué cree Ud. que muchas personas no votan?

Al tanto...

Here are some words and phrases to use when talking about the latest news, **las noticias de última hora**. See if you can guess their meaning from context.

En vivo y **en directo** desde...
Crece la tensión en...
En **la conferencia cumbre** se firmó **un acuerdo de paz** entre... y...
...cometió **un atentado** terrorista en...

martes 7

TVE-2
8.00 Con tu cuerpo.
8.15 Dibujos animados.
8.35 Cursos de idiomas.
9.05 El salero.
11.00 Nanny.
12.00 Las doce en punta.
13.00 Eurodiario.
13.30 La cometa blanca.
14.00 3 × 4.

15.00 Misterios sin resolver.
15.50 Tira de música.
16.45 Dona Beija.
17.35 El tiempo que vivimos.
18.30 La guerra de Jenny.
19.15 Mirador.
19.30 Cerca de las estrellas.
20.00 Noticias 2.
22.30 La casa por la ventana.
23.30 Yo, Claudio.
0.25 Tendido cero.
0.55 La noche.

¿Recuerda Ud.?

In Grammar Section 46, you will learn about and begin to use the forms of the past subjunctive. As you learn this new tense, you will be continually using the past tense forms you have already learned along with the new material, so this section presents many opportunities for review. The following brief exercises will help you get started.

A. To learn the forms of the past subjunctive, you will need to know the forms of the preterite well, especially the third person plural. Regular **-ar** verbs end in **-aron** and regular **-er/ir** verbs in **-ieron** in the third person plural of the preterite. Stem-changing **-ir** verbs show the second change in the third person: **servir (i, i)** → **sirvieron; dormir (ue, u)** → **durmieron**. Verbs with a stem ending in a vowel change the **i** to **y: leyeron, cayeron, construyeron**. Many common verbs have irregular stems in the preterite: **quisieron, hicieron, dijeron**, and so on. Three common verbs are totally irregular in this tense: **ser/ir** → **fueron, dar** → **dieron.**

Change these verbs to the third person plural of the preterite.

1. habla	5. pierde	9. estoy	13. traigo	17. digo
2. como	6. dormimos	10. tenemos	14. dan	18. destruimos
3. vives	7. río	11. vamos	15. sé	19. creo
4. juegan	8. leemos	12. visten	16. puedo	20. mantienen

B. The forms of the imperfect are relatively regular, and there are only three verbs with irregular imperfect forms: **dar, ir**, and **ser**. Give their first person singular and plural forms.

Las noticias de hoy

—¿Has oído las noticias de las cinco?
—No. ¿Qué pasó? Nada malo, espero.
—Pues, hubo un terremoto° en Centroamérica, pero no fue muy fuerte.   *earthquake*
—Menos mal. Siempre esperamos lo peor de los desastres naturales.

Austin, Texas

ESTRUCTURAS

· ·

46. ¡OJALÁ QUE PUDIÉRAMOS HACERLO!
Past Subjunctive

—VIEJOS VOTANTES. ¿Recuerda cuánto tuvimos que
discurrir° usted y yo antes de votar hace treinta años?   °to discuss

Aquéllos eran otros tiempos...
—¡Parece imposible que yo *dijera* eso! ¡Qué egoísmo!
—¡No es posible que *lucháramos* tanto!

Hace treinta años, era difícil que don Jorge y don Gustavo *hablaran* de las elecciones sin pelearse. Era imposible que se *pusieran* de acuerdo en política. ¡Qué lástima que *hubiera* tanta enemistad entre ellos!

Ahora es probable que no se acuerden de todas las peleas del pasado. También es posible que sus convicciones políticas sean menos fuertes... o simplemente que ahora tengan otras cosas de que hablar.

Hace diez años...

1. ¿de qué era difícil que Ud. hablara con sus padres?
2. ¿con quién era imposible que Ud. se pusiera de acuerdo?
3. ¿con quién era imposible que Ud. se comunicara?
4. ¿contra qué orden de sus padres era común que Ud. protestara?

Cuando Ud. era niño/a...

5. ¿era probable que discutiera (*you argued*) con alguien en la escuela primaria o en el barrio? ¿con quién?
6. ¿dónde le prohibían sus padres que jugara?
7. ¿qué era obligatorio que comiera o bebiera?
8. ¿de qué temía que sus padres se enteraran?

Although Spanish has two simple indicative past tenses (preterite and imperfect), it has only one simple subjunctive past tense, the *past subjunctive* (**el imperfecto del subjuntivo**). Generally speaking, this tense is used in the same situations as the present subjunctive but, of course, when talking about past events. The exact English equivalent depends on the context in which it is used.

Those were the days . . .   —It seems impossible that I said that. How selfish! —It's not possible that we fought that much!

Thirty years ago it was difficult for don Jorge and don Gustavo to talk about elections without fighting. It was impossible for them to come to any agreement about politics. What a shame that there was so much bad feeling between them!

Now it's probable that they don't remember all the fights of the past. It's also possible that their political convictions are less intense . . . or just that they have other things to discuss now.

Forms of the Past Subjunctive

PAST SUBJUNCTIVE OF REGULAR VERBS*		
hablar: hablarón	**comer: comierón**	**vivir: vivierón**
hablara habláramos	comiera comiéramos	viviera viviéramos
hablaras hablarais	comieras comierais	vivieras vivierais
hablara hablaran	comiera comieran	viviera vivieran

The past subjunctive endings **-a, -as, -a, -amos, -ais, -an** are identical for **-ar**, **-er**, and **-ir** verbs. These endings are added to the third-person plural of the preterite indicative, minus its **-on** ending. For this reason, the forms of the past subjunctive reflect the irregularities of the preterite.

Stem-Changing Verbs

-Ar and **-er** verbs: no change

> **empezar (ie):**   empezarón → **empezara, empezaras,** etc.
> **volver (ue):**   volvierón → **volviera, volvieras,** etc.

-Ir verbs: all persons of the past subjunctive reflect the vowel change in the third-person plural of the preterite.

> **dormir (ue, u):**   durmierón → **durmiera, durmieras,** etc.
> **pedir (i, i):**   pidierón → **pidiera, pidieras,** etc.

Spelling Changes

All persons of the past subjunctive reflect the change from **i** to **y** between two vowels.

> **i → y** (caer, construir, creer, destruir, leer, oír)
>
> **creer:** creyerón → **creyera, creyeras, creyera, creyéramos, creyerais, creyeran**

Verbs with Irregular Preterites

dar: dierón → **diera, dieras, diera, diéramos, dierais, dieran**

decir:	dijerón → **dijera**	**poner:**	pusierón → **pusiera**
estar:	estuvierón → **estuviera**	**querer:**	quisierón → **quisiera**
haber:	hubierón → **hubiera**	**saber:**	supierón → **supiera**
hacer:	hicierón → **hiciera**	**ser:**	fuerón → **fuera**
ir:	fuerón → **fuera**	**tener:**	tuvierón → **tuviera**
poder:	pudierón → **pudiera**	**venir:**	vinierón → **viniera**

---

*An alternate form of the past subjunctive (used primarily in Spain) ends in **-se**: **hablase, hablases, hablase, hablásemos, hablaseis, hablasen.** This form will not be practiced in *¿Qué tal?*.

Uses of the Past Subjunctive

The past subjunctive usually has the same applications as the present subjunctive, but is used for past events.

Quería que **jugaran** por la tarde.	*I wanted them to play in the afternoon.*
Sintió que no **estuvieran** allí.	*He was sorry (that) they weren't there.*
Dudábamos que se **equivocaran**.	*We doubted that they would make a mistake.*

In the preceding sentences, note the use of the subjunctive (1) after expressions of *influence, emotion,* and *doubt.* Remember that it is also used (2) after *nonexistent* and *indefinite antecedents* and (3) after certain *conjunctions* (**a menos que, antes [de] que, con tal [de] que, en caso de que, para que**).

No había nadie que **pudiera** resolverlo.	*There wasn't anyone who could (might have been able to) solve it.*
Los padres trabajaron **para que** sus hijos **asistieran** a la universidad.	*The parents worked so that their children might go to the university.*

[Práctica A–D]

Softening Requests or Statements

The past subjunctive forms of **deber, poder,** and **querer** are used to soften a request or statement.

Debieras estudiar más.	*You really should study more.*
¿**Pudieran** Uds. traérmelo?	*Could you bring it for me?*
Quisiéramos hablar con Ud. en seguida.	*We would like to speak with you immediately.*

[Práctica E–F]

—*Verás, quisiera un vaso de agua. Pero no te molestes, porque ya no tengo sed. Sólo quisiera saber si, en el caso de que tuviese otra vez sed, podría° venir a pedirte un vaso de agua.*

I could

Práctica

A. Recuerdos. Haga oraciones con una frase de cada grupo para describir los siguientes aspectos de su niñez.

Mis padres (no) querían que yo...
Mis maestros me pedían que...
Yo buscaba amigos que...
Yo siempre quería que los miembros de mi familia...

portarse bien, ser bueno/a,...
estudiar mucho, sacar buenas notas, ...
creer en Santa Claus, tener un árbol de Navidad muy alto, ...
ponerse la ropa vieja para jugar, no jugar en las calles, no luchar con mis amigos, traer animales a casa, ...
mirar mucho la televisión, comer muchos dulces, ...
vivir en nuestro barrio, tener muchos juguetes, venir a mi casa para jugar, ...
ir a la playa en verano, pasar juntos los días feriados, ...

¡EL MUNDO DEL MAÑANA YA ESTÁ AQUÍ!

LA NUEVA REVISTA
¡DINÁMICA Y DIFERENTE!

B.   Las últimas novedades. Cambie al pasado. Luego diga si la oración presenta un hecho (*fact*) o es sólo una opinión del locutor.

1. Los obreros quieren que les den un aumento de sueldo.
2. Es posible que los trabajadores sigan en huelga hasta las Navidades.
3. Es necesario que las víctimas reciban asistencia médica en la Clínica Sagrado Corazón.
4. Es lástima que no haya espacio para todos allí.
5. Los terroristas piden que los oficiales no los sigan.
6. Parece imposible que el gobierno escuche sus demandas.
7. Es necesario que el gobierno informe a todos los ciudadanos del desastre.
8. Dudo que la paz mundial esté fuera de nuestro alcance (*reach*).
9. Lee Iacocca prefiere que la nueva fábrica se construya en México.
10. Temo que el número de votantes sea muy bajo en las próximas elecciones.

C.   Escenas históricas. Dé una breve descripción de la historia de los Estados Unidos, haciendo oraciones según las indicaciones. Empiece en el pasado, pero tenga en cuenta (*keep in mind*) que la historia termina en el presente.

1. indios / temer / que / colonos / quitarles / toda la tierra
2. colonos / no / gustar / que / tener / pagar / impuestos / sin representación
3. parecía imposible / que / joven república / tener éxito (*success*)
4. los del sur / no / gustar / que / gobernarlos / los del norte
5. abolicionistas / no / gustar / que / algunos / no / tener / mismo / libertades
6. era necesario / que / declararse / en huelga / obreros / para / obtener / alguno / derechos
7. era terrible / que / haber / dos / guerra / mundial
8. para que / nosotros / vivir / en paz / es cuestión de / aprender / comunicarse / con / demás naciones
9. también / es necesario / que / haber / leyes / que / garantizar / derechos / todos

D.   El comienzo y el fin del delito perfecto. Combine las oraciones, usando las conjunciones entre paréntesis y haciendo otros cambios necesarios.

1. El ladrón (*thief*) no pensaba entrar en la casa. No oía ningún ruido. (a menos que)
2. No iba a molestar a los dueños. Encontraba dinero y objetos de valor. (con tal que)
3. Un amigo lo acompañaba. Había alguna dificultad. (en caso de que)
4. El amigo rompió la ventana. El ladrón pudo entrar. (para que)
5. El ladrón entró silenciosamente. Los dueños no se despertaron. (para que)
6. Salió. Los dueños pudieron llamar a la policía. (antes de que)

E. La situación es delicada... ¿Cómo se dice en español?

1. You really should drive more slowly.
2. Couldn't you think about others this time?
3. We would like you to do your household chores.
4. How would you like to pay, madam?
5. We really should protect their welfare first.

Notas comunicativas: I Wish I Could . . . I Wish They Would . . .

There are many ways to express wishes in Spanish. As you know, one of the most common is **ojalá (que)** with the subjunctive. The past subjunctive following **ojalá** is one of the most frequent uses of those verb forms.

Ojalá (que) pudiera acompañarlos, pero no es posible.	*I wish I could go with you, but it's not possible.*
Ojalá inventaran una máquina que hiciera todas las tareas domésticas.	*I wish they would invent a machine that would do all the household chores.*

F. Complete las oraciones lógicamente.

1. Ojalá que (yo) tuviera _____.
2. Ojalá que pudiera _____.
3. Ojalá pudiera _____ por _____.
4. Ojalá inventaran una máquina que _____.
5. Ojalá solucionaran el problema de _____.
6. Ojalá que en esta universidad fuera posible _____.

UN POCO DE TODO

A. Siempre los mismos problemas. Cambie por el pasado.

1. Es increíble que haya tantos problemas mundiales.
2. No creo que nadie sepa todas las soluciones.
3. Siento que no se pueda resolver todos los problemas.
4. Las autoridades siempre niegan que la culpa sea suya.
5. Los ciudadanos piden que alguien haga algo por ellos.

Siga con la historia, haciendo oraciones completas según las indicaciones.

6. ser / necesario / que / todos / cumplir (*to fulfill*) / con / responsabilidades / suyo
7. haber / suficiente / recursos / para que / nadie / sufrir / ninguno / privación
8. ¿haber / gobierno / que / ser / mejor / nuestro?
9. (yo) dudar / que / se / formar / nunca / sociedad / perfecto

10. (yo) sugerir / que / todo / ciudadanos / trabajar / junto / para / crear / mundo / mejor

B. El noticiero de las seis. Complete the following news flashes with the correct form of the words in parentheses, as suggested by the context. When two possibilities are given in parentheses, select the correct word. Use the past participle of infinitives indicated with an asterisk.

Trenton, New Jersey, Estados Unidos

Se reveló ayer que los comandantes de las bases navales de los Estados Unidos han (*recibir*)* órdenes «supersecretas» de (*intensificar²*) las medidas de seguridad.° Se (*creer³*) que terroristas (*pensar⁴*) sabotear instalaciones norteamericanas. Estas órdenes, (*emitir⁵*)* por el jefe de operaciones navales, (*mandar⁶*) que los comandantes (*aumentar⁷*) las medidas de seguridad para que no (*ocurrir⁸*) otra tragedia como el ataque contra el cuartel de los marinos en Beirut.

medidas… security measures
to issue

Moscú

Hoy todo Moscú se está (*preguntar⁹*) si el jefe del Estado y del Partido Comunista va a (*asistir¹⁰*) mañana sábado (*por/de¹¹*) la tarde a la solemne reunión (*organizar¹²*)* por el Kremlin para (*celebrar¹³*) el aniversario (*del/de la¹⁴*) revolución bolchevique. Hace varios meses que el jefe no (*aparecer¹⁵*) en público y es posible que (*ser/estar¹⁶*) gravemente enfermo. Hasta este momento, claro, la prensa soviética no (*haber decir¹⁷*) nada al respecto.° Mañana sábado, a las 17 horas, no sólo el cuerpo° diplomático y los periodistas (*extranjero¹⁸*), sino° también la población soviética (*ser/estar¹⁹*) ante° los televisores para (*ver²⁰*) si la directiva° del Partido hace su entrada° en la Sala de Congreso del Kremlin.

al… about it
corps
but / in front of
leadership / entrance

UN PASO MÁS: Situaciones

Hablando de las noticias

En la televisión

—¿Oíste lo del último accidente de aviación?

—¿Te refieres al accidente en que murieron cerca de 150 personas?

—Sí. Dicen que sucedió° por pura negligencia.

pasó

—Es difícil creerlo, ¿no? Parece imposible que el piloto no pudiera hacer nada para evitarlo.

—Bueno, hay que tomar en cuenta que es posible que el avión tuviera un desperfecto.°

¿ ?

—No creo que fuera eso… Si las autoridades se interesaran más por proteger al público…

—Bueno. Es cuestión de opiniones. Personalmente creo que sí se interesan.

—¡Pero no lo suficiente! Yo creo que…

En el periódico

—¿Algo nuevo?

—¡Qué va! Centroamérica está a punto de estallar,° la tensión sigue cre-   *explode*
ciendo° en el Golfo Pérsico, la situación en el Oriente Medio continúa   *¿ ?*
igual de catastrófica…

—Ya veo. Lo de siempre.

Después de las elecciones

—Te digo de verdad que nunca creí que hubiera alguien que apoyara° a ese   *¿ ?*
candidato.

—Ya lo ves. No les importó su postura° sobre el desarme nuclear.   *position*

—¿Qué le vamos a hacer, pues?

—Bueno… esperar las próximas elecciones.

Conversación

Con un compañero (una compañera), exprese dos opiniones distintas sobre
cada uno de los siguientes temas en diálogos de cinco a seis oraciones.
¡OJO!   *No* es necesario que expresen sus opiniones personales. Sólo deben
presentar dos puntos de vista opuestos.

- la pena de muerte: ¿castigo (*punishment*) inhumano o freno necesario
  para el crimen?
- la censura de las canciones rock: ¿tema «de moda» o es necesaria para
  proteger a la juventud?
- el desarme nuclear: ¿amenaza a la libertad o compromiso inteligente?

Notas culturales: Formas de gobierno

No es por casualidad que los hispanoamericanos llaman a España la «madre patria». Cuando los con-
quistadores llegaron al Nuevo Mundo, instalaron un
sistema de gobierno, controlado directamente desde
España, que duró casi doscientos años. Pero a pesar
de los vínculos (*in spite of the ties*) culturales, sociales
y religiosos que existen entre estos países y España,
ha habido también muchas diferencias entre ellos, sobre
todo en el área de la política.

España tiene una larga tradición monárquica,
empezando con la unificación política de la península
que ocurrió cuando se casaron la reina Isabel y el rey
Fernando en 1469. Esta tradición ha sido interrum-
pida sólo por dos períodos republicanos, una guerra
civil (1936–1939) y la dictadura del general Francisco
Franco (1939–1975). Según la Constitución Española
de 1978, «La forma política del Estado español es la
Monarquía parlamentaria.» El monarca actual, el rey
don Juan Carlos, se inclina por las reformas
democráticas.

En Hispanoamérica, el siglo XIX es la época de
las guerras de independencia y de los libertadores. Se
destaca (*stands out*) entre todos la figura de Simón Bolívar, quien es para Sudamérica lo que Jorge Washington es para los norteamericanos: el verdadero padre
de la independencia. En la actualidad todavía conti-
núan las luchas (*struggles*) en Hispanoamérica. Ha
habido—y sigue habiendo (*there continue to be*)—guerras de guerrillas en algunos países y verdaderas re-
voluciones en otros. El objetivo de éstas es lograr
(*achieve*) cambios políticos, económicos y sociales.

VOCABULARIO

Verbos

comunicarse (con) to communicate (with)
discutir to argue; to discuss
enterarse (de) to find out (about)
gobernar (ie) to govern, rule
informar to inform
luchar to fight
obedecer (obedezco) to obey
ofrecer (ofrezco) to offer
votar to vote

Las últimas novedades

el acontecimiento event, happening
el asesinato assassination
el barrio neighborhood

la bomba bomb
el canal (TV) channel
el choque collision
el desastre (natural) (natural) disaster
la (des)igualdad (in)equality
la esperanza hope, wish
la guerra war
la huelga strike (*labor*)
el ladrón, la ladrona thief
la libertad liberty, freedom
el noticiero newscast
el/la obrero/a worker
la paz peace
la prensa press
el/la reportero/a reporter
el/la testigo witness

El gobierno y la responsabilidad cívica

el/la ciudadano/a citizen
los demás others, other people
el derecho right
el/la dictador(a) dictator
la ley law

Palabras adicionales

tomar/tener en cuenta to keep/have in mind, take into account

---

Frases útiles para la comunicación

Ojalá + *past subjunctive*   I wish . . . could/would
  ¡Ojalá pudiera asistir!   I wish I could attend!
  ¡Ojalá llamaran esta noche!   I wish they would call tonight!

seguir + *pres. participle*   to keep on, continue (*doing something*)

30 años de vida
son muchos años de historia.
Hemos llenado toda una
página en la historia
de la televisión.
Reciban un saludo fraternal
de un nuevo año
con una nueva imágen...

PUNCH

30 AÑOS
DE IMAGEN
CON FUTURO

✕ EL DINERO

VOCABULARIO: EN EL BANCO

BANCO NACIONAL

el cajero

la libreta de ahorros

el talonario de cheques

la cuenta corriente

PRÉSTAMOS

la cuenta de ahorros

el préstamo

la tarjeta de crédito

el alquiler rent
la cuenta/factura bill
los gastos expenses
el presupuesto budget

ahorrar to save (*money*)
aumentar to increase
cargar (a la cuenta de uno) to charge (to someone's account)
cobrar to cash (*a check*); to charge (*someone for an
   item or service*)

devolver (ue) to return (*something*)
economizar to economize
gastar to spend (*money*)
ingresar (depositar)/sacar to put in, deposit/to
   take out, withdraw
pagar a plazos/en efectivo/con cheque to pay in
   installments/in cash/by check
prestar to lend
quejarse (de) to complain (about)

A. Indique una respuesta para cada pregunta o situación. Luego invente un contexto para cada diálogo. ¿Dónde están las personas que hablan? ¿en un banco? ¿en una tienda? ¿Quiénes son? ¿clientes? ¿cajeros? ¿dependientes?

1. ¿Cómo prefiere Ud. pagar? f.
2. ¿Hay algún problema? d.
3. Me da su pasaporte, por favor. Necesito verlo para que pueda cobrar su cheque. e.
4. ¿Quisiera usar su tarjeta de crédito? c.
5. ¿Va a depositar este cheque en su cuenta corriente o en su cuenta de ahorros? a.
6. ¿Adónde quiere Ud. que mandemos la factura? b

a. En la cuenta de ahorros, por favor.
b. Me la manda a la oficina, por favor.
c. No. Prefiero pagar en efectivo.
d. Sí, señorita, Ud. me cobró demasiado por la medicina.
e. Aquí lo tiene Ud. Me lo va a devolver pronto, ¿verdad?
f. Cárguelo a mi cuenta, por favor.

B. Situaciones. ¿Quiénes son estas personas? ¿Dónde están? ¿Qué van a comprar? ¿Cómo van a pagar? ¿Qué van a hacer después?

1.   2.   3.

C. Definiciones. Dé una definición de estas palabras en español.

1. el presupuesto
2. economizar
3. el préstamo
4. la factura
5. el alquiler
6. pagar a plazos

Ahora explique la diferencia entre una cuenta corriente y una cuenta de ahorros; entre un talonario de cheques y una libreta de ahorros; entre ingresar dinero en una cuenta y sacarlo.

D. De estas oraciones, ¿cuáles describen la situación económica suya?

1. Me resulta imposible ahorrar dinero. Siempre aumentan los gastos.
2. Uso demasiado mis tarjetas de crédito; por eso tengo muchas cuentas que pagar.
3. Es mejor pagar con dinero en efectivo que cargarlo todo a la cuenta.
4. Necesito dos empleos para poder pagar todas mis cuentas.
5. Si mi producto favorito sube un 50 por ciento de precio, dejo de comprarlo.
6. Si el dependiente de una tienda me cobra demasiado, me quejo en seguida.
7. Si no tengo dinero al final del mes, saco dinero de mi cuenta de ahorros.
8. En mi cuenta corriente siempre tengo mucho dinero al final del mes.
9. Siempre les pido dinero prestado (*borrow*) a mis amigos, pero nunca se lo devuelvo.
10. Tengo muchos amigos que no me devuelven nunca el dinero que les presto.

De 726 a 1.292 millones de pesetas.

Todos para usted. ¿Se imagina? Es muy fácil, sólo tiene que recortar del YA unos cupones que aparecerán diariamente (entre el 21 de mayo y el 21 de noviembre), completar una semana entera de domingo a sábado y remitirlos, en un sobre cerrado poniendo en el remite su nombre y dirección completa, a YA, Apartado de Correos no. 466-28080 de Madrid.

Al tanto...

Spanish, like English, has a number of colloquial terms that refer to money. Listen to these Hispanic friends as they negotiate who will pay the bill.

generalized usage	la plata	—Oye, ¿tú traes **plata**?	
Spain	la pasta	—Venga, hombre. Suelta° **la pasta**.	*Let go of*
	sin chavo (*a cent*)	—De verdad, estoy **sin chavo** hoy.	
Mexico	la lana	—Pues… yo tampoco tengo **lana**. ¿Qué vamos a hacer?	

ESTRUCTURAS

47. TALKING ABOUT THE FUTURE
Future Verb Forms

¡Hay que reducir los gastos! ¿Qué vamos a hacer?

MADRE: *Tomaré* el autobús en vez de usar el carro.
ANDRÉS: *Comeremos* más ensalada y menos carne y pasteles.
PADRE: Los niños no *irán* al cine con tanta frecuencia.
JULIETA: Yo *dejaré* de fumar.
MADRE: Los niños *gastarán* menos en dulces.
PADRE: Y yo no *cargaré* nada a nuestras cuentas. Lo *pagaré* todo en efectivo.
JULIETA: *Bajaremos* la calefacción.
GABRIELA: Y yo me *iré* a vivir con los abuelos. Allí *habrá* de todo como siempre, ¿verdad?

1. ¿Quién dejará de usar el carro? ¿de fumar?
2. ¿Qué comerá la familia? ¿Qué no comerá?
3. ¿Cómo gastará menos dinero el padre? ¿y los niños?
4. ¿Adónde irá a vivir Gabriela? ¿Por qué?

You have already learned to talk about the future in a number of ways. The forms of the present can be used to describe the immediate future, and the

---

It's necessary to cut down on expenses! What are we going to do?   MOTHER: I'll take the bus instead of using the car. ANDRÉS: We'll eat more salad and less meat and cake. FATHER: The kids won't go to the movies so much. JULIETA: I'll stop smoking. MOTHER: The kids will spend less on candy. FATHER: And I won't charge anything. I'll pay for everything in cash. JULIETA: We'll turn down the heat. GABRIELA: And I'll go to live with our grandparents. There they'll have (there will be) everything as usual, right?

ir + **a** + *infinitive* construction (Grammar Section 12) is very common in both spoken and written Spanish. The future can also be expressed, however, with future verb forms.

hablar		comer		vivir	
hablaré	hablar**emos**	comeré	comer**emos**	viviré	vivir**emos**
hablarás	hablar**éis**	comerás	comer**éis**	vivirás	vivir**éis**
hablar**á**	hablar**án**	comer**á**	comer**án**	vivir**á**	vivir**án**

In English, the future is formed with the auxiliary verbs *will* or *shall*: *I will/ shall speak*. In Spanish, the *future* (**el futuro**) is a simple verb form (only one word). It is formed by adding the future endings **-é, -ás, -á, -emos, -éis, -án** to the infinitive. No auxiliary verbs are needed.

The following verbs add the future endings to irregular stems.

decir:	**dir-**		
hacer:	**har-**		
poder:	**podr-**	
poner:	**pondr-**	
querer:	**querr-**	
saber:	**sabr-**	
salir:	**saldr-**	
tener:	**tendr-**	
venir:	**vendr-**	

**-é
-ás
-á
-emos
-éis
-án**

decir	
diré	diremos
dirás	diréis
dirá	dirán

The future of **hay** (**haber**) is **habrá** (*there will be*).*

¡OJO! Remember that indicative and subjunctive present tense forms can be used to express the immediate future. Compare the following:

Llegaré a tiempo. — *I'll arrive on time.*
Llego a las ocho mañana. ¿Vienes a buscarme? — *I arrive at eight tomorrow. Will you pick me up?*
No creo que Pepe **llegue** a tiempo. — *I don't think Pepe will arrive on time.*

¡OJO! When English *will* refers not to future time but to the willingness of someone to do something, Spanish uses a form of the verb **querer**, not the future.

¿**Quieres** cerrar la puerta, por favor? — *Will you please close the door?*
¿**Quisieras** cerrar la puerta? — *Would you close the door?*

---

*The future forms of the verb **haber** are used to form the *future perfect tense* (**el futuro perfecto**), which expresses what *will have* occurred at some point in the future. You will find a presentation of these forms in Appendix 2, Additional Perfect Forms (Indicative and Subjunctive).

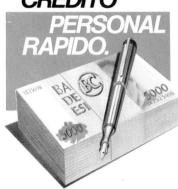

Práctica

A. **Un viaje en grupo.** Un grupo de amigos piensa hacer un viaje a México este verano. Imagine que Ud. forma parte de ese grupo y haga oraciones según las indicaciones para hacer algunos comentarios respecto al viaje.

1. yo
   - hablar sólo español
   - leer mucho en español: periódicos, revistas…
   - conocer a mucha gente joven
   - ver un programa del Ballet Folklórico

2. tú
   - levantarse temprano todos los días
   - comer comida típica
   - aprender mucho sobre la historia de México
   - visitar todos los museos

3. nosotros
   - cambiar mucho dinero en los bancos
   - escribir muchas tarjetas postales
   - comprar muchos recuerdos
   - regatear en los mercados

4. Uds.
   - no usar demasiado las tarjetas de crédito
   - querer pagarlo todo con dinero en efectivo
   - tratar de adaptarse a un presupuesto
   - regresar a los Estados Unidos con algún dinero

5. Gustavo
   - gastar todo su dinero muy pronto
   - pasar todo el tiempo con otros turistas
   - tener que volver pronto a los Estados Unidos
   - estar muy descontento con el viaje

¿Cierto o falso? Corrija las oraciones falsas.

1. Todos los miembros del grupo tendrán mucho cuidado con el dinero.
2. Nadie aprenderá nada sobre la cultura del país.
3. Todos harán por lo menos algunas de las cosas que siempre les interesan sobre todo (*especially*) a los turistas.

B. **Mi amigo Gregorio.** Describa Ud. las siguientes cosas que hará su compañero Gregorio. Luego indique si Ud. hará lo mismo (**Yo también… Yo tampoco…**) u otra cosa.

MODELO: no / gastar / menos / mes →
Gregorio no gastará menos este mes. Yo tampoco gastaré menos. (Yo sí gastaré menos este mes. ¡Tengo que ahorrar!)

1. pagar / tarde / todo / cuentas
2. tratar / adaptarse a / presupuesto
3. volver / hacer / presupuesto / próximo mes
4. no / ingresar / nada / en / cuenta de ahorros
5. quejarse / porque / no / tener / suficiente dinero
6. seguir / usando / tarjetas / crédito

7. pedirles / dinero / a / padres
8. buscar / trabajo / de tiempo parcial

¿Cuál de las siguientes oraciones describe mejor a su amigo?

1. Gregorio es muy responsable en cuanto a asuntos de dinero. Es un buen modelo para imitar.
2. Gregorio tiene que aprender a ser más responsable con su dinero.

C.   Para conseguir más dinero. What can you do to get extra cash or to save money? Some possibilities are shown in the following drawings. What are the advantages and disadvantages of each plan?

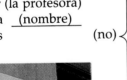

MODELO: dejar de tomar café → Si dejo de tomar café estaré menos nervioso/a, pero será más difícil despertarme por la mañana. ¡Pero realmente quisiera dejar de tomar café!

1. pedirles dinero a mis amigos
2. cometer un robo
3. alquilar un cuarto de mi casa a otras personas
4. dejar de fumar
5. buscar un trabajo de tiempo parcial
6. ¿ ?

D.   Imagine que Ud. es astrólogo/a y puede predecir (*predict*) el futuro. ¿Qué predicciones puede Ud. hacer usando una palabra o frase—en su forma correcta—de cada grupo? Use el futuro del verbo principal.

yo
el profesor (la profesora)
mi amigo/a   (nombre)
mis padres
¿ ?

(no)

conseguir
querer
tener
poder
ser
vivir
¿ ?

pagar todas las cuentas algún día
casarse, mudarse a, trabajar como _____, retirarse en _____
    (año)
un aumento de salario por fin
en un país hispánico, en _____
casado/a, soltero/a, rico/a, famoso/a, _____
ahorrar dinero para comprar _____
muchos/pocos/ningún hijo(s)
¿ ?

Entre amigos
—Oye, ¿me puedes prestar cien dólares?
—¡Hombre! Bueno... si me los devuelves lo antes posible.
—Cómo no. Pasado mañana a más tardar.°   a... *at the latest*
—¿Para qué necesitas tanto dinero?
—Tengo unas cuentas atrasadas° que quisiera pagar.   *late*

48. EXPRESSING FUTURE OR PENDING ACTIONS
Subjunctive and Indicative After Conjunctions of Time

eres

salir... decir que

Complete las oraciones según el dibujo.

PADRE: Cuando yo sea anciano, Mafalda me va a preguntar...
MAFALDA: Cuando yo sea grande, papá me va a decir que...

Talking about future events in a two-clause sentence often involves the use of conjunctions of time.

cuando	when	**hasta que**	until
después (de) que	after	**tan pronto como**	as soon as
en cuanto	as soon as		

In a dependent clause after these conjunctions of time, the subjunctive is used to express a future action or state of being, that is, one that is still pending or has not yet occurred from the point of view of the main verb. The events in the dependent clauses are conceptualized—not real-world—events.

PENDING ACTION (SUBJUNCTIVE)

Saldremos **en cuanto llegue** Felipe.

Anoche, íbamos a salir **en cuanto llegara** Felipe.

We'll leave as soon as Felipe arrives.

Last night we were going to leave as soon as Felipe arrived.

The indicative is used after conjunctions of time to describe a habitual action or a completed action in the past. Compare the following:

HABITUAL ACTION (INDICATIVE)

Siempre salimos **en cuanto llega** Felipe.

We always leave as soon as Felipe arrives.

PAST ACTION (INDICATIVE)

Anoche, salimos **en cuanto llegó** Felipe.	*Last night, we left as soon as Felipe arrived.*

The subject and verb are frequently inverted in the subordinate clause following conjunctions of time.

¡OJO! Remember that the time conjunction **antes de que** always requires the subjunctive (Grammar Section 44).

Práctica

A.   Hablando de dinero. Haga oraciones completas, usando el presente del subjuntivo de los verbos indicados.

1. Julio empezará a ahorrar más en cuanto… (darle [ellos] un aumento de sueldo; dejar de gastar tanto)
2. Pagaré todas mis cuentas tan pronto como… (tener el dinero para hacerlo; ser absolutamente necesario)
3. Susana dice que dejará de usar sus tarjetas de crédito tan pronto como… (encontrar un buen trabajo; recibir el sueldo del primer mes)
4. Mis compañeros pagarán la matrícula después de que… (sus padres mandarles un cheque; cobrar su cheque en el banco)
5. No podré pagar el alquiler hasta que… (sacar dinero de mi cuenta de ahorros; ingresar el dinero en mi cuenta corriente)
6. Los García no van a retirarse hasta que su hijo… (terminar sus estudios universitarios; establecerse y casarse)
7. Vamos a volver a hablarle a Ernesto cuando… (devolvernos los cien dólares que le prestamos; dejar de pedirnos más dinero)

B.   Dos momentos en la vida… Compare Ud. lo que pasó y lo que pasará en el futuro en la vida de Mariana.

1. Hace cuatro años, cuando Mariana (*graduarse*) en la escuela secundaria, sus padres (*darle*) un reloj. El año que viene, cuando (*graduarse*) en la universidad, (*darle*) un coche.
2. Cuando (*ser*) niña, Mariana (*querer*) ser enfermera. Luego, cuando (*tener*) 18 años, (*decidir*) que quería estudiar computación. Cuando (*terminar*) su carrera este año, yo creo que (*poder*) encontrar un buen trabajo como programadora.
3. Generalmente Mariana no (*escribir*) cheques hasta que (*tener*) los fondos en su cuenta corriente. Sin embargo (*However*), el año pasado, (*escribir*) un cheque antes de que sus padres (*mandarle*) su cheque mensual (*monthly*). Este mes tiene muchos gastos, pero no (*ir*) a pagar ninguna cuenta hasta que le (*llegar*) el cheque.
4. Cuando (*estudiar*) en la secundaria, los padres de Mariana no le permitían mirar la tele hasta que (*terminar*) la tarea. Mariana aprendió bien la lección. Ahora nunca (*dejar*) su trabajo hasta que lo (*haber*) terminado. Yo

creo que, cuando Mariana (*tener*) niños, les va a prohibir que vean la
tele hasta que (*haber*) hecho sus deberes.

C.   Preguntas

1. ¿Qué piensa Ud. hacer después de graduarse en la universidad? ¿Qué le
    van a regalar sus padres/amigos cuando Ud. se gradúe? ¿Qué recibió
    Ud. cuando se graduó en la escuela secundaria? ¿y en la primaria?
2. Cuando Ud. tenga el tiempo y el dinero, ¿adónde va a ir? ¿Adónde fue
    Ud. el año pasado cuando estaba de vacaciones? Cuando todavía vivía
    con su familia, ¿adónde iban Uds. de vacaciones?

**D.   ¿Qué piensa que pasará cuando se encuentre en estas situaciones en el
futuro? Dígalo con tantos detalles como posible.**

> MODELO: Cuando sea anciano, _____. → Cuando sea anciano, no me
> va a gustar la música que escuchan los jóvenes.

1. Cuando por fin tenga un puesto   3. Cuando sea anciano/a, _____.
    que me guste mucho, _____.
2. Cuando tenga 40 (65) años, _____.

UN POCO DE TODO

A.   Los planes de la familia Alonso. Haga oraciones completas según las
indicaciones. Use el futuro donde sea posible.

1. ser / necesario / que / (nosotros) ahorrar / más
2. yo / no / usar / tanto / tarjetas / crédito
3. mamá / buscar / trabajo / donde / (ellos) pagarle / más
4. (nosotros) pedir / préstamo / en / banco
5. ¿creer (tú) / que / nos / lo / dar ?
6. papá / estar / tranquilo / cuando / todos / empezar / economizar
7. (tú) deber / pagar / siempre / en efectivo
8. no / haber / manera / de que / (nosotros) irse / de vacaciones / este
    verano

Según los comentarios de las personas anteriores, ¿cree Ud. que la familia
Alonso está muy bien económicamente o no? Explique.

SOLICITE LA TARJETA DE
MAYOR PRESTIGIO EN EL MUNDO

B.   «La Tarjeta de Mayor Prestigio en el Mundo... » Lea la siguiente descripción de las ventajas de tener una Tarjeta American
Express y conteste las preguntas. ¡OJO!   Ud. no tiene que com-
prenderlo todo para poder contestar. Busque sólo la idea principal de cada ventaja.

¿Qué ventaja le interesará más a la persona... ?

1. que teme que le pase algún accidente mientras está viajando
2. a quien nunca le gusta pagarlo todo en efectivo

1.   **SIN LIMITES:** Usted puede utilizarla en España y en todo el mundo sin límite de gastos.* Miles de hoteles, restaurantes, establecimientos comerciales, líneas aéreas, compañías de alquiler de coches... aceptan la Tarjeta AMERICAN EXPRESS y dan la bienvenida a sus Titulares. Ya no necesitará llevar consigo importantes sumas de dinero.

2.   **LA PERDIDA NO ES PROBLEMA: Su tranquilidad está garantizada** si pierde o le roban la Tarjeta. Incluso aunque no haya podido avisar a tiempo, su responsabilidad está siempre limitada a un máximo de 8.000 Ptas. Además, obtendrá una nueva Tarjeta, rápida y gratuitamente, en cualquier parte del mundo.

3.   **UN SEGURO GRATUITO: Un Seguro de Accidentes de Viaje de 60.000.000 de Ptas.** ** Le protege gratuitamente a usted, su cónyuge y sus hijos menores de 23 años cada vez que adquieran sus billetes de viaje con cargo a la Tarjeta.

4.   **MAXIMA INFORMACION:** Verificará y controlará sus gastos fácilmente, al recibir todos los meses un Estado de Cuenta acompañado de las copias de todas las facturas.

3.   que tiene una familia grande
4.   que tiene miedo de las emergencias
5.   a quien siempre se le pierden las cosas
6.   a quien le gusta saber exactamente lo que ha gastado

Posteriormente, el cargo le será presentado en la cuenta bancaria que usted haya designado.

5.   **ASISTENCIA AMERICAN EXPRESS EN VIAJES:** Más de 1.200 Agencias de Viajes AMERICAN EXPRESS y sus Representantes en 160 países le prestarán la ayuda que necesite en sus planes de viaje o ante cualquier emergencia

6.   **SU FAMILIA TAMBIEN CUENTA:** Su familia también puede beneficiarse de todas estas ventajas, disponiendo de Tarjetas Suplementarias emitidas a su nombre.

UN PASO MÁS: Lectura cultural

¿CÓMO SE GANAN LA VIDA LOS ESTUDIANTES?

La preocupación financiera es algo compartido por los estudiantes en todo el mundo. Aun cuando el sistema universitario esté a cargo del Estado, o sea, que es gratuito—cosa que ocurre en la mayor parte de los países de habla española—hay que tener dinero para los gastos personales, sin hablar ya de cines, cassettes, cafeterías y otras diversiones.

¿Cómo te ganas la vida, siendo estudiante? O, ¿cómo te ganabas la vida en tu época universitaria? Éstas fueron las preguntas que se hicieron a un grupo de hispanohablantes. A continuación aparecen algunas de sus respuestas.

«Desde los trece años empecé a trabajar en una oficina para así poder pagar la colegiatura de mis estudios. Trabajaba de día y estudiaba de noche.»

Eva Martínez Torres, México

«Trabajaba como ayudante en las escuelas especiales, o sea en escuelas para estudiantes incapacitados.»

María Luisa Valencia, México

«Cuando era estudiante me ganaba la vida como fotógrafo. Sacaba fotos de casamientos, bautismos, fiestas de cumpleaños y en cualquier ocasión en la que alguien estuviera dispuesto a pagarme por fotografiar.»

Eduardo Cabrera, Uruguay

Algunos de los entrevistados ofrecieron comentarios más largos. A continuación hay algunos de los más interesantes.

«Yo estudié en los Estados Unidos, pero mi sobrina, que ahora estudia para contadora° pública y que vive en Ciudad Juárez, gana su dinero juntando ropa usada de la gente rica y vendiéndola en El Paso. Los domingos mi sobrina y

accountant

otras dos jovencitas alquilan un puesto° en un centro comercial y venden   *stand*
durante todo el día. Así ellas pagan su matrícula y gastos escolares.»
    Graciela Ramírez, México

«Ayudaba a enseñar a párvulos.° A los estudiantes en España, normalmente   *tots*
los padres les mantienen económicamente. Algunos trabajan, como por ejemplo: las chicas cuidan niños o ayudan en casa y los chicos trabajan en talleres.
Pero, es raro que si los padres tienen dinero, los hijos trabajen hasta que no
terminen su carrera.»
    Margarita Cuesta, España

«No olvidar que en la Argentina la enseñanza universitaria es gratuita. Si fuera
pagada, el dinero no alcanzaría jamás° para estudiar. Claro que de todos modos   *no… would never be enough*
los estudiantes siempre necesitan más de un trabajo y los padres ayudan con
lo que pueden. Muchos no se van a otras ciudades sino que viven con sus
padres y estudian en la universidad más cercana.»
    Marianela Chaumiel, Argentina

«En la actualidad muchos estudiantes quieren independizarse de sus familias
y desean vivir fuera de casa. Encontrar un trabajo es difícil para un estudiante
en un país con un índice de paro° muy alto. Sin embargo hay bastantes estu-   *unemployment*
diantes que trabajan fundamentalmente en bares, *pubs* o discotecas, y algunos
otros trabajos.
    «Otros estudiantes aprovechan la temporada turística (principalmente los
meses de verano, en que la universidad está cerrada) y trabajan para ganar
dinero para el curso escolar. También hay algunos que viajan a otros países
como Francia para trabajar en el campo u otras cosas y vuelven para estudiar.
    «En general hay que decir que es un poco más fácil para un hombre ganar
dinero que para una mujer, pues estamos en una sociedad en la que domina
el hombre a pesar de que la mujer se está igualando. Un ejemplo lo tenemos
es que en España es bastante difícil encontrar mujeres que sean camareras.»
    José Luis Suárez, España

Comprensión

Busque en la lectura por lo menos un trabajo que se relacione con las siguientes categorías.

1. algo relacionado con los niños
2. algo que tenga que ver con las diversiones
3. un trabajo para la persona a quien le gusta estar al aire libre
4. un trabajo ideal para una persona que sepa escribir a máquina
5. algo que demuestre cierta aptitud artística
6. algo que tenga que ver con la ropa

Para escribir

Aquí hay una lista de otros trabajos que hacen o han hecho otros estudiantes hispánicos. ¿Son trabajos que hacen también los estudiantes esta-

dounidenses? Haga una encuesta (*survey*) entre sus compañeros, dentro o fuera de clase, o entre sus amigos o parientes para saber si alguien ha tenido o tiene los siguientes trabajos. Debe averiguar también qué clase de trabajo tienen—o tenían—si no es uno de los siguientes. Algunos estudiantes…

_____ trabajan pintando paredes en casas particulares
_____ dan clases privadas a los niños que tienen problemas en la escuela
_____ dan clases de música
_____ trabajan en negocios de venta de ropa, de comida, de zapatos, etcétera
_____ trabajan en bibliotecas
_____ venden productos de «Tupperware» o «Avon» u otros artículos de venta a domicilio
_____ realizan encuestas
_____ reparten propaganda (*advertising*)
_____ pasan trabajos a máquina (o procesan textos)

Después de hacer la encuesta, describa los resultados organizándolos en forma de que se pueda hacer una comparación entre los trabajos de los estudiantes hispánicos y los de los estadounidenses.

VOCABULARIO

Una cuestión de dinero

ahorrar to save (*money*)
aumentar to increase
cargar to charge (*to an account*)
cobrar to cash (*a check*); to charge (*someone for an item or service*)
depositar to deposit
devolver (ue) to return (*something*)
economizar to economize
ingresar to put in, deposit
pedir (i, i) prestado/a to borrow

el banco bank
el/la cajero/a cashier

la cuenta account
la cuenta corriente checking account
la cuenta de ahorros savings account
la factura bill
los gastos expenses
la libreta de ahorros bankbook, passbook
el préstamo loan
el presupuesto budget
el talonario de cheques checkbook

a plazos in installments

con cheque by check
(con dinero) en efectivo cash

Conjunciones

después (de) que after
en cuanto as soon as
hasta que until
tan pronto como as soon as

Palabras adicionales

en vez de instead of
sobre todo above all, especially

Frases útiles para la comunicación

Me resulta imposible (difícil, …) + *inf.*   It's impossible (difficult, . . .) for me to (*do something*)

VOCES DEL MUNDO HISPÁNICO

España

Situada con Portugal en la Península Ibérica, España es de un gran interés histórico y turístico por su diversidad geográfica y cultural. A causa de la influencia de la larga presencia árabe (711–1492), su cultura es diferente de la de los otros países de Europa. Actualmente forma parte de la Comunidad Económica Europea y de la Organización del Tratado del Atlántico Norte (OTAN) y, además, mantiene muy buenas relaciones con los países de Hispanoamérica.

Políticamente España se divide en 17 comunidades autónomas. Se habla español en todas partes de España, pero se hablan otras lenguas en algunas comunidades. ¿En qué comunidad cree Ud. que se hablan estas lenguas?

el vascuence (euskera)   el gallego   el catalán

¿Qué comunidad se asocia con las siguientes frases?

la capital del país   Don Quijote   las naranjas

«La transición democrática española es un capítulo excepcional en la historia de nuestro país y una experiencia singular en el contexto nacional. Los últimos diez años de la política española han representado un giro° radical en el itinerario de nuestra vida colectiva en la época contemporánea. En el plano internacional el modelo español de transición pacífica a la democracia por su originalidad ejerce una profunda influencia en los complejos procesos de cambio por los que atraviesan° las sociedades iberoamericanas en la actualidad.»

turn

por... through which are passing

Felipe González, Presidente del gobierno socialista de España

La Familia Real Española

Plaza de Cataluña, Barcelona

CONSTITUCION

TITULO PRELIMINAR

Artículo 3.

1. El castellano es la lengua española oficial del Estado. Todos los españoles tienen el deber de conocerla y el derecho a usarla.

2. Las demás lenguas españolas serán también oficiales en las respectivas Comunidades Autónomas de acuerdo con sus Estatutos.

3. La riqueza de las distintas modalidades lingüísticas de España es un patrimonio cultural que será objeto de especial respeto y protección.

de la Constitución Española, aprobada por
las Cortes el 31 de octubre de 1978
Referéndum Nacional del 6 de diciembre

La otra cara de Euskadi

País Vasco

Euskadi prepara una ofensiva para cambiar en Europa su imagen de violencia

LAS autoridades del País Vasco quieren cambiar la imagen de desolación económica que desde 1985 ha provocado la desaparición del trece por ciento de las empresas vascas y del veintiséis por ciento de los empleos.

En los últimos cinco años se han perdido en Euskadi más de cuarenta mil puestos de trabajo y la tasa de desempleo, el veintidós por ciento de la población activa, es una de las más altas de España.

La violencia, el terrorismo y la crisis económica han hecho huir a los inversores extranjeros. El Gobierno autónomo ha lanzado una ofensiva a través de la Sociedad para la Promoción y Reconversión Industrial (SPRI) para cambiar, de cara al exterior, esta imagen negativa.

to flee

«Tenemos que dar una nueva visión del País Vasco —afirma Ramón Jáuregui, vicelendakari del Gobierno vasco—, no podemos seguir viviendo en el horror de la violencia y el conflicto permanente.»

TV-3

12.45	**Resum Calgary.**
13.00	**Esports.**
14.30	**Gol a gol.**
15.00	**Telenotícies migdia.**
15.30	**Batman.**
16.00	**Simon i Simon.**
16.50	**El signe dels quatre.**
18.30	**Bàsquet.**
20.00	**Gol a gol.**
20.30	**Telenotícies.**
21.00	**30 Minuts.**
21.30	**A cor obert.**
22.30	**Gol a gol.**

ETB

10.30	**Meza.**
11.30	**Hi heu.**
12.00	**Luzemetraia: ETA Robin Hood Deltzen Zloten.** "...Y le llamaban Robin Hood".
13.35	**Busterren mundua.** Telesaila.
14.00	**Gaur egun.** Albistegia.
14.15	**Filemon Katuaren mundu Harrigarria.**
14.40	**Don don kikilikor.**
15.40	**Bazkal osteko zinea.** *Gau ETA Egun.*
17.40	**Pottoklak.** Marrazki bizidunak.

18.05	**Aste ero.**
18.35	**Perry Mason.** Telesaila.
19.25	**Krimenaren Inguruan.** Dokumentala.
20.15	**Xanfarin eta andere king.** Telesaila.
21.00	**Gaur egun.** Albistegia.
21.15	**Ipuin Harrigarriak.** Telesaila.
21.45	**Cincinnati.** Telesaila.
22.10	**Kirolez kirol.**
23.40	**Azken Txokoa.**

TVG

11.30	**Mira de axuste.**
11.32	**Santa misa.**
12.00	**Deportes.** Baloncesto. Caixa Ourense-Cajamadrid.
13.30	**Deportes.** Campeonato de Natación.
14.00	**Sky Channel** (musical).
14.30	**Telexornal mediodía.**
15.00	**Deportes.**
15.30	**Viva o domingo** *(magazine).*
19.00	**Cine de domingo.**
20.50	**En xogo.**
21.00	**Telexornal serán.**
21.30	**Doutor Cándido Pérez,** médico de señoras.
22.00	**En xogo.**
24.00	**Sky Channel.**

TV-3 = Televisión Cataluña
ETB = País Vasco
TVG = Televisión Gallega

La tecnología del láser, Madrid

Paisaje cerca del pueblo de Riglos, en Aragón

El Alcázar, Segovia

Castilla miserable, ayer dominadora,
envuelta° en sus andrajos° desprecia cuanto ignora.   *wrapped / rags*
¿Espera, duerme o sueña? ¿La sangre derramada°   *spilled*
recuerda cuando tuvo la fiebre de la espada°?   *sword*
Todo se mueve, fluye, discurre,° corre o gira;°   *rambles / turns*
cambian la mar y el monte y el ojo que los mira.
Antonio Machado, «A orillas del Duero», *Campos de Castilla*

El Alcázar, Sevilla

Cantar° de Mío Cid   Poema

Mío Cid Ruy Díaz en Burgos entró,
sesenta pendones° lleva alrededor;   *banners*
salían a verle mujer y varón
y en cada ventana se escucha un clamor,
los ojos llorando cuenta su dolor.
De todas sus bocas sale un razón:°   *oración*
«¡Dios, qué buen vasallo, si tuviese buen señor°!»   *master*

«Tres músicos», del pintor español
Pablo Picasso

—Yo sé quién soy—respondió Don Quijote—,
y sé que puedo ser, no sólo los que he dicho,
sino todos los doce Pares de Francia,° y aun   *doce... French knights*
todos los nueve de la Fama, pues a todas las
hazañas° que ellos todos juntos y cada uno   *deeds, feats*
por sí hicieron se aventajarán° las mías.   *se... will surpass*
Miguel de Cervantes Saavedra, *El ingenioso
hidalgo Don Quijote de la Mancha*

Conjunto musical moderno, Madrid

EN BUSCA DE UN PUESTO

VOCABULARIO: ¿EN QUÉ QUIERES TRABAJAR?

llenar las solicitudes

caerle bien al entrevistador

DIRECCIÓN DE PERSONAL

graduarse

colocarse

¡renunciar al puesto!

caerle bien/mal a alguien to make a good/bad impression on someone
dejar to quit
entrevistar to interview
llenar to fill out (*a form*)
renunciar (a) to resign (from)

el/la aspirante candidate, applicant
el currículum resumé
el/la director(a) de personal director of personnel
la empresa corporation, business
la solicitud application (form)

¡Participa en el mundo que has soñado!

La Escuela Internacional Tuñon te prepara para la carrera de Técnico o de Azafata
en dos años de estudios.

• Una formación seria (cultura general, idiomas, informática).
• Numerosas prácticas en empresas durante la escolaridad.
• Posibilidad de intercambios entre las 23 escuelas durante el año.
• Múltiples salidas profesionales en los sectores del Turismo, Viajes, Hostelería...

Avenida Menendez Pelayo, 83 28007 MADRID Tel.: 433 80 48

ESCUELA INTERNACIONAL 23 Escuelas en el Mundo **TUÑON** Fundada en 1964 Enseñanzas Privada

Calle Tuset 23.25 08006 BARCELONA Tel.: 209 50 00

Imagine que Ud. solicitó un puesto recientemente. Usando los números del **1** al **14**, indique en qué orden ocurrió lo siguiente.

_____ Se despidió de Ud. cordialmente, diciendo que lo/la iba a llamar en una semana.

_____ Fue a la biblioteca para informarse sobre la empresa: su historia, dónde tiene sucursales (_branches_), etcétera.

_____ Ud. llenó la solicitud tan pronto como la recibió y la mandó, con el currículum, a la empresa.

_____ El secretario le dijo que Ud. se iba a entrevistar con la directora de personal.

_1_ Ud. necesitaba colocarse. En la oficina de empleos de su universidad, Ud. leyó un anuncio para un puesto en su especialización.

_____ Le dijo que le iba a mandar una solicitud para llenar y también le pidió que mandara su currículum.

_____ Cuando por fin lo/la llamó la directora, ¡fue para ofrecerle el puesto!

_____ Mientras esperaba para hablar con el entrevistador en la Dirección de Personal, Ud. estaba nerviosísimo/a.

_____ La directora le entrevistó con cuidado: cuándo se iba a graduar, qué cursos había tomado, etcétera.

_____ Llamó al teléfono que daba el anuncio y habló con un secretario en la Dirección de Personal.

_____ La mañana de la entrevista, Ud. se levantó temprano, se vistió con cuidado y salió temprano para la empresa para llegar puntualmente.

_____ Al entrar en la oficina de la directora, Ud. la saludó con cortesía, tratando de caerle bien desde el principio.

_____ También le pidió que hablara un poco en español, ya que la empresa tiene una sucursal en Santiago, Chile.

_____ En una semana lo/la llamaron para arreglar una entrevista.

> ## Al tanto...
>
> It is important *to make a good impression* in a job interview. To express that in Spanish you can use **caerle bien** or the following phrase.
>
> —¿Qué impresión tienes de la entrevista?
> —Pues, creo que **causé una buena impresión**.
>
> Another way to get a job is *to have "connections,"* expressed in Spanish with the phrase **tener enchufe** (= *electrical plug*).
>
> —No me lo explico. ¿Cómo es que Jorge consiguió el puesto con esa compañía? ¿Tiene enchufe?
> —Sí, hombre, es **un enchufado**. Está allí porque el jefe y su padre son muy amigos.

ESTRUCTURAS

49. EXPRESSING WHAT YOU WOULD DO
Conditional Verb Forms

La fantasía de la maestra de Mafalda

«¡Ya no aguanto este puesto! Creo que me *gustaría* ser abogada... *Pasaría* todo el día con tipos interesantes... *Ganaría* mucho dinero... *Viajaría* mucho, pues *tendría* clientes en todas partes del país... Me *llamarían* actores, actrices, políticos, hombres de negocios para consultar conmigo... También *haría* viajes internacionales para investigar casos en el extranjero... Todo el mundo me *respetaría* y me *escucharía*... »

Mafalda's teacher's fantasy   I can't take this job any more! I think I would like to be a lawyer . . . I would spend every day with interesting people . . . I would earn a lot of money . . . I would travel a lot, since I would have clients all over the country . . . Actors, actresses, politicians, businessmen would call me to consult with me . . . I would also take international trips to investigate cases abroad . . . Everyone would respect me and listen to me . . . .

Y Ud., siendo la maestra (el maestro) de Mafalda, ¿cómo sería? Use
no cuando sea necesario.

- estar contento/a → *Estaría* contento/a.
- ser un tipo (una tipa) coherente
- desorientar a los estudiantes
- mirarlos con ojos furiosos

- hacerlos morir de miedo (¡OJO!   **har-**)
- poner una cara de poco sueldo (¡OJO!   **pondr-**)
- hacer a los estudiantes llorar de lástima

hablar		comer		vivir	
hablaría	hablaríamos	comería	comeríamos	viviría	viviríamos
hablarías	hablaríais	comerías	comeríais	vivirías	viviríais
hablaría	hablarían	comería	comerían	viviría	vivirían

Like the English future, the English conditional is formed with an auxiliary
verb: *I would speak, I would write.* The Spanish *conditional* (**el condicional**),
like the Spanish future, is a simple verb form (only one word). It is formed
by adding the conditional endings **-ía, -ías, -ía, -íamos, -íais, -ían** to the infinitive. No auxiliary verbs are needed.

Verbs that form the future on an irregular stem use the same stem to
form the conditional.

decir: **dir-**
hacer: **har-**
poder: **podr-**   **-ía**
poner: **pondr-**   **-ías**
querer: **querr-**   **-ía**
saber: **sabr-**   **-íamos**
salir: **saldr-**   **-íais**
tener: **tendr-**   **-ían**
venir: **vendr-**

decir	
diría	diríamos
dirías	diríais
diría	dirían

The conditional of **hay** (**haber**) is **habría** (*there would be*).*

The conditional expresses what you would do in a particular situation,
given a particular set of circumstances.

¿**Hablarías** francés en México?	*Would you speak French in Mex-*
—No, **hablaría** español.	*ico? —No, I would speak*
	Spanish.

¡OJO!   When *would* implies *used to* in English, Spanish uses the imperfect.

| **Íbamos** a la playa todos los | *We would go (used to go) to the* |
| veranos. | *beach every summer.* |

---

*The conditional forms of the verb **haber** are used to form the *conditional perfect tense* (**el condicional perfecto**), which expresses what *would have* occurred at some point in the past. You will
find a presentation of these forms in Appendix 2, Additional Perfect Forms (Indicative and
Subjunctive).

Práctica

A.   ¿Es posible escapar? Cuente Ud. la fantasía de esta trabajadora social, dando la forma condicional de los verbos.

Necesito salir de todo esto… Creo que me (*gustar*) ir a Puerto Rico o a algún otro lugar exótico del Caribe… No (*trabajar*)… (*Poder*) nadar todos los días… (*Tomar*) el sol en la playa… (*Comer*) platos exóticos… (*Ver*) bellos lugares naturales… El viaje (*ser*) ideal…

Pero… , tarde o temprano, (*tener*) que volver a lo de siempre… a los rascacielos de la ciudad… al tráfico… al medio ambiente contaminado… al mundo del trabajo… (*Poder*) usar mi tarjeta de crédito, como dice el anuncio—pero, al fin y al cabo, ¡(*tener*) que pagar después!

¿Cierto, falso o no lo dice? Corrija las oraciones falsas.

1. Esta persona trabaja en una ciudad grande.
2. No le interesan los deportes acuáticos.
3. Puede pagar este viaje de sueños con dinero en efectivo.
4. Tiene un novio con quien quisiera hacer el viaje.

B.   ¿Qué harías si pudieras? Con un compañero (una compañera), haga y conteste preguntas según el modelo. Cambie los detalles, si quiere.

MODELO: estudiar árabe / japonés →
—¿Estudiarías árabe?
—No. Estudiaría japonés.

1. estudiar italiano / chino
2. renunciar a un puesto sin avisar / con dos semanas de anticipación
3. hacer un viaje a España / la Argentina
4. salir sin apagar el estéreo / nunca
5. seguir un presupuesto rígido / uno flexible
6. gastar menos en ropa / en libros
7. poner el aire acondicionado en invierno / en verano
8. alquilar un coche de lujo / uno económico

Ahora siga con el mismo modelo pero invente las respuestas.

9. dejar de estudiar / ¿ ?
10. vivir en otra ciudad / ¿ ?
11. ser presidente/a de los Estados Unidos / ¿ ?
12. gustarle conocer a una persona famosa / ¿ ?

C.   Entrevista. ¿Cómo será su futuro? ¿Qué hará? ¿Qué haría? Con otro/a estudiante, haga y conteste las siguientes preguntas. Después de la entrevista, cada estudiante debe preparar un retrato (*portrait*) del otro para presentar a la clase.

MODELO: ¿Dejarás de fumar algún día? →
•   ¡Ay, no! No dejaré de fumar nunca.
•   Pues, creo que sí. Dejaré de fumar algún día.

PREGUNTAS CON EL FUTURO

1. ¿Te graduarás en esta universidad (o en otra)?
2. ¿Vivirás en esta ciudad después de graduarte?
3. ¿Buscarás un empleo aquí?
4. ¿Te casarás pronto después de graduarte?
5. ¿Cuántos niños tendrás?
6. ¿Serás famoso/a algún día?
7. ¿Te pondrás gordo/a?
8. ¿Tendrás dificultades con la policía?

PREGUNTAS CON EL CONDICIONAL

1. ¿Te casarías con una persona de otra religión?
2. ¿Te mudarías con frecuencia?
3. ¿Estarías contento/a sin mirar la televisión?
4. ¿Ahorrarías el diez por ciento de tu sueldo?
5. ¿Vivirías en la misma ciudad para siempre?
6. ¿Te gustaría ayudar a colonizar otro planeta?
7. ¿Renunciarías a tu trabajo para viajar por el mundo?
8. ¿Podrías vivir sin usar nunca las tarjetas de crédito?

D. ¿Cómo sería el mundo si Ud. pudiera controlarlo todo? Haga oraciones con una palabra o frase de cada columna. También puede hacer oraciones con (**No**) **Habría…** y una frase de la tercera columna.

yo		usar	(las) guerras
la gente		tener	(las) bombas atómicas
el gobierno		quejarse de	(la) (des)igualdad
nosotros		vivir en	un gobierno mundial
los terroristas	(no)	ser	(el) petróleo, (la) gasolina, otros
alguien		eliminar	tipos de energía
(no) habría que		desarrollar	(la) esperanza para un futuro mejor
		matar	todos los dictadores
		destruir	(las) tarjetas de crédito

Bogotá, Colombia

Una preocupación universal

—Te digo que de verdad estoy preocupada. No he podido encontrar empleo todavía.
—¿No viste el anuncio en el Departamento de Lenguas? En dos semanas habrá puestos en la Compañía Palacios.
—¡No me digas! ¿Crees que pagarán bien?
—No lo dicen, pero piden varias lenguas y ofrecen la oportunidad de progresar y de viajar.

UN POCO DE TODO

A.   ¡Entendiste mal! Con un compañero (una compañera), haga y conteste preguntas según el modelo.

MODELO: llegar el trece de junio / tres →
- Llegaré el trece de junio.
- ¿No dijiste que llegarías el tres?
- ¡Que no! Dije que llegaría el trece. Entendiste mal.

1. estar en el bar a las dos / doce
2. estudiar con Juan / Juana
3. ir de vacaciones en julio / junio
4. verte en casa / en clase
5. comprar la blusa rosada / roja

B. Si el mundo fuera diferente... Adaptarse a un nuevo país o a nuevas circunstancias es difícil, pero también es una aventura interesante. ¿Qué ocurriría si el mundo fuera diferente?

MODELO: Si yo fuera la última persona en el mundo... →
- tendría que aprender a hacer muchas cosas
- sería la persona más importante—y más ignorante—del mundo
- me adaptaría fácilmente/difícilmente
- los animales y yo nos haríamos buenos amigos

1. Si yo pudiera tener solamente un amigo (una amiga), _____.
2. Si yo tuviera que pasar un año en una isla desierta, _____.
3. Si yo fuera (otra persona), _____.
4. Si el presidente fuera presidenta, _____.
5. Si viviera en la Argentina, _____.
6. Si fuera el año 2080, _____.
7. Si yo viviera en el siglo XIX (XV, etcétera), _____.
8. Si yo fuera la persona más poderosa (*powerful*) del mundo, _____.
9. Si los estudiantes fueran profesores y los profesores fueran estudiantes, _____.

• •

UN PASO MÁS: Situaciones

El mundo del trabajo

Hablando de la entrevista

—¿Qué tal te fue esta mañana?
—Pues no sé qué decirte. Me dijeron que me avisarían en una semana. ¿Y a ti?
—Lo mismo, pero no creo que me lo den. Tenían mucho interés en la experiencia que pudieran tener los candidatos, y como sabes, no tengo ninguna.

Hablando con los amigos

—¡Hola! ¿Ya tienes trabajo?
—¡Qué más quisiera! Me gustaría trabajar en lo mío,° pero de momento no hay nada.   lo... *mine (i.e., my field)*
—Por lo visto° los futuros biólogos no interesan demasiado...   Por... *Apparently*
—Hombre, a veces pienso que si volviera a entrar en la universidad, cambiaría de carrera, porque voy a tardar en colocarme de biólogo.
—Pues, no es sólo en lo tuyo.° No sé si te acuerdas, pero yo tardé medio   ¿ ?
año° en colocarme. ¡Y ahora llevo siete meses trabajando! O sea, ¡ánimo°!   yo... *it took me half a year* / ¿ ?

Notas comunicativas sobre el diálogo

The expression **tardar en** + *infinitive* expresses how long it takes to do something.

¿Cuánto tiempo **tardaste en llegar**? —Pues **tardamos dos horas**, por las malas condiciones en la carretera.

How long did it take you to get there? —Well, it took us two hours because of the bad conditions on the highway.

Conversación

Hágale preguntas a un compañero (una compañera) de clase que ya tiene empleo (o a su profesor[a]) para saber la siguiente información.

- el nombre exacto del trabajo que tiene
- la carrera que hizo en la universidad
- el tiempo que tardó en colocarse
- la experiencia que tenía en ese campo cuando se colocó
- el tiempo que lleva en el empleo

VOCABULARIO

En busca de un puesto

caerle bien/mal a alguien to make a good/bad impression on someone
colocarse to get a job
dejar to quit
entrevistar to interview
graduarse (en) (de) to graduate (from) (as a)

llenar to fill out (*a form*)
renunciar (a) to resign (from)

el/la aspirante candidate, applicant
el currículum resumé
la dirección de personal personnel, employment office
el/la director(a) de personal director of personnel

la empresa corporation, business
el/la entrevistador(a) interviewer
la solicitud application (form)
la sucursal branch (office)

Frases útiles para la comunicación

el tipo, la tipa   guy, gal; character

—¿Conoces al novio de Ceci? ¿Qué te parece?
—Es **un tipo** curioso, ¿no crees?

See also the words and phrases in **Notas comunicativas sobre el diálogo.**

HABLANDO DE CARRERAS

VOCABULARIO: PROFESIONES Y OFICIOS° *trades*

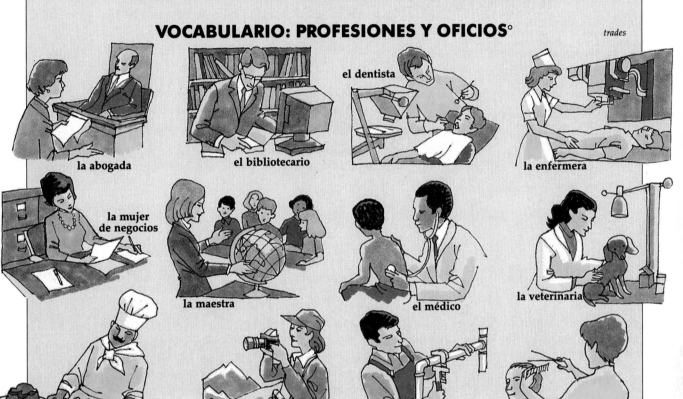

la abogada

el bibliotecario

el dentista

la enfermera

la mujer de negocios

la maestra

el médico

la veterinaria

el cocinero

la fotógrafa

el plomero

la peluquera

In the preceding chapters of *¿Qué tal?*, you have learned to use a number of the words for professions and trades that appear below. Learn to use the new terms that are important or interesting to you. Not all of these words will be considered "active vocabulary" that you will be expected to say or write spontaneously.

Profesiones

el/la analista de sistemas systems analyst
el/la contador(a) accountant
el/la ingeniero/a engineer
el/la médico/a doctor
el/la periodista journalist
el/la profesor(a) professor
el/la siquiatra psychiatrist
el/la trabajador(a) social social worker
el/la traductor(a) translator

Oficios

el/la cajero/a cashier, teller
el/la comerciante merchant, shopkeeper
el/la electricista electrician
el/la mecánico/a mechanic
el/la obrero/a worker, laborer
el/la secretario/a secretary
el soldado soldier
el/la técnico/a technician
el/la vendedor(a) salesperson

Las empresas norteamericanas buscan humanistas

Las humanidades están de moda en las universidades norteamericanas ante el interés de las empresas por contratar "administradores flexibles, críticos y capaces de aprender continuamente", gentes con "una educación liberal" según publica la revista "Nuestro Tiempo" de la Universidad de Navarra.

Los empresarios norteamericanos pretenden aumentar los contactos de graduados en Humanidades en un 20%, en tanto que los de graduados en áreas muy especializadas crecen menos del 1%.

Por otra parte, al decir de los rectores de estos centros hoy en auge, los estudiantes han "descubierto" los clásicos y se entusiasman con ellos.

A.   ¿A quién necesita Ud. en estas situaciones? ¿A quién llamará o con quién consultará?

1. Tiene problemas con la tubería (*plumbing*) de su cocina.
2. Ud. acaba de tener un accidente con el coche; el otro conductor dice que Ud. tuvo la culpa (*blame*).
3. Por las muchas tensiones y presiones de su vida profesional y personal, Ud. tiene serios problemas afectivos (*emotional*).
4. Ud. está en el hospital y quiere que alguien le dé una aspirina.
5. Ud. quiere que alguien le ayude con las tareas domésticas porque no tiene mucho tiempo para hacerlas.
6. Ud. quiere que alguien le construya una pared en el jardín.
7. Ud. conoce todos los detalles de un escándalo en el gobierno de su ciudad y quiere divulgarlos.

B.   Asociaciones. ¿Qué profesiones u oficios asocia Ud. con estas frases? Consulte las listas de **Profesiones** y **Oficios** y use las siguientes palabras también.

actor/actriz	camarero/a	pintor(a)
ama de casa	carpintero/a	poeta
(*homemaker*)	consejero/a	policía
arquitecto/a	cura/pastor(a)/	político/a
azafata/camarero	rabino/a	presidente/a
barman	detective	senador(a)

1. intelectual/aburrido
2. muchos/pocos años de preparación
3. sensible (*sensitive*)
4. mucho/poco dinero
5. mucho/poco poder (*power*)
6. mucha/poca responsabilidad
7. mucho/poco prestigio
8. mucha/poca prisa
9. mucho/poco peligro (*danger*)
10. mucho/poco trabajo
11. «de las nueve a las cinco»
12. en el pasado, sólo para hombres/mujeres
13. una carrera «nueva»
14. un programa de televisión

C.   ¿Qué preparación se necesita para ser… ? Imagine que Ud. es consejero universitario (consejera universitaria). Explíquele a un estudiante los cursos que debe tomar para prepararse para las siguientes carreras. Consulte la lista de cursos académicos de la página 43 y use la siguiente lista. Recomiéndele también lo que debe hacer durante los veranos y los trabajos de tiempo parcial que debe buscar para ganar experiencia en su campo.

Palabras útiles: la organización administrativa, la contabilidad (*accounting*), el márketing, la ingeniería, la pedagogía, el derecho (*law*), la sociología, la retórica (*speech*), las comunicaciones, la gerontología

1. traductor(a) en la ONU (Organización de las Naciones Unidas)
2. locutor(a) en la televisión, especializado/a en los deportes
3. contador(a) para un grupo de abogados
4. periodista en la redacción (*editorial staff*) de una revista de ecología

5. trabajador(a) social, especializado/a en los problemas de los ancianos
6. maestro/a de primaria, especializado/a en la educación bilingüe

---

Al tanto...

Career decisions have an enormous impact on our lives. Here are two ways to comment on them.

- ¿La medicina? Es **una carrera** { **con muchas salidas (opciones).**
  con mucho futuro.

- Quiero ser programadora para { **hacerme un porvenir.**
  hacerme un futuro.

D.   Entrevista. Con un compañero (una compañera), haga y conteste preguntas para saber la siguiente información.

1. la profesión u oficio de sus padres
2. lo que hacían sus abuelos
3. si tiene un amigo o pariente que ejerzca una profesión extraordinaria o interesante y el nombre de esa profesión
4. lo que sus padres (su esposo/a) quiere(n) que Ud. sea
5. lo que él/ella quiere ser
6. la carrera para la cual (*which*) se preparan muchos de sus amigos

Notas culturales: Los nombres de las profesiones

En el mundo de habla española hay poco acuerdo sobre las palabras que deben usarse para referirse a las mujeres que ejercen ciertas profesiones. En gran parte, eso se debe al hecho de que (*the fact that*), en muchos de estos países, las mujeres *acaban de empezar* a ejercer esas profesiones; por eso el idioma todavía está cambiando para acomodarse a esa nueva realidad. En la actualidad se emplean, entre otras, las siguientes formas:

- Se usa el artículo **la** con los sustantivos que terminan en **-ista.**

  el dentista → **la dentista**

- En otros casos se usa una forma femenina.

  el médico → **la médica**
  el trabajador → **la trabajadora**

- Se usa la palabra **mujer** con el nombre de la profesión.

  el policía → **la mujer** policía
  el soldado → **la mujer** soldado

Escuche lo que dice la persona con que Ud. habla para saber las formas que él o ella usa. No se trata de (*It's not a question of*) formas correctas o incorrectas, sólo de usos y costumbres locales.

¿Cuándo te gradúas?

—¿Qué hace tu hermano? Se graduó el año pasado, ¿verdad?

—Sí, se graduó de abogado, pero no tiene trabajo todavía. Mis padres quieren que solicite un puesto en el gobierno.

—Y tú, ¿cuándo te gradúas?

—Espero que en junio.

 # ESTRUCTURAS

Madrid, España

 ## 50. HYPOTHETICAL SITUATIONS: WHAT IF...?
Conditional Sentences

Una entrevista en la dirección del Canal 45

EL JEFE: ¿Qué *haría Ud. si hubiera* un choque entre un camión y un tren?

EL ASPIRANTE A REPORTERO: *Yo entrevistaría* a todos los testigos.

EL JEFE: ¿Y *si hubiera* una serie de bombas terroristas en algún país?

EL ASPIRANTE A REPORTERO: *Iría* al país y *me enteraría* de todos los detalles de la situación.

EL JEFE: ¿Y *si* aquí *hubiera* un terremoto?

EL ASPIRANTE A REPORTERO: *Me escondería* debajo de mi escritorio... ¡Los terremotos me inspiran más terror que los terroristas!

Complete las siguientes oraciones como si (*as if*) Ud. fuera el aspirante.

1. Si hubiera un choque de aviones, yo _____.
2. Si hubiera _____ en _____, yo iría al país para enterarme de los detalles.
3. Si hubiera un terremoto, yo _____.

An interview at Channel 45 headquarters   THE BOSS: What would you do if there were a collision between a truck and a train? THE ASPIRING REPORTER: I would talk with all the witnesses. THE BOSS: And if there were a series of terrorist bombs in a country? THE ASPIRING REPORTER: I would go to the country and find out all the details of the situation. THE BOSS: And if there were an earthquake here? THE ASPIRING REPORTER: I would hide under my desk . . . Earthquakes scare me more than terrorists!

DEPENDENT CLAUSE: *si* CLAUSE	INDEPENDENT CLAUSE
si + *imperfect subjunctive*	*conditional*
Si yo **fuera** tú, no **haría** eso.	*If I were you, I wouldn't do that.**
Si se levantaran más temprano, **podrían** llegar a tiempo.	*If they got up earlier, they would be able to arrive on time.*
Iría a las montañas **si tuviera** tiempo.	*He would go to the mountains if he had the time.*

When a clause introduced by **si** (*if*) expresses a contrary-to-fact situation, **si** is always followed by the past subjunctive. In such sentences, the verb in the independent clause is usually in the conditional, since the sentence expresses what one *would do or say* if the **si** clause were true.*

When the **si** clause refers to the present time or to a habitual action, the present indicative is used—not the present subjunctive.

Si tiene tiempo, **irá** (**va**) a las montañas.	*If he has time, he'll go (he goes) to the mountains.*

Como si (*As if, As though*) is always followed by the past subjunctive because it always indicates something contrary to fact.

Connie habla **como si fuera** española.	*Connie speaks as though she were Spanish.*

Práctica

A. ¿Qué haría Ud.? ¿Adónde iría? Complete las oraciones lógicamente.

1. Si yo quisiera comprar comida, iría a _____.
2. Si necesitara comprar un libro, iría a _____.
3. Si necesitara usar un libro, iría a _____.
4. Si tuviera sed en este momento, tomaría _____.
5. Si tuviera que emigrar, iría a _____.
6. Si quisiera ir a _____, viajaría en avión.
7. Si quisiera tomar _____, lo esperaría en la estación.
8. Si no funcionara(n) _____, compraría un coche nuevo.
9. Si me gustara(n) _____, iría a ver un concierto de Bruce Springsteen.
10. Si me gustara(n) _____, pasaría mucho tiempo mirando la televisión.

---

*The contrary-to-fact situations in these sentences express speculations about the present. The perfect forms of the conditional and the past subjunctive are used to speculate about the past: what *would have* happened if a particular event *had* or *had not occurred*.

Si hubiera tenido el dinero, **habría hecho** el viaje.	*If I had had the money, I would have made the trip.*

You will find a more detailed presentation of this structure in Appendix 2, Additional Perfect Forms (Indicative and Subjunctive).

B.   Si buscara un puesto... ¿Qué haría Ud. si necesitara un puesto? Haga oraciones según el modelo.

> MODELO: si / necesitar / puesto, / leer / anuncios / en / periódico →
>   Si necesitara un puesto, leería los anuncios en el periódico.

1.   si / encontrar / anuncio / interesante, / llamar / a / empresa
2.   si / empresa / mandarme / solicitud, / llenarla
3.   si / (ellos) pedirme / currículum, / mandárselo
4.   si / interesarme / salario, / pedir / entrevista
5.   si / (ellos) darme / entrevista, / tratar / caerle / bien / entrevistador
6.   si / él / hacerme / mucho / preguntas, / contestar / honestamente
7.   si / yo / tener / preguntas que hacer / sobre / empresa, / hacerlas / durante / entrevista
8.   si / (ellos) ofrecerme / puesto, / estar / muy / contento/a

C.   Su amiga Carlota exagera en todo. Describa sus exageraciones, usando oraciones que empiecen con **Habla como si...** , según el modelo. Incorpore las palabras sugeridas u otras si quiere.

> MODELO: Carlota es de una familia de la clase media. (rica) →
>   Habla como si fuera de una familia rica.

1.   Carlota vive en una casa bonita pero humilde. (palacio)
2.   Se equivoca con frecuencia porque tiene mala memoria. (recordarlo todo)
3.   No es experta en nada. (todo)
4.   Tuvo una entrevista ayer, pero no le han ofrecido el puesto todavía. (tenerlo ya)
5.   Tiene muy pocos amigos. (muchos)

D.   ¿Qué haría Ud. en estas situaciones? Explique su respuesta.

1.   Los señores Medina están durmiendo. De repente se oye un ruido. Un hombre con máscara y guantes (*gloves*) entra silenciosamente en la alcoba. **Si yo fuera** el señor (la señora) Medina, _____. **Si yo fuera** el hombre, _____.
2.   Celia está estudiando para un examen muy importante. Su compañera de cuarto se pone enferma y la tiene que llevar al hospital. No puede seguir estudiando para el examen y, a la mañana siguiente, no está lista para tomar el examen. **Si yo fuera** Celia, _____. **Si yo fuera** su compañera, _____.
3.   Los padres de Ana no quieren que se case con su novio Antonio, quien vive en otro estado. Un día, Ana recibe una carta de Antonio, la lee y de repente sale de la casa. Deja la carta abierta en la mesa. **Si yo fuera** Ana, _____. **Si yo fuera** el padre (la madre), _____.

E.   Entrevista. ¿Bajo qué circunstancias... ? Entreviste a otro/a estudiante según el modelo.

MODELO: comprar un coche nuevo →
—¿Bajo qué circunstancias comprarías un coche nuevo?
—Compraría un coche nuevo si tuviera más dinero.

1. dejar de estudiar en esta universidad
2. emigrar a otro país
3. estudiar otro idioma
4. no obedecer a los padres
5. votar por _____ para presidente/a
6. ser candidato/a para presidente/a
7. casarse
8. no decirle la verdad a un amigo

UN POCO DE TODO

Un exiliado cubano. Complete the following story with the correct form of the words in parentheses, as suggested by the context. When two possibilities are given in parentheses, select the correct word.

Miguel García es un médico excelente que vive y trabaja en Miami. Emigró de Cuba (*después de/después de que*[1]) la revolución de Fidel Castro. Miguel (*querer*[2]) mucho a su patria, pero no le (*gustar*[3]) el nuevo sistema político. Así (*salir: él*[4]) de Cuba en 1963 y (*llegar*[5]) con su familia a los Estados Unidos. El gobierno cubano no permitió que (*traer: ellos*[6]) muchos bienes personales; (*también/tampoco*[7]) les (*dejar*[8]) sacar dinero del país.

Ser un refugiado político es como empezar una nueva vida. Al° establecerse en los Estados Unidos, Miguel (*experimentar*[9]) muchos cambios difíciles. (*El/La*[10]) idioma, (*por/para*[11]) ejemplo, (*representar*[12]) un obstáculo para él. Ya (*saber*[13]) bastante° gramática (*inglés*[14]) porque la (*haber estudiar*[15]) en el colegio en Cuba. Pero nunca (*haber aprender*[16]) a hablarlo con facilidad, y (*también/tampoco*[17]) tenía muchos problemas en comprender (*al/a la*[18]) gente. Aunque Miguel (*haber ser*[19]) médico en Cuba, fue difícil encontrar trabajo. Tuvo que trabajar en una fábrica (*por/para*[20]) mantener° a su mujer° y a sus tres hijos. Mientras tanto,° hizo la residencia en un hospital y (*tomar*[21]) el examen en el estado de Florida. (*Por/Para*[22]) fin (*conseguir*[23]) un (*bueno*[24]) puesto en un hospital de Miami.

Además, era necesario que los García (*acostumbrarse*[25]) a una vida y a una cultura completamente diferentes. (*Decidir: ellos*[26]) adoptar una vida bilingüe: el español es (*que/lo que*[27]) usan en la casa, pero hablan inglés en el trabajo y en (*el/la*[28]) calle.

Hoy, después de muchos años de exilio, Miguel y su familia se (*haber acostumbrar*°[29]) a la forma de vida en los Estados Unidos. (*Ser/Estar: ellos*[30]) ciudadanos de (*este/esto*[31]) país, aunque muchas veces añoran° su tierra natal. Sin embargo, saben que si todavía (*estar*[32]) en Cuba, su vida (*ser*[33]) muy diferente.

Upon

a fair amount of

to support / esposa
Mientras... *Meanwhile*

they miss

¿Cierto, falso o no lo dice?

1. Miguel tuvo que salir de Cuba; no pudo escoger.
2. Miguel y su familia sufrieron más al principio que ahora.
3. A Miguel no le gustó trabajar en la fábrica.
4. Tuvo que estudiar mucho para aprobar sus exámenes.
5. Los hijos de los Sres. García son bilingües.
6. No hay ningún aspecto de la sociedad cubana que prefieran a su equivalente en los Estados Unidos.

UN PASO MÁS: Lectura cultural

El breve artículo siguiente es de una revista española. En el artículo una serie de personas que ejercen varias profesiones contestan la pregunta que da título a esta lectura.

¿CREES EN LO QUE HACES?

ENCUESTA

VIRGINIA MATAIX
(ACTRIZ)

Si no creyera no lo haría. Estoy muy satisfecha de mi trabajo como actriz y, ahora, como presentadora, donde también tengo que actuar. Soy muy entusiasta de lo que hago porque está muy relacionado con las emociones y la creatividad.

AMANDO DE MIGUEL
(SOCIOLOGO)

Qué pregunta más abstracta. Si no creyera sería como para volverse loco. Mi trabajo es muy apetecible°y, como no aspiro al poder, procuro hacer las cosas yo mismo y no delegar en los otros. Como sociólogo asimilo información, la digiero y luego la emito, procurando eliminar lo que me viene impuesto e imponer lo que me gusta.

tempting, attractive

ESPERANZA ROY
(ACTRIZ)

Absolutamente. Si no creyera en lo que estoy haciendo buscaría otra forma de creer, porque no me sentiría bien realizada.° Pienso que hay varias formas de realizarse en la vida, y una de ellas es creer en tu aportación personal.

fulfilled

FELIPE CAMPUZANO
(CANTANTE)

Hombre, claro que creo, porque sería absurdo no hacerlo, aunque fuera equivocadamente. Soy un Sagitario empedernido° y estoy seguro de que mi éxito se debe, en cierta forma, a creer en lo que hago.

stubborn

MAGDA ORANICH
(ABOGADA)

Sí, creo y mucho. A veces, demasiado. Pero no le veo un mérito especial, porque me resultaría muy difícil hacer algo si no creyera en ello. Tanto en el aspecto profesional, político, como en la vida cotidiana, mi actitud es tan importante para la sociedad como para mí misma. A veces me crea problemas pasajeros, pero la satisfacción de haber obrado° según mis convicciones supera cualquier otro inconveniente.

acted

MONCHO ALPUENTE
(PERIODISTA)

Creo en lo que hago, entre otras cosas, porque no tengo otro remedio. Nunca he cuestionado mi facultad fundamental, que es la de escribir, y lo hago instintivamente. Lo que sí me planteo° es su comercialización: qué escribo y para qué medio de comunicación.

me... I ask myself about

Comprensión

A. ¿Cierto, falso o no lo dice el artículo?

1. Todas las personas que aparecen en el artículo creen en lo que hacen.
2. La mayoría de ellos también afirman su profesión con entusiasmo.

B. De las personas del artículo, ¿quién... ?

_____ atribuye su satisfacción profesional a las características de su signo astrológico

_____ cree que contribuye al bienestar general de la sociedad con su trabajo

_____ cree que hace su trabajo casi sin pensar

_____ estaría loco si no creyera en lo que hace

_____ pone énfasis en la necesidad de poder contribuir con algo en esta vida

_____ pone énfasis en lo emocional y no en lo intelectual

Para escribir

Hágales la pregunta del artículo (¿Crees en lo que haces?) a una serie de amigos y parientes que ya ejercen una profesión o tienen un oficio. Si no son de habla española, hágales la pregunta en inglés. Luego escriba una serie de breves respuestas a la pregunta en español, siguiendo el modelo del artículo.

VOCABULARIO

Verbos

ejercer (ejerzo) to practice (*a profession*)

Profesiones y oficios

el/la abogado/a lawyer
el/la bibliotecario/a librarian
la carrera career
el/la comerciante merchant, shopkeeper

el hombre/la mujer de negocios businessman/woman
el/la plomero/a plumber
el/la trabajador(a) social social worker
el/la vendedor(a) salesperson

Frases útiles para la comunicación

como si + *past subjunctive*   as if . . .
Habla como si lo supiera todo.   He/She talks as if he/she knew
                                          everything.

EN MONTERREY SABEMOS DE NEGOCIOS...

DE VIAJE

VOCABULARIO: EN UN VIAJE AL EXTRANJERO

FRANCIA / ESPAÑA

ADUANA

cruzar la frontera

el viajero

declarar las compras

la inspectora
(de aduanas)

registrar las maletas

pagar los derechos/una multa

ir al extranjero to go abroad
tener algo que (declarar, decir, hacer) to have
   something to (declare, say, do)
viajar al/en el extranjero to travel abroad

la aduana customs
los derechos de aduana customs duty
la nacionalidad nationality
el pasaporte passport
la planilla (de inmigración) (immigration) form

A.   Definiciones. Dé una definición de las siguientes palabras.

1. la aduana
2. el pasaporte
3. los derechos de aduana
4. la frontera

5. la multa
6. registrar
7. la planilla de inmigración

B.   Pasando por la aduana. ¿Qué dice o pregunta el inspector en este diálogo?

INSPECTOR: ¿ _____?
  VIAJERA: Soy española, de Toledo.
INSPECTOR: ¿ _____?
  VIAJERA: Aquí lo tiene, señor.
INSPECTOR: ¿ _____?
  VIAJERA: Solamente estos libros y estos cigarrillos para uso personal.
INSPECTOR: ¿ _____?
  VIAJERA: Espere Ud. un momento. Mi esposo trae la llave.
INSPECTOR: ¡ _____!

  VIAJERA: ¡Oh, no! ¡No sabía que $\begin{cases} \text{tenía que declararlo!} \\ \text{era ilegal!} \end{cases}$

INSPECTOR: _____ .
  VIAJERA: ¿Cuánto tengo que pagar, pues?
INSPECTOR: _____ .

C.   Explíquele a su amigo Paul, que nunca ha viajado en el extranjero, lo que pasa cuando uno toma un vuelo internacional. Empiece desde el momento de subir al avión hasta el momento de salir de la Oficina de Inmigración. Si Ud. nunca ha hecho un viaje al extranjero, hágale preguntas a su profesor(a) para saber los detalles.

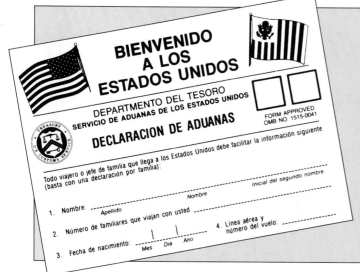

Al tanto...

The need to pass through airport security is a sign of the times. Here are the steps to follow.

- poner el equipaje de mano en la cinta (de rayos)
- pasar por el detector de metales

When you finally arrive at your destination, here is what you will do with your luggage.

- retirar la maleta de la cinta de equipaje
- buscar un maletero o un carrito para llevar el equipaje

ESTRUCTURAS

 51. *¿POR O PARA?*
A Summary of Their Uses

Antes de aterrizar

AZAFATA: Atención, *por favor*, señoras y señores. *Por fin* estamos empezando el descenso para aterrizar en Bogotá. Ha sido nuestro placer servirles durante el vuelo. En preparación *para* nuestra llegada, dentro de unos momentos el camarero Ortega y yo vamos a estar pasando *por* la cabina para entregarles las planillas de inmigración y de la declaración de aduana. *Por favor,* llénenlas antes de que aterricemos y ténganlas a mano con sus pasaportes. Se los van a pedir al pasar *por* inmigración y la aduana. Muchas gracias.

VIAJERO: Señorita, *por favor*. ¿Es necesario que declare las cámaras fotográficas y la grabadora? No son para vender...

AZAFATA: Con tal que no las traiga de regalo o *para* comerciar, no tiene que pagar derechos. *Por lo menos* esto es lo que yo tengo entendido. Pero declárelas *por si acaso*, aunque son *para* su uso personal.

VIAJERO: ¿Y hasta cuántas cámaras se permiten *para* uso personal?

AZAFATA: No sé exactamente, pero... ¡creo que menos de las diez que Ud. tiene! *Por eso* es mejor declararlas... *para* estar seguro.

¿Quién lo dijo? ¿Quién lo dirá? ¿la azafata, el camarero, el viajero o el inspector de aduanas?

1. Y ¿por qué trae Ud. estas diez cámaras?
2. Chicas, no van a creer lo que acaba de preguntarme uno de los pasajeros.
3. Pero... me dijo la azafata que se permitía entrar todo lo que fuera para uso personal...
4. Ya debes empezar el anuncio sobre las planillas, ¿no crees?

¿Quién será el viajero? ¿turista? ¿fotógrafo profesional? ¿contrabandista? ¿Qué cree Ud.? Explique.

Before landing ATTENDANT: Your attention, please, ladies and gentlemen. We are finally beginning our descent for landing in Bogotá. It has been our pleasure serving you during the flight. In preparation for our arrival, in just a few minutes Steward Ortega and I will be passing through the cabin to hand out the immigration and customs forms. Please fill them out before we land and have them within easy reach, along with your passports. You will be asked to produce them in immigration and customs. Thank you very much. TRAVELER: Please, miss. Is it necessary for me to declare my cameras and tape recorder? I don't intend to sell them . . . ATTENDANT: As long as you're not bringing them as a gift or for business reasons, you don't have to pay duty. That's what I understand anyway. But declare them just in case, even though they are for your personal use. TRAVELER: And (up to) how many cameras are permitted for personal use? ATTENDANT: I don't know exactly, but . . . I think fewer than the ten you have! That's why it's better to declare them . . . to be safe.

You have been using the words **por** and **para** right from the very beginning of your study of Spanish. The major uses of these two words have been presented gradually throughout the chapters of *¿Qué tal?*. Thus, the majority of the information in this section will be review for you, a chance to put together everything you have learned about them so far. As you read this section, keep in mind that, as with **ser** and **estar**, it is quite easy to determine whether to use **por** or **para** in most contexts, since both words have a number of clearly different areas of use.

Por

The preposition **por** has the following English equivalents.

- *by, by means of*

Vamos **por avión** (**tren, barco,** etcétera).	*We're going by plane (train, ship, and so on).*
Le voy a hablar **por teléfono**.	*I'll talk to him by phone.*

- *through, along*

¿No quieres caminar **por el parque**?	*Don't you want to walk through the park?*
Recomiendan que caminemos **por la playa**.	*They suggest that we walk along the beach.*

- *during, in* (the morning, afternoon, and so on)

Por la mañana juego al tenis.	*I play tennis in the morning.*

- *because of, on account of*

Estoy nervioso **por la entrevista**.	*I'm nervous because of the interview.*

- *for,* when *for* means the following:
  a. *in exchange for*

¿Cuánto me das **por este sombrero**?	*How much will you give me for this hat?*
Gracias por el regalo.	*Thanks for the gift.*

  b. *for the sake of, on behalf of*

Lo voy a hacer **por ti**.	*I'm going to do it for you (for your sake).*

  c. *for a period of time*

Elena manejó (**por**) tres horas esta tarde.	*Elena drove for three hours this afternoon.*

  Many native speakers of Spanish do not use **por** in this and similar sentences; **tres horas** implies *for three hours*.

Por is also used in a number of fixed expressions.

por Dios	for heaven's sake	**por lo general**	generally, in general
por ejemplo	for example	**por lo menos**	at least
por eso	that's why	**por primera/última vez**	for the first/last time
por favor	please	**por si acaso**	just in case
por fin	finally		

Para

The preposition **para** has many English equivalents, including *for*. Underlying most of them is reference to a goal or a destination.

- *in order to* + infinitive

Se quedaron en Andorra **para esquiar**.	*They stayed in Andorra to (in order to) ski.*
Sólo regresaron **para cenar**.	*They only came back to have dinner.*
Ramón estudia **para (ser) abogado**.	*Ramon is studying to be a lawyer.*

- *for*, when *for* means the following:
  a. *destined for, to be given to*

Le regalé un libro **para su hijo**.	*I gave him a book for his son.*
Todo esto es **para ti**.	*All of this is for you.*

  b. *for (by) a specified future time*

Para mañana estudien Uds. la página 72.	*For tomorrow, study page 72.*
Lo tengo que terminar **para la semana que viene**.	*I have to finish it by next week.*

  c. *toward, in the direction of*

Salieron **para Acapulco** ayer.	*They left for Acapulco yesterday.*

  d. *to be used for*

Es un vaso **para agua**.	*It's a water glass (a glass for water).*

¡OJO!   Compare the preceding sentence with this one:

Es un vaso **de agua**.	*It's a glass (full) of water.*

  e. *compared with others, in relation to others*

Para mí el español es fácil.	*For me Spanish is easy.*
Para (ser) extranjera habla muy bien el inglés.	*She speaks English very well for a foreigner.*

  f. *in the employ of*

Trabajan **para ese hotel**.	*They work for that hotel.*

La República Dominicana se desarrolla turísticamente con excelentes alternativas hoteleras en diferentes puntos del país. El clima cálido y fresco durante todo el año, sus costas bañadas por hermosas playas y la alegría del folklore dominicano son algunas de las razones que justifican visitarla repetidamente.

Práctica

A.   Preguntas. Conteste con oraciones completas, usando **por** y las expresiones entre paréntesis u otras, si quiere. Toda la clase debe llegar a un acuerdo sobre la respuesta más adecuada para cada pregunta.

1.   Supongamos que Uds. son muy ricos. ¿Cómo preferirían viajar? ¿En qué tipo de hotel preferirían quedarse? ¿Y si tuvieran que ahorrar? (barco, avión, autobús, …)

2.   ¿Cómo se enteran Uds. de lo que pasa en otros países? ¿Cómo se enteran de las noticias de su universidad (o su barrio)? ¿y de lo que les pasa a sus amigos? ¿Cuál es la mejor manera de enterarse en cada caso? (televisión, radio, teléfono, …)

3.   ¿A qué hora y por qué lugares les gusta a muchos hispanos dar paseos? ¿Por qué cree que pasean tanto? (las plazas, el centro, la noche, la tarde, …)

4.   ¿Cuándo es mejor estudiar? ¿ver la tele? ¿Es demasiado estudiar (por) 10 horas todos los días? ¿Es bueno ver la tele (por) media hora todos los días? (la mañana, la tarde, la noche, …)

5.   _____, un(a) estudiante en esta clase, está muy nervioso/a hoy. ¿Por qué será? (un examen, una cita con el dentista, su primera cita con alguien que le gusta de una manera especial, …)

6.   ¿Cuánto hay que pagar por una comida estupenda en esta ciudad? ¿por un almuerzo regular en esta universidad? ¿Cuál es el mejor sitio para cenar? ¿para almorzar? ¿y el peor? (más de 20 dólares, más de cinco dólares, …)

7.   De todos los profesionales, ¿cuáles cree Ud. que se sacrifican más por sus clientes? (médicos, enfermeros, bomberos [*firefighters*], …)

B.   Escoja una respuesta para cada pregunta o situación. Luego invente un contexto para cada diálogo. ¿Dónde están las personas que hablan? ¿Quiénes son? ¿Por qué dicen lo que dicen?

1.   ¡Huy! Acabo de jugar al básquetbol por dos horas.
2.   ¿Por qué quieres que llame a Pili y Adolfo? Nunca están en casa por la noche, sobre todo a estas horas.
3.   ¿No vas a comer nada? ¿por lo menos un sándwich?
4.   ¡Cuánto lo siento, don Javier! Sé que he llegado con una hora de retraso. No fue mi intención hacerle esperar.
5.   Es imposible que tome el examen hoy, por muchas razones.
6.   ¿No has oído? Juana acaba de tener un accidente horrible.
7.   ¡Pero, papá, quiero ir!
8.   Ay, Mariana, pensaba que sabías lo del terremoto. Murieron más de cien personas.

a.   ¡Por Dios! ¡Qué desgracia!
b.   Te digo que no, por última vez.
c.   No se preocupe, joven. Lo importante es que por fin está aquí.
d.   ¡Por Dios! ¿Qué le pasó?
e.   No, gracias. No tengo mucha hambre y además tengo que salir en seguida.
f.   ¿Por ejemplo? Dígame…
g.   Ah, por eso estás tan cansado.
h.   Llámalos de todas formas, por si acaso…

C. Imagine que Uds. están en los siguientes lugares. ¿Para qué están allí? Trabajando todos juntos, den todas las respuestas que puedan.

MODELO: en una playa de Acapulco → Estamos aquí para nadar...
para tomar el sol... para descansar...

1. en un banco, en Buenos Aires
2. en la Dirección de Personal de una empresa internacional
3. en la Ciudad de México
4. en un taller de automóviles

Notas comunicativas: Explaining Your Reasons

Here is a handy phrase to use when you are trying to explain your reasons for doing—or *not* doing—something.

La razón por la cual no pude asistir es que tuve que prepararme para un examen.

The reason why (for which) I couldn't attend is that I had to prepare for an exam.

Note the use of a similar structure to express *which* or *whom* in phrases like the following:

Una persona **por la cual**...
Un derecho **por el cual**...

A person for whom . . .
A right for which . . .

D. **Entrevista.** Con un compañero (una compañera), haga y conteste preguntas para ponerse de acuerdo sobre los siguientes temas. Luego dígales a los miembros de la clase lo que Uds. han acordado.

1. un lugar en esta ciudad por donde es peligroso (muy agradable) caminar
2. una persona con quien, por lo general, es difícil (fácil) comunicarse
3. un derecho por el cual Uds. (no) se sacrificarían
4. la forma más económica y a la vez más agradable de viajar
5. una cosa que—para los dos—es muy fácil (difícil) de hacer
6. la edad más apropiada para salir con un chico (una chica) por primera vez (para casarse)
7. una razón por la cual se disculpa (*it's O.K.*) faltar a clase (a un examen)
8. una cantidad de dinero que se considera excesiva cuando se trata de comprar un coche (una entrada para un partido importante)
9. la mejor manera de informarse de las noticias internacionales (del tiempo)
10. una razón por la cual (no) sería buena idea emigrar a otro país (inmigrar a este país)

Guadalajara, México

En la recepción
—¿Cuál es la tarifa de una habitación con pensión completa?
—¿Con o sin baño?
—Con baño privado, si es posible.
—Mil trescientos pesos la noche, señor.
—Está bien. Quisiéramos quedarnos dos noches.
—Muy bien, señor.

UN POCO DE TODO

A.   Complete las siguientes oraciones con el tiempo del verbo que sea apropiado.

1.   ¡Ay, Tomás está saliendo para el aeropuerto! Dígale que (*volviera/vuelva/ haya vuelto*) en seguida. Tiene una llamada urgente.
2.   Teníamos que encontrar la dirección de Luisa en Bogotá. Preguntamos por todas partes, pero no había nadie que (*sepa/haya sabido/supiera*) dónde vivía.
3.   ¿Su habitación (*room*)? La están preparando ahora mismo para que Uds. la (*puedan/hayan podido/pudieran*) ocupar en media hora.
4.   Es lástima que uno tarde tanto tiempo en pasar por la aduana. Ojalá que tus amigos no (*tienen/tenían/hayan tenido*) problemas.
5.   ¿No sabes el precio de la habitación? ¡Es imposible que no te lo (*digan/ han dicho/dicen*) todavía!
6.   Déjame explicarte lo que va a pasar cuando (*pasas/pases/pasaste*) por la aduana.

B.   El primer viaje a Guadalajara. Complete the following story with the correct form of the words in parentheses, as suggested by the context. When two possibilities are given in parentheses, select the correct word.

El día que salí para México, (*ser/estar*[1]) nublado. Iba a la Universidad de Guadalajara (*por/para*[2]) presentarme a un examen oral (*por/para*[3]) entrar en la Facultad de Medicina. Yo me (*haber preparar*[4]) con cuidado y (*esperar*[5]) saber todas las respuestas. Aunque en el pasado siempre (*haber sacar*[6]) buenas notas en ciencias, (*saber/conocer*[7]) que los profesores (*ser/ estar*[8]) muy exigentes. (*Tener: yo*[9]) miedo (*a/de*[10]) que me (*hacer: ellos*[11]) alguna pregunta imposible. —Si yo (*poder*[12]), me dije al despertarme (*por/para*[13]) la mañana, me (*quedar*[14]) en cama. Pero no (*ser/estar*[15]) así, y a las diez (*por/de*[16]) la mañana (*subir: yo*[17]) (*en el/al*[18]) avión.

Cuando (*llegar: yo*[19]) a Guadalajara, (*llover*[20]) ligeramente.° (*Ir: yo*[21]) al hotel y (*empezar*[22]) a repasar mis apuntes.° (*Leer*[23]) hasta las tres, cuando (*por/para*[24]) fin (*acostarse*[25]). (*Ser/Estar*[26]) tan cansada que (*dormirse*[27]) casi inmediatamente.

lightly

notes

Al día siguiente, después (*de/que*[28]) vestirme con cuidado, (*tomar*[29]) un taxi (*por/para*[30]) la Facultad. Los examinadores ya (*ser/estar*[31]) allí esperándome.

—(*Sentarse*[32]) Ud. aquí y no (*tener*[33]) miedo —me (*decir*[34]) ellos. —Aquí todos (*ser/estar: nosotros*[35]) amigos.—Y con esas palabras todos me (*sonreír*[36]).

Fue como si (*yo: tomar*[37]) un tranquilizante. (*Empezar*[38]) el examen y (*contestar: yo*[39]) como si (*tener*[40]) los libros (*abrir*[41]) en la mesa. Después, ellos me (*decir*[42]) que yo (*haber salido*[43]) muy bien y que todos (*esperar*[44]) verme allí el año siguiente. (*Regresar: yo*[45]) al hotel como si (*volar*[46]), casi sin (*tocar*[47]) el suelo. ¡Qué felicidad! ¡Y cómo (*brillar*[48]) el sol!

¿Cierto, falso o no lo dice? Si no lo dice, ¿qué cree Ud.? Explique.

1. La persona que habla es un hombre.
2. Es de los Estados Unidos.
3. Se ha preparado muy bien para el examen.
4. Creía que el examen iba a ser fácil.
5. Los examinadores lo/la trataron con cortesía y respeto.
6. Ya se ha graduado en la Facultad de Medicina.

UN PASO MÁS: Situaciones

Viajando en el extranjero

En la aduana argentina

—¿Su nacionalidad, por favor?
—Soy colombiana. Aquí tiene Ud. mi pasaporte.
—Muchas gracias. Y esa maleta... ¿es suya?
—Sí, señor, es mía, pero contiene solamente objetos de uso personal. No
tengo nada que declarar.
—Aunque sea así, ábrala, por favor. Es necesario que la registremos.
—Muy bien, señor.
—A ver, ropa... libros... nada de alcohol ni de cigarrillos... pues todo está
bien. Puede salir ahora, señorita.

En la fila° de inmigraciones, Uruguay   cola

—Pasaporte, por favor.
—Aquí lo tiene.
—¿Cuánto tiempo piensa quedarse?
—Dos semanas.
—Está bien. Le doy treinta días. Puede pasar.
—Gracias.

Entrando en un país extranjero

—Pasaporte. ¿En qué vuelo llegó? ¿Cuánto tiempo piensa permanecer° en el   ¿?
país?
—El número de vuelo está aquí, en el billete. Voy a quedarme cinco
semanas.
—¿Tiene una dirección aquí en la que se le pueda localizar°?   ¿?
—En casa de mis primos. Aquí tengo las señas.°   dirección
—¿Cuenta con dinero suficiente para cubrir sus gastos durante el tiempo
que permanezca en el país?
—Sí, señor. Aquí tiene los recibos° de los cheques de viajero que traigo   *receipts*
conmigo.
—Está bien. Eso es todo.

ENTRADA ARRIVAL ARRIVEE	USO OFICIAL OFFICIAL USE RESERVE A L'ADMINISTRATION	SALIDA DEPARTURE DEPART
Empresa y N° de vuelo o viaje Company and N° of flight or voyage Compagnie et N° de vol		**Empresa y N° de vuelo o viaje** Company and N° of flight or voyage Compagnie et N° de vol

Tarjeta internacional de entrada-salida - International card of arrival/departure - Carte internationale d'arrivée/départ

Para ser completado con letra de imprenta - Complete in block letters - Completer en lettres capitales

REPUBLICA ARGENTINA

Apellidos
Family Name
Nom

Nombres
Name
Prénom

Fecha de Nacimiento   Día   Mes   Año   Sexo   Uso oficial
Date of Birth   Day   Month   Year   Sex   Official use
Date de Naissance   Jour   Mois   Année   Sex   M   F   Reservé a l'Administ.

Nacionalidad
Nationality
Nationalité

Ocupación
Occupation
Profession

País de residencia habitual
Usual residence country
Domicile

Dirección en Argentina
Address in Argentina
Adresse en Argentina   _____

Tipo y N° de documento
Type and number of document
Clase et N° de document   _____

Expedido por - Issued by - Delivré par   _____

Conversación

Con un compañero (una compañera), haga los papeles de inspector(a) de aduanas y de viajero/a. A continuación se dan las preguntas.

MODELO: INSPECTOR: Su pasaporte, por favor. →
            VIAJERO/A: Sí, cómo no. *o* Claro. *o* Aquí tiene mi pasaporte. *o* Un momento, por favor. Está en esta maleta.

1. ¿Ciudadanía?
2. ¿Algo que declarar?
3. Hmm. Ud. trae muchos cigarrillos americanos.
4. ¿Son suyas todas estas maletas?
5. ¿Qué lleva en la pequeña?
6. ¿Cuánto tiempo va Ud. a estar en nuestro país?
7. Doscientos pesos, por favor.

VOCABULARIO

Verbos

aterrizar to land
cruzar to cross
declarar to declare
entregar to hand in, over
registrar to search, examine

Cruzando la frontera

la aduana customs
los derechos (de aduana) (customs) duty
la frontera border, frontier
la inmigración immigration
el/la inspector(a) (de aduanas) (customs) inspector
la nacionalidad nationality

la planilla form (*to fill out*)
el uso (personal) (personal) use
el/la viajero/a traveler

Palabras adicionales

al/en el extranjero abroad
tener algo que (decir, hacer, ...) to have something to (say, do, ...)

EN EL EXTRANJERO

VOCABULARIO: EL ALOJAMIENTO°

lodging

el hotel de lujo

la pensión

el hotel de primera (segunda) clase

Hotel Internacional

Hotel De La Paz

Pensión Fuentes

la recepción

la huéspeda

el botones/el mozo

los huéspedes

el huésped

confirmar to confirm
quedarse to remain, stay (*as a guest*)
reservar to reserve

los cheques de viajero traveler's checks
la habitación room
  para una persona single
  con/sin baño/ducha with(out) bath/shower
la pensión boarding house
  pensión completa room and full board (*all meals*)

media pensión room with breakfast and one other meal
la propina tip
la recepción front desk

con (_____ días de) anticipación (_____ days) in advance
desocupado/a vacant, unoccupied, free

Desayuno: de 8 a 10 horas	
Almuerzo:	**1.° Turno: 12,45 a 13,45**
	2.° Turno: 14,00 a 15,00
Cena:	**1.° Turno: 19,00 a 20,00**
	2.° Turno: 20,15 a 21,00

El día de salida les rogamos dejen libre su habitación antes de las 12 del medio día.

Las facturas se abonarán a su presentación.

No se aceptan cheques personales.

OBJETOS DE VALOR

La Dirección no se responsabiliza de los que no sean depositados en las cajas fuertes que al efecto existen en recepción.

REGLAMENTO INTERNACIONAL DE HOSTELERIA.

No se efectuará ninguna reducción a los clientes que efectúen comidas fuera del Hotel, si éstos están en pensión completa.

Está prohibido utilizar las toallas y otros objetos de la habitación fuera de la misma.

La corriente eléctrica es de 125 v.

Rogamos por respeto a los otros clientes no hacer ruido a partir de las 24 horas.

A.   ¿El Hotel María Cristina o la Pensión Libertad? De estas oraciones, ¿cuáles describen un hotel grande e internacional? ¿y una pensión pequeña y modesta?

1. Tiene todas las comodidades (*comforts*) que se encuentran en los mejores hoteles.
2. Los botones llevan el equipaje a la habitación.
3. Muchos de los huéspedes y del personal hablan solamente una lengua, el español, por ejemplo.
4. Hay que reservar una habitación con muchos días de anticipación.
5. Los dependientes confirman la reservación del huésped.
6. Generalmente se puede llegar sin reservaciones y encontrar una habitación desocupada.
7. Hay que gastar mucho dinero en propinas.
8. Los huéspedes suben (*carry up*) su equipaje, o el dueño los ayuda a subirlo.
9. Hablan muchos idiomas en la recepción.
10. Todas las habitaciones tienen ducha y, a veces, baño completo con ducha.
11. Se puede pedir una habitación con todas las comidas incluidas.
12. Generalmente es necesario compartir (*to share*) el baño con otros huéspedes.
13. Tiene un comedor grande y elegante.
14. Es posible que los huéspedes coman con la familia, en el comedor o en la cocina.

B.   ¿Qué se puede hacer? Si Ud. se encuentra en estas situaciones, ¿cómo va a resolver el problema? Hay más de una respuesta posible.

1. Ud. reservó una habitación, pero el recepcionista no puede encontrar la reservación.
   a. Me voy a otro hotel.
   b. Insisto en hablar con el gerente (*manager*).
   c. Me quejo en voz alta mientras el recepcionista la sigue buscando.
   d. ¿ ?
2. Ud. llega al único hotel del pueblo y encuentra que la única habitación desocupada cuesta muchísimo más de lo que quiere pagar.
   a. Regateo con el hotelero, pidiéndole que baje el precio.
   b. Busco a alguien para compartir el cuarto.
   c. Duermo en el coche.
   d. ¿ ?
3. Ud. está viajando con un amigo. Ud. quiere quedarse en un hotel de lujo con todas las comodidades—con aire acondicionado, televisor y refrigerador en la habitación—pero su amigo quiere quedarse en una pensión y prefiere una habitación sin baño porque es más barata.
   a. Lo dejo lo más pronto posible.
   b. Voy a la pensión pero me pongo de muy mal humor.

      c. Insisto en que nos quedemos en un hotel de lujo, pero pago más de la mitad (*half*) de la cuenta.

      d. ¿ ?

4. Ud. quiere pagar su cuenta y salir, pero sólo tiene cheques de viajero. El hotel no los acepta. Además, es domingo y los bancos están cerrados.

      a. Me quedo un día más.

      b. Salgo sin pagar.

      c. Le pido al gerente que me haga el favor de aceptar los cheques de viajero y lloro tanto que no me lo puede negar.

      d. ¿ ?

5. La pensión en que Ud. quiere quedarse ofrece tres posibilidades. ¿Cuál va a escoger? ¿Por qué?

      a. habitación sin comida

      b. pensión completa

      c. media pensión

Notas culturales: El alojamiento en el extranjero

En los países de habla española hay muchos tipos de hospedaje (*lodging*) entre los cuales el viajero puede escoger. Desde luego (*Of course*), un hotel de lujo ofrece todas las comodidades: piscina, canchas de tenis, restaurantes, discoteca, etcétera. Pero éstos son siempre muy caros. En cambio, los hoteles de segunda clase son más baratos y también muy buenos. Cada habitación tiene su baño, y hay comedor, bar y otras comodidades.

    Si uno va a pasar una temporada (*period of time*) larga en un lugar, es una buena idea buscar una pensión. En una pensión cada persona tiene su propio cuarto aunque puede ser necesario tener que compartir el baño con los demás huéspedes. Normalmente se sirve un desayuno sencillo y la cena. Todos los huéspedes viven como en una gran familia.

    Lo mejor para un estudiante que va a pasar un semestre o un año en una ciudad es tratar de hospedarse en la casa de una familia. Al principio puede ser necesario hacer un esfuerzo (*effort*) especial para adaptarse a la rutina y las costumbres de la familia, pues al fin y al cabo (*after all*) la casa es de ellos y uno sólo es un huésped. Pero no hay mejor forma de aprender otro idioma y conocer otra cultura.

ITINERARIO:

DIA PRIMERO.—CIUDAD DE ORIGEN - CANARIAS.
Presentación en el Aeropuerto, mostrador EUROIS-LAS, facturación del equipaje y recogida de la documentación y tarjeta de embarque. Subida al avión y salida hacia CANARIAS. Llegada, traslado a los hoteles y alojamiento.

DIAS INTERMEDIOS.—CANARIAS.
Estancia en los hoteles en el régimen de alojamiento elegido.
Días libres que podrán dedicar al descanso y a realizar las excursiones facultativas que nuestros guías en destino le ofrecerán.

DIA ULTIMO.—CANARIAS - CIUDAD DE ORIGEN.
Traslado al aeropuerto, facturación y embarque con destino a la ciudad de origen. Llegada y FIN DE NUESTROS SERVICIOS.

Al tanto...

The concept of being a tourist in a foreign country is not new. Centuries ago, Miguel de Cervantes had this advice for travelers: **«Allí donde fueres haz lo que vieres.»** What English saying makes the same recommendation? If you are not able to follow Cervantes' advice, people may say this about you: **Tiene pinta (= aspecto) de turista.**

— DESAYUNO Crillón —

Café americano	Jugo naranja	Fritos
American coffee	Orange juice	Fried
Café express	Jugo pomelo	Revueltos
Express coffee	Grapefruit juice	Scrambled
Café con leche	Jugo tomate	Omelette
Coffee with milk	Tomato juice	
Té	Jugo ananá	Con:
Tea	Pineapple juice	With:
Chocolate	Yoghurt	Panceta
		Bacon
Cereales	Huevos	Jamón
Corn flakes	Eggs	Ham
Ensalada de frutas	Pasados por agua	Salchicha
Fruit salad	Boiled	Sausage

Incluye: faturas, tostadas, manteca y mermelada
Rolls, toast, butter and marmalade included.
CON ESTE DESAYUNO SE SABOREA EL RICO CAFE "MARTINEZ"

Pedido especial ....
Special request ....

N° Hab.	Firma del cliente: ....
	Guest's signature: ....
ROOM NUMBER:	Aclaración de firma: ....

HOTEL
Crillón
BUENOS AIRES

C. Con un compañero (una compañera), haga el papel de un viajero (una viajera) que busca una habitación y el/la recepcionista del Hotel Crillón. El/La recepcionista le pregunta al viajero (a la viajera):

- si tiene una reservación
- la duración de la estancia (*stay*)
- el tipo de habitación reservado (o deseado)
- la forma de pagar

Más tarde, el huésped (la huéspeda) pide los siguientes servicios:

- el desayuno de mañana
- más toallas / jabón (*soap*) / información sobre _____
- subir / bajar la calefacción / el aire acondicionado

Por fin, el huésped (la huéspeda) pasa por la recepción para pagar la cuenta.

PREPARACIONES PARA UN AÑO EN EL EXTRANJERO

Ud. está considerando la posibilidad de pasar un año fuera de los EE.UU. Piensa que lo mejor para dominar una lengua es vivir en alguno de los países en que se habla. Y tiene razón. Pero... ¿en que país? El español se habla en muchos lugares. México y Centroamérica están fácilmente al alcance (*within reach*). ¿Y Sudamérica? Allí podría aprender español y conocer también la rica cultura precolombina. ¿Y España? ¿No le gustaría llegar a conocer la cultura y la tierra en donde nació el español? ¿No le atrae conocer cómo se mezclan lo hispano y lo europeo? En 1992 se conmemorará el

quinto centenario del descubrimiento de América. ¡Venga a descubrir el
Viejo Mundo!

Joe, un estudiante norteamericano, piensa pasar un año en España,
pero tiene algunas dudas y quiere hacer muchas preguntas. Para tantear (*to
feel out*) el terreno, le ha escrito a Maripepa, una amiga española que conoció en los EE.UU. cuando ésta estudiaba inglés en su universidad. Maripepa, que ahora vive en España, le contesta con entusiasmo.

Madrid, 7 de marzo

Querido Joe,

¡Cuánto me alegro de que por fin te hayas animado a escribirme y más
todavía por eso que me cuentas de que tal vez te decidas a pasar un año
en España! ¡Me parece genial! Has mejorado mucho tu español en estos
últimos meses y, desde luego,° un año en mi país sería perfecto.

desde... of course

Comprendo perfectamente todos tus temores. Alejarte° de tu familia,
de tus amigos, de tu país es siempre difícil, pero estoy segura de que te
alegrarás mucho de haber venido. Puede que al principio te cueste
acostumbrarte a nuestra manera de vivir y de ver la vida, pero verás
qué bien lo vas a pasar. Y no te preocupes tanto por la alimentación y la
asistencia médica... ¡que° aquí ya sabemos lo que es una vacuna°!

To distance yourself

for / shot, injection

Si vienes, tendrás ocasión de saborear la comida española, que por
cierto no tiene nada que ver con esas deliciosas enchiladas que
tomábamos allí. Y sinceramente España va a ser una cita obligatoria
muy pronto. ¿No recuerdas que en el 92 habrá una Feria Mundial en
Sevilla con motivo del quinto centenario del descubrimiento de
América? La Feria permanecerá abierta varios meses, y ya se están
celebrando numerosas actividades conmemorativas. Además, los Juegos
Olímpicos de 1992 tendrán lugar en Barcelona. ¡Qué más se puede pedir!
Tienes que venir pronto... ¡antes de que venga medio mundo!

Me resulta muy difícil decirte cuál es la mejor ciudad española para
pasar un año. Para mí, Madrid sería la mejor, pero probablemente no
estoy siendo imparcial. Vivo y estudio en Madrid, como sabes, y estoy
encantada. Además, como hace tan poco que regresé después de pasar
un año en los EE.UU., la nostalgia que tenía me hace verlo todo
maravilloso por aquí.

Madrid tiene unos 4 millones de habitantes. Es una gran ciudad
pero no agobiante,° bueno, si dejamos el tráfico de lado.° En los últimos
años las actividades culturales se han multiplicado por toda la ciudad.
Está llena de galerías de arte, de cafés-concierto, de salas especiales de
cine... Lo mismo puedes ir a una actuación de Tina Turner como a un
recital de Plácido Domingo. De verdad que Madrid tiene un ambiente
muy alegre y divertido, y eso que al principio los españoles te van a
parecer más serios que los mexicanos y los sudamericanos. El acento
castellano siempre resulta más seco.° (¿Recuerdas lo melodioso que te
parecía el acento de mi compañera colombiana y el de Carmen, la

overwhelming / de... out

terse

puertorriqueña?) Pero por otro lado Madrid sería la ciudad «crisol»°   *melting pot*
española por excelencia y creo que me entiendes. Aquí es muy difícil
sentirse extranjero. Hay gente procedente de todas las partes del país y
tal vez por eso es una ciudad muy acogedora.°   *welcoming*

Otra ventaja es que está en el centro del país, es decir que te puede
resultar mucho más fácil moverte desde aquí. Además hay un montón
de lugares interesantes en un radio de cien kilómetros: Toledo, Ávila,
Segovia, El Escorial, Aranjuez, ...*

Estoy de acuerdo contigo en que lo mejor es que asistas a la
universidad. Por cierto conozco a un chico que estudia en las
«Reunidas», una asociación de varias instituciones norteamericanas
que dan cursos para estudiantes estadounidenses en español y con
profesores españoles. Las clases son en la Universidad Complutense de
Madrid,† donde yo voy. Aquí te mando sus señas para que le escribas
con toda confianza. Él puede darte otras impresiones sobre la vida
madrileña.

Y otra cosa. Quedas invitado a pasar una temporadita° en mi casa.   *short while*
Así que decídete y vente unos días antes de que empiece el curso. Será
un placer volverte a ver. Hasta pronto. Recibe un abrazo de tu amiga.

---

*Toledo... "monument cities" close to Madrid where many historical buildings have been pre-
served. Among sights to be seen are: Toledo, paintings by El Greco and Moorish and Jewish
architecture from the Middle Ages; Ávila, home of Santa Teresa de Jesús, the mystic poet and
saint; Segovia, where a famous Roman aqueduct still brings water into the city from the sierra;
El Escorial, site of the famous monastery of the same name; Aranjuez, site of the summer palace of the Bourbon kings.
†La Universidad Complutense de Madrid, o Central, es la universidad más grande de España,
con un total aproximado de ciento treinta mil estudiantes. Madrid tiene dos universidades más:
la Politécnica y la Universidad Autónoma.

Ejercicio escrito final

Which of the preceding activities appeals to you the most? What parts of the Spanish-speaking world are you most interested in visiting? Express your preferences by writing paragraphs to complete the following statements.

1. Si yo estuviera en (Madrid, Buenos Aires, Cuernavaca, ¿ ?), …
2. Si yo pudiera viajar a cualquier lugar del mundo, …

VOCABULARIO

Verbos

compartir to share
confirmar to confirm
reservar to reserve

El alojamiento

el botones/el mozo bellhop
la comodidad comfort
el cheque de viajero traveler's check
el/la gerente manager
la habitación room (*in a hotel*)
  para una persona single

con/sin baño/ducha with(out) bath/shower
el hotel (de lujo) (deluxe) hotel
el/la huésped(a) guest
la pensión boardinghouse
  pensión completa room and full board
  media pensión room and breakfast plus one other meal
la propina tip (*to a bellhop, etc.*)
la recepción front desk
la reservación reservation

Adjetivo

desocupado/a unoccupied, vacant, free

Palabras adicionales

con (_____ días de) anticipación (_____ days) in advance

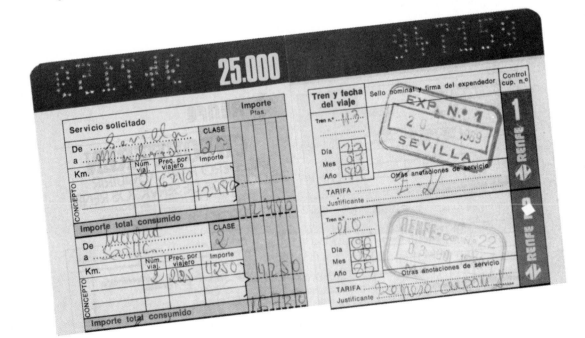

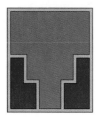

APPENDIX 1

USING ADJECTIVES AS NOUNS

Nominalization means using an adjective as a noun. Adjectives used as nouns are often called pronouns because they can take the place of a noun. In Spanish, adjectives can be nominalized in a number of ways. In most cases, these usages parallel those of English, although the English equivalent may be phrased differently from the Spanish.

Article + adjective (de + noun)

Simply omit the noun from an *article + noun + adjective* phrase.

> el **libro** azul → el **azul** (*the blue one*)
> la **hermana** casada → la **casada** (*the married one*)

Using the article with a *de + noun* phrase is a similar construction. Like the *article + adjective* phrase, it permits you to drop the noun.

> la **casa** de Julio → la **de Julio** (*Julio's*)
> los **coches** del Sr. Martínez → los **del Sr. Martínez** (*Mr. Martínez's*)

In both cases, the construction is used to refer to a noun that has already been mentioned. The English equivalent uses *one* or *ones*, or a possessive without the noun.

> —¿Necesitas el libro grande?
> —No. Necesito **el pequeño**.
> —*Do you need the big book?*
> —*No. I need the small one.*

> —¿Usamos el coche de Ernesto?
> —No. Usemos **el de Ana.**
> —*Shall we use Ernesto's car?*
> —*No. Let's use Ana's.*

Note that in the preceding examples the noun is mentioned in the first part of the exchange (**libro, coche**) but not in the response or rejoinder.

Note also that a demonstrative can also be used to nominalize an adjective: **este rojo** (*this red one*), **esos azules** (*those blue ones*).

Lo + adjective

As seen in **Capítulo 16**, **lo** combines with the masculine singular form of an adjective to describe general qualities or characteristics. The English equivalent is expressed with words like *part* or *thing*.

> lo mejor   *the best thing (part), what's best*

Article + stressed possessive adjective

The stressed possessive adjectives—but not the unstressed possessive—can be used as possessive pronouns: **la maleta suya → la suya.** The article and the possessive form agree in gender and number with the noun to which they refer.

> Éste es mi **banco.** ¿Dónde está **el suyo**?
> *This is my bank. Where is yours?*
> Sus **bebidas** están preparadas; **las nuestras**, no.
> *Their drinks are ready; ours aren't.*

Note that the definite article is frequently omitted after forms of **ser: ¿Esa maleta? Es suya.**

Demonstrative pronouns

The demonstrative adjective can be used alone, without a noun. In general, an accent mark is added to the demonstrative pronoun to distinguish it from the demonstrative adjectives (**este, ese, aquel**).

> Necesito este diccionario y **ése**.
> *I need this dictionary and that one.*
> Estas senoras y **aquéllas** son las hermanas de Sara, ¿no?
> *These women and those (over there) are Sara's sisters, aren't they?*

It is acceptable (though not yet the norm) in modern Spanish, per the **Real Academia Española de la Lengua**, to omit the accent on demonstrative pronouns when context makes the meaning clear and no ambiguity is possible.

APPENDIX 2

ADDITIONAL PERFECT FORMS (INDICATIVE AND SUBJUNCTIVE)

Some indicative verb tenses have corresponding perfect forms in the indicative and subjunctive moods. Here is the present system.

el presente: yo hablo, como, pongo
el presente perfecto: yo he hablado/comido/puesto
el presente perfecto del subjuntivo: yo haya hablado/comido/puesto

Other indicative forms that you have learned also have corresponding perfect indicative and subjunctive forms. Here are the most important ones, along with examples of their use. In each case, the tense or mood is formed with the appropriate form of **haber.**

El pluscuamperfecto del subjuntivo

yo hubiera hablado, comido, vivido, *etc.*
tú hubieras hablado, comido, vivido, *etc.*
Ud., él, ella hubiera hablado, comido, vivido, *etc.*
nosotros hubiéramos hablado, comido, vivido, *etc.*
vosotros hubierais hablado, comido, vivido, *etc.*
Uds., ellos, ellas hubieran hablado, comido, vivido, *etc.*

These forms correspond to **el pluscuamperfecto del indicativo (Capítulo 19).** They are most frequently used in **si** clause sentences, along with the conditional perfect. See examples below.

El futuro perfecto

yo habré hablado, comido, vivido, *etc.*
tú habrás hablado, comido, vivido, *etc.*
Ud., él, ella habrá hablado, comido, vivido, *etc.*
nosotros habremos hablado, comido, vivido, *etc.*
vosotros habréis hablado, comido, vivido, *etc.*
Uds., ellos, ellas habrán hablado, comido, vivido, *etc.*

These forms correspond to **el futuro (Capítulo 24).** They are most frequently used to tell what *will have already happened* at some point in the future. (In contrast, the future tells what *will happen.*)

Mañana **hablaré** con Miguel.
I'll speak to Miguel tomorrow.
Para las tres, ya **habré hablado** con Miguel.
By three, I'll already have spoken to Miguel.

El año que viene **visitaremos** a los nietos.
We'll visit our grandchildren next year.
Para las Navidades, ya **habremos visitado** a los nietos.
We'll already have visited our grandchildren by Christmas.

El condicional perfecto

yo habría hablado, comido, vivido, *etc.*
tú habrías hablado, comido, vivido, *etc.*
Ud., él, ella habría hablado, comido, vivido, *etc.*
nosotros habríamos hablado, comido, vivido, *etc.*
vosotros habríais hablado, comido, vivido, *etc.*
Uds., ellos, ellas habrían hablado, comido, vivido, *etc.*

These forms correspond to **el condicional (Capítulo 25).** These forms are frequently used to tell what *would have happened* at some point in the past. (In contrast, the conditional tells what one *would do.*)

Yo **hablaría** con Miguel.
I would speak with Miguel (if I were you, at some point in the future).
Yo **habría hablado** con Miguel.
I would have spoken with Miguel (if I were you, at some point in the past).

Note the use of the conditional to make suggestions about the present or future, the conditional perfect to make suggestions about the past.

Si clause: Sentences about the past

You have learned **(Capítulo 26)** to use the past subjunctive and conditional to speculate about the present in **si** clause sentences: what *would happen* if a particular event *were* to (or *were not* to) occur.

> Si **tuviera** el tiempo, **aprendería** francés.
> *If I had the time, I would learn French (in the present or at some point in the future).*

The perfect forms of the past subjunctive and the conditional are used to speculate about the past:

what *would have happened* if a particular event *would have* (or *would not have*) occurred.

> En la escuela superior, si **hubiera tenido** el tiempo, **habría aprendido** francés.
> *In high school, if I had had the time, I would have learned French.*

Dependent Clause: *Si* Clause	Independent Clause
si + imperfect subjunctive	conditional
si + past perfect subjunctive	conditional perfect

APPENDIX 3
VERBS

A. Regular Verbs: Simple Tenses

INFINITIVE PRESENT PARTICIPLE PAST PARTICIPLE	INDICATIVE					SUBJUNCTIVE		IMPERATIVE
	PRESENT	IMPERFECT	PRETERITE	FUTURE	CONDITIONAL	PRESENT	IMPERFECT	
hablar	hablo	hablaba	hablé	hablaré	hablaría	hable	hablara	
hablando	hablas	hablabas	hablaste	hablarás	hablarías	hables	hablaras	habla tú,
hablado	habla	hablaba	habló	hablará	hablaría	hable	hablara	no hables
	hablamos	hablábamos	hablamos	hablaremos	hablaríamos	hablemos	habláramos	hable Ud.
	habláis	hablabais	hablasteis	hablaréis	hablaríais	habléis	hablarais	hablemos
	hablan	hablaban	hablaron	hablarán	hablarían	hablen	hablaran	hablen
comer	como	comía	comí	comeré	comería	coma	comiera	
comiendo	comes	comías	comiste	comerás	comerías	comas	comieras	come tú,
comido	come	comía	comió	comerá	comería	coma	comiera	no comas
	comemos	comíamos	comimos	comeremos	comeríamos	comamos	comiéramos	coma Ud.
	coméis	comíais	comisteis	comeréis	comeríais	comáis	comierais	comamos
	comen	comían	comieron	comerán	comerían	coman	comieran	coman
vivir	vivo	vivía	viví	viviré	viviría	viva	viviera	
viviendo	vives	vivías	viviste	vivirás	vivirías	vivas	vivieras	vive tú,
vivido	vive	vivía	vivió	vivirá	viviría	viva	viviera	no vivas
	vivimos	vivíamos	vivimos	viviremos	viviríamos	vivamos	viviéramos	viva Ud.
	vivís	vivíais	vivisteis	viviréis	viviríais	viváis	vivierais	vivamos
	viven	vivían	vivieron	vivirán	vivirían	vivan	vivieran	vivan

B. Regular Verbs: Perfect Tenses

INDICATIVE								SUBJUNCTIVE			
PRESENT PERFECT		PAST PERFECT		PRETERITE PERFECT		FUTURE PERFECT		CONDITIONAL PERFECT		PRESENT PERFECT		PAST PERFECT	
he		había		hube		habré		habría		haya		hubiera	
has	hablado	habías	hablado	hubiste	hablado	habrás	hablado	habrías	hablado	hayas	hablado	hubieras	hablado
ha	comido	había	comido	hubo	comido	habrá	comido	habría	comido	haya	comido	hubieras	comido
hemos	vivido	habíamos	vivido	hubimos	vivido	habremos	vivido	habríamos	vivido	hayamos	vivido	hubiéramos	vivido
habéis		habíais		hubisteis		habréis		habríais		hayáis		hubierais	
han		habían		hubieron		habrán		habrían		hayan		hubieran	

C. Irregular Verbs

INFINITIVE PRESENT PARTICIPLE PAST PARTICIPLE	INDICATIVE					SUBJUNCTIVE		IMPERATIVE
	PRESENT	IMPERFECT	PRETERITE	FUTURE	CONDITIONAL	PRESENT	IMPERFECT	
andar andando andado	ando andas anda andamos andáis andan	andaba andabas andaba andábamos andabais andaban	anduve anduviste anduvo anduvimos anduvisteis anduvieron	andaré andarás andará andaremos andaréis andarán	andaría andarías andaría andaríamos andaríais andarían	ande andes ande andemos andéis anden	anduviera anduvieras anduviera anduviéramos anduvierais anduvieran	anda tú, no andes ande Ud. andemos anden
caer cayendo caído	caigo caes cae caemos caéis caen	caía caías caía caíamos caíais caían	caí caíste cayó caímos caísteis cayeron	caeré caerás caerá caeremos caeréis caerán	caería caerías caería caeríamos caeríais caerían	caiga caigas caiga caigamos caigáis caigan	cayera cayeras cayera cayéramos cayerais cayeran	cae tú, no caigas caiga Ud. caigamos caigan
dar dando dado	doy das da damos dais dan	daba dabas daba dábamos dabais daban	di diste dio dimos disteis dieron	daré darás dará daremos daréis darán	daría darías daría daríamos daríais darían	dé des dé demos deis den	diera dieras diera diéramos dierais dieran	da tú, no des dé Ud. demos den
decir diciendo dicho	digo dices dice decimos decís dicen	decía decías decía decíamos decíais decían	dije dijiste dijo dijimos dijisteis dijeron	diré dirás dirá diremos diréis dirán	diría dirías diría diríamos diríais dirían	diga digas diga digamos digáis digan	dijera dijeras dijera dijéramos dijerais dijeran	di tú, no digas diga Ud. digamos digan
estar estando estado	estoy estás está estamos estáis están	estaba estabas estaba estábamos estabais estaban	estuve estuviste estuvo estuvimos estuvisteis estuvieron	estaré estarás estará estaremos estaréis estarán	estaría estarías estaría estaríamos estaríais estarían	esté estés esté estemos estéis estén	estuviera estuvieras estuviera estuviéramos estuvierais estuviera	está tú, no estés esté Ud. estemos estén
haber habiendo habido	he has ha hemos habéis han	había habías había habíamos habíais habían	hube hubiste hubo hubimos hubisteis hubieron	habré habrás habrá habremos habréis habrán	habría habrías habría habríamos habríais habrían	haya hayas haya hayamos hayáis hayan	hubiera hubieras hubiera hubiéramos hubierais hubieran	
hacer haciendo hecho	hago haces hace hacemos hacéis hacen	hacía hacías hacía hacíamos hacíais hacían	hice hiciste hizo hicimos hicisteis hicieron	haré harás hará haremos haréis harán	haría harías haría haríamos haríais harían	haga hagas haga hagamos hagáis hagan	hiciera hicieras hiciera hiciéramos hicierais hicieran	haz tú, no hagas haga Ud. hagamos hagan

C. Irregular Verbs (continued)

INFINITIVE PRESENT PARTICIPLE PAST PARTICIPLE	INDICATIVE					SUBJUNCTIVE		IMPERATIVE
	PRESENT	IMPERFECT	PRETERITE	FUTURE	CONDITIONAL	PRESENT	IMPERFECT	
ir yendo ido	voy vas va vamos vais van	iba ibas iba íbamos ibais iban	fui fuiste fue fuimos fuisteis fueron	iré irás irá iremos iréis irán	iría irías iría iríamos iríais irían	vaya vayas vaya vayamos vayáis vayan	fuera fueras fuera fuéramos fuerais fueran	ve tú, no vayas vaya Ud. vayamos vayan
oír oyendo oído	oigo oyes oye oímos oís oyen	oía oías oía oíamos oíais oían	oí oíste oyó oímos oísteis oyeron	oiré oirás oirá oiremos oiréis oirán	oiría oirías oiría oiríamos oiríais oirían	oiga oigas oiga oigamos oigáis oigan	oyera oyeras oyera oyéramos oyerais oyeran	oye tú, no oigas oiga Ud. oigamos oigan
poder pudiendo podido	puedo puedes puede podemos podéis pueden	podía podías podía podíamos podíais podían	pude pudiste pudo pudimos pudisteis pudieron	podré podrás podrá podremos podréis podrán	podría podrías podría podríamos podríais podrían	pueda puedas pueda podamos podáis puedan	pudiera pudieras pudiera pudiéramos pudierais pudieran	
poner poniendo puesto	pongo pones pone ponemos ponéis ponen	ponía ponías ponía poníamos poníais ponían	puse pusiste puso pusimos pusisteis pusieron	pondré pondrás pondrá pondremos pondréis pondrán	pondría pondrías pondría pondríamos pondríais pondrían	ponga pongas ponga pongamos pongáis pongan	pusiera pusieras pusiera pusiéramos pusierais pusieran	pon tú, no pongas ponga Ud. pongamos pongan
querer queriendo querido	quiero quieres quiere queremos queréis quieren	quería querías quería queríamos queríais querían	quise quisiste quiso quisimos quisisteis quisieron	querré querrás querrá querremos querréis querrán	querría querrías querría querríamos querríais querrían	quiera quieras quiera queramos queráis quieran	quisiera quisieras quisiera quisiéramos quisierais quisieran	quiere tú, no quieras quiera Ud. queramos quieran
saber sabiendo sabido	sé sabes sabe sabemos sabéis saben	sabía sabías sabía sabíamos sabíais sabían	supe supiste supo supimos supisteis supieron	sabré sabrás sabrá sabremos sabréis sabrán	sabría sabrías sabría sabríamos sabríais sabrían	sepa sepas sepa sepamos sepáis sepan	supiera supieras supiera supiéramos supierais supieran	sabe tú, no sepas sepa Ud. sepamos sepan
salir saliendo salido	salgo sales sale salimos salís salen	salía salías salía salíamos salíais salían	salí saliste salió salimos salisteis salieron	saldré saldrás saldrá saldremos saldréis saldrán	saldría saldrías saldría saldríamos saldríais saldrían	salga salgas salga salgamos salgáis salgan	saliera salieras saliera saliéramos salierais salieran	sal tú, no salgas salga Ud. salgamos salgan

C. Irregular Verbs (continued)

INFINITIVE / PRESENT PARTICIPLE / PAST PARTICIPLE	PRESENT	IMPERFECT	PRETERITE	FUTURE	CONDITIONAL	PRESENT SUBJUNCTIVE	IMPERFECT SUBJUNCTIVE	IMPERATIVE
ser siendo sido	soy	era	fui	seré	sería	sea	fuera	
	eres	eras	fuiste	serás	serías	seas	fueras	sé tú, no seas
	es	era	fue	será	sería	sea	fuera	sea Ud.
	somos	éramos	fuimos	seremos	seríamos	seamos	fuéramos	seamos
	sois	erais	fuisteis	seréis	seríais	seáis	fuerais	
	son	eran	fueron	serán	serían	sean	fueran	sean
tener teniendo tenido	tengo	tenía	tuve	tendré	tendría	tenga	tuviera	
	tienes	tenías	tuviste	tendrás	tendrías	tengas	tuvieras	ten tú, no tengas
	tiene	tenía	tuvo	tendrá	tendría	tenga	tuviera	tenga Ud.
	tenemos	teníamos	tuvimos	tendremos	tendríamos	tengamos	tuviéramos	tengamos
	tenéis	teníais	tuvisteis	tendréis	tendríais	tengáis	tuvierais	
	tienen	tenían	tuvieron	tendrán	tendrían	tengan	tuvieran	tengan
traer trayendo traído	traigo	traía	traje	traeré	traería	traiga	trajera	
	traes	traías	trajiste	traerás	traerías	traigas	trajeras	trae tú, no traigas
	trae	traía	trajo	traerá	traería	traiga	trajera	traiga Ud.
	traemos	traíamos	trajimos	traeremos	traeríamos	traigamos	trajéramos	traigamos
	traéis	traíais	trajisteis	traeréis	traeríais	traigáis	trajerais	
	traen	traían	trajeron	traerán	traerían	traigan	trajeran	traigan
venir viniendo venido	vengo	venía	vine	vendré	vendría	venga	viniera	
	vienes	venías	viniste	vendrás	vendrías	vengas	vinieras	ven tú, no vengas
	viene	venía	vino	vendrá	vendría	venga	viniera	venga Ud.
	venimos	veníamos	vinimos	vendremos	vendríamos	vengamos	viniéramos	vengamos
	venís	veníais	vinisteis	vendréis	vendríais	vengáis	vinierais	
	vienen	venían	vinieron	vendrán	vendrían	vengan	vinieran	vengan
ver viendo visto	veo	veía	vi	veré	vería	vea	viera	
	ves	veías	viste	verás	verías	veas	vieras	ve tú, no veas
	ve	veía	vio	verá	vería	vea	viera	vea Ud.
	vemos	veíamos	vimos	veremos	veríamos	veamos	viéramos	veamos
	veis	veíais	visteis	veréis	veríais	veáis	vierais	
	ven	veían	vieron	verán	verían	vean	vieran	vean

D. Stem-changing and Spelling Change Verbs

INFINITIVE / PRESENT PARTICIPLE / PAST PARTICIPLE	INDICATIVE PRESENT	IMPERFECT	PRETERITE	FUTURE	CONDITIONAL	SUBJUNCTIVE PRESENT	IMPERFECT	IMPERATIVE
construir (y) construyendo construido	construyo	construía	construí	construiré	construiría	construya	construyera	
	construyes	construías	construiste	construirás	construirías	construyas	construyeras	construye tú, no construyas
	construye	construía	construyó	construirá	construiría	construya	construyera	construya Ud.
	construimos	construíamos	construimos	construiremos	construiríamos	construyamos	construyéramos	construyamos
	construís	construíais	construisteis	construiréis	construiríais	construyáis	construyerais	construyan
	construyen	construían	construyeron	construirán	construirían	construyan	construyeran	
dormir (ue, u) durmiendo dormido	duermo	dormía	dormí	dormiré	dormiría	duerma	durmiera	
	duermes	dormías	dormiste	dormirás	dormirías	duermas	durmieras	duerme tú, no duermas
	duerme	dormía	durmió	dormirá	dormiría	duerma	durmiera	duerma Ud.
	dormimos	dormíamos	dormimos	dormiremos	dormiríamos	durmamos	durmiéramos	durmamos
	dormís	dormíais	dormisteis	dormiréis	dormiríais	durmáis	durmierais	duerman
	duermen	dormían	durmieron	dormirán	dormirían	duerman	durmieran	

D. Stem-changing and Spelling Change Verbs (continued)

INFINITIVE PRESENT PARTICIPLE PAST PARTICIPLE	INDICATIVE					SUBJUNCTIVE		IMPERATIVE
	PRESENT	IMPERFECT	PRETERITE	FUTURE	CONDITIONAL	PRESENT	IMPERFECT	
pedir (i, i) pidiendo pedido	pido pides pide pedimos pedís piden	pedía pedías pedía pedíamos pedíais pedían	pedí pediste pidió pedimos pedisteis pidieron	pediré pedirás pedirá pediremos pediréis pedirán	pediría pedirías pediría pediríamos pediríais pedirían	pida pidas pida pidamos pidáis pidan	pidiera pidieras pidiera pidiéramos pidierais pidieran	pide tú, no pidas pida Ud. pidamos pidan
pensar (ie) pensando pensado	pienso piensas piensa pensamos pensáis piensan	pensaba pensabas pensaba pensábamos pensabais pensaban	pensé pensaste pensó pensamos pensasteis pensaron	pensaré pensarás pensará pensaremos pensaréis pensarán	pensaría pensarías pensaría pensaríamos pensaríais pensarían	piense pienses piense pensemos penséis piensen	pensara pensaras pensara pensáramos pensarais pensaran	piensa tú, no pienses piense Ud. pensemos piensen
producir (zc) produciendo producido	produzco produces produce producimos producís producen	producía producías producía producíamos producíais producían	produje produjiste produjo produjimos produjisteis produjeron	produciré producirás producirá produciremos produciréis producirán	produciría producirías produciría produciríamos produciríais producirían	produzca produzcas produzca produzcamos produzcáis produzcan	produjera produjeras produjera produjéramos produjerais produjeran	produce tú, no produzcas produzca Ud. produzcamos produzcan
reír (i, i) riendo reído	río ríes ríe reímos reís ríen	reía reías reía reíamos reíais reían	reí reíste rió reímos reísteis rieron	reiré reirás reirá reiremos reiréis reirán	reiría reirías reiría reiríamos reiríais reirían	ría rías ría riamos riáis rían	riera rieras riera riéramos rierais rieran	ríe tú, no rías ría Ud. riamos rían
seguir (i, i) (ga) siguiendo seguido	sigo sigues sigue seguimos seguís siguen	seguía seguías seguía seguíamos seguíais seguían	seguí seguiste siguió seguimos seguisteis siguieron	seguiré seguirás seguirá seguiremos seguiréis seguirán	seguiría seguirías seguiría seguiríamos seguiríais seguirían	siga sigas siga sigamos sigáis sigan	siguiera siguieras siguiera siguiéramos siguierais siguieran	sigue tú, no sigas siga Ud. sigamos sigan
sentir (ie, i) sintiendo sentido	siento sientes siente sentimos sentís sienten	sentía sentías sentía sentíamos sentíais sentían	sentí sentiste sintió sentimos sentisteis sintieron	sentiré sentirás sentirá sentiremos sentiréis sentirán	sentiría sentirías sentiría sentiríamos sentiríais sentirían	sienta sientas sienta sintamos sintáis sientan	sintiera sintieras sintiera sintiéramos sintierais sintieran	siente tú, no sientas sienta Ud. sintamos sientan
volver (ue) volviendo vuelto	vuelvo vuelves vuelve volvemos volvéis vuelven	volvía volvías volvía volvíamos volvíais volvían	volví volviste volvió volvimos volvisteis volvieron	volveré volverás volverá volveremos volveréis volverán	volvería volverías volvería volveríamos volveríais volverían	vuelva vuelvas vuelva volvamos volváis vuelvan	volviera volvieras volviera volviéramos volvierais volvieran	vuelve tú, no vuelvas vuelva Ud. volvamos vuelvan

VOCABULARIES

The **Spanish–English Vocabulary** contains all the words that appear in the text, with the following exceptions: (1) most close or identical cognates that do not appear in the chapter vocabulary lists; (2) most conjugated verb forms; (3) diminutives in **-ito/a**; (4) absolute superlatives in **-ísimo/a**; (5) most adverbs in **-mente**; (6) most vocabulary that is glossed in the text; and (7) much vocabulary from realia and authentic readings. Active vocabulary is indicated by the number of the chapter in which a word or given meaning is first listed (**P = Pasos preliminares**); vocabulary that is glossed in the text is not considered to be active vocabulary and is not numbered. Only meanings that are used in the text are given. The **English–Spanish Vocabulary** is based on the chapter lists of active vocab-

ulary. It includes all words and expressions necessary to do the translation exercises in the text and in the **Workbook** that accompanies the text.

The gender of nouns is indicated, except for masculine nouns ending in **-o** and feminine nouns ending in **-a**. Stem changes and spelling changes are indicated for verbs: **dormir (ue, u); llegar (gu).**

Words beginning with **ch, ll,** and **ñ** are found under separate headings, following the letters **c, l,** and **n,** respectively. Similarly, **ch, ll,** and **ñ** within words follow **c, l,** and **n,** respectively. For example, **coche** follows **cóctel, calle** follows **calor,** and **añadir** follows **anuncio.**

The following abbreviations are used:

adj.	adjective	*i.o.*	indirect object	*pl.*	plural
adv.	adverb	*inf.*	infinitive	*poss.*	possessive
approx.	approximately	*inv.*	invariable in form	*prep.*	preposition
col.	colloquial	*irreg.*	irregular	*pron.*	pronoun
conj.	conjunction	*L.A.*	Latin America	*refl. pron.*	reflexive pronoun
d.o.	direct object	*m.*	masculine	*s.*	singular
f.	feminine	*Mex.*	Mexico	*Sp.*	Spain
fam.	familiar	*n.*	noun	*sub. pron.*	subject pronoun
form.	formal	*obj. (of prep.)*	object (of a preposition)	*subj.*	subjunctive
gram.	grammatical term	*p.p.*	past participle	*v.*	verb

SPANISH–ENGLISH VOCABULARY

A

a to (P); at (*with time*) (P); **a la(s)** _____ at (hour) (P); **a menos que** unless (22); **a partir de** starting from; **¿a qué hora?** at what time? (10); **a tiempo** on time (10)
abajo below
abalanzarse (c) (sobre) to pounce (on)
abandonar to abandon
abandono abandonment
abarcar (qu) to cover (*a topic*)
abierto/a *p. p.* open(ed) (5)
abogado/a lawyer
abolicionista *m., f.* abolitionist
abrazar (c) to hug
abrazo hug
abrigado/a warm, heavy (*clothing*)
abrigarse (gu) to bundle up, dress warmly

abrigo coat (5)
abril *m.* April (7)
abrir (*p. p.* **abierto/a**) to open (4)
abstenerse (*like* **tener**) need not apply (*classified ad*)
abuelo/a grandfather/grandmother (4) *pl.* grandparents (4)
abundante abundant
abundar to be plentiful
aburrido/a bored (5); boring; **estar** (*irreg.*) **aburrido/a** to be bored; **ser** (*irreg.*) **aburrido/a** to be boring
acabar to finish (17); to put an end to; **acabar de** + *inf.* to have just (*done something*) (8); **acabarse** to run out of (17); **y se acabó** and that's that
académico/a academic
acampada camping

acampar to camp
acariciante *adj.* caressing
acaso: por si acaso just in case (27)
acceso access
accesorio accessory
accidente *m.* accident
acción *f.* action
aceite *m.* oil (18)
aceitoso/a oily, greasy
aceituna olive
acelerado/a fast, accelerated (20)
acelerador *m.* accelerator
acelerar to accelerate, speed up
acelga Swiss chard
acento accent
acentuación *f.* accentuation, stress
aceptación *f.* acceptance
aceptar to accept

acera sidewalk (21)
acerca de *prep.* about, concerning
acercar (qu) to bring nearer; acercarse (a) to approach, draw near (to)
aclaración: aclaración (*f.*) de firma print name (to clarify signature)
acné *f.* acne
acogedor(a) welcoming, friendly
acomodar to accommodate
acompañado/a accompanied
acompañar to accompany, go with (21)
acondicionado: aire (*m.*) acondicionado air conditioning
acondicionador *m.* air conditioner
aconsejar to advise
acontecer (zc) to happen
acontecimiento event (23)
acordarse (ue) (de) to remember (17)
acordeón *m.* accordion
acosar to chase, harass
acostar (ue) to put to bed (14); acostarse to go to bed (14)
acostumbrar(se) (a) to get used, accustomed (to); to be accustomed (to)
actitud *f.* attitude
activar to activate
actividad *f.* activity (11)
activo/a active
acto act, action
actor *m.* actor
actriz *f.* (*pl.* actrices) actress
actuación *f.* performance
actual *n. m.* the present (month, *etc.*); *adj.* current, present day, up-to-date
actualidad: en la actualidad at present, at the present time (20)
actuar to act
acuario aquarium (12)
acuático/a aquatic
acudir (a) to respond; to come (to), be present (at)
acuerdo agreement; de acuerdo agreed; de acuerdo con according to; (no) estar (*irreg.*) de acuerdo to (dis)agree (5); ponerse (*irreg.*) de acuerdo to reach an agreement
acumularse to accumulate
acústico/a acoustic
Ada Ada (a computer programming language)
adaptarse to adapt oneself
adecuado/a adequate
además besides (15)
adicional additional (P)
adiós good-bye (P)
adivinanza riddle
adivinar to guess
adjetivo adjective
adjunto/a attached (*to a letter*)
administración *f.* administration
administrador(a) administrator
admiración *f.* admiration
admirar to admire
admitir to admit; to accept
adolescente *adj.* adolescent
¿adónde? where (to)?

adopción *f.* adoption
adoptar to adopt
adornado/a adorned
adosado/a attached (*house*)
adquirir (ie) to acquire
adquisición *f.* acquisition
aduana customs (27); derechos (*m. pl.*) de aduana customs duty (27); inspector(a) de aduana customs inspector (27)
adulto/a adult
adverbio adverb
advertir (ie, i) to warn, advise
adviento navideño Advent (four weeks preceding Christmas)
aéreo/a *adj.* air
aeróbico/a aerobic
aerolínea airline
aeropuerto airport (10)
afectar to affect
afectivo/a affective, emotional
afecto affection
afeitadora shaver, razor
afeitar to shave (14); afeitarse to shave oneself (14)
afición *f.* enthusiasm
aficionado/a *n.* fan, enthusiast (22); *adj.* fond; aficionado/a a fond of
afirmar to affirm
afirmativo/a affirmative
africano/a African
afuera outside (7)
afueras: en las afueras in/on the outskirts (13)
agencia agency; agencia de empleos employment agency; agencia de viajes travel agency
agenda diary, appointment book
agente *m., f.* agent; agente de viajes travel agent
ágil agile
aglomeración *f.* multitude
agobiante overwhelming
agosto August (7)
agotamiento exhaustion
agotar to deplete; agotarse to exhaust oneself
agradable agreeable, pleasant
agradar to please
agradecer (zc) to thank
agregar (gu) to add
agresión *f.* aggression
agrícola *m., f.* agricultural
agricultura agriculture
agridulce bittersweet
agrio/a sour
agua *f.* (*but* el agua) water (7); agua mineral mineral water (9); cama de agua water bed (13)
aguantar to put up with, endure, tolerate
aguar to spoil (*a party, pleasure*)
agudo/a acute
aguinaldo Christmas gift
agujero hole
ahí there
ahora now (4); ahora bien well now; ahora mismo right now (5); de ahora en adelante from now on
ahorrar to save (money) (24)

ahorro saving, economy; *pl.* savings; cuenta de ahorros savings account (24); libreta de ahorros bankbook (24)
aire *m.* air (20); aire acondicionado air conditioning; aire acondicionador *m.* air conditioner (14); al aire libre open-air
aislado/a isolated
aislamiento isolation
ajedrez *m.* chess; jugar (ue) (gu) al ajedrez to play chess (21)
ajedrezado/a checkered
ajo garlic
ajustar to fit
al (*contraction of* a + el) to the; al + *inf.* upon, while, when + *verb form*; al (mes, año, etcétera) per (month, year, etc.)
alambre *m.* wire
albóndiga meatball
alcalde *m.* mayor
alcalino/a alkaline
alcance *m.* reach; al alcance within reach
alcanzar (c) to get up to; to reach
alcázar *m.* fortress; castle
alcoba bedroom (13)
alcohólico/a alcoholic
alegrarse (de) to be happy (about)
alegre happy (5); bright (*color*)
alegría happiness, joy
alejarse to keep away
alemán *m.* German (*language*) (2)
alemán, alemana German; perro pastor alemán German shepherd
Alemania Germany
alergia allergy
alérgico/a allergic
alfabetizado/a alphabetized
alfabeto alphabet
alfombra rug (13)
alfombrado *n.* carpeting
algo something, anything (8); *adv.* somewhat
algodón *m.* cotton (5)
alguien someone, anyone (8)
algún, alguno/a some; any (8); algún día some day; alguna vez once; ever
alianza alliance
alimentación *f.* food
alimentar (de) to feed, live (on)
alma *f.* (*but* el alma) soul
almacén *m.* department store (6)
almacenar to store
almorzar (ue) (c) to have lunch (7)
almuerzo lunch; noon meal (8)
aló hello (*on telephone*)
alojamiento lodging (2)
alquilar to rent (13)
alquiler *m.* rent (13)
alrededor de *prep.* around
alto/a tall (3); high
altura height
alumno/a student
alza: en alza rising, popular
allá there
allí there (4)
ama *f.* (*but* el ama) de casa housekeeper; housewife

amable kind, nice (3)
amante *m., f.* lover; sweetheart
amar to love
amarillo/a yellow (5)
Amazonas *m. s.* Amazon
ambición *f.* ambition
ambientación *f.* atmosphere, setting
ambiental environmental
ambiente *m.* environment; atmosphere; **medio ambiente** environment (20)
ambos/as both
ambulancia ambulance
amenaza threat
ameno/a pleasant
americano/a American; **fútbol** (*m.*) **americano** football
amigo/a friend (1)
amistad *f.* friendship (4)
amor *m.* love
amortiguador *m.* dimmer
amparo shelter, protection
amplio/a large, ample, spacious
amueblado/a furnished
análisis *m. s.* analysis
analizar (c) to analyze
ananá *m.* pineapple
anaranjado/a *adj.* orange (5)
anciano/a elderly person
ancho/a wide
anchoa anchovy
andar (*irreg.*) to go; to walk; **anda** come on, now; **¿cómo andas?** how are you?
andrajo rag
ángel *m.* angel
anglosajón, anglosajona Anglo-Saxon
angustia anguish
anillo ring
animación *f.* animation
animado/a animated; **dibujos** (*m. pl.*) **animados** cartoons
animal *m.* animal; **animal doméstico** pet
ánimo courage
aniversario anniversary
anoche last night (9)
anónimo/a anonymous; **sociedad** (*f.*) **anónima** corporation
ansiedad *f.* anxiety
antártico/a antarctic
Antártida Antarctica
ante *n. m.* suede; *prep.* before; **ante todo** first of all
anteayer *adv.* (the) day before yesterday (13)
antecedente *m.* antecedent (*of a pronoun*)
anteojos *m. pl.* (eye)glasses
antepasado/a *n.* ancestor
anterior previous, preceding
antes *adv.* sooner; before (19); **antes de** *prep.* before (9); **antes (de) que** *conj.* before (22); **lo antes posible** as soon as possible
antibiótico antibiotic (16)
anticipación: con (_____ días de) anticipación (_____ days) in advance (28)
anticuado/a antiquated
antiguo/a old, ancient

antigüedades *f. pl.* antiques
antipático/a unpleasant (3)
antojito appetizer; hors d'oeuvres
antónimo antonym
antropología anthropology
anualmente annually
anunciar to announce (10)
anuncio ad; announcement
añadir to add
año year (7); **año bisiesto** leap year; **Año Nuevo** New Year; **el año pasado** last year; **el año que viene** next year; **tener** (*irreg.*) _____ **años** to be _____ years old (4)
añorar to miss, long for
apagar (gu) to turn off (17)
aparato apparatus, appliance (14); **aparatos electrodomésticos** electrical home appliances
aparecer (zc) to appear
aparente apparent
apartado postal post office box
apartamento apartment; **casa de apartamentos** apartment house
apartar to take away
aparte (de) aside (from)
apellido surname, family name, last name (3)
apenas scarcely
apendicitis *f. s.* appendicitis
aperitivo aperitif, before-dinner drink
apetecer (zc) to crave, feel like (*eating*)
apetecible appealing
apio celery
aplicar (qu) to apply
aportación *f.* contribution
aporte *m.* contribution
apoyar to support
apoyo support
apreciar to appreciate, enjoy
aprehender to capture
aprender to learn (4)
aprendizaje *m.* learning
aprobar (ue) to pass (*an exam*)
apropiado/a appropriate
aproveche: ¡que aproveche(n)! enjoy your meal!
aproximado/a approximate
aptitud *f.* aptitude
apuntes *m. pl.* notes
aquel, aquella *adj.* that (*over there*) (4); **aquél, aquélla** *pron.* that one (*over there*); **en aquel entonces** back then, in those days (15); **en aquella época** at that time (16)
aquello that, that thing, that fact (4)
aquellos/as *adj.* those (*over there*) (4); **aquéllos/as** *pron.* those (ones) (*over there*)
aqueso/a *pron.* that (*poetic*)
aquí here (2); **aquí mismo** right here; **por aquí** around here
árabe *m.* Arabic (*language*); *adj. m., f.* Arabian
árbitro arbitrator; referee
árbol *m.* tree (15)
arco iris rainbow
archipiélago canario Canary Islands

archivar to file (19)
archivo *n.* file
ardilla squirrel
área *f.* (*but* **el área**) area
arena sand
argentino/a Argentine, Argentinian
armada navy
armado/a armed
armamento weaponry
armario closet
armónico/a harmonious
arquitecto/a architect
arquitectónico/a architectural
arquitectura architecture
arrancar (qu) to start (*a motor*) (18); to uproot
arrebatador(a) captivating
arreglar to fix, repair (13); to arrange
arriba above; on top; **boca arriba** face up
arriendo *n.* leasing
arrojar to throw; toss
arroyo stream
arroz *m.* rice (9)
arrugar (gu) to crumple
arruinar to ruin
arte *m., f.* art; **las artes liberales** liberal arts
artículo article
artista *m., f.* artist
artístico/a artistic
arveja pea (9)
asado grilled meat
asar to roast, grill
ascendencia heritage
ascendente rising
ascenso promotion; rise
asegurar to assure, guarantee
aseo cleanliness
asequible available
asesinar to murder, assassinate
asesinato murder, assassination (23)
asesino/a murderer
asfixiarse to suffocate
así so, thus; that way; **así así** so-so (P)
asiento seat (10)
asimilar to assimilate
asistencia aid, assistance
asistir (a) to attend, go (to) (*a class, play, etc.*) (4)
asociación *f.* association
asociado/a member; associate
asociar to associate; **asociarse (con)** to be associated (with)
aspecto aspect; appearance
áspero/a rough; harsh
aspereza asperity, roughness
aspiradora vacuum cleaner (14); **pasar la aspiradora** to vacuum (14)
aspirante *m., f.* candidate (*for a job*) (25)
aspirar to aspire
aspirina aspirin (17)
astigmatismo astigmatism
astrología astrology
astrológico/a astrological
astrólogo/a astrologist
astronomía astronomy

asumir to assume
asunto matter
atacar (qu) to attack
atasco obstruction; traffic jam
atención f. attention; poner (irreg.) atención to pay attention
atender (ie) to be attentive, heed
atentado n. attack
aterrizaje m. landing
aterrizar (c) to land (27)
atleta m., f. athlete
atlético/a athletic
átomo atom
átono/a unaccented, unstressed (gram.)
atracción f. attraction
atraco robbery
atractivo n. attractiveness
atractivo/a attractive
atraer (like traer) to attract
atrapar to trap
atrás adv. back
atrasado/a late, behind (10); estar (irreg.) atrasado/a to be late (10)
atraso backwardness
atravesar (ie) en to cross over
atrevido/a daring, bold
atribuir (y) to attribute
atún m. tuna (9)
auge: en auge in vogue
aumentar to increase (24)
aumento raise, increase (12)
aun adv. even
aún adv. still, yet
aunque although (12)
ausentarse to be absent
ausente absent
auspicioso/a promising, auspicious
auténtico/a authentic
autobús m. s. bus (11); estacion (f.) de autobuses bus station (11); parada de autobús bus stop
autoconsciente self-conscious
automático/a automatic
auto(móvil) m. car, auto(mobile) (18)
autonomía autonomy, freedom
autónomo/a autonomous
autopista freeway (18)
autor(a) author, writer
autoridad f. authority
autorización f. authorization
autorizado/a authorized
autostop: hacer (irreg.) autostop to hitchhike
auxiliar (m.) de vuelo flight attendant (10)
avance m. advance
avanzado/a advanced; late (hour)
ave f. (but el ave) bird; ave de corral poultry
avenida avenue
aventajarse to advance, get ahead
aventón m. ride; pedir (i, i) un aventón to hitchhike
aventura adventure
avergonzado/a embarrassed (15)
averiguar (gü) to find out
aviación f. aviation

aviador(a) flyer, pilot
avión m. plane (10)
avisar to advise, warn
aviso announcement; sign
ayer yesterday (13)
ayuda help, assistance
ayudante m., f. assistant
ayudar to help (9)
ayuntamiento city council
azafata female flight attendant (10)
azotea (flat) roof
azteca n. m., f. Aztec; adj. Aztec
azúcar m. sugar (7)
azul blue (5)

B

bacalao codfish
bachillerato course of studies equivalent to high school, junior college
bagazo pulp
bahía bay
bailar to dance (2)
baile m. dance
bajar to carry down (10); bajar (de) to get down (from) (10); to get off (of) (10)
bajo prep. under
bajo/a short (in height) (3); low; planta baja ground floor, first floor (13)
bajos m. pl. cuffs (of trousers)
balneario beach resort
balón m. ball
banana banana (9)
banca n. banking
bancario/a adj. banking
banco bank (24)
bandeja tray (8)
bandera flag
banquete m. banquet
bañador m. bathing suit
bañar to bathe (14); bañarse to take a bath (14)
bañera bathtub (13)
baño bathroom (13); bath; traje (m.) de baño bathing suit (5)
bar m. bar
baraja deck of cards
barato/a inexpensive, cheap (3)
barbacoa barbecue
bárbaro/a great, wonderful; barbaric
barbería barber shop
barbero barber
barco boat, ship (11)
barman m. bartender
barra bar (of metal, wood)
barrer (el suelo) to sweep (the floor) (14)
barrio neighborhood (23)
barullo uproar
basado based
basar to base; basarse (en) to be based (on)
base f. base; basis; en base basic
básico/a basic
básquetbol m. basketball (22)

bastante adv. rather, quite (16); adj. enough, sufficient; a lot (of) (16)
bastar to be enough
basto club (suit of cards)
basura garbage; sacar (qu) la basura to take out the garbage (14); triturador (m.) de basuras garbage disposal
batería battery (18); revisar la batería to check the battery
bautismo baptism
bautizo baptism
bebé m. baby
beber to drink (4)
bebida beverage, drink (9)
béisbol m. baseball (22)
Belén Bethlehem
Bélgica Belgium
belleza beauty
bello/a beautiful (20)
beneficiar to benefit
beneficio benefit
besar to kiss
Biblia Bible
biblioteca library (1)
bibliotecario/a librarian (26)
bici(cleta) f. bicycle (12); pasear en bicicleta to ride a bike (22)
bien n. m. good; adv. well (2); está bien it's okay (5); estar (irreg.) bien to be comfortable (in temperature) (7); muy bien very well, fine (P); pasarlo bien to have a good time (15); ¡qué bien! great!
bienes m. pl. possessions, property (12)
bienestar m. well-being (16)
bienvenida n. welcome; bienvenido/a adj. welcome (3)
bilingüe bilingual
bilingüismo bilingualism
billete m. ticket (10); billete de ida one-way ticket (10); billete de ida y vuelta round-trip ticket (10)
biología biology
biólogo/a biologist
bisiesto: año bisiesto leap year
bistec m. steak (9)
bisturí m. scalpel (surgical)
Blancanieves f. s. Snow White
blanco/a white (5); vino blanco white wine (9)
bluejeans m. pl. jeans (5)
blusa blouse (5)
blusón m. smock
boca mouth (16); boca arriba face up
bocadillo snack
bocina horn
boda wedding (4)
bodega wine cellar
bodeguero/a owner of a wine cellar
bolchevique adj. m., f. Bolshevik
boleto ticket (10); boleto de ida one-way ticket (10); boleto de ida y vuelta round-trip ticket (10); boleto de regreso return ticket, round-trip ticket
bolí m. (ballpoint) pen (col.)

boliche *m.* bowling
bolígrafo (ballpoint) pen (10)
bolillo bread roll (*Mex.*)
bolívar *m. monetary unit of Venezuela*
boliviano/a Bolivian
bolsa purse (5); bag
bomba bomb (23)
bombero/a firefighter
bonito/a pretty (3)
bordado/a embroidered
bordillo curb
bordo: a bordo on board
borrar to erase
borrasca storm, squall
bosque *m.* forest
bota boot (5)
botella bottle (8)
botones *m. s.* bellhop (28)
brasa ember, coal
Brasil *m.* Brazil
brasileño/a Brazilian
brazo arm (17)
brécol *m.* broccoli
breve short
brillante bright, brilliant
brillar to shine
brillo shine
brío spirit
brisa breeze
broma joke; **hacer** (*irreg.*) **bromas** to play tricks
bronce *m.* bronze
bronceado suntan
bronceador *m.* suntan lotion
bronceador: crema bronceadora suntan lotion
brusco/a abrupt, brusque
buen, bueno/a *adj.* good (2); **buenas noches** good evening/night (P); **buenas tardes** good afternoon/evening (P); **buenos días** good morning (P); **hace buen tiempo** it's good weather (7); **bueno** *adv.* well, okay; **lo bueno** the good news (16)
buganvilla bougainvillea (*a tropical vine with brilliant purple or red flowers*)
bujía spark plug
bulevar *m.* boulevard
bullicio hustle and bustle
buque (*m.*) **de vapor** steamboat
burla joke
burro donkey
busca: en busca de in search of (25)
buscar (qu) to look for (2)
butaca theater seat (21)

C

caballero gentleman
caballo horse (11); **montar a caballo** to ride horseback (11)
cabaña cabin
cabaret *m.* night club
cabello hair
cabeza head (16)

cabina cabin (*of ship*); booth
cabo: al fin y al cabo in the end; **llevar a cabo** to carry out
cacao cocoa
cacharro pot
cada *inv.* each, every (12)
cadena chain
caer (*irreg.*) to fall (17); **caer desvanecido/a** to fall in a faint; **caerle bien/mal a alguien** to make a good/bad impression on someone (25); **caerse** to fall down (17)
café *m.* coffee (6); café, coffee shop (6)
cafetera coffeepot (14)
cafetería cafeteria, café
caída *n.* fall
caja box
cajero/a cashier (24)
calado/a drenched
calcetines *m. pl.* socks (5)
calculadora calculator (1)
cálculo calculus
calefacción *f.* heating, heat
calendario calendar
calentar (ie) to heat
calentura fever, temperature
calidad *f.* quality
cálido/a warm, hot (*climate*)
caliente hot
calina haze
calor *m.* heat; **hace calor** it's hot (weather) (7); **tener** (*irreg.*) **calor** to be/feel warm/hot (7)
caloría calorie
calzoncillos *m. pl.* underpants, shorts
calzones *m. pl.* shorts
callado/a quiet
calle *f.* street (5)
cama bed (13); **cama de agua** water bed (13); **guardar cama** to stay in bed (16); **hacer** (*irreg.*) **la cama** to make the bed (14)
cámara camera
camarero/a waiter/waitress (8); flight attendant
camarones *m. pl.* shrimp (9)
cambiar (de) to change (12); **cambiar de idea** to change one's mind; **cambiar de lugar** to move (*something*)
cambio change; rate of exchange; **cambio de ritmo** change of pace; **cambio de rumbo** change of direction **en cambio** on the other hand (14); **transmisión** (*f.*) **de cambios** manual shift
caminante *m., f.* hitchhiker
caminar to walk (16)
camino road (18); way
camión *m.* truck
camioneta station wagon (3)
camisa shirt (5)
camisero/a clothed, covered
camiseta T-shirt (5)
campaña campaign; countryside; **tienda de campaña** tent
campeón, campeona champion
campeonato championship
campesino/a *n.* farm worker, peasant (20); *adj.* country

camping: hacer (*irreg.*) **camping** to go camping (11)
campo country(side) (12); area, field; (playing) field (22)
Canadá *m.* Canada
canal *m.* channel (*on TV*) (23)
canción *f.* song
cancha court (*sports*) (22)
candente red-hot
canela cinnamon
canicas *f. pl.* (game of) marbles
cansado/a tired (5)
cantante *m., f.* singer
cantar to sing (2)
cántaros: llueve a cántaros (*coll.*) it's raining cats and dogs
cantautor(a) singer
cantidad *f.* quantity, amount
canto song; **al canto del gallo** (*coll.*) at cock-crow, dawn
caña cane
cañón *m.* cannon; canyon
capa layer, cap
capacidad *f.* capacity
capaz (*pl.* **capaces**) capable
Caperucita Roja Little Red Riding Hood
capital *f.* capital (city)
capitán *m.* captain
capítulo chapter
capó hood (*of car*)
captura *n.* capture
capturar to capture
cara face
carácter *m.* (*pl.* **caracteres**) character; aspect
característica characteristic
caracterizarse (c) (por) to be characterized (by)
caramelo caramel; candy
cárcel *f.* jail
carecer (zc) to lack
cargar (gu) to charge (*to an account*) (24)
cargo post, position; charge; **estar** (*irreg.*) **a cargo de** to be in charge of
caribe *adj.* Caribbean
Caribe *n., m. + adj.* Caribbean
caribeño/a Caribbean
cariño affection
cariñoso/a affectionate (4)
carmín *m.* crimson (*dye*)
carne *f.* meat (9)
carnet *m.* identity card
caro/a expensive (6)
carpeta folder
carpintero/a carpenter
carrera course of study; career (26); race
carreta cart
carretera highway (12)
carro car
carta letter (4); menu; (playing) card; **jugar (ue) (gu) a las cartas** to play cards (21)
cartel *m.* poster (12)
cartera wallet (5)
cartón *m.* cardboard
casa house, home (3); **casa de apartamentos** apartment house; **en casa** at home (2);

regresar a casa to return home (2)
casada: nombre (*m.*) de casada married name
casado/a married (3)
casamiento wedding
casarse (con) to marry (15)
cáscara peel
casi almost (4)
caso case; en caso de que in case (22)
castaño/a (chestnut) brown
castellano Castilian; Spanish
castigar (gu) to punish
castigo punishment
castillo castle
casualidad: por casualidad by chance
catalán *m.* language of Catalonia
Cataluña Catalonia (*northeastern province of Spain*)
catarro head cold
catástrofe *f.* catastrophe
catastrófico/a catastrophic
catedral *f.* cathedral
categoría category
catolicismo Catholicism
católico/a Catholic
catorce fourteen (P)
caucho rubber
causa cause; a causa de because of, on account of
causar to cause
cautivante *adj.* captivating, entrancing
cautivo/a *adj.* captive
caza: avión (*m.*) de caza fighter plane
cazador(a) hunter
cebiche *m.* ceviche *raw fish marinated in lime juice*
cebolla onion
cebra zebra
ceguera blindness
celebración *f.* celebration
celebrar to celebrate (15)
célebre famous
cementerio cemetery
cena supper, dinner (8)
cenar to have/eat supper; to dine out
censura censorship
centenario *n.* centennial
central calefacción (*f.*) central central heating
céntrico/a central, focal
centro center; downtown (6); centro comercial shopping mall (6)
ceñido/a tight-fitting
cerámica ceramic, tile
cerca adv. near, close; cerca de *prep.* close to (9)
cercano/a close-by
cerdo pork; chuleta de cerdo pork chop (9)
cereal *m.* cereal
ceremonia ceremony
cero zero (P)
cerrado/a closed (5)
cerrar (ie) to close (7)
cervato: de cervato fawn-colored
cerveza beer (2)

césped *m.* lawn, grass
cetro scepter
cía. *abbreviation of* compañía
ciclismo cycling
ciclista *m.*, *f.* cyclist
ciego/a blind; cita a ciegas blind date
cielo sky; heaven
cien(to) one hundred (3); cientos hundreds; por ciento percent
ciencia science (2); ciencias naturales *pl.* natural sciences (2); ciencias policiales *pl.* police science; ciencias políticas *pl.* political science; ciencias sociales *pl.* social science (2)
científico/a scientific
cierto/a certain; true; es cierto it's true (18)
ciervo male deer, stag
cigarrillo cigarette
cimiento creator
cinco five (P)
cincuenta fifty (3)
cine *m.* cinema; movie theater (6)
cinta tape; strap; conveyor belt
cinturón *m.* belt (5); cinturón de seguridad seat belt, safety belt
circulación *f.* traffic (18)
circular to drive; to circulate
círculo circle
circunstancia circumstance; incident
cita date (4); appointment (4)
citado/a booked up, committed (5)
citar to cite
ciudad *f.* city (3)
ciudadanía citizenship
ciudadano/a citizen (23)
cívico/a civic (23)
civilización *f.* civilization
clamor *m.* wailing
clarinete *m.* clarinet
claro/a *adj.* clear; está claro it's clear/obvious (5); claro *adv.* of course
clase *f.* class (1); kind; clase alta upper class; clase baja lower class; clase media middle class; clase turística tourist class (10); primera clase first class (10)
clásico/a classical; classic
cláusula clause; cláusula subordinada dependent clause (*gram.*)
cliente *m.*, *f.* client (1)
clima *m.* climate (7)
clínica clinic
club *m.* club
cobrar to cash (*a check*) (24); to charge (*someone for something*) (24)
cobre *m.* copper
cocción *f.* cooking
cocer (ue) (z) to cook
cocina kitchen (13)
cocinar to cook (8)
cocinero/a cook, chef (8)
cocodrilo crocodile
coctel *m.* cocktail; coctel de camarones shrimp cocktail
coche *m.* car (3); coche descapotable convertible (12)

código list
cognado cognate
coherente coherent
cojín *m.* cushion
cola line; hacer (*irreg.*) cola to stand in line (10)
colaboración *f.* cooperation
colaborador(a) collaborator
colaborar to collaborate
colección *f.* collection
colectivo/a communal, collective
colega *m.*, *f.* colleague
colegiado/a high school student
colegiatura scholastic fees
colegio elementary or secondary school
colesterol *m.* cholesterol
colgar (ue) (gu) to hang
colilla cigarette butt
colisión *f.* collision, crash
colocar (qu) to place, position; colocarse to get a job (25)
colombiano/a Colombian
Colón: Cristóbal Colón Christopher Columbus
colonización *f.* colonization
colonizador(a) settler
colonizar (c) to colonize, settle
colono *m.* settler
coloquial colloquial
color *m.* color (5)
colorado: ponerse (*irreg.*) colorado/a to blush
columna column
collar *m.* necklace
comandante *m.* commander
combatir to fight, combat
combinación *f.* combination
combinar to combine
combustible *m.* fuel
comedia play (*theater*) (21); comedy (21)
comedor *m.* dining room (13)
comentar to comment (on); to discuss
comentario commentary, comment
comenzar (ie) (c) to begin
comer to eat (4); comerse to eat up
comercial *adj.* business; administración (*f.*) comercial business administration; centro comercial shopping mall (6)
comercialización *f.* commercialization
comerciante *m.*, *f.* merchant, shopkeeper (26)
comerciar to do business
comercio business (2)
cometer to commit
comí I ate (9)
cómico/a *n.* comedian/comedienne; *adj.* funny, amusing
comida food (7); midday meal; meal (8); comida rápida fast food
comió he/she/it ate (9)
comisión *f.* commission, committee
comiste you ate (9)
como as (a); like; since; como si + *past subj.* as if . . . (26); como si nada as if nothing were wrong; habla como si lo supiera todo he/she talks as if he/she knew everything (26); tan pronto como as soon as (24)

¿**cómo?** how?; what? I didn't catch that (6);
¿**cómo es** _____? what is _____ like?;
¿**cómo está(s)?** how are you? (P); ¡**cómo no!**
of course! (2); ¿**cómo que...** ? what do you
mean . . . ?; ¿**cómo se dice** _____ ? how
do you say _____?; ¿**cómo se llama Ud.?,**
¿**cómo te llamas?** what is your name? (P)
cómoda bureau, chest of drawers (13)
comodidad _f._ comfort (28); _pl._ conveniences
cómodo/a comfortable (6)
compa _m., f. coll._ friend; roommate
compact disc _m._ compact disc (player) (12)
compañero/a companion, friend;
  compañero/a de clase classmate;
  compañero/a de cuarto roommate (9)
compañía company
comparación _f._ comparison
comparar to compare
comparativo/a _adj._ comparative
compartir to share (28)
compasión _f._ compassion
compensación _f._ compensation
competencia competition
competente competent
competir (i, i) to compete
complejo/a complex
complemento object (_gram._)
completar to complete
completo/a complete; **pensión** (_f._) **completa**
  full room and board (28)
complicado/a complicated
componerse (_like_ **poner**) (**de**) to be composed
  (of)
comportamiento behavior
composición _f._ composition
compra _n._ purchase
comprador(a) shopper, customer
comprar to buy (2)
compras: ir (_irreg._) **de compras** to go shopping (6); to shop
comprender to understand (4)
comprensión _f._ comprehension
comprensivo/a _adj._ understanding
comprobar (ue) to try
compromiso _n._ appointment; something to
  do; compromise
compuesto/a _pp._ (**por**) composed (of)
computación _f._ computer science (2)
computador _m._ computer (_L.A._)
computadora computer (_L.A._) (12)
computerizado/a computerized
común common; **sentido común** common
  sense; **tener** (_irreg._) **en común** to have in
  common
comunicación _f._ communication (1); _pl._
  (study of) communications
comunicarse (qu) (con) to communicate
  (with) (23)
comunicativo/a communicative
comunidad _f._ community
comunista _m., f._ communist
comunitario: centro comunitario community
  center
con with (2); **con cheque** by check (24); **con
  frecuencia** frequently (2); **con permiso**

excuse me (P); **con tal (de) que** provided
  that (22)
conceder to concede
concentración _f._ concentration
concentrar to concentrate
concepto concept
concesión _f._ concession
concierto concert
conclusión _f._ conclusion
concreto/a specific
concurso contest
condición _f._ condition; **en buenas condiciones** in good condition
condicionador: aire (_m._) **condicionador** air
  conditioner
condicional _adj._ conditional (_gram._)
conducir (_irreg._) to drive (_a vehicle_); **conducir
  a la defensiva** to drive defensively
conducta conduct, behavior
conductor(a) driver (18)
conexión _f._ connection
conferencia lecture
conferenciante _m., f._ lecturer, speaker
confesión _f._ confession
confianza confidence; **tener** (_irreg._) **confianza**
  to trust
confirmación _f._ confirmation
confirmar to confirm (28)
conflicto _n._ conflict
conformar to form; **conformarse con** to
  resign oneself to
confort _m._ comfort
confrontación _f._ confrontation
confundido/a confused
congelado/a frozen
congelador _m._ freezer (14)
congestionado/a congested, stuffed-up (16)
conjugar (gu) to conjugate
conjunción _f._ conjunction (_gram._)
conjunto group, ensemble
conmemorar to commemorate
conmemorativo/a commemorative
conmigo with me (9)
conmiserarse to commiserate
conmutador: teléfono conmutador main telephone line
conocer (zc) to know, be acquainted with (8)
conotación _f._ connotation
conquista conquest
conquistador(a) conqueror
consecución _f._ acquisition
consecuencia consequence
conseguir (i, i) (g) to get, obtain (12)
consejero/a counselor, advisor (1)
consejo advice (6); counsel
conservación _f._ conservation
conservador(a) conservative
conservar to conserve, save (20)
consideración _f._ consideration
considerar to consider
consistir (en) to consist (of)
consorcio consortium, group
conspirar to conspire, plot
constante loyal; persevering
constantemente constantly

constipado/a stuffed-up (_with a head cold_)
Constitución _f._ Constitution
constituir (y) to constitute, make up
construcción _f._ construction
construir (y) to build (20)
consulado consulate
consulta consultation
consultar to consult
consultorio (medical) office (16)
consumidor(a) consumer
consumir to consume
contabilidad _f._ accounting
contacto contact; **lente** (_m._) **de contacto** contact lense
contado: al contado (in) cash (24)
contador(a) accountant
contaminación _f._ pollution; **hay (mucha/poca)
  contaminación** there's (a lot of/little) pollution, smog (7)
contaminante _m._ pollutant
contaminar to pollute (20)
contar (ue) to tell, relate (15); to count
contemporáneo/a contemporary, modern
contenedor _m._ container
contener (_like_ **tener**) to contain, hold (18)
contenido _n._ content
contento/a happy (5)
contestador (_m._) **automático** answering
  machine
contestar to answer (7)
contexto context
contigo with you (_fam._) (9)
continente _m._ continent
continuación: a continuación immediately
  after; below
continuar to continue
continuo/a continual
contra against; **contra viento y marea** against
  all odds
contraatacar (qu) to strike back
contrabandista _m._ smuggler
contraer (_like_ **traer**) **matrimonio** to get married
contrario contrary; **al contrario** to the contrary; **lo contrario** the opposite
contratar to hire
contrato contract
contribución _f._ contribution
contribuir (y) to contribute
controlar to control
convencer (z) to convince
convención _f._ convention
convencional conventional
conversación _f._ conversation
conversar to converse, talk
convertirse (ie, i) (en) to become
convicción _f._ conviction, belief
convivencia cohabitation
cónyuge _m., f._ spouse
copa glass, goblet (8); drink (_alcoholic_)
copia _n._ copy
coquí _m._ small frog native to Puerto Rico
corazón _m._ heart (16); **ataque** (_m._) **al corazón**
  heart attack
corbata necktie (5)

cordialmente cordially, warmly
cordillera mountain range
corral: ave (*f.* but **el ave**) **de corral** poultry
correcto/a right, correct
corregir (i, i) (j) to correct
correo mail
correr *n. m.* running, jogging; *v.* to run (11); **correr (el) peligro (de)** to be in danger (of)
correspondencia correspondence, mail; **mantener** (*like* **tener**) **correspondencia** to correspond (*by letter*)
corresponder (a) to correspond (to), match
corrida (de toros) bullfight
corriente common, everyday; recent; **cuenta corriente** checking account (24)
corte *m.* cut, fit (*clothing*)
cortés courteous
cortesía courtesy (P)
corto/a short (*in length*) (3); **pantalones cortos** shorts
cosa thing (1)
cosilla little (insignificant) thing
cosmética *sing.* cosmetics
cosmopolita *m., f.* cosmopolitan
costa coast
costar (ue) to cost
costarricense *m., f.* Costa Rican
costumbre *f.* custom; **como de costumbre** as usual; **por costumbre** habitually
cotidiano/a *adj.* daily, everyday (21)
cotillón *m.* cotillion, formal dance
creación *f.* creation
creador(a) creator
crear to create
creatividad *f.* creativity
crecer (zc) to grow
crecimiento growth
crédito credit; **tarjeta de crédito** credit card (24)
creencia belief
creer (y) (en) to think (1); to believe (in) (4); **creo que sí (no)** I (don't) think so (1)
crema cream; cream-colored
criado/a servant/maid (13)
criatura creature; baby
crimen *m.* crime
criminal *m., f.* criminal
criminología criminology
crisis *f. s.* crisis
crisol *m.* melting pot
cristal *m.* crystal
cristiano/a Christian
criticar (qu) to criticize
crítico/a critical; decisive
crónica history, story
croqueta croquette, fritter
cruce (*m.*) **para peatones** crosswalk
crucero cruise (11)
cruciletras *m. s.* crossword puzzle
cruzar (c) to cross (27)
cuaderno notebook (1)
cuadro square; picture; **de cuadros** checkered, plaid (5); **cuadros escoceses** plaid
cual: cada cual each one; **la razón por la cual** the reason that; **lo cual** which (*thing*)

¿cuál? what?, which? (P); **¿cuáles?** which (ones)?
cualquier *adj.* any
cualquiera *indefinite pron.* anyone
cuando when; **cuando pueda** whenever you have a second (can) (8); **de vez en cuando** from time to time (16)
¿cuándo? when? (P)
cuanto: en cuanto *conj.* as soon as (24); **en cuanto a** *prep.* with regard to, regarding
¿cuánto/a? how much? (P); **¿cuántos/as?** how many? (P); **¿cuánto pagaste por _____?** how much did you pay for _____? (6)
cuarenta forty (3)
cuartel *m.* barracks
cuartilla page (of manuscript)
cuarto *n.* room (1); **compañero/a de cuarto** roommate (9); fourth; quarter; **(las dos) menos cuarto** a quarter to (two) (P); **(las dos) y cuarto** (two)-fifteen, a quarter after (two) (P); **en cuarto menguante** on the wane
cuarto/a *adj.* fourth (18)
cuatro four (P)
cuatrocientos/as four hundred (6)
cubano/a Cuban
cubanoamericano/a Cuban American
cubierto/a *adj.* overcast; *p. p.* covered
cubo pail, bucket
cubrir (*p. p.* **cubierto/a**) to cover (19)
cuchara spoon (8)
cucharada tablespoon
cucharita teaspoon (8)
cuchillo knife
cuenta bill (8); account (24); **cuenta corriente** checking account (24); **cuenta de ahorros** savings account (24); **darse** (*irreg.*) **cuenta de** to realize; **tomar/tener** (*irreg.*) **en cuenta** to keep/have in mind (23)
cuentakilómetros *m.s.* odometer (*in kilometers*)
cuento story
cuero leather
cuerpo body (16); **cuerpo diplomático** diplomatic corps
cuestión *f.* question; matter (24)
cuestionar to question
cueva cave
cuidado care; **¡cuidado!** be careful!; **con cuidado** carefully; **tener** (*irreg.*) **cuidado** to be careful (21)
cuidadoso/a careful
cuidar to take care of; **cuidarse** to take care of oneself (16)
culpa blame; **tener** (*irreg.*) **la culpa** to be guilty
cultivo cultivation
culto cult; worship
culto/a cultured; educated
cultura culture
cumpleaños *m. s.* birthday (7)
cumplir to accomplish; **cumplir con** to fulfill (*an obligation*)
cuna cradle
cuota fee

cupón *m.* ticket
cura *m.* priest
curar to cure, heal
curiosidad *f.* curiosity
curioso/a curious
currículum *m.* résumé (25)
cursivas: letras cursivas italics
curso course (2)
curva curve
cuyo/a whose

CH

champán *m.* champagne
champiñón *m.* mushroom
chandal *m.* sweatshirt
chaperón, chaperona chaperone
chaqueta jacket (5)
charro cowboy (*Mex.*)
¡chau! ciao!, good-bye!
chavo: estar (*irreg.*) **sin chavo** to be broke
cheque *m.* check (12); **cheque de viajero** traveler's check (28); **con cheque** by check (24); **talonario de cheques** checkbook (24)
chibcha *m., f.* Chibcha Indian (*Colombia*)
chicano/a *n., adj.* Mexican American
chico/a boy/girl; *pl.* children; boys/girls; *adj.* small
chileno/a Chilean
chino Chinese (*language*) (2)
chisme *m.* gossip
chiste *m.* joke (15)
chocar (qu) (con) to run into, collide (with), hit (18)
chocolate *m.* chocolate
choque *m.* collision, crash (23)
chorizo sausage
chubasco shower (*weather*)
chuleta (de cerdo) (pork) chop (9)
chulo/a pretty

D

dama lady, woman; **dama de honor** bridesmaid
danza dance
danzar (c) to dance
danzarín *m.* dancer
daño: hacerse (*irreg.*) **daño** to hurt oneself (17)
dar (*irreg.*) to give (10); **dar a conocer** to make known; **dar una fiesta** to give a party (15); **dar un paseo** to take a walk (21); **dar un aventón** to give a lift, ride; **darse con** to run, bump into; **darse la mano** to shake hands; **(eso) me da igual** (that's) it's all the same to me (17)
dato fact
de *prep.* of; from (P); **¿de dónde es Ud.?** where are you from?; **de joven** as a youth (16); **de la mañana/tarde/noche** in the morning/afternoon/evening (P); **de nada** you're welcome (P); **de niño/a** as a child (16); **¿de quién?** whose?; **de repente** sud-

denly (16); **de verdad** really; **de vez en cuando** from time to time (16)

debajo de *prep.* under(neath), below (9)

deber *n. m.* duty, responsibility, obligation; *v.* to owe; **deber** + *inf.* should, must, ought to (*do something*) (4)

debido/a a due to, because of

débil weak

década decade

decenio decade; 10-year period

decibelio decibel

decidir to decide

décimo/a *adj.* tenth (18)

decir (*irreg.*) to say, tell (10); **dime** (*fam. command*) tell me (17); **es decir** that is to say; **(eso) quiere decir** that means

decisión *f.* decision

decisivo/a decisive

declaración *f.* declaration

declarar to declare (27); **declararse en huelga** to strike

decoración *f.* (interior) decoration, decor

decorar to decorate

decorativo/a decorative

dedo finger; **hacer** (*irreg.*) **dedo** to hitchhike

deducir (**zc**) to deduce, infer

defecto defect

defender (**ie**) to defend; **defenderse** to defend oneself

defensiva: conducir (**zc**) **a la defensiva** to drive defensively

deficitario/a deficient, lacking

definición *f.* definition

definido/a definitive; **artículo definitivo** definite article (*gram.*)

dejar to leave (behind) (12); to quit (25); to let, allow; **dejar de** + *inf.* to stop (*doing something*) (16)

del (*contraction of* **de** + **el**) of the; from the

delante (**de**) in front (of) (9)

delantero/a *adj.* front

delegar (**gu**) to delegate

delgado/a thin (3)

delicado/a delicate

delicioso/a delicious

delito crime (20)

demanda demand

demás other, rest of; **los/las demás** the others (23)

demasiado *adv.* too, too much (14)

demasiado/a *adj.* too much

democracia democracy

demócrata *n. m., f.* democrat

democrático/a democratic

demonio devil; **¿qué demonios?** what the devil?

demora delay (10)

demostración *f.* demonstration

demostrar (**ue**) to demonstrate

demostrativo/a demonstrative

denso/a dense, thick (20)

dentista *m., f.* dentist

dentro *adv.* within; **dentro de** *prep.* inside of, within

departamento department

depender (**de**) to depend (on); **depende** it depends

dependiente/a clerk (1)

deportar to deport

deporte *m.* sport (16)

deportista *adj.* sports-minded, athletic (21)

deportivo/a *adj.* sports

depositar to deposit (24)

depresión *f.* depression

deprimente depressing

derecha: a la derecha (**de**) to the right (of) (9)

derecho *n.* right (23); **derechos** (*pl.*) **de aduana** customs duty (27); *adv.* (straight) ahead (11); **seguir** (**i, i**) (**g**) **todo derecho** to go straight ahead

derivarse (**de**) to derive from; to tend toward

derramar to spill

desafío challenge

desagradable disagreeable

desagüe *m.* drain, sewerage

desaparecer (**zc**) to disappear

desaparición *f.* disappearance

desarme *m.* disarmament

desarrollar to develop (20)

desastre *m.* disaster (23)

desastroso/a disastrous, miserable

desayunar to eat breakfast (8)

desayuno breakfast (8)

descalzo/a barefoot

descansar to rest (5)

descanso *n.* rest; sleep

descapotable: coche (*m.*) **descapotable** convertible (12)

descartable disposable

descartar to discard

descendencia descent

descendente descending, downward

descenso descent

desconectar to disconnect, unplug

desconfiado/a distrustful

desconocido/a unknown

descontento/a unhappy, discontented

descortés discourteous, impolite

descripción *f.* description

descubierto/a *p. p.* discovered; uncovered

descubrimiento discovery

descubrir (*p. p.* **descubierto/a**) to discover (19)

descuidado/a careless

descuidar to neglect

desde *prep.* from; **desde que** *conj.* since; **desde luego** of course

desdentado/a toothless

desear to want (2)

desempleo unemployment

deseo desire, wish

desesperado/a desperate

desesperante desperate

desfile *m.* parade

desgracia: ¡qué desgracia! what a shame! (27)

desgraciadamente unfortunately

deshacerse (*like* **hacer**) **de** to get rid of

desierto desert (11)

desierto/a deserted

designar to designate, specify

desigualdad *f.* inequality (23)

desinflado: llanta desinflada flat tire (18)

desinteresado/a altruistic, selfless

deslizarse (**c**) to glide

deslumbrante dazzling

desobedecer (**zc**) to disobey

desocupado/a vacant, free (28)

desolación *f.* desolation; distress

desordenado/a disorganized; disorderly

desorientar to disorient, confuse

despacio *adv.* slowly

despechado/a peeved; spiteful

despedida leave-taking, good-bye

despedir (**i, i**) to fire (12); **despedirse** (**de**) to say good-bye (to), take leave (of) (14)

despegar (**gu**) to take off (*airplane*) (10)

despejado/a clear (weather)

despensa pantry

desperdicios *m. pl.* waste, garbage

desperfecto defect

despertador *m.* alarm clock (14)

despertar (**ie**) to wake (*someone*) (14); **despertarse** to wake up (14)

despistado/a scatter-brained

desplazar (**c**) to shift, move

despreciable contemptible

despreciar to scorn

después *adv.* later, afterward (14); **después de** *prep.* after (9); **después (de) que** *conj.* after (24)

destacarse (**qu**) to stand out

destinar to allot, earmark (*money*)

destino destination

destronar to dethrone, overthrow

destruir (**y**) to destroy (20)

desvanecido: caer desvanecido/a to fall in a faint

desventaja disadvantage (18)

detalle *m.* detail (8)

detective *m., f.* detective, private investigator

detener (*like* **tener**) to detain; to stop; **detenerse** to stop

deteriorar to spoil, damage; **deteriorarse** to deteriorate

deterioro deterioration, destruction

determinante *m.* determinant, factor

determinar to determine

detestar to detest

detrás de *prep.* behind (9)

deuda debt

devengado/a earned, taken in

devoción *f.* devotion

devolver (**ue**) (*p. p.* **devuelto/a**) to return (*something*) (24)

día *m.* day (1); **al día** per day; **buenos días** good morning (P); **con (_____ días de) anticipación** (_____ days) in advance (28) **día festivo** holidays (15); **hoy en día** nowadays; **todos los días** every day (2)

dibujo illustration, sketch; **dibujo animado** cartoon

diccionario dictionary (1)

diciembre *m.* December (7)
dictador(a) dictator (23)
dictar to dictate
dicho *n.* saying
dicho/a *p. p.* said, aforementioned
diecinueve nineteen (P)
dieciocho eighteen (P)
dieciséis sixteen (P)
diecisiete seventeen (P)
diente *m.* tooth
diestramente skillfully
dieta: estar (*irreg.*) **a dieta** to be on a diet (9)
dietético/a *adj.* diet, dietetic
diez ten (P)
diferencia difference
difícil difficult, hard (5)
dificultad *f.* difficulty
difunto/a dead person
digestión *f.* digestion
dígito digit, number
dignidad *f.* dignity
dignificar (qu) to dignify
digno/a worthy
dime (*fam. command*) tell me (17)
Dinamarca Denmark
dinámico/a dynamic
dineral *m.* fortune (*money*)
dinero money (1); **dinero en efectivo** cash (8)
Dios *m. s.* God; **por Dios** for heaven's sake
diplomático: cuerpo diplomático diplomatic corps
diptongo diphthong
diputado deputy
dirección *f.* address (13); direction; **Dirección de Personal** personnel/employment office (25); **libreta de direcciones** address book
directo/a direct
director(a) director (12); **director(a) de personal** personnel manager (25)
dirigir (j) to direct; **dirigirse** to make one's way
disc: compact disc *m.* compact disc (player) (12)
disciplina discipline
disco (phonograph) record (3); computer disc (19); **disco duro** hard disc; **frenos** (*m. pl.*) **de disco** disc brakes
discoteca disco(theque)
discreto/a discreet
disculpa excuse, apology
disculparse to excuse oneself, apologize; **discúlpeme** excuse me (17)
discurrir to discuss
discurso speech
discutir to argue (23); to discuss (23)
diseñar to design; **diseñar programas** to design, write programs (19)
diseño design
disfrazado/a de disguised as
disfrutar (de) to enjoy
disgustar to annoy
disgusto annoyance, irritation
disimular to disguise, cover up

disimulo/a dissimilar
disminuir (y) to reduce
disparar to fire, shoot
disperso/a scattered
disponer (*like* **poner**) to dispose, arrange
disponible available
dispositivo mechanism
dispuesto/a *p. p.* **(a)** disposed (to)
disputar to debate, argue
distancia distance
distinto/a distinct, different
distracción *f.* distraction
distraído/a distracted, absent-minded (17)
distribuidor(a) distributor
diversidad *f.* diversity
diversión *f.* diversion, entertainment
diverso/a diverse
divertido/a fun, amusing
divertir (ie, i) to amuse, entertain (14); **divertirse** to enjoy oneself, have a good time (14); **que te diviertas** (I hope you) have a good time (21)
dividir to divide
divino/a divine
divorciado/a divorced
divorcio *n.* divorce (4)
divulgar (gu) to expose, reveal
doblado/a dubbed (21)
doblar to dub; to turn (11)
doble double
doce twelve (P)
docena dozen
doctor(a) doctor
documental *n. m.* + *adj.* documentary
documento document
dólar *m.* dollar
doler (ue) to hurt, ache (16)
dolor *m.* pain; **dolor de estómago** stomach-ache; **tener** (*irreg.*) **dolor (de)** to have a pain (in) (16)
doméstico/a domestic, home; **aparato doméstico** home appliance (14); **quehacer** (*m.*) **doméstico/tarea doméstica** household chore (14)
domicilio residence; **a domicilio** at home
dominador(a) dominant
dominar to master
domingo Sunday (6)
Dominicana: la República Dominicana Dominican Republic
don *m. title of respect used with a man's first name*
donde where
¿dónde? where? (P); **¿adónde?** where (to)?; **¿de dónde es Ud.?** where are you from?; **¿dónde estará?** where can it be?, I wonder where it is? (24); **¿dónde estaría?** where could it be? (25)
dondequiera wherever
doña *title of respect used with a woman's first name*
dorado/a gold(en)
dormir (ue, u) to sleep (7); **dormirse** to fall asleep (14)

dormitorio bedroom
dos two (P)
doscientos/as two hundred (6)
drama *m.* drama, play
dramático/a dramatic
dril *m.* duckcloth
droga drug
ducha shower
duda doubt; **no hay duda** there's no doubt; **sin duda** undoubtedly
dudar to doubt (18)
dudoso/a dubious, doubtful
dueño/a owner (8); landlord/landlady
dulce *adj.* sweet
dulces *m. pl.* sweets, candy
duración *f.* duration, length
durante during (9); for (*a period of time*)
durar to last
duro/a hard

E

e and (*used instead of* **y** *before words beginning with stressed* **i** *or* **hi**)
ecología ecology
ecológico/a ecological
economía economy
económico/a economic(al)
economizar (c) to economize (24)
ecuatoriano/a Ecuadorean
echar to throw, fling; **echarse una siesta** to take a nap
edad *f.* age; **mayoría de edad** adult status, full legal age
edición *f.* edition
edificio *n.* building (1)
educación *f.* education
educado/a well-mannered, cultured; **mal educado/a** badly behaved, rude
educativo/a educational
efectivamente indeed; in fact
efectivo: dinero en efectivo cash (8); **pagar (gu) en efectivo** to pay cash
efecto effect; **en efecto** in fact
eficiente efficient
egocéntrico/a egocentric
egoísmo selfishness
egoísta *m., f.* egotistical, selfish
ejecutivo/a *n.* + *adj.* executive
ejemplar *adj.* model, exemplary
ejemplo example; **por ejemplo** for example
ejercer (z) to exert; to practice (*a profession*) (26)
ejercicio exercise (3); **hacer** (*irreg.*) **ejercicio** to exercise (16)
ejército army
el the (*m. definite article*)
él *sub. pron.* he; *obj. of prep.* him
elección *f.* choice; election
electricidad *f.* electricity
electricista *m., f.* electrician
eléctrico/a electric

electrodoméstico: aparato electrodoméstico electrical home appliance
electrólisis *f. s.* electrolysis
electrónico/a electronic
elefante *m.* elephant
elegante elegant
elegir (i, i) (j) to select, choose
elemental: educación (*f.*) **elemental** primary/elementary education
elemento element
elevar to raise
eliminar to eliminate
eludir to avoid
ella *sub. pron.* she; *obj. of prep.* her
ello it, that
ellos/as *sub. pron.* they; *obj. of prep.* them
embarazada pregnant
embarcación *f.* boat
embargo: sin embargo however, nonetheless
embarque: puerta de embarque loading gate
emborracharse to get drunk
embotellamiento traffic jam
emergencia emergency; **sala de emergencias** emergency room (16)
emigrar to emigrate
emisión *f.* emission
emitir to issue; to declare
emoción *f.* emotion
emocional emotional
emocionante exciting
empastar una muela to fill a tooth
empaste *n. m.* filling (*for a tooth*)
empedernido/a diehard, confirmed
emperador *m.* emperor
empezar (ie) (c) to begin (7); **empezar a +** *inf.* to begin to (*do something*) (7)
empleado/a employee (12)
emplear to use; to employ
empleo job, employment; **agencia/oficina de empleos** employment agency/office
empresa corporation, business (25)
empresariales: estudiante (*m., f.*) **de Empresariales** Business student
empresario/a *n.* business person; *adj.* business
empujar to push
en in; on; at (P)
enamorado/a sweetheart; **Día** (*m.*) **de los Enamorados** Valentine's Day
enamorarse (de) to fall in love (with)
enanito/a dwarf
encabezar (c) to head, lead
encajar to circle
encantado/a delighted; pleased to meet you (P)
encantador(a) charming
encantar to enchant (20); **me encanta(n)** _____ _____ is/are exciting to me (12)
encanto *n.* charm
encargado/a (de) charged (with), in charge (of)
encender (ie) to light
encendido/a fiery
encima de on top of (9)

encontrar (ue) to find (11); **encontrarse (con)** to meet (someone)
encuesta survey
enchilada rolled tortilla filled with meat, cheese, etc., and covered with sauce
enchufado/a *n.* person holding a position because of connections
enchufar to plug in (19)
enchufe *m.* plug (*electrical*); **tener** (*irreg.*) **enchufe** to have connections
enemistad *f.* enmity
energía energy (20)
enero January (7)
énfasis: poner (*irreg.*) **énfasis en** to place emphasis on
enfático/a emphatic; stressed (*gram.*)
enfermarse to get sick (16)
enfermedad *f.* sickness (16)
enfermería infirmary, hospital
enfermero/a nurse (14)
enfermo/a sick (5)
enfrentarse (con) to face, confront
engaño deceit
engañoso/a deceptive
engordar to fatten, make fat; to gain weight (9)
enojarse to get angry (15)
enorme enormous
ensalada salad (9)
ensamblaje *m.* joining
ensayo essay
enseñanza *n.* teaching
enseñar to teach (2)
entender (ie) to understand (7)
enterarse (de) to find out (about) (23)
entero/a entire, whole
entonces then, in that case; **en aquel entonces** at that time, in those days (15)
entrada first course; ticket (*for an event or performance*) (21); entrance
entrar (en, a) to enter, go (in)
entre between, among (9)
entrega delivery
entregar (gu) to deliver, hand over (27)
entremés *m. s.* appetizer (15)
entrenamiento *n.* training
entresemana: días (*m. pl.*) **de entresemana** weekdays
entretención *f.* amusement, entertainment
entrevista interview
entrevistador(a) interviewer (25)
entrevistar to interview (26)
entusiasmarse (con) to become enthusiastic (about)
entusiasmo: con entusiasmo enthusiastically
entusiasta enthusiastic
enunciado statement
envenenado/a poisoned
enviar to send
envidia envy
envío shipment
envoltorio wrapper
envuelto/a *p. p.* wrapped
episodio episode

época era; time period
equilibradamente in a balanced manner
equipaje *m.* luggage (10)
equipamento equipment
equipo team (22); equipment; **equipo estereofónico** stereo equipment (12); **equipo fotográfico** photographic equipment (12)
equivalente *m.* equivalent
equivocadamente mistakenly
equivocarse (qu) to be wrong, make a mistake (17)
era era, age
eres (*from* ser) you (*fam. s.*) are
erosión *f.* erosion
error *m.* error
erupción *f.* eruption
es (*from* ser) you (*form. s.*)/he/she/it is; **es de...** it is made of . . . (5); **es la una** it's one o'clock (P)
escala stopover; **hacer** (*irreg.*) **escalas** to make stops (11); **sin escalas** nonstop
escaldadura *n.* scalding
escalera ladder (17)
escándalo scandal
escapar(se) to escape
escasez *f.* (*pl.* escaseces) lack, scarcity (20)
escena scene
escenario scenery
escoceses: cuadros (*m. pl.*) **escoceses** plaid
escoger (j) to choose, select
escolar *adj.* of or pertaining to school
escolaridad *f.* course of study
esconderse to hide
escribiente *m., f.* writer
escribir (*p. p.* **escrito/a**) to write (4); **escribir a máquina** to type (19); **máquina de escribir** typewriter (12)
escrito/a *p. p.* written
escritor(a) writer
escritorio desk (1)
escuchar to listen (to) (8)
escuela school (16); **escuela primaria** elementary school; **escuela secundaria** high school
escultor(a) sculptor/sculptress
escultura sculpture
escurrirse to sneak away
ese/a *adj.* that (4); **ése/a** *pron.* that (one)
esencial essential
esfuerzo effort
esmero care
eso that, that thing, that fact (4); **eso es** that's right; **por eso** therefore, that's why (3)
esos/as *adj.* those (4); **ésos/as** *pron.* those (ones)
espacial *adj.* space, spatial
espacio space
espada sword
espaguetis *m. pl.* spaghetti
espalda back (*of body*)
España Spain
español *m.* Spanish (*language*) (2)
español(a) Spanish; **de habla española** Spanish-speaking
espárragos *m. pl.* asparagus

especial *adj.* special
especialidad *f.* specialty
especialista *m., f.* specialist
especializarse (c) to specialize; to major (*in a subject*)
especie *f.* species; type, kind
específico/a specific
espectacular spectacular
espectáculo spectacle; performance, show
espectador(a) spectator
especulación *f.* speculation, venture
espejo mirror
espera: sala de espera waiting room (10)
esperanza hope (23)
esperar to wait (for) (8); to hope (8); to expect
esplendor *m.* splendor
espolvorear to dust; to sprinkle
esposa wife (4); handcuff
esposo husband (4); *pl.* spouses; handcuffs
esquí *m.* skiing; ski (22)
esquiar to ski (11)
esquina street corner (18)
estable *adj.* stable
establecer (zc) to establish; establecerse to establish oneself, settle down
establecimiento establishment
estación *f.* season (7); station (11); estación de autobuses bus station (11); estación de gasolina gas station (18); estación del tren train station (11)
estacionamiento parking (lot)
estacionar(se) to park (18)
estadio stadium (22)
estadista *m.* statesman
estado state; Estados Unidos *pl.* United States
estadounidense *m., f.* person from the United States
estallar to explode
estallido outbreak (*of conflict, war, etc.*)
estampado *n.* print (design)
estancia stay, visit
estante *m.* bookshelf (13)
estar (*irreg.*) to be (5); to be located (P); está bien it's okay (5); está claro it's clear (5); está nublado it's cloudy (7); estar a dieta to be on a diet (9); estar aburrido/a to be bored (5); estar atrasado/a to be late (10); estar bien to be comfortable (*temperature*) (7); estar cogidos/as de las manos to hold hands; (no) estar de acuerdo (con) to (dis)agree (with) (5); estar de vacaciones to be on vacation (11); estar en alza to be rising (*in popularity*); estar listo/a (para) to be ready, prepared (to) (12); estar seguro/a to be certain (18)
estatal *adj.* state
estatuilla statuette
estatura height
estatuto statute
este *m.* east
este/a *adj.* this (3); éste/a *pron.* this (one); en este momento right now (5); esta noche tonight; este uh, um (*vocalized pause*)

estéreo stereo
estereofónico/a stereophonic; equipo estereofónico stereophonic equipment (12)
estereotipo stereotype
estética *s.* aesthetics
estilizar (c) to highlight, play up
estilo style
estimación *f.* estimation
estirar to stretch
esto this, this thing, this matter (4); por esto for this reason
estómago stomach (16); dolor (*m.*) de estómago stomachache
estos/as *adj.* these (3); éstos/as *pron.* these (ones)
estrecho/a narrow; tight
estrella star
estreno premiere
estricto/a strict
estructura structure
estudiante *m., f.* student (1)
estudiantil *adj.* of or pertaining to student(s)
estudiar to study (2)
estudio *n.* study; *pl.* studies, schoolwork
estudioso/a studious
estufa stove (14)
estupendo/a stupendous, marvelous
estúpido/a stupid
etcétera et cetera
ética *s.* ethics
etiqueta label, tag; fiesta de etiqueta formal ball
étnico/a ethnic
Europa Europe
europeo/a European
evaluación *f.* evaluation
evaluar to evaluate
evanescente *adj.* disappearing
evaporación *f.* evaporation
evento event
evitar to avoid (20)
exacto/a exact
exageración *f.* exaggeration
exagerar to exaggerate
exaltarse to get excited, worked up
examen *m.* exam (3)
examinador(a) examiner
examinar to examine (16)
excavación *f.* excavation
excavar to dig
exceder to exceed
excelencia: por excelencia par excellence, above all other
excelente excellent
excepción *f.* exception
excepcional exceptional
excesivo/a excessive
exceso excess; en exceso to excess
exclamar to exclaim
exclusivo/a exclusive
excursión *f.* excursion, trip; hacer (*irreg.*) una excursión to take a trip (11)
excursionista *m., f.* excursionist, tourist
exhibir to show

exigencia demand
exigente *adj.* demanding
exigir (j) to demand
exiliado/a *n.* exiled person
exilio exile
existencia existence
existente existing, current
existir to exist
éxito success; tener (*irreg.*) éxito to be successful
exótico/a exotic
expansión *f.* expansion
expedido/a shipped
experiencia experience
experimentar to experience
experimento experiment
experto/a *n.* + *adj.* expert
explicación *f.* explanation
explicar (qu) to explain (10)
exploración *f.* exploration
explosión *f.* explosion
explosivo *n.* explosive
explotación *f.* exploitation
explotar to exploit (20)
exponencial *adj.* exponential
exponer (*like* poner) to expose
exportar to export
exposición *f.* exhibition
expresar to express
expresión *f.* expression (P)
expreso express train
exquisito/a exquisite
extender (ie) to stretch; to spread
extenso/a extensive
exterior *m.* outward appearance
externo/a external
extranjero: en el/al extranjero abroad (27)
extranjero/a *n.* foreigner (1); *adj.* foreign
extrañar to miss (*someone or something*)
extraño/a strange; ¡qué extraño! how strange (12)
extraordinario/a extraordinary
extremo/a extreme
extrovertido/a extroverted

F

fábrica factory (20)
fabricante *m.* manufacturer
fabuloso/a fabulous
fácil easy (5)
facilidad *f.* ease; *pl.* facilities, conveniences; con facilidad easily
facilitar to facilitate
factor *m.* factor
factura bill, invoice (24)
facturar to check (*baggage*) (10)
facu, facul *f.* campus; department (*of a university*) (*coll.*)
facultad *f.* campus; department (*of a university*)
falda skirt (5)
falso/a false

falta lack; **sin falta** without fail
faltar to miss (*a class, work*); to be lacking (15)
fallar to fail, falter
fama fame
familia family (4)
familiar *n. m.* relative, member of family; *adj.* family, familial (4)
famoso/a famous
fango mud
fantasía fantasy
fantasma *m.* ghost
fantástico/a fantastic
farmacéutico/a pharmacist
farmacia pharmacy (16)
farmacología pharmacology
farsa farce, comedy
fascinante fascinating
fatal terrible; unlucky
fauna animal life
favor *m.* favor; **favor de + inf.** please (*do something*); **favor de repetir** please repeat (6); **por favor** please (P)
favorito/a favorite
fe *f.* faith
febrero February (7)
fecha date; **¿cuál es la fecha?** what is the date? (7)
felicidad *f.* happiness; *pl.* congratulations (15)
feliz (*pl.* **felices**) happy (15); happily; **Felices Pascuas/Feliz Navidad** Merry Christmas
femenino/a feminine
fenomenal phenomenal
fenómeno phenomenon
feo/a ugly (3)
feria fair
feriado: día (*m.*) **feriado** holiday
feroz (*pl.* **feroces**) ferocious
ferruginoso/a containing iron
festival *m.* festival
festivo: día (*m.*) **festivo** holiday (15)
fiebre *f.* fever (16)
fiel loyal; faithful
fiesta party (2); feast; holiday; **dar** (*irreg.*)/ **hacer** (*irreg.*) **una fiesta** to give a party (15)
figura figure
figurar to figure, appear
fijar to stick, attach; **fijarse (en)** to pay attention (to), concentrate (on)
fijo/a fixed, set
fila line, queue
filme *m.* film, movie
filología philology
filosofía philosophy
fin *m.* end; goal; **a fin de** in order to; **en fin** in summary; **fin de semana** weekend (2); **por fin** finally, at last (14)
final *n. m.* end; **al final de** at the end of; *adj.* final
finalizar (c) to finish
finalmente finally (14)
financiación *f.* financing
financiamiento financing
financiero/a financial

finca farm, ranch (20)
fino/a fine
firma signature
firmar to sign
firme firm, solid
física *s.* physics
físico physique, appearance
físico/a physical
flan *m.* caramel custard (9)
flor *f.* flower (10)
floreado/a flowered
florecer (zc) to bloom
Florida: Pascua Florida Easter (15)
flota fleet
flotar to float
fluir (y) to flow
flujo *n.* flow
foco *n.* light
folio page
folklore *m.* folklore
folleto pamphlet
fondo fund; foundation; *pl.* funds, money; **en el fondo** to the rear
fonógrafo phonograph
forestal *adj.* pertaining to forests
forma form; manner; **en forma** in good shape (16)
formación *f.* formation; education, upbringing
formalidad *f.* formality
formalizar (c) to formalize; to settle
formar to form
formato format
foto(grafía) *f.* photography; photo(graph) (3); **sacar (qu) una foto** to take a picture (12)
fotografiar to photograph
fotográfico/a photographic; **equipo fotográfico** photographic equipment (12)
fotógrafo/a photographer
fracasado/a failed
fracción *f.* fraction
fractura break, fracture
francés *m.* French (*language*) (2)
francés, francesa *adj.* French
frasco bottle, flask
frase *f.* phrase (1)
frazada blanket
frecuencia frequency; **con frecuencia** frequently (2); **¿con qué frecuencia?** how often? (4)
frecuentado/a visited, frequented
frecuente frequent; common
frenar to restrain, limit
freno restraint; *pl.* brakes (18); **frenos de disco** disc brakes
frente *n. m.* front; **frente a** *prep.* facing, in front of; with regard to
fresco/a cool; fresh; **hace fresco** it's cool (*weather*) (7)
fricasé *m.* fricassee, stew
frijol *m.* bean (9)
frío/a cold; **hace (mucho) frío** it's (very) cold (*weather*) (7); **tener** (*irreg.*) **(mucho) frío** to be/feel (very) cold (7)

frito/a fried; **papa frita** French fried potato (9)
frontera border, frontier (27)
fronterizo/a *adj.* border
frustrado/a frustrated
fruta fruit (9)
fue (*from* **ir, ser**) he/she/it went (11); **fue una ganga** it was a bargain (6); **fue sin querer** it was unintentional (17)
fuego fire
fuente *f.* source
fuera *adv.* out, outside (9); **fuera de** *prep.* out of, away from
fuerte strong; heavy, large (meal); **plato fuerte** main course
fuerza *n.* force
fui (*from* **ir**) I went (11)
fuiste (*from* **ir**) you went (11)
fumador(a) smoker
fumar to smoke (10); **sección** (*f.*) **de (no) fumar** (non)smoking section (10)
función *f.* show, performance (21); function
funcionar to function (12); to run, work (*with machines*) (12)
funcionario/a official (person)
fundar to found, establish
funeral *m.* funeral
furioso/a furious (5)
fútbol *m.* soccer (22); **fútbol (norte)americano** football (22)
futuro *n.* future
futuro/a *adj.* future

G

gabardina raincoat
gafas *f. pl.* (eye)glasses (16)
galaxia galaxy
galería gallery
gallego language of Galicia (*in northwestern Spain*)
galleta cookie (9)
gallo rooster; **al canto del gallo** at dawn
gama gamut, full range
gambas *f. pl.* shrimp
ganador(a) winner
ganar to earn (12); to gain; **ganarse la vida** to earn a living
ganas: tener (*irreg.*) **ganas de + inf.** to feel like (*doing something*)
ganga bargain; **fue una ganga** it was a bargain (6)
garaje *m.* garage (13)
garantía guarantee
garantizar (c) to guarantee
garganta throat (16)
gas *m. s.* gas (13); heat (13)
gasolina gasoline; **estación** (*f.*) **de gasolina** gas station (18)
gasolinera gas station (18)
gastar to use, expend (18); to spend (*money*) (6)
gastos *m. pl.* expenses (24)
gato/a cat (3)

generación *f.* generation
general general; **en general** in general, generally; **por lo general** in general, generally
generalizado/a generalized; common
género genre, type
generoso/a generous
genial funny; pleasant
gente *f. s.* people (8)
gentil genteel; polite
geografía geography
geográfico/a geographic
gerente *m., f.* manager (28)
germánico/a Germanic
gerontología gerontology
gerundio present participle (*gram.*)
gesto gesture
gimnasio gymnasium (22)
gimnástico/a gymnastic
girafa giraffe
girar to revolve, turn
giro turnover; **giro postal** money order
gobernador(a) governor
gobernar (ie) to govern (23)
gobierno government (12)
golf *m.* golf (22)
golfo gulf
golpista *adj:* pertaining to a *coup d'état*
goma rubber
gordo/a fat, plump (3)
gozar (c) to enjoy
grabación: equipo de grabación recording equipment
grabador (*m.*) **de vídeo** video recorder, VCR (12)
grabadora tape recorder
gracias thanks (P); **Día** (*m.*) **de Gracias** Thanksgiving Day; **muchas gracias** thank you very much (P)
gracioso/a funny
grado degree; grade (*school*)
graduado/a graduate
graduarse (en) to graduate (from) (25)
gramática grammar
gran, grande large, big (3); great (3)
granada grenade
granizo hail (*weather*)
grasa grease
gratis *inv.* free, gratis
grato/a pleasant
gratuito/a free of charge
grave serious
gravedad *f.* gravity, seriousness
gravoso/a costly; onerous
greca decorative border
griego/a Greek
gripe *f.* flu, cold
gris gray (5)
gritar *n.* to scream, shout
grito scream, shout
grotesco/a grotesque
gruesa: mar (*f.*) **gruesa** heavy sea
grupo group
guagua bus (*in Cuba and Puerto Rico*)
guajolote *m.* turkey

guantes *m. pl.* gloves
guapo/a handsome, good-looking (3)
guarachera singer of **guarachas** (*Cuban songs*)
guardar to save (*a place*) (10); to guard, watch over (10); **guardar cama** to stay in bed (16)
guardia: farmacia de guardia all-night pharmacy
guatemalteco/a Guatemalan
guayabera man's loose embroidered shirt
guerra war (23)
guía *m., f.* guide; **guía** (*f.*) **telefónica** telephone book
guiar to drive
guisante *m.* pea
guitarra guitar
gustar to be pleasing (10); **¿le/te gusta _____?** do you like _____? (P); **¡me gusta muchísimo!** I like it a lot! (9) **me gustaría** + *inf.* I would really like (*to do something*) (10); **no, no me gusta _____** no, I don't like _____ (P); **¡no me gusta (para) nada!** I don't like it at all (9); **sí, me gusta _____** yes, I like _____ (P)
gusto pleasure; taste; *pl.* likes (P); **a gusto** at ease, comfortable; **¡cuánto gusto!** what a pleasure!; **mucho gusto** pleased to meet you (P)

H

ha viajado he, she, it has traveled (11)
haba *f.* (*but* **el haba**) bean
Habana Havana
haber (*irreg.*) *inf. form of* **hay**; to have (*auxiliary*); **va a haber** there's going to be; **había (habías, había,...**) + *p. p.* I (you, he/she/it) had (*done something*) (19); **he, has, ha viajado** I, you have traveled, he/she/it has traveled (11)
había + *p. p.* I/he/she/it had (*done something*) (19)
habías + *p. p.* you had (*done something*) (19)
habilidad *f.* ability
habitación *f.* room (*in hotel, pension*) (28)
habitante *m., f.* inhabitant
hábito habit
habla *f.* (*but* **el habla**) speech (*language*); **de habla española** Spanish-speaking
hablar *v.* to speak (2); to talk (2); *n. m.* dialect, speech
hace + *period of time* (+ *preterite*) (*period of time*) ago (15); **hace** + *period of time* + **que** + *present tense* to have been (*doing something*) for (*a period of time*)
hacer (*irreg.*) (*p.p.* **hecho/a**) to do (7); to make (7); **hace buen/mal tiempo** it's good/bad weather (7); **hace calor/fresco/frío/sol/ viento** it's hot/cool/cold/sunny/windy (7) **hacer** *camping* to go camping (11); **hacer cola** to stand in line (10); **hacer ejercicio** to exercise (16); **hacer escalas** to have/make stopovers (11); **hacer la cama** to make the bed (14); **hacer las maletas** to pack one's

suitcases (11); **hacer planes para** + *inf.* to make plans to (*do something*) (21); **hacer un viaje** to take a trip (7); **hacer una excursión** to take a trip (11); **hacer una fiesta** to give a party (15); **hacer una pregunta** to ask a question (7); **hacerse** to become (15); **hacerse daño** to hurt oneself (17); **¿qué tiempo hace?** what's the weather like? (7)
hacia toward
hacienda ranch (20)
halago flattery
hallar to find
hambre *f.* (*but* **el hambre**) hunger; **tener** (*irreg.*) **(mucha) hambre** to be (very) hungry (9)
hamburguesa hamburger (9)
harina flour
has viajado you have traveled (11)
hasta *adv.* even; *prep.* until (7); **hasta luego** until then, see you later (P); **hasta mañana** see you tomorrow (P); **hasta que** *conj.* until (24)
hay there is, there are (P); **hay contaminación** there is pollution (7); **hay que** + *inf.* it's necessary to (*do something*) (19); **no hay más remedio** nothing can be done about it
hazaña heroic deed, exploit
he viajado I have traveled (11)
hebreo/a Hebrew
hecho *n.* fact; event; **de hecho** in fact
hecho/a *p. p.* made, done
helado ice cream (9)
hemisferio hemisphere
heraldo herald
heredero/a heir
herencia inheritance
herida *n.* wound
herido/a wounded
hermano/a brother/sister (3); *m. pl.* siblings, brothers and sisters
hermoso/a beautiful
héroe *m.* hero
hervir (ie, i) to boil
hidalgo gentleman
hidrógeno hydrogen
hielo ice (7)
hierba grass
hierro iron; **óxido de hierro** rust-colored
higiene *f.* hygiene, cleanliness
higiénico: papel (*m.*) **higiénico** toilet paper
hijo/a son/daughter (4); child; *m. pl.* children (4)
himno anthem
hipopótamo hippopotamus
hispánico/a Hispanic
hispano/a *n.* Hispanic (*person*); *adj.* Hispanic
Hispanoamérica Latin America
hispanoamericano/a Latin American
hispanohablante *m.* Spanish speaker
historia history (2); story
histórico/a historic(al)
historieta comic strip
hockey *m.* hockey (22)
hogar *m.* home, house

hoguera campfire
hoja sheet; leaf; **hoja de inscripción** enrollment form
hola hi, hello (P)
hombre *m.* man (1); **¡hombre!** man!, well!; **hombre de negocios** businessman (26)
hombrillo shoulder (of road)
hombro shoulder
hondo/a deep
hondureño/a Honduran
honestamente honestly
honor: dama de honor bridesmaid
honrado/a honorable, honest
honrar to honor
honroso/a honorable
hora hour; **¿a qué hora?** (at) what time? (P); **(es) hora de** + *inf.* time to (*do something*); **¿qué hora es?** what time is it? (P)
horario schedule
horizonte *m.* horizon
hornacina vaulted niche
horno oven (14)
horror *m.* fear, horror
hortaliza vegetable
hospedaje *m.* lodging, housing
hospedarse to lodge, stay
hospital *m.* hospital
hotel *m.* hotel (28); **hotel de lujo** luxury, first-class hotel (28)
hotelero/a hotelkeeper
hoy today (P); **de hoy** daily; **hoy (en) día** nowadays
huelga *n.* (labor) strike (23)
huella *n.* trace, track
hueso bone
huésped(a) guest (28)
huevo egg (9)
huir (y) to flee
humanidad *f.* humanity; *pl.* Humanities
humanista *m., f.* humanist; Humanities major
humano/a human
humilde humble
humo *n.* smoke (10)
humor *m.* humor
huracán *m.* hurricane

I

Ibérico/a Iberian
ida: boleto/billete (*m.*) **de ida** one-way ticket (10); **de ida y vuelta** round-trip (10)
idea idea; **cambiar de idea** to change one's mind
idealista idealistic
idéntico/a identical
identificación *f.* identification
identificar (qu) to identify
ideología ideology, belief
idioma *m.* language
iglesia church (4)
ignorante ignorant
ignorar to be ignorant of

igual equal; **(eso) me da igual** (that's) all the same to me (17); **igual que** the same as; **por igual** equally
igualar to match, be equal to
igualdad *f.* equality (23)
igualmente likewise (P)
ilegal illegal
ilimitado/a unlimited
iluminar to illuminate
ilusión *f.* illusion; dream
ilusionista *m., f.* conjurer, magician
imagen *f.* image
imaginar to imagine
imaginario/a imaginary
imaginativo/a imaginative
imitar to imitate
impaciente impatient (11)
imparcial impartial
impedir (i, i) to prevent
imperfecto/a imperfect
imperio empire
impermeable *m.* raincoat (5)
implicar (qu) to imply
imponer (*like* **poner**) to impose
importado/a imported
importancia importance
importante important
importar to import; to matter; **no (me) importa (nada)** it doesn't matter (to me) (at all) (17)
imposible impossible
imprenta: letra de imprenta print(ing)
imprescindible indispensable
impresión *f.* impression; printing
impresionante impressive
impresionar to impress
impresora printer (12); **impresora matricial** dot-matrix printer
imprevisto/a *p. p.* unforeseen
improvisar to improvise
impuesto tax (12)
impulsar to throw, launch
impulsivo/a impulsive
inagotable inexhaustible
inalámbrico: teléfono inalámbrico cordless telephone
inauguración *f.* inauguration
inca *n. m., f.* Incan
incaico/a *adj.* Inca, Incan
incalculable inestimable, incalculable
incapacitado/a disabled
incendio fire
incidente *m.* incident
inclinarse to be inclined
incluir (y) to include
inclusive including
incluso *adv.* even, including
incompleto/a incomplete
inconveniente *m.* drawback, inconvenience
incorporar(se) to incorporate
incorrecto/a wrong
increíble incredible (12)
indefinido/a indefinite
independencia independence

independiente independent
independizarse (c) to become independent
indicación *f.* suggestion
indicado/a indicated
indicar (qu) to indicate
indicativo indicative (mood) (*gram.*)
índice (*m.*) **de paro** unemployment rate
indígena *adj. m., f.* indigenous, native
indio/a *n.* + *adj.* Indian
indirecto/a indirect
indiscreto/a indiscreet
individuo individual, person
industria industry
inesperadamente unexpectedly
inevitable unavoidable
infancia infancy
infantil *adj.* children's
infección *f.* infection
inferior lower; inferior
infierno hell
infinidad *f.* infinity
infinitivo infinitive (*gram.*)
inflación *f.* inflation
inflamado/a inflamed
influencia influence
influir (y) to influence
información *f.* information, data; **archivar la información** to store data (19)
informar to inform (23); **informarse** to find out
informática data processing (19)
informativo *n.* news broadcast
informe *m.* report
infracción *f.* violation (*of law*)
ingeniería engineering
ingeniero/a engineer
ingenio skill
ingenioso/a ingenious, clever
ingenuo/a naive
Inglaterra England
inglés *m. s.* English (*language*) (2)
inglés, inglesa *adj.* English
ingresar to put in, deposit (24)
inicio: agente (*m.*) **de inicio** instigating element
inmediato/a immediate
inmejorable unbeatable
inmenso/a immense
inmigración *f.* immigration (27)
inmigrante *n. m., f.* + *adj.* immigrant
inmigrar to immigrate
innecesario/a unnecessary
innovación *f.* innovation
inocente *m., f.* naive person, fool; **Día** (*m.*) **de los Inocentes** April Fools' Day
inolvidable unforgettable
inquilino/a tenant, renter (13)
inscripción: hoja de inscripción enrollment form
insecto insect
inseguro/a insecure
insistir en + *inf.* to insist on (*doing something*) (4)
insólito/a unusual

insomnio insomnia
inspector(a) (de aduanas) (customs) inspector (27)
inspirar to inspire
instalación f. installation; plant
instalar to install
instantáneo/a instantaneous
instintivamente instinctively
institución f. institution
instituto institute; secondary school
instrucción f. instruction
instrumento instrument
insuficiencia scarcity, lack
intelectual intellectual
inteligente intelligent
intención f. intention
intensidad f. intensity
intensificar (qu) to intensify, step up
intensivo/a intensive
intentar to attempt
intercambio exchange
interés m. s. interest
interesante interesting
interesar to interest; me interesa(n) _____
_____ is/are interesting to me (12)
interior n. m. interior
intermedio middle
internacional international
interpretación f. interpretation
interpretar to interpret, construe
interrogativo/a interrogative (P)
interrumpir to interrupt
interruptor m. switch (electrical)
intocable untouchable
introvertido/a introverted
inútil useless
invadir to invade
invasión f. invasion
invención f. invention
inventar to invent
inventario inventory (12)
invento invention
inventor(a) inventor, creator
investigación f. research
investigar (gu) to investigate
invierno winter (7)
invitación f. invitation
invitado/a n. guest; adj. invited
invitar to invite
inyección f. injection, shot; ponerle (irreg.) una inyección to give (someone) a shot (16)
ir (irreg.) to go (6); fui, fuiste, fue I went, you went, he/she/it went (11); ir a + inf. to be going to (do something) (6); ir al extranjero to go abroad; ir de compras to go shopping (6); ir de vacaciones to go on vacation (7); irse to leave, go away (14)
irrealizable unattainable
irregularidad f. irregularity
irresponsable irresponsible
irritado/a irritated
irrumpir to erupt
isla island
Italia Italy

italiano Italian (language) (2)
italiano/a Italian
itinerario route; schedule, timetable
izquierda n. left (direction); a la izquierda de to the left of (9)
izquierdo/a adj. left; levantarse con el pie izquierdo to get up on the wrong side of the bed (17)

J

jabón m. soap
jamás never (8)
jamón m. ham (9)
Japón m. Japan
japonés m. s. Japanese (language) (2)
jarabe m. (cough) syrup (16)
jardín m. garden
jarrita small jug
jarro jug, pitcher (8)
jaspeado/a marbled
jefe/a boss (12); jefe/a subrogante acting chief
jerarquía hierarchy
jerez m. sherry
jirafa giraffe
joven n. m., f. young person; adj. young (3); de joven as a youth (16)
jubilado/a retired (from work)
judía green bean
juego (board, card) game (22); gambling; card playing; juego electrónico video game
jueves m. s. Thursday (6)
juez m. (pl. jueces) judge
jugador(a) n. player (22)
jugar (ue) (gu) (a) to play (a sport, game) (7); jugar a las cartas/al ajedrez to play cards/ chess (21)
jugo juice (9)
juguete m. toy (13)
julio July (7)
junio June (7)
juntar to collect
junto a along with
juntos/as together (8)
jurídico/a legal
justicia justice
justificar (qu) to justify
justo/a just, fair; precise
juvenil youthful
juventud f. youth
juzgar (gu) to judge

K

kilo(gramo) kilogram (about 2.2 pounds)
kilometraje m. mileage
kilómetro kilometer (about two-thirds of a mile)

L

la the (f. definite article); d. o. you (form. s.), her, it (f.)

labor f. labor, work
laborable adj. workable
laboratorio lab; laboratorio de lenguas language lab
lado side; a un lado out of the way; de lado aside; por otro lado on the other hand
ladrar to bark
ladrón, ladrona thief (23)
lagarto alligator
lago lake
laguna lagoon
lamentar to be sorry
lámpara lamp (13)
lana wool (5); perro de lanas poodle
langosta lobster (9)
lanzar (c) to launch; to throw
lapicero pencil holder
lápiz m. (pl. lapices) pencil (1)
largo/a long (3)
las d. o. you (form. pl.), them (f.)
lástima n. pity; es lástima it's a shame (12); ¡qué lástima! what a shame! (12)
lata (tin) can; ¡qué lata! what a bore!
latín m. Latin (language)
latino/a Latin (person)
Latinoamérica Latin America
latinoamericano/a Latin American
lavado/a laundry, wash
lavadora washing machine (14)
lavaplatos m. s. dishwasher (14)
lavar to wash (13); lavarse to wash oneself (14)
le i. o. (to/for) you (form. s.), him, her, it
leal loyal
lección f. lesson
lectura reading
leche f. milk (9)
lechuga lettuce (9)
leer (y) to read (4)
legendario/a legendary
legua league (distance)
lejos de prep. far from (9)
lengua language (2); tongue; laboratorio de lenguas language lab
lenguaje m. (computer) language (19)
lenteja lentil bean
lente (m.) de contacto contact lens (16)
lento/a slow
leña (fire)wood
león m. lion
les i. o. to/for you (form. pl.), them
lesionado/a injured
letra letter (of alphabet); letra de imprenta print(ing); typing; letras cursivas italics
leucocito white blood cell
levantar to lift, raise (14); levantarse to get up (14); to stand up (14); levantarse con el pie izquierdo to get up on the wrong side of the bed (17)
ley f. law (23)
liberado/a liberated
libertad f. liberty, freedom (23)
libertador(a) liberator
libra pound

libre free; **al aire libre** *adj.* outdoor (6); **un rato libre** a few free minutes (21); **ratos libres** free, spare time (21)
librería bookstore (1)
libreta small book; **libreta de ahorros** bankbook (24); **libreta de direcciones** address book
libro book (1); **libro de texto** textbook (1)
licencia license (18); **licencia de manejar/conducir** driver's license
liceo high school
licor *m.* liqueur
líder *m.* leader
liga (sports) league
ligero/a light (*in weight*); slight
limitación *f.* limitation
limitar to limit
límite *m.* limit; **límite de velocidad** speed limit
limón *m.* lemon
limonada lemonade
limosnas *pl.* alms
limpiar to clean (13)
limpieza cleanliness
limpio/a clean (5)
lindo/a pretty
línea line; **línea aérea** airline
lingüístico/a linguistic
linterna lantern
liquidación *f.* sale
líquido liquid
liso/a smooth
lista list
listado/a striped
listo: estar (*irreg.*) **listo/a** to be ready (12); **ser** (*irreg.*) **listo/a** to be smart
litera train berth
literatura literature (2)
lo *d. o.* you (*form. s.*), him, it (*m.*); **lo que** what, that which (11); **lo** + *adj.*, *m. s.* the _____ thing/part/news (16); **lo bueno/ malo** the good/bad news (16); **lo siento** I'm sorry (5); **lo suficiente** enough (16)
lobo wolf
local *n. m.* place; *adj.* local
localidad *f.* place, location
localizar (c) to find, locate
loco/a crazy; **volverse (ue) loco/a** to go crazy
locutor(a) announcer (media)
lógico/a logical
lograr to achieve; **lograr** + *inf.* to manage to (*do something*)
lona canvas
Londres *m. s.* London
lotería lottery
lubricación *f.* lubrication
lubricante lubricant, cream
lubricar (qu) to grease, lubricate
lucir (zc) to dress to advantage; to shine; to show off
lucha *n.* fight
luchar to fight (23)
luego then, next (1); **desde luego** of course; **hasta luego** until then, see you later (P)

lugar *m.* place (1); **cambiar de lugar** to move (*something*); **tener** (*irreg.*) **lugar** to take place, occur
lujo: de lujo *adj.* luxury (27)
lujoso/a luxurious
luminoso/a bright
luna moon; **luna de miel** honeymoon (4)
lunares *m. pl.* polka dots
lunes *m. s.* Monday (6)
luz *f.* (*pl.* **luces**) light (13); electricity (13)

LL

llamar to call (8); **llamarse** to be called, named (14); **¿cómo se llama Ud.?, ¿cómo te llamas?** what's your name? (P); **me llamo _____** my name is _____ (P)
llamativo/a loud, bright (*of clothes*)
llanta tire (18); **llanta desinflada** flat tire (18); **llanta radial** radial tire
llave *f.* key (17)
llegada arrival (10)
llegar (gu) to arrive (4); **llegar a ser** to become (15); **llegar tarde/a tiempo** to be late/on time
llenar to fill (up) (18); to fill out (*a form*) (25)
lleno/a full
llevar to carry (5); to wear (5); to take (*someone or something somewhere*) (5); to remain (*somewhere for a period of time*); **llevar una vida _____** to live a _____ life (16)
llorar to cry (15)
llover (ue) to rain (7); **llueve a cántaros** it's raining cats and dogs
lluvia rain (7)
lluvioso/a rainy

M

madera wood
madrastra stepmother
madre *f.* mother (3)
madrileño/a *adj.* of Madrid
madrugador(a) early riser
madrugar (gu) to rise early (20)
maduro/a mature
maestro/a teacher
magia magic
mágico/a magic(al)
magnífico/a magnificent
mago: Reyes (*m. pl.*) **Magos** Magi, Three Wise Men
mal *n. m.* evil
mal *adv.* badly (2); **pasarlo mal** to have a bad time (15)
mal, malo/a *adj.* bad (3); **hace mal tiempo** the weather's bad (7); **lo malo** the bad news (16); **¡qué mala suerte!** what bad luck! (17)
maldad *f.* wickedness
maldición *f.* curse
maleducado/a ill-mannered, rude; poorly brought up

maleta suitcase (10); **hacer** (*irreg.*) **las maletas** to pack one's suitcases (11)
maletero porter
maletín *m.* small suitcase
malévolo/a malevolent
malgastar to waste
malvado/a evil, wicked
mamá mom, mother (4)
mamoncillo honey berry (*kind of fruit*)
manchar to stain
mandar to send (10); to order (12)
mandato command
manejar to drive (11); to use, operate (*a machine*) (19); **licencia de manejar** driver's license
manejo operation, use (*of a machine*) (19)
manera way, manner; **de todas maneras** in any case
manifestación *f.* (*political*) demonstration; manifestation
manifestarse (ie) to show oneself
mano *f.* hand (17); **bordado/a a mano** hand-embroidered; **darse** (*irreg.*) **la mano** to shake hands; **escalera de mano** ladder; **escrito/a a mano** handwritten; **hecho/a a mano** handmade; **meter mano en** to have a hand in
manteca butter
mantel *m.* tablecloth (8)
mantenimiento maintenance
mantener (*like tener*) to maintain; to support; **mantenerse** to keep, maintain oneself
manual *m.* handbook, manual
manzana apple (9)
mañana *n.* morning; *adv.* tomorrow (P); **de la mañana** in the morning (P); **hasta mañana** until tomorrow, see you tomorrow (P); **pasado mañana** day after tomorrow (6); **por la mañana** in the morning (2)
mapa *m.* map
máquina machine; **escribir a máquina** to type (19); **máquina de escribir** typewriter (12)
mar *m., f.* sea
maratón *m.* marathon
maravilla marvel, wonder
maravilloso/a marvelous
marca brand, make
marcador (*m.*) **de lectura** bookmark
marcar (qu) to mark out; to indicate
marco setting
marcha: poner (*irreg.*) **en marcha** to set in motion
marea: contra viento y marea against all odds
mareado/a nauseated (16)
marejada groundswell
marfil *m.* ivory
margen *f.* border; edge
marido husband
marihuana marijuana
marino *n.* member of Marines
marino/a *adj.* sea
mariscos *m. pl.* shellfish (9)
marítimo/a *adj.* sea; maritime
marrón *m.* brown

Marruecos *m. s.* Morroco
martes *m. s.* Tuesday (6)
marzo March (7)
más more (2); most; **más _____ que** more _____ than (6); **sus más y sus menos** its/his/her good and bad points
masaje *m.* massage
máscara mask
masculino/a masculine
matar to kill
matasanos *m. s.* quack, unskilled doctor
matemáticas *f. pl.* mathematics (2)
materia matter; (*school*) subject (2)
material *n. m. + adj.* material (5)
materialista materialistic
materno/a maternal
mates *f. pl.* math (*colloquial*)
matricial: impresora matricial dot-matrix printer
matrícula *s.* tuition (27); registration
matrimonio marriage (4); married couple
máximo/a maximum
maya *m., f.* Maya(n)
mayo May (7)
mayor older (7); greatest, greater
mayoría majority; **mayoría de edad** adult status, full legal age
mayorista *adj.* wholesale
mazo bundle
me *d. o.* me; *i. o.* (to/for) me; *refl. pron.* myself
mecánico/a *n.* mechanic (18); *adj.* mechanical
mecanismo mechanism
mecedora: silla mecedora rocking chair
medalla medal
mediante by means of
medias *f. pl.* stockings (5)
medicamento medicinal product
medicina medicine (16)
médico/a *n.* doctor (16); *adj.* medical
medida measurement; measure, extent; **a la medida de** to suit
medio *n.* means; *pl.* means (11); **medio ambiente** environment (20)
medio/a *adj.* middle; intermediate; average; half; **clase** (*f.*) **media** middle class; **(las tres) y media** half past (three) (P); **media pensión** (*f.*) room with two meals; (28) **Oriente** (*m.*) **Medio** Middle East
mediodía *m.* noon, midday
medir (i, i) to measure; to be _____ tall
mejor better (7); best (3); **lo mejor** the best thing
mejorar to improve
melanocito dark pigmentation cell
melodioso/a melodious
memoria memory (19)
mencionar to mention
menguante: en cuarto menguante on the wane
menor *n. m.* minor, underage person; *adj.* younger (7); least
menos less; least; minus; **(las dos) menos cuarto** a quarter to (two) (P) **más o menos** more or less; **menos _____ que** less _____ than (6); **a menos que** unless (22); **por lo**

menos at least (27); **sus más y sus menos** its/his/her good and bad points
mensaje *m.* message
mensual monthly
mentira lie
menú *m.* menu (8)
mercado (al aire libre) (outdoor) market(place) (6)
mercantil *adj.* business, commercial
merendar (ie) to snack
merienda snack
mermelada marmelade
mes *m. s.* month (7); **al mes** monthly, per month (4)
mesa table (1); **poner** (*irreg.*) **la mesa** to set the table (14)
meseta *n.* plain
Mesías *m. s.* Messiah
mesita end table (13)
mesón *m.* inn; tavern
metal *m.* metal
meter to put into; **meter mano** to lend a hand; **meter la pata** to put one's foot in one's mouth
método method
metro subway
metrópoli *f.* city, metropolis
mexicano/a Mexican
mexicanoamericano/a Mexican American
mezcla mixture
mezclar to mix
mezclilla tweed
mezquita mosque
mi(s) *poss.* my (6)
microcomputadora microcomputer (19)
microondas *m. s.* microwave (14)
microordenador *m.* microcomputer
miedo fear; **tener** (*irreg.*) **miedo (de)** to be afraid (of) (5)
miel *f.* honey; **luna de miel** honeymoon (4)
miembro member
mientras while (13)
miércoles *m. s.* Wednesday (6)
migra immigration authority (*col.*)
mil *m.* one thousand (6)
militar *adj.* military
milla mile (18)
millón (de) *m.* one million (6)
mina *n.* mine
mineral: agua (*f.* but **el**) **mineral** mineral water (9)
minifalda miniskirt
mínimo/a minimal
ministerio ministry
ministro: primer ministro prime minister
minuto *n.* minute (*time*)
mío/a(s) *poss.* my, of mine
miopía myopia, nearsightedness
mirar to look (at) (4); to watch (4)
miscelánea miscellany, assortment
miserable wretched, unfortunate
misión *f.* (religious) mission, establishment
mismo/a self; same; **ahora mismo** right now (5); **consigo mismo/a** with oneself; **sí mismo/a** oneself

mitad *f.* half
mobilidad *f.* mobility
mochila backpack (1)
moda fashion; **estar** (*irreg.*) **de moda** to be in style; **¡está muy de moda!** it's the latest style! (5)
modalidad *f.* variety, type
modelo model
moderación *f.* moderation
moderado/a moderate
moderarse to restrain oneself
moderno/a modern
modesto/a modest, unassuming
modismo idiomatic expression
modo manner; **de modo que** so that; **de todos modos** anyway
mojado/a wet
mole (*m.*) **poblano** *Mexican dish of meat cooked in sauce of spices, peppers, and bitter chocolate*
molestar to bother; **molestarse** to get upset
molestia *n.* bother
momentito just a minute/second
momento moment; **de momento** right now, for the time being; **en este/ese momento** at this/that very moment (5)
monarca *m.* monarch, sovereign
monarquía monarchy
monárquico/a monarchical
monitor *m.* monitor, screen (19)
mono (*male*) monkey
monocromo/a monochromatic
monótono/a monotonous
monóxido de carbón carbon monoxide
montaña mountain (11)
montar to ride; **montar a caballo** to ride horseback (11)
monte *m.* mountain
montón *m.* large pile, heap
monumento monument
morado/a purple (5)
morcilla blood sausage
morder (ue) to bite
moreno/a brunet(te) (3)
morir(se) (ue, u) (*p. p.* **muerto/a**) to die (14)
moro/a *n.* Moor
mosca fly
mostrador *m.* counter (*in a shop*)
mostrar (ue) to show, exhibit
moteado/a speckled
motivo: con motivo de because of
moto(cicleta) *f.* motorcycle (12)
motor *m.* motor, engine
movimiento movement
mozo bellhop (28)
muchacho/a young man/woman; boy/girl
muchachón *m.* big boy
mucho/a *adj.* a lot of (4); *pl.* many; *adv.* much, a lot (2); **muchas gracias** many thanks (P); **muchas veces** often; **mucho gusto** pleased to meet you
mudarse to move (*from one home to another*) (20)
mueblería furniture store
muebles *m. pl.* furniture (13); **sacudir los muebles** to dust the furniture (14)

muela molar (tooth)
muerte f. death; **pena de muerte** death penalty
muerto/a n. dead person; p.p. killed; died; adj. dead
mujer f. woman (1); **mujer de negocios** businesswoman (26)
multa fine, penalty (17); traffic ticket
multiplicar (qu) to multiply, increase
mundial adj. world, worldwide
mundo n. world
municipio municipality
muñeca doll
muñeco puppet
mural m. mural
muralista m., f. muralist
museo museum
música music
músico/a musician
muy very (2); **muy bien** very well, fine (P); **muy buenas** good afternoon/evening

N

nácar m. mother-of-pearl
nacer (zc) to be born
nacido/a born
nacimiento birth (15)
nación f. nation
nacional national
nacionalidad f. nationality (27)
nada nothing, not anything (8); **como si nada** as if nothing were wrong; **de nada** you're welcome (P); **nada más** nothing else, no more; **¡no me gusta (para) nada!** I don't like it at all! (9); **no (me) importa nada** it doesn't matter (to me) at all (17)
nadar to swim (11)
nadie no one, not anyone, nobody (8)
naranja n. orange (fruit) (9)
naranjo/a orange-colored
nariz f. nose (16)
narración f. narration, story
natación f. swimming (22)
natal adj. native, of birth
nativo/a native
natural adj. natural; **recurso natural** natural resource (20)
naturaleza nature (20)
navegar (gu) en barco to travel by boat (11)
Navidad f. Christmas (15); pl. Christmas holidays; **Feliz Navidad** Merry Christmas
navideño/a adj. Christmas
neblina fog
necesario/a necessary
necesidad f. necessity, need
necesitar to need (2)
negar (ie) (gu) to deny (18); to refuse
negativo/a negative
negligencia negligence
negocio business (20); **hombre** (m.)/**mujer** (f.) **de negocios** businessman/businesswoman (26)

negro/a black (5)
nervioso/a nervous (5)
neurótico/a neurotic
neutrónica: bomba neutrónica neutron bomb
nevar (ie) to snow (7)
nevera refrigerator
ni neither; nor; not even; **ni _____ ni _____** neither _____ nor _____; **ni siquiera** not even
nicaragüense n. m., f. + adj. Nicaraguan
nido nest
niebla fog
nieto/a grandson/granddaughter (4); m. pl. grandchildren
nieve f. snow (7)
ningún, ninguno/a no, none, not any (8); **de ninguna manera** no way
niñez f. (pl. **niñeces**) childhood
niño/a little boy/girl; child (1); **de niño/a** as a child (16); m. pl. children
nivel n. m. level
no no (P); not; **¿no?** right?, don't they (you, etc.)? (5); **no hay** there is/are not (P)
nocturno/a adj. night
noche f. night (1); **buenas noches** good evening/night (P); **de la noche** in the evening/at night (P); **de noche** at night; **esta noche** tonight; **Noche Vieja** New Year's Eve (15); **por la noche** in the evening/at night (2); **todas las noches** every night
Nochebuena Christmas Eve (15)
nombrado/a named, appointed
nombrar to name
nombre m. (first) name (3)
noreste m. northeast
norma norm, rule
normal regular, ordinary
noroeste m. northwest
norte m. north
Norteamérica North America
norteamericano/a North American (4); from the United States (4); **fútbol** (m.) **norteamericano** football (22)
nos d. o. us; i. o. (to/for) us; refl. pron. ourselves
nosotros/as sub. pron. we; obj. of prep. us
nota note; grade (in a class); **sacar (qu) una buena/mala nota** to get a good/bad grade
noticia notice, piece of news (15); pl. news (15)
noticiero newscast (23)
novecientos/as nine hundred (6)
novedades f. pl. news (23)
novela n. novel
novelista m., f. novelist
noveno/a adj. ninth (18)
noventa ninety (3)
noviazgo engagement (4)
noviembre m. November (7)
novio/a boyfriend/girlfriend (4); fiancé(e) (4); groom/bride (4); m. pl. lovers; engaged couple
nube f. cloud
nublado/a cloudy; overcast; **estar** (irreg.) **nublado** to be cloudy/overcast (7)

nuboso/a cloudy
nuestro/a(s) poss. our (6); (of) ours
nueve nine (P)
nuevo/a new (3); **Año Nuevo** New Year
nuez f. (pl. **nueces**) nut
numerario member
número number (P)
numeroso/a numerous, many
nunca never (4)

O

o or (P)
obedecer (zc) to obey (23)
objeto object; **objeto volador no identificado (OVNI)** UFO
obligación f. obligation
obra work (of art, literature, construction)
obrar to act, proceed
obrero/a worker, laborer (23)
observar to observe
obsesión f. obsession
obstáculo obstacle
obtener (like **tener**) to obtain, receive
obvio/a obvious
ocasión f. occasion
ocasionar to cause
océano ocean
octavo/a adj. eighth (18)
octubre m. October (7)
oculista m., f. eye doctor
ocultar to hide
ocupación f. occupation
ocupado/a busy, occupied (5)
ocupar to occupy; **ocuparse de** to attend to
ocurrir to happen, occur
ochenta eighty (3)
ocho eight (P)
ochocientos/as eight hundred (6)
odiar to hate
oeste m. west
ofender to offend
ofensiva n. offensive, plan of attack
oficina office (1)
oficio trade (work) (26)
ofrecer (zc) to offer (23)
oiga(n) hey (you, form.), listen
oír (irreg.) to hear (8)
ojalá God willing; **ojalá + (que)** past subj. I wish _____ could/would (23); **ojalá (que)** + present subj. I wish/hope that (something happens) (11)
ojo eye (16); **¡ojo!** watch out!
ola n. wave
Olimpíada s. Olympic Games
olvidar to forget (11); **olvidarse (de)** to forget (about) (15); **olvidarse de + inf.** to forget to (do something)
olla pot
once eleven
opaco/a opaque; dull
opción f. option
opcional optional

operación *f.* operation
opinar to think, have an opinion
opinión *f.* opinion
oponerse (*like* **poner**) to oppose
oportunidad *f.* opportunity
optimismo optimism
optimista optimistic
opuesto/a *p. p.* opposing; **lo opuesto** the opposite (*thing*)
oración *f.* sentence (*gram.*)
orden *m.* order, sequence; *f.* order, command
ordenador *m.* computer (*Sp.*) (12)
ordenar to put in order
organización *f.* organization
organizar (c) to organize
oriental eastern; oriental
oriente *m.* east; **el Medio Oriente** the Middle East
origen *m.* origin
originalidad *f.* originality
originario/a de originating from
orilla (*river*) bank
oriundo/a de native of
oro gold; playing card representing a coin
orquesta orchestra
ortodoxo/a orthodox, conventional
ortográfico/a *adj.* spelling
os *d. o.* you (*fam. pl., Sp.*); *i. o.* (to/for) you (*fam. pl., Sp.*); *refl. pron.* yourselves (*fam. pl., Sp.*)
oscuridad *f.* darkness; obscurity
oscuro/a *adj.* dark
oso bear
ostentar to boast; to flaunt
ostra oyster
otoño autumn (7)
otro/a other, another (3); **otra vez** again; **por otro lado** on the other hand
OVNI (objeto volador no identificado) UFO
óxido de hierro iron oxide
oye hey (*you, fam. s.*), listen
ozono: capa de ozono ozone layer

P

paciencia patience
paciente *n. m., f.* patient (16); *adj.* patient
pacífico/a peaceful
padecer (zc) to suffer
padre *m.* father (3); *pl.* parents (3)
padrino godfather; *pl.* godparents
paella *Spanish dish of saffron rice with shellfish, chicken, and sausage*
pagar (gu) to pay (for) (2); **¿cuánto pagaste por _____?** how much did you pay for _____? (6); **pagar al contado/en efectivo** to pay cash (24); **pagar a plazos** to charge, pay for over time (24)
página page
pago payment
país *m. s.* country, nation (3)
paisaje *m.* countryside, landscape

pájaro bird (12)
palabra word (P)
palacio palace
palillos *m. pl.* castanets
palma palm tree, palm
palmera palm tree
palomitas *f. pl.* popcorn
pampa extensive plains, pampas
pan *m.* bread (9); **pan dulce** sweet roll; **pan tostado** toast (9)
pana corduroy
panameño/a Panamanian
pandilla group of friends
pantalón *m.* trousers; **pantalones** trousers, pants (5); **pantalones cortos** shorts
pantalla screen (19)
papa *f.* potato (*L. A.*) (9); **papa frita** French fried potato (9)
papá *m.* dad, father (4)
papel *m.* paper (1); role; **jugar (ue) (gu)/hacer** (*irreg.*) **un papel** to play a role; **papel higiénico** toilet paper
papelería stationery store
paquete *m.* package; packet
par *m.* pair (5)
para *prep.* (intended) for (1); in order to (1); **no es para tanto** it's no big deal; **para que** *conj.* so that (22)
parada stop; **parada del autobús** bus stop; **parada de taxis** taxi stand
paraguayo/a Paraguayan
paraíso paradise
paralizado/a paralyzed
parar to stop (18)
parcial: de tiempo parcial part-time (12)
pardo/a brown (5)
parecer (zc) to seem, appear (11); **¿qué te/le parece?** what do you think?
parecido/a similar
pared *f.* wall (13)
pareja couple; dancing partner
paréntesis *m. s. + pl.* parenthesis; **entre paréntesis** within parentheses
pariente/a *n.* relative (4)
paro: índice (*m.*) **de paro** unemployment rate
parque *m.* park (7)
párrafo paragraph
parrilla: a la parrilla grilled, barbecued
parroquia parish
parte *f.* part (13); **en/por todas partes** everywhere; **por parte de** on the part of
participante *m., f.* participant
participar to participate
participio pasado past participle (*gram.*)
partícula particle
particular private; particular
partido (*sports*) match, game (22); (*political*) party
partir: a partir de starting from
párvulo small child, tot
pasado *n.* past
pasado/a past; last (*in time*); **pasado mañana** day after tomorrow (6)
pasaje *m.* (*travel*) ticket, passage; **pasaje de**

ida y vuelta round-trip ticket
pasajero/a passenger (10)
pasaporte *m.* passport (10)
pasar to happen; to pass (*by*); to spend (*time*) (4); **pasar a** to go to; **pasar la aspiradora** to vacuum (14); **pasarlo bien/mal** to have a good/bad time (11); **pasar por** to stop by; **pase(n) Ud(s).** come in; **que lo pases bien** have a good time (21)
pasatiempo pastime (21)
Pascua (Florida) Easter (15); **Felices Pascuas** Merry Christmas
pasear to take a walk; **pasear en bicicleta** to go for a bike ride (22)
paseo excursion; route; stroll; **dar** (*irreg.*) **un paseo** to go for a walk (21)
pasillo hallway
pasión *f.* enthusiasm
paso step; crossing
pasta money (*coll.*)
pastel *m.* pastry; cake (9)
pastilla pill (16)
pasto pasture; fodder
pastor(a) pastor, minister; **perro pastor alemán** German shepherd dog
pata foot (*of animal*); **meter la pata** to put one's foot in one's mouth
patata potato (*Sp.*)
paterno: apellido paterno father's family name
patinar to skate (22)
patio patio (13); yard (13)
patito baby duck
patria native land
patrimonio heritage
patrón: santa patrona patron saint
pavimentar to pave
pavo turkey
payasito little clown
paz *f.* (*pl.* **paces**) peace (23)
peatón, peatona pedestrian; **cruce** (*m.*) **para peatones** pedestrian crosswalk
peculiar *adj.* characteristic
pedagogía *n.* teaching
pedido *n.* order; purchase
pedir (i, i) to ask for, order (7); **pedir prestado/a** to borrow (24)
pegar (gu) to hit, strike (17)
pegatina (bumper) sticker
pelea fight, argument
pelearse to fight, argue (*with someone*)
película film, movie (5)
peligro danger
peligroso/a dangerous (15)
pelo hair; **tomarle el pelo a alguien** to pull someone's leg
pelota ball (22)
peluquería hairdresser shop
peluquero/a hairdresser
pena punishment; **no vale la pena** it's not worth it (17); **pena de muerte** death penalty
pendiente *n. m.* earring; *adj.* hanging
pendón *m.* banner

penicilina penicillin
península peninsula
pensamiento *n.* thought
pensar (ie) to think (7); **pensar + *inf.*** to intend to (*do something*); **pensar de** to think of, have an opinion about; **pensar en** to think about; **pienso que...** I think . . . (7); **¿qué piensas de _____?** what do you think of _____? (7)
pensión *f.* inn; boarding house (28); **media pensión** room plus two meals (28); **pensión completa** room plus all meals (28)
peor worse (7); worst; **lo peor** the worst part/thing
pequeño/a small, little (3)
perder (ie) to lose (7); to miss (*a bus, plane, social event, etc.*) (7)
perdido/a lost
perdón pardon me, excuse me (P)
perdonar to pardon
perdone pardon (17)
peregrino/a pilgrim; traveler
perezoso/a lazy (3)
perfeccionado/a perfected
perfecto/a perfect
perfil *m.* profile, shape
perfume *m.* perfume
perfumería perfume shop
periódicamente periodically
periódico newspaper (4)
periodismo journalism
periodista *m., f.* journalist
período period of time
perla pearl
permanecer (zc) to remain, stay; to reside
permanente permanent
permisible permissible
permiso permission; **con permiso** excuse me (P)
permitir to permit, allow (12)
pero *conj.* but (1)
perro/a dog (3); **perro pastor alemán** German shepherd dog; **perro de lanas** poodle
persona *f.* person (1)
personaje *m.* character (*in a book, play*)
personal *n. m.* personnel; **dirección (*f.*) de personal** personnel/employment office (25); *adj.* personal (12)
personalidad *f.* personality
perspectiva perspective
pertenecer (zc) to belong; to relate
perteneciente *adj.* belonging
pertinente relevant
peruano/a Peruvian
pesado/a boring (15)
pesar: a pesar de in spite of
pesca fishing
pescado (*cooked*) fish (9)
pesebre *m.* manger
peseta *monetary unit of Spain*
peso weight; *monetary unit of Bolivia, Colombia, Cuba, Chile, Mexico, the Dominican Republic, and Uruguay*
petróleo oil; petroleum

pez *m.* (*pl.* **peces**) (*live*) fish (12)
picante spicy
picar (qu) to nibble; to itch
picnic *m.* picnic
pie *m.* foot (17); **de pie** standing; **levantarse con el pie izquierdo** to get up on the wrong side of the bed (17)
piedra stone
piel *f.* skin; *pl.* furs
pierna leg (17)
pieza piece (*of art, music*)
piloto/a pilot (10)
pimienta pepper
pingüino penguin
pino pine tree
pinta *n.* mark
pintar to paint
pintor(a) painter
pintura painting (12)
piña pineapple
piñata *hanging pot filled with candies and gifts*
pirámide *f.* pyramid
pisar to step on
piscina swimming pool (11)
piso floor; apartment, flat; **primer piso** second floor (first floor up) (13)
pista (de baile) (dance) floor
piza pizza
pizarra chalkboard (1)
placer *m.* pleasure
plan *m.* plan; **hacer (*irreg.*) planes para + *inf.*** to make plans to (*do something*) (21)
plancha iron
planchar to iron (14)
planear to plan
planeta *m.* planet
planilla form (*to fill out*) (27)
plano/a plane; level; flat
planta plant; floor (*of a building*); **planta baja** ground floor, first floor (13)
plantear to pose (*a question*)
plasmarse to come into being
plástico *n.* plastic
plata *n.* silver
plateado/a silvery
platillos *children's game* (*similar to marbles*) *played with bottle caps*
plato plate (8); dish (*cuisine*) (8); **plato del día** daily special
playa beach (7)
plaza square; place, space; **plaza de toros** bullring
plazo time limit; **pagar (gu) a plazos** to pay on time/in installments (24)
pleno/a full, complete; **pleno de** full of; **luces (*f.*) plenas** high beams
plomero/a plumber (26)
población *f.* population (20)
pobre poor (3)
pobreza poverty
poco *adv.* little (2); **poco a poco** little by little; *n.* **un poco de** a little of
poco/a *adj.* little, few (4)
poder *n. m.* power
poder (*irreg.*) to be able, can (5); **cuando**

pueda whenever you have a second/can; **¿podría Ud.... ?** could you . . . ? (19); **puede que + *subj.*** it's possible that (28)
poderoso/a powerful
poema *m.* poem
poeta *m., f.* poet
poético/a poetic
policía *f.* police force; *m., f.* police officer (18); **ciencias policiales** criminology
política *s.* politics
político/a *n.* politician; *adj.* political; **ciencias políticas** *pl.* political science
polución *f.* pollution
polvo dust; powder
pollo chicken (9)
ponche *m.* punch (*beverage*)
poner (*irreg.*) to put, place (7); to turn on (*appliances*) (7); to set (*the table, a clock*) (14); **poner inyecciones** to give shots (16); **poner una multa** to give a fine/ticket; **ponerse** to put on (*clothing*) (14); to become, get (15); **ponerse colorado/a** to blush; **ponerse de acuerdo** to reach an agreement
por *prep.* in (*the morning, etc.*) (2); because of; for; per; by; through; during; on account of; for the sake of; **por ciento** percent; **por completo** completely; **por Dios** for heaven's sake; **por ejemplo** for example; **por eso** therefore, that's why (3); **por favor** please (P); **por fin** finally (14); **por hora** per hour; **por la manana/tarde/noche** in the morning/afternoon/evening (2); **por lo general** generally; **por lo menos** at least (13); **por parte de** on behalf of; **por primera/última vez** for the first/last time; **por si acaso** just in case; **por supuesto** of course; **por último** finally
porcelana porcelain
porción *f.* part, portion
¿por qué? why? (3)
porque because (3)
portarse to behave (oneself) (15)
portátil portable
portero/a building manager (13); doorperson (13)
portugués *m. s.* Portuguese (*language*)
portugués, portuguesa Portuguese
posada: dar (*irreg.*) **posada** to give refuge, hospitality
posadas Christmas festivities
poseer (y) to possess
posesivo/a possessive (*gram.*)
posibilidad *f.* possibility
posible possible
posición *f.* position
postal: tarjeta postal postcard; **giro postal** postal money order
posterior(a) *adj.* rear, back
posteriormente previously
postre *m.* dessert (9); **de postre** for dessert
postura position
potencia power
potente powerful
potingue *m.* concoction, potion
practicante *m., f.* practitioner; type of nurse or intern

practicar (qu) to practice (2); to participate in (*sports*) (16)
práctico/a practical (3)
pragmático/a pragmatic, practical
precio price (6); **precio fijo** fixed price (6)
precipitación *f.* rainfall
preciso/a necessary (12)
precoces: medidas (*f. pl.*) **precoces** precautionary measures
precolombino/a pre-Columbian, before Columbus
predecir (*like* **decir**) to predict
predicar (qu) to preach
predicción *f.* prediction
preferencia preference (P)
preferible preferable (12)
preferir (ie, i) to prefer (5); **prefiero** + *inf.* I prefer to (*do something*) (2)
pregunta question; **hacer** (*irreg.*) **una pregunta** to ask a question (7)
preguntar to ask, inquire (10)
preliminar beginning, preliminary
premio prize; **Premio Nobel** Nobel Prize
prensa press (23); news media
preocupación *f.* worry; concern
preocupado/a worried (5)
preocuparse (por) to worry (about) (13); **no te preocupes** (*fam.*) don't worry (13)
preparación *f.* preparation
preparar to prepare (14)
preparativos *m. pl.* preparations
preparatorio/a preparatory
preposición *f.* preposition (*gram.*)
presencia bearing; appearance
presentar to present; to introduce
presente *adj.* current, present
presidente/a president
presidir to preside, govern
presión *f.* pressure, tension (17); **sufrir muchas presiones** to be under a lot of pressure (17)
prestado: pedir (i, i) prestado/a to borrow (24)
préstamo *n.* loan (24)
prestar to lend (10)
prestigio prestige
presupuesto budget (24)
pretender to try (to get)
pretérito preterite (*gram.*)
prevención *f.* warning
prevenir (*like* **venir**) to prevent
preventivo/a preventive; warning
previamente beforehand
primaria: (escuela) primaria primary/elementary school
primavera spring (7)
primer, primero/a *adj.* first (18); **primer piso** second floor (first floor up) (13); **el primero de _____** the first of (*month*) (7); **por primera vez** for the first time; **primera clase** first class (10); **primero** *adv.* first (of all)
primo/a cousin (4)
princesa princess
principal main; **plato principal** main course
príncipe *m.* prince

principio beginning; **al principio** at first
prisa haste, hurry; **de prisa** hurriedly; **tener** (*irreg.*) **prisa** to be in a hurry (5)
privación *f.* deprivation
privado/a private
privar to deprive
probador *m.* fitting room
probar (ue) to try; to taste; to prove
problema *m.* problem (1)
procedente de coming from
procesador (*m.*) **de textos** word processor
procesar textos to do wordprocessing
proceso process
procurar to try; to manage
producción *f.* production
producir (*irreg.*) to produce
producto product
profe *m., f.* professor (*coll.*)
profesar to profess (*a faith*)
profesión *f.* profession (26)
profesional *n. m., f.* + *adj.* professional
profesionalizado/a professionalized
profesor(a) professor (1)
profundizarse (c) to deepen
profundo/a profound
programa *m.* program
programación *f.* (computer) programming
programador(a) (computer) programmer
progresar to get ahead
progresivo/a progressive (*gram.*)
progreso progress
prohibir to prohibit, forbid (12)
prometer to promise
promoción *f.* promotion
pronombre *m.* pronoun (*gram.*)
pronóstico forecast
pronto soon; **tan pronto como** as soon as (24)
pronunciación *f.* pronunciation
pronunciar to pronounce
propenso/a predisposed
propiedad *f.* property, quality
propina tip (*given to a waiter, etc.*) (28)
propio/a *adj.* (one's) own; same, aforementioned
proponer (*like* **poner**) to propose
propósito purpose; **a propósito** by the way
próspero/a prosperous
protagonista *m., f.* protagonist, main character
protección *f.* protection
protector(a) protective
proteger (j) to protect (20)
protestar to protest
protón *m.* proton
proveer (y) to provide
provocar (qu) to provoke; to cause
próximo/a next (*in time*) (6); **la próxima vez** the next time
proyección *f.* projection
proyecto project
prueba proof; quiz (7); **poner** (*irreg.*) **a prueba** to put to the test
psicología psychology
publicidad *f.* publicity

público/a *adj.* public (20)
pueblo town; people
puede que + *subj.* it's possible that (28)
puerta door (13); **puerta de embarque** loading gate
puertorriqueño/a Puerto Rican
pues well . . . (2)
puesto *n.* position, place (*in line*) (10); job (12); **cambiar de puesto** to change jobs
pulmones *m. pl.* lungs (16)
pulpo octopus; pulp
pulsera bracelet
punto point; dot; **a punto** in good shape; **en punto** on the dot, exactly (*time*) (P); **punto de vista** point of view
puntual punctual
puñado handful
puro/a pure (20)

Q

que that, who (P); **lo que** what, that which; **que** + *subj.* I hope + *verb form* (21); **¡que aproveche(n)!** enjoy your meal
¿qué? what?, which? (P); **¿por qué?** why? **¡qué!** + *n.* what a _____!; **¡qué bien!** great!; **¡qué extraño!** how strange! (12); **¡qué lástima!** what a shame! (12); **¿qué tal?** how are you (doing)? (P)
quechua *m.* ancient Peruvian language; *m., f.* Quechuan person
quedar to remain, be left (17); **no queda(n)** there isn't any (are none) left; **quedar mal** to make a bad impression; **quedarse** to stay (14)
quehacer *m.* chore, task (14)
quejarse (de) to complain (of/about) (15)
quemadura *n.* burn
querer (*irreg.*) to want (5); to love (*a person*); **fue sin querer** it was unintentional (17); **(no) quiero** + *inf.* I (don't) want to (*do something*) (2)
querido/a dear, beloved (5)
queso cheese (9)
quetzal *m.* monetary unit of Guatemala
quien who
¿quién(es)? who? (P); whom? (P); **¿de quién?** whose?; **¿quién será?** who can that be? (24)
quijotada act or deed typical of don Quixote
química chemistry
quina tree bark producing quinine
quince fifteen (P)
quinceañera *party celebrating a girl's fifteenth birthday*
quinientos/as five hundred (6)
quinto/a *adj.* fifth (18)
quisiera + *inf.* I would like to (*do something*) (19)
quitar to remove, take away (14); **quitar el polvo** to dust; **quitarse** to take off (*clothing*) (14)
quizá(s) perhaps

R

rábano radish
rabino/a rabbi
racional rational
radiador *m.* radiator
radial: llanta radial radial tire
radical *n. m.* root (*gram*); *adj.* radical
radicar (qu) en to stem from
radio radio (set) (7); radius; **radio portátil**
  portable radio (12); *f.* radio (*broadcasting
  medium*)
radiografía X-ray
radiología radiology
rail *m.* rail, track
raíz *f.* (*pl.* **raíces**) root; **a raíz de** as a result of
ramo bouquet
ranchero/a rancher (20)
rancho ranch (20)
rápido/a *adj.* rapid, fast; *adv.* rapidly; **comida
  rápida** fast food
raqueta racket (22)
ráquetbol *m.* racketball
raro/a strange; unusual, rare
rascacielos *m. s.* skyscraper (20)
rasgo *m.* trait, characteristic
raspadura scraping
rato short period of time; **un rato libre** a few
  free minutes (21); **ratos libres** *pl.* free time (21)
ratón *m.* mouse
rayas: de rayas striped (5)
rayos: cinta de rayos X-ray belt (*in an airport*)
razón *f.* reason; **la razón por la cual** the reason why, for which; **(no) tener** (*irreg.*)
  razon to be right (wrong) (5)
razonable reasonable
reacción *f.* reaction
reaccionar to react
real royal; real
realidad *f.* reality; **en realidad** really
realista realistic
realizar (c) to bring about, realize
realzar (c) to heighten
rebaja bargain, sale (6)
rebelde rebellious
rebozo shawl
recado message
recámara bedroom
recepción *f.* (*formal*) reception; pick-up; front
  desk (*of hotel*) (28)
recepcionista *m., f.* receptionist
receta recipe; prescription (16)
recetar to prescribe
recibir to receive (4)
recibo receipt
reciclaje *m.* recycling
recién + *adj.* recently + *adj.*
reciente recent
recipiente *m.* container
recíproco/a reciprocal
recital *m.* performance, recital
recitar to recite
recobrar(se) to recover
recoger (j) to pick up (13)

recomendable recommendable
recomendación *f.* recommendation
recomendar (ie) to recommend (12)
reconocer (zc) to recognize
reconstruido/a rebuilt
récord *m.* record
recordar (ue) to remember (14)
recorrer to cover (*miles, territory*) (20)
recrear to recreate
recreo recreation
recto/a straight
rector *m.* president of a university
recuerdo memory; souvenir
recuperar to recover, regain
recurso recourse; **recurso (natural)** (natural)
  resource (20)
red *f.* net (22)
redacción *f.* writing
redactar to write (*fiction, nonfiction*)
redada roundup
redondo/a round
reducción *f.* reduction
reducido/a reduced, discounted
reducir (*like* **producir**) to reduce
reembolso reimbursement
referirse (ie, i) (a) to refer (to)
refinado/a refined
reflejar to reflect
reflexivo/a reflexive (*gram*)
refrán *m.* proverb
refresco soft or cold drink (7); *pl.* refreshments (15)
refrigerador *m.* refrigerator (14)
refugiado/a refugee
refugio refuge
regalar to give (as a gift) (10)
regalo present, gift (3)
regañar to scold
regatear to bargain (6)
regeneración *f.* renewal
régimen *m.* regime, rule
región *f.* region
registrar to examine, search (27)
regla rule
reglamentario/a regulatory
reglamento *s.* regulations
regresar to return (2); **regresar a casa** to go
  home (2)
regreso *n.* return; **boleto de regreso** return
  ticket
regulador *m.* regulator; control (knob)
regular *v.* to regulate; *adj.* normal; okay
rehén *m.* hostage
reina queen
reírse (i, i) (de) to laugh (about, at) (14)
relación *f.* relation; relationship (4)
relacionar to connect, relate; **relacionarse** to
  get acquainted
relativo/a *adj.* relative
relevancia relevance
religión *f.* religion
religioso/a religious
reloj *m.* clock; watch (5)
relucir (zc) to shine

remate *m.* auction
remedio solution; **no hay más remedio**
  there's nothing else to do
remover (ue) to stir
rendición *f.* surrender
rendido/a surrendered
renegar (ie) (gu) to renounce
renovado/a renovated
renta income
renunciar (a) to resign (from), quit (25)
reparación: en reparación under repair
reparo misgiving, doubt
repartir to deal; to distribute
repasar to review
repaso *n.* review
repente: de repente suddenly (16)
repetición *f.* repetition
repetir (i, i) to repeat; **repite** (*fam.*) repeat (6);
  favor de repetir please repeat (6)
reportero/a reporter (23)
representación *f.* representation
representante *m., f.* representative
representar to represent
reproche *m.* reproach
reproducción *f.* reproduction
reproductor (*m.*): **vídeo-reproductor** VCR
república republic
republicano/a republican
requisito requisite, requirement
res: carne (*f.*) **de res** beef
resbaladizo/a slippery
reseco/a dried-out
reserva reservation
reservación *f.* reservation (28)
reservar to reserve (28)
resfriado head cold (16)
resfriarse to catch a cold (16)
residencia residence; dormitory (1); **residencia estudiantil** dormitory
residencial residential
residuo residue
resignación *f.* resignation
resolver (ue) (*p. p.* **resuelto/a**) to resolve (19)
respectivo/a respective
respetar to respect
respeto *n.* respect
respiración *f.* breathing
respirar to breathe (16)
responder to answer, respond
responsabilidad *f.* responsibility (23)
responsable responsible
respuesta response (8)
restante *m.* remainder
restaurante *m.* restaurant (8)
resto rest, remainder
restringir (j) to restrict
resuelto/a *p. p.* resolved
resultado result
resultar: me resulta imposible (difícil,...) +
  inf. It's impossible (difficult, . . .) for me to
  (*do something*) (24)
resumen *m.* summary
retablo series of paintings
retirado/a retired (*from work*)

retirar to take away; **retirarse** to retire (*from work*)
retórica rhetoric
retraso: de retraso late
retratar to depict
retrato portrait
reunión *f.* meeting
reunir to reunite; to join together; **reunirse (con)** to get together (with) (21)
revelar to reveal
reverente reverent
reverso reverse, opposite
revisar to check, examine (18)
revista magazine (6)
revolución *f.* revolution
revolucionario/a revolutionary
revueltos: huevos revueltos scrambled eggs
rey *m.* king; **Reyes Magos** Wise Men
rico/a rich (3); delicious
ridículo/a ridiculous
rígido/a rigid
riguroso/a rigorous
rincón *m.* (*inside*) corner
río river
riqueza richness; variety
ritmo rhythm (20); **cambio de ritmo** change of pace
robar to steal
robo robbery
robot *m.* robot
rodadura tire track
rodear to surround
rodilla knee
rojo/a red (5)
rollo *n.* bore (*coll.*)
romántico/a romantic
rompecabezas *m. s.* jigsaw puzzle
romper (*p. p.* **roto/a**) to break (17)
ropa clothing (5)
rosado/a pink (5)
roto/a *p. p.* broken (18)
rubio/a blond(e) (3)
rueda wheel
ruido noise (5)
ruidoso/a noisy
ruinas ruins
rumbo: cambio de rumbo change of direction
rumor *m.* rumor, gossip
ruso Russian (*language*) (2)
rutina routine

S

sábado Saturday (6)
saber (*irreg.*) to know (8); **saber** + *inf.* to know how to (*do something*)
sabor *m.* taste; flavor
saborear to taste, savor
sabotear to sabotage
sacar (**qu**) to take out, remove; to get, receive (*with grades*); **sacar fotos** to take photographs (12); **sacar la basura** to take out the

garbage (14); **sacar la lengua** to stick out one's tongue (16)
saco de dormir sleeping bag
sacrificar (**qu**) to sacrifice
sacudir los muebles to dust the furniture (14)
sagrado/a sacred
sajón, sajona (Anglo)-Saxon
sal *f.* salt
sala room; **sala (de estar)** living room (13); **sala de emergencias** emergency room (16); **sala de espera** waiting room (10)
salado: agua (*f. but el*) **salada** salt water
salar to salt
salario salary, wages; **aumento de salario** raise
salchicha sausage
salida exit; departure (10)
salir (*irreg.*) to leave, go out (7); to turn out
salmón *m.* salmon (9)
salón *m.* room
salsa sauce; **salsa picante** hot sauce
saltar to jump
salud *f.* health (16)
saludar to greet (15)
saludo greeting (P)
salvación *f.* salvation
salvadoreño/a Salvadorean
salvaje savage, wild
salvo except (for)
sanar to heal, restore
sandalia sandal (5)
sándwich *m.* sandwich (9)
sangre *f.* blood
sanitario/a sanitary
sano/a healthy (16)
santo/a saint; **día** (*m.*) **del santo** saint's day
saquear to plunder
satisfacción *f.* satisfaction
satisfacer (*like* **hacer**) to satisfy
satisfecho/a satisfied
saxofón *m.* saxophone
se (*impersonal*) one; *refl. pron.* yourself (*form.*)/ himself/herself/yourselves (*form.*)/ themselves
sea: o sea in other words
secadora clothes dryer (14)
secarropa clothes dryer
sección *f.* section; **sección de (no) fumar** (non)smoking section (10)
seco/a dry
secre *m., f.* secretary (*coll.*)
secretario/a secretary (1)
secreto *n.* secret
secuencia sequence, series
secundaria: (escuela) secundaria high school
sed *f.* thirst; **tener** (*irreg.*) (**mucha**) **sed** to be (very) thirsty (9)
seda silk (5)
sede *f.* headquarters
seductor(a) seductive
sefardí *m., f.* Sephardic Jew
seguida: en seguida right away, immediately
seguir (**i, i**) (**g**) to follow (11); to continue (11); **seguir** + *pres. participle* to keep on, continue (*doing something*) (23)

según according to
segundo *n.* second (*time*)
segundo/a *adj.* second (18); **Segunda Guerra Mundial** World War II; **segundo piso** third floor (second floor up) (13)
seguridad *f.* safety, security; **cinturón** (*m.*) **de seguridad** seat belt
seguro *n.* insurance; **seguro médico** health insurance
seguro/a sure, certain; safe; **estar** (*irreg.*) **seguro/a** to be sure (18); **es seguro que** it's certain that (18); **seguro que** of course
seis six (P)
seiscientos/as six hundred (6)
selección *f.* team
seleccionar to choose
selva jungle
semáforo traffic signal (18)
semana week (2); . . . **a la semana** . . . a week (4); **fin** (*m.*) **de semana** weekend (2); **la próxima semana** next week (6); **la semana que viene** next week; **Semana Santa** Easter Week
semblanza biographical sketch
semejante similar
semejanza similarity
semestre *m.* semester
senador(a) senator
sencillo/a simple
sendero path, way
sentar (**ie**) to seat, lead to a seat (14); **sentarse** to sit down (14)
sentido sense; meaning; **sentido común** common sense
sentimiento feeling, emotion
sentir (**ie, i**) to regret (12); to feel sorry (12); **sentirse** to feel (15); **lo siento** I'm sorry (5)
señor (Sr.) *m.* Mr., sir (P); gentleman
señora (Sra.) Mrs. (P); lady
señores (Sres.) *m. pl.* Mr. and Mrs.; gentlemen
señorita (Srta.) Miss (P); young lady
se(p)tiembre *m.* September (7)
séptimo/a *adj.* seventh (18)
ser (*irreg.*) to be (3); **es la/son las _____** it's _____ o'clock (P); **fue una ganga** it was a bargain (6); **llegar** (**gu**) **a ser** to become (15); **¿quién será?** who can that be? (24); **ser en** + *place* to take place in/at (*place*) (15); **ser listo/a** to be smart; **serán las ocho** it must be eight o'clock (24); **sería** it would be (18); **soy, eres, es** I am, you (*fam.*) are, he/she/it is (P)
serie *f. s.* series
serio/a serious
serpiente *f.* snake
servicio service (18); **estación** (*f.*) **de servicio** gas station; **servicios humanos** human services; **servicios públicos** public services (20); **servicios** restrooms
servilleta napkin (8)
servir (**i, i**) to serve (7)
sesenta sixty (3)
sesión *f.* session

setecientos/as seven hundred (6)
setenta seventy (3)
sevillana *lively dance typical of Seville*
sexo sex
sexto/a *adj.* sixth (18)
si if (2); **como si** + *past subjunctive* as if (26)
sí yes (P)
siamés, siamesa Siamese
sicología psychology (2)
SIDA *m.* AIDS
siempre always (2); **siempre que** whenever (22)
siento: **lo siento** I'm sorry (5)
siesta nap; **dormir (ue, u)/echarse una siesta** to take a nap
siete seven (P)
siglo century
significado *n.* meaning
significar (qu) to mean
signo sign
siguiente following, next (7); **al día siguiente** the next day; **lo siguiente** the following
sílaba syllable
silencioso/a silent
silla chair (1)
sillón *m.* armchair (13)
simpático/a nice (3)
simulado/a simulated
simultáneamente simultaneously
sin *prep.* without (9); **fue sin querer** it was unintentional (17); **sin chavo** broke (*coll.*); **sin duda** undoubtedly; **sin embargo** nevertheless; **sin falta** without fail; **sin que** *conj.* without
sincero/a sincere
sinfónico/a symphonic
singular *adj.* unique; singular (*gram*)
sino but (rather)
sinónimo synonym
sinopsis *f. s.* synopsis, résumé
síntoma *m.* symptom (16)
siquiatra *m., f.* psychiatrist
siquiera: **ni siquiera** not even
sistema *m.* system
sitio site, place
situación *f.* situation
situado/a located; situated
sobre *n. m.* envelope; *prep.* about; above; on; **sobre todo** above all, especially (24)
sobrevivido/a survived
sobrino/a nephew/niece (4)
social social (4); **trabajador(a) social** social worker (26)
socialista *adj.* socialist
sociedad *f.* society
socio/a member
sociología sociology
sociólogo/a sociologist
socorro *n.* help
sofá *m.* couch (13)
sol *m.* sun; **hace sol** it's sunny (7); **tomar el sol** to sunbathe (11)
solamente *adv.* only
solapa lapel (*of a coat*)

soldado soldier; **la mujer soldado** female soldier
soledad *f.* solitude (20)
solemne solemn, serious
solicitar to solicit, ask for
solicitud *f.* application form (25)
solitario/a solitary
sólo *adv.* only (2)
solo/a *adj.* alone
solomillo sirloin steak
soltar (ue) to toss; to free up, let go (of)
soltero/a single, unmarried (3)
solución *f.* solution
sombrero hat (5)
sombrío/a somber
sometido/a submitted
son las _____ it is _____ o'clock (P)
sonar (ue) to ring
sonido *n.* sound
sonreír (i, i) to smile (14)
soñar (ue) (con) to dream (about)
sopa soup (9)
sorprendente surprising
sorprender to surprise; **me (te, le...) sorprende** it is surprising to me (you, him . . .) (12)
sorpresa surprise (15)
soy (*from* ser) I am (P)
su(s) *poss.* his/her/its/your (*form. s., pl.*)/their (6)
suave soft
suavidad *f.* softness
suavizar (c) to soften
subdesarrollado/a underdeveloped
subir (a) to rise; to go up (into/onto); to get on/in (*a vehicle*) (10); to carry up
subjuntivo subjunctive (*gram.*)
subordinada: **cláusula subordinada** dependent clause (*gram.*)
subrogante: **jefe/a subrogante** acting chief
subterráneo/a subterranean
suburbio suburb
suceder to happen
sucio/a dirty (5)
sucursal *f.* branch (office) (25)
sudadera sweatshirt
Sudamérica South America
sudamericano/a South American
sudar to sweat
sudoeste *m.* southwest
Suecia Sweden
suegros in-laws
sueldo salary (12); **aumento de sueldo** raise
suelo floor
suelto/a loose
sueño dream; **tener** (*irreg.*) **sueño** to be sleepy (5)
suerte *f.* luck; **buena suerte** good luck; **¡qué mala suerte!** what bad luck! (17); **tener** (*irreg.*) **suerte** to be lucky
suéter *m.* sweater (5)
suficiente enough; **lo suficiente** enough (16)
sufijo suffix (*gram.*)
sufrir to suffer (17); **sufrir muchas presiones** to be under a lot of pressure (17)
sugerencia suggestion

sugerido/a suggested
Suiza Switzerland
sujeto *n.* subject (*gram*); estar (*irreg.*) **sujeto/a a** to be subject to; *p. p.* held, grasped
suma sum; **en suma** in short
sumamente highly, extremely
sumar to total
sumario summary
superar to exceed
superlativo *n.* superlative (*gram.*)
superligero/a superlight
supermercado supermarket (6)
supersensible supersensitive
supiera: **habla como si lo supiera todo** he/she talks as if he/she knew everything
suplementario/a additional
suponer (*like* poner) to suppose
supuesto/a *p. p.* supposed; **por supuesto** of course
sur *m.* south
suroeste *m.* southwest
surtido supply
suscribir a (*p. p.* suscrito/a) to subscribe to
suscripción *f.* subscription
suspenso failing grade
sustantivo noun (*gram.*)
sustituto *n.* substitute
suyo/a(s) *poss.* your, of yours (*form. s., pl.*); his/her/its/their; of his/hers/theirs

T

tabaco tobacco
tabla chart, table
tacón *m.* heel
tal such (a); **con tal (de) que** provided that (22); **de tal forma** in such a way; **¿qué tal?** how are you doing? (P); **tal vez** perhaps
talonario de cheques checkbook (24)
talla size
taller *m.* (repair) shop (18); workshop
tamaño size
también also (P)
tampoco neither, not either (8)
tan as, so; **tan _____ como** as _____ as (6); **tan pronto como** as soon as (24)
tanque *m.* tank (18)
tanto/a as much; **tanto/a _____ como** as much _____ as (6); **tanto** *adv.* as, so much; **al tanto** up to date; **no es para tanto** it's no big deal
tantos/as as many; so many
tapa snack; hors d'oeuvres (*Sp.*)
tapizado/a upholstered with tapestry
taquilla ticket office (21)
tardar (en) to be late (in); to take time (in); **a más tardar** at the latest
tarde *n. f.* afternoon/evening (1); **buenas tardes** good afternoon/evening (P); **de la tarde** in the afternoon/evening (P); **por la tarde** in the afternoon/evening (2); **todas las tardes** every afternoon/evening; *adv.* late (2); **más tarde** later; **tarde o temprano** sooner or later

tarea homework (16); chore; **tarea doméstica** household chore

tarifa cost, rate

tarjeta card (8); **tarjeta de crédito** credit card (8); **tarjeta postal** postcard

tasa rate; **tasa de estacionamiento** parking fine

taxi *m.* taxicab (11); **parada de taxis** taxi stand

taxista *m., f.* taxicab driver

taza cup (17)

te *d. o.* you (*fam. s.*); *i. o.* (to/for) you (*fam. s.*); *refl. pron.* yourself (*fam. s.*)

té *m.* tea (9)

teatro theater (21)

teclado keyboard

tecla key (*of computer, typewriter, etc.*) (19)

técnica technique

técnico/a technician

tecnología technology

tecnológico/a technological

techo ceiling; roof

tejado roof

tela cloth

telediario/a TV newsprogram

telefonear to telephone

telefónico/a *adj.* telephone; **guía telefónica** telephone book

teléfono telephone; **teléfono inalámbrico** cordless telephone

telégrafo telegraph

telegrama *m.* telegram

telenovela soap opera

tele(visión) *f.* television, TV

televisor *m.* television set (7)

tema *m.* theme, topic

temer to fear (12)

temeroso/a fearful

temor *m.* fear

temperatura temperature (16)

templado/a temperate, mild

temporada season; period of time

temporal temporary

temprano/a early (2); young; **tarde o temprano** sooner or later

tendido/a stretched, lying down

tenedor *m.* fork (8)

tener (*irreg.*) to have (5); **tener _____ años** to be _____ years old (4); **tener algo que decir/hacer** to have something to say/do (27); **tener calor/frío** to be/feel warm/cold (7); **tener cuidado (de)** to be careful (about) (21); **tener dolor de _____** to have pain in (16); **tener en cuenta** to keep/have in mind, take into account (23); **tener ganas de** + *inf.* to feel like (*doing something*) (5); **tener hambre** to be hungry (9); **tener lugar** to take place; **tener miedo (de)** to be afraid (of) (5); **tener prisa** to be in a hurry (5); **tener que** + *inf.* to have to (*do something*); **tener que ver con** to have to do with; **(no) tener razón** to be right (wrong) (5); **tener sed** to be thirsty (9); **tener sueño** to be sleepy (5)

tengo I have (4)

tenis *m. s.* tennis (22); *pl.* tennis shoes

tenista *m., f.* tennis player

tensión *f.* tension

tentativa *n.* attempt

tercer, tercero/a third (18); **tercer piso** fourth floor (third floor up) (13)

terminación *f.* ending (*gram.*)

terminar to finish, end; **terminar con** to put an end to

termómetro thermometer

termostato thermostat

terraza veranda

terremoto earthquake

terreno land, earth; **tantear el terreno** to get the lay of the land

territorio territory

terrorismo terrorism

terrorista *m., f.* terrorist

tersura smoothness

tertulia group of friends that meet on a regular basis

tesoro: Departamento de Tesoro Treasury Department

testigo/a witness (23)

tétano tetanus

texto text; **libro de texto** textbook (1)

ti *obj. of prep.* you (*fam. s.*)

tía aunt (4)

tiempo tense (*gram.*); time; weather (7); **a tiempo** on time (10); **de tiempo parcial** part-time (12); **hace buen/mal tiempo** it's good/bad weather (7); **¿qué tiempo hace?** what's the weather like? (7)

tienda shop, store (5)

tiene he/she/it has (4); you (*form. s.*) have (4)

tienes you have (*fam. s.*) (4)

tierra land, earth (19)

tigre *m.* tiger

timbre *m.* bell, buzzer

tímido/a timid, shy

tinta ink

tinto: vino tinto red wine (9)

tío uncle (4); *pl.* aunts and uncles

tipa gal (25); character (25)

típico/a typical

tipo type, kind; character (25); guy (25)

titulado/a with an academic degree

titular *m.* cardholder

título title, name; degree

toalla towel

tobillo ankle

tocar (qu) to touch; to play (*a musical instrument*) (7); to be obliged; **tocarle a uno** to be someone's turn (14)

todavía still, yet (5)

todo/a *n.* whole; all, everything; *pl.* everybody, all (of them); **de todo** everything (6); **sobre todo** above all; *adj.* all, every (3); **de todos modos** anyway; **todas las tardes/noches** every afternoon/evening; **todo derecho** straight ahead (11); **todo ello** all that; **todos los días** every day (2)

tolerante tolerant

tomar to take (2); to drink (2); to eat; **tomar el sol** to sunbathe (11); **tomar en cuenta** to take into account (23); **tomarle el pelo a alguien** to pull someone's leg; **tomarle la temperatura a alguien** to take someone's temperature

tomate *m.* tomato (9)

tonelada ton

tónico *n.* tonic, pick-me-up

tónico/a stressed, accented (*gram.*)

tono tone

tontería foolish thing (4)

tonto/a silly, foolish (3); stupid

torcer (ue) (z) to twist

tormenta storm

toro bull; **corrida de toros** bullfight; **plaza de toros** bullring

torpe clumsy (17)

torpeza clumsiness

torta cake

tortilla omelet (*Sp.*); round, flat, corn or wheat bread (*Mex., Central America*)

tortuga tortoise

tos *f. s.* cough (16)

toser to cough (16)

tostadas *f. pl.* toast

tostado/a brown; **pan** (*m.*) **tostado** toast

tostadora toaster (14)

total *m.* total; **en total** in all; **total que** the upshot is

toxina toxin

trabajador(a) *n.* worker; *adj.* hard-working (3); **trabajador(a) social** social worker (26)

trabajar to work (2)

trabajo work, job (12); written work (12); (term) paper (12)

tradición *f.* tradition

tradicional traditional

traducción *f.* translation

traducir (*like* **producir**) to translate

traductor(a) translator, interpreter

traer (*irreg.*) to bring (8)

tráfico traffic (18)

tragedia tragedy

trágico/a tragic

traje *m.* suit (5); **traje de baño** swim suit (5)

trama plot (*of play or novel*) (21)

tranquilidad *f.* tranquility

tranquilizante *m.* tranquilizer

tranquilo/a calm, peaceful (11)

transeúnte *n. m., f.* pedestrian

transición *f.* transition

tránsito traffic

transmisión *f.* transmission

transparente transparent

transpirar to perspire

transporte *m.* (means of) transportation (20)

tras after

trasladado/a transferred

traslado *n.* transfer

tratamiento treatment (16)

tratar to treat; **tratar de** + *inf.* to try to (*do something*); **tratarse de** to be a matter of

trato manner

través: a través de through, by means of

travieso/a mischievous

trayectoria path, course

trébol *m.* clover

trece thirteen (P)
treinta thirty (P)
tren *m.* train (11); **estación** (*f.*) **del tren** train station (11)
tres three (P)
trescientos/as three hundred (6)
tribu *f.* tribe
trigo wheat
trimestre *m.* (*school*) quarter
triste sad (5)
tristeza sadness
triturador (*m.*) **de basuras** garbage disposal
trofeo trophy (12)
trompeta trumpet
tu(s) *poss.* your (*fam. s.*) (6)
tú *sub. pron.* you (*fam. s.*); **¿y tú?** and you? (P)
tubería plumbing
tuerca: nut (*mechanical*)
tumba tomb
túnica tunic
turismo tourism
turista *n. m., f.* tourist
turístico/a *adj.* tourist; **clase** (*f.*) **turística** tourist class (10)
turno turn; **por turno** in turn
tuyo/a(s) *poss.* your, (of) yours (*fam. s.*)

U

u or (*used instead of* **o** *before words beginning with* **o** *or* **ho**)
ubicar (qu) to locate, place
últimamente lately
último/a *n.* the last one; *adj.* latest (23); last; final; **de última moda** the latest style; **la última vez** the last time; **por último** finally
un, uno/a one (P); a, an (*indefinite article*); **cada uno/a** each one
único/a unique; only
unido/a united; **los Estados Unidos** United States
unificación *f.* unification
unión *f.* union
unir to unite
universidad *f.* university (1)
universitario/a *adj.* university
urbanismo *n.* city planning
urbanístico/a *adj.* city planning
urbano/a urban
urbe *f.* city
urgencia emergency; **sala de urgencia** emergency room (16)
urgente urgent (12); **es urgente** it's urgent (12)
uruguayo/a Uruguayan
usado/a *p. p.* used
usar to use; to operate (*a machine*) (19)
uso *n.* use (19); **uso personal** personal use (27)
usted (Ud., Vd.) *sub. pron.* you (*form. s.*); *obj. of prep.* you (*form. s.*); **¿y usted?** and you? (P)
ustedes (Uds., Vds.) *sub. pron.* you (*form. pl.*); *obj. of prep.* you (*form. pl.*)
utensilio utensil (8)

útil useful; helpful; *pl.* equipment
utilizar (c) to use

V

vaca cow
vacación *f.* vacation; **estar** (*irreg.*) **de vacaciones** to be on vacation (11); **ir** (*irreg.*) **de vacaciones** to go on vacation (7)
vacilar: sin vacilar without hesitation
vacío/a empty
vacuna shot, vaccination
vainilla vanilla
válido/a correct, valid
valiente brave
valioso/a valuable
valor *m.* value
valle *f.* valley
vanidad *f.* vanity
vano: en vano in vain
vapor: buque (*m.*) **de vapor** steamboat
variación *f.* variation
variar to vary
variedad *f.* variety
varios/as various; several
varón *m.* male
vasallo vassal, servant
vasco/a Basque; **País** (*m. s.*) **Vasco** Basque region of Spain
vascuence *m.* Basque language
vaso (drinking) glass (8); **vaso para agua** water glass
vecino/a neighbor (13)
vegetación *f.* vegetation; plants
vegetariano/a vegetarian
vehículo vehicle
veinte twenty (P)
vela candle (8)
velocidad *f.* speed (18)
vemos: ¡nos vemos! (*from* **ver**) see you around! (5)
vendedor(a) salesperson (26)
vender to sell (5)
venezolano/a Venezuelan
venganza revenge
venir (*irreg.*) to come (5); **el año que viene** next year
venta sale
ventaja advantage (18)
ventana window (14); **lavar las ventanas** to wash the windows (14)
ventanilla small window (*in car, train, etc.*)
ventilación *f.* ventilation
ver (*irreg.*) to see (8); **a ver** let's see; **tener** (*irreg.*) **que ver con** to have to do with; **¡nos vemos!** see you around! (5)
veraneante *m., f.* vacationer
veraneo: de veraneo *adj.* summer (vacation)
veraniego/a *adj.* summer
verano summer (7)
verbo verb
verdad *f.* truth; **de verdad** really; **¿verdad?** right?, don't they (you, *etc.*)? (5)
verdadero/a real, true
verde green (5)

verdura vegetable (9)
verificar (qu) to verify
vermút *m.* vermouth
versánico/a insane, mad
versión *f.* version
verter (ie, i) to pour
vestido dress (5)
vestimenta *s.* attire, clothes
vestir (i, i) to dress (14); **vestirse** to get dressed (14)
veterinario/a veterinarian
vez *f.* (*pl.* **veces**) time, occasion; **a la vez** at the same time (18); **a veces** at times, sometimes (4); **de vez en cuando** from time to time; **dos veces** twice (4); **en vez de** instead of (24); **la primera/última vez** the first/last time; **muchas veces** frequently, a lot; **otra vez** again; **por primera vez** for the first time; **tal vez** perhaps; **una vez (a la semana/al mes)** once (a week/a month) (4)
vía road, route
viajar to travel (7); **viajar al/en el extranjero** to travel abroad; **he, has, ha viajado** I/you (*fam. s.*) have traveled, he/she/it has traveled (11)
viaje *m.* trip (10); **agente** (*m., f.*) **de viajes** travel agent; **de viaje** on a trip; **hacer** (*irreg.*) **un viaje** to take a trip (7)
viajero/a traveler (27)
via road, route
vibrar to vibrate
víctima *m., f.* victim
vida life (47); **llevar una vida _____** to lead a _____ life (16)
vídeo video; **equipamento de vídeos** video equipment; **grabador** (*m.*) **de vídeo** video recorder, VCR (12)
viejo/a *n.* old man/woman (3); *adj.* old (3); **Noche** (*f.*) **Vieja** New Year's Eve (15)
viene: el año que viene next year; **la semana que viene** next week
viento wind; **contra viento y marea** against all odds; **hace viento** it's windy (7)
viernes *m. s.* Friday (6)
vietnamita *m., f.* Vietnamese
vigilancia vigilance, patrolling
villanía villany
vínculo tie, link
vino (blanco/tinto) (white/red) wine (9)
violencia violence
violento/a violent
violín *m.* violin
violinista *m., f.* violinist
violoncelo cello
virgen *f.* virgin; *adj.* untouched
visado visa (*Sp.*)
visión *f.* vision
visita visit; visitor, guest (13)
visitante *m., f.* visitor
visitar to visit (21)
vista view (13); **punto de vista** point of view
vitamina vitamin
viudo/a widower/widow
vivienda *n.* housing (20)
vivir to live (4)
vivo/a lively; clever; live (*broadcast*)

vocabulario vocabulary
vocal *f.* vowel
volador: objeto volador no identificado (OVNI) UFO
volante *m.* steering wheel; **al volante** at the wheel
volar (ue) to fly (11)
volcán *m.* volcano
vólibol *m.* volleyball (22)
volumen *m.* volume (*sound*)
voluntad *f.* will; choice; desire
volver (ue) (*p. p.* **vuelto/a**) to return (7); **volver a** + *inf.* to do (*something*) again (8); **volverse loco/a** to go mad
vosotros/as *sub. pron.* you (*fam. pl., Sp.*); *obj. of prep.* you (*fam. pl., Sp.*)

votante *m., f.* voter
votar to vote (23)
voz *f.* (*pl.* **voces**) voice; **en voz alta** in a loud voice
vuelo flight (10)
vuelto/a *p. p.* returned; **dar** (*irreg.*) **una vuelta** to take a walk; **de ida y vuelta** round-trip
vuestro/a(s) *poss.* your (*fam. pl., Sp.*) (6); (of) yours (*fam. pl., Sp.*)

Y

y and (P)
ya already (5); now; **ya no** no longer (5); **ya que** since, seeing that

yate *m.* yacht
yelmo helmet
yerba grass; herb
yoga *m.* yoga
yogur *m.* yogurt

Z

zanahoria carrot (9)
zapatería shoe store
zapato shoe (5)
zona zone, area
zoo zoo

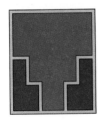

ENGLISH-SPANISH VOCABULARY

A

able: to be able **poder** (*irreg.*)
above all **sobre todo**
abroad **en el/al extranjero**; to travel abroad **viajar en el/al extranjero**
absent: to be absent (lacking) **faltar**
absent-minded **distraído/a**
accelerated **acelerado/a**
accompany **acompañar**
account **cuenta**; checking account **cuenta corriente**; savings account **cuenta de ahorros**; to take into account **tomar, tener** (*irreg.*) **en cuenta**
ache *v.* **doler (ue)**
activity **actividad** *f.*
additional **adicional**
address *n.* **dirección** *f.*
advance: (. . . days) in advance **con (... días) de anticipación**
advantage **ventaja**
advice **consejo**
advisor **consejero/a**
aerobic: to do aerobic exercises **hacer** (*irreg.*) (*p.p.* **hecho/a**) **ejercicios aeróbicos**
affectionate **cariñoso/a**
afraid: to be afraid (of) **tener** (*irreg.*) **miedo (de)**
after *prep.* (*with time*) **después de**; *conj.* **después (de) que**
afternoon **tarde** *f.*; good afternoon **buenas tardes**; in the afternoon **de/por la tarde**
afterward **después**

again **otra vez**; to do (*something*) again **volver (ue) a** (+ *inf.*)
ago: (*time*) ago **hace** + (*time*) (+ *preterite*)
agreement: to be in agreement (with) **estar** (*irreg.*) **de acuerdo (con)**
ahead: straight ahead **todo derecho**
air **aire** *m.*
air conditioner **aire acondicionado** *m.*
airplane **avión** *m.*
airport **aeropuerto**
alarm clock **despertador** *m.*
all *adj.* **todo/a**
allow **permitir**
almost **casi**
already **ya**
also **también**
although **aunque**
always **siempre**
among **entre**
amuse **divertir (ie, i)**
and **y**
angry **furioso/a**; to get angry **enojarse**
announce **anunciar**
another **otro/a**
answer *v.* **contestar**; *n.* **respuesta**
antibiotic **antibiótico**
any **algún, alguno/a**
anything: not anything **nada**
apple **manzana**
appliance **aparato**; household appliance **aparato doméstico**
applicant **aspirante** *m., f.*
application (form) **solicitud** *f.*

appointment: to have an appointment **estar** (*irreg.*) **citado/a**
April **abril** *m.*
aquarium **acuario**
argue **discutir**
arm **brazo**
armchair **sillón** *m.*
arrival **llegada**
arrive **llegar (gu)**
as: as . . . as **tan ... como**; as if **como si** + *past subj.*; as much/many . . . as **tanto/a/os/as ... como**; as soon as **en cuanto, tan pronto como**
ask **preguntar**; to ask a question **hacer** (*irreg.*) (*p.p.* **hecho/a**) **una pregunta**; to ask for **pedir (i,i)**
asleep: to fall asleep **dormirse (ue, u)**
aspirin **aspirina**
assassination **asesinato**
at **en**; (*with time*) **a**; at least **por lo menos**
attend **asistir (a)**
August **agosto**
automobile **automóvil** *m.*
avoid **evitar**

B

back then **en aquel entonces**
backpack *n.* **mochila**
bad **mal, malo/a**; it's bad weather **hace mal tiempo**; what bad luck! **¡qué mala suerte!**
badly **mal**
bag (suitcase) **maleta**

baggage **equipaje** *m.*
ball **pelota**
ballpoint pen **bolígrafo**
banana **banana**
bank **banco**
bankbook **libreta de ahorros**
bargain *v.* **regatear;** *n.* **ganga;** It was a bargain. **Fue una ganga.**
baseball **béisbol** *m.*
basketball **básquetbol** *m.*
bathe **bañar;** to take a bath **bañarse**
bathroom **baño**
bathtub **bañera**
battery **batería**
be **ser** *(irreg.);* **estar** *(irreg.);* to be _____ years old **tener** *(irreg.)* _____ **años;** to be (feel) hungry/thirsty **tener hambre/sed**
beach **playa**
bean **frijol** *m.*
beautiful **bello/a**
because **porque**
become **hacerse** *(irreg.)* *(p.p.* **hecho/a);** **ponerse** *(irreg.);* *(p.p.* **puesto/a)** **llegar (gu) a ser**
bed **cama;** to go to bed **acostarse (ue);** to make the bed **hacer** *(irreg.)* *(p.p.* **hecho/a) la cama;** to put to bed **acostar (ue);** to stay in bed **guardar cama;** water bed **cama de agua**
bedroom **alcoba**
beer **cerveza**
before *(with time) prep.* **antes de;** *conj.* **antes (de) que**
begin **empezar (ie) (c);** to begin to *(do something)* **empezar a** + *inf.*
behave (well/badly) **portarse (bien/mal)**
behind *prep.* **detrás de**
believe (in) **creer (y) (en)**
bellhop **botones** *m. s.;* **mozo**
beloved **querido/a**
belt **cinturón** *m.*
besides **además (de)**
best **mejor**
better **mejor**
between **entre**
beverage **bebida**
bicycle **bicicleta**
big **gran, grande**
bike: to ride a bike **pasear en bicicleta**
bill *(restaurant)* **cuenta; factura**
bird **pájaro**
birth **nacimiento**
birthday **cumpleaños** *m. s.*
bit: a little bit **un poco**
black **negro/a**
blond(e) *adj.* **rubio/a**
blouse **blusa**
blue **azul**
board: room and full board **pensión** *(f.)* **completa;**
boardinghouse **pensión** *f.*
boat **barco**
body **cuerpo**
bomb **bomba**
book **libro;** textbook **libro de texto**
bookshelf **estante** *m.*

bookstore **librería**
boot **bota**
border *(political)* **frontera**
bored **aburrido/a**
boring **pesado/a**
borrow **pedir (i, i) prestado/a**
boss **jefe/a**
bottle **botella**
box office **taquilla**
boy **niño**
brakes **frenos**
branch (office) **sucursal** *f.*
bread **pan** *m.*
break **romper** *(p.p.* **roto/a)**
breakfast **desayuno;** to have breakfast **desayunar**
breathe **respirar**
bring **traer** *(irreg.)*
broken **roto/a**
brother **hermano**
brown **pardo/a**
brunette *adj.* **moreno/a**
budget *n.* **presupuesto**
build **construir (y)**
building **edificio;** building manager **portero/a**
bump into **darse** *(irreg.)* **con**
bureau *(furniture)* **cómoda**
bus **autobús** *m. s.;* bus station **estación** *(f.)* **de autobuses**
business (enterprise) **comercio; empresa**
businessman/woman **hombre** *(m.)* **/mujer** *(f.)* **de negocios**
busy **ocupado/a**
but **pero**
buy **comprar**
by **por;** by check **con cheque**

C

café **café** *m.*
cake **pastel** *m.*
calculator **calculadora**
call *v.* **llamar**
called: to be called **llamarse**
calm **tranquilo/a**
camping: to go camping **hacer** *(irreg.)* *(p.p.* **hecho/a)** *camping*
can *v.* **poder** *(irreg.)*
candidate **aspirante** *m., f.*
candle **vela**
car **automóvil** *m.,* **coche** *m.*
card **tarjeta;** credit card **tarjeta de crédito;** postcard **tarjeta postal;** play cards **jugar (ue) (gu) a las cartas**
career **carrera**
careful: to be careful **tener** *(irreg.)* **cuidado**
carrot **zanahoria**
carry **llevar;** to carry down **bajar**
cash *v. (a check)* **cobrar;** (in) cash **(con) dinero en efectivo**
cashier **cajero/a**
cat **gato/a**
catch a cold **resfriarse**
celebrate **celebrar**

certain: it's certain **es cierto;** to be certain **estar** *(irreg.)* **seguro/a**
chair **silla**
chalkboard **pizarra**
change *v.* **cambiar (de);** to change *(location/ residence)* **mudarse**
channel *(T.V.)* **canal** *m.*
character **tipo/a**
charge *v. (someone for an item or service)* **cobrar;** *(to an account)* **cargar (gu)**
cheap **barato/a**
check *v.* **revisar;** *(baggage)* **facturar;** *n.* **cheque** *m.;* *(traveler's)* check **cheque de viajero;** *(restaurant)* **cuenta;** by check **con cheque**
checkbook **talonario de cheques**
checking account **cuenta corriente**
cheese **queso**
chef **cocinero/a**
chess: to play chess **jugar (ue) (gu) al ajedrez**
chicken **pollo**
child: **hijo/a; niño/a;** as a child **de niño/a**
Chinese *(language)* **chino**
chop: (pork) chop **chuleta (de cerdo)**
chore (household) **quehacer** *m.* **(doméstico)**
Christmas **Navidad** *f.;* Christmas Eve **Nochebuena**
citizen **ciudadano/a**
city **ciudad** *f.*
civic **cívico/a**
class **clase** *f.;* first class **primera clase;** tourist class **clase turística**
clean *v.* **limpiar;** to clean the (whole) house **limpiar la casa (entera);** *adj.* **limpio/a**
clear: it's clear **está claro**
clerk **dependiente/a**
clever **listo/a**
client **cliente** *m., f.*
climate **clima** *m.*
clock: alarm clock **despertador** *m.*
close *v.* **cerrar (ie);** *prep.* close (to) **cerca (de)**
closed **cerrado/a**
clothes dryer **secadora**
clothing *n.* **ropa**
cloudy: it's cloudy (weather) **está nublado**
clumsy **torpe**
coat *n.* **abrigo**
coffee **café** *m.;*
coffee shop **café** *m.*
coffeepot **cafetera**
cold *(illness)* **resfriado;** it's cold (weather) **hace frío;** to be cold **tener** *(irreg.)* **frío;** to get/catch a cold **resfriarse**
collide (with) **chocar (qu) (con)**
collision **choque** *m.*
color **color** *m.*
come **venir** *(irreg.);* come in **pase(n) Ud(s).** *form.*
comedy **comedia**
comfort **comodidad** *f.*
comfortable **cómodo/a;** to be comfortable (temperature) **estar** *(irreg.)* **bien**
committed (booked up) **citado/a**
communicate (with) **comunicarse (qu) (con)**
compact disc (player) **compact disc** *m.*
complain (about) **quejarse (de)**

computer (*L.A.*) **computadora**; (*Sp.*) **ordenador** *m.*; computer disc **disco**; computer language **lenguaje** *m.*
computer science **computación** *f.*
conditioner: air conditioner **aire acondicionador** *m.*
confirm **confirmar**
congested **congestionado/a**
congratulations **felicidades**
conserve **conservar**
contact lens **lente** (*m.*) (**de contacto**)
contain **contener** (*like* **tener**)
contaminate **contaminar**
content *adj.* **contento/a**
continue **seguir (i,i) (g)**; to continue (*doing something*) **seguir** + *present participle*
convertible *adj.* (*with cars*) **descapotable**
cook *v.* **cocinar**; *n.* **cocinero/a**
cookie **galleta**
cool: it's cool (weather) **hace fresco**
corporation **empresa**
cost *v.* **costar (ue)**
cotton **algodón** *m.*
cough *v.* **toser**; *n.* **tos** *f.*; cough syrup **jarabe** *m.*
could you . . . ? **¿podría Ud.... ?**
country **país** *m. s.*; country(side) **campo**
course **curso**; of course **cómo no**
court: (tennis) court **cancha**
cover *v.* **cubrir** (*p.p.* **cubierto/a**); to cover (territory, miles) **recorrer**
cracker **galleta**
credit card **tarjeta de crédito**
crime **delito**
cross *v.* **cruzar (c)**
cruise **crucero**; cruise ship **crucero**
cry **llorar**
cup **taza**
custard **flan** *m.*
customs **aduana** *s.*; customs duty **derechos** (*pl.*) **de aduana**; customs inspector **inspector(a) de aduanas**

D

daily **cotidiano/a**
dance *v.* **bailar**
dangerous **peligroso/a**
data processing **informática**
date (*calendar*) **fecha**; to have a date **estar** (*irreg.*) **citado/a**
daughter **hija**
day **día** *m.*; day after tomorrow **pasado mañana**; day before yesterday **anteayer**; every day **todos los días**
dear **querido/a**
December **diciembre** *m.*
declare **declarar**
delay *n.* **demora**
deluxe hotel **hotel** (*m.*) **de lujo**
dense **denso/a**
deny **negar (ie) (gu)**
department store **almacén** *m.*

deposit *v.* **ingresar, depositar**
desert **desierto**
design programs **diseñar programas**
desk **escritorio**; front desk (*hotel*) **recepción** *f.*
dessert **postre** *m.*
destroy **destruir (y)**
detail **detalle** *m.*
develop **desarrollar**
dictator **dictador(a)**
dictionary **diccionario**
die **morir(se) (ue, u)** (*p.p.* **muerto/a**)
diet: to be on a diet **estar** (*irreg.*) **a dieta**; to eat a well-balanced diet **comer equilibradamente**
difficult **difícil**
dining room **comedor** *m.*
dinner **cena**; to have dinner **cenar**
director **director(a)**; director of personnel **director(a) de personal**
dirty **sucio/a**
disadvantage **desventaja**
disaster **desastre** *m.*
disc: compact disc (player) **compact disc** *m.*; computer disc **disco**
discover **descubrir** (*p.p.* **descubierto/a**)
discuss **discutir**
dish **plato**
do **hacer** (*irreg.*) (*p.p.* **hecho/a**); to do (*something*) again **volver (ue) a** (+ *inf.*)
doctor (*medical*) **médico/a**
dog **perro/a**
door **puerta**
doorperson **portero/a**
dormitory **residencia**
doubt *v.* **dudar**
downtown **centro**
dress *v.* **vestir (i, i)**; *n.* **vestido**
dressed: to get dressed **vestirse (i, i)**
drink *v.* **beber; tomar**; *n.* **bebida**; soft drink **refresco**
drive *v.* **manejar; conducir** (*irreg.*)
drugstore **farmacia**
dryer: clothes dryer **secadora**
dubbed **doblado/a**
during **durante**
dust *v.* **sacudir**
duty: customs duty **derechos** (*pl.*) **de aduana**

E

each **cada** (*inv.*)
early **temprano/a**; to get up early **madrugar (gu)**
earn (*a salary*) **ganar**
earth **tierra**
Easter **Pascua (Florida)**
easy **fácil**
eat **comer**; to eat a well-balanced diet **comer equilibradamente**
economize **economizar (c)**
egg **huevo**
eight **ocho**
eighteen **dieciocho**
eighth **octavo/a**

eighty **ochenta**
either: not either **tampoco**
electricity **luz** *f.* (*pl.* **luces**)
eleven **once**
embarrassed **avergonzado/a**
emergency room **sala de emergencias/urgencia**
employee **empleado/a**
employment office **Dirección** (*f.*) **de Personal**
enchant **encantar**
end table **mesita**
energy **energía**
English (*language*) **inglés** *m.*
enjoy: to enjoy oneself **divertirse (ie, i)**; enjoy your meal **que aproveche(n)** *form.*
enough **lo suficiente**
entertain **divertir (ie, i)**
enthusiast **aficionado/a**
environment **medio ambiente** *m.*
equality **igualdad** *f.*
especially **sobre todo**
Eve: Christmas Eve **Nochebuena**; New Year's Eve **Noche** (*f.*) **Vieja**
evening **tarde** *f.*; **noche** *f.*; good evening **buenas tardes/noches**; in the evening **de/por la tarde/noche**
event **acontecimiento**
every *adj.* **cada** *inv.*; **todo/a**; every day **todos los días**
everything **de todo**
examine **examinar**; (*search*) **registrar**
excellent **excelente**
exciting: to be exciting to one **encantarle a uno**
excuse me (*to apologize*) **perdón**; (*to get through*) **con permiso**
exercise *v.* **hacer** (*irreg.*) (*p.p.* **hecho/a**) **ejercicio**; to do aerobic exercises **hacer ejercicios aeróbicos**; *n.* **ejercicio**
expend **gastar**
expense **gasto**
expensive **caro/a**
explain **explicar (qu)**
exploit **explotar**
eye **ojo**

F

factory **fábrica**
fall *v.* **caer** (*irreg.*); to fall asleep **dormirse (ue, u)**; to fall down **caerse**; *n.* (*season*) **otoño**
family *n.* **familia**; *adj.* **familiar**
fan (*enthusiast*) (*of*) **aficionado/a (a)**
far from **lejos de**
farm *n.* **finca**
farm worker **campesino/a**
fat *adj.* **gordo/a**
father **padre** *m.*
fear *v.* **temer**
February **febrero**
feel **sentirse (ie, i)**; to feel like (*doing something*) **tener** (*irreg.*) **ganas de** (+ *inf.*); to feel sorry **sentir**
fever **fiebre** *f.*
few **poco/a**

field (playing) **campo**
fifteen **quince**
fifth **quinto/a**
fifty **cincuenta**
fight *v.* **luchar**
fill (up) **llenar**; to fill out (*a form*) **llenar**
finally **finalmente**
find **encontrar (ue)**; to find out (about) **enterarse (de)**
fine *n.* **multa**; *adv.* it's fine **está bien**
finish **acabar**
fire *v.* (dismiss) **despedir (i, i)**
first *adj.* **primer, primero/a**; first class **primera clase** *f.*; first name **nombre** *m.*; the first of . . . **el primero de...**
fish (*alive*) **pez** *m.* (*pl.* **peces**); (*prepared as food*) **pescado**
five **cinco**
fix **arreglar**
fixed price **precio fijo**
flat tire **llanta desinflada**
flight **vuelo**
flight attendant **auxiliar** (*m.*) **de vuelo**; **azafata**
floor: ground floor, first floor **planta baja**
flower **flor** *f.*
fly *v.* **volar (ue)**
follow **seguir (i, i) (g)**
following *adj.* **siguiente**
food **la comida**
foolish **tonto/a**
foot **pie** *m.*
football **fútbol** (*m.*) **norteamericano**
for **para**; **por**
forbid **prohibir**
foreigner **extranjero/a**
forget **olvidar**; to forget (about) **olvidarse (de)**
fork **tenedor** *m.*
form **forma**; (application) **solicitud** *f.*; (*to fill out*) **planilla**
forty **cuarenta**
four **cuatro**
fourteen **catorce**
fourth **cuarto/a**
free **desocupado/a**
free time **ratos libres**
freedom **libertad** *f.*
freeway **autopista**
freezer **congelador** *m.*
French (*language*) **francés** *m. s.*; French fried potato **papa frita**
frequently **con frecuencia**
Friday **viernes** *m. s.*
friend **amigo/a**
from **de**; from time to time **de vez en cuando**
front: in front of **delante de**
front desk (*hotel*) **recepción** *f.*
frontier **frontera**
fruit **fruta**
fun *adj.* **divertido/a**
function *v.* **funcionar**
furniture **muebles** *m. pl.*

G

gain weight **engordar**

game (card, board) **juego**; (match) **partido**
garage **garaje** *m.*
gas **gas** *m. s.*; gas station **estación** (*f.*) **de gasolina, gasolinera**
gasoline **gasolina**
German (*language*) **alemán** *m.*
get (obtain) **conseguir (i, i) (g)**; (become) **ponerse** (*irreg.*) (*p.p.* **puesto/a**); to get a job **colocarse (qu)**; to get married (to) **casarse (con)**; to get off, down (from) **bajar (de)**; to get on (*a vehicle*) **subir (a)**; to get sick **enfermarse**; to get together (with) **reunirse (con)**; to get up **levantarse**; to get up early **madrugar (qu)**; to get up on the wrong side of the bed **levantarse con el pie izquierdo**
girl **niña**
give **dar** (*irreg.*); to give (*as a gift*) **regalar**; to give a party **dar/hacer** (*irreg.*) (*p.p.* **hecho/a**) **una fiesta**; to give (*someone*) a shot, injection **ponerle** (*irreg.*) (*p.p.* **puesto/a**) **una inyección** (f.)
glass (drinking) **vaso**
glasses (prescription) **gafas**
go **ir** (*irreg.*); to be going to (*do something*) **ir a** (+ *inf.*); to go away **irse**; to go home **regresar a casa**; to go on vacation **ir de vacaciones**; to go out **salir** (*irreg.*); to go shopping **ir de compras**; to go to (*a class, function*) **asistir (a)**; to go to bed **acostarse (ue)**
goblet **copa**
golf **golf** *m.*
good **buen, bueno/a**; it's good weather **hace buen tiempo**
good-bye **adiós**; to say good-bye (to) **despedirse (i, i) (de)**
good-looking **guapo/a**
govern **gobernar (ie)**
government **gobierno**
graduate (from) (as a) **graduarse (en) (de)**
grandfather **abuelo**
grandmother **abuela**
grandparents **abuelos**
gray **gris**
great **gran, grande**
green **verde**
greet **saludar**
ground **tierra**
guest **huésped(a)**
gym, gymnasium **gimnasio**

H

half: it's half past . . . **es la.../ son las... y media**
ham **jamón** *m.*
hamburger **hamburguesa**
hand *n.* **mano** *f.*; to hand in/over **entregar (gu)**
handsome **guapo/a**
happening *n.* **acontecimiento**
happy **feliz** (*pl.* **felices**); **alegre, contento/a**
hard (difficult) **difícil**
hard-working **trabajador(a)**

hat **sombrero**
have **tener** (*irreg.*); to have a date/appointment **estar** (*irreg.*) **citado/a**; to have a bad time **pasarlo mal**; to have a good time **pasarlo bien**; **divertirse (ie, i)**; to have a pain (in) **tener dolor (de)**; to have a party **dar** (*irreg.*)/**hacer** (*irreg.*) (*p.p.* **hecho/a**) **una fiesta**; to have breakfast **desayunar**; to have dinner **cenar**; to have in mind **tomar/tener en cuenta**; to have just (*done something*) **acabar de** (+ *inf.*); to have lunch **almorzar (ue) (c)**; to have something to (say, do) **tener algo que (decir** (*irreg.*) (*p.p.* **dicho/a**), **hacer)**; to have stopovers **hacer escalas**; to have to (*do something*) **tener que** (+ *inf.*)
he **él**
head **cabeza**
health **salud** *f.*
healthy **sano/a**
hear **oír** (*irreg.*)
heart **corazón** *m.*
heat(ing) **gas** *m. s.*
hello **hola**
help *v.* **ayudar**
her *poss.* **su(s)**
here **aquí**
highway **carretera**
him **él**
his *poss.* **su(s)**
history **historia**
hit **pegar (gu)**
hockey **hockey** *m.*
hold **contener** (*like* **tener**)
holiday **día** (*m.*) **festivo**
home **casa**: at home **en casa**; to go home **regresar a casa**
homework **tarea**
hope **esperar**; I hope that (*something happens*) **ojalá (que)** + *present subj.*; I hope you have a good time **que lo pases bien**; **que te diviertas**; *n.* **esperanza**
hors d'oeuvres **tapas**
hot: it's hot (weather) **hace calor**
to be/feel hot **tener** (*irreg.*) **calor**
hotel **hotel** *m.*; deluxe hotel **hotel de lujo**
hour **hora**
house **casa**
household *adj.* **doméstico/a**
housing *n.* **vivienda**
how **¿cómo?**; how are you? **¿cómo está(s)?**; **¿qué tal?**; how many **¿cuántos/as?**; how much **¿cuánto/a?**;
hundred **cien, ciento**
hungry: to be hungry **tener** (*irreg.*) **hambre**
hurry: to be in a hurry **tener** (*irreg.*) **prisa**
hurt **doler (ue)**; to hurt oneself **hacerse** (*irreg.*) (*p.p.* **hecho/a**) **daño**
husband **esposo**

I

ice **hielo**
ice cream **helado**
if **si**
illness **enfermedad** *f.*

immediately **en seguida**
immigration **inmigración** *f.*
impatient **impaciente**
important **importante**
impression: to make a good/bad impression on someone **caerle** (*irreg.*) **bien/mal a alguien**
in **en;** in case **en caso de que;** in front of **delante de;** in order to **para**
increase *v.* **aumentar;** *n.* **aumento**
incredible **increíble;** it is incredible **es increíble**
inequality **desigualdad** *f.*
inexpensive **barato/a**
inform **informar**
injection **inyección** *f.;* to give (*someone*) a shot **ponerle** (*irreg.*) (*p.p.* **puesto/a**) **una inyección**
insist: to insist (*on doing something*) **insistir** (**en** + *inf.*)
inspector (customs) **inspector(a) (de aduanas)**
installments: in installments **a plazos**
instead of **en vez de**
intend to (*do something*) **pensar (ie)** (+ *inf.*)
interesting: to be interesting to (*someone*) **interesarle a uno**
interrogative **interrogativo/a**
interview *v.* **entrevistar**
interviewer **entrevistador(a)**
inventory **inventario**
iron *v.* **planchar**
is (*located*) **está**
Italian (*language*) **italiano**

J

jacket **chaqueta**
January **enero**
Japanese (*language*) **japonés** *m. s.*
jeans **bluejeans** *m. pl.*
job **trabajo, puesto;** to get a job **colocarse (qu)**
joke **chiste** *m.*
juice **jugo**
July **julio**
June **junio**
just: to have just (*done something*) **acabar de** (+ *inf.*)

K

keep in mind **tomar/tener** (*irreg.*) **en cuenta;** keep on (*doing something*) **seguir (i, i) (g)** + *pres. participle*
key **llave** *f.;* (*of computer, typewriter*) **tecla**
keyboard **teclado**
kind *adj.* **amable**
kitchen **cocina**
knife **cuchillo**
know **conocer (zc)** (*someone*); **saber** (*irreg.*) (*a fact; how to*)

L

lacking: to be lacking **faltar**
lamp **lámpara**

land *v.* **aterrizar (c)**
landlady **dueña**
landlord **dueño**
language **lengua;** computer language **lenguaje** *m.*
large **gran, grande**
last *adj.* (*in time*) **pasado/a;** last name **apellido;** last night **anoche**
late: to be late **llegar (gu) tarde;** *adv.* **tarde;** *adj.* **atrasado/a**
later **más tarde; después**
latest (*most recent*) **último/a**
laugh (at) **reírse (i, i) (de)**
law **ley** *f.*
lawyer **abogado/a**
lazy **perezoso/a**
lead: to lead a . . . life **llevar una vida... ;** to lead to a seat **sentar (ie)**
learn **aprender**
least: at least **por lo menos**
leave **salir** (*irreg.*); **irse** (*irreg.*); to leave (*behind*) **dejar; quedar**
left: to be left **quedar;** to the left of **a la izquierda de**
leg **pierna**
less . . . than **menos... que**
lettuce **lechuga**
liberty **libertad** *f.*
librarian **bibliotecario/a**
library **biblioteca**
life **vida**
lift *v.* **levantar**
light *n.* **luz** *f.* (*pl.* **luces**)
like **gustarse;** do you like . . . ? **¿te (le) gusta... ?;** no, I don't like . . . **no, no me gusta... ;** yes, I like . . . **sí, me gusta... ;**
likeable **simpático/a**
line **cola;** to stand in line **hacer** (*irreg.*) (*p.p.* **hecho/a**) **cola**
listen (to) **escuchar**
literature **literatura**
little *adv.* **poco;** *adj.* (*amount*) **poco/a;** a little bit **un poco**
live *v.* **vivir**
living room **sala**
loan *n.* **préstamo**
lobster **langosta**
lodging **alojamiento**
long **largo/a**
longer: no longer **ya no**
look (at) **mirar;** to look for **buscar (qu)**
lose **perder (ie)**
lot: a lot *adv.* **mucho; bastante;** a lot of *adj.* **mucho/a**
luck: what bad luck! **¡qué mala suerte!**
luggage **equipaje** *m.*
lunch **almuerzo;** to have lunch **almorzar (ue) (c)**
lungs **pulmones** *m. pl.*

M

madam **señora (Sra.)**
made: it is made of . . . cotton/silk/wool **es de... algodón** *m.***/seda/lana**

magazine **revista**
maid **criada**
make **hacer** (*irreg.*) (*p.p.* **hecho/a**); to make a good/bad impression on someone **caerle** (*irreg.*) **bien/mal a alguien;** to make a mistake **equivocarse (qu);** to make plans to (*do something*) **hacer planes para** (+ *inf.*); to make stopovers **hacer escalas;** to make the bed **hacer la cama**
mall: shopping mall **centro comercial**
man **hombre** *m.*
manager **gerente** *m. f.;* **director(a);** building manager **portero/a**
many: how many? **¿cuántos/as?**
March **marzo**
market(place) **mercado;** outdoor marketplace **mercado al aire libre**
married **casado/a**
marry **casarse (con)**
match (*game*) **partido**
material **material** *m.*
mathematics **matemáticas** *f. pl.*
matter *n.* **cuestión** *f.*
May **mayo**
meal **comida;** enjoy your meal **que aproveche(n)** (*form.*); room and breakfast plus one other meal **media pensión** *f.*
means of transportation **medios de transporte** *m.*
meat **carne** *f.*
mechanic **mecánico/a**
medical office **consultorio**
medicine **medicina**
meet **conocer (zc)**
memory **memoria**
menu **menú** *m.*
merchant **comerciante** *m., f.*
microcomputer **microcomputadora**
microwave oven **(horno de) microonda**
milk **leche** *f.*
million **millón** *m.*
mind: to have in mind **tomar/tener** (*irreg.*) **en cuenta**
mineral water **agua** *f.* (*but* **el**) **mineral**
mirror **espejo**
miss *v.* (*a function*) **perder (ie);** *n.* (*title*) **señorita (Srta.)**
mistake: to make a mistake **equivocarse (qu)**
model **modelo**
mom **mamá**
Monday **lunes** *m. s.*
money **dinero**
monitor **monitor** *m.*
month **mes** *m. s.;* once a month **una vez al mes;** twice a month **dos veces al mes**
more **más;** more . . . than **más... que**
morning: good morning **buenos días;** in the morning **de/por la mañana**
mother **madre** *f.*
motorcycle **motocicleta**
mountain **montaña**
mouth **boca**
move **mudarse**
movie **película;** movie theater **cine** *m.*
Mr. **señor (Sr.)** *m.*
Mrs. **señora (Sra.)**

much **mucho**; how much? **¿cuánto/a?**
murder **asesinato**
museum: to visit a museum **visitar un museo**
must (*do something*) **deber** (+ *inf.*)
my *poss.* **mi(s)**; my name is . . . **me llamo...**

N

name (first) **nombre** *m.*; (last) **apellido**; my
  name is . . . **me llamo...**
named: to be named **llamarse**
napkin **servilleta**
nation **país** *m. s.*
nationality **nacionalidad** *f.*
natural disaster **desastre** (*m.*) **natural**
natural resource **recurso natural**
nature **naturaleza**
nauseated **mareado/a**
near *prep.* **cerca de**
necessary **preciso**; it is necessary **es preciso**
need *v.* **necesitar**
neighbor **vecino/a**
neighborhood **barrio**
neither **tampoco**
nervous **nervioso/a**
net **red** *f.*
never **nunca, jamás**
new **nuevo/a**
New Year's Eve **Noche** (*f.*) **Vieja**
news **noticias** *f. pl.*; **novedades** *f. pl.*; newscast **noticiero**; piece of news **noticia**; the
  bad news **lo malo**; the good news **lo bueno**
next *adv.* **luego**; (*in order*) **siguiente**; *adj.* (*in
  time*) **próximo/a**; next week **la próxima
  semana**; next (Tuesday, *etc.*) **el próximo
  (martes, etcétera)**
nice **amable**; **simpático/a**
night **noche** *f.*; at night **de/por la noche**; good
  night **buenas noches**; last night **anoche**
nine **nueve**
ninety **noventa**
ninth **noveno/a**
no *adv.* **no**; *adj.* **ningún, ninguno/a**; no longer
  ya no; no one *pron.* **nadie**
nobody **nadie**
noise **ruido**
none **ningún, ninguno/a**
nonsmoking section **sección** (*f.*) **de no fumar**
North American *n.* + *adj.* **norteamericano/a**
nose **nariz** *f.*
not any **ningún, ninguno/a**; not anybody
  nadie; not anything **nada**; not either
  tampoco
notebook **cuaderno**
nothing **nada**
noun **sustantivo**
November **noviembre** *m.*
now **ahora**; right now **en la actualidad; ahora
  mismo**
nurse **enfermero/a**

O

obey **obedecer (zc)**
obtain **conseguir (i,i) (g)**

ocean **océano**
o'clock: it's . . . o'clock **es la... /son las... en
  punto**
October **octubre** *m.*
of **de**; of course **cómo no**
offer **ofrecer (zc)**
office **oficina**; box office **taquilla**; branch
  office **sucursal** *f.*; employment office
  Direccion (*f.*) **de Personal**; medical office
  consultorio
oil **aceite** *m.*
okay: it's okay **está bien**
old **viejo/a**
older **mayor**
on: on the other hand **en cambio**; on time **a
  tiempo**; on top of **encima de**
once **una vez**; once a week **una vez a la
  semana**; twice a week **dos veces a la
  semana**
one **un, uno/a**
one-way ticket **billete** (*m.*) **/boleto de ida**
only *adv.* **sólo**
open *v.* **abrir** (*p.p.* **abierto/a**)
open(ed) *adj.* **abierto/a**
operate **funcionar**; (*a machine*) **manejar, usar**
operation (*of a machine*) **manejo, uso**
or **o**
orange *n.* **naranja**; *adj.* **anaranjado/a**
order *v.* **pedir (i, i)**; **mandar**
ordinal (adjective) (adjetivo) **ordinal**
other *adj.* **otro/a**; others *pron.* **los/las demás**
ought to (*do something*) **deber** (+ *inf.*)
out *adv.* **fuera**
outdoor marketplace **mercado al aire libre**
outside *adv.* **afuera**
outskirts **afueras**
oven **horno**; microwave oven **horno de
  microonda**
overcast: it's overcast (*weather*) **está nublado**
owner **dueño/a**

P

pace **ritmo**
pack: to pack one's suitcases **hacer** (*irreg.*)
  (*p.p.* **hecho/a**) **las maletas**
pain: to have a pain (in) **tener** (*irreg.*) **dolor
  (de)**
painting **pintura**
pair **par** *m.*
pants **pantalones** *m. pl.*
paper **papel** *m.*; term paper **trabajo**
pardon **perdón**; pardon me **perdone, discúlpeme** (*form. s.*)
parents **padres** *m. pl.*
park *v.* **estacionar(se)**; *n.* **parque** *m.*
part **parte** *f.*
part-time **de tiempo parcial**
party **fiesta**; to give/have a party **dar** (*irreg.*) /
  hacer (*irreg.*) (*p.p.* **hecho/a**) **una fiesta**
pass through **recorrer**
passage (*ticket*) **pasaje** *m.*
passbook **libreta de ahorros**
passenger **pasajero/a**

passport **pasaporte** *m.*
past *adj.* **pasado/a**
pastime **pasatiempo**
patient **paciente** *m., f.*
patio **patio**
pay **pagar (gu)**
pea **arveja**
peace **paz** *f.* (*pl.* **paces**)
peasant **campesino/a**
pen **bolígrafo**
penalty **multa**
pencil **lápiz** *m.* (*pl.* **lápices**)
people **gente** *f. s.*
performance (*show*) **función** *f.*
permit *v.* **permitir**
person **persona** *f.*
personal **personal**; personal use **uso
  personal**
personnel office **Dirección** (*f.*) **de Personal**
personnel director **director(a) de personal**
pharmacy **farmacia**
photo(graph) **foto(grafía)** *f.*; photographic
  equipment **equipo fotográfico**; to take photographs **sacar (qu) fotos**
piano **piano**
pick up **recoger (j)**; to pick (someone) up at
  . . . **pasar por alguien a...**
pictures: to take pictures **sacar (qu) fotos**
pie **pastel** *m.*
piece of paper **papel** *m.*
pill **pastilla**
pilot **piloto/a**
pink **rosado/a**
pitcher **jarro**
place *v.* **poner** (*irreg.*) (*p.p.* **puesto/a**); *n.* **lugar**
  m.; (*in line*) **puesto**
plaid **de cuadros**
plan: to make plans to (*do something*) **hacer**
  (*irreg.*) (*p.p.* **hecho/a**) **planes para** (+ *inf.*)
plane **avión** *m.*; by plane **en avión**
plate **plato**
play *v.* (*a game, sports*) **jugar (ue) (gu) (a)**;
  (*music*) **tocar**; to play cards **jugar a las cartas**; to play chess **jugar al ajedrez**; *n.* (*in a
  game*) **juego**; (*theater*) **comedia**
player **jugador/a**
please **por favor**; pleased to meet you **mucho
  gusto; encantado/a; igualmente**
pleasing: to be pleasing **gustar**
plot (*of a play or novel*) **trama**
plug in **enchufar**
plumber **plomero/a**
police officer **policía** *m.*
pollution: there's pollution **hay contaminación** *f.*
poor **pobre**
population **población** *f.*
pork chop **chuleta de cerdo**
portable radio **radio** (*f.*) **portátil**
position (job) **puesto**
possession *n.* **bien** *m.*
possible: it's possible that **puede que**
  (+ *subj.*)
postcard **tarjeta postal**
poster **cartel** *m.*
potato **papa**; French fried potato **papa frita**

practical **práctico/a**
practice **practicar (qu)**; (*a profession*) **ejercer (z)**
prefer **preferir (ie, i)**
preferable **preferible**; it is preferable **es preferible**
prepare **preparar**
prepared **listo/a** (*with estar [irreg.]*)
preposition **preposición** *f.*
prescription **receta**
present: at the present time **en la actualidad**
press *n.* **prensa**
pressure **presión** *f.*; to be under a lot of pressure **sufrir muchas presiones**
pretty *adj.* **bonito/a**
price **precio**; fixed price **precio fijo**
printer **impresora**
problem **problema** *m.*
profession **profesión** *f.*
professor **profesor(a)**
prohibit **prohibir**
protect **proteger (j)**
provided (that) **con tal (de) que**
psychology **sicología**
public *adj.* **público/a**
pure **puro/a**
purple **morado/a**
purse **bolsa**
put **poner** (*irreg.*) (*p.p.* **puesto/a**); to put in **ingresar, depositar**; to put on (*clothing*) **ponerse**; to put to bed **acostar (ue)**

Q

quarter: it's a quarter past . . . **es la... /son las... y cuarto**; it's a quarter to . . . **es la ... /son las... menos cuarto**
question **pregunta**; (*matter*) **cuestión** *f.*; to ask a question **hacer** (*irreg.*) (*p.p.* **hecho/a**) **una pregunta**
quit **dejar**
quite **bastante**
quiz **prueba**

R

racket **raqueta**
radio (set) **radio**; portable radio **radio portátil**
rain *v.* **llover (ue)**; *n.* **lluvia**
raincoat **impermeable** *m.*
raise *v.* **levantar**; *n.* **aumento**
ranch **hacienda; rancho**
rancher **ranchero/a**
rather **bastante**
read **leer (y)**
ready **listo/a** (*with estar [irreg.]*)
receive **recibir**
recommend **recomendar (ie)**
record (*phonographic*) **disco**
red **rojo/a**
reduction (sale) **rebaja**
refreshments **refrescos**
refrigerator **refrigerador** *m.*

refuse **rehusar**
regret **sentir (ie, i)**
relative (*family*) **pariente** *m.*
remain **quedar(se)**
remember **acordarse (ue) (de); recordar (ue)**
remove **quitar**
rent *v.* **alquilar**; *n.* **alquiler** *m.*
renter **inquilino/a**
reporter **reportero/a**
reservation **reservación** *f.*
reserve **reservar**
resign: to resign (from) **renunciar (a)**
resolve **resolver (ue)** (*p.p.* **resuelto/a**)
resource: natural resource **recurso natural**
responsibility **responsabilidad** *f.*
rest *v.* **descansar**
restaurant **restaurante** *m.*
résumé **currículum** *m.*
return **volver (ue)** (*p.p.* **vuelto/a**); to return (*to a place*) **regresar**; to return (*something*) **devolver (ue)** (*p.p.* **devuelto/a**)
rhythm **ritmo**
rice **arroz** *m.*
rich **rico/a**
ride: to ride a bike **pasear en bicicleta**; to ride horseback **montar a caballo**
right *n.* (*political*) **derecho**; right? **¿no? ¿verdad?**; right now **en la actualidad, ahora mismo, en este momento**; to be right **tener** (*irreg.*) **razón**; to the right of **a la derecha**
ring (*telephone*) **sonar (ue)**
road **camino**
room **cuarto**; (*in a hotel*) **habitación** *f.*; emergency room **sala de emergencias/urgencia**; room and breakfast plus one other meal **media pensión** (*f.*); room and full board **pensión** (*f.*) **completa** room with(out) bath/shower **habitación con/sin baño/ducha**; single room **habitación para una persona**
roommate **compañero/a de cuarto**
round-trip ticket **billete** (*m.*)**/boleto de ida y vuelta**
rug **alfombra**
run: to run into (*collide*) **darse** (*irreg.*) **con; chocar (qu) (con)**; to run out of **acabar**
Russian (*language*) **ruso**

S

sad **triste**
salad **ensalada**
salary **sueldo**
sale **rebaja**
salesperson **vendedor(a)**
salmon **salmón** *m.*
same: at the same time **a la vez**
sandal **sandalia**
sandwich **sándwich** *m.*
Santa Claus **Papá Noel**
Saturday **sábado**
save **conservar**; (*a place*) **guardar**; (*money*) **ahorrar**
savings account **cuenta de ahorros**
say **decir** (*irreg.*) (*p.p.* **dicho/a**); to say goodbye (to) **despedirse (i, i) (de)**

scarcity **escasez** *f.* (*pl.* **escaseces**)
school **escuela**
science **ciencia**
screen monitor *m.*; **pantalla**
sea **mar** *m., f.*
search *v.* **registrar**; in search of **en busca de**
season **estación** *f.*
seat *v.* **sentar (ie)**; *n.* **asiento**; (*in a theater*) **butaca**
second *adj.* **segundo/a**
secretary **secretario/a**
see **ver** (*irreg.*) (*p.p.* **visto/a**); see you around **nos vemos**; see you later **hasta luego**; see you tomorrow **hasta mañana**
seem **parecer (zc)**
sell **vender**; they sell (have) everything **venden de todo**
send **mandar**
September **se(p)tiembre** *m.*
servant **criado/a**
serve **servir (i, i)**
service **servicio**
set: to set the table **poner** (*irreg.*) (*p.p.* **puesto/a**) **la mesa**
seven **siete**
seventeen **diecisiete**
seventh **séptimo/a**
seventy **setenta**
shame **lástima**; it is a shame **es (una) lástima**; what a shame! **¡qué desgracia!**
shape: in good shape **en forma**
share *v.* **compartir**
shave (*oneself*) **afeitar(se)**
she **ella**
shellfish **mariscos** *m. pl.*
ship **barco**; cruise ship **crucero**
shirt **camisa**; T-shirt **camiseta**
shoe **zapato**
shop: repair shop **taller** *m.*
shopkeeper **comerciante** *m., f.*
shopping: to go shopping **ir** (*irreg.*) **de compras**; shopping mall **centro comercial**
short (*in height*) **bajo/a**; (*in length*) **corto/a**
shortage **escasez** *f.* (*pl.* **escaseces**)
shot **inyección** *f.*; to give (*someone*) a shot **ponerle** (*irreg.*) (*p.p.* **puesto/a**) **una inyección**
should (*do something*) **deber** (+ *inf.*)
show (performance) **función** *f.*
shrimp **camarones** *m. pl.*
sick **enfermo/a**; to get sick **enfermarse**
sidewalk **acera**
silk **seda**
silly **tonto/a**
sing **cantar**
single (*not married*) **soltero/a**; single room (*in a hotel*) **habitación** (*f.*) **para una persona**
sister **hermana**
sit: to sit down **sentarse (ie)**
six **seis**
sixteen **dieciséis**
sixth **sexto/a**
sixty **sesenta**
skate *v.* **patinar**
ski *v.* **esquiar**; *n.* **esquí** *m.*
skirt **falda**

skyscraper **rascacielos** *m. s.*
sleep *v.* **dormir (ue, u)**
sleepy: to be sleepy **tener** (*irreg.*) **sueño**
slender **delgado/a**
slowly **lentamente**
small **pequeño/a**
smart **listo/a**
smile *v.* **sonreír (i, i)**
smog: there's smog **hay contaminación** *f.*
smoke *v.* **fumar;** *n.* **humo**
smoking: (non)smoking section **sección** (*f.*) **de (no) fumar**
snow *v.* **nevar (ie);** *n.* **nieve** *f.*
so *adv.* **así;** so much **tanto;** so-so **así así;** so that *conj.* **para que**
soccer **fútbol** *m.*
social worker **trabajador(a) social**
socks **calcetines** *m.*
sofa **sofá** *m.*
soft drink **refresco**
solitude **soledad** *f.*
solve **resolver (ue)** (*p.p.* **resuelto/a**)
some **algún, alguno/a**
someone **alguien**
something **algo**
sometimes **a veces**
son **hijo**
soon: as soon as **en cuanto, tan pronto como**
sorry: I'm sorry **lo siento;** to feel sorry **sentir (ie, i)**
soup **sopa**
soupspoon **cuchara**
Spanish (*language*) **español** *m.*
spare time **ratos** (*m. pl.*) **libres**
speak **hablar**
speed *n.* **velocidad** *f.*
spend (*money*) **gastar**
spoon **cuchara**
sport **deporte** *m.;* sports-minded *adj.* **deportista**
spring (*season*) **primavera**
stadium **estadio**
stairs, stairway **escalera**
stand: to stand in line **hacer** (*irreg.*) (*p.p.* **hecho/a**) **cola;** to stand up **levantarse**
start *v.* **comenzar (c);** (*motor*) **arrancar (qu)**
station **estación** *f.;* bus station **estación de autobuses;** gas station **gasolinera, estación de gasolina;** station wagon **camioneta;** train station **estación del tren**
stay *v.* **quedarse;** to stay in bed **guardar cama**
steak **bistec** *m.*
stereo equipment **equipo estereofónico**
stick: to stick out (*tongue*) **sacar (qu)**
still *adv.* **todavía**
stockings **medias**
stomach **estómago**
stop *v.* **parar;** to stop (*doing something*) **dejar de** (+ *inf.*)
stopovers: to have/make stopovers **hacer** (*irreg.*) (*p.p.* **hecho/a**) **escalas**
store *n.* **tienda;** *v.* to store information **archivar la información**
stove **estufa**
straight (ahead) **(todo) derecho**

strange: it is strange **es extraño;** how strange **qué extraño**
street **calle** *f.*
strike *v.* (*hit*) **pegar (gu);** *n.* (*labor*) **huelga**
striped **de rayas**
student **estudiante** *m., f.*
study **estudiar**
style: it's the latest style **está muy de moda**
subject (*school*) **materia**
suburbs **afueras**
suddenly **de repente**
suffer **sufrir**
sugar **azúcar** *m.*
suit **traje** *m.*
suitcase **maleta;** to pack one's suitcases **hacer** (*irreg.*) (*p.p.* **hecho/a**) **las maletas**
summer **verano**
sunbathe **tomar el sol**
Sunday **domingo**
sunny: it's sunny (*weather*) **hace sol**
supermarket **supermercado**
supper **cena**
sure: to be sure **estar** (*irreg.*) **seguro/a;** it's a sure thing **es seguro**
surprise *n.* **sorpresa**
surprising: to be surprising to one **sorprenderle a uno**
sweater **suéter** *m.*
sweep (the floor) **barrer (el suelo)**
swim *v.* **nadar**
swimming **natación** *f.*
swimsuit **traje** (*m.*) **de baño**
symptom **síntoma** *m.*
syrup: cough syrup **jarabe** *m.*

T

table **mesa;** end table **mesita**
tablecloth **mantel** *m.*
take **tomar; llevar;** to take a bath **bañarse;** to take a trip **hacer** (*irreg.*) (*p.p.* **hecho/a**) **un viaje, hacer una excursión;** to take a walk **dar** (*irreg.*) **un paseo;** to take away **quitar;** to take care of oneself **cuidarse;** to take into account **tomar, tener** (*irreg.*) **en cuenta;** to take leave (of) **despedirse (i,i) (de);** to take off (*an airplane*) **despegar (gu);** to take off (*clothing*) **quitarse;** to take out the garbage **sacar la basura;** to take pictures, photographs **sacar (qu) fotos;** to take place **tener lugar, ser en** (*place*)
talk **hablar**
tall **alto/a**
tank **tanque** *m.*
taste *n.* **gusto**
tax *n.* **impuesto**
taxi **taxi** *m.*
tea **té** *m.*
teach **enseñar**
teaspoon **cucharita**
television set **televisor** *m.*
tell **decir** (*irreg.*) (*p.p.* **dicho/a**); tell me (something, one thing) **dime (algo, una cosa)** (*fam.*); to tell about **contar (ue)**

temperature **temperatura**
ten **diez**
tenant **inquilino/a**
tennis **tenis** *m. s.;* tennis court **cancha**
tenth **décimo/a**
term paper **trabajo**
terminal **terminal** *m.*
test **examen** *m.*
textbook **libro de texto**
than **que**
thank you **gracias;** thank you very much **muchas gracias**
that *adj.* **ese/a;** *pron.* **eso, aquello** *conj.* **que;** that which **lo que;** that's why **por eso**
theater **teatro**
then **luego**
there **allí;** there is, are **hay;** there is not, are not **no hay**
these *adj.* **estos/as**
thief **ladrón, ladrona**
thin **delgado/a**
thing **cosa**
think **creer (y); pensar (ie);** I think so **creo que sí;** I don't think so **creo que no**
third **tercer, tercero/a**
thirsty: to be thirsty **tener** (*irreg.*) **sed**
thirteen **trece**
thirty **treinta**
this *adj.* **este/a;** *pron.* **esto**
three **tres**
throat **garganta**
Thursday **jueves** *m. s.*
ticket **billete** (*m.*), **boleto;** (*for a performance*) **entrada;** one-way **billete de ida;** (*passage*) **pasaje** *m.;* round-trip **billete de ida y vuelta**
tie *n.* **corbata**
time **hora; tiempo; vez,** *f.* (*pl.* **veces**); at that time **en aquel entonces, en aquella época;** at the present time **en la actualidad;** at the same time **a la vez;** free time/spare time **ratos libres;** from time to time **de vez en cuando;** on time **a tiempo;** what time is it? **¿qué hora es?**
tip (*to a bellhop, etc.*) **propina**
tire *n.* **llanta;** flat tire **llanta desinflada**
tired **cansado/a**
to **a**
toast **pan** (*m.*) **tostado**
toaster **tostadora**
today **hoy**
together *adj.* **juntos/as;** to get together (with) **reunirse (con)**
tomato **tomate** *m.*
tomorrow **mañana;** day after tomorrow **pasado mañana**
tongue **lengua**
tonight **esta noche**
too/too much **demasiado**
top: on top of **encima de**
tourist class **clase** (*f.*) **turística**
toy **juguete** *m.*
trade (*job*) **oficio**
traffic **tráfico**
train **tren** *m.;* train station **estación** (*f.*) **del tren**

tranquil **tranquilo/a**
transportation **transporte** *m.*; means of transportation **medio de transporte**
travel **viajar;** to travel by boat **navegar (gu) en barco**
traveler **viajero/a**
tray **bandeja**
treatment **tratamiento**
tree **árbol** *m.*
trip **viaje** *m.*; to take a trip **hacer** (*irreg.*) (*p.p.* **hecho/a**) **un viaje, hacer una excursión**
trophy **trofeo**
try: to try to (*do something*) **tratar de** (+ *inf.*)
T-shirt **camiseta**
Tuesday **martes** *m. s.*
tuition **matrícula**
tuna **atún** *m.*
turn (*a corner*) **doblar;** to be someone's turn **tocarle (qu) a uno;** to turn off (*lights, appliances*) **apagar (gu);** to turn on (*appliances*) **poner** (*irreg.*) (*p.p.* **puesto/a**)
TV set **televisor** *m.*
twelve **doce**
twenty **veinte**
twice **dos veces;** twice a week **dos veces a la semana;** twice a month **dos veces al mes**
two **dos**
type *v.* **escribir** (*p.p.* **escrito/a**) **a máquina**
typewriter **máquina de escribir**

U

ugly **feo/a**
under(neath) **debajo de**
understand **comprender; entender (ie)**
unintentional: it was unintentional **fue sin querer**
university **universidad** *f.*
unless **a menos que**
unoccupied **desocupado/a**
unpleasant **antipático/a**
until **hasta (que)**
urgent **urgente;** it is urgent **es urgente**
U.S.: from the U.S. **norteamericano/a**
use *v.* (*expend*) **gastar;** (*a machine*) **manejar, usar;** *n.* (*of a machine*) **manejo, uso;** personal use **uso personal**
utensil **utensilio**

V

vacant **desocupado/a**
vacation: to be/go on vacation **estar** (*irreg.*) **ir** (*irreg.*) **de vacaciones**
vacuum *v.* **pasar la aspiradora;** vacuum cleaner **aspiradora**

VCR **grabador** (*m.*) **de vídeo**
vegetables **verduras**
verb **verbo**
very **muy**
view **vista**
visit: to visit a museum **visitar un museo**
vocabulary **vocabulario**
volleyball **vólibol** *m.*
vote **votar**

W

wait (for) **esperar;** to wait in line **hacer** (*irreg.*) (*p.p.* **hecho/a**) **cola**
waiter **camarero**
waiting room **sala de espera**
waitress **camarera**
wake **despertar (ie);** to wake up **despertarse (ie)**
walk: to take a walk **dar** (*irreg.*) **un paseo**
wall **pared** *f.*
wallet **cartera**
want **querer** (*irreg.*)**;** **desear**
war **guerra**
warm: to be/feel warm **tener** (*irreg.*) **calor**
wash (oneself) **lavar(se);** to wash the windows **lavar las ventanas**
washing machine **lavadora**
watch *v.* **mirar;** to watch over **guardar;** *n.* **reloj** *m.*
water **agua** *f.* (*but* **el agua**); water bed **cama de agua**
wear **llevar**
weather **tiempo;** what's the weather like? **¿qué tiempo hace?**
Wednesday **miércoles** *m. s.*
week **semana;** next week **la próxima semana;** once a week **una vez a la semana;** twice a week **dos veces a la semana**
weekend **fin** (*m.*) **de semana**
welcome **bienvenido/a**
welfare **bien**
well **bien;** very well **muy bien;** well . . . **pues...**
well-being **bienestar** *m.*
what (that which) **lo que;** what? **¿qué?;** **¿cómo?;** (at) what time . . . ? **¿a qué hora... ?;** what's your name? **¿cómo te llamas?** *fam.;* **¿cómo se llama usted?** *form.*
when **cuando;** when? **¿cuándo?**
whenever **siempre que**
where **donde;** where? **¿dónde?**
which *conj.* **que**
which? **¿cuál(es)?;** while **mientras (que)**
white **blanco/a**

who **quien;** who? **¿quién?;** *pl.* **¿quiénes?**
whole **entero/a**
why **¿por qué?;** that's why **por eso;** why not? **¿por qué no?**
wife **esposa**
win **ganar**
windy: it's windy (*weather*) **hace viento**
wine **vino;** red (white) wine **vino tinto (blanco);** wine glass **copa**
winter **invierno**
wish: *n.* **esperanza;** I wish that . . . **ojalá (que)** (+ *subj.*)
with **con;** with me **conmigo;** with you **contigo**
without **sin**
witness *n.* **testigo** *m., f.*
woman **mujer** *f.*
wool **lana**
word **palabra**
work *v.* **trabajar;** (*machines*) **funcionar;** *n.* **trabajo**
worker **obrero/a;** farm worker **campesino/a**
worried **preocupado/a**
worry: don't worry **no te preocupes** (*fam. s.*)
worse **peor**
write **escribir** (*p.p.* **escrito/a**); to write programs **diseñar programas**
written work **trabajo**
wrong: to be wrong **equivocarse (qu);** no **tener** (*irreg.*) **razón**
would: I would like to (*do something*) **quisiera** (+ *inf.*); it would be **sería**

Y

yard **patio**
year **año;** to be _____ years old **tener** (*irreg.*) _____ **años**
yellow **amarillo/a**
yes **sí**
yesterday **ayer;** day before yesterday **anteayer**
yet **aún**
you *sub. pron.* **tú** *fam. s.;* **usted (Ud.)** *form. s.;* and you? **¿y tú?** *fam. s.;* **¿y usted?** *form. s.*
young **joven**
younger **menor**
you're welcome **de nada**
your *poss.* **tu(s)** *fam. s.;* **su(s)** *form. s.;* **vuestro/a(s)** *fam. pl. Sp.*
youth: as a youth **de joven**

Z

zero **cero**

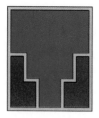

INDEX

In this index, *Study Hints* and vocabulary topic groups are listed by individual topic as well as under those headings. **A propósito...**, **Al tanto...**, and **Notas comunicativas sobre el diálogo** sections appear only as a group, under those headings.

OCÉANO ATLÁNTICO

Barranquilla
Cartagena
Lago de
Maracaibo
Caracas

VENEZUELA

Río Orinoco

GUAYANA

SURINAM

GUAYANA FRANCESA

Manizales

Río Magdalena

Bogotá

Cali

COLOMBIA

ECUADOR

Otavalo

Quito

ECUADOR

Iquitos

Río Amazonas

Cajamarca

PERÚ

BRASIL

Machu Picchu

Pisac

Lima

Cuzco

Ayacucho

BOLIVIA

Brasilia

Lago
Titicaca

La Paz

Sucre

Potosí

PARAGUAY

Río Paraná

Salta

Asunción

Río de Janeiro

OCÉANO PACÍFICO

Iguazú

Río Uruguay

URUGUAY

Santiago

Buenos Aires

Montevideo

Punta del Este

OCÉANO ATLÁNTICO

CHILE

ARGENTINA

Río de la Plata

Temuco

Estrecho de Magallanes

TIERRA DEL FUEGO

América del Sur

| 0 | 200 | 400 | 600 | 800 Millas |

| 0 | 200 | 400 | 600 | 800 Kilómetros |